a gift from the

JAN KARSKI
Educational
Foundation

www.jankarski.net

The Great Powers and Poland

The Great Powers and Poland

From Versailles to Yalta

Anniversary Edition

Jan Karski

ROWMAN & LITTLEFIELD
Lanham • Boulder • New York • Toronto • Plymouth, UK

Published by Rowman & Littlefield
4501 Forbes Boulevard, Suite 200, Lanham, Maryland 20706
www.rowman.com

10 Thornbury Road, Plymouth PL6 7PP, United Kingdom

British Library Cataloguing in Publication Information Available

Library of Congress Cataloging-in-Publication Data
Karski, Jan, 1914–2000.
[Great Powers & Poland, 1919–1945]
The great powers and Poland : from Versailles to Yalta / Jan Karski. — Anniversary edition.
pages cm
Originally published as: The Great Powers & Poland, 1919–1945. Lanham, MD : University Press of America, c1985.
Includes bibliographical references and index.
ISBN 978-1-4422-2664-7 (cloth : alk. paper) — ISBN 978-1-4422-2665-4 (electronic)
1. Poland—Foreign relations—1918–1945. 2. Europe—Politics and government—1918–1945. 3. Paris Peace Conference (1919–1920) 4. Yalta Conference (1945) 5. United States—Foreign relations—Poland. 6. Poland—Foreign relations—United States. I. Title.
DK4402.K37 2014
943.8'04—dc23
2013030897

Printed in the United States of America

This book is dedicated to
PETER F. KROGH
in appreciation of his leadership in the School of Foreign Service,
Georgetown University

Contents

Preface

The study pursued on the following pages has not been structured as to convey any message or judgment. It reflects what has been found in the documentary/archival records, memoirs of the main statesmen, and various fragmentary studies by recognized scholars in the field. The study took many years of research, particularly frustrating when confronting the plethora of memoirs. Most of them are self-serving. Therefore, only otherwise verified portions have been used.

The main theme of the study deals with the policies of the Great Powers toward Poland during the years 1919–1945. At the time of the Versailles Peace Conference, these were France, Great Britain, and the United States. Italy and Japan were not active in Polish problems, while Tsarist Russia, Austria-Hungary, and Germany played either a momentary or a marginal role. During the interwar period Germany, the Soviet Union, France, and Great Britain became essential. During World War II, the Soviet Union, Great Britain, and the United States were crucial. Because of the personal power they exercised in their own countries, that specifically meant Joseph Stalin, Winston S. Churchill, and Franklin D. Roosevelt.

It seems that from Poland's resurrection at the end of World War I to its demise following World War II, only once were the Poles able to determine their own fate by themselves. That was during the Polish-Bolshevik war of 1919–1920. Only once—at the Versailles Peace Conference—did a Great Power, the United States, throw its support on behalf of Poland for reasons other than its own interest. In all other instances Poland was unable to play an independent and effective role in the international arena, regardless of the merits or demerits of its policies. Essentially, its fate depended on the Great Powers—their short- or long-range goals and their interrelations. The Poles were never strong enough to change that reality.

The interrelations of the Great Powers were far from stable. On the contrary, for a variety of reasons they had been fluctuating or shifting. Because of its geopolitical location between expansionist Germany and Russia, Poland always had been affected—favorably or unfavorably.

In the final analysis, Poland was not much more than an object in the policies of the Great Powers, and its fortunes were a function of their changeable interrelations.

Abbreviations

AANA	*Auswärtiges Amt Archives* (microfilm). National Archives, Washington, DC.
AANP-Zespoly MSZ	*Archiwum Akt Nowych, Zespoly Ministerstwa Spraw Zagranicznych* (New Records' Archives, Folders of the Ministry of Foreign Affairs). Warsaw: National Archives.
BBB	Great Britain, Foreign Office. *Documents Concerning German-Polish Relations and the Outbreak of Hostilities between Great Britain and Germany on September 3, 1939.* New York: Farrar and Rinehart, 1939. (*The British Blue Book.*)
DBFP	E. L. Woodward and R. Butler, eds. *Documents on British Foreign Policy, 1919–1939.* London: H. M. Stationery Office.
DDF	*Documents Diplomatiques Français, 1932–1939.* Paris: Imprimerie Nationale.
DGFP	Department of State. *Documents on German Foreign Policy.* Washington, DC: US Government Printing Office.
DPSR, 1939–1945	General Sikorski Historical Institute. *Documents on Polish-Soviet Relations, 1939–1945.* 2 vols. London: Heinemann, 1961–1967.

FO   Foreign Office Records. London: Public Records Office.

FRUS   *Foreign Relations of the United States*. Washington, DC: US Government Printing Office.

GWB   German Foreign Office. *Documents on the Events Preceding the Outbreak of the War*. New York: German Library of Information, 1940. (*The German White Book*.)

LJF   Ministère des Affaires Étrangères. *Le Livre Jaune Français*. Paris: Imprimerie Nationale, 1939.

PSZ   *Polskie Sily Zbrojne w Drugiej Wojnie Swiatowej* (The Polish Armed Forces in the Second World War). London: General Sjkorski Historical Institute, 1950–1951.

PWB   Republic of Poland. *Official Documents Concerning Polish-German and Polish-Soviet Relations*. London: Hutchinson Co., 1940. (*The Polish White Book*.)

SDANA   State Department Archives. National Archives, Washington, DC.

TMWC   *The Trial of the Major War Criminals Before the International Military Tribunal*. 42 vols. Nuremberg: 1947–1949.

Part I

The Great Powers and Poland between the Two World Wars (1919–1939)

Chapter One

The Polish Question during World War I

For over one hundred years, Poland was partitioned among Prussia, Russia, and Austria—a tie that kept the three occupying powers strongly bound together. The subjugated Poles, always hoping for the reestablishment of independence, conspired and fought to break the solidarity of their oppressors. World War I was an answer to their prayers and dreams: at last the partitioning powers were at each other's throats. True, the war brought innumerable suffering upon the Polish people. They were at the center of a holocaust, the front lines repeatedly crossed their territories, and the advancing or withdrawing armies usually marked their moves by destruction, forcible deportations of inhabitants, or political repression. The Poles had to fight in three different armies, with members of the same families often fighting against each other. In the first year of the war, one million Poles—and by the end of the war, more—wore German, Austrian, or Russian uniforms. But the war was to fulfill their hopes, offering them great opportunities which they learned to exploit.

The partitioning powers needed the loyalty and support of a subjugated nation occupying a strategic position, and they wooed the Poles. Although the promises or commitments were usually equivocal, vague, and made at the expense of the enemy, they were bound to advance the Polish cause.

In the West, particularly in France and the United States, Polish aspirations were popular, and many considered the emergence of a free Poland an act of justice and a natural outcome of the war. But to Allied governments, Poland represented a grave political issue related to their own interests and

3

the security of postwar Europe. All agreed that the Poles should have an opportunity to lead their own national life and should be accorded self-government. But should Poland be reconstituted as a genuinely sovereign state, or should it form an autonomous unit bound to Russia, the indispensable ally in the war? Should the future Poland be added to the Hapsburg Empire in the event that Austria abandoned the German camp and concluded a separate peace? Would not an independent Poland unavoidably become a hindrance to the stability of Europe by cutting Russia off from the encirclement of Germany? The answers to these questions were not easy and in many instances depended on the changing fortunes of war.

As the Allied statesmen differed or vacillated, so did the Poles themselves. Some were loyal to the partitioning powers. Some looked for the defeat of the Central Powers and for a union with Russia under the aegis of the Romanovs. Some, particularly those living in Austrian Galicia, argued that a united Poland should cast its lot with the Hapsburg Empire, which was more liberal than either Germany or Russia and capable of checking the imperialism of both. Others, not many, wanted a unified Poland to become an autonomous part of the German empire. [1] There were also those who rejected all "orientations" altogether, arguing that since the three oppressing powers were bound to weaken each other in the course of the war, the Poles might be able to create faits accomplis, provided they had their own military forces. Consequently, they would concentrate all their efforts on organizing, training, and equipping the youth in all Polish-inhabited areas, secretly or, whenever possible, openly. Still others decided to work and fight in the West, gambling on an Allied victory, casting their lot with the Western powers, seeking sympathy, understanding, and recognition of the Poland to come. They hoped their activities would make their voices heard in Allied councils and at the peace conference.

THE POLICIES OF THE CENTRAL POWERS

The first public act dealing with the Polish issue came from the Central Powers. On August 9, 1914, the Austro-Hungarian and German military commands, whose armies had just crossed the Russian borders into the Polish-inhabited areas, appealed to the Poles for war support and cooperation. [2] In lofty language they spoke about a deliverance from "the Muscovite yoke," about liberty and independence for Poland, about Oriental barbarism and common Western civilization. The liberated Poles were asked to join the "liberating" armies and to "chase the Asiatic hordes beyond the frontiers of Poland." The appeal did not contain any mention of when, under what guarantees, and within what boundaries "free" Poland would arise. In addition, the appeal had no political meaning, since it did not come from governments but from military headquarters only.

By the autumn of 1915, the Central Powers had pushed the Russian armies not only out of ethnic Poland but out of the large areas formerly part of what had been the Polish-Lithuanian Commonwealth. On August 5 Warsaw had been taken, and by September the front extended to the Vilna-Pinsk line. Without delay, the German and Austrian authorities began an energetic reorganization of the newly conquered territories and were soon able to claim some successes in reducing the war's destructive effects and in bringing about some degree of normality. They divided the conquered areas into two parts—the northern, with Warsaw as the capital, headed by a German, General Hans Hartwig von Beseler; and the southern, over which an Austrian general, Karl von Kuk, was given authority, with residence in Lublin.

The extension of control over all Polish-inhabited territories and public appeals for military volunteers required some program for the future of Poland, mutually agreed upon by Berlin and Vienna. It was not an easy task, however.

In Germany, many voices in political, economic, and intellectual quarters claimed that historical necessity demanded Germany's eastward as well as southward expansion. The concept of a German-dominated Mitteleuropa, including the Baltic, Polish, and Balkan areas, as well as Turkey, was widely known and popular.[3] The conservative and nationalist parties justified the necessity of expansion by economic needs and military security. As early as May 1915, powerful business organizations submitted a public petition to the government, demanding a "considerable extension of Imperial and Prussian frontiers in the east," that is, the Baltic areas and "those territories which lie to the South [of the Baltic Sea]."[4] If implemented, those demands would deny freedom not only to the German Poles but also to those who had just become "liberated."

The strongest pressure for eastern expansion was exercised by the military, particularly by two generals—Paul Beneckendorf von Hindenburg and Erich von Ludendorff.[5] Their views carried weight because of the positions they held and the power they exercised. In September 1916 Hindenburg became chief of the general staff and Ludendorff first quartermaster general. The two shared the highest responsibility for the conduct of the war.

The attitude of the Austrian authorities was more moderate but by no means clear. To placate the Poles they indicated that a future Poland might contain not only the Russian part but also Austrian Galicia. They were ambiguous, however, in clarifying the status of Poland in relationship to the Hapsburg monarchy. In their secret discussions with the Germans, they vacillated and compromised. In October 1915 Vienna suggested a unification of the Austrian and Russian Polish-inhabited provinces and then their incorporation into the Dual Monarchy as an autonomous unit. But on August 12, 1916, Austria's foreign minister, Count Stephan Burian von Rajecz, reached a general understanding with German Chancellor Theobald von Bethmann-Hollweg that the future Poland should consist of only the Russian part, with Germany and Austria having a right to detach certain areas. Poland was to be reconstituted as a monarchy under equal control of both Germany and Austria-Hungary. The German High Command would control its army. The question of the dynasty was left open.[6]

In the second half of 1916 the Polish issue emerged as part of a larger problem, namely, a compromise peace between the Central Powers and Russia. By that time, strong pressures to end the war had developed on both sides. In Germany, liberal and socialist circles pressed for peace, and in Austria, apprehensions were growing as to the future of the Dual Monarchy, while in Russia, the newly appointed head of the cabinet, Boris Stürmer, advocated a separate peace.[7]

Hindenburg and Ludendorff opposed these tendencies, still believing in victory on the western as well as on the eastern fronts. Both realized, however, that they needed more manpower for the war effort because of recent military setbacks. In April 1915 Italy joined the Allied powers; in June 1916 General Alexei Brusilov won important victories over Austro-Hungarian armies, and soon after, Romania entered the Allied camp. Ludendorff was particularly eager to get Polish volunteers, even at the price of important political concessions. "The Pole is a good soldier. . . . Let us make a Grand Duchy of Poland out of Warsaw and Lublin and then make a Polish army under German command," he recommended in July 1916.[8] He had a supporter in Beseler, an advocate of a formally independent, but in practice German-controlled, Poland.

As a result of these pressures and war events, on November 5, 1916, Emperors William II of Germany and Franz Joseph of Austria-Hungary issued a joint manifesto addressed to the Poles.[9] They solemnly proclaimed the creation of a Polish state in the territories "snatched with heavy sacrifices from Russian power." Poland would become an autonomous state, a constitutional and hereditary monarchy; its frontiers would be determined later. The wording of the manifesto indicated that no German or Austrian areas would be included in the envisaged kingdom, the word "sovereign" was carefully avoided, and the question of the dynasty was not even mentioned.

From the standpoint of the German High Command, probably the most important item was the reference to the "glorious tradition of the Polish army of former times." That tradition, together with the "memory of our brave Polish fellow-combatants in the great war of the present, will continue to live." The manifesto announced the creation of the Polish army. Its "organization, training, and command," however, were to be "regulated by mutual agreement" sometime in the future.

Whatever the motives for the manifesto, its importance in enhancing the Polish cause was undeniable. For, unlike the previous proclamation, it was signed by heads of state and represented a formal, albeit vague, commitment. Clearly aiming at Russia, it could not but destroy whatever chances existed for a compromise peace.

Subsequently, the manifesto became one of the most controversial and criticized documents of World War I. Prince von Billow called it a "crazy project," "a most lamentable blunder," and a "crime committed against all Germany."[10] In Petrograd it was considered an "outrage," an "insult to the emperor."[11] The Russian ambassador in Washington, Boris Bakhmetov, labeled it as being "in contempt of the law of nations" in a formal letter to Secretary of State Robert Lansing.[12] Both the British and the French governments protested that the formation of a Polish army in the conquered territories was contrary to the Hague Convention.[13]

THE POLICIES OF TSARIST RUSSIA

When World War I broke out, Russia controlled some three-quarters of ethnic Poland. Consequently, the policies of the Russian governments were of particular importance to the Poles. These policies were carefully observed in Paris and London as well because Russia was a powerful ally whose confidence and loyal participation in the war seemed necessary. As long as Russia, whether tsarist or even revolutionary, fought at the side of the Western allies, they considered it imprudent to initiate any policy of their own concerning the future of Poland.

Because the Polish-inhabited areas formed the initial war theater, the loyalty and support of the Poles were valuable to the Russian government. Thus, as early as August 14, 1914, Generalissimo Grand Duke Nicholas Nikolayevich appealed to the Polish people. [14] He grandiloquently announced that the dreams of the Polish nation would soon come true, for although the living body of Poland had been cut into pieces a century and a half before, its soul did not die, and the "sword which beat the foe at Grünewald had not rusted." [15] At long last a fraternal Polish-Russian reconciliation would be achieved, and a reborn Poland would become free in its religion, language, and autonomy under the scepter of the tsar. Like the joint appeal of the German and Austrian commands, issued five days earlier, the proclamation lacked any precision, and the references to the scepter of the tsar were most significant.

The proclamation of the grand duke, the tsar's uncle, evoked a favorable response from those Poles who adhered to the so-called Russian orientation, who sought reconstitution of prepartition Poland under the Romanov dynasty. It was received with considerable satisfaction in the Allied capitals as well, because it implied that the tsarist government intended to abandon its autocratic rule, thus making the issue of democracy and freedom versus "Teutonic aggression" clearer than ever. [16]

In reality, the grand duke's proclamation aimed at not much more than securing the war support of the Polish population, the loyalty of some half million soldiers of Polish origin, and a further expansion of the empire. Only one month after its issuance, the French ambassador in Petrograd, Maurice Paleologue, informed the Quai d'Orsay that the tsarist government intended to annex eventually not only the German-held territories on the lower Nemen River but also the eastern part of Galicia. The future Poland, as envisaged by Petrograd, would consist of no more than the severely curtailed Polish-inhabited areas that belonged to Germany and Austria before the war. Even that Poland, the ambassador emphasized, would remain under Russian control. [17]

That the French ambassador was well informed became evident after the Russian armies temporarily occupied a part of Austrian Galicia in the autumn of 1914. Without delay, the Russian minister of the interior, Nicholas Maklakov, informed the governors in a secret circular that the proclamation did not apply to any Russian-held lands but only to those Polish-inhabited territories which the grand duke would eventually "conquer." A few months later, on March 30, 1915, the Imperial Council of Ministers formally decided to detach the province of Chelm from Galicia and incorporate it into Russia proper.[18]

Years later, Alexander Kerensky, the hapless premier of the Russian provisional government, described the proclamation as no more than a cover for tsarist "imperialism."[19] Essentially, it was just that. On March 8, 1916, Foreign Minister Sergei D. Sazonov informed his ambassador in Paris, Alexander Izvolsky, that Poland had to be excluded from any Allied discussion. He instructed the ambassador to "oppose every attempt to place the future of Poland under the control and guarantee" of the Western powers.[20] Soon after, he warned Ambassador Paleologue that any Western intervention—"even a discreet intervention"—in Polish matters would place Allied unity in real "danger."[21] Sazonov's warning was of particular significance because fears then existed in Allied quarters that Russia, having suffered painful reverses, might seek a separate peace. Sazonov, himself a supporter of the war, enjoyed confidence in both Paris and London.

Although Sazonov did consider the Polish question Russia's exclusive domain, he also saw a need for concessions to the Poles and sought a positive solution. Subsequently, at his urging, in July 1916, Nicholas II ordered a "draft manifesto proclaiming the autonomy of Poland" to be submitted for his signature "without delay." The future Poland was to consist of the "Polish Kingdom"[22] and the Austrian and German Polish-inhabited areas. It was to have a viceroy as the tsar's representative, its own council of ministers, and two legislative chambers. The country was to be autonomous, except for foreign policy, army, customs, finance, and railways of strategic importance. All of these would remain under direct imperial control.[23]

The manifesto was never issued, because Sazonov had to resign soon thereafter, and the ultrareactionary Stürmer took his place. The latter aimed at a compromise peace with the Central Powers, and that naturally could mean, at best, the prewar status quo for the Poles. Consequently, the intended manifesto had to be put aside—but not for long. In the meantime, the war party prevailed in Germany, and on November 5, 1916, the Two Emperors' Manifesto was issued. Its provisions naturally closed the door to a compromise peace between the Central Powers and Russia. This time Petrograd could not remain silent, and on November 15, the tsar communicated to the Duma his "resolve to reunite the territories of Poland in an autonomous kingdom."[24] A few weeks later, on December 25, he issued an order of the day announcing the creation of "free Poland composed of her three partitions" as one of Russia's war aims.[25] Although the announcement lacked any

data as to the boundaries, government, or international status of "free Poland," nevertheless it obviously further enhanced the Polish cause in the
international arena.

POLES UNDER THE CENTRAL POWERS

Although generally the Poles hoped for the eventual unification and independence of their country, they differed over the ways of achieving their goals.
The most radical among them believed in military-revolutionary action, hoping that one day a conflict between the partitioning powers would offer them
a chance.

Their main area of activities was Russia, because it controlled the greater
part of the Polish population and because its government was the most op-
pressive. Passed on from generation to generation, the idea of armed struggle
for independence had become a national tradition.

In Russia, they had to act secretly. Eventually, however, Austria offered
them opportunities to organize openly and to prepare in safety.

In the Austrian part of Poland, Galicia, the government was more liberal
than in either Germany or Russia, and the Poles enjoyed greater administrative, cultural, and economic autonomy than anywhere else. Austria was also
a traditional enemy of Russia, and Vienna saw in the anti-Russian Poles a
potential weapon. Thus, as early as the end of the nineteenth century, the
Poles in Galicia founded numerous organizations, some extending their activities into Russian-controlled Poland as well. After 1908,[26] when the Aus-
trian-Russian conflict became more acute than ever, the Austrian authorities
began to tolerate if not encourage even paramilitary Polish groups.

Among the Poles active in Galicia on the eve of and during World War I,
Józef Piłsudski played the most fateful role. An extraordinary man, he was
destined to influence the history of his nation more than any other individual.
Born in 1867 in the Russian-held Vilna province, he grew up in a family of
landed gentry where patriotism and revolutionary tradition marked daily life.
As a student of medicine in Kharkov, he joined the socialist revolutionary
movement. In 1887 at the age of twenty, he was arrested by the tsarist police
and deported to Siberia for five years. Released, he joined the Polish Socialist party (PPS), just organized in Paris. At twenty-five, he became chief
editor of the party's underground paper, *Robotnik* (The Worker). But his luck
deserted him, and in 1900 he was arrested again. This time he escaped, left
Russia, and went to the Austrian part of Poland, then to London, then back to

Russia, everywhere and at all times promoting the independence of his country.

After the outbreak of the Russo-Japanese War in 1904, Pilsudski went to Tokyo, hoping to receive aid and arms for his organization and proposing to form military units of Russian war prisoners of Polish nationality.[27] Unsuccessful, he returned to the Russian part of Poland determined to organize secret cadres for the future army. In the meantime, the PPS split, and he became the leader of its Revolutionary Faction, which made an armed struggle for Poland's independence its principal goal. Taking advantage of the growing conflict between Russia and Austria-Hungary, Pilsudski took command (together with his closest collaborator, Kazimierz Sosnkowski) of the paramilitary Association of Riflemen, obtained its legalization in Galicia, and from there secretly extended its operation to Russia.

He considered Russia Poland's principal and natural enemy and the destruction of Russian imperialism a precondition for Poland's independence. For years he hoped for and expected a war in which the occupying powers would clash. He wanted the Poles to take part in that war—but under their own banners and command. Then, when the enemies had exhausted each other, Pilsudski planned to enforce the establishment of a united and independent Polish state.

When the war did break out, the Austrian government agreed to the formation of Polish semiautonomous units and to the establishment of the Supreme (Polish) National Committee with administrative jurisdiction over them. Three brigades were formed, called the Polish Legions, and Pilsudski obtained command of the First Brigade. By that time, he already enjoyed considerable popularity all over Poland, and the distinguished war record of his legionnaires increased his prestige. Although a part of the committee, he and his brigade remained aloof because, at least initially, the committee thought in terms of a future Poland reconstituted from the Russian and Austrian provinces and attached to the Hapsburg Empire.[28] Pilsudski opposed that as well as all other "orientations" and took precautions not to be identified with any of them.

Pilsudski's cooperation with the Central Powers was neither harmonious nor lasting, because he modified his policy soon after the German-Austrian occupation of all Russian-dominated Poland. Instead of building up the Legions, he now began to channel volunteers into the secret Polish Military Organization (POW), which he controlled. He distrusted the Central Powers, did not believe they could be victorious, and did not intend to assist them in their exploitation of the Polish people for their own purposes. Essentially, he saw in the Legions a sort of military school for the cadres of a future independent Polish army. The unwillingness of Berlin and Vienna to assume formal obligations with regard to the future Poland only strengthened his boldness. Eventually, on July 25, 1916, he resigned as brigadier.

His resignation very effectively diminished Polish cooperation with the Central Powers because the Socialist and Peasant parties as well as some democratic groups supported Pilsudski's opposition to the Supreme National Committee. It was to secure the loyalty of the Poles that a few months later, in November 1916, the Two Emperors' Manifesto was issued.

Whatever its inadequacies, the manifesto did represent an important gain for the Poles, and many of them responded favorably, in some quarters even enthusiastically. The general consensus was to make immediate use of it. When, soon after, General Beseler brought to life the Provisional State Council in Warsaw, twenty-five prominent Poles agreed to join it. The council had no more than some rather undefined advisory powers, and all its members were appointed by the Austrian and German governors. Its membership consisted of predominantly right-wing politicians, but some left-of-center political leaders joined too, and Pilsudski agreed to head its department of defense.

The hopes raised by the apparent reconciliation and cooperation between the Poles and the Central Powers were short-lived—understandably so, because essentially neither party (official declarations of good faith notwithstanding) was loyal to the other. The Poles thought of their future and not of the war effort, and the State Council wanted real rather than nominal power. Berlin and Vienna were primarily interested in getting manpower and mass support for the war. As a result, the Central Powers did not take adequate steps to turn the administration of the country over to the council, nor did the council make serious efforts to levy an army. As Hindenburg bitterly complained, instead of the expected hundreds of thousands of volunteers or recruits, only a few thousand reported.[29]

In time both the German and the Austrian governments became increasingly suspicious of the Legions' loyalty as well as of Pilsudski's maneuvering and took measures that provoked a crisis. In March 1917 they demanded a public oath of "fidelity in arms" from all the legionnaires as a demonstration of the "community of aims." Pilsudski, by that time determined to break with the Central Powers altogether, made the issue a matter of principle, vehemently and publicly opposed the demand, and instructed his followers to refuse the oath. He contended that the legionnaires owed their allegiance to the Polish nation and to no one else.

Pilsudski's challenge was only partially successful. The State Council, hard-pressed and anxious to survive, complied with the Austrian-German demand, as did a sizable part of the Legions. But the First Brigade and some other units—altogether over five thousand men—refused. Soon after, on July 22, Pilsudski was arrested and imprisoned in the fortress of Magdeburg; others were either interned (if formerly Russian citizens) or incorporated into Austrian military units.

The July crisis killed any prospects for levying a large Polish army fighting on the side of the Central Powers and gave Pilsudski and his First Brigade an aura of heroism and martyrdom—an important factor in postwar Polish politics. His arrest did not diminish his role, for he left behind him thousands of men and women secretly organized in the POW and fanatically devoted to him. Convinced that Germany would be defeated, they waited for an opportunity to seize power and place it in the hands of their commandant.

THE DECLARATION OF THE RUSSIAN PROVISIONAL GOVERNMENT

Pilsudski timed his challenge well, because in the spring of 1917 the war situation changed dramatically, and the Polish question assumed a new international dimension. The Romanov dynasty collapsed, the United States joined the Allies, the fortunes of Germany and Austria-Hungary became at best uncertain, and the provisional government of Prince Georgi E. Lvov took a step that advanced Poland's cause more than any other previous declaration or act.

In a powerful wave of reaction against tsarist imperialist policies, most of the revolutionary groups in Russia demanded self-determination for non-Russian nationalities, Poles included. On March 28, 1917, the Petrograd Soviet passed a resolution to the effect that "Poland [had] the right to complete independence in national and international affairs," and two days later the provisional government issued a formal declaration on this subject. The "creation of an independent Polish state comprised of all the lands in which the Polish people [constituted] a majority of the population" was defined as a historical necessity and a "reliable guarantee for lasting peace in the new Europe." The frontiers of this reconstituted Poland, the government announced, would be determined by the future Russian constituent assembly, and the new country would enter into a "free military union" with Russia.[30]

As could be expected, the declaration was well received by the Poles, whether in Russia, in German-Austrian controlled Poland proper, or in the West. But its last two provisions aroused criticism, which was well expressed by the Warsaw State Council in April. Poland's right to independence, the council argued, could not be conditioned by military or other commitments. As for Poland's boundaries, not only the will of the future Russian constituent assembly but also the historic interests of Poland and the will of the inhabitants (that is, Ukrainians and Byelorussians) would have to be considered.[31]

The Russian declaration opened new vistas for the Poles. Until then the subject of Poland's future had been rather avoided in both Paris and London, where Poland was considered essentially a domain of Russia, which no one wanted to antagonize. Now, the Russian government itself had publicly and formally recognized the Poles' right to be united and independent. Until then, a number of statesmen in the West had been raising doubts as to whether Poland's independence was altogether in the interest of European stability. Their arguments were now appearing somewhat superfluous.[32]

The apprehensions as to Poland's independence were particularly strong in Great Britain. As a rule, British politicians seemed to agree that the Poles should be accorded self-government; as early as November 15, 1915, the secretary of state for the colonies, Bonar Law, had mentioned in the House of Commons that Poland had a right to be restored as a nation.[33] He cautiously failed to state, however, whether Poland had a right to full independence.

First Lord of the Admiralty Arthur J. Balfour, looking far into the future, saw a genuinely sovereign Poland as a possible hindrance rather than an asset to the interests of France and Britain. In a formal memorandum to the war cabinet on November 13, 1916—just one week after the issuance of the Two Emperors' Manifesto—he argued against the idea of an independent Poland. He thought such a Poland would "relieve" Germany "of all fear of pressure from Russia" by geographically separating the two countries and making it possible for Germany "to turn her whole strength towards developing her Western ambitions." Should this happen, Balfour said, France and Great Britain might become "sufferers." Furthermore, he argued, Russia might increase its interest or expansion in the Far East if it were cut off from western Europe by an independent Poland. This should also be avoided. "The more Russia is made a European power rather than an Asiatic power, the better for everybody," he maintained. "The solution of the Polish question which would best suit our interests," he concluded, "would be the constitution of Poland endowed with a large measure of autonomy while remaining an integral part of the Russian Empire." Otherwise, the future Poland, "far from promoting the cause of European peace would be a perpetual occasion for European strife." He strongly emphasized that an independent Poland could never become an "efficient" buffer state between Germany and Russia.[34]

As late as March 1917—a few days before the Russian provisional government formally recognized Poland's right to independence—Balfour still argued before the war cabinet that a fully sovereign Poland would weaken the chances of the Western powers vis-à-vis Germany. By the nature of things, he reasoned, such a state was bound to "protect" Germany against Russia. Would this be in the interest of the Western powers? he asked.[35]

Balfour's views carried great weight because since December 1916 he had occupied the post of foreign minister and also because others shared them, and not just the British. On the contrary, until the collapse of the Romanov dynasty, official French quarters considered the Franco-Russian alliance a historical necessity and an autonomous but Russia-bound Poland the most effective means for encircling and containing Germany. On the eve of the Russian Revolution in March, in a secret exchange of opinions and notes between Paris and Petrograd, a secret understanding was reached. The tsarist government promised to support France's territorial claims against Germany and the Quai d'Orsay recognized Russia's freedom in establishing its western boundaries. According to this understanding, the future Poland would consist of no more than areas formerly belonging to Germany and Austria and would be attached to Russia as an "autonomous" unit.[36]

It was in the still-neutral United States rather than in any Allied country that the Poles found their first open, direct support. The efforts of several million Americans of Polish descent on behalf of the "old country," President Woodrow Wilson's idealism and his belief in the principle of national self-determination, as well as the untiring efforts of the widely respected artist and statesman Ignacy Paderewski, contributed to the popularity of the Polish cause. Paderewski gained the ear of Wilson's influential advisor Colonel Edward M. House and through him that of the president. Subsequently, less than three months after the publication of the Two Emperors' Manifesto (and before the Russian provisional government's declaration), the president took a public stand in Polish matters. In his "Peace without Victory" address of

January 22, 1917, he included a statement that resounded throughout the world:

> No peace can last, or ought to last, which does not recognize and accept the principle that governments derive all their just powers from the consent of the governed, and that no right anywhere exists to hand peoples about from sovereignty to sovereignty as if they were property. I take it for granted, for instance, if I may venture a single example, that statesmen everywhere are agreed that there should be a united, independent and autonomous Poland.[37]

Although Wilson's assertion that "statesmen everywhere agreed" certainly could be disputed, the declaration, coming from the head of a powerful nation, created a sensation and immense enthusiasm among the Poles.

THE WESTERN ALLIES AND THE "AUSTRIAN SOLUTION"

In the second half of 1917, Allied policy on Poland shifted again, this time because of the military situation. In July the Russian provisional government committed itself to a general offensive against the Central Powers and failed, causing disappointment in the Allied capitals and pessimism about the future of the new regime. The reliability and strength of the Kerensky government began to be widely questioned and Russia's future effectiveness in the war seriously doubted.

The worsening situation in Russia had its impact on the Polish question, and in the Allied chanceries a new argument emerged: namely, that the future Poland should be considered in the *Austrian* rather than the Russian context. If Poland was offered to the Hapsburgs, they might be able to check postwar Germany more effectively than could the new, unstable Russia. Besides, such an offer, together with other concessions, might induce Austria-Hungary to withdraw from the war and conclude a separate peace.

From July to August 1917 some informal and unofficial conversations took place between Count Abel Armand, an officer of the Second Bureau of the French General Staff, and Count Nicholas Revertera, who represented the Austrians. Armand suggested that Poland, "restored to its frontiers prior to Partitions of 1772," might be attached to the Hapsburg monarchy in a personal union. The French General Staff favored such a solution, hoping that Poland, so reconstituted, would be "irreconcilably hostile" to revolutionary Russia. Should Poland become a part of the powerful multinational empire, it might also be able to check Germany in the east, thus providing for stability and a balance of power in Europe.[38]

The informal negotiations were carried out in utter secrecy, and the Russian provisional government had no knowledge of them. Years later the exiled Kerensky would complain bitterly, condemning the Allies for what he considered two-faced diplomacy and worse.[39]

Nothing came of the Franco-Austrian conversations because of Emperor Charles's attitude. Like his government, he wanted to end the war, but he was also unwilling to abandon his German ally. He wanted peace but would seek it only in tandem with Germany. Since it was evident that in order to buy peace Germany would have to renounce at least Alsace-Lorraine, the emperor decided to recompense his ally with his own possessions. Using the German crown prince as intermediary, Emperor Charles let it be known that if Germany were to renounce Alsace-Lorraine, he was prepared to renounce all Austrian-held Polish territories and "help to incorporate the kingdom so formed with Germany." In return for a "slice" of its territory in the west, "Germany would gain a Kingdom in the East," he argued.[40]

The emperor's offer proved futile because German military leadership still hoped for victory. The Polish issue continued to be used as bait, however, this time by Great Britain.

The Bolshevik seizure of power in Russia on November 7, 1917, finally ended any British support for the "Russian solution" to the Polish question. Lenin's principal slogan was "a separate peace," and his regime was looked upon with contempt in London. As a result, plans to break up the solidarity of the Central Powers assumed greater importance than ever before. British prime minister Lloyd George hastily instructed the Foreign Office to "take advantage of every overture which might lead to a separate peace with Austria."[41] Without delay, in mid-December 1917 Whitehall established high-level secret contacts with Austrian authorities, impressing upon them the advantages of an early and separate peace. Jan C. Smuts acted as spokesman for Britain, and the former Austrian ambassador to Britain, Count Mensdorff, represented Foreign Minister Count Ottokar Czernin.

As on so many other occasions, Poland's future was part of the negotiations. Discussing the advantages to Austria of a compromise peace, Smuts observed that the Allies were "pledged to an independent Kingdom or State of Poland." However, the future Poland "should not have a German orientation," he added. If Austria were willing to break away from Germany, the Allies, Great Britain included, would not "exclude" the attachment of Poland to the Hapsburg Empire either on the basis of a personal union or in some other way. Since Russia had disintegrated, Smuts reasoned, a strong Austria would be needed in postwar Europe. The British government realized this and did not intend to weaken or partition Austria; on the contrary, it wanted the Hapsburg monarchy to be strong so it could play a salutary role in European affairs. He concluded that the Austro-Hungarian Empire might and should play the same stabilizing role in Central Europe that the British Empire had been playing "for the rest of the world."[42]

The British initiatives failed because—against all odds—Vienna decided to stand by Germany to the bitter end. The Treaty of Brest-Litovsk was signed soon afterward, on March 3, 1918, by Austria-Hungary and Germany on one side and Bolshevik Russia and Ukraine on the other, thus sealing the solidarity of the Central Powers. But the treaty also offered tremendous opportunities to the Poles and their cause.

THE POLES IN THE WEST

The Russian provisional government's declaration of March 1917, together with the improved fortunes of the Allies, brought to the fore those Poles who were active in the West and led by Roman Dmowski.

Born in 1864 in the Russian part of Poland, Dmowski led the rightist National Democratic Party before the war. A member of the Duma, he became one of the most prominent leaders of the Polish deputies. He was a nationalist, striving to unify all Polish areas. He considered Germany Poland's main enemy and, unlike Pilsudski, believed that Polish-Russian understanding and cooperation were necessary conditions for Poland's security. Initially—before the war and during its early stages—he saw the future Poland as being in some sort of union with Russia through the Romanov dynasty.

Even before the war Dmowski and his party commanded a considerable following among the Poles, not only in Russia but in Germany and Austria as well. The National Democrats emphasized political "realism." Their social program was marked by moderation, and they gave priority to "organic" work—building schools, organizing cooperatives, and establishing industries and commerce, thus strengthening Poles culturally, economically, and socially. They wanted to create a Polish middle class. Strongly nationalistic, they viewed with hostility Jewish influence on and contributions to Polish society. Followers of free-market economy, they also opposed the Socialists because of their revolutionary activities and Marxism. Until the end of his life (January 2, 1939), Dmowski was an implacable opponent and rival of Pilsudski.

The grand duke's proclamation of August 1914 was in line with Dmowski's policies, and, like many other Poles, he reacted positively. At that time he expected that the tsarist government would proclaim the restoration of prepartition Poland. When he realized that Petrograd did not intend to accomplish this, and when Russia lost all Polish-inhabited territories to the Central Powers, he went to the West—first to London, then to Switzerland, and finally to Paris. There, together with other prominent, and mostly right-wing, compatriots, he fostered well-organized, effective international activities on behalf of Poland.

Once in the West, Dmowski and his organization pinned all their hopes on Allied victory. They saw in their undivided support of the Allied cause the best guarantee for a restored Poland. Before long they established excellent contacts with British, French, and American officials, as well as gaining support from Polish communities throughout Europe and the United States. Eventually, they extended their activities to all major Allied countries, considering themselves the only free representatives of Poland's interests. In time most of the Allied officials recognized them as such. Dmowski also won respect for his loyalty to the Allied cause, and his views were listened to attentively.[43] Besides, he had the wholehearted support of Paderewski, who, because of his international fame and the admiration he inspired, had access to the most influential Allied leaders.

Although Dmowski's organization did enjoy respect and sympathy, its chances were at first limited because the Allies did not want to antagonize the tsarist government. The emergence of the Russian provisional government, however, and its March declaration, served to internationalize the Polish question and gave the Poles a powerful argument for official recognition. Observing the growing enthusiasm among the Poles dispersed in western Europe, Canada, and the United States, and realizing the importance of the military factor, Dmowski also decided to seek volunteers for a Polish army to take part as a national unit in Allied war operations. In the United States, Paderewski appealed for one hundred thousand men.

The French government was the first to respond to the military request. On June 4, 1917, it officially decreed the organization of an "autonomous Polish army" led by Polish officers and fighting under Polish banners, although subordinate to the supreme French command. Polish volunteers from France, Canada, and the United States, as well as German and Austrian war prisoners of Polish extraction, were allowed to join the ranks. Interestingly, this move had been recommended by the Russian provisional government,[44] which, like its predecessors, considered the Polish issue a sensitive one, had greater confidence in France (Russia's traditional ally) than in other countries, and was particularly apprehensive of the American interest in Polish matters.

Soon after, on August 15, the Polish National Committee reconstituted itself as an official "representation of Polish interests." Dmowski became its chairman and Paderewski its official representative in the United States. On September 20 France was the first Allied government to formally recognize the committee. Great Britain recognized it on October 15 and Italy on October 30, and the United States followed suit on December 1.

Formal recognition of the committee still did not mean a formal commitment to restore a fully sovereign Polish state. The Bolshevik seizure of power, however, and Lenin's announcement of withdrawal from the war changed the situation. Dmowski could now argue not only that such a commitment would result in weakening the Central Powers in the Polish-inhabited areas but that an independent Poland might replace a hostile Russia in checking Germany in the east. He impressed upon the Allies that unless the Poles were reunited as an independent nation, they might fall under Bolshevik influence. By the same token, he reasoned, a strong Poland would become a natural barrier against Bolshevik expansion. The last argument was bound to appeal to the Allies, for at that time, anti-Bolshevik intervention was contemplated in some quarters, and the use of Polish military forces, particularly those in Russia, seemed attractive.

Dmowski pressed for an official commitment from the principal Allies to "reconstitute an independent Polish state comprising Polish territories which before the war belonged to Russia, Germany, and Austria."[45] The Quai d'Orsay responded favorably. At the insistence of Lloyd George, the Inter-Allied Conference decided against the appeal. Lloyd George contended that a declaration of such scope should be left to individual governments without binding others, counseling that the Allies should avoid any final commitments or final political decisions "which would risk the prolongation of the war."[46] Lloyd George's objections turned out to be quite understandable, for while they debated at the conference, General Smuts was engaged in secret negotiations for a separate peace with Austria—the "Austrian solution" of the Polish question constituted a part of the bargain.

Individual declarations on Poland's future soon followed. On December 12 the Italian prime minister, Vittorio Orlando, referred to Poland's independence in parliament. On December 27 the French foreign minister, Étienne Pichon, formally stated in the Chamber of Deputies that Poland "united, independent, indivisible, with all guarantees of free political, economic, and military development"[47] was his government's goal. One month later, on January 5, 1918, the British prime minister publicly, though less formally, asserted that "an independent Poland, comprising all those genuinely Polish elements who desire to form a part of it, is an urgent necessity for the stability of Western Europe." Then, President Wilson proclaimed his historic Fourteen Points in the Senate of the United States. The thirteenth, dedicated to the Polish issue, was more precise and went further than any other war declaration: "An independent Polish state should be erected which should include the territories inhabited by indisputably Polish population, which should be assured a free and secure access to the sea, and whose political and economic independence and territorial integrity should be guaranteed by international covenant."[48]

The tremendous power and prestige commanded by President Wilson, support from the Quai d'Orsay, as well as Vienna's decision to stand by Germany finally cleared the way for a long-sought joint Allied declaration issued at Versailles on June 3: "The question of a united and independent Polish state, with free access to the sea, constitutes one of the conditions for a just and durable peace and rule of rights in Europe."[49]

Once the official Allied declaration was issued, the status of the Polish National Committee in Paris was changed. On June 22 the First Division of the Polish army swore its allegiance to Poland in a formal public ceremony. On September 28 the committee's full authority over the "autonomous, allied, and cobelligerent" Polish forces commanded by General Józef Haller was recognized.[50] By then, the committee had become the official representative of the Polish nation in the West and was strong enough to secure for Poland the status of a full-fledged ally of the victorious powers.

THE EMERGENCE OF AN INDEPENDENT POLAND

While in the West Dmowski's committee was increasingly successful in its dealings with the Allies, in the homeland Poles were gaining more and more control over their own destinies.

Pilsudski's demonstration and his arrest in July 1917 further undermined whatever confidence the Poles had in the Central Powers. Discontent grew and the March Russian Revolution did not fail to have an influence on the radical elements. The State Council became unpopular and soon resigned. Eager to calm the Poles and still hoping for some cooperation, the German and Austrian governments created a seemingly more attractive body. On September 12 the Regency Council was established in Warsaw by imperial decrees to act in the name of the future Polish monarchy. The council, comprising three nationally known personalities—Archbishop Alexander Kakowski, Prince Zdzislaw Lubomirski, and Count Józef Ostrowski—was given a sort of semisovereign status. It did not obtain, however, clearly defined powers.

On December 7 the Regency Council appointed a cabinet headed by a prominent historian, Jan Kucharzewski. Although the new quasi-government depended heavily on the German governor, General Beseler, and through him on Berlin, it succeeded in promoting extensive activities, particularly in public education, justice, finance, and social affairs. From its inception it aimed at reorganization and polonization of as many sectors of public life as possible and at laying foundations for the Polish state structure. Its mere existence, as well as its patriotism and organizational efforts, were of undisputed value.[51] The Central Powers largely tolerated this state of affairs, eager to preserve tranquility in the rear guard. Faced with the growing certainty of their losing the war, they probably also considered the ersatz kingdom a possible bargaining point at the future peace conference.

After August 1918 it became evident that Germany and Austria were going down to defeat. In September Hindenburg and Ludendorff informed the emperor that, militarily, the war could not be won. For the Regency Council, the approaching collapse of the Central Powers meant an opportunity to strengthen its authority and formally register Poland's aspirations. In a widely circulated manifesto of October 7, the council expressed the will of the nation to have full independence, to recover all lands lost in the partitions, and to acquire free access to the sea. The manifesto also announced preparations for national elections to the Sejm, which would assume fully sovereign powers.[52]

Whatever its qualities and the efforts of its staff, the council lacked popularity in many quarters, notably among the Socialists. They were critical of its German-Austrian antecedents and considered it a stronghold of monarchism and reaction. When invited to join its cabinet, they refused, thinking more of its overthrow than of cooperation. Their hostility did not diminish even with the appointment of Pilsudski—at that time still interned in Magdeburg—as minister of defense. On the contrary, on November 7 the Socialists and several leftist factions suddenly formed a provisional people's government in Lublin, thus directly challenging the council and creating conditions for civil war. Pilsudski's followers formed the backbone of this rival government.

The resulting confusion lasted but a few days. One day before Germany signed the armistice, November 10, Pilsudski, by now a legendary figure, was released from internment and returned to Warsaw. He commanded such popularity and prestige that within hours the Regency Council dissolved itself altogether and transferred its civilian authority to him. At that time many expected him to support the Lublin government, but he did not. Instead, he made the group dissolve itself. Then he assumed the role of temporary head of state; publicly announced that social reforms as well as the form of government would be decided by Sejm; appointed one of his trusted companions, Socialist Jedrzej Moraczewski, head of government; and decreed general elections for January 26, 1919. He also let it be known that once the Sejm was elected, he would place himself at its disposal.

At that time, Pilsudski's main concern was not political issues or social reforms but the formation of a unified, strong national army. For, while November 1918 inaugurated peace in western Europe, in Poland it inaugurated a new two-front war that came from the east. The representatives of the victorious powers who gathered at Versailles two months later could neither stop nor control it. Poland had to fight alone both for its political future and for its eastern boundaries.

NOTES

1. Leon Grosfeld, *Polityka Panstw Centralnych wobec Sprawy Polskiej w Latach 1914–1918* (*The Policy of the Central Powers Toward the Polish Question in 1914–1918*) (Warsaw: Panstwowe Wydawnictwo Naukowe, 1962), 18–29, 39–42, 47–50, 58–60, 89–92.

2. For the full text, see Stanislas Filasiewicz, ed., *La Question Polonaise pendant la Guerre Mondiale* (Paris: Section d'Études et Publications Politiques du Comité National Polonais, 1920), 5.

3. For the role Poland was supposed to play in the proposed Mitteleuropa, see Grosfeld, *Polityka Panstw Centralnych*, 54–69.

4. Ralph Haswell Lutz, *The Fall of the German Empire*, 2 vols. (Stanford, CA: Stanford University Press, 1932), 1:316.

5. Gordon A. Craig, *The Politics of the Prussian Army, 1640–1945* (New York: Oxford University Press, 1956), 318–20.

6. Graf Stephan Burian von Rajecz, *Austria in Dissolution* (London: E. Senn, 1925), 96–162; also Prince Bernhard von Bülow, *Memoirs of Prince Bülow*, 3 vols. (Boston: Little Brown and Co., 1932–1936), 3:274.

7. Bülow, *Memoirs*, 3:278–79; also Sir George Buchanan, *My Mission to Russia*, 2 vols. (London: Cassell and Co., 1923), 2:19.

8. Ralph Haswell Lutz, ed., *The Causes of the German Collapse in 1918* (Stanford, CA: Stanford University Press, 1934), 281.

9. For the text, see Lutz, *The Fall of the German Empire*, 1:760.

10. Bülow, *Memoirs*, 3:17, 28, and 279, respectively.

11. Maurice Paleologue, *An Ambassador's Memoirs*, 3 vols. (London: Hutchinson & Co., 1923–1925), 3:83.

12. US Department of State, *Foreign Relations of the United States* (Washington, DC: US Government Printing Office, 1916), supp. 1, 797. Hereafter cited as *FRUS*.

13. See the report of the American ambassador, dated December 5, 1916, *FRUS*, 1916, supp. 1, 798; also David Lloyd George, *War Memoirs*, 6 vols. (London: Ivor Nicholson & Watson, 1933–36), 2:958.

14. For the text, see Frank A. Golder, ed., *Documents on Russian History, 1914–1917* (Gloucester, MA: Peter Smith, 1964), 37.

15. Reference to the famous Polish Lithuanian victory over the forces of the Teutonic Knights in 1410.

16. *Times* (London), September 25, 1914, 3.

17. See Paleologue's dispatch of September 14, 1914, Golder, *Documents on Russian History*, 57.

18. Filasiewicz, *La Question Polonaise*, 14 and 20, respectively.

19. Alexander Kerensky, *The Crucifixion of Liberty* (New York: John Day, 1934), 163.

20. Filasiewicz, *La Question Polonaise*, 42.

21. Paleologue, *An Ambassador's Memoirs*, 2:261.

22. Established at the Congress of Vienna in 1815 as an autonomous unit, it consisted of the central part of the Polish-inhabited areas and through a personal union was attached to the Romanov empire. After the unsuccessful Polish uprisings against Russia in 1830 and 1863, its autonomy had been abolished, and for all practical purposes, the area became a province of the Russian empire.

23. Paleologue, *An Ambassador's Memoirs*, 2:297–98.

24. Ibid., 3:91.

25. For the text, see Golder, *Documents on Russian History*, 52.

26. The year of the Austrian annexation of Bosnia and Herzegovina.

27. For an exhaustive study on this subject, see Jerzy J. Lerski, "A Polish Chapter in the Russo-Japanese War," *The Transactions of the Asiatic Society of Japan*, third series, vol. 7 (Tokyo, 1959), 69–97.

28. Grosfeld, *Polityka Panstw Centralnych*, 23, 58–60, 62–64.

29. Bülow, *Memoirs*, 3:274–75.

30. Robert P. Browder and Alexander F. Kerensky, eds., *The Russian Provisional Government 1917: Documents*, 3 vols. (Stanford, CA: Stanford University Press, 1961), 1:321–23.

31. For the full text of the declaration, see Browder and Kerensky, *The Russian Provisional Government 1917*, 1:326–27.

32. Roman Dmowski, *Polityka Polska i Odbudowanie Panstwa* (*Polish Policy and the Reconstitution of the State*) (Warszawa: Perzynski, Niklewicz, 1925), 207–8, 218.

33. *5 Parliamentary Debates*, Commons, 75 (1915), 1563.

34. Blanche E. C. Dugdale, *Arthur James Balfour* (New York: G. P. Putnam's Sons, 1937), 330–331.

35. See Balfour's memorandum dated May 18, 1917, to Secretary of State Robert Lansing: US Department of State, *Papers Relating to the Foreign Relations of the United States, The Lansing Papers, 1914–1920*, 2 vols. (Washington, DC: US Government Printing Office, 1939), 2:28. Hereafter cited as *The Lansing Papers*.

36. F. Seymour Cocks, ed., *The Secret Treaties and Understandings* (London: Union of Democratic Control, 1918), 67–74.

37. *US Congressional Record*, 62nd Congress, 2nd Sess. (1917), 54, part 2, 1742. Hereafter cited as *Congressional Record*.

38. G. de Manteyer, *Austria's Peace Offer, 1916–1917* (London: Constable & Co., 1921), 219–32.

39. Kerensky, *The Crucifixion of Liberty*, 338.

40. Charles's letter dated August 20, 1917, see Manteyer, *Austria's Peace Offer*, 227–30.

41. Lloyd George, *War Memoirs*, 5:2498.

42. Ibid., 5:2464.

43. See Balfour's comments on March 26, 1917, *FRUS, The Lansing Papers*, 2:28.

44. Marian Kukiel, *Dzieje Polski Porozbiorowej, 1795–1921* (*The Post-Partitions History of Poland, 1795–1921*) (London: B. Swiderski, 1961), 535–36.

45. *FRUS* (1917), 1, suppl. 2, 787–89.

46. Tytus Komarnicki, *Rebirth of the Polish Republic* (London: William Heinemann, Ltd., 1957), 181.

47. *Chambre des Deputés*, Debats, 1917, session ordinaire, 3795.

48. *Congressional Record*, Senate, 56, part 1, 681.

49. Reddaway, *The Cambridge History of Poland*, 488–89.

50. Dmowski, *Polityka Polska i Odbudowanie Panstwa*, 382.

51. Roman Debicki, *Foreign Policy of Poland, 1919–1939* (New York: Frederick A. Praeger, 1962), 8–9.

52. Kukiel, *Dzieje Polski Porozbiorowej*, 534–44.

Chapter Two

The Versailles Peace Conference, January 18–June 28, 1919

The task of making major decisions at the Versailles Peace Conference, which convened on January 18, 1919, belonged to the Supreme Council, comprising representatives from France, Great Britain, Italy, Japan, and the United States. When the council began its deliberations, the Polish state was already in existence, owing to the disintegration of the German armies and faits accomplis created by Pilsudski. The country, however, had no fixed boundaries.

By the end of the war, Germany occupied a large part of Eastern Europe—the Baltic regions, Byelorussia, Ukraine, and all of Poland. Because of the region's instability and the fear that Bolshevism might spread, the Allies provided in Article 12 of the armistice that the German forces would remain in the territories previously belonging to Russia until further orders.[1] This decision proved unworkable in Poland. On November 11 a spontaneous uprising broke out in Warsaw and other areas, and the Germans were disarmed. Then, three days later, Pilsudski, acting as both the head of state and the commander in chief, reached an agreement with the German soldiers' councils, on the basis of which German armies began immediate withdrawals. On January 26 general elections were held—the first in postwar Europe. On February 10 the Sejm—the first independent Polish parliament since 1795—met in Warsaw. By that time, the evacuation of the German forces was completed, and the authority of the Warsaw government extended from Poznan to Grodno and from Cracow to Lvov.

Poland still had no definite boundaries because the task of defining them formally belonged to the Supreme Council. In addition, from the very first day of the armistice, there was fighting in the east. The Galician Ukrainians, striving for their own independence, rose up in arms and seized Lvov and large areas of eastern Galicia. The Polish-Ukrainian War resulted. The Bolshevik forces tried to fill the vacuum left by the Germans, attempting to extend the revolution as far west as possible. They soon occupied large portions of the Baltic region, seizing Vilna. Pilsudski mobilized all national resources and energies to meet the threat with force, resulting in the Polish-Bolshevik war. Civil war raged in Russia, and for a long time no one could foresee the outcome of the turmoil.

The position of the Poles in Paris was no clearer. The emergence of Pilsudski as head of state aroused some anxiety and misgivings among the Allies. He fought with the Central Powers and was known for his view that Poland should extend far to the east both territorially and politically, resuming the federalist tradition of the prepartition multinational Jagellonian Commonwealth. He was a Socialist and an old political antagonist of Dmowski who, together with Paderewski, enjoyed the full confidence of the Allies and whose National Committee had been formally recognized as the only voice for the Polish nation before the war ended.[2] Pilsudski, a pragmatist, solved the problem in a singular fashion: he appointed Dmowski to head the Polish delegation to the peace conference; Paderewski was appointed premier and foreign minister. Both agreed to serve, thus recognizing Pilsudski's position and, in a way, legitimizing his authority in the West. The moves proved effective. On January 15 the Polish delegation received an official invitation to take part in the conference, and on February 21 the Polish government was formally recognized by the Supreme Council.[3]

In its attempts to determine the boundaries of the new state, the Supreme Council encountered tremendous difficulties and achieved unanimity only rarely. What territories should be detached from the conquered nations for the benefit of the new state? How should Polish aspirations to the commonwealth lands be reconciled with the Wilsonian concept of national self-determination? Should the new state contain only ethnically Polish areas? Should historical, strategic, cultural, and economic considerations be discarded? What form should the reborn state take in order to serve peace and contribute to postwar Europe in a manner consonant with the divergent interests of the major victors, particularly France and Great Britain? How could the future role of Germany and Russia be envisioned so that the Allies might take an intelligent attitude toward the Polish territorial claims? These were only a few of the questions that the Supreme Council had to answer.

The council's legal authority over Polish territorial issues was also unclear. Both Germany and Austria understood from the beginning that they would have to recognize the Allies' decisions regarding their postwar boundaries. Accordingly, in Article 87 of the Treaty of Versailles, the council reserved to itself the right to trace the Polish frontiers on the previously German territories.[4] Galician territory proved more complicated. Although in Article 91 of the Treaty of Saint-Germain-en-Laye Austria had recognized the council's right to dispose of its possessions,[5] the decision regarding Galicia was problematic. Although Poland's acquisition of western Galicia, a purely Polish area, was not questioned, opinions differed as to eastern Galicia which, although historically Polish, had a two-thirds Ukrainian majority.[6] The Ukrainians wanted independence. The Poles claimed the whole region on historical grounds. The Russians—both the Whites and the Bolsheviks— wanted to incorporate the Galician Ukrainians into the Russian Ukraine and to rule them from Moscow.

The most difficult task was the establishment of a boundary in the formerly Russian territories. Historic Poland (before the first partition of 1772) included large areas in the east—Lithuania, part of Latvia, Byelorussia, and the Ukraine up to the Dnieper River—while ethnic Poland was hundreds of miles to the west. Areas of mingled nationalities, creeds, and languages lay in between. The Polish cultural and historical claims to large parts of these areas aroused many apprehensions. Russia had belonged to the Allied camp until the Bolsheviks seized power and, afterward, did not fight the Allies. Thus, although Russia did not participate in the formulations of the peace treaties and was not represented in the Supreme Council, the Council was extremely cautious in disposing of Russia's prewar possessions; to do so could cause grave complications for the future.

This view was strongly advocated by the Political Conference, an unofficial representative group of non-Bolshevik Russians. Headed by Sazonov, it consisted of prominent Russian statesmen such as Socialist Boris Savinkov, former prime minister Prince Lvov, and former cabinet member Maklakov. They did recognize Poland's right to independence and reconciled themselves to the idea of some autonomy for other Russian-dominated nations, but they never wavered in their stand on the "one and indivisible Russia" and defended the legality of the western frontiers as established by the third partition of Poland in 1795.[7] They even demanded eastern Galicia, although it had no Russian population and had never belonged to the tsarist empire.[8] They also threatened that, after the Bolsheviks' collapse, the new government would not recognize any decisions violating Russia's territorial integrity.

Their arguments carried weight because the situation in Russia was very fluid in the early postwar period, and no one could predict what kind of a regime would be established permanently. During 1918 and most of 1919 the Bolsheviks still faced armed resistance led by General Nicolai Yudenich in the Baltic area, Admiral Alexander Kolchak in Siberia and the Ural regions, and General Anton Denikin in the south. If the Bolsheviks were defeated, the future of Russia might become a stabilizing factor in Europe, a natural check on German imperialism. As such, it should not be antagonized or weakened. If the Bolsheviks won, a strong Poland, forming a bastion between Communism and western Europe, seemed desirable. On the other hand, the idea of finding some modus vivendi with Bolshevik Russia, in case the White forces collapsed, also seemed attractive, particularly to the British.

The Polish position was defined officially for the first time by Dmowski at the meeting of the Supreme Council on January 29, 1919,[9] and a few weeks later, on February 28 and March 3, by his memoranda concerning the future boundaries of Poland.[10] He argued that a formal link should be established between the historic and the reborn Polands. The Allies should take the 1772 Polish boundaries as "the point of departure" and "rectify" them according to the new conditions. The principle of an ethnic Poland should be discarded. The long process of denationalization (carried out primarily by Germany and Russia) should be kept in mind, and Poland's centuries-old cultural sway over these lands, together with its economic and strategic needs, should be recognized. Religious preferences should also be taken into consideration, especially in the east. For while the majority of non-Poles in these historically Polish lands were Orthodox or Jewish, most Ukrainians in Galicia belonged to the Uniate Church, which, though of the Eastern rite, recognized the authority of Rome. The Polish, Ukrainian, Byelorussian, and Jewish nationalities were so mixed, Dmowski argued, that the establishment of an ethnic frontier would be impossible anyway. Besides, the council had hardly questioned Russia's multinational composition, and amid the confusion and lawlessness of war, a plebiscite was out of the question.

All the leading statesmen at the Versailles conference—Lloyd George, Clemenceau, and Wilson—recognized that the ethnic consideration, which was used to determine the council's policies and the Polish-German boundaries, was inapplicable in the east. They concluded that an arbitrary decision, based on extensive studies, would have to decide the issue. For this purpose, a special Commission on Polish Affairs (headed by the former French ambassador to Germany, Jules Cambon) was created on February 12, 1919, to conduct the necessary studies and present its findings to the council. Soon, in a unanimous report, the commission confirmed the prevailing opinion and concluded that the settlement of the Polish-Russian frontier on ethnic grounds alone was indeed impossible.[11]

The Versailles Peace Conference was dominated by three powerful personalities—the Father of Victory and premier of France, Georges E. Clemenceau; the prime minister of Great Britain, David Lloyd George; and the president of the United States, Woodrow Wilson. The eighty-year-old Clemenceau, a passionate, obstinate, and at times ruthless man (*le tigre*, as he was called), centered all his policies on and conducted all his activities with the thought of providing maximum security for France. France, after all, had suffered two million casualties and tremendous material losses. Representing the formidable power of the United States, the idealistic Wilson enjoyed unprecedented prestige and personified the hopes of many formerly foreign-dominated nations. For Wilson the key to peace and security lay in a League of Nations, effective and strong because he believed the United States would join it. But he was better at visions than at diplomacy and was not always able to counteract the behind-the-scenes maneuvers of the European politicians. Consequently, it was the dynamic, pragmatic, changeable, self-assured Lloyd George who most often exercised decisive influence—which, as a rule, he used against what the Poles considered their rightful interests.

Throughout the conference Lloyd George argued against the Polish demands and ambitions. Essentially, he was skeptical of the principle of national self-determination for small nations and of the wisdom of creating new states in central-eastern Europe. The attitude of the entire British delegation, according to a contemporary American historian, "was one of sharp impatience with the small powers because they were troublemakers and costly, and so long as they would not settle down, there could be no return to peace, and no revival of normal trade and commerce in which the British (and to a lesser degree Americans) were vitally interested."[12]

From the very beginning, the British prime minister took a negative stand on Polish territorial demands and, above all, on the concept of a "historical Poland." As he expressed it: "These memories of a greater Poland were destined to give trouble to those who sought to settle national boundaries on

ethnological and traditional principles. . . . Their [Polish] claims were by
every canon of self-determination extravagant and inadmissible."[13]

As a result, Lloyd George insisted that the new country be as homogenous
as possible, fearing that a Poland containing large German, Ukrainian, and
Byelorussian minorities, extending too far both westward and eastward,
would have no future.[14] Instead of becoming a center of stability, it would
instead bring about a German-Russo cooperation aimed at Poland's reparti-
tion. He thought that Polish arguments were self-defeating and was vehemently opposed to the idea of Poland as a multinational state. He favored
impartial plebiscites to determine Polish-German boundaries, opposed the
inclusion of Ukrainians and Byelorussians, and usually argued against the
curtailment of Germany and Russia.

Lloyd George's adherence to the traditional balance-of-power policy in
Europe no doubt also influenced his stand. Convinced that the Poles would
become natural satellites of France, whose hegemony in Europe he feared, he
pursued policies that secured a strong position for Germany and, at times,
Russia. This of course had to adversely affect his attitude toward Poland.

Last but not least, the British prime minister was not devoid of idiosyn-
crasies. Harold Nicolson, British participant and later historian of the Versailles conference, noted that Lloyd George "had never been guilty of pro-
Polish sentiments."[15]

Clemenceau favored a different policy, based on what Lloyd George disapprovingly called a "military strategy."[16] Obsessed with a possible revival
of Germany's strength and German revanche, he sought to weaken the old
enemy economically through substantial war reparations; militarily, through
disarmament; and territorially, through reincorporating the Saar and establishing the Ruhr as an independent state. He also wanted to secure new allies
east of Germany who, together with France, would be sufficiently strong to
check the Reich.[17] To France, this represented a matter of vital importance,
he argued, since the old Franco-Russian alliance might no longer be possible.

Clemenceau argued that owing to its geographical position and traditions,
the new Poland, together with Czechoslovakia, Yugoslavia, and Romania,
could replace Russia in the anti-German security system. Poland seemed to
be an ideal partner, and throughout the conference Clemenceau made great
efforts to recreate a strong Polish state at the expense of Germany. He criticized the British delegation because, as he put it, "Great Britain did not take
sufficient interest in Poland. A strong Poland was the best way to avoid a war
between Germany and the Allies."[18] Without his support, the western boun-

daries of Poland would certainly look different, and the Poles knew it. "All that we achieved . . . we owe primarily to France,"[19] wrote Dmowski years later.

Clemenceau's views on Polish-German frontiers largely coincided with the findings of the Commission on Polish Affairs. In March it recommended that Poland receive a part of West Prussia, certain localities in East Prussia, almost all of Upper Silesia, the province of Poznan, and Danzig (Gdansk). The commission opposed Polish demands for the incorporation of the Allenstein (Olsztyn) and Marienwerder (Kwidzyn) districts in East Prussia, recommending instead plebiscites, in agreement with Lloyd George's wishes.[20]

Wilson was essentially for an ethnic Poland. He had no illusions as to Clemenceau's policies. "The only real interest of France in Poland is in weakening Germany by giving Poland territory to which she has no right," he commented in April 1919.[21] Because of his conviction that the League of Nations would become an all-powerful regulator of international justice, he was skeptical about the historical, strategic, or military arguments of the Poles. Neither did he favor plebiscites, preferring instead firm and final decisions by the council, based on impartial, competent, and scholarly studies. But he also had great sympathy for the Poles. Wilson considered the partitions of Poland a crime, viewed Poland's revival as a triumph of justice, and was thus anxious to accommodate the Poles. His friend, collaborator, and intimate confidant, Colonel House, catered to his chief's sympathies, he himself believing in a strong Poland. Professor Robert H. Lord, the leading expert on eastern European affairs in the American delegation, more than shared Colonel House's views. Lloyd George called them all "fanatical pro-Poles."[22]

The differences between the British and the French policies toward the new Poland were accentuated by their divergent views on international security and Russia. The French considered that Britain, a maritime power, had already obtained maximum security and advantages through Germany's loss of its navy, merchant fleet, colonies, and foreign trade, while France failed to obtain treaty guarantees from Britain and the United States.[23] Clemenceau had little confidence in the League of Nations' ability to prevent future wars and was very conscious of the fact that the Bolsheviks had replaced the tsarist government in Moscow, thus ending Russia's role as a traditional French ally. Therefore, he considered the creation of a new Poland—a buffer against both German and Bolshevik expansion—a necessity.[24]

Supporting the Poles fully in their claims against Germany, Clemenceau was cautious, however, on Poland's eastward territorial aspirations. He regarded the Bolsheviks with invariable enmity and at times even advocated using an Allied military expedition to crush them.[25] When that became impossible, he still hoped that the Bolshevik regime would sooner or later collapse. Consequently, Clemenceau wanted to avoid any serious territorial curtailment of what he hoped would be a non-Bolshevik Russia, a decisive force in checking Germany from the east. Essentially, he favored an ethnic Poland in the formerly Russian-controlled areas.

Lloyd George was pragmatic and flexible. Russia was, first of all, a valuable market for British industrial products and an unlimited source of cheap raw materials. To do business with Russia, Britain needed political stability there, not turmoil. Because the Bolsheviks were troublemakers, he did not wish them well. But once he came to the conclusion that the White forces had no chance either to seize or to maintain power, he wanted regular relations with the Bolsheviks. In January 1919 he opposed Clemenceau's policy of a cordon sanitaire against the Bolsheviks.[26] The temporary successes of the White armies changed his mind in May. But, by the end of the year he decided to stop all aid to the disintegrating White forces, incongruously advocating both a "barbed-wire fence" and trade relations with the new regime. "The moment trade was established with Russia, communism would go,"[27] he confidently assured the Supreme Council on January 14, 1920.

As a result of those divergent views and positions, compromise decisions on Polish-German boundaries were the only ones reached by the Supreme Council,[28] while the situation in Russia and developments in eastern Europe precluded final and enforceable decisions on Poland's eastern frontiers altogether. Thus, Poland received Poznan Province (and the so-called *corridor*, which provided access to the sea) and separatist Prussia from Germany proper. In two provinces of East Prussia, Allenstein and Marienwerder, plebiscites were to be held. A plebiscite also was to decide the future of Upper Silesia. Danzig was declared a free city under the protection of the League of Nations and was included in the Polish customs system. Poland was accorded unrestricted use of the harbor and political representation of the city in international affairs. It was a compromise decision reluctantly approved by the French and Americans. Lloyd George vehemently opposed giving Danzig to Poland unconditionally.

In addition to the decisions concerning the Polish-German boundaries, the Supreme Council requested that the Polish delegation (as well as the delegations of Czechoslovakia, Yugoslavia, Romania, Greece, Bulgaria, Hungary, and Turkey) sign a convention for the protection of national and religious minorities. The members of those minorities were to have a right to send their complaints to the League of Nations for consideration and redress. Since the convention somewhat limited the sovereignty of the countries in question, all of them, Poland included, only reluctantly complied.[29]

The provisions of the Treaty of Versailles were subsequently criticized in many quarters. Giving Poland access to the Baltic while denying it unrestricted control of the Vistula estuary would never work, and to Danzig's dissatisfaction, the Poles eventually decided to build their own port, Gdynia. Nor did the plebiscites satisfy everyone. The plebiscites in East Prussia were held on July 11, 1920, when the Red Army stood at the gates of Warsaw and the fate of Poland seemed uncertain. The overwhelming majority voted for Germany, thus deciding the future of the area. The plebiscite in Upper Silesia took place on March 20 of the following year, with over 60 percent voting for Germany. Because the plebiscite was carried out by the communes and some of the communes proved to be predominantly Polish, the area was partitioned according to ethnic lines. This solution, insisted upon by the French, dissatisfied Lloyd George, who thought the entire province should be kept by Germany.[30] The Germans and the Poles were not satisfied, either. While the latter accused Germany of pressuring the population at the time of the electoral campaign, the Germans bitterly criticized the partition of a province which had formed an entity for centuries. As to the obligations toward national minorities, the Poles resented them, particularly since Germany, with a considerable Polish population, was not required to assume equal responsibilities.

Because the Allies had no power of enforcement in that area, Poland's eastern boundaries were not included in the Treaty of Versailles. Instead, the Supreme Council reserved for itself the right to make a decision later, at some unspecified date. For all practical purposes, this left Poland and Russia to settle the question either through war or through negotiations. They would make use of both.

NOTES

1. For the text: US Department of State. *Papers Relating to the Foreign Relations of the United States. The Paris Peace Conference, 1919*, 13 vols. (Washington, DC: US Government Printing Office, 1943), 2:4. Hereafter cited as *US Paris Peace Conference.*

2. On November 13, 1918, the French government even recognized the National Committee as the Polish government de facto. See M. Leczyk, *Komitet Narodowy Polski a Ententa i Stany Zjednoczone, 1917–1919* (*Polish National Committee, the Entente and the United States*) (Warsaw: Panstwowe Wydawnictwo Naukowe, 1966), 260–62.

3. Only the Japanese member temporarily demurred. See David Hunter Miller, *My Diary at the Conference of Paris, with Documents*, 21 vols. (New York: Appeal Printing Co., 1924), 15:509–10.

4. Harold W. V. Temperley, ed., *A History of the Peace Conference of Paris*, 6 vols. (London: Frowde, Hodder & Stoughton, 1920–1924), 2:207–15.

5. Ibid., 4:134–35.

6. Great Britain, Foreign Office, *Documents on British Foreign Policy, 1919–1939*, ed. Ernest Llewellyn Woodward and Rohan Butler, 1st series, 5 vols. (London: H. M. Stationery Office, 1946–55), 2:736; 3:350. Hereafter cited as *DBFP*.

7. Sergei Dmitrievich Sazonov, *Vospominanya* (*Memoirs*) (Paris: E. Cyaliskoy, 1927), 371–72.

8. Memorandum by the Russian Political Council of March 9 and May 10, 1919, Miller, *My Diary*, 17:408 ff; 18:274.

9. David Lloyd George, *The Truth about the Peace Treaties*, 2 vols. (London: Victor Gollancz Ltd., 1938), 1:313; 2:972–76.

10. For the text, see Dmowski, *Polish Policy*, 617–22 and 623–25, respectively.

11. Temperley, *History of the Peace Conference*, 6:242–44; also Edward M. House, ed., *What Really Happened in Paris* (New York: Charles Scribner's Sons, 1921), 84.

12. Ray S. Baker, *Woodrow Wilson and World Settlement*, 3 vols. (Garden City, NY: Doubleday, Page & Co., 1922), 1:398–99.

13. Lloyd George, *The Truth about the Peace Treaties*, 2:72.

14. Ibid., 1:405–09.

15. Harold Nicolson, *Curzon: The Last Phase, 1919–1925* (Boston: Houghton Mifflin & Co., 1934), 203.

16. Lloyd George, *The Truth about the Peace Treaties*, 1:311; 2:978–1000.

17. Edouard Briault, *La Paix de la France, les Traités de 1918–1921* (Paris: Librairie du Recueil Sirey, 1937), 33f; also Winston Churchill, *The Great War*, 3 vols. (London: G. Newness, Ltd., 1933–1934), 3:1434.

18. *DBFP*, 1st series, 2:736.

19. Dmowski, *Polish Policy*, 264.

20. For the meetings of the Supreme Council on March 19, June 2, and June 3, see *US Paris Peace Conference*, 4:413–19 and 6:138–46, 147–55, respectively.

21. Baker, *Woodrow Wilson and World Settlement*, 2:60.

22. Lloyd George, *The Truth about the Peace Treaties*, 1:311; 2:991.

23. George Clemenceau, *Grandeur et misères d'une victoire* (Paris: Plon, 1930), 194–95.

24. *DBFP*, 1st series, 2:736–37, 745.

25. Lloyd George, *The Truth about the Peace Treaties*, 1:320, 356–58; also Nicolson, *Curzon: The Last Phase*, 208.

26. *DBFP*, 1st series, 2:744, 748.

27. Ibid., 874.

28. See Temperley, *History of the Peace Conference*, 6:246–65.

29. For the text, see German Foreign Office, *Documents on the Events Preceding the Outbreak of the War* (New York: German Library of Information, 1940) (*The German White Book*), 5–7. Hereafter cited as *GWB*.

30. For a documented treatment of the issues involved in the French and British policies, see Piotr S. Wandycz, *France and Her Eastern Allies, 1919–1925: French-Czechoslovak-Polish Relations from the Paris Peace Conference to Locarno* (Minneapolis: University of Minnesota Press, 1962), 225–37.

Chapter Three

The Polish-Bolshevik War and the Curzon Line[1]

As early as August 29, 1918, the Council of People's Commissars, headed by Lenin, "annulled forever" all agreements pertaining to the partitions of Poland and formally recognized the "inalienable right of the Polish nation to decide its own fate and to become united."[2] There were many indications, however, that Lenin thought of a Communist, not a "bourgeois," Poland, and that the Red Army's westward drive was to ensure the success of his policy. Besides, to Lenin, Poland was a corridor leading to Germany, where revolutionary forces seemed to be in ascendancy. He hoped that once the Bolsheviks joined hands with German Communists, "bourgeois-capitalist" Europe would collapse.[3]

In trying to push the Bolshevik forces eastward, Pilsudski pursued two goals. He certainly wanted to seize areas that had belonged to prepartition Poland. But he also wanted to create conditions that would enable the non-Russian nations to break away from Moscow.

Pilsudski feared that a Poland sandwiched between Germany and Russia might be unable to secure its independence. Consequently, he aimed at reducing Russia's territorial holdings. He strongly believed that Russian domination over the multiple nationalities of the defunct tsarist empire had to be ended. For him the best guarantee of Poland's security was in having Russia—any Russia, Red or White—confined to the ethnically Russian lands. He always viewed with sympathy the struggle for independence of the Balts, the Byelorussians, the Ukrainians, and the Caucasus nations, and saw Poland's interest in their success. He also nurtured far-reaching plans of bringing a

39

free Poland, Lithuania, Byelorussia, and the Ukraine into some form of coop-eration—federation, confederation, or alliance—thus creating a bloc of coun-tries between the Baltic and Black Seas strong enough to withstand both German and Russian expansion. In fighting the Bolsheviks, he even refused to cooperate with the White generals because they strove toward the goal of a "one and indivisible" Russia.[4]

For some time there was also fiery fighting between the Poles and the Galician Ukrainians. On November 1, 1918—just at the time of the final disintegration of the Austro-Hungarian armies—the Ukrainian regiments oc-cupied the main centers of eastern Galicia and soon after proclaimed the Western Ukrainian People's Republic. Their initial successes were short-lived, however, because the Poles offered effective resistance, particularly in the ethnically Polish city of Lvov.[5] In May 1919 the Poles started a general offensive and by July had driven the Ukrainians beyond the Zbrucz River, the eastern border of prewar Austria. In the wake of these military successes, the Polish administration took uneasy possession of all territories once seized by Austria through partitions of Poland.

These developments were observed closely by the Supreme Council, which at that time sought, above all, stability in Galicia, particularly because of events in neighboring Hungary. There, on March 21, 1919, Béla Kun seized power and established a Communist regime. Less than three months later, on June 16, the Slovak Soviet Republic was proclaimed. When Kun's authority began to disintegrate, he appealed to Moscow for military aid. The Bolsheviks were expected to respond favorably to Kun's appeal, which meant that Russian assistance would flow through Galicia. Thus, the stabil-ization and strengthening of the region was imperative. As a result, even the British, who consistently opposed the inclusion of eastern Galicia into Po-land, recognized the urgent need for at least temporary Polish military con-trol over the province.[6] That, in turn, required a decision concerning the area's political future.

The Commission on Polish Affairs was charged with making the prelimi-nary study of the Polish-Ukrainian problem and with recommending work-able solutions. The inquiries took some three months, and on June 17 the commission presented the Council of Foreign Ministers with three alternate solutions: (1) establishment of a mandate over the Galician Ukrainians, to be administered by the League of Nations or by one of the great powers; (2) incorporation of the area into Poland, unconditionally or under a special autonomous statute; or (3) creation of a provisional authority to take over until a plebiscite could be carried out. Although no one particular solution seems to have been favored by the commission, independence for the Galician Ukrainians was not recommended. Most members of both the Supreme Council and the commission considered the inhabitants of the area unready for independence, chiefly because of their high illiteracy rate and general backwardness.[7] Ceding the region to Russia was also not contemplated: Galicia had never been part of the Russian empire and had few if any ethnic Russian inhabitants.

Whatever the solution, a boundary had to be drawn between western (indisputably Polish) and eastern (predominantly Ukrainian) Galicia. The commission therefore traced two boundaries, leaving the eventual adoption of one of them to the Supreme Council.[8] Line A assigned Lvov, Drohobycz, and the rich oil fields to the Ukrainian area, while Line B left them in what was considered Poland proper. If Line A were approved, approximately 1,700,000 Poles would find themselves on the Ukrainian side. If Line B were accepted, approximately 1,000,000 Poles would be separated from Poland proper while roughly equivalent numbers of Ukrainians would reside within the Polish borders. In the event the Supreme Council decided to separate eastern Galicia from Poland permanently, the American, French, and Italian members of the commission declared themselves in favor of Line B, while the British member favored Line A, which was less advantageous to the Poles. None of the solutions proposed by the commission was conclusive or binding upon the Supreme Council, and, naturally, they had no legal international character. Besides, with the exception of the British, all delegations to the Supreme Council "were strongly in favor of assigning the whole territory as a natural unit to Poland in some form or other."[9]

The issue was discussed by the foreign ministers of the Supreme Council on June 18 and again on June 25, resulting in a unanimous compromise decision authorizing the Poles to introduce and maintain their own administration over *all* of eastern Galicia up to the Zbrucz River to "safeguard the integrity of persons and property of the peace-loving population . . . against dangers arising from Bolshevik gangs." The Poles were to ensure autonomy for eastern Galicia and, at some unspecified time, to hold a plebiscite that would finally determine the future of the area. Thus, the Polish administration was to have only a provisional character.[10]

The council's decision could not but arouse wide dissatisfaction among Poles. In military terms it meant no more than a confirmation of the status quo. In June 1919 most of the province was occupied by the Polish forces anyway, and Polish administration functioned almost everywhere. Making that administration provisional and subject to future plebiscite was considered unfair. Protests followed in Warsaw and Paris, and they did educe either sympathetic response or outright support from both the French and the American delegations.[11] Lloyd George, however, continued to oppose permanent inclusion of the province in Poland under any circumstances, and his will prevailed. Subsequently, on November 21 the Supreme Council itself voted the so-called Statute of Eastern Galicia, implementing the views of the British prime minister. Poland would have a "mandate" over the disputed area for a period of twenty-five years. Then, the Council of the League of Nations would "maintain, revise or modify" the statute on the basis of a plebiscite.[12]

The council's decision was made under unusual circumstances, and eventually it lost its validity. First, the chairman of the Commission on Polish Affairs, Jules-martin Cambon, voiced his opposition. Then, the American delegation formally registered its misgivings in a memorandum entitled "Summary of American Position Regarding Eastern Galicia."[13] The Poles were not informed about the decision and were not asked to accept it formally. It nevertheless became known in Warsaw, and vehement opposition was raised. Pilsudski even hinted to the British envoy, Horace Rumbold, that should the Allies persist in their policy he might stop fighting the Bolsheviks and come to an understanding with them.[14] Clemenceau, after second thoughts, considered the decision imprudent. At that time he was advancing his ideas of building a cordon sanitaire to separate Bolshevik Russia from western Europe; a strong, confident, anti-Bolshevik Poland seemed to him indispensable. Consequently, on December 11 he asked Lloyd George to reconsider his stand. The latter reluctantly agreed, and on December 22 the council decided that "the decision recently taken at Paris, granting to Poland a mandate of twenty-five years over Eastern Galicia, ought to remain in suspense and be the subject of a new examination to be conducted later."[15] Thus, the Polish claim to all of Galicia was to be held in abeyance until a definitive council decision. That decision was never to be reached, although the matter would reappear later.

While there was no agreement among the Allies regarding the Polish boundary line in the formerly Austrian Galicia, a unanimous decision concerning the previously *Russian-held* territories was reached and announced at the beginning of December 1919. By then the Polish-Bolshevik war had subsided somewhat,[16] and in Russia, the Bolsheviks won spectacular victories over the White armies of Denikin in the south and Yudenich in the Baltic areas. The diminishing chances of the counterrevolution caused Lloyd George to change his attitude toward Lenin's regime, and on November 17 he indicated in the House of Commons that his government had decided to stop aiding the anti-Bolshevik forces. In agreement with Clemenceau, he now pressed for a policy of a "barbed-wire fence" around Communist Russia. The purpose of such a policy was to bring peace with Moscow on conditions somewhat acceptable to the latter, to contain Communism within Russia itself and then wait either for its collapse or its evolution. [17]

The Supreme Council's formal decision concerning the Polish-Russian boundary was taken on December 8, 1919:

> The Principal Allied and Associated Powers, recognizing that it is important as soon as possible to put a stop to the existing conditions of political uncertainty in which the Polish nation is placed, and without prejudging the provisions which must in the future define the Eastern frontiers of Poland, hereby declare that they recognize the right of the Polish government to proceed according to the conditions previously provided by the treaty with Poland of June 28, 1919, to organize a regular administration of the territories of the former Russian Empire situated to the west of the line described below. . . . [A detailed description of the line follows.] The rights that Poland may be able to establish over the territories situated to the East of the said line are expressly reserved. [18]

The line described by the council corresponded roughly to the boundary of imperial Russia after the third partition of Poland in 1795. Formal as it was, the decision contained significant qualifications. First, it applied only to the territories that had belonged to Russia; no reference was made to Galicia. Second, the *final* frontier had yet to be decided. The Supreme Council did not consider the line specified in the resolution as a permanent frontier but, on the contrary, explicitly reserved Poland's right to territories "situated in the east." Significantly, great caution was exercised in deciding not to reveal the declaration to the public. At that time, the Bolshevik armies stood no less than 250 miles east of the line recommended by the council. [19]

In the meantime, Lenin's government, probably fearing that Pilsudski might join forces with the already disintegrating White armies of Denikin, informally approached the Poles offering territorial concessions and peace negotiations. The first official proposals were issued on December 22 by Georgi Chicherin, the people's commissar for foreign affairs. Then, on January 28, 1920, new proposals—signed by Lenin, Chicherin, and Trotsky—

followed. After having condemned the "extreme imperialists" for their attempts to "draw Poland into a baseless, senseless and criminal war with Soviet Russia," the Bolsheviks offered an armistice line much farther to the east than the one proposed by the Supreme Council.[20] On February 2 the All-Russian Central Executive Committee sent another appeal, directed this time to the "Polish nation."[21] All these notes and appeals, rather general in nature, were replete with heavy-handed Communist propaganda. Pilsudski had no confidence in them, particularly since he had evidence that the Bolsheviks were preparing for a new offensive.[22]

Whatever his plans and political visions, Pilsudski had to proceed cautiously. His armies were in dire need of weapons and supplies. Many of his compatriots—notably, the National Democrats—favored negotiations and criticized his policies. He was also well aware of the mistrust he inspired in London and Paris. Finally, the secret and exploratory peace talks to which he agreed proved unproductive.[23] As a result, at the end of January 1920 he sent his new foreign minister, Stanislaw Patek, to London and Paris to consult with the Allies and to learn what guarantee or help, if any, they were willing to offer.

The consultations proved fruitless because there was no Allied consensus as to what the Poles should do. The Supreme Council limited itself to generalities.[24] Lloyd George recommended withdrawal from the ethnically non-Polish areas and speedy conclusion of peace.[25] The French were in favor of continuing the war against the Bolsheviks but did not offer any immediate military aid. As for the American minister in Warsaw, he had no instructions on the matter and withheld his opinion altogether.[26]

A few weeks later, on March 27, Moscow rather unexpectedly received a note from Warsaw to the effect that Poland was ready to enter into formal peace negotiations. Without delay, the Bolshevik government answered positively and asked for an immediate suspension of all military activities on all fronts. Pilsudski refused, however, agreeing to no more than a local armistice until the outcome of the negotiations. Furthermore, he demanded Moscow's explicit renunciation of all rights to territories belonging to the historic Polish-Lithuanian Commonwealth. Then, he argued, Poland would determine the commonwealth's future according to the wishes of the population. Moscow refused and an exchange of notes and mutual recriminations followed. The formal peace negotiations never got underway. They could not, because Pilsudski no longer sought peace. On the contrary, in greatest secrecy, he was preparing a military expedition to wrest the Ukraine from Bolshevik control, to establish it as an independent country, and to gain an ally in the east.

Taking advantage of revolutionary conditions, the Russian Ukrainians proclaimed the Ukrainian People's Republic on November 19, 1917, and set up their national government in Kiev. Soon after, on January 22, 1918, they announced their secession from Russia. For a while it seemed that Lenin had genuine sympathy for the national aspirations of the second-largest Slavic nation, but it soon became obvious that he would tolerate only a Communist Ukraine. Subsequently a Bolshevik-Ukrainian war broke out. The Ukrainians tried to get some help from French-supported General Denikin, who fought against the Bolsheviks in the same regions. But he refused to recognize their secession, and as a result the insurgents faced not only the overwhelming Red forces but also the White armies. Against these odds, their cause faltered. Kiev fell to the Bolsheviks on February 19, 1919, and the Ukrainian armies withdrew to the west.

Warsaw viewed these events with grave apprehension and on May 24 concluded a Polish-Ukrainian provisional agreement.[27] According to its terms, the Poles recognized the formerly Russian Ukraine as an independent state and declared that, if formally requested, they would help the Ukrainians militarily. The Ukrainians renounced their claims to eastern Galicia and western Volhynia. In exchange, the Poles promised autonomy to their ethnically Ukrainian citizens. Both governments guaranteed property and equality of rights to their respective national minorities. A special military convention, specifying the extent of mutual military aid, was to be concluded in the future. The terms of the agreement (signed, on the Polish side, by Paderewski) were general, and neither party ratified the accord at that time.

The Ukrainians started a new offensive shortly thereafter, and on August 31 they reoccupied Kiev, only to lose it this time to the advancing White forces of General Denikin, weakening the chances of the nationalist army commanded by Semen Petlura. Before long, the Bolsheviks recovered, won important victories, and again occupied Kiev. Withdrawing westward, the Ukrainians eventually took refuge in Polish-held areas. In a formal declaration issued December 2, the Ukrainians asked the Polish government for military support.[28]

The ensuing negotiations resulted in perhaps one of Pilsudski's most dangerous decisions: to undertake a military expedition aimed at liberating the Bolshevik-controlled Ukraine. Many factors influenced him. Petlura, the central figure in the Ukrainian government and also the commander in chief, convinced the Poles that he had the support of his people, who would rise against the Bolsheviks and assist the liberating forces. The argument seemed plausible; a general Ukrainian uprising did seem likely. But recent Bolshevik victories over the White armies of Kolchak and Denikin and the constantly growing strength of the Red Army concerned Pilsudski, as did the changing attitudes of London and Paris toward Lenin's regime.[29] Pilsudski never trusted Lenin's peaceful declarations, believing that Lenin was playing for time; regardless of any negotiations, Pilsudski assumed the Bolsheviks would eventually resume their westward offensive. Still, confident of his own military superiority, he decided to take advantage of the momentary exhaustion of the Red Army and deliver a deadly blow to Russian imperialism. The emergence of an independent, nationalist Ukraine might strengthen the drive for independence in Byelorussia and other non-Russian nations. It would also enable him to carry out his far-reaching federalist policies. Independent Ukraine, Byelorussia, and Lithuania all allied with Poland—as he envisioned—might change the course of history and eliminate Russia as the dominant power in the east.

After more than four months of secret negotiations and military planning, Pilsudski concluded a formal alliance with Petlura on April 21, 1920. Three days later he signed a secret military convention.[30] Then, without delay, he started a general offensive in the direction of Kiev.

By the terms of the agreements, Poland recognized Ukrainian sovereignty over the territories that belonged to the Polish Commonwealth before 1772 and were seized by tsarist Russia. In exchange, the Ukraine formally recognized Poland's sovereignty over eastern Galicia. The military convention committed the Poles to assist Ukrainians in restoring the independence of their country, defined the conditions and forms of military cooperation, and provided for overall Polish command in war operations. However, Polish assistance and military cooperation were to apply only to the areas belonging to prepartition Poland. Once those areas had been freed and Ukrainian sovereignty over them secured, the Polish forces were to return to Poland and the Ukrainians were to be left to themselves.

Pilsudski's historic decision inaugurated a new phase in Polish-Russian relations and also brought the resurrected state to the brink of collapse. The initial successes seemed impressive: within two weeks, on May 8, the Polish-Ukrainian forces entered Kiev, and soon after Pilsudski received a triumphant, ecstatic reception in Warsaw. The triumph was short-lived; reverses brought the campaign to near disaster. Pilsudski evidently had underestimated the strength of the Bolsheviks, overestimated his own strength, and miscalculated Petlura's military and political resources. The Ukrainian masses failed to actively support the Polish-led expedition. Already on June 11, Kiev had to be evacuated and a general withdrawal ordered. Within the next three weeks, the northern wing of the Red Army took Vilna, the southern wing marched toward Lvov, while the center forced its way toward Warsaw, threatening the very existence of Poland.[31] By the end of July a provisional Revolutionary Committee of Poland, headed by the most prominent Polish Communists, was formed in the rear of the Red Army. Felix Dzierzynski, the dreaded chief of the Bolshevik Cheka, was listed as one of its members. In a proclamation, the Revolutionary War Council forecast a Communist victory in western Europe "across the corpse of White Poland," while Lenin impressed upon the delegates to the Second Congress of Comintern, then in session in Moscow, that the fall of Poland would be a prelude to Communist world victory.[32] Suddenly, more than Poland was at stake. The prospect that the Red Army might join forces with the German Communists hung heavily over the continent.[33]

While Pilsudski was desperately maneuvering at the front, confusion and fear reigned in Warsaw. The government fell on June 9. Politicians wrangled for two long weeks over the composition of a new cabinet. Finally, on June 25, the rightist government of Wladyslaw Grabski was installed. For Pilsudski it meant a political setback, because rightist opinion (led by Dmowski's National Democratic Party, traditionally hostile to Pilsudski and vehemently opposed to his federalist ideas) condemned his Ukrainian expedition and demanded his resignation. Without delay the new government dispatched a delegation—headed by Grabski himself—to Spa, Belgium, where the Supreme Council was deliberating, to request immediate military assistance or ask for mediation.

Although the Communist danger did generate considerable anxiety in Great Britain and France, Poland was generally considered an aggressor against Russia. Particularly in Great Britain, condemnation was widespread. There, the people sought peace, not war, and as to the Foreign Office and Lloyd George, they were always opposed to any idea of carving new states out of Russia. They considered Pilsudski's federalist ideas at best as adventurous, shortsighted, and dangerous to European stability.[34]

On May 18 Comintern appealed to the workers of all countries to oppose aid to the "Polish imperialists."[35] The appeal deepened the indignation that already existed. On June 17 the Belgian government prohibited the sale of arms and even of food to the Poles.[36] On July 20 the German government declared neutrality and forbade passage over its territory of war materiel headed for the Polish front.[37] In Great Britain, Ernest Bevin, together with other prominent trade union leaders, condemned the shipping of aid to Poland, and in August a "Council of Action" threatened Lloyd George with a strike to obstruct any assistance efforts.[38] War transports proceeding through Czechoslovakia were stopped, searched, and refused passage. On August 7 Czechoslovakia officially announced neutrality. Eager to protest the Allies' decisions concerning the "corridor," German workers in Danzig refused to unload shipments destined for Warsaw.[39]

At Spa, it was Lloyd George who played the leading role in the Supreme Council. France was represented by Premier Alexandre Millerand instead of Clemenceau, who retired shortly after the French general elections of November 1919. Millerand, although critical of Pilsudski's expedition, was strongly anti-Bolshevik and unwilling to involve France in any direct relations with Moscow. He preferred to follow Lloyd George's lead.[40] The Italian delegation had no interest in eastern European affairs. The Americans by that time had withdrawn from the European scene for all practical purposes.

The British prime minister fully realized the seriousness of the situation resulting from what he considered Pilsudski's unwise adventure.[41] But he also saw an opportunity to implement his policy toward eastern Europe. For now, the hard-pressed Poles would have to reconcile themselves to a purely ethnic Poland. Then, once the Polish-Bolshevik war ended, with Great Britain acting as intermediary, Anglo-Russian diplomatic and trade relations could be established. The Bolshevik trade mission, headed by Leo Kamenev and Leonid Krassin, had been negotiating in London since May 1920.

After tortuous negotiations, Grabski—who did not conceal his own opposition to Pilsudski's policies—agreed on July 10 to all of Lloyd George's demands in exchange for assurances that the council would either obtain an immediate armistice or, if Moscow rejected the terms, would accord aid to Poland. The armistice line was to be the one that had been provisionally laid down by the council on December 8, 1919; the Polish army was to withdraw to that line and the Bolsheviks were to stop fifty kilometers east of it; in east Galicia, both armies were to stand on the line which they would hold "on the date of the armistice" and then withdraw ten kilometers each. Should the Soviets refuse the armistice and invade ethnic Poland, the Allies were to give Poland all "possible" aid.[42] In addition, Grabski committed his government to abide by the council's decisions concerning the Teschen area, the future of east Galicia, and the status of Danzig. Vilna was to belong to Lithuania.

The terms, as agreed to by Grabski, were harsh. But he felt helpless. An immediate armistice seemed of vital importance, and he realized that no better terms could be obtained. The British prime minister had nothing but contempt for Polish policies. He attacked Polish "imperialism." He castigated the Poles for marching into Russia and occupying territories "containing between 20,000,000 and 30,000,000 Russians [*sic*]." Again and again he repeated that he had always opposed the inclusion of east Galicia in Poland. [43]

Since neither France nor Italy maintained diplomatic relations with Moscow at the time, the British Foreign Office was charged with forwarding the peace proposals. An unsolved mystery still lies behind the story of the British message. [44] The cable was sent the next day, July 11, and, as was later revealed, the foreign secretary, Lord Curzon, had little to do with its wording—he merely signed it as it was handed to him. According to the council's decision, the armistice line consisted of two parts, the northern and the southern. The northern part, running across the territories previously held by the Russian empire, was described according to the council's decision of December 8, 1919. As for the southern part, which ran through Galicia, the proposals stipulated that both armies should remain where they stood on the day of the armistice. By then, that is, mid-July, the Polish-Bolshevik front line was on the River Zbrucz, and all of east Galicia was still held by Polish troops. The reading of Curzon's telegram to Moscow shows an important though hardly noticeable change in the text of the proposal, namely, an additional description of the southern part of the armistice line, coinciding with Line A, the *alternate* line recommended by the Commission on Polish Affairs on June 18, 1919. [45] But the British government had no authorization either from the council or from the Polish delegation to make the change. Moreover, since the actual front was far to the east of the line described, the provision was practically irreconcilable with that clause of the proposal (correctly inserted) which stipulated that "in eastern Galicia both armies shall stand on the line which they occupy on the date of the armistice." The incident has never been fully explained.

The line described in Lord Curzon's telegram, which eventually became known as the Curzon Line, was based on a mystifying error, because the cession of Lvov to Russia had never been decided, either at the Versailles Peace Conference or during the conference at Spa. Besides, the agreement at

Spa lost its validity. Warsaw's observation of the agreement depended on the council's successful mediation for an armistice—a condition not destined to materialize.

Only one week later, on July 17, the Soviet government rejected the proposals, condemned British "interference" in Polish-Russian relations, and expressed willingness "to agree to a territorial frontier more favorable for the Polish people" than that proposed by Curzon.[46] Three days later, a proclamation signed by Lenin offered Poland boundaries "to the east of the frontier marked out by the imperialists of London and Paris."[47] Apparently, the Bolsheviks, confident of their military superiority, preferred to deal with the Poles directly.

The second part of July and the first part of August 1920 marked the most critical period in the life of the young republic. In the West, the Poles were regarded as imperialists and widely criticized for their invasion of Russia. Comintern and the Bolsheviks were appealing for peace, national self-determination, and freedom for all. Moscow procrastinated on armistice negotiations. The Red Army was pushing toward Warsaw. As for the Allied governments, instead of sending the arms and equipment the Poles desperately needed, they dispatched an inter-Allied inquiry mission to Warsaw with D'Abernon and Jules Jusserand as the civilian representatives and General Sir Henry Radcliffe and General Maxime Weygand as their military counterparts.[48]

On July 20 the Foreign Office informed Moscow that the Poles had been urged to come to terms but that Britain would come to Poland's aid if the Red Army passed the line specified in the dispatch of July 11. Two days later the Poles radioed a message to the Soviets asking for immediate armistice negotiations.[49] But the Red Army did not stop its offensive. On July 24 it passed the northern part of the line;[50] on August 1 it took Brest-Litovsk and then crossed the Bug River. Neither France nor Great Britain moved. As became known later, neither of them seriously contemplated dispatching arms or men to Poland.[51]

At the beginning of August the Red Army approached Warsaw, and it seemed that the fate of Poland was about to be sealed. Lloyd George lost no time in adapting his policy to the new situation. On August 10, during the historic debate on Poland in the House of Commons,[52] he declared that regardless of circumstances, he would not involve Great Britain in a war with Russia. He again castigated the Poles for their "attack upon Russia" and declared that the Soviets were entitled to demand from Poland guarantees that would render impossible any similar attack in the future. Having mentioned the importance of an independent, "ethnographical" Poland, he urged the Poles to accept the Soviet terms, unless they were "absolutely inconsistent with the independence and existence of Poland as a free nation." He praised the Poles for being "brave" and making "fine soldiers" but criticized Polish "statesmanship." Having made it clear that Allied troops would not be sent to Poland, he observed rather ambiguously that, should the Soviets present demands incompatible with the independence of Poland, military equipment, advice, guidance, economic pressure, and naval action would be used to help the Poles.

At the end of the debate, the prime minister informed the House that he had just received Moscow's peace proposals, which he read aloud. Moscow demanded the frontier specified in Curzon's telegram of July 11; reduction of Polish military strength to fifty thousand men, including no more than ten thousand officers; organization of a "citizen's militia" with unnamed prerogatives; demobilization of Polish forces within one month; delivery of all arms exceeding the needs of the reduced Polish army and militia to the Red Army; dismantling of war industries; and, finally, prohibition of troops or materiel shipments into Poland. The terms read more like a statute for a satellite than an armistice agreement between two sovereign nations.

Lloyd George did not consider the terms incompatible with the independence of Poland. On the contrary, he immediately notified Warsaw that should Poland reject them, Great Britain would not attempt to obtain better ones.[53] The British representative in Warsaw, D'Abernon, commented later: "These terms were so extravagant that I cannot conceive any Polish government taking them into consideration."[54] It had become evident that Lloyd George was reconciled to Russia's control over Poland. The situation seemed so critical that the French government, which considered the Soviet terms entirely unacceptable, disassociated itself altogether from the British, decided to give its full support to Poland, and informed the Poles accordingly.[55]

The course of events changed because of the unexpected Polish victory at the gates of Warsaw. On July 24, a new Polish government emerged, headed by a prominent peasant leader, Wincenty Witos. The product of a coalition of all important political parties, the government succeeded in mobilizing the public for an all-out national effort. Then the advancing Red Army apparently overextended itself, a fatal error in view of the ever-increasing hostility of the local population. Then, in mid-August, Pilsudski suddenly outflanked the enemy in a masterful maneuver, launched a general offensive, and in the critical Battle of Warsaw forced the Bolsheviks to retreat.

Within the next few weeks, the Polish armies pushed the enemy far to the east. But they were exhausted, and the Warsaw government proposed negotiations. Its only condition was that they be conducted away from the war area, in some neutral country. This time Moscow promptly complied, and on September 21, the negotiations were reopened in Riga, the capital of neutral Latvia. The Supreme Council had no part either in the negotiations or in the subsequent conclusion of the Polish-Russian peace treaty.

The Polish victory over the Bolshevik forces in 1920 was to be viewed by many as one of the most important events in the early postwar years. D'Abernon considered it one of the eighteen most decisive battles in world history.[56] As for Lenin, less than three weeks after the Polish-Soviet war operations ended (on October 8, 1920), he stated publicly in Moscow: "If Poland had become Soviet, if the Warsaw workers had received from Russia the help they expected and welcomed, the Versailles Treaty would have been shattered, and the entire international system built up by the victors would have been destroyed."[57]

NOTES

1. For a comprehensive study on the subject, see Norman Davies, *White Eagle, Red Star: The Polish-Soviet War, 1919–1920* (New York: St. Martin's Press, 1972), 318 pages.

2. For the full text, see General Sikorski Historical Institute, *Documents on Polish-Soviet Relations, 1939–1945*, 2 vols. (London: Heinemann, 1961–1967), 1:1. Hereafter cited as *DPSR, 1939–1945*.

3. For the contemporary Polish secret reports on the activities of the Communist-oriented German troops in the Baltic area, see *Archiwum Akt Nowych, Zespoly Ministerstwa Spraw Zagranicznych* (*New Record's Archives, Folders of the Ministry of Foreign Affairs*) (Warsaw: National Archives), 4475, 64–78, 85, 94–100. Hereafter cited as *AANP-Zespoly MSZ*.

4. For a documented study on Pilsudski's federalist ideas and plans, see M. K. Dziewanowski, *Joseph Pilsudski: A European Federalist, 1918–1922* (Stanford, CA: Hoover Institution, 1969), 379 pages.

5. For the Polish character of Lvov, *US Paris Peace Conference*, 4:409.

6. For Balfour's memorandum on eastern Galicia, ibid., 4:828, 837–39.

7. For the report of the Commission, *DBFP*, 1st series, 3:829–41; for Lansing's and Balfour's views, as expressed at the Council of Foreign Ministers on June 18, 1919, ibid., 844–49.

8. Ibid., 836–41.

9. Temperley, *History of the Peace Conference*, 6:271.

10. *DBFP*, 1st series, 3:844–61.

11. For Dmowski's note of August 25, 1919, ibid., 882–84; for the American memorandum proposing the elimination of the clauses concerning the plebiscite and provisional character of the Polish administration, ibid., 1:784–87.

12. Ibid., 2:378.

13. Ibid., 1:784–86 and 2:383, respectively.

14. For Rumbold's report, ibid., 3:633–36.

15. Ibid., 582; 3:908–09.

16. See *5 Parliamentary Debates*, Commons, 121 (1919), 721–26.

17. *DBFP*, 1st series, 2:744–48.

18. For a full text, ibid., 446–47.

19. The Poles occupied Pinsk on March 8, 1919, Vilna on April 19, Minsk on August 22, and Polotsk on August 28. See William P. Coates and Zelda K. Coates, *Armed Intervention in Russia 1918–1922* (London: Victor Gollancz, 1935), 99.

20. Jane Degras, ed., *Soviet Documents on Foreign Policy, 1917–1941*, 3 vols. (London: Oxford University Press, 1951–1953), 1:177–78 and 179–80, respectively. Hereafter cited as Degras, *Soviet Documents*.

21. For the text, Polska Akademia Nauk, *Dokumenty i Materialy Do Historii Stosunkow Polsko-Radzieckich* (*Documents and Materials on Polish-Soviet Relations*) (Warszawa: Ksiazka i Wiedza, 1961), 2:572–74. Hereafter cited as Polska Akademia Nauk, *Dokumenty i Materialy*.

22. For documentation, see Josef Korbel, *Poland between East and West: Soviet and German Diplomacy toward Poland, 1919–1933* (Princeton, NJ: Princeton University Press, 63), 26–33.

23. Piotr S. Wandycz, "Secret Soviet-Polish Peace Talks in 1919," *Slavic Review* 24 (September 1965): 425–49.

24. Temperley, *History of the Peace Conference*, 6:319.

25. *DBFP*, 1st series, 3:803–05.

26. Polska Akademia Nauk, *Dokumenty i Materialy*, 2:594.

27. For the text, ibid., 2:259–60.

28. For the text, ibid., 2:461–63.

29. See Bonar Law's comments in the House of Commons on May 20, 1920: *5 Parliamentary Debates*, Commons, 129 (1920), 1696–1702.

30. For the texts, as well as critical evaluation of the campaign, see John S. Reschetar Jr., *The Ukrainian Revolutions 1917–1920: A Study in Nationalism* (Princeton, NJ: Princeton University Press, 1952), 300–14.

31. Edgar V. D'Abernon, *The Eighteenth Decisive Battle of the World, Warsaw, 1920* (London: Hodder & Stoughton, 1931), 47.

32. See Vladimir Illich Lenin, *Sotchinenya* (*Works*), 3rd ed. (Moscow: Gosudarstvennoye Izdatelstvo, 1935), 25:398.

33. See *Times* (London), July 29, 1920, 12; *Manchester Guardian*, June 21, 1920, 6.

34. See Zygmunt Gasiorowski, "Joseph Pilsudski in the Light of British Reports," *The Slavic and East European Review* (London) 50, no. 121 (October 1972): 558–69.

35. Jane Degras, ed., *The Communist International 1919–1943: Documents*, 2 vols. (London: Oxford University Press, 1956, 1960), 1:91–92. Hereafter cited as Degras, *The Communist International*.

36. Jacques Bardoux, *De Paris à Spa* (Paris: Librairie Felix Alcan, 1921), 385.

37. Adam Przybylski, *La Pologne en luttre pour ses frontières* (Paris: Gebethner & Wolff, 1929), 139. The author erroneously gives the date as July 25.

38. Nicolson, *Curzon: The Last Phase*, 204. See also Winston S. Churchill, *The Aftermath* (New York: Charles Scribner's Sons, 1929), 280–81.

39. Louis Fisher, *The Soviets in World Affairs*, 2 vols. (Princeton, NJ: Princeton University Press, 1951), 1:237, 264–65; also Ian D. Morrow, *The Peace Settlement in the German-Polish Borderlands* (London: Oxford University Press, 1936), 69–70.

40. *DBFP*, 1st series, 8:506.

41. Nicolson, *Curzon: The Last Phase*, 203–6.

42. For the full text, see Kazimierz W. Kumaniecki, *Odbudowa Panstwowosci Polskiej, Najwazniejsze Dokumenty, 1912–Styczen 1924* (*The Reconstruction of the Polish Statehood, Basic Documents, 1912 January 1924*) (Krakow: Ksiegarnia Powszechna, 1924), 291–92.

43. *DBFP*, 1st series, 8:505, 740.

44. For documentary review of the subject, see W. Sworakowski, "An Error Regarding Eastern Galicia in Curzon's Note to the Soviet Government," *Journal of Central European Affairs*, University of Colorado, 4, no. 1 (April 1944): 1–26.

45. Supra, 48–49. For a full text of the telegram, see *5 Parliamentary Debates*, Commons (1920), 2372–74.

46. For the text, see Degras, *Soviet Documents*, 1:194–97.

47. *Times* (London), July 22, 1920, 11.

48. Nicolson, *Curzon: The Last Phase*, 205.

49. Korbel, *Poland between East and West*, 51.

50. See *Times* (London), July 27, 1920, 14.

51. For the conference on July 16 between Lloyd George, Alexandre Millerand, Field-Marshal Sir Henry Wilson, and Marshal Ferdinand Foch, see Major General Sir C. E. Callwell, *Field-Marshal Sir Henry Wilson, His Life and Diaries*, 2 vols. (New York: C. Scribner's Sons, 1927), 2:253.

52. See *5 Parliamentary Debates*, Commons, 133 (1920), 253–355.

53. *Times* (London), August 14, 1920, 10; see also Bonar Law's statement in the House of Commons on August 16 concerning the government's stand on the Soviet terms to Poland, *5 Parliamentary Debates*, Commons, 133 (1920), 57–73.

54. D'Abernon, *The Eighteenth Decisive Battle of the World*, 73–74.

55. Alexandre Millerand, "Au secours de la Pologne," *Revue de France* (Paris) 12 année, 4 (1932), 587–91.

56. D'Abernon, *The Eighteenth Decisive Battle of the World*, 11–12 and passim.

57. Degras, *Soviet Documents*, 1:218.

Chapter Four

Poland's Eastern, Northern, and Southern Boundaries

A Profile of the Reborn State

THE TREATY OF RIGA, MARCH 18, 1921

The preliminary armistice between the Polish and the Bolshevik armies was signed on October 12, 1920, and one month later, on November 14, formal peace negotiations began in Riga. They were concluded with the signing of the so-called Treaty of Riga on March 18, 1921.[1] At the time of the negotiations, both sides were exhausted, both needed peace badly, and both were ready for a compromise.[2]

According to the stipulations of the treaty, the final frontier between the two countries was agreed upon, peace was established, and the principle of nonaggression and noninterference in the internal affairs of the other party was solemnly proclaimed. Both countries renounced all claims to war damages. Libraries and archives as well as works of art appropriated by Russia at the time of the partitions were to be returned to Poland. Both countries committed themselves not to support any "foreign military action against the other Party." Particularly significant was the mutual commitment not to support any organizations aimed at provoking armed conflict or at overthrowing the social or political form of government in either country. This meant that the Poles gave in to Soviet insistence and agreed to recognize the Moscow-controlled Ukrainian government in Kiev, to disarm the Ukrainian nationalist forces, and to withdraw all support from those Ukrainians and Byelorussians who were still striving for independence from Bolshevik rule. It also meant that Pilsudski's federalist ideas, so essential to his vision of Poland's future, had been formally repudiated. In exchange for the Polish concessions, the Bolsheviks declared their disinterest in the Polish-Lithuanian dispute over Vilna.

Historically speaking, the treaty represented a compromise on the part of Poland, who abandoned its claims to almost half of the territories, approximately 120,000 square miles, belonging to it at the close of the eighteenth century. More than one million Poles were left in the Soviet Union, and approximately 150,000 Russians remained in Poland.[3] The agreement pushed the frontier thirty to sixty miles farther than that proposed by the Bolsheviks in January 1920.

The treaty also represented a compromise on the part of Moscow. Poland gained approximately 42,471 square miles containing a population of four million beyond the line agreed upon by the Supreme Council on December 8, 1919, as well as all of Galicia. The new frontier—running from the Dvina River and the Soviet Latvian border down the Zbrucz River to its junction with the Dnester River—followed rather closely the line of the second partition of Poland in 1793.

Two years later, on March 15, 1923, the Conference of Ambassadors, representing the Supreme Council, recognized the boundaries agreed upon at Riga in execution of Article 87 of the Treaty of Versailles and Article 91 of the Treaty of Saint-Germain. The United States gave its official recognition on April 5, 1923.[4]

Although a compromise, the treaty was viewed in Moscow as a Soviet diplomatic and political victory. That was Lenin's opinion[5] and the official opinion of his successors. As late as 1940, the *Great Soviet Encyclopedia*, an official government publication, concluded the chapter "Polish-Soviet War 1920" as follows:

> On March 18, 1921, the Peace Treaty was signed. In accordance with its provision, Poland kept Galicia and part of White Ruthenia. However, the new Polish-Soviet frontier meant for the White Poles much worse conditions in comparison to those which the Soviet Government suggested to Poland in order to maintain the peace in April 1920. The frontier determined after the Polish-Soviet war runs 50 to 100 kilometers to the West of the line which was suggested at the beginning of the war. This means that Soviet Russia emerged victorious also from this struggle against the forces of counterrevolution.[6]

THE INCORPORATION OF VILNA, 1922

At the end of the fourteenth century Poland and the Grand Duchy of Lithuania (an empire stretching from the Baltic to the Black Sea) were united in what became known as the Polish-Lithuanian Commonwealth. The union lasted almost four hundred years, ending with the partitions of Poland.

In the course of the centuries-long association between the two countries, Polish culture made deep inroads in the grand duchy. Many Polish statesmen, poets, and scientists, as well as much of the nobility, were of Lithuanian ancestry. The same process took place in Vilna (Wilno, Vilnius). [7] In time, it acquired a predominantly Polish character, with Poles and Jews forming the strongest ethnic groups. After the partitions, it emerged as an important patriotic center of Polish resistance against Russia's domination, and it became in the eyes of the Poles an integral part of Poland. The Lithuanians, however, never ceased to see in Vilna the ancient capital of their once independent and powerful country.

In 1915 the Lithuanian areas, together with Vilna, were occupied by the advancing German armies, and the occupation lasted almost until the end of the war. But the eventual collapse of Germany and the disintegration of Russia offered the Lithuanians the same chances the Poles had. They took advantage of them, and just before the surrender of the Central Powers—on November 2, 1918—the Republic of Lithuania was proclaimed.

On January 5, 1919, the Red Army entered Vilna and a Communist regime took over. Because the Bolsheviks lacked the military strength to occupy the entire country, the provisional government moved to the western provinces, having established its temporary headquarters in Kaunas.

On April 19, 1919, the Poles pushed the Bolsheviks out of the city. By then Pilsudski, acting as head of state and commander in chief, still hoped that Lithuania, the Ukraine, and perhaps even Byelorussia, all free and independent from Moscow, could be brought together with Poland into some form of federation, confederation, or alliance. He decided to use the new situation to gain that end and on April 22 issued a proclamation to the "inhabitants of the Grand Duchy" reaffirming the principle of self-determination and announcing that the population would get a chance to decide their political future in secret, equal, universal, and direct elections. [8] He also tried to gain support for his plans from the Lithuanian provisional government. To his disappointment, it firmly refused to revive the old union, fearing a stronger and more populous Poland.

In July 1920 the Bolshevik forces, on the offensive against the Poles, occupied the city again and then "returned" Vilna to the Lithuanians in a formal treaty signed July 12. In exchange, they obtained Lithuania's neutrality in their war with Poland. Warsaw complained to the League of Nations, holding that Moscow had no right to dispose of the city. But the complaint did not fall on friendly ears. The Western powers, particularly Great Britain, had always thought Vilna should belong to Lithuania unconditionally. Furthermore, the Polish prime minister, Grabski, had just agreed to Lloyd George's demand at Spa.

In August Polish forces broke through the Bolshevik front line and advanced far to the east. They bypassed Vilna because Pilsudski forbade them to seize it by force. He still hoped that the Lithuanians could be won over to his federalist policies and realized that an open war against the much weaker neighbor would ruin his plans. Instead, on September 5, 1920, Warsaw asked the League of Nations to act as an intermediary in the Polish-Lithuanian conflict.

Without delay the Council of the League appointed and dispatched to Poland a special commission headed by Colonel Pierre Chardigny, charged with the task of arranging an armistice and establishing a demarcation line between the two countries.[9] Tortuous negotiations followed, but eventually, on October 7, an armistice between Poland and Lithuania was concluded. The demarcation line mutually agreed upon left Vilna on the Lithuanian side. The agreement was to be implemented on October 9, with the League of Nations supervising.

Just as the armistice was to take effect, on October 8/9, General Lucjan Żeligowski occupied Vilna in a sudden move and established a supposedly independent but in reality Polish-controlled "Central Lithuania." He was one of Pilsudski's officers, and his division consisted mostly of Poles from Vilna and adjacent provinces. He was reported to have acted on his own, out of local patriotism, eager to secure the interests of the Polish inhabitants. But it was generally understood that Żeligowski acted on Pilsudski's secret orders. Pilsudski was willing to leave Vilna to Lithuania within the framework of a Polish-Lithuanian federation or confederation. However, faced with opposition, he decided to take the city by force, speculating perhaps that the move might enable him to bring the Lithuanians into some eventual association with Poland. Interestingly enough, the government in Warsaw disassociated itself from Żeligowski's action. The then foreign minister, Prince Eustachy Sapieha, even referred to it as a "mutiny."[10]

Both Paris and London were aware of Pilsudski's scheme and disapproved of it. Four days before Żeligowski's move, Lord Curzon, who sympathized with the notion of a Polish-Lithuanian federation, recommended that the Quai d'Orsay issue a joint warning that the British and French diplomatic representatives would be recalled from Poland in the event Vilna were forcibly occupied by Poland.[11] Soon after, on October 12, the French minister in Warsaw and the British chargé d'affaires, Sir Percy Lorraine, visited Pilsudski, protesting and demanding the return of Vilna to the Lithuanians.[12]

Neither the protest nor the demand produced any results. Pilsudski threatened to resign and go to Vilna as a "plain citizen" in order to protect the interests of "his soldiers" and the Polish inhabitants. At that time, just after his victories over the Bolsheviks, Pilsudski enjoyed tremendous prestige in Poland. Both diplomats concurred that if he carried out his threat, the consequences would be incalculable. So, acting upon the recommendations of their diplomats, Paris and London reconciled themselves to the fait accompli.

The semi-independence of "Central Lithuania" ended in circumstances bound to poison Lithuanian-Polish relations permanently. On January 8, 1922, a general election was ordered. Kaunas protested vehemently, and all Lithuanians as well as many Jewish and Byelorussian inhabitants boycotted the election as an illegal and Polish-controlled affair. Sixty-four percent of those eligible to vote, however, did vote. Shortly afterward, on February 20, the elected deputies almost unanimously called for an unconditional accession to Poland, and a few weeks later the Polish parliament formally voted to incorporate Vilna.[13]

A year later, on March 15, 1923, the Conference of Ambassadors formally recognized Poland's eastern boundaries, and the permanent Polish control of Vilna was no longer an issue. Moscow, however, objected. On March 14, 1923, and then again on April 5, 1923, Georgi V. Chicherin, commissar for foreign affairs, notified Warsaw that Moscow would recognize only a Polish-Lithuanian agreement, not a unilateral decision.[14] The Lithuanians never became reconciled to what they considered an unlawful seizure of their capital. All diplomatic and economic relations between the two countries were broken by Kaunas. There was no transportation or communication over the frontier, and Lithuanians refused to conclude a formal peace treaty with Poland. Vilna was described in the Lithuanian constitution as the capital, and its recovery became the country's most important national goal.

Although Pilsudski's determination secured Vilna for Poland, it was in many ways a personal tragedy and a political failure. He himself was of

Lithuanian stock. Born and raised in Lithuania, he was always conscious of his Lithuanian heritage. His lifelong dream was to bring the two nations together, and he had failed. Clearly, the Lithuanians, like the Ukrainians, considered a close association with Poland a hindrance to their national interests.

THE POLISH-CZECH CONFLICT OVER TESCHEN

Although Poland was partly successful in imposing its will on Lithuania, it failed to protect its own interests against Czechoslovakia. The issue was the city and the province of Teschen.

The coal-rich duchy of Teschen (Cieszyn, Tesin) belonged to the Polish crown until 1335 and then passed to Bohemia. In 1526, together with Bohemia, it became a part of the Hapsburg domains. Once the Czechs became independent, they claimed the 880-square-mile province as their own. The Poles objected on the basis of the ethnic character of the duchy—according to the Austrian census of 1910, there were some 234,000 Poles, 116,000 Czechs, and 77,000 Germans living in the area. Furthermore, just before the final disintegration of Austria-Hungary, on November 5, 1918, the two local political organizations—the Polish National Council and the Czech National Committee—agreed on temporary delimitation of the boundaries on an ethnic basis. Prague, however, refused to recognize the agreement.

On January 23, 1919, Czech troops occupied the entire area just three days before the Polish general elections, in which the Poles of the Teschen province were supposed to participate. Warsaw's protests and a formal appeal to the Supreme Council followed. The council responded favorably to the appeal and pressured the Czechs to withdraw. Subsequently, on February 5, an armistice agreement cut the area in two almost equal parts, and the Poles soon reoccupied their part. Prague protested this time, and the matter went to the council again. In September the Supreme Council decided to determine the future of the province by a plebiscite.

For several months a state of uncertainty prevailed, marked by clashes, riots, and the mutual hostility of the local Czechs and Poles. The conflict reached its climax in July 1920, when the Polish-Bolshevik war took a dangerously unfavorable turn for Poland. On July 10 the Polish prime minister, Grabski, hard-pressed by circumstances, agreed at Spa that the judgment of the council rather than a plebiscite would determine the division of the province. Less than three weeks later, on July 28, the Conference of Ambassadors made a decision, acting in the name of the Supreme Council. Some 490 square miles, including the rich Karvina coal basin, an important railroad center, and some 140,000 Poles were given to Czechoslovakia. No Czechs were left in the area assigned to Poland.

The end of July 1920 marked one of the most critical moments in Polish history. The fast-advancing Red Army already occupied Poland's eastern provinces. The Polish forces seemed inadequate, Warsaw itself was in danger, and the whole future of the young republic seemed to hang in the balance. This time, the Poles could not but comply with the Supreme Council's decision. The resentment, however, was great, and the Czechs, rather than the Allies, were blamed for the loss of what the Poles considered rightfully theirs. The resentment was that much deeper because, as mentioned before, the Czechoslovak government condemned Pilsudski's expedition to Kiev and refused any aid, direct or indirect, to Poland.

All this could not help but poison Warsaw-Prague relations for many years to come.

A PROFILE OF THE REBORN STATE

The recognition of Poland's boundaries by the Conference of Ambassadors in March 1923 formally concluded the process of establishing the reborn state. The new Poland covered an area of 150,041 square miles, inhabited by more than twenty-seven million people. It was the sixth most populous European country and the fifth largest.

From the outset of their national independence, the people of Poland were confronted with tremendous difficulties and wracked with inherent weaknesses.

The country emerged ravaged and poverty-stricken from the war. Almost three-fourths of the territory had been torn up in battles. The eastern front swayed back and forth for several years, each withdrawal marked by new devastation. Some three thousand bridges, nearly two million buildings, and over nine hundred railway stations were destroyed. A large part of the industrial equipment and most of the railroad rolling stock were removed by either German or Russian troops. Approximately one-fifth of all arable land lay wasted. At least two million people were forced to leave their homes because of war operations or measures taken by temporary occupants.

The material losses caused by the war had been estimated at two billion gold dollars and represented proportionately more than the value of the losses suffered by either France or Belgium. However, those countries received German reparations; Poland received none. On the contrary, Poland had to pay a part of Austria's reparations and debts. [15]

As a whole, the country was backward economically. For over 125 years its economic life had been substantially subordinated to the needs of Prussia, Austria, and Russia, which in many respects were more interested in extracting wealth from the acquired areas than in developing them. As a result, some exceptions notwithstanding, the Poles were not affected by the nineteenth-century Industrial Revolution that exerted such a powerful influence in many European nations. When the new state emerged in 1919, the standard of living of the masses was appallingly low, and the economy, until then oriented in three different directions, was unprepared to function as a cohesive entity.

There were no unified laws, no national currency, no adequate foreign or domestic capital. The nation began to rebuild amid ruins, poverty, and backwardness, with inflation assuming monstrous proportions.

Nor did the Poles form a modern entity socially or culturally. Approximately one-third of the entire population could not read or write. The standard of living, rate of literacy, and political coherence were the highest in the formerly German-occupied areas. The tradition of self-government, organizational forms of public life, and higher learning were most developed in the formerly Austrian area. The formerly Russian-controlled provinces in the east were the most handicapped. At the end of the war, some 65 percent of all inhabitants in the eastern provinces and 71 percent of all children from ten to fourteen years of age were illiterate. They had no tradition of enlightened self-government; on the contrary, hostility toward the state organs and officials was considered a patriotic duty.

The country was divided along ethnic, religious, and linguistic lines. Some one-third of its inhabitants belonged to Ukrainian, Byelorussian, Jewish, or German minorities. According to the 1931 census, some 69.0 percent of the population spoke Polish; 13.8 percent, Ukrainian; 8.2 percent, Yiddish and Hebrew; 3.2 percent, Byelorussian; and 2.3 percent, German. Approximately 65 percent were Roman Catholic; 12.0 percent, Greek Orthodox; 10.3 percent, Greek Catholics; 9.5 percent, Jewish; and 2.7 percent, Protestant. [16]

Though the country was so diversified, ethnic Poles had no basic agreement on government policy toward minorities. Pilsudski's federalist ideas were dead—a casualty of the Polish-Bolshevik war and Treaty of Riga. The Socialist, Peasant, and other left-of-center political groups concentrated on economic and social progress. The National Democrats, led by Dmowski, wanted to assimilate the Slavic minorities but opposed assimilation of the Jews. The Moscow-controlled Communists, not numerous but active, wanted the eastern territories to be joined to the Soviet Ukrainian and Byelorussian republics. The center and right-of-center political parties had a majority in the Sejm, and Polish nationalism seemed in ascendancy, threatening to further split the multiethnic society. Nationalism was to grow among the Ukrainians and Byelorussians as well, and attempts to assimilate them into the new nation encountered vigorous and often violent opposition. As for the Jews, the Nationalists' program meant either their permanent alienation or a total exodus of more than three million citizens—both clearly impossible.

The Poles began building their state structure in a political and administrative vacuum. Except for Austrian Galicia and the lowest levels of government, there were neither trained administrators nor well-established, Polish-manned state agencies. The situation was all the more serious since conditions urgently demanded a particularly competent and efficient leadership able to command popular support.

The constitution was adopted on March 17, 1921, and established state and political structures modeled after the French multiparty parliamentary democracy. The all-powerful Sejm was divided into numerous clubs. In time their numbers and political atomization increased. The parties were frequently formed not only according to their programs and ideologies but according to the nationality of their membership.

The Upper House, or Senate, had no power, and the president of the republic was no more than a figurehead. The government was weak and responsible at all times and in all matters to the Sejm. No one political party ever had, or was expected to have, a majority, and only a coalition government could command majority support in the Sejm. The coalitions were short-lived and the party alliances were changing, each change bringing the downfall of the current cabinet. As in France, frequent changes in party coalitions were not always due to important or valid reasons. The multitude of parties, the shapelessness and instability of government coalitions, and the absence of well-defined responsibilities and controls were bound to have a demoralizing effect on the entire society. The French system—so arduous in well-established, homogenous France—encountered even greater obstacles in the multiethnic, young Polish state.

The international picture was no brighter. In the west, the Germans never reconciled themselves to post-Versailles territorial losses. In the east, Moscow-controlled international Communism gave Russia a new and powerful weapon. In the south, because of Teschen, the Poles cast a jaundiced eye upon the Czechs. In the north, because of Vilna, the Lithuanians considered themselves at war with Poland.

All these difficulties and weaknesses made many foreign observers—friends and foes alike—wonder about Poland's future. Friends looked upon the young republic with concern. The foes saw in the new Poland a *Saison-staat*—a country for a season.

NOTES

1. For the full text, see Leonard Shapiro, ed., *Soviet Treaty Series*, 2 vols. (Washington, DC: Georgetown University Press, 1950), 1:105–16.

2. For the Polish stand and views, see the remarks of Stanislaw Grabski, member of the Polish delegation at Riga, Grabski, *The Polish-Soviet Frontier*, 34–36.

3. S. Konovalov, ed., *Russo-Polish Relations: An Historical Survey* (Princeton, NJ: Princeton University Press, 1945), 83.

4. For the texts: *DPSR, 1939–1945*, 1:8–11 and *Polish-Soviet Relations 1918–1943, Official Documents* (Washington, DC: Polish Embassy, 1944), 83.

5. Lenin, *Sotchinenya*, 25:412.

6. *Bolshaya Sovietskaya Enceeklopedya, 1940* (Moscow: Gosudarsviennyi Institut, 1940), 46:247.

7. For a documentary study of the Vilna question, see Alfred Erich Senn, *The Great Powers, Lithuania, and the Vilna Question* (Leiden, Netherlands: E. J. Brill, 1966).

8. For interesting data on Pilsudski's policies at the time, see M. K. Dziewanowski, "Joseph Pilsudski, the Bolshevik Revolution and Eastern Europe," in *Essays on Poland's Foreign Policy, 1918–1939*, ed. Thaddeus V. Gromada (New York: Joseph Pilsudski Institute of America, 1970), 13–29.

9. Piotr S. Wandycz, *France and Her Eastern Allies, 1919–1925: French-Czechoslovak-Polish Relations from the Paris Peace Conference to Locarno* (Minneapolis: University of Minnesota Press, 1962), 181.

10. See his note to Lord Curzon, *DBFP*, 1st series, 11:595–96.

11. Ibid., 641–42, 583–84 respectively.

12. For Lorraine's report, see ibid., 605–7.

13. For statistical and other data, see Waclaw Chocianowicz, "Sejm Wilenski w 1922 roku" (Vilna Sejm in 1922), *Zeszyty Historyczne* 1 (August 1963): 24–44.

14. For the text, see Degras, *Soviet Documents*, 1:379–80 and 382–83, respectively.

15. See Polish Information Center, *The Truth about Poland* (New York: n.p., 1943), 10.

16. Polish Ministry of Information, *Concise Statistical Yearbook of Poland September 1939–June 1941* (Glasgow: Robert Maclehose & Co., 1941), 8. Hereafter cited as *Concise Statistical Yearbook of Poland*.

Chapter Five

German-Soviet Secret Understanding, 1919–1932

Pre-Nazi Germany had no government nor any major political party that favored stable relations with Poland. The prevailing opinion was that Poland would not survive as an independent state and that its early collapse should be taken for granted. The establishment of the Corridor and the Free City of Danzig, as well as Poland's territorial acquisitions in Silesia, were regarded as bleeding wounds, and Germany's eastern frontier was termed *die brennende Grenze*. German enmity toward the *Saisonstaat* was equaled only by their scorn for Poland as an inferior nation and unable to govern itself. Politically, the new state was considered a French satellite, a link in the French system of encirclement. Destruction or dismemberment of Poland—the creation of the *Versailles Diktat*—represented an avowed goal of all pre-Nazi governments and most of the major German political parties.[1]

After the conclusion of the armistice, but prior to the signing of the peace treaty, General Wilhelm Gröner, an influential member of the postwar cabinet, put forward a plan against Poland. He wanted to establish a military collaboration between Germany and the Allies to combat the Bolsheviks; the reestablishment of the prewar German eastern boundary was his condition. On the eve of the signing of the Versailles treaty, he urged President Friedrich Ebert to organize a "*deutsche Irredenta*" in the lost provinces "immediately."[2]

The determination to change Germany's eastern boundaries became a constant factor in Berlin's foreign policy and eventually produced the so-called eastern orientation. Its proponents argued that, as in the past, cooperation with Russia, any Russia, was needed in order to encircle Poland and either break it down or, at least, curtail it territorially. General Hans von Seeckt, who since November 1919 had been head of the Heeresleitung, the camouflaged version of the general staff, subscribed to that orientation. Believing that Communism could be successfully opposed in Germany proper, Seeckt favored the Bolsheviks' westward expansion. "If we cannot for the time being help Russia with the reestablishment of the boundaries of her old empire, we should certainly not hamper her," he wrote on January 31, 1920.[3] On February 9 of the same year, in a conference with his staff officers and departmental chiefs, Seeckt advanced the idea of moving against Poland, establishing contacts with Russia, and, after jointly crushing Poland, marching together with the Red Army against France and Britain.[4]

At the time of the victorious Bolshevik offensive on Warsaw in the crucial summer months of 1920, Seeckt nurtured schemes of an invasion of Poland. But he also realized the risk involved, and when sometime later Bolshevik officials suggested informally active and immediate cooperation, he offered no more than a "benevolent" neutrality in the event of Russia's attack on Poland.[5] Nevertheless, he remained steadfast in his views that a German-Russian collaboration against Poland was a historical necessity. In his memorandum of September 11, 1922, sent to Chancellor Joseph Wirth, he wrote:

> When we speak of Poland, we come to the kernel of the eastern problem. Poland's existence is intolerable and incompatible with Germany's vital interests. It must disappear, and will disappear through its own weakness and through Russia with our aid. . . . The attainment of this objective must be one of the firmest guiding principles of German policy, as it is capable of achievement—but only through Russia or with her help. A return to the frontiers of 1914 should be the basis of agreement between Russia and Germany.[6]

Seeckt was not alone in holding these views. Powerful personalities, particularly in the Auswärtiges Amt and in the Ministry of Defense, considered German-Soviet collaboration mandatory, and for the same reason.[7] On July 5, 1920, just after the Bolsheviks launched their powerful offensive against the Poles, the German cabinet decided formally that "any support of the Poles against the Bolsheviks was out of the question" and declared neutrality, which, in practice, resulted in occasional aid to the Red Army. On August 11 Pilsudski's chief of staff, General Tadeusz Rozwadowski, supplied French,

British, and American military missions with documentation concerning German-Bolshevik cooperation on military intelligence.[8]

Soon after, on July 22, Foreign Minister Walter Simons wrote Chicherin, proposing "resumption of normal relations" between both countries and asking for reassurance that the Red Army in its march through Poland would respect the German boundaries of 1914. He received a favorable reply.[9] On July 24, 1922, Chancellor Wirth, briefing Count Ulrich Brockdorff-Rantzau (who was soon to be German ambassador to Russia), agreed with General Seeckt's view that the Polish problem had to be resolved, either peacefully or by force if necessary. "Poland has to be finished off," he concluded. On October 16 Wirth further elaborated on his views, telling Rantzau that a common boundary with Russia and destruction of Poland should be the goal of German foreign policy.[10]

These opinions were of great significance, because the disarming of Germany following the war had not fulfilled the Versailles treaty's specifications. Large forces remained intact in East Prussia and Silesia and later were even strengthened, while German industrial potential not only did not diminish but expanded quickly, in good measure owing to loans from former adversaries. By September 1921 Germany had 150,000 men in the Sicherheitspolizei, 150,000 in the Zeitfreiwilligen, and 350,000 in the Einwohnerwehr—all armed with grenades, machine guns, and rifles.[11] In addition, numerous volunteer military organizations—the Freikorps—sprang up throughout the country. Socialist leader Hugo Haase told the National Assembly at Weimar that there were more than a million men in these groups.[12]

In the spring of 1922 the eastern orientation found expression in a formal rapprochement between Germany and Russia. Berlin's determination to weaken the strong position of the Western powers, and its hostility toward the new Poland, prevailed over the fear of domestic and Russian Communism. The recently concluded Franco-Polish alliance was generally interpreted as an encirclement of Germany, both politically and militarily. Subsequently, most German political groups, even strongly anti-Communist organizations, agreed that German-Russian cooperation directed against France and its Polish ally should be considered.[13] As a result, the Moscow-initiated German-Soviet Rapallo Agreement was concluded on April 16, 1922. As could be expected, the agreement aroused serious apprehension in Poland, where it appeared especially ominous in view of the US isolationist course and the growing rift between Britain and France.

The Rapallo Agreement corresponded with Seeckt's schemes; in the minds of the Poles it revived memories of Russo-Prussian collaboration against Poland in the eighteenth century. This time the collaboration seemed even more intimate, particularly in military matters.[14] Eventually, and in great secrecy, German pilots and tank experts were allowed to circumvent the restrictions laid down by the Versailles peace provisions and began to train their crews in the Soviet Union. German munitions, aircraft, and chemical factories were constructed and operated on Russian soil. The Soviets, in turn, sent their officers to the War Academy in Berlin to be trained in modern tactics and weaponry.[15] In time, the military cooperation assumed such proportions that secrecy could no longer be preserved. Once bits of information leaked to the public, the whole matter aroused criticism or open opposition, notably among German Socialists. They considered such extended and close cooperation risky and dangerous. Not only was it bound to strengthen Bolshevik Russia but also, they argued, it would enable it to undermine Germany from within through the Communist party. On December 16, 1926, Phillip Scheidemann, a prominent Socialist leader, publicly denounced the Auswärtiges Amt and gave detailed accounts of clandestine dealings between German and Soviet military forces.[16]

Although the Rapallo spirit more or less prevailed in German-Soviet relations until Hitler's accession to power, those relations were neither harmonious nor free from mutual suspicion. The Soviet government, isolated for the most part, feared any German tendencies to gain a rapprochement with the Western powers. On the other hand, many German leaders suspected or feared Moscow-directed Communist international activities. Whatever the nature and intensity of momentary conflicts between these two countries, however, hostility toward Poland was a constant unifying factor.[17]

The first occasion for implementing the Rapallo spirit presented itself at the beginning of 1923, when on January 11 French and Belgian troops occupied the Ruhr to enforce German postwar reparations. The move was not popular in Great Britain or the United States, and France was momentarily isolated. As a result, in May Marshal Ferdinand Foch visited Warsaw and Prague seeking support. The Warsaw visit and the enthusiasm it evoked in Poland prompted public charges in Berlin that the Poles were planning to occupy East Prussia. The Soviet government threatened without delay that should Poland make such a move, Russia would not stay neutral. Although there is no evidence that the Poles were planning such a move, the well-publicized charges together with Moscow's vociferous diplomatic intervention aroused sympathy in many quarters for Germany's revisionist policy, thus weakening Poland's international standing.[18]

On August 13, 1923, Gustav Stresemann was appointed Germany's foreign minister. The so-called Stresemann era, marked by Germany's spectacular successes on the international scene, followed.

By August 1924 the Dawes Plan had substantially eased war reparations, allowing German industry considerable British and American capital and raw materials and opening new markets to the Allies' former foe.

In October 1925 the Locarno pacts stabilized relations between Germany on one side and France and Belgium on the other, with Britain and Italy as guarantors. By having formally recognized and guaranteed only Germany's western frontiers, Rome and London indirectly sanctioned a peaceful German revisionism in the east. By that time Stresemann stated clearly that his government had no intention of recognizing the eastern boundary. On March 19, 1925, he sent a long memorandum—instructions to Rantzau in Moscow informing him about his long-range policy,[19] simultaneously informing Paris and London that his government did not consider Germany's eastern boundary as permanent, would not guarantee it, and, in time, would change it "peacefully."[20]

Six months after the conclusion of the Locarno pacts, on April 24, 1926, a German-Soviet nonaggression pact, the so-called Treaty of Berlin, was signed by Stresemann and the Soviet ambassador in Berlin, Nikolai Krestinsky. Mitigating Moscow's uneasiness about Germany's rapprochement with the West, it reaffirmed the bonds of friendship provided by the Treaty of Rapallo and secured the continuity of political, military, and economic cooperation between the two countries.

Soon after, on September 8 of the same year, Germany was admitted to the League of Nations and awarded a permanent seat on its council. Poland applied for the same privilege and, although supported by France, Italy, and Great Britain, met with effective German opposition.[21] Thus, only eight years after Germany's defeat, it had not only stabilized relations with both the West and the East but was receiving considerable aid and support from both: Great Britain and the United States, in particular, had been providing open economic assistance; Bolshevik Russia had provided secret opportunities for rearmament. Germany's position in the League of Nations was soon recognized as prominent.

These developments were scrutinized by the Poles, who watched Stresemann's activities with growing anxiety. His conciliatory gestures toward

France and Britain were greeted most favorably, and he became extremely popular in many quarters as one of the great architects of peace. He eventually received a Nobel Peace Prize. With regard to Poland, however, he was uncompromising, believing Germany's eastern postwar frontiers were a permanent obstacle to peace. [22] True, he did not propose to change them by war. But both publicly and in his secret diplomatic dealings, Stresemann insisted that his unalterable goal was to modify them.

Stresemann wanted to have his policy toward Poland clearly understood not only in Germany but in Moscow, the Western capitals, and Warsaw. At the beginning of April 1925, during the preliminary negotiations leading to the Locarno pacts, he publicly stated that "peaceful modification" of Germany's eastern frontier represented one of the most basic goals of his policy. On May 18 he again declared in the Reichstag that "nobody" in Germany considered the eastern boundary as "definite." On September 7 of the same year, less than two months before the conclusion of the Locarno pacts, he wrote to the former crown prince of Germany that "the third great task of Germany is the readjustment of our Eastern frontiers, the recovery of Danzig, the Polish Corridor and a correction of the frontier of upper Silesia." In December 1927 he again declared that since "the removal of the Corridor by war was impossible," peaceful means of achieving Germany's unalterable goal would have to be found. [23]

Stresemann was no less outspoken to Moscow. Rapprochement with the Western powers notwithstanding, he did not intend to break with the Soviet Union; he considered both countries' interest in Poland a durable, common bond. On December 13, 1924, Ago von Maltzan, undersecretary in the Auswärtiges Amt, instructed Rantzau to inform the Narkomindel that Germany's contemplated entry into the League of Nations should not be interpreted as Berlin's renunciation of territories lost to Poland or a guarantee of Poland's eastern boundary. "Theoretically" Germany would be committed to Article X of the League's covenant "to respect Poland's territorial integrity." However, the instruction pointed out that this commitment "is no guarantee and hardly has any practical meaning respecting Poland's eastern border" because before entering the League of Nations, the German government would "ensure" its "right to preserve neutrality" in the event of an international conflagration involving the Soviet Union. This, the instruction implied, would give Moscow a free hand toward Poland and "make a League's action nearly illusory." As to Poland's western borders, membership in the League would only help to keep Germany's claims alive, particularly since world public opinion realized that the "present situation is in the long run untenable."[24] Rantzau informed Chicherin nine days later about his government's stand, intimating that the "solution of the Polish question by Germany and Russia lie in forcing Poland back to her ethnographic borders."[25]

On April 5, 1925, Stresemann himself assured Krestinsky that Germany's coming rapprochement with the Western powers would not deprive it of "freedom of action" with regard to the eastern frontier. During the negotiations of the Berlin treaty, he informed Chicherin that should Moscow enter into any agreement recognizing or guaranteeing Poland's boundaries, the German-Soviet treaty could not be concluded.[26]

While securing Russia's cooperation, Berlin carried on a well-planned diplomatic campaign in the West to prove that the revision of the German-Polish boundary was in everyone's interest, including the Poles. Even the line of argumentation was prepared and meticulously defined. On June 30, 1925, the Auswärtiges Amt issued a secret memorandum several pages long; it was to serve as guidance in diplomatic "private talks."

Poland, the memorandum stated, asked for and received access to the sea for economic, not ethnographic or political, reasons. Once German-Polish relations became friendly, the economic reasons lost their validity because Poland's vital trade with Germany "moves overwhelmingly over the dry borders" anyway.

From the military standpoint, the Corridor was indefensible because it was too narrow. It was therefore bound to feed Polish aspirations to incorporate the southern part of East Prussia and detach the rest of the area from Germany in one form or another. Consequently, the Corridor endangered peace.

Because the situation was untenable, the memorandum continued, new solutions had to be found. A plebiscite would not do because of the influx of the Poles and the expulsion of the German population. Merging Danzig with the Corridor to create an independent "neutral state"—suggested in certain British quarters—was impractical because both the Polish and German populations would regard such a solution temporary.

The only practical recourse was the incorporation of the Corridor, together with Danzig and Upper Silesia, into Germany. This would not affect Polish interests adversely because the German government would offer the Poles a free port in Danzig, guarantee them all economic facilities in Stettin and Königsberg, and accord other concessions or rights as necessary for

Poland's healthy development. If circumstances allowed, Poland could even seek and receive recompensations in Memel and Lithuania.

The memorandum recognized that the Poles would see little virtue in the above arguments and anticipated that "pressure" would have to be brought to bear. German-Russian cooperation was the most important element in such a campaign; second in importance would be "pressure" from the Anglo-Saxon countries, from whom Poland needed financial aid and who could make such aid contingent on Poland's "sacrifice in the interest of general peace."

With territorial revision accomplished, the Poles would have a good neighbor in Germany because the Germans no longer wished either to weaken or to partition Poland. On the contrary, they wanted Poland to be prosperous and "in certain circumstances" would even be ready to renounce all other claims, such as Posen (Poznan), inhabited by Germans. [27]

Berlin's revisionist campaign had some prospect of success because at that time, politically and economically, Poland seemed to be on the edge of collapse. From November 1918 to May 1926, fourteen cabinets fell. [28] The governments depended on the parliamentary majority, which in turn had to be built on the shifting sands of ever-changing party coalitions and maneuverings. Antagonism among the numerous parties was rife not only because of their conflicting ideologies and programs but because of their differing ethnic makeup—an extremely important factor in a country with more than 30 percent of the population belonging to various national minorities: Ukrainian, Byelorussian, Jewish, and German.

On December 16, 1922, Gabriel Narutowicz, the first president of the republic, was murdered by a nationalist fanatic, and soon afterward the government passed into the hands of a rightist coalition. By then, Pilsudski had limited his activities to military matters. A passionate opponent of the constitution, he refused to serve as president of the republic, although the Sejm initially offered him the post. Disgusted, he resigned as chief of the general staff in May 1923 and left Warsaw with a final blast of angry criticism and warning, ostensibly retiring from public service. He would return three years later—a different man, in a different role.

The country seemed to be on the verge of economic disintegration. Inflation could not be stopped, and the foreign trade sector was in deficit. The successive governments could not balance the budgets or control prices and wages. The national currency, the zloty, set up in 1924, originally had an official dollar parity of 5.16, yet by March–April 1926, after much depreciation, some twenty banks failed to meet the demands for panicky withdrawals.

By then the official dollar-zloty rate was 1 dollar to 9.9 zloty, while the dollar brought twelve zloty in the free market. With more than one-third of the industrial labor force unemployed, street demonstrations and riots increased. Poland's chances of obtaining foreign loans became almost nonexistent.

Poland's internal situation accommodated Stresemann's policy of peaceful revisionism, as evinced by the ensuing Polish-German "tariff war."[29] According to the Treaty of Versailles, for a period of five years—until January 1925—there was to be a free flow of products into the Reich from those Polish provinces previously a part of Germany, devised to avoid economic breakdowns in those areas. The Geneva Economic Convention, which was concluded between Poland and Germany on May 15, 1922, determined that certain products, particularly coal, could be exported to Germany duty-free for three years. As a result, approximately 45 percent of all Polish exports went to the Reich. When the convention was about to expire, Berlin announced its willingness to conclude a new agreement, but only if the Poles would accept numerous political conditions. When Warsaw rejected these conditions in June 1925, Germany halted duty-free imports of Silesian coal. Retaliating, Poland passed a series of laws that, although apparently designed to correct the trade balance and stabilize the currency, also blocked many German imports. Berlin then placed prohibitive tariffs on many Polish imports, including foodstuffs, timber, petroleum, and zinc, simultaneously withdrawing German capital from Polish banks. Warsaw escalated the conflict by imposing still further prohibitions and restrictions on German imports. A sort of economic warfare resulted.

The Poles eventually found new markets at home, in Great Britain, in Scandinavia, and in the Baltic countries. Their trade balance, previously in the red, became favorable, and Germany proved to be the heavier loser.[30] Still, the years 1925 and 1926 were extremely difficult. Loss of the German market seriously upset the Polish economy for some time.

The situation in Poland was well known in the West and aroused apprehensions in not a few quarters. Poland's economic collapse, it was argued, might provide an opportunity for militant Communism and thus undermine general security in Europe. These apprehensions were particularly strong in Great Britain where, since the end of 1924, the Soviet government and the Comintern had become extremely unpopular because of their policies vis-à-vis the Far East and western Europe. Many argued that Polish-German reconciliation and cooperation would increase international stability, and thus the Poles should be induced to accept the necessary territorial revisions.

In January 1925 the German embassy in London reported that the British and American governments probably would help the Poles, with the proviso that Poland reach "an economic understanding" with Germany. The report seemed well founded because one year later, on February 27, 1926, the British ambassador in Berlin, D'Abernon, agreed with Stresemann that good German-Polish relations were in everyone's interest, that they required territorial readjustments, and that, in spite of Polish "chauvinism," the "absurd" Polish-German boundary would have to be changed "as soon as possible." D'Abernon well realized the extent of Berlin's claims because Dirksen—complying with Stresemann's secret memorandum of June 30, 1925—briefed him on the subject shortly beforehand.[31]

The assumption that Poland's economic stability was conditioned by Germany's cooperation and aid eventually led to an initiative by the governor of the Bank of England, Montagu Norman. He approached the German ambassador, Friedrich Sthamer, in March 1926 to explore the possibility of German financial assistance to Poland in exchange for modified German-Polish boundaries. He also forwarded his plan to the president of the Reichsbank, Hjalmar Schacht.[32]

The initiative, certainly unauthorized by Warsaw, brought a reaction indicative of Stresemann's long-range attitude. Informed about the conversations, he refused to pursue the matter, arguing that the situation was not yet ripe for such an initiative. He welcomed Britain's support of Germany's territorial claims, considered it valuable, and wanted Germany to have a "hand in the game in order to influence its development to our [German] taste." However, he said that "unless Poland's economic and financial crisis has reached an extreme degree and has brought Poland's entire body politic to a condition of impotence," no Polish government would agree to territorial changes. Besides, he thought Germany's international position was still too weak for such a plan. He reiterated that the Corridor, Danzig, Upper Silesia, and certain parts of Central Silesia would have to return to Germany, concluding: "Only the unconditional restoration of sovereignty in the areas in question can satisfy us."[33]

Stresemann's arguments apparently appealed to Norman, for he even contemplated using his influence "to prevent" Poland from receiving *any* foreign loans until the Poles agreed to "earnestly deliberate the Danzig Corridor and the Upper Silesia question."[34]

At that time—May 1926—Pilsudski seized power through a military coup.[35] Convinced that the parliamentary democratic system of government would provide neither political coherence nor national unity, he finally decided to impose both by force. The greater part of the officers' corps was devoted to him, and he enjoyed immense moral prestige. Besides, the government and the political parties wanted to avoid a bloody civil war. As a result, after some three days of fighting in Warsaw, he seized power and held the reins of Polish politics until his death nine years later.

Pilsudski well realized the dangers of Poland's international situation, and, having always considered Russia to be his country's primary enemy, he was eager to reach some accommodation with Germany. Several approaches toward Berlin followed, all unsuccessful—territorial issues remained an insurmountable obstacle.

On December 10, 1926, Poland's new foreign minister, August Zaleski, met Stresemann in Geneva with a proposal to end the tariff war. There could be no normalization in German-Polish relations unless a "solution of the frontier problem" was found, answered the German statesman in straightforward language. To avoid any misunderstanding, he specified Danzig, Upper Silesia, and the Corridor as the "problems" in question.[36]

Having failed with a direct approach, Pilsudski tried an indirect method. At the end of 1927 the Polish delegation to the League of Nations introduced a motion proposing nonaggression agreements between *all* members with disputes. Stresemann gained French and British support to oppose the motion, and it was defeated.

In December 1927 Pilsudski himself went to Geneva to meet Stresemann. He assured him of his goodwill toward Germany and of his desire to establish good relations.[37] This time he was not entirely unsuccessful, and shortly thereafter negotiations began, resulting in a number of technical conventions. On the essential points, however—liquidation of the tariff war and a political détente—the negotiations proved unproductive. They were broken off six times, and finally, in March 1930, when the long-negotiated treaty was signed, the Reichstag refused to ratify it.

The principal theme in Berlin's policy toward Poland—avoidance of normalization and refusal to conclude agreements that implied recognition of the existing boundaries—prevailed until 1933, regardless of who headed the government or the Auswärtiges Amt. In February 1930 Stresemann's successor, Julius Curtius, impressed upon the cabinet that German-Soviet relations should not be allowed to deteriorate in view of the Polish question. On July 3 he told the British ambassador, Sir Horace Rumbold, "in particularly energetic terms" that his country would never renounce its claim to the lost territories. [38]

Germany's entry into the League of Nations and its permanent membership in the League's council afforded Berlin ample opportunities to attack Poland diplomatically, particularly on the issues of Danzig and the German minority. [39] The Polish-Danzig convention, concluded under the patronage of the Supreme Council on November 9, 1920, resulted only in a continuous tension between the Free City and Warsaw. Because Danzig was under the League's protection, nearly one hundred disputes, many of them trivial, went to Geneva for decision. The increasingly Berlin-oriented and highly organized German minority in Poland of some 800,000 also had the right to bring complaints to the League's council because of Poland's obligations resulting from the convention for protection of national minorities. Those disputes and complaints multiplied after Germany took its seat in the League's council, and they were usually interpreted by the German representatives as evidence that radical territorial changes in Poland were unavoidable. [40]

At that time Germany's domestic situation began to change rapidly. In 1929 the worldwide economic depression struck Germany with growing unemployment, decreasing wages, desertion of foreign capital, multiple bankruptcies, and economic chaos. In the winter of 1931 almost six million Germans were unemployed, and several key banks had to suspend payments. The economic crisis resulted in the growth of the extremist parties (National Socialist and Communist), increasing political instability, excesses, and demagoguery.

The Nazis became particularly abusive and violent, condemning the "Versailles Diktat" and calling for the revision of Germany's boundaries. Their press campaigns concentrated on the necessity and inevitability of an early recovery of territories lost to Poland. They also initiated numerous revisionist mass demonstrations throughout the country.

The Nazi campaign became so effective and brought such a favorable public response that high government officials and non-Nazi political leaders deemed it necessary to associate themselves with it. On August 10, 1930, Gottfried Treviranus, leader of the People's Conservative Party and a cabinet member, publicly called for the "unification of all Germans" in the east through the revision of the Polish-German boundary. His statement shocked Warsaw and Paris, but the German press praised it almost unanimously. On December 29 Chancellor Heinrich Bruening assured the representatives of the German minority in Poland that one day they would again belong to

Germany. Several months later he spoke publicly for the revision of Germany's eastern frontiers.[41]

The general elections in September 1930 brought great political change to Germany: the Nazis increased their seats in the Reichstag from twelve to 107. Hostility toward Poland became so intense and widespread that the Auswärtiges Amt refused to renew even minor Polish-German conventions nearing expiration.[42] The 1932 election campaigns were accompanied by such vitriolic anti-Polish agitation (based on the theme of a supposedly impending "Polish aggression") that Warsaw felt forced to supply several countries, including the United States, with a special aide-mémoire.[43]

Pilsudski, however, did not give up hope, instructing his minister in Berlin, Alfred Wysocki, to conduct a special study of the "attitudes" of the main political parties and to report on any possibilities for improving Polish-German relations. Wysocki replied that territorial concessions alone would satisfy the German public opinion and open the road toward any kind of rapprochement.[44]

The revisionist campaign paralleled secret, persistent efforts to keep the Polish issue alive in German-Soviet relations. In 1931–1932, these efforts seemed particularly timely because Polish-Soviet negotiations for a nonaggression pact were in progress.

In the middle of October 1931 Ambassador Dirksen drew Litvinov's attention to the fact that the pact would represent "far-reaching concession" to the Poles, neither necessary nor unavoidable. On November 4 the undersecretary, Bernhard Wilhelm von Billow, instructed Dirksen to inform the Narkomindel that if the Polish-Soviet pact contained any direct or indirect "guarantee of the Polish territory," this would directly affect German-Russian relations and bring about an "open serious discrepancy" in the joint German-Soviet policy toward Poland. Dirksen was instructed to declare that Germany would "never acquiesce in the present territorial position of Poland."[45] Transmitting the instructions to Krestinsky, Dirksen warned him that any "stipulation on respecting the integrity of the other State" would be considered by Berlin as indirectly meaning a "territorial guarantee" to Poland. Litvinov argued that the envisaged pact would only preclude the use of military force in Soviet-Polish relations without "guaranteeing" Poland's boundaries, which evoked disapproval from Richard Meyer, deputy director of the eastern European department in the Auswärtiges Amt.[46]

In the middle of 1932 the Soviet leaders finally succeeded in convincing Berlin that the nonaggression pact with Poland would not affect their Rapallo orientation. By then, however, they themselves feared that the growing forces of Nazism might change the course of German policy vis-à-vis Russia and thus asked for reassurances. And so, on June 29, 1932, Reichswehrminister General Kurt von Schleicher told the Soviet ambassador that "friendly relations" with Russia, particularly in the military field, were his government's main goal. Six months later he and Litvinov agreed that regardless of momentary differences between the German and the Soviet foreign policies, "the vital necessities of both states [would] prove themselves stronger" than any treaty commitments with third countries.[47] This exchange of views was of particular significance because Schleicher now occupied the post of chancellor and the Polish-Soviet nonaggression pact had just been ratified.

Six weeks after the Schleicher-Litvinov conversation, Adolf Hitler became chancellor. To everyone's surprise, his accession to power, instead of deepening the conflict between Germany and Poland, brought their rapprochement.

NOTES

1. For a comprehensive study on the subject, see Janusz Sobczak, *Propaganda Zagraniczna Niemiec Weimarowskich Wobec Polski* (*International Propaganda of the Weimar Republic Against Poland*) (Poznan: Instytyt Zachodni, 1973).

2. *General Wilhelm Gröner's Papers* (Cambridge, MA: Harvard University, Houghton Library), reel 7, stack 26, as cited by Korbel, *Poland between East and West*, 69–71.

3. Friedrich von Rabenau, *Seeckt, Aus seinem Leben, 1918–1936* (Leipzig: Verlag Hase & Koehler, 1940), 252.

4. John Wheeler-Bennett, *The Nemesis of Power: The German Army in Politics, 1918–1945* (London: Macmillan Co., 1953), 71, 122–23.

5. Rabenau, *Seeckt*, 297, 309; also Edward H. Carr, *The Bolshevik Revolution 1917–1923*, 3 vols. (New York: Macmillan Co., 1935), 3:364.

6. Rabenau, *Seeckt*, 295, 316; also Wheeler-Bennett, *The Nemesis of Power*, 136.

7. Kurt Rosenbaum, *Community of Fate: German Soviet Relations, 1922–1928* (Syracuse, NY: Syracuse University Press, 1965), 13–15, 52.

8. See *AANP-Zespoly MSZ*, 4477, 13–17; also 34, 38, 96–100.

9. For German policies during the Polish-Bolshevik war, see Korbel, *Poland between East and West*, 79–93.

10. Rosenbaum, *Community of Fate*, 34, 45, respectively.

11. M. Epstein, ed., *Statesman's Yearbook 1922* (London: Macmillan Co., 1922), 948.

12. Robert G. L. Waite, *Vanguard of Nazism: The Free Corps Movement in Postwar Germany, 1918–1923* (Cambridge, MA: Harvard University Press, 1952), 39.

13. Ruth Fisher, *Stalin and German Communism* (Cambridge, MA: Harvard University Press, 1948), 533–34.

14. For a documented study see Hans W. Gatzke, "Russo-German Military Collaboration during the Weimar Republic," *American Historical Review* 68, no. 3 (April 1958): 565–97.

15. See E. H. Carr, *German-Soviet Relations between the Two World Wars, 1919–1939* (Baltimore, MD: Johns Hopkins University Press, 1951), 47–80; also Gustav Hilger and Alfred G. Meyer, *The Incompatible Allies: A Memoir-History of German-Soviet Relations, 1914–1941* (New York: Macmillan Co., 1953), 187–208.

16. Hilger and Meyer, *The Incompatible Allies*, 203–4; also Gatzke, "Russo-German Military Collaboration," 584.

17. Gatzke, "Russo-German Military Collaboration," 596–97; also Harvey Leonard Dyck, *Weimar Germany and Soviet Russia, 1926–1933: A Study in Diplomatic Instability* (New York: Columbia University Press, 1966), 27ff.

18. See Franz von Papen, *Memoirs* (New York: E. P. Dutton & Co., 1953), 119ff; see also Richard Breyer, *Das Deutsche Reich and Polen, 1932–1937: Aussenpolitik und Volksgruppen-fragen* (Würzburg: Holzner Verlag, 1955), 17, 19–24, 30–37.

19. Zygmunt J. Gasiorowski, "The Russian Overture to Germany of December 1924," *Journal of Modern History* 30, no. 2 (June 1958), 110–11.

20. Gustav Stresemann, *Vermächtnis*, 3 vols. (Berlin: Ullstein Verlag, 1932–1933 , 68ff.

21. Eventually a compromise was adopted; on September 11, Poland was elected to the council by forty-six out of forty-nine voting members as a nonpermanent member with a right to unlimited reelections to a three-year term.

22. For informative essays on the subject, see Zygmunt J. Gasiorowski, "Stresemann and Poland before Locarno," and "Stresemann and Poland after Locarno," *Journal of Central European Affairs* 18, no. 1 (1958): 25–47, and no. 3:292–317, respectively.

23. Eric Sutton, ed., *Gustav Stresemann, His Diaries, Letters and Papers*, 3 vols. (London: Macmillan Co., 1935–1937), 2:266, 503.

24. Telegram from Maltzan to Moscow, December 13, 1924, *AANA*, 4562H/2313/E154874-76; also Rosenbaum, *Community of Fate*, 123.

25. Rantzau's telegram dated December 22, 1924, *AANA*, 4562H/2313/E154905.

26. Rosenbaum, *Community of Fate*, 138, 209; also Korbel, *Poland between East and West*, 194–95.

27. For the text, see *AANA*, 4556/2301/E149414-34; also Korbel, *Poland between East and West*, 168.

28. For the situation in Poland prior to Pilsudski's seizure of power, see Joseph Rothschild, *Pilsudski's Coup d'Etat* (New York: Columbia University Press, 1966), 3–24.

29. See Tadeusz Kunicki, "Problemy Polsko-Niemieckie, 1920–1939" (Polish-German Problems, 1920–1939), *Niepodleglośc* (London), 1952, 113–15. Kunicki was for many years one of the leading Polish diplomatic experts on Germany; also Charles Kruszewski, "The German Polish Tariff War (1925–1934) and Its Aftermath," *Journal of Central European Affairs* 3 (October 1943): 294–315.

30. Royal Institute of International Affairs, *Survey of International Affairs 1925* (London: Oxford University Press, 1925), 2:239–41.

31. For Stresemann's memorandum on the conversation, see *AANA*, 4569/2339/E168487-89; also *AANA*, 4556/2301/E149515-19.

32. Ibid., 4569/2339/E168640-43.

33. Christian Holtje, *Die Weimarer Republik und das Ostlocarno-Problem 1919–1934* (Würtzburg: Holzner Verlag, 1958), 254–56, as cited by Dyck, *Weimar Germany and Soviet Russia*, 30–31.

34. *AANA*, 4569/2339/El68643.

35. For details, see Rothschild, *Pilsudski's Coup d'Etat*, 47–154.

36. Gasiorowski, "Stresemann and Poland after Locarno," 300, 305. For pertinent reports, see *AANP-Zespoly MSZ*, 4014, 23–24; 4503, 156–7, 203–08.

37. Joseph Beck, *Dernier Rapport: Politique Polonaise, 1926–1939* (Neuchatel, Switzerland: Éditions de la Baconniere, 1952), 4–5.

38. Dyck, *Weimar Germany and Soviet Russia*, 188; *DBFP*, 2nd series, 1:490, respectively.

39. See Dirksen's note, dated March 4, 1926, "For a talk with Chamberlain over questions of Germany's policy toward Poland," *AANA*, 4569/2339/E168519-23.

40. F. P. Walters, *A History of the League of Nations* (London: Oxford University Press, 1952), 1:407–9; also Gasiorowski, "Stresemann and Poland after Locarno," 315–17.

41. See the report of the British ambassador in Berlin: *DBFP*, 2nd series, 1:491–93.

42. Tadeusz Cieslak, *Historia Polskiej Dyplomacji w Latach 1926–1939* (*History of the Polish Diplomacy in the Years 1926–1939*), part 2 (Warszawa: n.p., 1960), 26.

43. For various pertinent reports and data, see *AANP-Zespoly MSZ*, 4503, 49–52, 111–13, 127–30; 4618, 2–121.

44. Józef Lipski, "Przyczynki do Historji Polsko-Niemieckiej Deklaracji o Nieagresji" (Addenda to the history of the Polish-German Declaration of Nonaggression), *Bellona* (London) (January–June 1951), 32. See also the second part of the article in *Bellona* (July–September 1951). Hereafter cited as Lipski, "Addenda," part 1, and Lipski, "Addenda," part 2, respectively.

45. See Dirksen's report of October 19, 1931, *AANA*, K290/3933/K101530; 35–36, respectively.

46. For the pertinent reports, see *AANA*, K290/3933/K101535-36; 45–48; 33; 60.

47. *AANA*, 6609H/3082/E496711; 929–30, respectively.

Chapter Six

Poland in the Foreign Policy of France, 1921–1932

France's main concern after World War I and the conclusion of the peace treaties was Germany—defeated but potentially stronger. The US abandonment of the League of Nations and withdrawal from European affairs increased French fears. So did Britain's policy of opposing anti-German solutions or even, at times, supporting Germany as a natural counterbalance to possible French supremacy on the continent. Tsarist Russia, a traditional ally of France, no longer existed, and Moscow-dominated Communism was considered a danger.

These concerns or fears prompted Paris to establish a system of alliances with Poland and the countries of the Little Entente (Czechoslovakia, Romania, and Yugoslavia). Poland by its very nature and geographical position seemed destined to play a dual role—as an eastern check on Germany and as a cordon sanitaire against Communist westward expansion. Poland's military successes in the war against the Bolsheviks somewhat improved its international position, and Pilsudski, who had never inspired confidence in French government circles, enjoyed at least respect, if not popularity, in the early 1920s.[1]

Collaboration between France and Poland was considered even more important to the Poles than to the French. Germany viewed the reborn state with open enmity, and the Bolsheviks regarded their western neighbor as no more than a bridge that they intended to cross in order to spread the proletarian revolution. The French-sponsored Versailles system—containment of Germany and Russia and the maintenance of the status quo—seemed to offer the best guarantee for the new state, making France a natural and effective ally.

The two countries formalized relations in February 1921 during a state visit to Paris by the then chief of state, Pilsudski, accompanied by his foreign minister, Prince Eustachy Sapieha, and the minister of war, General Kazimierz Sosnkowski.[2] The French side was represented by President Alexandre Millerand, Foreign Minister Aristide Briand, and War Minister Louis Barthou. Short negotiations, marked by mutual understanding, led to the February 19 Accord[3]—usually referred to as an alliance—which became a cornerstone of Polish foreign policy for several years.

Under the terms of the alliance, the two governments committed themselves to consult each other on all international problems of mutual concern, particularly if either intended to enter into new engagements in central and eastern Europe. Article 2 laid the groundwork for economic cooperation by announcing an economic convention to be signed sometime in the future, while Article 3, the heart of the accord, provided for mutual assistance in case of unprovoked aggression: "If, notwithstanding the sincerely peaceful views and intentions of the two contracting states, either or both of them should be attacked without giving provocation, the two governments shall take concerted measures for the defense of their territory and the protection of their legitimate interests within the limits specified by the préamble."

Significantly, the alliance, according to Article 5, was to become effective only after the economic convention had been signed. This stress on economic factors was prompted primarily by French interests in Poland. French capital investment in the Polish textile, oil, and mining industries was substantial. In exchange for the alliance and a military convention, to be signed two days later, France expected from Poland economic concessions and, of course, internal stability.

A secret military convention of February 21 stipulated that if the internal German situation endangered either nation or if execution of the Treaty of Versailles demanded concerted action, the two governments would synchronize their military preparations.[4] In case of German aggression against either or both of them, the two countries would aid each other according to the terms of their agreement. In the event that Russia attacked Poland, France committed itself to help its ally by safeguarding land and sea communications between the two nations. If war broke out or aggression seemed imminent, France was to supply Poland with materiel and technical personnel, though it was not obliged to send troops. Poland undertook to maintain nine peacetime cavalry brigades, a minimum of thirty infantry divisions, and appropriate reserve units. The convention specified France's financial aid to equip the Polish army. Finally, permanent collaboration between the Polish and French general staffs was to be established.[5]

Soon afterward—on March 3, 1921—again because of Pilsudski's initiative, a Polish-Romanian convention providing for mutual "unconditional" assistance in the event of unprovoked aggression "from the east" was concluded.[6] For several years those agreements, and particularly the Polish-French accord, formed a foundation on which Poland's security system rested.

But the alliance, so natural in 1921, was wrought with inherent weaknesses. First, there were many in France—particularly the military—who argued, as Balfour did in 1916, that Poland would be unable to fulfill its role in the long run. Then, in the event of any Franco-German or Franco-Russian rapprochement, France's commitments to Poland were bound to become a hindrance. And the French were mindful of their role in the rebirth of Poland, their contribution to Poland's security, the risks involved in their commitments, and Poland's dependence on their power. They expected the Poles to be satisfied with a status of junior partner, or an appreciative follower. This in time could hardly be popular with the Poles, increasingly eager to free themselves from French tutelage. On the other hand, the Poles interpreted France's obligations in the broadest sense, expecting the French to adapt their policies to the exigencies of Poland's security—a difficult task for a world power which in a continuously changing international situation had to think primarily of its own interests.

The alliance was strongly supported by Millerand, Briand, and Barthou. But military circles, headed by Marshal Foch, feared or even opposed it, considering Poland a poor, if not risky, substitute for Russia.[7] Poland, they reasoned, was vulnerable, being dangerously flanked by both a revisionist Germany and an expansionist Russia; it was in conflict with both its northern and its southern neighbors; its western and eastern frontiers were indefensible; and the national minorities were bound to weaken the state from within. Thus, Poland might involve France in an unwanted conflict. The alliance, they argued, was more of an unnecessary liability than an asset. Because of their unshakeable views, no plans were ever made for joint military action in the event of war, and it was not until 1939 that any serious collaboration between the French and the Polish general staffs came to pass. From the military standpoint, the alliance was never more than symbolic.

As time passed, Paris grew more uneasy about the extent of its commitments to Poland. The Rapallo treaty, concluded by Germany and Russia in April 1922, was partly responsible. When Marshal Foch visited Warsaw a few weeks later, he suggested a review of the military obligations existing between the Polish and French armies, hoping to modify the alliance by limiting its applicability to German aggression and by excluding Russia from its provisions. He argued that since Poland had recently concluded a peace treaty with Moscow and the Polish-Soviet frontiers had been formally recognized by the Council of Ambassadors, the Poles had nothing to fear from the east. His hosts, considering Russia no less dangerous than Germany, disagreed, and the alliance was left unchanged. [8]

French attempts to weaken the alliance did not mean that France's interest in central-eastern Europe had diminished. On the contrary, France tried to strengthen Poland and the Little Entente countries, viewing them as natural allies in the face of a common danger, Germany. In time, however, Paris grew less interested in their role as a barrier against Russia. With militant Communism on the decline, Paris began to think of a détente with Moscow.

In May 1924 general elections took place in France, and the National Bloc, in power since 1919, was defeated. A coalition of the left, the so-called Cartel des Gauches, formed the new government. Édouard Herriot, the new prime minister who took the reins of foreign policy as well, believed in bringing Russia into European politics and initiated a rapprochement with Moscow. Soon afterward, on October 28, 1924, France formally recognized the Soviet government.

In Warsaw, the French move could only be considered a dangerous setback, because Poland pursued the opposite course, trying to keep Russia out of European politics. A new foreign minister, Count Alexander Skrzynski, was subsequently charged with strengthening Warsaw's relations with Paris. He apparently met with some success. Before long, the legations of both countries were raised to embassy rank. A Franco-Polish consortium was established to construct Gdynia, a new port on the Baltic—an event of much greater than economic importance. [9] Cultural exchanges increased. Franco-Polish political relations suffered, however, for it was apparent that Poland's role as a barrier against Communist Russia was losing its allure to the new French government.

In less than a year Franco-Polish relations underwent another setback, although this time it was more direct and the implications graver because Germany was involved. When the Herriot cabinet fell in April 1925, the new cabinet—headed by Paul Panlevé—included the brilliant and enthusiastic pacifist Aristide Briand as foreign affairs minister. Shortly before, the Auswärtiges Amt, headed by Gustav Stresemann, initiated a political détente between Germany and its western neighbors, based on a recognition of the territorial status quo and framed so as to bring Great Britain and Italy into the agreement. Briand responded favorably to Stresemann's overture and soon became a strong partisan of the proposed system, seeing in it an excellent vehicle for political stability in western Europe. By that time, opinion prevailed in the Quai d'Orsay that because Germany's economic and political resurgence could not be avoided, France should quickly establish a modus vivendi with the still-weak Germany rather than face it in the not-too-distant future as both hostile and stronger than itself. [10] Multinational conferences thus ensued at Locarno in early October and resulted in the signing of a series of treaties known as the Locarno pacts. [11]

The essential element in the Locarno system was the treaty of mutual guarantee concluded among Germany, France, and Belgium and "guaranteed" by Great Britain and Italy. The signatories recognized the Franco-Belgian-German boundaries as permanent and inviolable, committed themselves not to wage war against each other, and agreed to submit all disputes to arbitration or conciliation. In case of aggression, the victim was to be assisted by guarantees contained in the covenant of the League of Nations (Articles 15, 16, and 17) and also by automatic and immediate aid from Great Britain and Italy. As an additional assurance of peace and security, the demilitarization of the Rhineland was formally confirmed by all.

France, in deference to its alliance with Poland, tried to extend the territorial guarantees to Germany's eastern frontiers, but Berlin, London, and Rome refused. Stresemann made it clear from the start that Germany did not consider the eastern frontiers as permanent, nor would it include Poland or Czechoslovakia in the system. Great Britain and Italy refused to guarantee Germany's eastern borders on the grounds that they were unstable. Faced with German opposition and British veto, France finally gave in and agreed to a compromise. [12] Germany indicated that it would conclude separate treaties with Poland and Czechoslovakia providing for the peaceful solution of all disputes through the good offices of international tribunals and arbitration. In case of aggression, the guarantees contained in the covenant of the League of Nations would apply—the permanence of the postwar boundaries, however, would not be mentioned and there would be no British and Italian guarantees.

Having no other choice, Warsaw agreed to the compromise, although the treaties caused considerable dissatisfaction. The Poles viewed Germany's free hand in the east as the price paid for a détente and recognition of the western European status quo. The Polish press severely criticized both France and Great Britain.[13] If the covenant of the League of Nations provided security sufficient to neutralize possible German aggression, the Poles argued, then British-Italian guarantees of the Franco-German and Belgian-German boundaries were superfluous. If, however, such guarantees were thought necessary for the preservation of Europe's territorial status quo, then adequate provision for Polish-German boundaries had not been made.

To appease Polish public opinion and to reconcile France's obligations toward Poland with its newly assumed obligations toward Germany, the Franco-Polish guarantee treaty was signed in London on December 1, 1926. According to its provisions, in case of unprovoked German aggression against either party, the League of Nations' covenant imposing compulsory arbitration by its council was to be applied. If the council were unable to achieve a unanimous decision, the two countries were obliged to come to each other's aid. In the event of a unanimous decision, France and Poland would be bound by it.[14]

As was commonly known, the League's machinery moved slowly and was not expected to be effective if and when war broke out. The League's prestige and popularity were not high in Warsaw. Even more important, however, was a possibility that the treaty might be interpreted as an amendment to the *automatic* operation of the alliance. From that time, in answer to a German attack on Poland, France might either declare war on Germany immediately, as required by the alliance, or, applying the Locarno system, merely mobilize and then dump the entire matter in the complicated procedural lap of the League. Briand was quite aware of the ambiguities and so informed his colleagues in Paris.[15] And indeed, in the years to come, the Quai d'Orsay would use this argument in its dealings with Warsaw.

That the Locarno pacts indirectly opened the question of Germany's eastern frontier was widely acknowledged in Europe and was so interpreted at the time by several prominent German jurists and statesmen, Chancellor Luther and Stresemann included.[16] In the eyes of the Germans, the pacts and Germany's subsequent entry into the League of Nations provided new means of recovering the territories lost to Poland. The Auswärtiges Amt, in particular, had good reasons to be optimistic. Numerous French statesmen, including Briand himself, accepted the notion that Polish-German boundaries eventually would have to be changed peacefully.[17] Stresemann thus concluded that the desired territorial changes might be obtained in cooperation with the Western powers, including France.[18]

France's role at Locarno was judged severely by the Pilsudski regime, and Pilsudski himself noted that "every decent Pole spits when he hears the word [Locarno]."[19] He never forgave Skrzynski for adhering to the Locarno system, and from 1925 on, Polish governmental circles became ultrasensitive to the problems of Poland's security and suspicious of the Quai d'Orsay. They resented Poland's ancillary role in French foreign policy and accused France of abandoning its commitments in order to gain German cooperation. For them, the Locarno pacts symbolized France's willingness to sacrifice their vital interests.

Conversely, in France criticism of Poland was now widespread. Public opinion overwhelmingly disapproved of Pilsudski's coup d'état and regarded the Polish leader as less than a friendly ally. French disfavor intensified when Pilsudski began his harsh campaign against domestic political opposition and separatist factions. In 1930 several prominent opposition leaders were arbitrarily arrested, illegally sent to the fortress of Brest-Litovsk, and subjected to mistreatment and humiliation. Some of these men—such as the peasant leader and former prime minister Wincenty Witos or Christian Democratic party leader Wojciech Korfanty—were held in high esteem throughout Europe. Others, such as peasant leaders Wladyslaw Kiernik and Kazimierz Baginski, or Socialists like Norbert Barlicki, Adam Ciolkosz, Herman Liberman, Zygmunt Mastek, and Adam Pragier, held leading positions in their parties.[20] Three years later, in October 1933, they were convicted by the government-pressured courts. In some cases charges were never formulated (e.g., Karol Popiel). Eventually, Witos, Korfanty, Liberman, and others went to Czechoslovakia to carry out an anti-Pilsudski campaign from exile. They had many sympathizers in France.

In September 1930 police and military units, retaliating against the terroristic acts of the Organization of Ukrainian Nationalists (OUN), carried out a "pacification program" that resulted in mass brutalities. Protests to the League of Nations and other international organizations followed.

The November 1930 general elections gave the government an absolute majority in the Sejm; however, there were charges of extensive voting irregularities.

A year later, anti-Semitic demonstrations occurred at several universities, with nationalistic students demanding *numerus clausus* for the Jews. In February 1932 the Socialist party tried to organize mass strikes in Silesia, Gdynia, Cracow, and Lodz but instead brought about government-imposed restrictions on freedom of assembly and judicial independence. All these incidents received extremely unfavorable worldwide publicity, diminishing Poland's prestige and popularity. In Paris, organizations and individuals of great prestige intervened at the Polish embassy. [21]

From the moment of Germany's entry into the League of Nations, the Auswärtiges Amt won one political victory after another, while tired, pacifist France sought to preserve the status quo, [22] trying to maintain the newly won détente as the most essential requirement for general peace and national security. Poland could not contribute to that détente; in fact, the frequent Polish-German disputes and frictions in the League of Nations represented an annoying dissonance, especially since Warsaw usually expected full support from its French ally. Once a valuable eastern check on a hostile Germany, Poland now became a hindrance to Franco-German rapprochement.

The meaning of France's commitments vis-à-vis Poland also changed because of Great Britain's attitude toward Germany's eastern neighbors. It was generally assumed that Great Britain would defend France in the event of a German attack but would not necessarily if France declared war on Germany as a result of its obligations to its eastern allies. The British considered the Rhine River their security frontier but would go no further in their commitments. Paris was informed of that stance on several occasions, in answer to its inquiries. [23] Until the spring of 1939 Austen Chamberlain's paraphrase of Bismarck, "for the Polish Corridor, no British government ever will or ever can risk the bones of a British grenadier," [24] sounded like a motto for the British attitude vis-à-vis eastern Europe. As a result, France's commitments to Poland became yet another hindrance, this time to Franco-British cooperation.

The task of adapting the alliance to the post-Locarno situation was entrusted to the newly appointed French ambassador in Warsaw, Jules Laroche. In 1927, only one year after his arrival, he suggested pertinent negotiations. In case of German aggression, the French wanted formal replacement of the automatic operation of the alliance by the procedures of Articles 15, 16, and 17 of the covenant of the League of Nations. They also proposed that France's specific obligations in case of a Soviet attack upon Poland be eliminated altogether. The Polish government stood firmly by the terms of the alliance and rejected the suggestion. [25]

Exploratory conferences between the representatives of the French and Polish general staffs took place soon afterward. On those occasions, the French representatives tried to weaken the provisions for mutual military aid. Only because of the stern Polish opposition did the military convention remain unchanged. During the discussions, the chief of the Polish mission, General Kutrzeba, declared officially that if France were attacked by Germany, Poland would mobilize immediately and go to France's aid. Then he asked what the French reaction would be if Germany attacked Poland. General Marie Eugene Debeney, French chief of staff, gave an evasive answer in which he conditioned his country's reaction by citing Great Britain's stand and France's military situation. [26]

The change in France's attitude toward Poland was a result in no small measure of its domestic situation. In 1927 the construction of the Maginot Line began—a purely defensive measure. Military service was reduced to one year the year after, and special legislation stipulated that the military forces had to have a defensive character. The general staff subsequently adopted a purely defensive strategy. [27]

The year 1928 brought new hopes in Paris for permanent security and peace and, strangely enough, marked a further weakening of France's interest in Poland. At that time, the American secretary of state Frank B. Kellogg initiated what eventually became known as the Briand-Kellogg Pact. Signed in Paris by fifteen countries on August 27, 1928, it provided a solemn renunciation of war as an instrument in settling international disputes. The pact contained no sanctions against transgressors and, as the future would show, it never played an important role in international politics. But it did strengthen France's self-confidence and its belief that peace and security would continue as long as Franco-German relations were not embroiled by a third party or side issues. In addition, since growing stability in the West did not reduce the tensions in German-Polish relations, so the argument that the Polish alliance represented a liability and not an asset gained strength. Again the French tried to weaken their treaty obligations, and again the Poles stood fast. [28] Before long, the American ambassador in Moscow, John N. Willys, signaled to Washington that "France would joyfully be rid of responsibility in respect to the Polish Western frontiers," that the Poles "doubtless" had knowledge of these intentions, and that, as a result, they became "suspicious" and "cautious." Their caution applied to the American attitudes toward Germany as well, he added. [29]

The Poles had good reasons to be suspicious. By that time the French leaders no longer believed that the Polish-German boundaries, particularly the Corridor, could long remain unchanged, and their skepticism was shared by the American government. In October 1931, French prime minister Pierre Laval visited Washington for an extensive exchange of views with President Herbert Hoover and Secretary of State Henry L. Stimson. Both "urged" Laval "to do something about the frontiers of Central Europe"—the cause of "political unrest" and the "root of all political and financial difficulties" in Europe. Those frontiers, they believed, were "indefensible" and had to be revised. Laval agreed that the "Polish corridor was a monstrosity." Nothing, however, could be done at the moment, he said, because the Poles "would rather have war than agree to any modification" of their western boundaries.[30]

The disarmament conference that opened in Geneva in February 1932 further deepened the rift between Paris and Warsaw. After several months of complex negotiations, Germany withdrew from the conference. To bring it back, France—together with Great Britain, Italy, and the United States—agreed on December 11 to a compromise resolution of Equality of Rights. Those were days of turmoil in Germany, of violent anti-Versailles outbursts and the Nazi revisionist campaigns. Concessions to Germany aroused anxiety in Russia, Czechoslovakia, Romania, Yugoslavia, Turkey, and, more than anywhere else, in Poland. Pilsudski considered Germany's disarmament as prescribed by Part 5 of the Versailles Treaty a "permanent element of the European security." He vigorously opposed any compromise in this matter and did not conceal his profound misgivings about French foreign policy. "To allow [Germany] to have arms means a lost game," the Polish foreign minister told Laroche bluntly.[31]

An important shift occurred in the Polish foreign ministry at the end of 1932. On November 3, August Zaleski,[32] whom Pilsudski considered too pro-French and too favorably disposed toward the League of Nations, was replaced by the marshal's confidant and disciple Colonel Jozef Beck.[33]

Beck occupied the post until the outbreak of World War II, and his personality was to weigh heavily on the conduct of Poland's foreign policy. Born in 1894 to an upper-middle-class family of Flemish ancestry, he received a somewhat peripatetic and incomplete education at the Lvov Polytechnic School and the Vienna Foreign Trade Academy. He joined Pilsudski's legions, fought with distinction, embarked upon a military career, and eventually landed in the intelligence school. In January 1922, at the age of twenty-eight, he was sent to Paris as a military attaché, remaining there for eighteen months. There were rumors, albeit unproved, that he resorted to irregular methods in his work.[34] After active participation as a lieutenant colonel in Pilsudski's coup of 1926, he became intimately associated with the marshal and won his confidence—along with high positions, responsibilities, and honors. In 1926, at the age of thirty-two, he became chief of cabinet in the national defense ministry headed by Pilsudski. Four years later he became vice premier and went to the ministry of foreign affairs as undersecretary of state shortly afterward. When appointed foreign minister, he was not yet thirty-eight years old.

An ardent patriot, Beck was also blindly devoted to Pilsudski. To him, as to so many others, Pilsudski was the embodiment of wisdom, and his ideas were the final formulas of the Polish raison d'état. Beck's competence was never seriously questioned in Polish governmental quarters because he had Pilsudski's personal sympathy and confidence. It was not seriously questioned even after Pilsudski's death in 1935, because as the marshal's disciple, he and his policies supposedly represented the marshal's legacy. Departing from the scene on September 17, 1939, he was the dean of all European foreign ministers, having remained in power for almost seven uninterrupted years.

From the beginning of his career to the end of his life in inhospitable Romania, on June 5, 1944, he saw his role as that of a torchbearer and executor of Pilsudski's ideas and methods. Since he had been his commandant's choice, he acquired great self-confidence and a sense of personal assurance and political durability. Once appointed, he shaped the ministry and its personnel in his own image and soon became the real master of Poland's foreign policy.

Beck's former post of undersecretary of state went to Count Jan Szembek, for six years head of the Polish legation in Bucharest. Szembek, a professional of great experience, refinement, and diplomatic expertise, had Pilsudski's respect. But, together with other high-ranking diplomats, he also acknowledged Beck's leadership and faithfully executed Beck's policies. Thus, for the successes and failures of these policies, more than anyone else, Beck has to bear historical responsibility.

NOTES

1. Leon Noël, *L'Aggression allemande contre la Pologne. Une ambassade à Varsovie, 1935–1939* (Paris: Flammarion, 1946), 98. Leon Noël was French ambassador to Poland in the years 1935–1939. See also Jules A. Laroche, *La Pologne de Pilsudski: Souvenir d'une Ambassade 1926–1935* (Paris: Flammarion, 1953), 12–13.

2. For detailed treatment of the alliance, see Wandycz, *France and Her Eastern Allies*, 211–37.

3. For the text, see Ministère des Affaires Étrangères, France, *Le Livre Jaune Français, Documents Diplomatiques, 1938–1939* (Paris: Imprimerie Nationale, 1939), 419. Hereafter cited as *LJF*.

4. For the reconstructed text, see Wandycz, *France and Her Eastern Allies*, appendix 3, 394–95.

5. General Maurice Gustave Gamelin, *Servir*, 3 vols. (Paris: Plon, 1946–1947), 2:225, 467. Also Komisia Historyczna Polskiego Sztabu Głównego w Londynie, *Polskie Sily Zbrojne w Drugiej Wojnie Swiatowej* (*The Polish Armed Forces in the Second World War*), 3 vols. (London: General Sikorski Historical Institute, 1950–1951), 1, part 1, 88. This is a history of the Polish armed forces prepared by the Polish general staff in London. Hereafter cited as *PSZ*.

6. For the text, Arnold J. Toynbee, *Survey of International Affairs, 1920–1923* (London: Oxford University Press, 1925), 504–5. On January 5, 1931, the convention had been changed into a regular treaty of mutual assistance, with validity until March 1941. See *PSZ 1*, part 1, 106–7.

7. Noël, *L'Aggression allemande contre la Pologne*, 100–102; Laroche, *La Pologne de Pilsudski*, 13–15.

8. Noël, *L'Aggression allemande contre la Pologne*, 101; also *PSZ 1*, part 1, 88.

9. Wandycz, *France and Her Eastern Allies*, 314–16; 324.

10. Richard D. Challener, "The French Foreign Office: The Era of Philippe Berthelot," in *The Diplomats, 1919–1939*, ed. Gordon A. Craig and Felix Gilbert (Princeton, NJ: Princeton University Press, 1953), 77–79.

11. For background and analysis, see Wandycz, *France and Her Eastern Allies*, 312–68.

12. Henry Ashby Turner Jr., *Stresemann and the Politics of the Weimar Republic* (Princeton, NJ: Princeton University Press, 1963), 203, 212.

13. For a contemporary treatment from the Polish standpoint, see Stronski, op. cit., 492–504.

14. For the text, see *LJF*, 420–21.

15. George Bonnet, *Défense de la paix*, 2 vols. (Geneva: Les Éditions du Cheval Ailé, 1946–1948), 1:102; also Noël, *L'Aggression allemande contre la Pologne*, 101–2.

16. Alexandre Bregman, *La Politique de la Pologne dans la Societé des Nations* (Paris: Librarie Felix Alcan, 1952), 207–9.

17. For documentation, see Korbel, *Poland between East and West*, 216, 242.

18. Ibid., 243; also Gasiorowski, "Stresemann and Poland after Locarno," 312–13.

19. Joseph Beck, *Dernier rapport. Politique polonaise 1926–1939* (Neuchatel: Éditions de la Baconnière, 1951), 268.

20. See Hans Roos, *A History of Modern Poland* (London: Eyre and Spottiswoode, 1966), 114–22.

21. See Ambassador Chlapowski's report, dated December 9, 1931; *AANP-Zespoly MSZ* 3789, 222–26.

22. See Breyer, *Das Deutsche Reich and Polen*, 19–25.

23. Georges Bonnet, *Le Quai d'Orsay sous trois republiques, 1870–1961* (Paris: Arthème Fayard, 1961), 132.

24. Challener, "The French Foreign Office," 82.

25. Laroche, *La Pologne de Pilsudski*, 17; also Tytus Komarnicki, "Pilsudski a Polityka Wielkich Mocarstw Zachodnich" (Pilsudski and the Policy of the Western Powers), *Niepodleglosc* 4 (1952): 81–84; also Noël, *L'Aggression allemande contre la Pologne*, 256.

26. Gamelin, *Servir*, 2:467; also Wladyslaw Pobog-Malinowski, *Najnowsza Historja Polityczna Polski 1864–1945* (Modern Political History of Poland), 2 vols. (London: B. Swiderski, 1967), 2:700.

27. See France, Assemblée Nationale, *Les événements survenus en France de 1933 à 1945*, 9 vols. (Paris: Imprimerie Nationale, 1947–1951), 4:1674 (General Maxime Weygand's testimony). Hereafter cited as France, *Les événements*.

28. *Diariusz i Teki Jana Szembeka* (ed. Tytus Komarnicki) (*Diaries and Portfolios of Jan Szembek*), 4 vols. (London: Polish Research Center, 1964–1972), 2:14–16. Hereafter cited as Szembek, *Diariusz*. This much enlarged and extensively documented publication superseded the earlier French edition edited by the former French ambassador to Poland, Leon Noël: Comte Jean Szembek, *Journal, 1933–1939* (Paris: Plon, 1952), 504 pages. Hereafter cited as Szembek, *Journal*. Because of language, as a rule, the French edition will be used. However, whenever the content requires it, the *Diariusz* will be cited.

29. *Foreign Relations of the United States: Diplomatic Papers* (Washington, DC: US Government Printing Office), 1931, 1:598. Hereafter cited as *FRUS*.

30. *DBFP*, 2nd series, 2:307.

31. Laroche, *La Pologne de Pilsudski*, 111–13, 118, 135, 145; also the report of Colonel d'Arbonneau, French military attaché in Warsaw, concerning his conversation with Pilsudski on October 25, 1932, France, Ministère des Affaires Etrangères, *Documents Diplomatiques Français, 1932–1939* (Paris: Imprimerie Nationale, 1963–1966), Ier Série, 1:592–94. Hereafter cited as *DDF*.

32. For a factual and detached study on Zaleski, see Piotr Wandycz, "August Zaleski, Minister Spraw Zagranicznych RP 1926–1932 w swietle wspomnien i dokumentdw" (August Zaleski, foreign minister of Poland 1926–1932, in the light of memoirs and documents) *Zeszyty Historyczne* 52 (1980).

33. For a spirited characterization of Beck as a man and a diplomat, see Viscount Templewood (Sir Samuel Hoare), *Nine Troubled Years* (London: Collins, 1954), 346–47; for an exhaustive, documented study, see Craig and Gilbert, *The Diplomats, 1913–1939*, chapter 19, "The Diplomacy of Colonel Beck," by Henry L. Roberts, 579–614.

34. Roberts, "Diplomacy of Colonel Beck," 580.

Chapter Seven

Two-Faced Eastern Neighbor, 1921–1932

From the time of its birth, Communist Russia followed a twofold foreign policy. One, conducted in the name of the government, professed peace and international collaboration. The other, carried out by the Comintern, aimed at the destruction of the "capitalistic bourgeois" states through agitation, violence, and revolution. On the highest level, both policies were directed from the Kremlin, a fact which put most governments, all Polish governments included, on guard.[1]

After the civil war ended, it was only gradually that the Bolsheviks succeeded in establishing diplomatic relations with other countries: in 1920 with Finland, Estonia, Latvia, and Lithuania; in 1921 with Poland, Turkey, Persia, and Afghanistan. In 1924–1925 the Union of the Soviet Socialist Republics was recognized by Great Britain, France, Italy, and Japan. Of the great powers, only the United States of America demurred.

Diplomatic recognition notwithstanding, Moscow was distrusted throughout Europe; its influence, particularly political, was feared. The Baltic states, Poland, Romania, and to some extent the Balkan countries, were looked upon by many as a barrier to Bolshevik expansion, a "barbed-wire fence" or cordon sanitaire. The Soviet leaders certainly realized this and suspected that one day the Western powers might embark upon a policy aimed at the destruction of Communism in Russia, using these countries as a springboard. They considered Poland an outpost of aggressive "capitalist imperialism."

Poland emerged the strongest of the states on Russia's western borders, and its governments and peoples were vehemently anti-Communist. They saw in Communist activities an invasion of an alien ideology and a cover for traditional Russian expansion. They remembered the war against the Bolsheviks in 1919–1920 and the role of the Polish Communists. Furthermore, there was evidence that Moscow tried to stir the Ukrainian and Byelorussian national minorities, which made the Poles fear that Russia might eventually embark upon revisionist policies. The Communist party of Western Ukraine and the Communist party of Byelorussia, both active in Poland, officially put forth the program of joining Polish eastern territories to the Soviet Ukraine and Byelorussia.[2]

As for the Soviet leaders, Pilsudski's federalist ideas, though frustrated by the 1920 campaign and formally renounced in the Riga treaty, were certainly not forgotten. They were not entirely forgotten in Poland, either. Some groups did advocate Poland's "mission" in the east, propagandizing the national aspirations of the Russian Ukrainians, Byelorussians, and the Caucasian nations.[3] To be sure, the government dissociated itself from them, but their mere existence could not fail to arouse suspicion in Moscow. Furthermore, a considerable number of White émigrés were active in Poland, causing frequent Soviet protests. Last but not least, since the conclusion of the Treaty of Riga, both governments continuously accused each other of maintaining armed bands in the frontier zones.[4]

Apparently the Soviet leaders never reconciled themselves to the idea that the Riga treaty represented a final settlement with Poland, because on several occasions they officially registered their interest in the areas inhabited by Ukrainians and Byelorussians. As early as March 13, 1923—the eve of the final recognition of Poland's eastern boundaries by the Conference of Ambassadors—Chicherin addressed a note to the British, French, and Italian governments emphasizing that the Treaty of Riga did not "in any way imply that the fate of these territories is a matter of indifference to Russia and (Soviet) Ukraine." Soon after, on September 22, 1924, he warned Warsaw that the Soviet Union could not "under any circumstances consider the Eastern Galician question as an internal affair of the Polish government and [continued] to look upon it as an international problem not finally settled."[5]

It was not the Soviet unilateral declarations, however, but its cooperation with Germany that constituted the real threat to the young state. Lenin was an eager proponent of that cooperation. He considered it a necessity both because the Reichswehr could help him reorganize the Red Army and because he believed Poland had to be destroyed. According to him: "An independent Poland is very dangerous to Soviet Russia; it is an evil which, however, at the present time has also its redeeming features; for while it exists, we may safely count on Germany, because the Germans hate Poland and will at any time make common cause with us in order to strangle Poland. . . . Germany wants revenge and we want revolution. For the moment our aims are the same."[6]

These words were not just Lenin's opinions, they were long-range guidelines for Soviet policy. As early as 1920, prominent Bolsheviks Karl Radek and Leonid B. Krassin established contacts with General Seeckt, proposing German-Soviet collaboration against Poland. One year later the Soviet chief of staff, P. Lebedev, told the head of the German military mission in Moscow, Colonel Otto Hasse, that the Red Army might attack Poland if the Germans made "all-out efforts" to rebuild Russia's war industry. As much as the Soviets' approaches fit into his own conceptions, Seeckt considered Germany too weak to make any commitments at that time, and the matter was left open.[7]

The Western orientation of German foreign policy, initiated by Stresemann in 1924, again brought Poland into the focus of Soviet-German relations. In order to make Germany turn away from its intended course, Moscow used the Polish issue as bait. Poland had to be reduced to its ethnic borders, and for that purpose Germany and Russia should continue the Rapallo cooperation—this was the essence of Chicherin's arguments. Germany was to reincorporate Danzig, the Corridor, and Silesia, while the Soviets were to take the Ukrainian- and Byelorussian-inhabited areas.[8]

On December 4, 1924, Victor Kopp, director of the Department of Baltic and Polish Affairs in the Narkomindel, pointed out to Rantzau that Russia's and Germany's interests in Poland were so similar that a mutual long-range agreement was a necessity. The two assured each other that their governments had not and would not in the future renounce their territorial claims on Poland. On the contrary, an "exchange of ideas" would have to take place, and an understanding would have to be reached on how to keep Poland under continuous pressure.[9] That same month Rantzau, acting under instructions, agreed with Chicherin that the "pressure" on Poland should be maintained independently of Germany's position in the West.[10] Six months later in a conversation with Stresemann, Litvinov, then vice commissar for foreign affairs, clearly hinted at secret cooperation against Poland. On September 30 Chicherin proffered the same hint to the German foreign minister.[11]

While assuring the Soviet leaders that a German-Russian understanding directed against Poland was a historical necessity, Stresemann pursued rapprochement with the Western powers, which resulted in the Locarno pacts and Germany's entry into the League of Nations. Moscow could only view these events as serious setbacks. For while Berlin began to enjoy greater freedom of action than at any time since the end of the war, Russia could find itself totally isolated, should the German government so decide. Such an eventuality spelled real danger because Russia's international position had visibly deteriorated.

True, in 1924, Great Britain, France, and Italy established diplomatic relations with Moscow, but they were motivated by hopes for economic advantages and expectations of changes in Russia rather than by sympathy for or confidence in Soviet policies. In numerous instances, those policies were openly castigated or successfully challenged. In the spring of 1924 the French parliament, despite Moscow's protests, ratified an agreement recognizing Romania's incorporation of Bessarabia. Furthermore, the collision of British and Russian interests in Persia, Afghanistan, and Turkey weakened Russia's influence in the region. Following unsuccessful Communist uprisings in China, Sino-Soviet relations became strained and would eventually be broken off altogether. Comintern's activities were widely and critically commented upon in the European press. The famous "Zinoviev Letter" of October 1924 caused an uproar in Great Britain. Though most probably the whole affair originated in a forgery, it resulted in a well-publicized campaign against Comintern's interference in Britain's domestic policies. Abortive Communist attempts to seize power in Bulgaria (September 1923) and Estonia (December 1924) were criticized all over Europe. Since April 1925 the Bulgarian government had publicly accused Moscow of fomenting subversion and violence.[12] In 1925 Polish authorities discovered that members of the Soviet legation and commercial missions had engaged in espionage and strikes in Silesia. A note of protest sent to Moscow produced accusations that the Poles, in cooperation with the British, had been preparing a "war" against the Soviet Union.[13] The Polish revelations, however, received wide and sympathetic international press coverage.

At that time, just prior to the conclusion of the Locarno pacts, the Soviet government made some moves apparently aimed at improving relations with Poland. In September 1925 Chicherin rather unexpectedly visited Warsaw, where he met with the press and had a discussion with Foreign Minister Skrzynski. In his press interview he spoke about mutual advantages that would result from improved Polish-Soviet relations, particularly in the economic field.[14] In his conversation with Skrzynski, he went as far as to suggest a nonaggression pact.

Chicherin's initiative may have been a bona fide attempt to break Russia's isolation and acquire some freedom of action vis-à-vis Germany, or (the matter is not entirely clear) it could have been just an exercise in pressuring Berlin, registering Moscow's displeasure with Stresemann's Western policies. In any case, it failed. Suspicious of Communist Russia, the Poles were less than enthusiastic about defying the trend. The security of Poland, it was reasoned in Warsaw, rested on the support of the Western powers. Although not opposed to a rapprochement in principle, the Polish government raised conditions that made it unacceptable to Moscow.

The conditions, in part, concerned Poland's Baltic policies. Russia's western neighbors—the Baltic countries and Romania—feared and distrusted it no less than the Poles did. They considered their domestic Communism to be more dangerous than it was elsewhere because they had no natural frontiers protecting them against Soviet-Communist infiltration. Furthermore, all of the Baltic states, large areas of Poland, and Romanian Bessarabia had been Russian provinces in the past—another reason to fear that Moscow might try to recover its old possessions. They well remembered that in 1918 the Red Army and the Bolshevik government openly supported their Communist parties and even proclaimed Finland, Latvia, Estonia, and Lithuania Soviet republics. Memories and circumstance thus resulted in a tendency among the Baltic states to create some regional organization to strengthen their security.

Poland supported, and in several instances initiated, concrete actions to that end. Formation of a Baltic bloc might not only create a new balance of power in central-eastern Europe but, because of Poland's size and potential, could secure a leading position for it.

Attractive and advantageous as the idea seemed, it had systemic weaknesses and never produced meaningful results. Finland, although in principle favoring the design, considered itself a Scandinavian nation and gravitated toward Sweden and Norway rather than toward its southern neighbors. Lithuania, waging its undeclared "war" against Poland over the issue of Vilna, refused to cooperate with Warsaw. Without Lithuania, a security arrangement with Poland looked less attractive to Latvia and Estonia. And, of course, all countries had to be on guard not to arouse too much displeasure in Moscow.

Eventually, on March 17, 1922, Finland, Estonia, Latvia, and Poland concluded a rather loose agreement not to enter into any coalitions directed against each other. Ensuing conferences produced some vague declarations of "common interest and concern," and, on November 1, 1923, Estonia and Latvia concluded a mutual defense treaty, the only significant step in the otherwise flimsy "Baltic bloc."

When Chicherin offered Poland a nonaggression pact, he was confronted with a demand that it include the Baltic states as well, *all acting together*. He categorically rejected this as a move to form an anti-Soviet bloc, led by Poland and covertly by the British.

Even before Chicherin's visit to Warsaw, Alexis I. Rykov, chairman of the Council of People's Commissars, branded the Baltic efforts to establish a bloc as anti-Soviet in his May 1925 report to the Third Soviet Congress. On April 6, 1926, Chicherin publicly accused Great Britain of enticing Poland into an anti-Soviet orientation and of "hindering the prospect of a rapprochement." Several days later Litvinov pointed out in his report to the Central Executive Committee that the Soviet government would not deal with Poland as a "manager" for the Baltic states, nor would it recognize "Poland's protectorate, open or concealed, over the Baltic." The Soviet ambassador in Paris, Khristian Rakovsky, argued that acquiescing to the Polish demand would practically mean "ourselves creating an anti-Soviet coalition."[15]

As could be expected, the Chicherin-initiated rapprochement with Poland produced a dissonance in German-Soviet relations. In March 1926 he explained his policy to Rantzau, pointing out that Russia needed stability on its western frontier and had to frustrate British plans for using Poland as part of its anti-Soviet policies. As a result, he said, Russia should anticipate a three- to five-year nonaggression pact with Poland, recognizing the Treaty of Riga boundaries. The German ambassador vehemently disagreed, emphasizing that even a temporary agreement along these lines would be irreconcilable with the imminent German-Soviet treaty.[16] Soon afterward, on March 27, Stresemann instructed Rantzau to inform the Narkomindel that any agreement between Russia and Poland—nonaggression, neutrality, or arbitration—would be "incompatible" with the negotiated German-Soviet treaty.[17]

It is a matter of conjecture whether Chicherin's initiative, if accepted by Warsaw, would have significantly affected German-Soviet relations—already strained in any event by the Locarno pacts. As the situation developed, Russia and Germany concluded the Treaty of Berlin on April 24, 1926. At face value it provided for each state's neutrality in case the other was attacked. In practice, however, its importance was much greater. In a special exchange of letters attached to the treaty, the Soviet government received assurance that should Russia be involved in a war and should the League of Nations declare it an aggressor, Germany would still be free not to comply with the League's decision to apply sanctions.[18] There was nothing illegal in the assurance, because at the time of Germany's entry into the League, the council did recognize its right to declare neutrality in case sanctions provided by Article 16 were applied.[19] The meaning of the document, however, was evident; Germany implicitly recognized the possibility of Russia's expansion in central-eastern Europe, particularly in Poland.

That this was the meaning of the exchange of letters can be deduced from the arguments used in preliminary negotiations. In December 1925 Chicherin demanded and obtained assurance from Stresemann that should Russia find itself at war with Poland or Romania, Germany would remain neutral.[20] During formal negotiations they also reached an understanding that in the future neither party would conclude any agreement explicitly recognizing or guaranteeing Poland's boundaries.[21]

Pilsudski's May 1926 coup d'état had to be carefully watched by Moscow because of Pilsudski's past, his personality, and his well-known vision for Poland. During World War I he fought, albeit temporarily, on the side of Germany. He fought against Bolshevik Russia and as commander in chief of Polish forces defeated the Red Army at the gates of Warsaw. He believed that in the final analysis the security of central-eastern European countries, notably Poland, was conditioned by the independence of non-Russian nations dominated by Moscow. It was this belief that led him to Kiev in April 1920. He saw Poland as a natural leader of smaller nations situated between Germany and Russia and in the past had professed Poland's "historical mission." Terminating the unstable period of the parliamentary system of government, his rule guaranteed cohesion in Poland's foreign policy. He enjoyed great popularity in his country, and nothing indicated that his regime would be short-lived. His emergence as the unchallenged master of Polish politics created a new situation that had to be reckoned with.

Moscow must have considered Pilsudski's seizure of power particularly dangerous because of domestic and international developments. On the domestic scene, all signs indicated an approaching crisis. The struggle for power between Stalin, Trotsky, and other prominent Bolshevik leaders weakened the Soviet Union's political structure. Economic difficulties appeared insurmountable, industry seemed incapable of steady growth, and the agricultural sector was constantly at odds with the cities. The standard of living was dangerously low. Many expected a collapse of the entire system.

In the international arena, Russia's isolation became almost complete. In October 1925 several Communist leaders were arrested in Great Britain, and numerous compromising documents were found in their homes and offices. In June of the following year the British government offered these documents as proof of the British Communist party's subversive character. The Soviet Trade Unions' open political and financial support of the coal miners' strike in the summer of 1926 led to renewed accusations of Moscow's interference in Britain's domestic affairs. Demands for a rupture of diplomatic relations with Russia multiplied.

On June 19, 1926, France and Romania signed a treaty of guarantee, a move viewed as a challenge by Moscow because of Russia's never-abandoned claim to Bessarabia. A sharply worded Soviet protest followed. A few months later Italy concluded a similar treaty. The Soviet press made accusations, and there was another diplomatic protest. [22]

The Anglo-Russian conflict had meanwhile reached a critical stage. In February 1927 the Foreign Office threatened to suspend diplomatic relations with Moscow, and in May British police raided both the Anglo-Soviet commercial company ARCOS (All Russian Cooperative Society) and the Soviet trade delegation's premises, holding its personnel incommunicado for several days. Eventually, on May 26, 1929, Great Britain did break off diplomatic relations with Russia.

Shortly thereafter, the Soviet minister in Warsaw, Peter L. Voykov, was murdered by a Russian political émigré, Boris Koverda. The incident provoked an extremely strong reaction in Moscow and prompted an accusation that Polish authorities supported "terrorist acts and bandit raids" against Soviet citizens and territory. [23] The Communist press launched a campaign using Voykov's murder as new evidence that an international anti-Soviet conspiracy existed and that Pilsudski's government was taking an active part in its operations.

On July 28, 1927, Stalin wrote about a "real and material threat of a new war in general, and a war against the U.S.S.R. in particular." He specifically accused the "English bourgeoisie and its fighting staff, the Conservative party," in power since the end of 1925, of "initiating" and "creating a united imperialist front against the U.S.S.R." Two weeks later, on August 10, the Narkomindel issued an official statement accusing the British press of inciting a war against Russia and preparing a "moral atmosphere" for it. [24] Apparently believing that an anti-Soviet, British-led international front was in the making, the Soviet leaders feared that Pilsudski's regime might become its outpost.

To neutralize the new Polish regime's expected hostility, Moscow took three steps. First, it sought and received assurance from Berlin that the Rapallo spirit would continue to guide German-Soviet relations. Second, it undermined Poland's Baltic policies. Third, it approached the Poles, again offering détente.

Chicherin assessed the situation in Poland soon after Pilsudski staged his coup. Although convinced of Pilsudski's hostility and having the "greatest interest in the maintenance of a certain opposition against Pilsudski within Poland,"[25] he told Rantzau that Russia would not intervene. Pilsudski was anti-French and pro-British, and because of Poland's economic situation, he might try some accommodation with Germany. In view of his anti-Russian orientation, such an accommodation would mean that he wanted a free hand in the east. The commissar for foreign affairs concluded that the Soviet government would watch his activities with caution. Six months later Chicherin confirmed this evaluation in a talk with Stresemann. Both agreed that Poland should be kept under "pressure" from the west, meaning Germany.[26]

In attacking Warsaw's Baltic policies, Moscow offered each Baltic state a *separate* neutrality treaty. Estonia and Latvia rejected the offer, insisting on collectivity, with the inclusion of Poland. Lithuania, however, accepted it because of Russia's stand on the Vilna question, and on September 28, 1926, a Lithuanian-Soviet treaty was signed. In the official exchange of letters, Chicherin declared on behalf of his government that the "violation of the Lithuanian frontiers which has taken place against the will of the Lithuanian people" had never been recognized by the Soviet Union and, in consequence, had not prejudiced Lithuania's rights.[27] Although not mentioning Poland, the declaration evidently referred to the Polish seizure of Vilna in 1920.

The Soviet move proved adroit and effective. It deepened the Lithuanian-Polish conflict, made Russia a champion of a small country, and inserted a powerful wedge between Poland and the Baltic community of states. As could be expected, it also resulted in recriminations between Warsaw and Moscow. August Zaleski, Polish foreign minister since Pilsudski's coup, publicly stated that the agreement was directed against Poland and was contrary to the Treaty of Riga.[28] His denunciation drew Soviet protest, accompanied by an open press campaign. On October 10 the Soviet minister in Kaunas stated in a press interview that his government would recognize "any settlement" of the Vilna question, provided it was arrived at "by voluntary agreement between Poland and Lithuania." It would not recognize, however, any solution imposed "against the will of the Lithuanian people." Five weeks later, on November 19, Chicherin sent a note to Warsaw accusing the Polish government of violating the Treaty of Riga.[29]

The third Soviet step—normalization of relations with Poland—culminated in a formal proposal on August 24, 1926, to conclude a neutrality and nonaggression pact. Without directly rejecting the offer, Warsaw again insisted on the principle of collectivity of all Baltic states. Moscow's reaction was negative, as before. On April 18, 1927, Rykov, chairman of the Council of People's Commissars, reported to the Fourth Soviet Congress that the goal of establishing good treaty relations with each of the Soviet Union's western neighbors occupied a "large place" in Soviet foreign policy. The Poles, however, stood in Russia's way and, for the moment at least, the Soviet government was helpless. Rykov complained that "Poland wanted to be guardian or surety for all other Baltic states and has tried to create from Romania to Finland an unbroken chain of states negotiating with us through Poland and with Poland's help." Such a stand—unacceptable to the Soviet government—became the "chief" obstacle in reaching an agreement, he concluded.[30]

Formal stabilization of relations with Russia's neighbors apparently played an increasing role in Moscow's foreign policy, because nearly two years later, Warsaw was approached again. This time the Briand-Kellogg Pact served as a vehicle. It may be recalled that on August 27, 1928, Poland, together with fourteen other countries, signed the Briand-Kellogg Pact, "condemning" war as a means of solving international disputes and "renouncing" it as an "instrument of national policy." Justifiably, the Soviet government originally criticized the pact's vagueness, lack of sanctions, lack of provisions for disarmament, and so on, but eventually adhered to it. A few weeks later, it became the first of all signatories to obtain its ratification.

The Briand-Kellogg Pact could enter into force only upon ratification by all signatories. Since those ratifications were not forthcoming, Litvinov sent a formal note to Warsaw on December 29 with an offer difficult to reject. He recalled earlier Soviet proposals for a neutrality and nonaggression pact and expressed regret that the negotiations proved "fruitless." He reasserted his government's "unchanging readiness" to sign such a pact if Poland were willing. Since both Poland and the Soviet Union had signed the Briand-Kellogg Pact, since none of its original signatories had ratified it, and since no one could foresee when all the ratifications would be in, Litvinov proposed a separate Polish-Soviet agreement implementing the pact's provisions between the two countries "immediately."[31] The Poles could hardly reject the proposal without compromising their participation in the original Briand-Kellogg Pact and without opening themselves to accusations of nurturing some anti-Soviet plans. But again they imposed the old condition that the agreement also should be proposed to and signed by the Baltic states and Romania, all acting together.

Pressed by international and domestic difficulties, and probably anxious to break its dangerous isolation, Moscow, after complex negotiations, finally gave in. The agreement, known as the Litvinov Protocol, was signed in Moscow on February 9, 1929, by the USSR on the one side and Estonia, Latvia, Poland, and Romania on the other.[32] Finland refused to participate, while Lithuania (and, eventually, Turkey and Persia) signed a separate agreement later on.

Warsaw considered the event a diplomatic victory. It seemed that Pilsudski, apprehensive of French policies and confronted with Germany's hostility, had taken an important step toward making secure Poland's position in the east. Apparently, the optimism was somewhat exaggerated. Moscow did want a détente with its neighbors but did not intend to depart from the Rapallo course. When the Auswärtiges Amt asked if the protocol meant that Russia recognized Poland's frontiers, Litvinov repeatedly assured Dirksen that, since the agreement contained no territorial guarantees, German apprehensions were baseless.[33]

The times, however, and an inexorable turn of events undermined Berlin-Moscow relations. Allied troops evacuated the Rhineland on July 3, 1930, another sign of Germany's improving international position vis-à-vis the Western powers and its decreasing dependence on Russian cooperation. The growth of the Nazi movement's virulently anti-Communist party could not but affect the Rapallo spirit adversely. And finally, the great protagonists of the German-Soviet cooperation—Rantzau, Stresemann, and Chicherin—departed from the scene. Rantzau died in 1928 and Stresemann the year after. In the middle of 1930, Chicherin, afflicted by a long illness, resigned. Rantzau had had great influence in Germany and sincerely believed that cooperation between Germany and Russia was a historical necessity. Essentially, it was he more than anybody else in Berlin who had been the "center" of the eastern orientation.[34] He succeeded in establishing friendly, durable relations with Chicherin. Both of them had similar aristocratic backgrounds and tastes, and they respected and understood each other. Stresemann, the grand old man of German politics, enjoyed enough prestige at home and abroad to guarantee the continuity of the Rapallo course, in spite of momentary adversities or political zigzags. With his departure, domestic politics was to influence the Auswärtiges Amt.[35]

In the meantime, Russia's international and domestic difficulties became worse, making its isolation more and more dangerous. In the Far East, the Japanese invaded Manchuria in September 1931, threatening the Soviet position in Outer Mongolia, undermining the status of the Trans-Siberian Railway, and rendering Japanese aggression a new and unwelcome challenge. With the increasing strength of the Nazi party, anti-Soviet propaganda picked up speed. On the domestic front, the harshness of the first Five-Year Plan and desperate outbursts of the forcibly collectivized peasantry brought government terror and famine in many areas, particularly in the Ukraine. To offset these dangers and to improve Russia's international and internal situation, the government increased efforts to break through the walls of isolation. This time, Moscow proposed a rapprochement with France, renewed its offer of nonaggression pacts with all Russia's neighbors, and intensified its campaign for foreign capital. On March 19, 1930, *Izvestya*, the official government organ, called for a further improvement in Soviet-Polish relations and a Soviet-Polish nonaggression pact.

The Soviet initiative found cautious support in Pilsudski. His wariness derived from his wish to prevent Russia from entering European politics. But distrusting France and seeing Germany's growing revisionism, he feared that Poland might be stranded in the event of a Polish-Soviet conflict. He also wanted to demonstrate freedom of action for his foreign policy and argued that formal stabilization of relations with Russia was bound to brace Poland's security and decrease Poland's dependence on France. Thus, after some delay, at the end of 1931, he instructed Beck, then undersecretary of state in the ministry of foreign affairs, to take personal charge of the task.[36]

The ensuing negotiations were long, complex, and marked by suspicion and recriminations. For while Pilsudski, a hard bargainer, tried to extract as many commitments from Moscow as possible, the Soviet leaders, though anxious to conclude the agreement, did not wish to weaken further their already deteriorating relations with Germany. The fact that they were simultaneously negotiating a nonaggression pact with France made for further complications.

Pilsudski demanded confirmation of Poland's territorial status quo in a manner not allowing different interpretations; an agreement on an unequivocal definition of aggression; a provision for arbitration of disputes; and, finally, Moscow's agreement that the negotiations would be carried out and the pact signed by all of Russia's neighbors, acting as a bloc.

At the outset of negotiations a compromise had already been reached: the Poles dropped their demand for collectivity, and Moscow agreed to negotiate and conclude *similar* pacts with its western neighbors, separately but at approximately the same time. This procedure soon revealed the lack of solidarity and confidence among the negotiating countries. The Baltic states—Finland, Estonia, and Latvia—signed first and quickly ratified the pacts without waiting for Poland, which made Warsaw uneasy. Romania delayed its signature because the Russians were adamant about formally recognizing the loss of Bessarabia. The Poles signed without waiting for the Romanians, thus producing resentment in Bucharest. Signaling its disapproval of Poland's attitude, Paris made Romania's signature a condition for its own. Warsaw then accused Paris of interfering in Poland's relations with its southern ally.[37]

The Soviet leaders also encountered difficulties. They wanted to commit Russia's western neighbors to good-neighborly relations, but they did not want to lose Germany's confidence and tried hard to keep the Rapallo spirit alive. This proved to be a difficult task, particularly in reference to Poland, because the Auswärtiges Amt opposed any agreement that would guarantee Poland's boundaries. Knowing that Pilsudski insisted on clear recognition of "territorial integrity," Berlin took the stand that Moscow's approval of such a clause would constitute an "indirect" guarantee of Poland's boundaries. This, they argued, would be contrary to the spirit of the German-Soviet secret cooperation against Poland.[38]

At that time, the Treaty of Berlin—concluded in 1926 for five years—came up for extension. German negotiators seized the opportunity to pressure Moscow for a confirmation of the existing "understanding" on Poland. One day before the Protocol for an Extension was signed, on June 23, 1931, Dirksen (who succeeded Rantzau in Moscow in 1929) obtained assurance from Krestinsky, then vice commissar for foreign affairs, that the Soviet Union would not abandon the existing German-Soviet policy toward Poland.[39] Litvinov, the commissar for foreign affairs since 1930, took great pains to impress upon the German officials that his government still adhered to and would adhere to the Rapallo line. The nonaggression pact by its very nature would have to contain a clause precluding an attack on the territory of the other party, but "a far-reaching interpretation" that such a clause would mean a "guarantee" of Poland's boundaries "could not be imputed," he told

Dirksen in November 1931. Soon after, he advised the German government to "give up misgivings" about the pact. True, it would prohibit aggression, but this "by all means" should not be interpreted as "establishing the borders" of the territory in question.[40]

Since Berlin was still apprehensive, Stalin himself decided to take a public stand. On December 11, 1931, in the middle of Soviet-Polish negotiations, he accorded a public interview to the well-known German writer Emil Ludwig. Discussing Soviet foreign policy, he mentioned "certain dissatisfaction and alarm" with the German statesmen who "fear" that the Soviet Union "gives its sanction to, or guarantees the possessions and frontiers of Poland." He refuted those fears in strong language, stating: "Such fears are groundless. We never have been guarantors for Poland and never shall be, just as Poland never has been, and never will be guarantor of our frontiers. Our friendly relations with Germany will remain what they have been hitherto."[41]

The interview was a sort of double-talk. Technically Stalin was correct and, being formally outside the government, he did not speak for it, anyway. However, in speaking about "guarantees," he did not mention Poland's eastern boundaries resulting from the Polish-Soviet Treaty of Riga. Were they or were they not "guaranteed" by Moscow? The interview and its timing probably aimed at the Auswärtiges Amt.

Stalin's public pronouncement did not calm all the apprehensions of Berlin, which consistently considered the pact to be a liability in German-Soviet relations. However, following numerous assurances by Litvinov and "a row of other [Soviet] personalities," the German ambassador in Moscow eventually concluded that, pact or no pact, Moscow had no intention of abandoning the Rapallo line.[42] In June 1932 this belief obtained the official approval of the Auswärtiges Amt.[43]

The Polish-Soviet nonaggression pact was signed on July 25, 1932, by Stanislaw Patek, the Polish minister in Moscow, and Krestinsky.[44] The two countries recognized the Treaty of Riga as the "basis" of their relations. They committed themselves to refrain from "any aggressive action against or invading the territory of the other party" and from reaching any understanding with a third country directed against each other. They agreed to settle all disputes between themselves by conciliation and to maintain neutrality in case of aggression against the other signatory. In case one of the signatories engaged in aggression against any other country, the other signatory had the right to denounce the pact. The agreement was not to "limit or change" any previous obligations assumed by either party and, if not extended, was to expire after a three-year period.

In Warsaw's eyes, the pact meant diplomatic victory. Although the Soviet government never directly questioned Russia's frontiers with Poland, there were many voices in the West—probably with some inspiration from Moscow—suggesting that one day Russia would claim what she had lost at Riga. Now relations between the two countries seemed to be stabilized on the basis of the territorial status quo. The much-discussed and much-argued clause recognizing "the integrity and inviolability of the territory," inserted in Article 1, seemed to strengthen Poland's international position, particularly vis-à-vis Germany, where revisionism had meanwhile become one of the leading political slogans. To accentuate the détente, both governments ratified the agreement exceptionally quickly, on November 26, and the ceremonies were accompanied by favorable commentary in the press.

Understandably, the conclusion of the pact aroused criticism and ire in Berlin. Soviet assurances notwithstanding, many in the Auswärtiges Amt considered the pact and Moscow's obligations vis-à-vis Poland unnecessary, motivated by false fears and calculations. Apparently the Soviet government wanted to improve its image in Europe, the deputy director of the Eastern Europe Department, Richard Meyer, wrote to Dirksen.[45] In view of multiple domestic difficulties, it also wanted to secure Russia from the West. Through a rapprochement with France, it hoped for much-needed financial aid and trade. Above all, seeing the growth of Nazism, it sought reassurance against Germany. Meyer considered Soviet motives and fears "unsound," "unfounded," and "ridiculous." He thought that the new trend in Moscow's foreign policy was unjustified because Germany would not change its policy toward Russia and because German-Russian cooperation was profitable to both. "The Russians appear to me like someone who, in fearing death, secretly commits suicide," he concluded.

It soon became evident that the German diplomats, not the Soviet leaders, failed to be realistic, for in Moscow the prospect of a Nazi reorientation of Germany's foreign policy was considered a distinct probability. On June 3, 1932, *Pravda* editorialized that "insofar as the National Socialists will play an important role in any government which should be formed in the future, their influence on German foreign policy will also grow." On November 9, Dirksen reported that all the leading Soviet diplomats, including Litvinov, were alarmed by the growth of the Nazi party.[46]

Less than three months later, on January 30, 1933—the most important date in the history of interwar Europe—Hitler became chancellor. With his accession to power, Russia's erstwhile Rapallo partner had suddenly become its mortal enemy. Hitler had his own vision of Germany's future, Germany's role in the world, and German-Soviet relations. In his vision, and in his far-reaching plans, Poland assumed a new and fateful significance.

NOTES

1. For a comprehensive study on the subject, see Piotr S. Wandycz, *Soviet-Polish Relations, 1917–1921* (Cambridge, MA: Harvard University Press, 1969).

2. See M. K. Dziewanowski, *The Communist Party of Poland: An Outline of History* (Cambridge, MA: Harvard University Press, 1959), 105 and passim.

3. See Bohdan B. Budurowycz, *Polish-Soviet Relations, 1932–1939* (New York: Columbia University Press, 1963), 36–37.

4. See the Soviet note to Poland of September 22, 1921, and Chicherin's report to the Central Executive Committee on October 18, 1924, Degras, *Soviet Documents*, 1:254–57, 467, respectively.

5. Ibid., 378–79, 458, respectively.

6. *Ost-Information* (Berlin), no. 81, as quoted by Wheeler-Bennett, *The Nemesis of Power*, 126–27.

7. Rabenau, *Seeckt*, 309; also Carr, *The Bolshevik Revolution, 1917–1923*, 3:363–64.

8. See Hans Gatzke, "Von Rapallo nach Berlin: Stresemann and die Deutsche Russlands Politik," *Vierteljahrshefte für Zeitgeschichte* (Stuttgart) 5, no. 1 (January 1956): 1–29.

9. See Rantzau report dated December 5, 1924, *AANA*, 4562H/2313/E154862-63; also Rosenbaum, *Community of Fate*, 121–23.

10. Gasiorowski, "The Russian Overture to Germany of December 1924," 103.

11. Stresemann, *Vermächtnis*, 2:516–18; also Dyck, *Weimar Germany and Soviet Russia*, 31.

12. For Chicherin's statement of April 21, see Degras, *Soviet Documents*, 2:24–25; for his telegram of August 3, 1926, ibid., 126–27.

13. Beck, *Dernier rapport*, 309.

14. Degras, *Soviet Documents*, 2:55–57.

15. Degras, *Soviet Documents*, 2:32–33, 103, 112, 139, respectively.

16. For Brockdorff-Rantzau's report, see *AANA*, 294S/1426/D572119-21; also Dyck, *Weimar Germany and Soviet Russia*, 34–35; also Korbel, *Poland between East and West*, 193–94.

17. For Stresemann's instructions, see Dyck, *Weimar Germany and Soviet Russia*, 35; also Korbel, *Poland between East and West*, 194–95.

18. For the texts, see Shapiro, *Soviet Treaty Series*, 1:317–18.

19. For the text of the German memorandum, addressed to the League's council and the latter's reinterpretation of Article 16, see Henry L. Bretton, *Stresemann and the Revision of Versailles: A Fight for Reason* (Stanford, CA: Stanford University Press, 1953), 140–41.

20. For documentation, see Korbel, *Poland between East and West*, 188–89.

21. For documentation, see Rosenbaum, *Community of Fate*, 205–6, 209; also Dyck, *Weimar Germany and Soviet Russia*, 33–36.

22. Degras, *Soviet Documents*, 2:136–37, 137–38, respectively.

23. For Litvinov's note of June 11, 1927, see Degras, *Soviet Documents*, 2:228–31.

24. Ibid., 2:233–37, 244, respectively.

25. For Rantzau's report dated May 22, 1926, see *AANA*, 4569/2339/El68754-55; also Dyck, *Weimar Germany and Soviet Russia*, 38.

26. Korbel, *Poland between East and West*, 214; also Rosenbaum, *Community of Fate*, 227.

27. For the text, see Shapiro, *Soviet Treaty Series*, 1:323–24.

28. Cieslak, *Historia Polskiej Dyplomacji w Latach*, 6, 16.

29. Degras, *Soviet Documents*, 2:140, 142–43, respectively.

30. Ibid., 2:190–91.

31. Ibid., 2:356–58.

32. For the text, see *DPSR, 1939–1945*, 1:12–14.

33. Dyck, *Weimar Germany and Soviet Russia*, 113.

34. For his spirited description, see Herbert von Dirksen, *Moscow-Tokyo-London: Twenty Years of German Foreign Policy* (Norman: University of Oklahoma Press, 1952), 47–50.

35. Dyck, *Weimar Germany and Soviet Russia*, 182–84; 234.

36. Beck, *Dernier rapport*, 10.

37. See William Evans Scott, *Alliance against Hitler* (Durham, NC: Duke University Press, 1962), 56–58, 6406; also Beck, *Dernier rapport*, 11–12, 283.

38. For German arguments and suggestions see Dirksen's report, dated January 5, 1932, regarding his conversation with Litvinov, *AANA*, K290/3933/K101869-80; also Dyck, *Weimar Germany and Soviet Russia*, 245.

39. Dyck, *Weimar Germany and Soviet Russia*, 240.

40. For Dirksen's telegrams of November 29 and December 6, see *AANA*, K290/3933/K101593, 2860/1417/D562267, respectively.

41. For extracts, see Degras, *Soviet Documents*, 2:517–18.

42. For Dirksen's report dated February 4, 1932, see *AANA*, K290/3933/K102128-36.

43. See Meyer's memorandum dated June 10, 1932, *AANA* 6609H/3082/E4496729-31.

44. For the text, *DPSR, 1939–1945*, 1:14–16.

45. For Meyer's letter to Dirksen, dated January 6, 1932, see *AANA*, K290/3933/K101842-45.

46. See Dirksen's report dated November 9, 1932, *AANA*, 6609H/3082/E496877-80.

Chapter Eight

The Crucial Year, 1933

PILSUDSKI'S "INITIATIVE"

After 1930 the Nazis increasingly dominated the German political scene. In 1929 approximately eight hundred thousand Germans voted for them, but by 1930 the Nazis polled 6,400,000 votes (18.3 percent). On April 11, 1932, Hitler received 13.4 million votes for president. On July 31 of the same year, his party received 13,700,000 votes (37.4 percent) with 230 out of 608 seats in the Reichstag, making the Nazis the strongest party. But the Communist vote also increased substantially. The appeal of these extremist parties, both dedicated to the destruction of the democratic system of government and understandably hostile to each other, deeply undermined the structure of the Weimar Republic. The Nazis lost some two million votes and thirty-four seats in the subsequent elections, held on November 6, 1932. However, on January 30, 1933, Adolf Hitler was appointed chancellor. Overnight, his slogans of scrapping the "Versailles Diktat," rebuilding Germany's military power, territorial revisionism, and demands for Lebensraum became official policy. The powerful and delirious torchlight parade, which took place the same night in Berlin, signified the opening of a new era for Germany.

The elections of March 5, 1933, gave the Nazis 17,266,000 votes (43.9 percent) and 288 seats in the Reichstag. That meant that with the support of the Nationalists (52 seats) they could control the majority in a house of 647 deputies. On March 23 Hitler was granted extraordinary powers through the well-known Enabling Act. The way was cleared for his total control of Germany.

But, strong as Hitler seemed to be in the spring of 1933, he was not yet fully established, and the opposition was still considerable. His first cabinet included only two other Nazis—Hermann Göring and Wilhelm Frick. And Germany was still militarily weak compared to other powers. The numerous paramilitary organizations notwithstanding, there were no more than one hundred thousand regular soldiers. There was no artillery, no air force, no panzer divisions. Austria and Czechoslovakia were independent, and Italy was far from the Nazi camp. In the event of war, Göring confessed later on, France by itself could have defeated Germany at that time.[1] The Reich's foreign minister, Baron Konstantin von Neurath, grimly warned the chancellor at a cabinet meeting on April 7 that these factors might spell grave danger should Germany's new leadership provoke an international conflict with impetuous policies.[2]

It was then that the much-disputed "Pilsudski's initiative" to undertake preventive action against Hitler's regime supposedly took place. There is no evidence that he contemplated a preventive war, nor is there any direct documentary evidence of specific proposals forwarded to Paris or London. Nevertheless, many of his contemporaries believed that Pilsudski suggested some concerted international action. Others thought his initiative was nothing but a myth created by his admirers.[3] The issue is of some importance, because if such an initiative really took place and was rejected, it might offer a key to Pilsudski's subsequent policies.

In the second half of 1932 and in the spring of 1933 several significant incidents of Pilsudski's making took place. In 1932 the Warsaw-Danzig convention (allowing Polish warships to enter the Free City freely) was to expire, and Danzig's senate refused to renew it. The violent anti-Polish propaganda was then at its peak in Danzig, and local Nazis were loudly professing their determination to unite the city with the Vaterland. Just by coincidence, on June 14 three British destroyers paid an official visit to the Free City. Suddenly, and in defiance of Danzig's prerogatives, Pilsudski sent the warship *Wicher* to act as a host to the visitors. The Nazi-controlled senate fiercely complained to the League's council but to no avail. Then, realizing its helplessness, the senate agreed to renew the convention. According to one of Pilsudski's closest collaborators, the marshal, disappointed by the passivity of the Western powers, wanted to show to Paris, London, and Rome that the German "tiger" was still without teeth and that some military action could still be effective.[4]

A few months later another, more serious, incident (also created by Pilsudski) took place. Soon after his appointment as chancellor, Hitler dissolved the Reichstag and ordered new elections. The electoral campaign, more violent than ever before, was marked by anti-Polish utterances. On February 12 the London *Sunday Express* quoted Hitler as declaring in an interview that the Polish Corridor was a "hideous injustice" and would have to be returned to Germany. Although the chancellor's statement was denied the next day by the Wolff Agency, the European press quoted the interview as authentic. Three days later Beck pointedly observed in a major speech before the Sejm that "so far no one managed to change frontiers with words." As if in reply, the Danzig senate announced that from then on the special harbor police were to be replaced by its own forces. Apparently, Danzig's authorities, impressed by Hitler's appointment, decided to deny Poland's special rights guaranteed by the Warsaw-Danzig agreement of 1923. The declaration provoked rumors that Berlin was preparing a coup d'état in the Free City, to be followed by its incorporation into the Reich.[5]

For three weeks Warsaw did not react in any meaningful way. Then, on the eve of the election day—March 4—Hitler flew to Danzig over the Corridor. Pilsudski waited until the elections took place and then, on March 6, sent military reinforcements to the Polish garrison at Westerplatte in Danzig, mobilized the border division, and ordered a great military parade to be held in Vilna on April 21. Belligerent articles appeared in the progovernment Warsaw press. Ignacy Matuszewski, an important member of Pilsudski's group, wrote in the semiofficial *Gazeta Polska* that "for the Western territories Poland can and will speak only with the voice of her cannons." Anti-Nazi street demonstrations took place, and the German legation had to be guarded day and night. The French ambassador, Jules Laroche, was "convinced" that the government in Warsaw "favored" the general excitement.[6] As eventually became known, Pilsudski had prepared a draft of a decree entitled "In Case of War with Germany," countersigned by the president of the republic, and held it ready in his personal, most secret safe.[7]

By ordering the reinforcement of the garrison at Westerplatte, Pilsudski violated Poland's international obligations. Poland was not allowed to take such a step without authorization from the League of Nations, and many thought that Pilsudski provoked the incident, purposely offering an occasion for the Western powers to take a stand against Nazi Germany. If so, the move failed, because the incident caused consternation and condemnation, particularly in Paris and London. The League of Nations' high commissioner in

Danzig, Helmer Rosting, refused to approve the action, demanded the immediate withdrawal of Polish forces, and referred the matter to the League's
council. Immediately, Poland filed its own complaint, protesting the action of
the Danzig senate of February 16, and a week later the matter ended in a
compromise. Under strong French and British pressure, the council ordered
the restoration of the status quo as of February 15, 1933. Poland complied,
but Pilsudski took notice that the Western powers would not associate themselves with any significant action directed against Germany.

According to official German sources, the possibility of a preventive war
was being taken quite seriously in Berlin. The German ambassador in Rome
and the German minister in Prague reported on the subject. The then German
minister in Warsaw, Hans von Moltke, in a memorandum of several pages,
informed Berlin that he had observed no war preparations, public or secret, in
Poland. He suspected, however, that the Polish government either wanted to
pressure the new German regime into a public renunciation of the territorial
claims or aimed at producing pretexts for a military action. [8]

On April 7 the matter was raised by Neurath at the cabinet meeting, where
he warned Hitler that Poland was "playing with the idea of preventive war."
On April 25 the subject was discussed again by the cabinet at an emergency
session. Neurath considered the situation "tense" and recommended that
"provocations from our side must under all circumstances by avoided." Distrustful of Warsaw's intentions, he even instructed the German ambassador
in Moscow to sound out possible Soviet attitudes in the event of a Polish-
German conflict. [9] On October 25 General Werner von Blomberg ordered the
armed forces to make special secret preparations for war. [10]

Years later, in July 1947, former German chancellor Heinrich Bruening
confirmed that in 1933 Berlin had seriously considered Pilsudski's intentions
regarding military action. This explains why the Socialists in the Reichstag
went so far as to vote with the Nazis on a resolution expressing the unanimous will of all Germans to defend the Reich in the "hour of danger." In his
public letter dated November 5, 1949, Bruening stated further that:

> According to our military and diplomatic information, Pilsudski made steps to
> see if France was ready to exercise military pressure on Germany in common
> with Poland. I was urgently asked at that time by the Reichswehr as well as by
> our Ministry of Foreign Affairs to show to Hitler the magnitude of danger.
> Hitler himself had asked for a conversation. The speech, which he made later
> in the Reichstag [on May 17] went too far in assurances to the Polish Govern-

ment, especially since at the time of the Reichstag's session our information from Paris indicated that France hesitated to accept Pilsudski's proposal. [11]

Otto Meissner, the former secretary of state in the Reich chancellery, mentioned in his memoirs that at the beginning of 1933 Hitler learned from Moltke that Poland proposed to France a joint preventive military action against Germany. As a result, Hitler, afraid that the proposal might be received favorably in French rightist circles, stressed in his speech of May 17 his peaceful intentions. According to Meissner, Hindenburg himself intervened with the chancellor in this matter. [12]

Pilsudski's "initiative" had been accepted as a fact on the British side by Sir Robert Vansittart, the then permanent undersecretary in the Foreign Office. He was informed by the British ambassador in Berlin, Sir Horace Rumbold, that "there is no doubt that Poland is now being held back by France, but would invade Germany in the case of preventive war." [13]

In the Soviet *History of Diplomacy*, A. M. Pankratova mentioned that in March 1933 Pilsudski briefed the French government about Germany's rearmament and preparations for revenge. The Polish army was ready to march provided France rendered its support. The French, however, reacted negatively. One month later the Polish ambassador presented a new memorandum in Paris proposing negotiations on the subject of a "preventive war" in order to guarantee maintenance of the Versailles system. Daladier again rejected the Polish initiative. [14]

Pilsudski's alleged proposals were not corroborated by the French statesmen in office at that time. When General Maxime Weygand, head of the French army, was asked for comment in 1953, he observed curtly that he "never heard of such an initiative by Pilsudski." Foreign minister Joseph Paul-Boncour; prime minister Édouard Daladier; and General d'Arbonneau, military attaché in Warsaw, also stated years later that they were unaware of any Polish proposals for military action. The denials by the military leaders seemed genuine. Even if the incident did take place, they might not have been informed. The denial by Paul-Boncour, however, arouses some doubt. According to Tytus Komarnicki, then the Polish representative to the League of Nations, Paul-Boncour told him in Geneva, in 1933, that the Polish proposals for preventive action against Germany had been discussed in a secret meeting of the French parliamentary commission and were rejected almost unanimously. [15]

As for the Polish diplomats in office at the time, Beck did not mention the "initiative" in his memoirs; Szembek did not believe in its existence;[16] and Józef Lipski, suggesting its existence, offered no evidence.

The existence of Pilsudski's initiative was taken for granted by numerous contemporary political writers and historians. Louis Fisher, generally critical of Polish policies, regarded France's rejection of Pilsudski's proposals for a "preventive war" as the genesis of what he considered Poland's extremely pro-German foreign policy.[17] Similar opinions were expressed by Alexander Werth, the well-informed French political commentator Genevieve Tabouis, prominent British historian Louis B. Namier, and several others.[18] Pankratova and Tabouis believed that Pilsudski's proposals were no more than a pretext for his imminent cooperation with Nazi Germany.

Reports of those who did consider Pilsudski's "initiative" a fact abound in irreconcilable contradictions. The search for documentary evidence has so far failed to produce conclusive results, so the matter is still far from certain. In any event, the search for evidence would probably be fruitless—Pilsudski rarely acted in orthodox ways or through orthodox channels. Before the First World War he joined the Socialist party and soon became its prominent leader. Once Poland became independent, he abandoned Socialism. During the war, he sided with the Central Powers, though he did not believe in their cause, and then abandoned them when the opportunity arose. He went to war against Bolshevik Russia in 1920 in alliance with the Ukrainians. He abandoned the Ukrainians in 1921 when circumstances dictated such a course.

He retired in 1923 and let the parliamentary democracy, based on a multi-party system, disintegrate. When he judged the situation ripe for his military seizure of power, he created such a public image of his personality and views that the Socialists and—paradox of paradoxes—the Communists supported his coup. He had no love for democratic processes but always wanted to be known as a man of law. Having seized power, he let himself be constitutionally elected as president of the republic. He then spurned the formal position, preferring an informal, paternalistic dictatorship. To the end of his life, he was secretive, elusive, and pragmatic, delighting in surprises, evasions, and indirect actions. He maneuvered men and events—cunningly and often ruthlessly—making them serve the only fixed and unchangeable goal he had: the interest of Polish statehood as he understood it.

Pilsudski's memoranda and records of direct offers in 1933 may not even exist. He maneuvered so as to make Paris and London *believe* he was ready for a concerted international action against the Nazi regime. He certainly realized that with the Nazis in power, Germany's revisionist policy, having received a powerful impetus, aimed at Poland. But the policy also aimed at the Western powers. So he indicated to the West—through his *acts*, not memoranda—that, if they were willing and ready, Poland would take part in preventive action. Apparently, at approximately that time, or shortly before, he even approached Edward Beneš suggesting a Polish-Czechoslovak alliance.[19]

But, as so often in the past, he played more than one game at a time. Pilsudski also knew that Germany was still weak and Hitler's power not yet firmly established. So he secretly approached him as well, proposing an accommodation. Already in April—only one month after his military demonstration in Danzig—Pilsudski instructed the Polish minister in Berlin, Alfred Wysocki, to ask for a top-secret conference with the chancellor himself.

Soon it became obvious that the Western powers would not respond to Pilsudski's approaches. But Hitler did. Thus, the foundation for German-Polish rapprochement was laid down.

THE FOUR-POWER PACT

Whatever plans Pilsudski may have made against Nazi Germany in 1933, they were doomed to failure. The French ambassador in Berlin, André François-Poncet, was thinking not of preventive action against the Nazi regime but rather of a mutual-assistance pact with Germany. As for the Czechs, they not only rejected Pilsudski's secret offer but "circles close to [President Thomas G.] Masaryk" informed Berlin that "they [reckoned] seriously in Prague with Polish intention of preventive military action at the German eastern border."[20] By that time the Wilhelmstrasse also learned that the Quai d'Orsay did not consider Germany's demands vis-à-vis Poland nonnegotiable.

On January 29 and 30, 1933, on the eve of Hitler's appointment, informal conversations among prominent French, German, Belgian, and Luxembourg industrialists took place in Paris. The purpose of the meeting was to obtain a consensus on the conditions for a durable peace. The German participants demanded complete "abolition of the Corridor"; cession by Poland to Germany of all territories north to the Berlin-Danzig line, including Danzig; and "rectification" of the frontiers in Upper Silesia in Germany's favor. In exchange, Poland would get the Lithuanian-held harbor Memel, recompensation for the construction of Gdynia, free zones in Danzig, an advantageous economic agreement, and a guarantee of its frontiers.

Soon afterward, the Germans were informed that the French government sympathized with their demands. Still, nothing came out of these rather unorthodox dealings because Neurath disapproved strongly of the entire affair. He did not believe that the conversations were well timed and, more important, he thought his compatriots' demands were modest.[21]

If the Quai d'Orsay's reaction to the Paris incident was a serious breach of the Polish-French alliance, the attitude of the French ambassador in Warsaw, Jules Laroche—whose official duty was to safeguard Polish-French solidarity—seemed even more astonishing. Three weeks after Hitler became chancellor, Moltke reported that Laroche "repeatedly" spoke to him about Polish-German relations, expressing his conviction that sooner or later Poland, "in her own interest," would have to cede the Corridor to Germany. As he told Moltke, he "was careful not to bring up this subject with Polish politicians." Nevertheless, he himself was always convinced that the Corridor was "untenable."[22]

These incidents were taking place behind the screen of diplomatic secrecy and could not be known in Warsaw. On March 16, however, the British Draft Convention conceded Germany's right to increase its army to two hundred thousand men; on May 5 the German-Soviet treaty was extended; on July 20 the German government concluded a concordat with the Vatican; and then—most important—the ill-famed Four-Power Pact was signed. All of these acts, particularly the last, were bound to give Pilsudski food for thought.

The Four-Power Pact was presaged by Mussolini in his speech at Turin on October 23, 1932, and was formally presented by him to British prime minister Ramsay MacDonald and his foreign secretary, Sir John Simon, in Rome on March 18, 1933.[23] It was initialed June 7 and finally signed by Italy, France, Great Britain, and Germany in Rome on July 15. Mussolini's interest originated in his fears that international tensions resulting from the Nazi seizure of power might culminate in a preventive war against Germany. He thought that the Poles, as well as French military circles, wanted such a war.[24]

The pact contained several significant clauses. It recognized for Germany equal rights in armaments. All four signatories committed themselves to pursue a common policy in all matters "political and nonpolitical." The decisions of the great powers were to bind the lesser countries in certain circumstances, and the principle of revision of treaties as specified in Article 19 of the Covenant of the League of Nations was reaffirmed. The original draft even contained a provision for connecting East Prussia with the rest of Germany through the Corridor, but, upon British and French insistence, this and other similarly drastic provisions were deleted.[25] The intention, however, remained. Encouraging Germany to join the pact, Mussolini solemnly assured Neurath that he "fully recognized and would support the claims of Germany to have East Prussia connected again with the Reich through elimination of the dividing corridor." A possibility of territorial changes was also implied by Paul-Boncour in his June 15 conversation with the German ambassador in Paris.[26]

That the Four-Power Pact aimed at territorial revisionism was widely assumed. The French ambassador in Rome, Henri de Jouvenel, and the Italian delegate to the League of Nations, di Sorragna, did not bother to conceal their intention to apply the principle of territorial revisionism to Poland.[27] Speculation about an imminent partition of Poland even found an echo in the House of Commons, where several prominent MPs—Austen Chamberlain, Clement Attlee, Winston Churchill, and others—sharply criticized the proposed "directorate of the great powers" as well as the intended concessions to Nazi revisionism.[28] Churchill's words, in particular, were marked by sympathy toward Poland. Even in France, many deputies as well as a sizable part of the press were critical of the pact.[29]

Like the Locarno treaties, the Four-Power Pact was considered in Warsaw another threat to Poland, dangerous and far-reaching. It seemed that the great Western powers had undertaken the creation of a new international body, somehow above the League of Nations, in order to control the destinies of small countries and to reward the new Germany for its good behavior in the West at the expense of others. On March 24, a few days after Mussolini's initiative became known, the newly appointed Polish ambassador to Italy, Count Jerzy Potocki, resigned ostentatiously, while Beck canceled his visit to Paris. On March 25 the Little Entente countries registered an official protest. True, upon an amendment of the pact and French formal assurances of its interpretation, they eventually reversed their stand in a joint communiqué.[30] But this did not change Warsaw's hostile attitude. It only provoked sharp criticism of the Little Entente.

On April 6, Édouard Daladier—premier since January 31, 1933, and an ardent supporter of the pact—observed publicly that "no treaty is eternal," in an obvious reference to the treaties that had established the Polish-German boundary. His observation elicited an acid riposte from Beck who, on the same day, warned Laroche: "If a state, alone or with others, wants to take possession of a single square meter of our territory, the cannons will speak. They know this in Berlin. I am afraid that this is not known well enough in London and in Rome, or even in Paris."[31]

On June 3 Beck publicly declared that his government would not cooperate with the four powers as an international body and would not recognize, directly or indirectly, nor be bound by any decisions of the signatories concerning the Polish Republic. He pointed out that the signing of the pact might result in a crisis within the League of Nations, thus implying the possibility of Poland's withdrawal from that organization.[32] His declaration had been preceded by Warsaw street demonstrations hostile to the pact. The Polish press, without exception, severely criticized the pact.

The Four-Power Pact was never ratified, principally because Hitler withdrew from the disarmament conference and the League of Nations in October 1933. It was he who closed the matter, Daladier and Paul-Boncour having been the pact's ardent supporters to the end.[33] To Pilsudski, the whole affair probably furnished decisive proof that a direct Polish-German understanding, if at all feasible, was the only way to strengthen Poland's security. As a contemporary British historian saw it: "Once convinced that, far from taking direct action to destroy the members of National Socialism, France and Britain were actually negotiating secretly with Germany and Italy for an understanding at the expense of Poland, the Marshal did not hesitate to take his own measures. He flung himself into the vanguard of the race for appeasement and won by a short head, at the same time nullifying the immediate efforts of his competition."[34]

NEW ORIENTATIONS IN GERMAN-SOVIET, FRANCO-SOVIET, AND GERMAN-POLISH RELATIONS

In 1933 fundamental changes took place in relations among Germany, France, Poland, and the Soviet Union. Relations between Germany and the USSR changed against the wishes of the Soviet leaders, who on numerous occasions tried to impress the new German leadership with the need to pursue the Rapallo course.

On February 28 Krestinsky assured Ambassador Dirksen that although the Soviet government nurtured misgivings concerning Germany, it did "not want to undertake any re-orientation of its own policy."[35] In April, after a cabinet meeting during which the rumors about Poland "playing with the idea of a preventive war" were discussed, Neurath instructed Dirksen to make inquiries in Moscow. The latter was assured by Litvinov that should the German-Polish "clash" occur, "there would be no question of change in the standpoint of the Soviet government."[36]

On April 28 the Soviet ambassador officially appealed to Hitler to continue the established policy toward the USSR. Less than a month later, Litvinov again assured the German ambassador that the Soviet Union was ready to cooperate with the new Germany. He pointed out two "basic" fields in which the past cooperation could and should be maintained—the "fight" against the Versailles system and a joint posture vis-à-vis Poland. Interestingly, the reference to Poland was made less than one year *after* the conclusion of the Soviet-Polish nonaggression pact and in the midst of convention negotiations on the definition of aggression. It must have sounded to the Auswärtiges Amt like an ardent appeal to continue the Rapallo policy against all odds and appearances. In August, Molotov impressed upon Dirksen that his government sought friendly relations with Germany "regardless of [its] internal structures."[37] Four months later he made a similar, public statement.[38]

Nor did Hitler's accession to power make the Soviet leaders discontinue *military* cooperation with Germany. At that time, at secret stations near Kazan, Lipetzk, and Saratov, German and Soviet officers still jointly conducted courses and carried on experiments in the field of aviation as well as in mechanized and chemical warfare. In May 1933 Lieutenant General Alfred von Bockelberg, chief of the Army Ordnance Office, visited Russia and met with a "pronouncedly friendly" reception. Marshal Mikhail N. Tukhachevsky told him that he "wished to see Germany have an air force of 2,000 bombers as soon as possible in order to get out of the difficult political situation." Other Soviet officials emphasized that they desired a military cooperation. Not until the end of September 1933 were the military stations definitely closed. Even then, however, key Soviet military leaders "had intimated" that they "hoped" for a "re-establishment of closer military relations again shortly." On January 10, 1934, Marshal Clementi Voroshilov, at the time commissar of defense, "dwelt a particularly long time on *Mein Kampf*" in a conversation with Dirksen's successor, Rudolf Nadolny. Voroshilov suggested that Soviet confidence would be restored by "two words of the Chancellor's in public" making clear that the "anti-Soviet tendency of the book" had no more validity. Three days later, the chief of staff of the Red Army, A. Yegorov, "unofficially" invited the German highest-ranking military leaders to Moscow for a "frank conversation."[39]

The Soviet efforts did not move Hitler; the essence of his policy was irreconcilable with the Rapallo spirit. His lifelong ambition and, as he thought, his destiny, was to lay the foundation for the Thousand-Year Reich, master of the European continent. This Reich had to have its Lebensraum, where the Deutschtum would find unlimited opportunities to expand, to rule, and to prosper. Lebensraum, as he had stated in *Mein Kampf*, was to be found in Russia.[40] The conquest of Russia represented for him an absolute condition for the fulfillment of his dreams, and any policy that might strengthen Russia's position was considered inimical to Germany's long-range interests. Because of Germany's economic situation, he would not object to the long-overdue ratification of the Protocol of 1931, and for a long time, he was to take precautions not to provoke Russia. Even his own Auswärtiges Amt may not have been aware, until much later, of just how deadly serious his Russian policy was. But from the very outset of his rule, Hitler sought the destruction of Russia.

Hitler's attitude could only push the Soviet leaders into reorienting their foreign policy, particularly in view of the situation in the Far East, where Japanese expansion threatened Russia's vital interests. For years an enemy of the Versailles system, Russia would soon become a staunch supporter of the territorial status quo. An enemy of the League of Nations, it would soon join it. So far content with the nonaggression pacts, it would now launch a diplomatic offensive for higher goals and assume a new role on the international scene.

In early 1933 Litvinov proposed to all Russia's neighbors an agreement, eventually known as the London Convention for the Definition of Aggression. The convention[41] defined "direct" as well as "indirect" attack, launched with or without the declaration of war, by "regular" armed forces or "irregular" armed bands. It specified that neither internal disorders nor a government's domestic or foreign policies could ever be used as pretexts for aggression. Political and economic sovereignty, as well as territorial integrity of all signatories, were explicitly recognized. After brief negotiations, the convention was signed in London by the Soviet Union, Estonia, Latvia, Poland, Romania, Persia, Turkey, and Afghanistan on July 3, 1933. Faithful to its tradition of not taking part in any activity together with Poland, Lithuania signed separately on July 5.

In all countries concerned, the convention received an extremely good reception as an important step toward collective security, especially since Russia concluded similar conventions with the Little Entente countries

(Czechoslovakia, Romania, and Yugoslavia), none of whom at the time had diplomatic relations with the Soviet government. Those events, too, received a wide and sympathetic coverage in the international press. With Hitler already in power, Moscow's emphasis on peace contributed to the popularity of and confidence in the Soviet Union. On November 16 the United States accorded its de jure recognition and was followed by Austria, Bulgaria, Czechoslovakia, Hungary, and Romania. Nazi "anti-Bolshevik" propaganda only increased the Soviet Union's popularity, and many began to look upon it as a bastion of international stability and progress against the Nazi reaction and the expected adventurism of the new Germany.

The second Soviet move, of even greater importance, concerned France. In July and August 1933 Litvinov and the Soviet ambassador in France, Valerian Dogalevsky, made preliminary suggestions for "furthering" the "political and economic rapprochement."[42] The initiative fell on fertile ground. Hitler's initial successes; the sharp and publicly announced increase in Germany's military budget; Germany's imminent withdrawal from the disarmament conference and from the League of Nations; the weakness of France's eastern European allies; and, finally, France's own domestic instability made many in Paris believe that only close cooperation with Russia could bolster its undermined national security. The military particularly emphasized the need for Franco-Soviet cooperation.[43] The tradition of Franco-Russian alliance was deeply rooted in France. Improved relations between the Soviet Union and its neighbors had an equal impact. The latter factor, it was thought, might enable Poland and the Little Entente countries to join France and the Soviet Union and eventually produce a powerful system of security aimed at containing Hitler's Germany on both sides.

Although the Quai d'Orsay officially shunned negotiations for several weeks, in an October 31 conversation with Litvinov, Paul-Boncour forwarded the idea of an alliance. He also outlined the procedure: Russia would have to enter the League of Nations, and a future Franco-Soviet alliance would have to be "coordinated" with existing French alliances, notably the one with Poland.[44] The Soviet government readily agreed to both points. Soon thereafter, Stalin publicly hinted that the Soviet Union might join the League of Nations,[45] and negotiations for the so-called Eastern Locarno, or Eastern Pact, got underway.

The third Moscow initiative was aimed at Poland. With the hostile Nazis in power, Poland suddenly assumed a new significance. No longer a prospective victim of Soviet-German cooperation, it now became a corridor through which Germany might one day attack Russia with or even without the cooperation of the Poles. Thus, bringing Poland into the Soviet security system became a matter of grave importance.

In approaching the Poles, the Soviet leaders followed the pattern that governed their past relations with Germany—territorial expansion. They knew of Poland's interest in the Baltic area and probably suspected that Pilsudski still nurtured some ideas not exactly friendly toward Lithuania's independence. They apparently decided to exploit these factors. Twice— once informally through Radek, and formally a few months later—the Polish government received two Soviet proposals. The first was a Soviet-Polish "joint protection"; the second, a Soviet-Polish "guarantee" of the Baltic states. On the face of it, the proposals were directed against Germany, but Beck saw them as an attempt to establish a Polish-Soviet protectorate, a sort of "zone of interest." Strengthened in that belief because of Moscow's insistence on secrecy, he did exactly the opposite and informed Tallin and Riga, which understandably opposed the whole idea. The matter was dropped.[46]

The failure of the direct approach evidently did not discourage the Soviet leaders. They probably still expected that Poland eventually might join a collective security system via France. Whatever the motives, they tried to create as friendly an atmosphere between both countries as possible. In March, a Soviet art exhibition opened in Warsaw. In April, the editor of the semiofficial *Gazeta Polska*, Boguslaw Miedzinski, visited Moscow, and soon the editor of *Izvestya*, Radek, returned the visit. In May, the Soviet trade mission arrived in Warsaw, followed by a courtesy visit of army, navy, and air force officers. All these events were widely and sympathetically publicized. By the end of the year (two months after the Paul-Boncour–Litvinov conversation), the commissar for foreign affairs reported to the Central Executive Committee on the growing "mutual confidence and understanding" between the Soviet Union and Poland and about the "community of interest arising from common dangers and common anxieties."[47]

Soviet initiatives to establish a close cooperation with Poland in 1933 failed because Pilsudski still considered Russia a more imminent danger than Germany. He saw advantages in the nonaggression pact and agreed to exchange courtesies, but he would go no further.

This was because Pilsudski saw in recent developments an unexpected opportunity for Poland. He had never relied on the League of Nations, he did not trust France, and he had just discovered that the Western powers were ready to cooperate with Hitler through the Four-Power Pact. He feared that in the event of any Polish-German crisis, Poland might be left alone, flanked by a distrusted Russia. On the other hand, however, the new Germany was still weak and needed time for reconstruction. Hitler himself needed time to consolidate the situation domestically and internationally. As an Austrian, Pilsudski thought, Hitler was probably free of the traditional Prussian anti-Polish bias. As a dictator, Hitler could control public opinion and initiate policies that no other politician ever dared initiate before him. His accession to power could represent a "unique" chance for Poland to normalize its relations with Germany, at least temporarily.

The Polish-German rapprochement also must have seemed attractive to Pilsudski because the Rapallo policy, so dangerous to Poland, seemed buried by Hitler. Consequently, an accommodation with Germany would give Poland an enviable position of balance between its two neighbors, powerful but antagonistic toward each other. Poland's security might be strengthened and its international standing enhanced. Pilsudski concluded that he should approach Hitler.

On April 4 Wysocki received highly secret instructions to arrange a conference of "utmost importance" between Hitler and Szembek, undersecretary in the foreign affairs ministry. Simultaneously, Beck, in a conversation with Moltke, hinted at direct German-Polish negotiations.[48] Eventually, the project to send Szembek was abandoned; instead Warsaw decided to use Wysocki. On April 18 Wysocki received new and detailed instructions for his meeting with Hitler. He immediately asked for an audience and was invited for May 2.[49]

Only three days after Pilsudski sent his first set of instructions to Wysocki, Neurath presented the Auswärtiges Amt views on Germany's eastern policies at a cabinet meeting.[50] He emphasized that since Germany's "main objective" should be, as before, the "revision of the eastern border," an understanding with Poland was "neither possible nor desirable." Tension in German-Polish relations should be maintained so that the world would not forget Germany's claims. He did not believe that territorial revision could take place in less than five years, because Germany needed that much time for military and economic recovery.

While making his exposé, Neurath obviously did not yet realize the fateful significance of Hitler's accession to power. If Neurath's exposé made any impression on Hitler at all, it must have made him realize how little the Auswärtiges Amt understood his thinking and how vital was his personal direction of Germany's foreign policy. Neither the 754 square miles of Danzig nor some 6,300 square miles of the Corridor were the "main objective" of his eastern policy. His main objective was Russia, the only real Lebensraum in Europe for his future Reich. He did not want to maintain tensions between Poland and Germany; on the contrary, he wanted Poland's cooperation. He needed Poland's neutrality while he consolidated Germany's power, and he needed Poland as a corridor to Russia. The differences between Poland and Germany seemed of secondary importance to him, and one day, so he apparently thought, a peaceful settlement could be reached. He himself would choose the proper moment, as well as the terms of the settlement. The Poles, he expected, would approve of both, because he decided to reduce Germany's territorial claims on Poland to a minimum never before advocated by postwar German leaders.

In Hitler's view, once Germany recovered the position due Germany in Europe under his providential leadership, Poland would certainly become more amenable. Once his Russian policy succeeded—and about that the Führer had no doubts—by the nature of things, Poland would become Germany's vassal, dependent on his will. He could not go wrong in seeking rapprochement with Poland. "If only we could come to an agreement with Poland! But Pilsudski is the only man with whom that would be possible,"[51] he told Dirksen, who visited Berlin at the beginning of 1933. Hitler did not have to make the first move. Pilsudski did.

NOTES

1. Comte Jean Szembek, *Journal, 1933–1939*, preface by Leon Noël (Paris: Plon, 1952), 162.

2. *DGFP*, series C, 1:256.

3. For an analysis and documentation tending to prove that Pilsudski *did* suggest to France a joint preventive action against the Nazi regime, see Hans Roos, "Die Präventive Kriegspläne Pilsudskis von 1933," *Vierteljahrshefte für Zeitgeschichte* 3 (October 1955): 344–63. For the opposite view, Zygmunt J. Gasiorowski, "Did Pilsudski Attempt to Initiate a Preventive War in 1933?" *Journal of Modern History* 27 (June 1955). For the most recent collection of data tending to prove the existence of the "initiative," see Waclaw Jedrzejewicz, "The Polish Plan for a 'Preventive War' Against Germany in 1933," *The Polish Review* 11, no. 1 (Winter 1966): 62–91.

4. Miedzinski, "Pakty Wilanowskie" (Wilanow Pacts), *Kultura* (Paris), no. 8/190 (July–August 1963): 122–23.

5. See Jaroslaw Jurkiewicz, *Pakt Wschodni* (*Eastern Pact*) (Warsaw: Ministerstwo Obrony Narodowej, 1963), 41.

6. Pobóg-Malinowski, *Najnowsza Historja Polityczna Polski*, 2:733; Laroche, *La Pologne de Pilsudski*, 124–45.

7. It was found there upon Pilsudski's death, May 12, 1935. Pobóg-Malinowski, *Najnowsza Historja Polityczna Polski*, 2:740; also reported by Mieczyslaw Lepecki, Pilsudski's adjutant, *Świat* (Warsaw), no. 37 (582) (September 16, 1962), as cited by Szembek, *Diariusz*, 1:58.

8. For pertinent reports, see *DGFP*, series C, 1:325, 343, 328–33, respectively.

9. *DGFP*, series C, 1:259, 343, 364 respectively.

10. G. Meineck, *Hitler und die deutsche Aufrüstung 1933–1937* (Wiesbaden, 1959), 50–51, as cited by Jurkiewicz, *Pakt Wschodni*, 44.

11. For the full text, see S. Sopicki, "Przyczynki do Polskiej Akcji Prewencyjnej" (Footnotes to the Polish preventive action), *Niepodległość* (London) 4 (1952): 169–70.

12. Otto Meissner, *Stattssekretär unter Ebert-Hindenburg-Hitler* (Hamburg: Hoffman und Campe Verlag, 1950), 335, 338.

13. Lord Vansittart, *The Mist Procession* (London: Hutchinson and Co., 1958), 468–69; *DBFP*, 2nd series, 5, 28, respectively.

14. Potemkin, *Istoriia Diplomatii*, 3:471–73.

15. Konstanty Jelenski, "Wywiad z Generalem Weygand" (An interview with General Weygand), *Kultura* (Paris), no. 668 (June 1953): 87; Alexander Bregman, "Legenda czy Fakt Historyczny" (Legend or a historical fact), *Dziennik Żolnierza* (London), January 4, 1954, 2; Komarnicki, "Pilsudski a polityka wielkich mocarstw zachodnich," 90, respectively.

16. Szembek's letter to Edward Raczyński, dated August 31, 1942, Szembek, *Diariusz*, 2:4–10.

17. Louis Fisher, "Poland and Peace," *The New Statesman and Nation* (London), new series, 11 (268), April 11, 1936, 557–58; also Louis Fisher, *Men and Politics* (New York: Harper and Row, 1941), 285.

18. See Alexander Werth, *The Last Days of Paris* (London: Hamish Hamilton, 1940), 218–19; Geneviève Tabouis, *They Called Me Cassandra* (New York: Charles Scribner's Sons, 1942), 166–67; Lewis B. Namier, *Diplomatic Prelude, 1938–1939* (London: Macmillan Co., 1948), 10–15, 439.

19. See confidential conversation between Beneš, Prime Minister James MacDonald, and Foreign Secretary Sir John Allsebrook Simon in Geneva on March 13, 1933, *DBFP*, 2nd series, 4:520–21.

20. *DGFP*, series C, 1:20–21, 325, respectively.

21. Ibid., 2–5, 41, 38–41, respectively.

22. *AANA*, 5964/2802/E438393-94.

23. For the text of Mussolini's draft, see *DGFP*, series C, 1:162–63.

24. See the memorandum of Germany's foreign minister of March 14, 1933, and the reports of the German ambassador in Italy of March 15, March 28, and April 12, 1933; *DGFP*, series C, 1:160–62, 166–68, 227–29, 280–82, respectively.

25. *FRUS*, 1933, 1:396–98.

26. *DGFP*, series C, 1:160–62, 569, respectively.

27. Pobóg-Malinowski, *Najnowsza Historja Polityczna Polski*, 741; see also Marian Wojciechowski, *Stosunki Polsko-Niemieckie 1933–1938* (*Polish-German Relations 1933–1938*) (Poznan: Instytut Zachodni, 1965), 25–28.

28. See debate in the House of Commons on April 13, 1933, *5 Parliamentary Debates*, Commons, 276 (1933), 2739–48; 2755–59; 2786–800.

29. Paul-Boncour, *Entre deux guerres*, 2:342.

30. Ibid., 351.

31. Laroche, *La Pologne de Pilsudski*, 123.

32. Beck, *Dernier rapport*, 42; Noël, *L'Aggression allemande contre la Pologne*, 69.

33. See Paul-Boncour, *Entre deux guerres*, 2:356–57.

34. John Wheeler-Bennett, *Munich: Prologue to Tragedy* (New York: Duell, Sloan and Pierce, 1948), 284.

35. For Dirksen's telegram, dated February 28, 1933, see *AANA*, 2860/1417/D562413-14.

36. *DGFP*, series C, 1:364.

37. Ibid., 357, 450, 717, respectively.

38. Edward H. Carr, *German Soviet Relations between the Two Wars 1919–1939* (Baltimore, MD: Johns Hopkins University Press, 1951), 110; for extracts, see Degras, *Soviet Documents*, 3:46, 54–57.

39. Degras, *Soviet Documents*, 2:338, 377; see also James E. McSherry, *Stalin, Hitler and Europe: The Origins of World War II, 1933–1939* (Cleveland, OH, and New York: World Publishing Co., 1968), 31.

40. Adolf Hitler, *Mein Kampf* (New York: Reynal & Hitchcock, 1940), 961.

41. For the text: *DPSR, 1939–1945*, 1:16–19.

42. Scott, *Alliance against Hitler*, 117–21.

43. Gamelin, *Servir*, 2:130–33; also Paul-Boncour, *Entre deux guerres*, 2:371.

44. Paul-Boncour, *Entre deux guerres*, 2:362.

45. For Stalin's interview with the *New York Times* correspondent, see Degras, *Soviet Documents*, 3:45.

46. Beck, *Dernier rapport*, 35–36; 279–80.

47. Degras, *Soviet Documents*, 3:53.

48. For Moltke's report dated April 19, 1933, see *DGFP*, series C, 1:306–10.

49. For the text of instructions, see Józef Lipski, *Diplomat in Berlin 1933–39: Papers and Memoirs*, ed. Waclaw Jedrzejewicz (New York: Columbia University Press, 1968), 73–74.

50. For the minutes of the meeting see *DGFP*, series C, 1:256–60; also "Unsigned Memorandum," ibid., 2:139–41.

51. Dirksen, *Moscow, Tokyo, London*, 110.

Chapter Nine

The Polish-German Declaration of Nonaggression, January 26, 1934

The Hitler-Wysocki conference of May 2, 1933, was the first formal act in the Polish-German rapprochement. At the outset of his exposé, the Polish envoy stated that revisionist propaganda concerning Danzig and the Corridor was harmful, and that the Poles would defend their access to the sea. He asked the chancellor whether, instead of prolonging the tension, he would not prefer to reduce it by affirming publicly "in any form he considers suitable" that neither he nor his government had any desire to encroach upon Poland's rights and interests in the Free City. Such an affirmation would bring some normality to the relations between Germany and Poland.

Hitler understood that, although Wysocki's exposition was a veiled threat, it was mainly a proposal for a détente, and without hesitation gave the Polish minister all desired assurances. He expressed his surprise about the "concern of the public opinion in Poland," because "neither he nor any of the members of his Government has said or done anything that would justify this concern." He assured Wysocki that his government had not the "least intention" of violating either the treaties or Germany's obligations. He explained that he was a "pacifist," stressed the possibilities of economic exchange between the two countries, and emphasized that since he was "such a fervent nationalist," he fully understood Polish nationalism. If the Versailles peace conference gave Poland "access to the sea further eastward from Danzig, instead of tearing up German territory," he said, if not for that "malicious and senseless" decision, Germany and Poland would be able to solve all difficulties. He also pointed to the growing danger of Russia, an unmistakable sign that he did not intend to pursue the Rapallo course. In order to prove his goodwill, he agreed to issue a special communiqué asserting his intention to abide by the existing German-Polish treaties. [1]

If Pilsudski still had doubts about Hitler's response to his initiative, they must have disappeared two weeks later, after the chancellor's speech in the Reichstag on May 17. [2] He spoke about Poland without hostility or scorn. Poland was Germany's neighbor and "no imaginable historical event could change this reality." His government wanted peace and was ready "to take part in any solemn pact of nonaggression." He complained about the Treaty of Versailles, which had not succeeded in "solving" the German-Polish difficulties; however, "no German government will break an agreement . . . unless it is replaced by a better one," he added.

The détente was soon implemented. Without delay Beck informed Moltke that steps would be taken to stop anti-German propaganda and, particularly, attacks directed against "the person of the Reich Chancellor."[3] Pilsudski received a German military attaché on May 8, and seven days later the National Socialist Party in Danzig issued a declaration advocating collaboration between the Free City and Poland. On July 5 the Nazi president of the Danzig Senate, Herman Rauschning, paid a visit to Warsaw and was received by Pilsudski. On August 30, Moltke suggested to Berlin a cessation of the German-Polish customs war that had been going on for eight years. He judged that this would have "especially far-reaching political importance" and would ease tension between Germany and Poland "in accordance with principles proclaimed by the German Chancellor."[4] On September 23 he received Berlin's approval of his suggestion and was instructed to discuss the resumption of economic exchange between the two countries.

Beck pursued the matter with no less zeal. In September, attending the council meeting in Geneva, he met with Neurath and Goebbels, the latter certainly the most unpopular denizen of the League's corridors. Beck impressed them both with his friendly behavior. Neurath reported that the Polish minister greeted him "most amiably . . . , contrary to his conduct heretofore," and said that Poland "was tired of always letting itself be played off against Germany." The Poles wanted to regulate relations with their neighbors "themselves" and he, Beck, was "firmly resolved not to let the direct wire to Berlin break off again."[5]

The new era of German-Polish relations called for a new envoy in Berlin, and Pilsudski chose Józef Lipski for the task. Sent to Berlin as head of the legation in October 1933, Lipski served there until the outbreak of the war.

Born in the formerly German part of Poland, he had an extensive knowledge of Germany and its people, language, and problems. Before this appointment, he had headed the German division in the ministry of foreign affairs. A skilled diplomat, he was reputed to be a particularly gifted negotiator. Thirty-eight years old—Beck's age—he also enjoyed Pilsudski's confidence. On November 5 he received very detailed instructions from the marshal as to his mission in Berlin.[6]

The first conversation between Hitler and Lipski took place on November 15, one month after Germany's withdrawal from the Disarmament Conference and from the League of Nations. The new envoy used these two events as a point of departure for his arguments. Marshal Pilsudski, he said, wished to improve Polish-German relations through *direct* negotiations. This seemed the most practical in view of Germany's break with the League, which eliminated provisions for Poland's security contained in the League's covenant. And, he went on, since the marshal was responsible for Poland's security, he would have to take "necessary measures." Before doing this, however, the marshal wanted to ask the chancellor whether he "did not see any possibility" of compensating the reduction of Poland's security by improving *direct* German-Polish relations. He suggested a public statement by the chancellor expressing his peaceful intentions toward Poland.

As in the case of Wysocki's exposé of May 2, Hitler again chose not to notice the veiled threat contained in Lipski's statement and unhesitatingly gave his approval to the idea of rapprochement. He spoke about his peaceful intentions and expressed his appreciation for the "marshal's initiative." Although the Treaty of Versailles aimed at making German-Polish relations "difficult," he had no intention "of affecting any changes" by war. On the contrary, he recognized that Poland was a "reality," and that Germany and Poland were "obliged to live side by side." Then he agreed to issue a joint communiqué to the effect that the meeting revealed a "complete agreement" between the German and the Polish governments to seek direct negotiations and to "renounce all application of force in Polish-German relations."[7]

Once Hitler became sure that Warsaw really sought a rapprochement, he seized the initiative. Only nine days after Lipski's overture, Moltke received a draft of a German-Polish agreement to be presented to Pilsudski. He fulfilled his mission three days later, and the formal negotiations began. Pilsudski kept them strictly secret because, according to Lipski, until the last moment he still hoped for some concerted international action *against* Germany: "I [Lipski] was instructed by Colonel Beck to keep the matter strictly secret, and that also toward the *corps diplomatique*. Pilsudski, who personally dealt with the problem, would not sign a pact with the Germans before sounding Paris once more about jointly taking decisive action against Hitler, which was a further reason for his instructing me to preserve absolute silence."[8]

The Polish-German agreement, known as a pact of nonaggression, took the form of a declaration and was signed by Neurath and Lipski in Berlin on January 26, 1934.[9] The two parties declared that they would maintain peace through direct relations, affirmed their adherence to the Briand-Kellogg Pact of 1928, renounced the use of force in solving disputes, and committed themselves to not interfering in each other's internal affairs. The agreement was to bind the signatories for ten years and then remain valid unless renounced on six months' notice.

The form of the agreement—a declaration instead of a formal and precise treaty—was suggested by the Auswärtiges Amt, and with good reason. According to comments prepared for internal use and Moltke's information, the text of the declaration "could not only omit recognition of the present eastern boundaries of Germany but on the contrary give expression to the idea that the declaration is to provide a basis for the solution of all problems including therefore the territorial problem."[10] Lipski realized the meaning of the formula and warned Beck about it. Pilsudski, however, did not attach great importance to the form and had a dislike for "paragraphs." He raised no objections. That settled the matter.

As soon as the declaration was signed, a general détente in relations between the two countries began. The Nazi press ceased its attacks on Poland, and demands for the revision of Germany's eastern frontiers were silenced. By March 7 an economic convention was concluded, thus ending the customs war. Soon after, Beck assured Moltke that a congress of international Jewish organizations scheduled to meet in Warsaw in April would not be allowed to meet.[11] In June Goebbels, at the invitation of the Polish Intellectual Union, lectured in Warsaw on an intricate subject, "National Socialist Germany as an Element of European Peace." He was received by Pilsudski, an honor rarely accorded foreign visitors. Shortly after, Göring paid a visit. The Polish press restrained itself from attacking Hitler. On November 1, 1934, diplomatic representations of both countries were raised to the rank of embassies.

In international quarters, the declaration created a sensation and became a source of controversy from the outset. The French in particular argued that Poland had saved Nazi Germany from the diplomatic isolation that resulted from Germany's withdrawal from the Disarmament Conference and the League of Nations. The international press was full of speculation and rumors.

In Poland, although the declaration aroused criticism in some quarters, the government considered it a diplomatic victory. The declaration, together with Hitler's enmity toward Communism, seemed to confirm the end of the Rapallo policy. One of the most immediate dangers—German territorial claims—seemed to have been eliminated for at least ten years. Danzig's frequent, and at times highly embarrassing, complaints to the League of Nations stopped. The Polish economy, in dire need of markets, suddenly found new opportunities.

The triumph seemed even more remarkable because the advantages were gained with Poland's existing alliances left intact. Only three days after the signing of the declaration, Pilsudski personally told Laroche that the Polish-French alliance, of which Hitler had been informed, would bind both countries as strongly as before.[12] It appeared as though the marshal succeeded in accomplishing with Germany exactly what the Western powers themselves had tried before. "They would have sold us for two pounds and thirteen shillings,"[13] commented Beck, referring to a situation where Great Britain and France might have come to an understanding with the new Germany before Poland did. For him, and no doubt for many other Poles, the declaration represented Poland's belated answer to France's policy at Locarno. In 1925 France had secured its frontier with Germany without great regard for Polish interests. Now, nine years later, the Poles succeeded in doing the same for themselves, without French tutelage and, which seemed of even greater importance, without releasing France from its obligations toward Poland.

The initiation of the rapprochement did not mean that Pilsudski had either sympathy for or confidence in the new rulers of Germany. On the contrary, he realized that Hitler was playing for time but believed that Poland also needed time. He weighed all aspects of the situation carefully. In two conferences with close collaborators, on October 21, 1933, and April 12, 1934, he ordered a special study of German armaments and requested a source evaluation as to which of Poland's two great neighbors was the most dangerous. The evaluation was to be based not only on the military strength of Germany and Russia but also on political, diplomatic, social, and economic factors. He himself always considered Russia the more dangerous and permanent enemy. "In the event of our war with Russia we may very probably be left to ourselves," he cautioned.[14] As could be expected, his thinking prevailed, and the

Polish general staff eventually adopted a strategy based on the assumption of Soviet rather than German aggression.[15]

As the future would show, the agreement produced consequences more far-reaching than the Polish-German rapprochement, for it gave birth to what later on Beck would consider Pilsudski's political legacy. Skeptical of its French ally and placed between two potentially dangerous powers whose enmity was apparently irreconcilable, Poland had to rely chiefly on itself. To do this successfully, it had to maintain good neighborly relations with both Germany and Russia, based on reciprocity and bilateral nonaggression pacts. It had to maintain a balance between Moscow and Berlin, avoiding collective security schemes, particularly if they were directed against either of its neighbors. Finally, it had to preserve its freedom from foreign influences or pressures.[16]

As the future would demonstrate, the last point meant freedom of action vis-à-vis France.

NOTES

1. Republic of Poland, *Official Documents Concerning Polish-German and Polish-Soviet Relations* (*The Polish White Book*) (London: Hutchinson Co., 1940), 12. Hereafter cited as *PWB*.

2. For extracts, *PWB*, 13–15.

3. *DGFP*, series C, 1:470.

4. *GWB*, 50.

5. *DGFP*, series C, 1:840.

6. For Pilsudski-Beck-Lipski conversation on November 5, see Lipski, *Diplomat in Berlin*, 94–98.

7. See *PWB*, 16–19; *DGFP*, series C, 2:128–39.

8. L. B. Namier, *Europe in Decay: A Study in Disintegration, 1936–1940* (London: Macmillan Co., 1950), 282. From letter written by Lipski to the author.

9. For the full text: *PWB*, 20–21.

10. *DGFP*, series C, 2:145.

11. *AANP-Zespoly MSZ*, 4621, 2a–2b.

12. Laroche, *La Pologne de Pilsudski*, 148–50.

13. Szembek, *Journal*, 41.

14. Szembek, *Diariusz*, 1:153–56; Beck, *Dernier rapport*, 61–66.

15. *PSZ*, 1, part 1, 67–68, 89, 257.

16. Beck, *Dernier rapport*, 37–38.

Chapter Ten

Franco-Polish Relations, 1933–1936

The Polish-German declaration of nonaggression had a disturbing impact on Poland's relations with the Western powers, particularly France. Throughout his negotiations with Berlin, Beck kept the French ambassador uninformed. Although this emphasized the independence of his policy, it also made France uneasy. Rumors spread that behind the facade of open text were secret clauses providing for collaboration between Warsaw and Berlin. That Hitler could have renounced Germany's claims to Danzig and the Corridor without some serious concessions on the part of Poland seemed implausible, and Warsaw's assurances that the pact contained no secret understanding did not dispel suspicion. On the contrary, the ostentatious way in which both the Germans and the Poles began to emphasize their common interests, and the repeated visits of Nazi dignitaries to Poland—especially Marshal Göring's—only strengthened suspicion. Moreover, Beck acquired a reputation of disliking France—not the least important factor in the growing discomfort between the two allies.[1]

Economic issues contributed to political tension. French capital investments in Poland were greater than those of any other nation, and French financiers often were unduly zealous for fast and exorbitant profits. Their practices had been arousing the ire of Polish political circles and government authorities for years. In the early 1930s, strikes and scandals broke out in the large textile factory of Żyrardów, owned mostly by the French. Incidents involving two suicides and charges of bribery in high places led to the arrest of French managers and provoked an extremely hostile public reaction. The semiofficial *Gazeta Polska* castigated the "dirty methods" of French investors who treated Poland like a "colony."[2] Szembek, speaking with Laroche on February 3, 1935, bitterly criticized the "scandalous" profits of French investments.[3]

In Paris, the Polish attitude was considered unjustified and a part of an anti-French policy. Laroche suspected that the Żyrardów affair had been fabricated by "Pilsudski's men" for political purposes and saw in the press attacks a Polish "xenophobia" and a nationalist "inferiority complex." Poland represented a serious risk to foreign investors, therefore they were entitled to increased profits. Laroche's reports to Paris argued that since the country could not industrialize via its own means, it had to accept the "inconveniences" of foreign financing.[4] Eventually, in retaliation, the influx of French credits was suspended, and thousands of Polish miners had to leave France.

Domestic politics in the two countries was another factor in their estrangement. For while the French regarded the Pilsudski government as an unfriendly dictatorship, Polish governmental circles had no respect for or confidence in the French parliamentary democracy.

By 1933–1934, the position of France had deteriorated both internally and internationally. Belatedly, the country was hit hard by the world economic crisis. The budget could not be balanced, gold reserves were diminishing, and unemployment was growing. Politically, there was confusion approaching anarchy; no cabinet was able to survive more than a few months, sometimes only a few weeks. During 1933, five governments fell, causing anxiety and unfavorable comments in the international press. In December 1933 the Stavisky affair revealed corruption in high official circles and became a national scandal. There were numerous outbreaks of violence in the provinces, and the cabinet of the Cartel des Gauches, headed by Camille Chautemps, fell on January 27, 1934. His successor, Édouard Daladier, had to deal with a violent campaign of rightist elements who, on February 6, organized antigovernment mass demonstrations in Paris. Several participants were killed and more than one hundred wounded. On February 9 the Communists led a powerful street demonstration and clashed with the police. Daladier, unable to control the situation, resigned, and a right-of-center cabinet of the Union Nationale was formed by Gaston Doumergue. Hostility between extreme political groups did not subside, however, and occasional outbursts continued. In Warsaw, France seemed not only politically unreliable but on the verge of internal disintegration.

At this time, the Quai d'Orsay launched a diplomatic offensive aimed at concluding the so-called Eastern Locarno, or Eastern Pact. It may be recalled that Litvinov's proposal of a Franco-Soviet alliance, addressed to Paul-Boncour in October 1933, found a favorable response, contingent, however, on Russia entering the League of Nations and on "coordinating" the proposed alliance with the existing French system of alliances. The Soviet government readily agreed, and in May 1934 Litvinov renewed his proposal to Barthou, who in the meantime had become France's foreign minister.

Barthou not only approved of the proposal but soon adopted it as his own diplomatic project. He was exceptionally well qualified for the task. Seventy-two years old and a veteran of seventeen cabinets, he had some forty-five years of experience, first in the Chamber of Deputies and then in the Senate. He enjoyed great prestige, having always been an ardent partisan of France's military strength. As minister of war, Barthou had negotiated the Franco-Polish alliance of 1921, and the military convention bore his signature. He was a sincere supporter of the French alliances with the countries of central-eastern Europe, fiercely opposed further concessions to Germany, and believed that only strength could check Nazi aggression. But he also wanted to bring Russia into the collective security system.[5]

The Eastern Pact followed the pattern of the Locarno agreements and, in a way, was supposed to be its eastern extension. The Soviet Union, Poland, Czechoslovakia, the Baltic states, and Germany were to conclude a collective mutual-assistance pact. In case of aggression by one signatory against another, all were to come to the assistance of the victim. France was to conclude a mutual-assistance pact with the Soviet Union, and if Berlin desired it, with Germany as well. Thus, already bound by its alliances with Poland and Czechoslovakia, France would become a "guarantor" of the entire system. In exchange, Russia would join the western Locarno as its "third guarantor." The entire system was to be incorporated into the League of Nations' mechanism; Russia would enter that organization, and in case Germany acceded to the scheme, it too would reenter.[6]

Because of the structure of the proposed system and political conditions in central-eastern Europe, Barthou (and after his tragic death in October 1934, Pierre Laval) had to carry out negotiations on three levels: conclusion of the Eastern Pact; bringing the Soviet Union, and possibly Germany, into the League of Nations; and concluding a Franco-Soviet mutual-assistance pact.

The Eastern Pact, salutary as it seemed, did not materialize for several reasons. First, neither Great Britain nor Italy intended to join it as "guarantors," unwilling to be committed in the distant and unstable areas of eastern

Europe. Nor did they welcome Russia's participation in the western Locarno.[7] Berlin, as could be expected, viewed the entire project as an attempt to encircle Germany, and rejected it in its entirety. Poland, crucial for the project because of geography, adopted dilatory tactics. Although not rejecting the offer formally, the Poles registered reservations serious enough to preclude their participation.[8] They refused to assume any obligations toward Lithuania, which still had no diplomatic relations with Warsaw, or toward Czechoslovakia, which they considered too pro-Soviet.[9] They also made Germany's participation a *conditio sine qua non* of their own adherence.

The exchange of arguments between Paris and Warsaw, for and against the pact, revealed fundamentally different evaluations of German and Soviet roles. It was that divergence, sometimes bluntly stated, sometimes only hinted at, which made the Poles oppose the pact and caused yet another crisis in Franco-Polish relations.

As far as France was concerned, Germany was a natural enemy and Russia a natural ally. The postwar alliances with Poland and the Little Entente represented for the French not a choice but dire necessity resulting from the nature and policies of the early Bolshevik regime. That system of security worked until Hitler came to power. It was then argued in the Quai d'Orsay that it could and had to be improved. It could be because Hitler, having discarded the Rapallo policy, forced the Soviet Union to seek security in cooperation with France and its allies. That cooperation should be established, argued the French, both to preclude a possible revival of the Rapallo orientation and to deter Hitler from adventurism. France's international security had to be strengthened, the French insisted, because alone, or even together with its eastern allies, it might not be able to contain or oppose the new aggressive Nazi Germany.

None of this meant that the men who steered the French policy were sympathizers of the Soviet regime. Paul-Boncour, a Socialist; Barthou, a conservative known for his anti-Communist measures while minister of justice; Laval, a partisan of rapprochement with Germany and Italy—all of them considered closing ranks with the Soviet Union a strategic and not an ideological issue.[10]

The Poles argued that for them the best guarantee of security was not only stabilization of relations with their two great neighbors and the continuation of the Franco-Polish alliance but also avoidance of collective security systems. In concluding nonaggression agreements with both Moscow and Berlin, they kept repeating, Poland had established a solid equilibrium between them which should be preserved for as long as possible. Germany opposed the pact, and in Beck's opinion, Hitler might interpret Poland's adherence as violating the spirit of the recently signed declaration. By adhering to the pact, he argued, Poland might undermine the valuable détente with Germany and possibly push Hitler toward a resumption of Rapallo. On July 13, 1934, Neurath informed Lipski that Germany would not join the pact. The same day Beck firmly assured Moltke that he would not jeopardize advantages resulting from the Polish-German rapprochement. [11]

The other factor dividing Poland and France was the appraisal of Russia. Pilsudski distrusted Moscow and considered the Soviet Union a greater danger than Germany. Poland's memory of the war of 1919–1920 was vivid, and Communism was more than unpopular. The containment of that danger through recently concluded agreements guaranteeing the territorial status quo and noninterference in domestic affairs was viewed in Warsaw as useful, but going any further was considered imprudent—it might destroy the delicate balance Poland had been maintaining between Moscow and Berlin. It might limit Poland's freedom of action or offer opportunities to interfere in Poland's internal affairs. Above all, it might open the door to the Red Army bringing "assistance" to Poland or passing through in order to assist Lithuania or Czechoslovakia. The Red Army in Poland, it was feared, involved a risk, if not a certainty, of Poland losing eastern territories and giving Communism an upper hand in national life.

This Polish attitude had to be considered unacceptable by the French because, if shared by others, it would effectively and permanently eliminate the Soviet Union from the anti-Nazi defense system. And indeed, in a way, this was what Beck wanted. He and Pilsudski hoped that with Hitler in power, the "Prussian" anti-Polish spirit might subside in Germany. If it did not, the Polish leaders apparently believed that the Franco-Polish alliance would suffice to guarantee the security of both countries.

This reasoning was well expressed in Szembek's conversation with Laroche in mid-July 1934. He asked: "Do you see a German-Russian war and the Russian troops demanding a passage through our territories? It was in such a way that the partitions of Poland started." Laroche responded with a hypothesis of his own: "But what if Germany demands such a passage?" to which the Polish undersecretary of state replied: "We shall refuse it, too." But Laroche persisted: "What if Germany breaks the commitments toward you?" Szembek rejoined that "Poland has her alliance with France. She does not need any guarantee of Russia." [12] Six months later the counselor of the

Polish embassy in Paris, Feliks Frankowski, argued that the Eastern Pact was totally useless. Germany and Russia could not attack each other because they had no common frontier. Poland kept them apart. Being strong enough to enforce its neutrality between Berlin and Moscow, Poland by the nature of things effectively guaranteed peace and stability in eastern Europe. The Eastern Pact was a result of "unjustified fears," Lukasiewicz—an ardent opponent of the pact—told the British ambassador in Moscow.[13]

The attitude of the Polish government threatened to paralyze what had been viewed in Paris as a major political initiative. Poland's adherence was so crucial that Barthou personally and officially requested the British government to use their influence in Warsaw (and Berlin) on behalf of the pact. The Foreign Office complied, but in vain. On September 11, 1934, Paul-Boncour "explained" to Komarnicki that it was the French military strategy, defensive by law, that "dictated" cooperation with Russia. In the event of war, France, its treaty obligations notwithstanding, would be unable to wage an offensive against Germany. Consequently, he reasoned, Russia became necessary not only to France but to Poland.[14] In mid-January 1935, Paul Bargeton, director of the Political Department in the Quai d'Orsay, admonished the Polish diplomats for their policy, declaring that it eventually would produce German-Soviet cooperation or a German attack on Russia. In either case, he said, Poland would lose. On January 16 of the same year, Laval, in a discussion with Beck, criticized the Polish attitude toward the Eastern Pact. Three months later he again warned the Polish ambassador that the Eastern Pact was a "necessity." Without it, peace in Europe would be seriously endangered. The French ambassador in Moscow, Hervé Alphand, warned Lukasiewicz that failure to bring Russia into the European security system would sooner or later open the way for a Nazi-Soviet cooperation.[15] As for Ambassador Laroche, he developed contempt for Polish diplomacy. "In this matter you are marching hand in hand with Germany," he told Szembek, hinting that one day France, pressured by public opinion, might denounce the alliance with Poland altogether. His innuendo had a grave meaning. At that time Bargeton denied that in case of war the alliance called for "automatic" mutual military aid.[16]

As the more and more bitter exchange of arguments between Paris and Warsaw continued, French suspicions of Polish-German collusion deepened. For while the Nazi press unanimously praised Poland for its "independent stand," eventually most of the other central-eastern European countries gave their support to the French plan. Estonia, Latvia, and Lithuania approved of it "in principle," and the council of the Little Entente passed a resolution on April 18, 1935, recommending the "early conclusion" of treaties provided by the Eastern Locarno project.[17]

Warsaw was unimpressed. Of all the countries recommending or approving the Eastern Pact, none had boundaries with *both* Germany and Russia, and of the Little Entente or Balkan countries, only Romania bordered the Soviet Union. They did not have to face the problem of the Red Army's passage through their territories. Besides, except for Czechoslovakia, none had actually concluded the mutual-assistance pact with Russia they urged Poland to conclude.

Polish distrust of French policies soon increased even more because of the Quai d'Orsay's renewed attempts to loosen the bonds of the Franco-Polish alliance. On April 22–24, 1934, Barthou visited Warsaw, where he urged his hosts to join the Eastern Pact, simultaneously suggesting a revision of the Polish-French military convention. The suggestion, refused by Pilsudski, created a bad impression. As the French ambassador in Warsaw well knew, the marshal wished to reinforce the alliance, hoping to establish Polish-French military collaboration. Two months later, on June 24, General Marie-Eugène Debeney, on a special mission to Poland, renewed the attempt, again without success.[18] In both instances, the distinguished visitors wanted to eliminate France's obligations toward Poland in the event of a Soviet-Polish conflict.

By then, the Poles became more determined than ever that they should continue their "policy of equilibrium," convinced that, if implemented, it would ensure success. Thus, France should not be released from its treaty obligations, nor should Russia be allowed to replace Poland in France's eastern security system. Since, without Poland, any Franco-Soviet agreement had no military significance, consequently, the more "independent" Polish foreign policy was to be, the more earnestly France would have to seek Poland's cooperation.

Soon after the conclusion of the pact with Germany, Pilsudski instructed one of his trusted diplomats in Paris, Anatol Mühlstein, to sound out the French government on the subject of German rearmament. Pact or no pact, Pilsudski opposed military concessions and considered the problem a responsibility of the Western powers. In pursuing his mission, Mühlstein saw Barthou, but their conversation was more humorous than constructive. Mühlstein observed: "You know perfectly well that Germany began to arm. You also know that in two, three years Germany will become the greatest military power on the European continent. Marshal Pilsudski would like to know what France intends to do about it." Minister Barthou answered literally: "France knows that Germany is arming and France will not use force to stop it. However, France will not legally approve those armaments." Mühlstein, unable to "restrain" himself, observed that in Warsaw they consider illegal cannons firing not worse than legal ones.[19] When, a few weeks later, Barthou visited Pilsudski in Warsaw to win him over to the idea of the Eastern Pact, he was treated with more sarcasm. Pilsudski thought that *military* superiority was needed to contain Germany and argued for closer Franco-Polish military cooperation. Barthou sought *political* solutions, assuring the marshal that France was not going to make concessions to Hitler. This only irritated the marshal. "Vous céderez, Messieurs, vous céderez. Vous ne seriez pas ce que vous êtes si vous ne cédiez pas" (You yield, gentlemen, you yield. You would not be who you are if you do not yield),[20] he said.

Pilsudski's bitterness and apprehension seemed justified, because in February 1935 France, Great Britain, Italy, and Belgium offered Germany the cooperation of their air forces. One month later, on March 16, Hitler decreed military conscription, in open violation of Part 5 of the Versailles Treaty. At the resulting Stresa conference on April 14, France, Great Britain, and Italy condemned Germany's action and agreed to defend Austria in the event of Germany's encroachment, but they went no further. On June 18, 1935, Britain and Germany signed a naval agreement that gave Germany the right to a navy stronger than that accorded France or Italy on the basis of the 1922 Washington convention. The agreement, severely criticized in Paris and Rome, had a special meaning for Poland because it was bound to make Germany a decisive power in the Baltic.

These events became a source of increasingly reproachful arguments between Paris and Warsaw. The Western powers tolerated Germany's growing military strength and even contributed to it; how could Poland be expected to expose itself by entering a clearly anti-German combination? reasoned the Poles. For the French, Germany's defiance and its growing power made the Eastern Pact and Poland's adherence to it even more crucial.

Warsaw's opposition to the Eastern Pact eventually paved the way for the Franco-Soviet and Czechoslovak-Soviet alliances signed in May 1935.[21] For all practical purposes, the alliances were less than ideal solutions for France—again because of Poland. In case Germany attacked France, and Russia wanted to fulfill its obligations, how could France expect Russia to help it? For France only a multilateral Eastern Pact could guarantee an effective defense system against Germany's possible expansion—and Poland made it impossible.

While Paris criticized the Polish attitude, Warsaw's progovernment and much of the antigovernment press criticized the Franco-Soviet alliance as dangerous. Pilsudski, already a dying man, was deeply concerned. Laval, passing through Warsaw on his way to Moscow, told the Poles that he himself was rather unhappy. The Eastern Pact would be a much better solution. Should Warsaw decide to revive the pact, such an initiative would be welcome in Paris, he concluded. [22]

Pilsudski, who had governed Poland since 1926, died on May 12, 1935. Consumed by cancer, he was an old, tired, used man in the last years of his life. The power passed to his Legionnaires, "Pilsudski-ites," who readily announced to one and all that they would not relinquish it because they had to preserve and enrich the marshal's "heritage." They kept their word, and until World War II Poland was ruled with—or without—public consent, in the name of the man who was no longer there.

Pilsudski's death was a terrible blow to Poland because it soon became evident that, except for ardent patriotism, personal disinterestedness, condemnation of chauvinism, and priority accorded the state interests over any national group, he had left no "heritage" to guard. He was never an ideologue, a reformer like Lenin, Salazar, Mussolini, or Hitler. His paternalistic dictatorship, at times benevolent, at times ruthless, rested on no social, political, or economic system of his own making but on his personality, on his tremendous prestige, and, when neither sufficed, on force. Without him the "camp," as his successors called themselves, became not only leaderless but also sterile and uprooted. Power became a goal in itself.

Through legislative or administrative measures, they succeeded in depriving the opposition of proper parliamentary representation and of the responsibilities of power. That freed the "camp" from democratic control, but it also impoverished the life of the nation. For they themselves were unable to provide a comprehensive ideology or program. Essentially, Poland was ruled by clerks.

Soon coteries and rivalries appeared within the "camp," some purely personal, others based on "orientations." There was no uniform economic policy—a dangerous shortcoming in a country poor in capital, overpopulated, and essentially underdeveloped. There was no uniform policy toward national minorities—local government officials implemented their own views. There was no defined political, social, or economic program—the government was a "nonparty" organization.

Before long, the centrifugal forces surfaced. Ukrainian nationalism, ruthlessly suppressed in Russia, found ways and means to grow in Poland. Extremist groups resorted to subversion and violence, aiming at separation from Poland. High-ranking officials were murdered. The German minority was gradually falling under the spell and organizational control of the new Germany. And the three and a half million Jews, most of them living in abject poverty and alienated from the cultural and social life of the nation by a cruel past, became victims of growing anti-Semitism. For totalitarianism did not corrupt only German, Italian, or Russian societies—it had its influence on others as well. The National Democratic Party, which as early as 1928 dropped the "Democratic" from its name, began to champion militant nationalism and hierarchical, authoritarian leadership.²³ Still, for the young extremist elements, this was not enough. In March 1934 they formed their own organization, the National-Radical Camp (ONR).

The members of the ONR were no doubt patriotic—but in their own way. Antidemocratic and chauvinistic, they shouted for reforms, for cleansing public life, for protection of Poland's interests, supposedly endangered by national minorities, Masonry, international capital, liberal ideologies, Communism, western democracies, and, above all, the Jews. Repulsive anti-Semitic incidents were reported with increasing frequency, particularly at the universities. The ONR—influential in some cities, universities, and young intelligentsia circles—never formed more than an insignificant fraction of the population. They were defacing the centuries-old tradition of Poland, a haven for persecuted European Jewry since the fourteenth century. But they were noisy, fortified by fanaticism. Their violent excesses were commented upon from Moscow to Paris. In June 1934, when Pilsudski was still alive, the government instituted an "isolation" camp at Bereza Kartuska. The first to be sent there (by administrative rather than judicial decisions) were ONR and Ukrainian extremists. Soon the press in Paris, London, Moscow, and New York began to treat Poland as a semifascist state *in statu nascenti*.²⁴

There were three men in post-Pilsudski Poland who eventually succeeded in getting recognition within their "camp" as the official successors to the marshal's authority. One was the president of the republic, Ignacy Mościcki, an internationally known scientist whom Pilsudski had chosen for the post in 1926. The new constitution, adopted in April 1935, gave him great powers: not responsible to the parliament, he could issue important decrees without government countersignature. The other was Pilsudski's Legionnaire Edward Śmigly-Rydz, inspector general of the armed forces and commander-in-chief designate. According to the constitution, he was responsible only to the president of the republic and was free from parliamentary and even cabinet control. Before too long, it became evident that he also had political ambitions. The third successor, in matters of foreign policy, was Beck.

As has been said, Józef Beck took from Pilsudski his ideas as well as his methods, determined to apply them faithfully. This was bound to limit his horizons, not infrequently led him to wrong decisions, and at times inculcated him with prejudice. For Pilsudski was a free spirit, unrestrained by any fixed orientations, policies, or imponderabilities. He was a man of vision but also a pragmatist. Only a man of equally free mind and equally great vision could "continue" his foreign policy. And Beck, as one not-unfriendly contemporary described him, was "in all things the Marshal's adjutant"—even after the marshal passed away.[25]

Beck's distrust of France was caused not only by what he considered its pro-Soviet policy but even more by the growing Communist influence within its borders. On February 12, 1934, Socialists and Communists marched side by side in Paris in a powerful demonstration against the government, and six months later, on July 27, the two parties signed a formal agreement, forerunner of the well-known Popular Front. On May 5 and 12, 1935, in the municipal elections, the Communists gained control in ninety towns with populations of more than five thousand, thus doubling their influence. In July of the same year the Radical-Socialists acceded to the Popular Front, and on July 14, in a powerful demonstration, Édouard Daladier, Leon Blum, and Maurice Thorez marched together.

On August 20, 1935, the Seventh Congress of the Comintern formally initiated its new course of collaboration with the Socialist, "progressive," and "liberal" parties against Fascism, thus enabling the Communists to intensify their campaign of penetrating non-Communist organizations. The general elections of April 26 and May 2, 1936, gave victory to the political left and deeply divided the country. The Socialists obtained 146 seats in the Chamber of Deputies (an increase of 49), while the Communists won 73 seats, doubling their vote to an impressive one and a half million. Four weeks later, on June 4, Leon Blum formed his Popular Front government. By that time, Beck thought, "Today [French] policy is but an instrument in the hands of the Comintern."[26]

The internal division of France and the incapacity of its leadership, as well as the mechanism of Beck's "independent" policy, were demonstrated during the dramatic events of the spring of 1936. On March 7 Hitler formally announced the remilitarization of the Rhineland, citing as the reason for his action the Franco-Soviet mutual-assistance pact then being processed in Paris. He considered the pact a breach of the Locarno obligations on the part of France and an attempt to encircle Germany. Remilitarization of the Rhineland was his answer. The Nazi fait accompli was in direct violation of Articles 42, 43, and 44 of the Treaty of Versailles, as well as the Locarno pacts, and momentarily created one of the most serious crises in Europe since World War I.

Only a few hours after Hitler's speech, Beck summoned the newly appointed French ambassador, Leon Noël, and declared "solemnly" that "under the circumstances Poland [wanted] to assure France that should the situation require it, she will be faithful to the obligations which exist between the two countries." He explained that no Polish-German agreement could affect Poland's "general policy" and that Hitler well understood the significance of the Franco-Polish alliance. He asked Noël for the closest possible contacts and exchange of information "in the spirit of the alliance and in conformity with its goals." The entry of German troops into the Rhineland, he said, might "in certain circumstances" result in a Franco-German conflict. If that occurred "dans les conditions conformes à l'esprit de l'alliance, la Pologne n'hésiterait pas à remplir son devoir d'alliée." "This time it is serious," he said.

Noël considered Beck's declaration extremely important, a "historic" act. Within an hour he dispatched his report to Pierre-Étienne Flandin, who headed the Quai d'Orsay. He emphasized Beck's firmness. "Never before did he speak in such firm terms about the Franco-Polish relations and the alliance," he concluded, asking for immediate instructions.[27] The same day, Beck informed the Belgian minister in Warsaw, Paternotte de la Vaillée, that if Belgium marched against Germany, Poland would follow.[28]

The next day, March 8, the semiofficial news agency, *Iskra*, and the semiofficial *Gazeta Polska* published commentaries somehow condoning Germany's action. Without losing any time, Noël went to see Beck, protesting against what seemed to him two-faced diplomacy.[29] He obtained assurances that Poland would honor the alliance but did not receive any satisfactory explanation of the incident.

On March 10 the American ambassador, John Cudahy, called on Noël and obtained confirmation of Beck's declaration. Perplexed and anxious to inform Washington correctly on Poland's position, he visited Szembek the next day. The latter again confirmed that "Foreign Minister Beck had made a solemn promise to Ambassador Noël that Poland would remain faithful to its commitments under the Franco-Polish alliance." But he also explained how the Rhineland crisis fit into the alliance.

> He [Szembek] said that the Polish government did not construe the occupation of the demilitarized zone by German troops as an aggressive action against France demanding military assistance from Poland under the alliance, that an actual invasion of French soil would be necessary before Poland would be bound to act. He said that if France were to send troops into the demilitarized zone in an effort to eject German military occupation, such an action on the part of France would not be regarded as defensive under the terms of the Franco-Polish alliance and that Poland did not feel under obligation to render assistance to France under these circumstances.

Concluding his report, Cudahy defined Beck's position probably more precisely than Noël did and certainly more clearly than Beck did in his memoirs: "In the opinion of the [American] Embassy, every attempt will be made to achieve every national advantage and obtain all possible prestige by an avowal of the alliance with France with the hope that no demand will be made for the fulfillment of obligations under the alliance."[30]

The fact and the seriousness of Beck's declaration to Noël were essentially established by the French postwar Parliamentary Commission, created by the National Assembly to investigate the policies, motives, and events from 1933 to 1945. Paul-Boncour and Noël testified and confirmed it, while Flandin and Georges Bonnet concurred in their memoirs.[31] Premier Albert Sarraut, however, omitted Poland from a list of those countries that offered to help France in March 1936, while Flandin accused Beck of bad faith.

In the light of the available documents, Beck's position during the Rhineland crisis was, indeed, ambiguous to say the least. First, the crisis did not take him by surprise. He was skeptical about maintaining the demilitarized zone and told Noël so on February 1, 1936. On February 2 and 26, he discussed the approaching crisis with Szembek, who noted in his diary on both occasions that Beck thought the remilitarization of the Rhineland would *not* create a *casus foederis* under the terms of the Franco-Polish treaties. He expressed the same opinion to Szembek again on March 7, just a few hours *after* his declaration to Noël.[32]

As Cudahy was making his inquiries on March 10, Beck informed his ambassadors in Berlin and London about Poland's position in the Rhineland crisis, writing that only "in the event of an aggression against French territory Poland will fulfill her obligations resulting from the Franco-Polish alliance." On the same day he told Szembek that "Poland will fulfill her treaty obligations vis-à-vis France, but only when a *casus foederis* will take place." He emphasized that "Germany's violation of the Rhineland zone [did] not constitute [for Poland] a *casus foederis*."[33] He went further and instructed Flandin himself. This, of course, could not but make Flandin conclude that on March 7 Beck had acted in bad faith.

A few days later Beck went to London to attend the League of Nations' council, convoked for the deliberation over Hitler's fait accompli. There he noticed, and so informed Warsaw, that while pressing Poland to support France more strongly in the Rhineland crisis, French diplomats contemplated strengthening the Locarno system of security in the West.[34] In their dispirited discussions with Flandin and Paul-Boncour, Beck and his subordinates commented on the situation. The Poles would support France against the Nazi fait accompli only if France engaged in "action." They would not expose themselves, however, if France engaged in no more than "*coups d'épingles*." By then the Quai d'Orsay became hypercritical of Beck, considering him both unreliable and unfriendly toward France.[35]

It appears that in the spring of 1936 Beck used the remilitarization of the Rhineland as an occasion to confirm Poland's adherence to the alliance. He did it probably to obligate France and put some backbone into French diplomacy. But, obviously, he did not consider France's defense of the Rhineland as obligating Poland to military assistance and qualified his declaration to Noël so as to have a free hand in the event the crisis deepened. Either at the time he made his declaration or within hours thereafter, he concluded, rightly, that France *would not* act, and thus the ambiguity of his stand could be pinned down. Then, through the *Iskra* commentary, he made a condoning gesture toward Berlin so that Hitler would appreciate what an understanding foreign minister there was in Warsaw. Then, in London, he gave the French a lesson in how "realistic" his foreign policy was and how difficult the French were to deal with.

The passivity of France convinced Hitler that it was weak and the League of Nations impotent. Evidently, it also convinced him that the method of faits accomplis offered great possibilities. It has been established since the war that the remilitarization of the Rhineland was a large-scale bluff, whose success encouraged the Nazi dictator to attempt others. According to General Jodl, Germany occupied the area with no more than one division. "I can only say that, considering the situation we were in, the French covering army alone could have blown us to pieces,"[36] he stated at the Nuremberg Trials. Many of the high-ranking German officials actually expected military action by France and Great Britain and could not understand their inactivity. By the same token, Hitler's success strengthened his prestige in military quarters at home. Afterward he spoke with unshakable authority.

The crisis of March 1936 proved to be psychologically and politically important because, as Churchill stated, everybody came to believe that in case of an international conflagration, "France would not fight and England would hold her back even if she would."[37] According to the French ambassador in Warsaw:

> From the international point of view our failure of March 1936 inseminated an uncertainty among our allies and our friends; if France does not react when her own basic interests are concerned, will she not be even more passive if our interests are in danger and how can we expect her to fulfill her engagements towards us? Such was the language many were inclined to use and which was used only too often in Brussels, as well as in Warsaw, in Bucharest, as well as in Belgrade, and even in Prague otherwise stubbornly faithful to France.[38]

German remilitarization and the subsequent fortification of the Rhineland affected the security of all central-eastern Europe, particularly Poland. Soon the powerful Siegfried Line would be erected, which meant that in the event of a conflict, the Nazis, who were secure in the west, could engage more troops in the east. Beck, most critical of France's ineffective and vacillating policies, realized that the Locarno system—discriminatory to Poland but still the most powerful regional security system in existence—had irreversibly collapsed. That meant to him that Poland could not count on any future collective security schemes. Nor could it count on France. Nor could it count on the guarantees of the League of Nations. He left London at the end of March 1936, probably more than ever convinced that he should avoid antagonizing Hitler and instead try to take advantage of the progressing confusion and disintegration of the European order. Before long, his diplomacy would be described as an "undignified imitation of small fish that seek their meat in the wake of a shark."[39]

NOTES

1. Laroche, *La Pologne de Pilsudski*, 137, 142, 148–50; Noël, *L'Aggression allemande contre la Pologne*, 73, 104, 509; Francois-Poncet, *Souvenirs d'une ambassade à Berlin*, 164–66.

2. See *Gazeta Polska* (Warsaw), January 14, 1933; March 10, 1933.

3. Szembek, *Diariusz*, 1:227–29.

4. *DDF*, Ire Série, 1:668–70; Laroche, *La Pologne de Pilsudski*, 175–76.

5. Scott, *Alliance against Hitler*, 162–69.

6. For the text of the pact, see *DBFP*, 2nd series, 6:827–28. The plan also provided at some unspecified future for a similar system in the Mediterranean area (comprising Yugoslavia, Greece, Romania, Turkey, Bulgaria) with France, Russia, and Italy as guarantors, see ibid., 759–60, 809.

7. Scott, *Alliance against Hitler*, 177–78.

8. For the text of the Polish note to Paris, see Beck, *Dernier rapport*, 335–38; also Beck's conversation on October 4, 1934, *AANP-Zespoly MSZ*, 4621, 3–4.

9. Debicki, *Foreign Policy of Poland*, 88–89.

10. Scott, *Alliance against Hitler*, 167–68.

11. For Lipski's complete report, see *AANP-Zespoly MSZ*, 3623, 170–73; also *AANA/6695/H100307*.

12. Laroche, *La Pologne de Pilsudski*, 170.

13. *AANP-Zespoly MSZ*, 3244, 262; and 3247, 206.

14. Paul-Boncour, *Entre deux guerres*, 2:372–75.

15. *AANP-Zespoly MSZ*, 3244, 259–64; 5211, 75–76; 3244, 279; 41–43, respectively.

16. Szembek, *Diariusz*, 1:469–71.

17. See Degras, *Soviet Documents*, 3:86–88, 97.

18. Szembek, *Diariusz*, 1:153–54, 158; 2:16–17; also *PSZ*, 1, part 1, 91–92.

19. Anatol Mühlstein, "Świadectwo Ambasadora Laroche" (The testimony of Ambassador Laroche), *Kultura* (Paris), no. 6/68 (June 1953): 131.

20. Beck, *Dernier rapport*, 59; also Laroche, *La Pologne de Pilsudski*, 159.

21. For the texts of the Franco-Soviet and Czechoslovak-Soviet alliances, see McSherry, *Stalin, Hitler and Europe*, 259–67.

22. *AANP-Zespoly MSZ*, 3246, 191–93; 247–53.

23. For a positive evaluation of the National movement and Dmowski's role written by the latter's disciple and successor in the party's leadership, see Tadeusz Bielecki, *W Szkole Dmowskiego. Szkice i Wsponmienia* (*In Dmowski's School: Essays and Souvenirs*) (London: Polska Fundacja Kulturalna, 1968).

24. For the gory conditions in the "concentration camp" at Bereza Kartuska, as reported by Ambassador Kennard, see *FO* 371/17788/4973/664/55 and *FO* 371/17788/7895/664/55. For a study on Polish domestic politics, see Edward D. Wynot, *Polish Politics in Transition: The Camp of National Unity and Struggle for Power 1935–1939* (Athens, GA: University of Georgia Press, 1974).

25. Sir Anthony Eden, *Facing the Dictators: The Memoirs of Anthony Eden* (Boston: Houghton Mifflin Co., 1962), 190.

26. Szembek, *Journal*, 180; also Beck, *Dernier rapport*, 142.

27. For Noël's complete report to Paris, see *DDF*, 2e Série, 1:415–16.

28. Beck, *Dernier rapport*, 114; also Noël, *L'Aggression allemande contre la Pologne*, 125–26.

29. Noël, *L'Aggression allemande contre la Pologne*, 136–37.

30. For Cudahy's report, *FRUS*, 1936, 239–41.

31. Assemblée Nationale, *Les événements*, 80–81; 3:805; 4:849; also Pierre-Etienne Flandin, *Politique Française 1919–1940* (Paris: Les Editions Nouvelles, 1947), 155, 203, 206, 208–11; also Bonnet, *Quai d'Orsay sous trois républiques*, 159.

32. Szembek, *Journal*, 159; 163; 166.

33. Szembek, *Diariusz*, 2:403, 113.

34. *AANP-Zespoly MSZ*, 3251, 210.

35. For the French report, see *DDF*, 2e Série, 1:570–71.

36. *The Trial of the Major War Criminals before the International Military Tribunal, Nuremberg, November 14, 1945–October 1, 1946*, 42 vols. (Nuremberg, Germany: 1947), 5:352. Hereafter cited as *TMWC*.

37. Churchill, *The Gathering Storm*, 199.

38. Noël, *L'Aggression allemande contre la Pologne*, 134.

39. *DBFP*, 3rd series, 1:431.

Chapter Eleven

The Era of Appeasement, 1937–1938

The policy of appeasement pursued by Great Britain and France in the last prewar years has usually been interpreted as shortsightedness, unawareness of Hitler's goals and strategy, or lack of principles on the part of its main spokesmen. Such an approach, however, does not fully explain the problem. Other important factors also seem to have influenced the thinking and decisions of the Western leaders.

First, the prospect of war for the sake of Austria's independence or Czechoslovakia's territorial integrity was viewed by many in the Western democracies with abhorrence. As a result, French and British statesmen considered it their duty to seek compromises, and in those fateful years this meant appeasing Hitler. Their condemnation of Nazi methods notwithstanding, key statesmen in Western government circles, particularly Great Britain, such as Chamberlain, Halifax, the influential Sir Horace Wilson, John Simon, Home Secretary Samuel Hoare, Lord Lothian, Lord Runciman, and many others did not consider German demands for the incorporation of Austria or of the Sudetenland unjustifiable.

There was also distrust of the Soviet Union and fear that a war would strengthen the USSR and international Communism. Once hostilities between the Western powers and Germany started, it was argued, Moscow would find reasons to stay out and "have the last laugh."[1] In France many suspected that the Kremlin actually might welcome a war for its own ends. Coulondre told the German ambassador Schulenburg in August 1938: "You know as well as I do for whom we are working if we get at loggerheads."[2] Georges Bonnet, foreign minister since April 1938, believed that "Russia's one wish is to stir up general war in the troubled waters of which she will fish." The influential American ambassador in Paris, William Bullitt, fully agreed with him.[3]

Another factor that influenced Western leaders was the military situation. Both France and Great Britain were lagging in military preparedness, while Germany appeared united, dynamic, and strong. Particularly, Germany's progress in building up a powerful air force was immeasurably greater than that made by either of the two Western powers. The Foreign Office informed the French in the middle of the Czechoslovak crisis that during the first six or eight months of war, Britain could offer France no more than two nonmotorized divisions and no more than 120 to 150 planes.[4]

For the British and French democracies, domestic politics made it hard to embark upon a program of armaments. Since the late 1920s the French military budget had been closely watched by the parliament, and a defensive military strategy was required by law. In Great Britain prior to 1937, Prime Minister Stanley Baldwin went as far as to deny that any excessive German rearmament was going on in order to avoid substantial increases in military expenditure. He believed that the voters would back only that government which stood for minimum army, navy, and air force budgets. Churchill's pleas and warnings were in vain. Lord Robert Vansittart, permanent undersecretary at the Foreign Office, thought it necessary to leak information on German rearmament in order to arouse the public.[5]

As a result of these considerations, it was not confrontation but accommodation with Germany that Western leaders sought. They saw in it the best, if not the only, guarantee for peace and stability.[6] As late as January 1939 the German ambassador in London, Herbert Dirksen, described Chamberlain, prime minister since May 1937, as a fervent adherent of the idea that the great powers—Great Britain, France, Germany, and Italy—should assume the primary responsibilities of shaping the fate of Europe.[7] The ill-fated Four-Power Pact of 1933 was still much alive in the minds of many leading British statesmen. Those who opposed concessions to, or cooperation with, Nazi Germany (like Vansittart) were removed.

While London sought appeasement, the French resigned themselves to British leadership in foreign policy. Grave reasons prompted this attitude. The French realized that they were no match for Germany by themselves. France was terribly weakened by World War I. In 1936 her population was two-thirds that of Germany. Because of losses in 1914–1918, the number of men coming to draft age in the 1930s was half the normal quota and one-third to one-quarter of Germany's capability. French production represented no more than one-third of what Germany produced. The industrial units were usually small, family-run businesses, difficult to adapt to sudden war requirements. France's political instability made it next to impossible to conduct a comprehensive foreign policy, and French public opinion was overwhelmingly pacifist. To challenge Germany, France needed strong and reliable allies.

But France's eastern allies—Poland and the countries of the Little Entente—no longer seemed able to perform the tasks expected of them in the early postwar years. There was no effective cooperation among them: Poland was antagonistic to Czechoslovakia; the Little Entente countries were going their separate ways, except for their common stand against Hungarian revisionism; Warsaw was oriented more toward Berlin than Paris; Belgrade was seeking guidance in Rome; and Czechoslovakia, the only one never wavering in her support of France, was unable to reconcile with Germany or with Poland and Hungary.

The Quai d'Orsay could not establish meaningful political and military cooperation with Russia, a formal ally since 1935. Such cooperation would certainly alienate Britain and Russia's western neighbors as well. It might also destroy, it was feared, any chances for an agreement with Germany and Italy. Furthermore, French government leaders themselves had not much confidence in Moscow. Besides, without the cooperation of Poland and Romania, the effectiveness of Soviet commitments was either greatly reduced or nil. And neither of Russia's western neighbors could be brought to cooperate politically or militarily with Moscow.

The most valuable ally seemed to be Great Britain—democratic, commanding the tremendous resources of its empire, and traditionally interested in the preservation of the status quo. British support in any confrontation with Germany was considered absolutely necessary by the French military. But London pursued its own course, not always consistent with Paris's wishes or interests. Moreover, Great Britain was not committed to France's aid in all circumstances. By 1937–1938, London still was unwilling to assume commitments on behalf of any central-eastern European country. As a result, French government leaders feared to make any important step without the explicit and prior approval of London. For all practical purposes, France accepted Britain's leadership in a policy aimed at preserving peace in Europe.[8]

All of these factors were known and carefully scrutinized in Warsaw, where it looked as though Great Britain and France might withdraw from central-eastern Europe, leaving the area vulnerable to Nazi pressures. Many doubted that France would risk a conflict over her eastern European allies, and not a few feared that the Western powers, if pressed by circumstances, would try to appease Germany at the expense of Poland. That fear, a constant companion of Polish diplomacy since the conclusion of the Locarno pacts, made Beck extremely adamant about embarking upon any policies, demonstrations, or protests that might antagonize Hitler or be futile anyway. By that time the balance of strength between Poland and Germany had tipped decidedly in favor of Germany. Antagonizing Hitler presented a much greater risk in 1938 than in 1933 or even 1936.

Of course, seeing Nazi expansion unchallenged by the Western powers, Poland could remain passive. But passivity was not in Beck's nature. Doubting that the Versailles system could be saved, he was determined to take advantage of its progressive disintegration.

INCORPORATION OF AUSTRIA BY GERMANY, MARCH 12, 1938

On July 12, 1936, Germany and Austria concluded an agreement which, though ostensibly aimed at easing tensions between the two countries, actually became a prologue to the Nazi seizure of power in Vienna. According to the agreement, mutual hostilities were to be stopped; commercial relations between the two countries restored; the ban on the German press in Austria lifted; the swastika authorized; and the restoration of the Hapsburg monarchy once and for all forgotten. The agreement opened the way for peaceful Nazi penetration of Austria and—probably because of this—was well received in many European capitals, particularly in London. By that time, British official circles held the position that a union of Germany and Austria was inevitable and therefore should not be opposed.[9]

By the middle of 1937 British statesmen were making quite clear that London would not oppose a peaceful liquidation of Austria. In May Lord Lothian told Hitler that "Britain had no primary interests in Eastern Europe." In November Lord Halifax, then lord president of the council, visited Berlin and told Neurath that Britain would not object to the Anschluss. "People in England would never understand why they should go to war only because two German countries wish to unite," he said. He even went further, speaking to Hitler on November 19. "The Englishmen were realists and were perhaps more convinced than others that mistakes had been made in the Treaty of Versailles which had to be put right," he declared, adding that "on the English side it was not necessarily thought that the status quo must be maintained under all circumstances." He clearly stated that the status of Austria, Czechoslovakia, and Danzig might eventually be "altered," concluding that the changes would obtain English approval if executed peacefully. [10]

Halifax's views still were moderate compared to those of Sir Nevile Henderson, since April 1937 British ambassador to Germany. According to the latter: "Germany under Hitler is renewing Bismarck's policy of annexing all European peoples of German descent, Austria, Czechoslovakia and other countries. . . . Germany must dominate the Danube-Balkan zone which means that she is to dominate Europe. England and her Empire is to dominate the sea along with the United States. England and Germany must come into close relations, economic and political, and control the world. . . . France is a back number and unworthy of support." [11]

A few weeks before Halifax's November visit to Berlin, Henderson spoke to the German ambassador in Vienna, Franz von Papen. "England fully understood the historical need for a solution of this [Austrian] question in the Reich-German sense," he said. His only qualification was that Germany refrain from "rushing" the otherwise inevitable solutions. Chamberlain himself held no different views. It was at that time, in November 1937, that he noted in his diary: "I don't see why we shouldn't say to Germany, 'Give us satisfactory assurances that you won't use force to deal with the Austrians and Czechoslovakians and we will give you similar assurances that we won't use force to prevent the changes you want, if you can get them by peaceful means.'" [12]

Three months later, on February 21, 1938, Simon stated in the House of Commons that Great Britain had "never given special guarantees" regarding the independence of Austria. The next day Chamberlain said openly that Austria could not count on protection from either Britain or the League of Nations. [13] All these statements and opinions were of particular consequence since they were made *after* Eden resigned in protest of the appeasement policy.

The attitude of the Quai d'Orsay was not much different. Visiting Paris in November 1937, Papen was "amazed" to learn from the French premier, Camille Chautemps, that a "reorientation" of French policy in central Europe was "open to discussion," provided the "extension of German influence in Austria" would be effected peacefully. [14]

Aware of these trends and attitudes, Hitler did not fear taking risks. On November 5, 1937, in conference with the highest state dignitaries, he outlined the future course of the Reich's foreign policy. The German nation needed Lebensraum, living space. Its final acquisition could be achieved only by force. In the meantime Germany would have to proceed cautiously, step by step. Neither Austria nor Czechoslovakia could provide Germany with Lebensraum. Their destruction represented no more than preliminary steps to the final solutions. These steps, he thought, could be made without risking war. Great Britain "certainly" and France "probably" had "tacitly written off the Czechs and were reconciled to the fact that this question would be cleared up in due course by Germany." The same, he said, applied to the German annexation of Austria.[15] He was so sure of his judgment that in February 1938 when Neurath, the minister of war; Field Marshal Werner von Blomberg; and the commander in chief of the army, Colonel General Baron von Fritsch, differed, he had them dismissed, thus terminating the "conservative" period of his regime. On February 4 he himself assumed the supreme command of the armed forces and appointed Joachim von Ribbentrop foreign minister.

Subsequent events confirmed that Hitler was correct in his evaluation of British and French policies. When on March 11, 1938, the day before the Anschluss, the Austrians, faced with the Nazi ultimatum, appealed to London for help, the British government limited itself to a diplomatic protest in Berlin. As for France, it was in one of its usual governmental crises. Chautemps's government resigned on March 9, and Leon Blum's cabinet was not formed until March 13, the day after Austria fell. When Kurt von Schuschnigg, the Austrian chancellor, asked for help, the French acquiesced on condition that the British and Italians participate. Then they issued another diplomatic protest. Soviet pleas in Paris for some sort of concerted and effective action against Germany were rebuffed.[16]

POLAND'S ULTIMATUM TO KAUNAS

The fall of Austria did not weaken the Polish-German détente. In fact, it enhanced it. Pilsudski never thought Austria would survive for long. He was, instead, considering the advantages Poland could get by not opposing the Anschluss. As early as 1933 he informed the Polish ambassador in Rome that although Mussolini opposed the Anschluss, he, Pilsudski, would agree "to sell it" for "a good price."[17] For Beck, the marshal's opinion in all probability represented a "legacy."

In January 1938 Beck paid what he considered a highly successful visit to Berlin. All conversations with the chancellor and other highly placed Nazi officials were gratifying; neighborly relations between Poland and Germany seemed secured. While in Berlin he learned from Göring on January 13 that the Anschluss was imminent. He did not fail to assure the Nazi leader that Poland's interest in Austria was strictly economic. As he observed in his memo, Göring "understood" his comment. The same day Beck assured Neurath that Poland had no political interest in Austria.[18] Upon his return to Warsaw, Beck argued that since the annexation was unavoidable, it could not but contribute to European stability.[19] He thought Hitler meant to direct Germany's expansion southward rather than eastward, and the prospect of the Anschluss seemed to vindicate his theory.

Just before the Nazi coup in Austria, Beck decided to visit Rome. Only a few months before, in November 1937, Italy joined the Anti-Comintern Pact, withdrew from the League of Nations, recalled her ambassador to France, and then began a noisy propaganda campaign claiming Nice, Corsica, Djibouti, Tunisia, and a part in the Suez Canal administration. Noël tried hard to dissuade Beck from making the trip, which would have been interpreted as an anti-French gesture. Although there was no urgency whatsoever, Beck did go. In Rome, he showed such a "lack of interest" concerning the Anschluss that it surprised Ciano. He also repeatedly observed that "the alliance with France [would] not operate in the event of a war provoked by the Czech problem."[20]

With the fall of Austria, one more pillar of the Versailles structure crumbled, unsupported by both the Western democracies and Poland. On March 13, one day after the Anschluss, Szembek hastened to assure Moltke that the Polish government considered "developments" in Austria an "internal Austrian affair."[21] Simultaneously, according to Nazi sources, the Polish government informed Berlin it was "in sympathy" with Germany's success.[22]

Then Beck had his own triumph. He found it in Lithuania, which, it may be recalled, had had no diplomatic relations with Poland since 1920.

On March 11, the eve of the Anschluss, a Polish soldier, Stanislaw Serafin, was killed by Lithuanian border guards. The incident provoked anti-Lithuanian demonstrations in several Polish localities. Military circles became particularly agitated. Beck, evidently taking advantage of the general confusion caused by the Austrian crisis, decided to act.

On March 17, after a violent propaganda campaign, Warsaw dispatched a forty-eight-hour ultimatum to Kaunas demanding the establishment of diplomatic relations by March 31. The ultimatum was accompanied by government-instigated mass demonstrations in several cities. Some military units were ordered to the Polish-Lithuanian frontier zone. The ultimatum, which took all of Europe by surprise, was an unqualified success. Lithuania, a small country of some two and a half million inhabitants, duly complied with the demand.

Warsaw's move was well timed: Lithuania could not expect effective support from any country. Besides, the ultimatum—demanding only the establishment of diplomatic relations—seemed moderate if not justified. The high-handed method, however, as well as the timing, brought wide criticism and aroused new suspicions about cooperation between Beck and Hitler. Both the French and the British ambassadors intervened in Warsaw. In Moscow, Litvinov threatened that should Poland invade Lithuania, the Soviet-Polish nonaggression pact would be abrogated.[23]

There is no evidence of Polish-German collusion in March 1938. On the contrary, Berlin was taken as much by surprise as Paris, London, and Moscow. Nor does the ultimatum seem to have been premeditated. It represented instead Beck's reaction to Hitler's move in Austria. It was caused by a desire to show off Poland's strength and to focus international attention on Warsaw. Beck considered that in view of Hitler's fait accompli, it would be "dangerous" for Poland "to remain entirely passive."[24] He apparently wanted to demonstrate that the Poles were alert, prepared for all contingencies, and strong enough to create their own faits accomplis.

Domestic considerations probably played a role as well. Beck's policies, severely criticized in France and Great Britain as pro-German, were unpopular in many Polish quarters, even among some members of the government. He probably wanted to show all those who felt uneasy about the recent Nazi triumph that his diplomacy brought "success" as well. Thanks to general confusion, it did.

PARTITION OF CZECHOSLOVAKIA

In February 1938 Yves Delbos, the French foreign minister, publicly assured Czechoslovakia that in case of German invasion France would honor her obligations resulting from the mutual-assistance treaty signed on October 18, 1925. This assurance was repeated the following month by his successor,

Paul-Boncour, and then by Prime Minister Leon Blum. The declarations aroused great anxiety in the Chambre des Deputés and even caused the fall of Blum's cabinet in the middle of April. By then the French military commanders had informed civilian authorities that France was unprepared for a war.[25]

Although officially London sided with France, the Foreign Office let the new cabinet of Édouard Daladier know that England would go to war only if France were attacked. It would reserve decision, however, if France attacked Germany because of Nazi aggression against Czechoslovakia. Eventually, and on numerous occasions from March to September 1938, British officials repeated the warning.[26]

The British were of the opinion that, as a matter of principle, Prague should agree peacefully to a far-reaching compromise. Already in March, just three days after the Austrian Anschluss, Sir Basil Newton, British minister in Prague, advised London that Czechoslovakia should not get either encouragement or all-out support from Great Britain; on the contrary, Prague should be eased into making concessions. If France desired to defend her eastern ally, it should do it on its own, he recommended. Chamberlain agreed with Newton, and in order to expedite what he considered the unavoidable outcome, he decided to exercise his own initiative, a decision that suited the French. Georges Bonnet followed British diplomatic leadership in the Czechoslovak crisis, having taken for granted that without Britain's cooperation France would be unable to defend the Czechs anyway.[27]

The direct result of Austria's collapse was the intensification of separatist activities by the Nazi-led Sudeten Germans. Chamberlain did not delay in clarifying his position publicly. On March 27 he declared in the House of Commons that Great Britain would continue to lend her influence to the revision of relations between nations, whether by treaty or otherwise, if such a review would contribute to stability and peace. The British government, he continued, would exert every effort to solve in a peaceful and orderly manner all disputes that might arise. He assured the Czechs of Britain's good offices. But he also excluded British military action in defense of their country. He urged upon Prague the use of peaceful diplomacy and recommended measures to be taken in order "to meet the reasonable wishes of the German minority."[28]

The prime minister restated his position a month later during the London conference with Daladier and Bonnet.[29] All participants agreed that in the interest of peace and Czechoslovakia's own internal stability, Prague should make concessions. Soon after, on May 7, in the midst of the Czechoslovak-German "May crisis," both the British and the French ministers in Prague formally notified the Czechoslovak officials that their governments considered peaceful solution of the Sudetenland problem and substantial Czech concessions unavoidable. Berlin, Moscow, and Warsaw were so informed.[30] These events took place after the publication of Henlein's Karlsbad declaration (April 24), the content of which was irreconcilable with Czechoslovakia's sovereignty.

As in the case of the Austrian crisis, Hitler closely followed the policies of London and Paris and drew his own conclusions. On June 18, 1938, having ordered his generals to prepare plans for military action against Prague, he also assured them that he would succeed in avoiding war: "I will decide to take action against Czechoslovakia only if I am convinced, as in the case of the demilitarization zone and the entry into Austria, that France will not march, and that therefore, England will not intervene."[31]

Soon after, Sir Horace Wilson indicated to Theodore Kordt of the German embassy in London that Downing Street would not oppose the Nazi demands even if France stood by her ally. Lord Runciman, sent to Prague on a special mission, expressed the same views.[32]

In the meantime, the French, caught between their treaty commitments vis-à-vis Czechoslovakia and the position of the British government, vacillated continually. Behind the walls of diplomatic secrecy, they urged the Czechs to yield. In public, they supported Prague and appealed for peace. Daladier's public speech on July 12, 1938, is a good example. He reaffirmed France's support of Czechoslovakia but at the same time praised Germany's peaceful aspirations. Immediately after, he informed the British embassy that his speech did not mean he intended to slacken pressure on the Czechs, but that he did not want the Germans to think that he was becoming too compliant to their demands, either.[33] Evidently French diplomacy aimed more at preserving the appearance of adhering to France's obligations to Czechoslovakia than at fulfilling them.

As for the Soviet Union, Litvinov and other Soviet leaders repeatedly called for collective measures, expressing readiness to fulfill their international commitments. However, the Czechoslovak-Soviet mutual-assistance pact of May 1935 was operative only if France first came to Czechoslovakia's aid militarily. Litvinov emphasized that point to the League of Nations Assembly.[34] Furthermore, Russia had no effective way of helping the Czechs. It had no common frontier with either Czechoslovakia or Germany, and all of its western neighbors were unwilling to let the Red Army pass through their territories. The position taken by Warsaw represented a particularly insoluble problem. Poland was the only country that shared borders with Russia, Germany, *and* Czechoslovakia, an extremely important factor in military planning. And the Poles were more vehement than others in their refusal, maintaining the same stand they had adopted four years before, at the time of the negotiations for the Eastern Pact. As early as the first part of May 1938, Bonnet learned from Beck in Geneva that should Soviet troops cross the Polish border under any circumstances, Poland would declare war on Russia. In a conversation with Bullitt on May 21, the Polish ambassador in Paris, Lukasiewicz, echoed Beck's words. Even Soviet planes flying over Polish areas would be attacked, he declared.[35] Naturally, Warsaw's stand could only provide an additional argument for those in London who pressed for a compromise with Hitler.

The well-known Munich conferences of September 29–30, 1938, were portrayed by Chamberlain as a diplomatic success. Upon his return to London, he waved the Munich declaration from the window of his office and spoke to the enthusiastic crowds the much-quoted words: "This is the second time there has come back from Germany to Downing Street peace with honour. I believe it is peace in our time." His evaluation of Hitler's policy and his optimism were shared by most British as well as French politicians. The House of Commons approved the prime minister's role in Czechoslovakia's crisis by a vote of 366 to 14. Approval was even more overwhelming in France. With only 75 members in opposition, 543 members of the Chambre des Deputés approved Daladier's policy, an unusual success for any government in that politically divided country.[36]

Almost immediately after the conference, Dr. Walter Funk, German minister of economy, made an extensive tour of southeastern Europe. Upon his return to Berlin he stated that Germany had "great economic construction plans" for the Balkan countries. The plans were such that, if executed, most of central and southern Europe would be changed into German economic satellites. Attlee, leader of the Opposition, raised this point in the House of Commons on November 1, 1938. In reply, Chamberlain admitted that indeed Germany had acquired a "dominating position" in the region.[37]

As for the French, they went even further, because soon after, on December 6, the Franco-German Declaration of Friendship was signed in Paris. Because of its general nature, the declaration had no practical meaning, but the Auswärtiges Amt could not but conclude that the French had reconciled themselves to Nazi predominance in eastern Europe.[38]

POLAND'S ULTIMATUM TO PRAGUE

The Munich agreement was of tremendous importance to all of Europe— Poland in particular. The Western democracies had, in effect, agreed to the partition of a staunch supporter of the Versailles system, the League of Nations, and stability in central-eastern Europe. For all practical purposes France had sacrificed and lost its faithful ally. The Little Entente lost its significance, and the European balance of power was seriously affected. The agreement disoriented and demoralized not only large segments of European public opinion but also government circles. Most important, it convinced Hitler that the leaders of the Western democracies were no match for his ingenious policy of expansion. Talking to his generals a few months later, he described Chamberlain and Daladier as "poor worms."[39]

It was in Poland's interest to preserve Czechoslovakia, with its strong air force and its well-trained army. Of course, in 1938 the Poles had no way of helping their hapless neighbor either politically or militarily. In fact, the Polish government not only failed to observe neutrality, it actually joined the ranks of Czechoslovakia's enemies. Warsaw acted against Prague from the outset of the German-Czech conflict.

There were several reasons for this. First, Polish government circles considered Beneš and his government pro-Soviet. Prague provided a haven for Communist organizations and propaganda. Besides, Polish subversive and antigovernment political exiles fled to the Czech capital.[40] Second, Beck was convinced, rightly, that France and Britain were not ready or even willing to oppose Germany by force—which in 1938 seemed the only way to stop the Nazis. Conscious of the past, he feared that if Warsaw joined British and French diplomatic representations on behalf of Prague, Polish-German relations would be compromised without any practical results. During the May crisis, when the French government proposed that Poland join France and Great Britain in warning Germany against the use of force, Beck recalled the events of March 13, 1936, when Poland "was ready to honor her obligations as an ally of France,"[41] while France refused to act.

Another factor that prompted Beck's policy was Poland's claim to the Teschen area, inhabited by some 150,000 ethnic Poles and incorporated by Czechoslovakia during the Polish-Bolshevik war. He did not want to do anything that might be interpreted as an indirect renunciation of Poland's claim. Instead, he demanded for the Polish population the same treatment as that accorded the Sudeten Germans.

Beck's uncritical attachment to his late master apparently also played some role. Pilsudski never thought Czechoslovakia would survive; he also disdained the Czechs and did not bother to hide it. The Poles neither "respected nor loved" them, he told Göring in January 1935. For Beck, Pilsudski's opinion, and even prejudice, was law. He considered the Czechoslovak state "absurd." Beck actually believed, and so informed Eden in March 1936, that the Little Entente, led by Prague, wanted "hegemony" in eastern Europe and "advocated" Soviet influence there. Until the end of his life, he actually believed that interwar Czechoslovakia—the *only* country in central-eastern Europe where a democratic form of government survived—was a "classic police state."[42]

Beck publicly demanded in January 1938 that the Polish minority in Czechoslovakia be accorded the same rights as the German minority.[43] His declaration was more significant than it appeared, because on January 13 Neurath had told him (in reference to Czechoslovakia) that "wird dieser Blinddarm früher oder später ausgeschnitten werden müssen" (this appendix will need to be cut sooner or later).[44] Pressed hard by circumstances and trying desperately to localize the conflict, the Czechoslovak government formally agreed. Informed about the agreement, the Quai d'Orsay approved, convinced that a new status for national minorities in Czechoslovakia had become unavoidable and that Poland should not be pushed further into Germany's arms.

Nevertheless, French government circles and the press were more than critical of the Polish stand. Suspicions proliferated that Warsaw and Berlin had some understanding as to their policies against Prague. These suspicions seemed to be justified. On May 26 Lukasiewicz, on Beck's instruction, notified Bonnet that Poland would not fail to fulfill her obligations as an ally of France. He added, however, that the Poles were committed to come to the aid of France only after an unprovoked German attack. The alliance would *not* apply if France became involved in a war as a result of her support of Czechoslovakia. He suggested "clarifying" discussions on the subject.[45]

As time passed, criticism of the Polish government increased in Western capitals. Many argued that whatever the merits or demerits of French and English policies, Poland should not contribute to the crisis and indirectly strengthen the Nazi position but should withhold her claims until a more propitious moment. Resigned to concessions to Germany, London and Paris wanted to save rather than weaken further a loyal ally of France and a faithful supporter of the League of Nations. But they also wanted to keep Poland away from Germany as much as possible; this necessitated some consideration of Polish claims.[46]

Poles themselves were unwittingly provoking Western public opinion. The sometimes intemperate declarations of Polish officials, the violently anti-Czech propaganda led by the progovernment press, as well as public outbursts in several cities became known and were widely disapproved. By August both the French and the British governments intervened in Warsaw, appealing for moderation.[47]

Until the middle of September Warsaw was invoking self-determination and demanded a plebiscite in the Polish-inhabited areas. However, as a result of the Chamberlain-Hitler conference in Berchtesgaden on September 15, Great Britain, France, and, after concerted Franco-British pressure, Czechoslovakia agreed that the predominantly German areas should be ceded to the Reich on the basis of *delimitation* rather than *plebiscite*. Thus, on September 19, with great dispatch, Beck instructed Lipski to inform the Auswärtiges Amt that Warsaw would seek the same solution of its own claim.[48]

Beck knew very well that his note would be well received in Berlin. Göring had assured him three weeks before the Austrian Anschluss that Germany recognized Polish interests in Morayska Ostrava, an area much larger than the Poles had ever asked for, and in August the field marshal told Lipski that should Germany decide to occupy the Sudetenland by force, the Poles might do the same in the areas of their "interest." Three days before Beck's notification, Göring "strongly advised" Lipski to utilize "all possible means; press, agitation, etc.," as well as "representations" to the Western powers. Hitler himself assured Lipski that Germany would not guarantee Czechoslovakia's new frontiers before Polish (and Hungarian) demands were satisfied and that in the event of a Polish-Czechoslovak military conflict, the Reich would side with Poland.[49]

On September 21 the Polish government publicly denounced the convention on national minorities it had concluded with Czechoslovakia in 1925, and the Polish ambassador in Prague, Kazimierz Papée, formally demanded cession of the Teschen district.[50] The move seemed well timed because it preceded the second Chamberlain-Hitler conference by two days. Hitler shocked the prime minister during this conference with new demands and threatened to attack Czechoslovakia unless Prague met them by September

26. He also refused to guarantee Czechoslovakia's new frontiers unless recent Polish (and Hungarian) demands were met.[51] Chamberlain could not but conclude that the Polish-German collusion was a fact.

By then, the government-inspired anti-Czech press, radio, and diplomatic campaign—open and camouflaged—reached its peak in Poland. Polish organizations in the Teschen area—not without discreet instigation from Warsaw—intensified their activities and demanded outright incorporation by Poland. The Polish government simultaneously called up a considerable number of reservists and ordered a concentration of troops on the Czech border. All these moves were generally interpreted as further evidence of German-Polish cooperation.[52]

The military measures seemed especially significant, making Noël assume that a secret Warsaw-Berlin understanding indirectly affected France's security. The troops shifted to the Czech border came from Poland's western garrisons. As a result, he reasoned, in case of war the German military units stationed in the east would automatically become available on the French front. Since the French were not consulted on the matter, he considered the Polish-French military convention to have been violated by the Poles.[53]

On September 23, at Prague's request, the Soviet government warned Warsaw that a Polish attack on Czechoslovakia could not be reconciled with the Polish-Soviet nonaggression pact. Should such an attack take place, the pact would be rescinded.[54]

French and Soviet suspicions about Beck's intentions do not seem to have been entirely groundless. On September 19 Lipski was told to inform Hitler that Poland "paralyzed the possibility of Soviet intervention . . . in the Czechoslovak problem," that Soviet "intervention in European affairs" was considered "intolerable" in Warsaw, and that Polish military maneuvers on the Soviet frontier constituted a "warning" to Moscow. Furthermore, Beck sent Lipski a "private" letter on September 27 instructing him to obtain a promise from Ribbentrop that Warsaw would be informed about "the start of any possible military action" by Germany. Poland had enough military forces ready for "action" as well, he wrote. These forces "could take prompt action following the outbreak of a German-Czech conflict." Any attempt on the part of the Soviet Union to intervene on behalf of Czechoslovakia would be opposed by Poland, he concluded. The implications of Beck's instructions were so grave that Lipski used his better judgment and, as he stressed in his memoirs, never executed them.[55]

The Czechoslovak government tried to avoid both outright surrender and outright refusal of Polish demands. It also wanted to break the Polish-German solidarity and to secure at least Poland's neutrality in case of war. Subsequently, on September 22, Beneš wrote a personal letter to Moscicki (delivered in Warsaw four days later) in which he recognized the principle of territorial changes on behalf of Poland. He did it partly as a result of pressure from Paris, which was anxious to avoid an international conflict in which France and Poland might take opposite sides. [56]

Still the Poles were unsatisfied. On September 27 Beneš received a second, bolder note, as well as Moscicki's reply. Warsaw demanded an agreement both to the immediate occupation of unquestionably Polish-inhabited areas and to plebiscites in areas with a mixed population. Prague sent an extremely conciliatory reply, again agreeing to the territorial transfer but still trying to avoid overt surrender. Again both Great Britain and France intervened in Warsaw, warning the Poles against resorting to violence or collusion with Germany.

Things were happening fast. On September 29–30, Chamberlain, Daladier, and Mussolini met at Munich and accepted Hitler's demands, agreeing to the partition of Czechoslovakia. But they failed to make any definite decision concerning Polish claims. A special declaration on the subject left the issue open. "The Heads of Governments of the four Powers declare that the problems of the Polish and Hungarian minorities in Czechoslovakia, if not settled within three months by agreement between the respective governments, shall form the subject of another meeting of the Heads of Governments of the Four Powers here present." [57]

Beck had no choice but to view the Munich agreement as a setback. Poland was not invited to take part in the conferences, which could only mean that France and Great Britain did not consider her on their side and that Germany and Italy did not consider her presence important enough. The Poles found themselves isolated and reminded of their secondary role—certainly a painful reminder to Beck. He probably began to suspect that the delay in satisfying the Polish claims might lead to their enforced reduction or even denial. Even more important was a possibility that the conferences might revive the Four-Power Pact—a prospect that endangered Poland's territorial integrity.

There was also evidence that the Germans intended to seize a valuable part of the highly industrialized Teschen district themselves. When Hitler met Chamberlain on September 22, he handed the British prime minister a map on which the German demands were marked. They included Bohumin, an important transportation center of the Teschen district.[58] Having learned of the meeting, Beck immediately instructed Lipski to ask for assurance that Germany's territorial aims were drawn incorrectly on the map. The matter went to Hitler himself, who, showing his goodwill, accommodated the Poles. Still distrustful and hoping to prevent a fait accompli, the Poles decided to act immediately and on their own.

Just before midnight of September 30, Warsaw sent a twelve-hour ultimatum to Prague, demanding the outright cession of Teschen within ten days and negotiations on other border areas. Orders were issued to occupy Teschen by force in case a positive response was not received by noon of October 1.[59]

Pleased with the ultimatum, Ribbentrop and Göring hastened to assure the Polish ambassador of their sympathy and of Germany's support in the event of either Polish-Czechoslovak or Polish-Soviet conflict. Göring, in particular, was delighted with the "very bold action performed in excellent style." Ribbentrop told Lipski that the chancellor himself "expressed to his entourage great appreciation for Poland's policy."[60] Reciprocating, Beck assured the German ambassador in Warsaw, Moltke, that the value of Polish-German agreement was increasingly understood in Poland and that the "foresighted policies of Marshal Pilsudski" were appreciated more and more.[61]

As could be expected, Warsaw's high-handed performance shocked Western public opinion. The press in Paris, London, New York, and Moscow generally condemned it, while the French and British governments were thinking of ways to check the escalation of conflict. They pressed the Poles once more for moderation, but they also "advised" the Czechs to comply, which the Czechs did.[62] Poland thus acquired some four hundred square miles of territory with a population of 215,000, the majority of them Polish, the rest Czechs, Germans, and other ethnic groups. Beck had won another diplomatic "victory."

Poland emerged from the Munich crisis morally diminished. Her foreign policy was discredited in London, and, in Paris, Daladier was convinced that Polish-German cooperation was prearranged and spoke vituperatively of Beck's diplomacy. Gamelin thought the Poles betrayed the spirit of the alliance and deserved whatever was coming to them.[63]

The documentary evidence does not reveal such cooperation, but it does reveal Beck's modus operandi, which he explained to the government leaders in Warsaw in the midst of the May crisis. His entire policy was based on two assumptions: first, that Czechoslovakia would not fight, and, second, that neither France nor Great Britain would support her on the issue of the Sudetenland. He thus considered it his duty to advance Poland's immediate interests. He pointed out that if his assumptions "were contradicted by the facts, it would be necessary, within twenty-four hours, to modify Polish policy completely, since in the case of a real European war against Germany, [Poland] could not be on the side of the latter, even indirectly."[64]

Successful as Beck seemed to be, he must have realized how imperiled Poland's position was. Politically isolated and generally distrusted, the country found itself alone vis-à-vis Germany. Beck therefore looked for new allies, concentrating on Hungary and Romania.

Beck thought of making Hungary and Romania cooperate and of establishing a common Polish-Hungarian boundary. Hungary was a traditional friend of Poland, and a common frontier, he reasoned, would strengthen both countries. Hungary and Romania were traditional enemies over the issue of Transylvania. Making them cooperate would contribute to the stabilization of central-eastern Europe. Such a plan, however, required the further partition of Czechoslovakia, because Beck envisioned that the Czechoslovak Carpatho-Ukraine would be divided between Hungary and Romania. He apparently thought that sharing in the spoils might provide a common bond for Poland, Hungary, and Romania.

On October 19 Beck went to Bucharest "offering" the Romanians a slice of Carpatho-Ukraine and proposing Polish-Hungarian-Romanian cooperation.[65] But Foreign Minister Nicolae Petrescu Comnene realized that it was not in his country's interest to further weaken its natural ally nor to augment Russian, Bulgarian, and Hungarian claims on Romania by grabbing some insignificant real estate. He lectured Beck on the "sacred duties" of the Little Entente, condemned the recent German-Polish partition of Czechoslovakia, and prophesized that "before long" Czechoslovakia would recover what it had just lost. As Beck reported in his memoirs, he could not understand what his host was talking about, concluded that he was dealing with a "*parfait imbecile*," and went on with his plan to the king.[66] Not successful there, he returned to Warsaw to learn—four days later—that Ribbentrop had confronted Lipski with Germany's demands on Poland.

As for the Polish-Hungarian frontier, within five months events brought Beck a success—but a dubious one. Hungary was understandably eager to recover the areas it lost after World War I. But it also knew that to do this, the support of Hitler and Mussolini, not Beck, was paramount. When Hungary did seize the Carpatho-Ukraine in March 1939—an event hailed in Warsaw as another diplomatic triumph for Beck—it was already in the Fascist-Nazi orbit. On February 2, 1939, Hungary joined the Anti-Comintern Pact.[67]

NOTES

1. See the report of the secretary of the German embassy in Moscow on his conversation with the counselor of the French embassy, Payart, on August 30, 1938: *DGFP*, series D, 2:667.

2. For Schulenburg's report, see *DGFP*, series D, 2:602.

3. *DBFP*, 3rd series, 2:219–20 and *FRUS*, 1938, 1:57–59, respectively.

4. Gamelin, *Servir*, 2:319–28; also France, *Les événements* 9:2634–36; 2642–43 (Bonnet's testimony); 4:964–65 (Lebrun's testimony).

5. Churchill, *The Gathering Storm*, 71, 110–29; and Vansittart, *The Mist Procession*, 9, respectively.

6. For a documented description of the mechanism of appeasement in Great Britain, see A. L. Rowse, *Appeasement: A Study in Political Decline, 1933–39* (New York: W. W. Norton & Co., 1961); also Martin Gilbert and Richard Gott, *The Appeasers* (London: Weinfeld & Nicolson, 1963).

7. *DGFP*, series D, 4:357ff.

8. See Ambassador Lukasiewicz's report on his conversation with Bonnet in April 1939: Juliusz Lukasiewicz, *Papers and Memoirs: Diplomat in Paris, 1936–1939*, ed. Waclaw Jedrzejewicz (New York: Columbia University Press, 1970), 71–77; also *PSZ*, 1:40.

9. Arnold Wolfers, *Britain and France between Two Wars* (New York: Harcourt Brace & Co., 1940), 271.

10. Gilbert and Gott, *The Appeasers*, 53; also Ministry of Foreign Affairs of the USSR, *Documents and Materials Relating to the Eve of the Second World War*, 2 vols. (Moscow: Foreign Languages Publishing House, 1948), 1:34.

11. William E. Dodd, *Ambassador Dodd's Diary, 1933–1938* (New York: Harcourt Brace & Co., 1941), 421.

12. *DGFP*, series D, 2:427–28, and Feiling, *The Life of Neville Chamberlain*, 333, respectively.

13. *Parliamentary Debates*, Commons, 332 (1938), 8–9, 227.

14. *DGFP*, series D, 1:44.

15. *DGFP*, series D, 1:35.

16. See C. G. Haines and R. J. S. Hoffman, *The Origins and Background of the Second World War* (London: Oxford University Press, 1943), 248.

17. See Wojciechowski, *Stosunki Polsko Niemieckie*, 375.

18. *AANP-Zespoly MSZ*, 4624, 36–50; 6–7, respectively.

19. Noël, *L'Aggression allemande contre la Pologne*, 181.

20. Galeazzo Ciano, *Ciano's Hidden Diary, 1937–1938* (New York: E. P. Dutton & Co., 1953), 85.

21. *DGFP*, series D, 5:41.

22. Axel von Freytagh-Loringhoven, *Deutschlands Aussen Politik, 1933–1940* (Berlin: O. Stollberg, 1940), 148, as quoted by Noël, *L'Aggression allemande contre la Pologne*, 185.

23. Szembek, *Journal*, 293–95; Potemkin, *Istoriia Diplomatii*, 3:625, respectively.

24. Beck, *Dernier rapport*, 149.

25. France, *Les événements*, 3:801–2 (Paul-Boncour testimony); also Gamelin, *Servir*, 2:322–28.

26. *DBFP*, 3rd series, 1:95–97, 140–43, 346–47, 601–3; 2:328; also France, *Les événements*, 4: 964–87 (testimony by President Lebrun); 9:217–20 (testimony by Bonnet).

27. *DBFP*, 3rd series, 1:55–56; also Noël, *L'Aggression allemande contre la Pologne*, 202–3.

28. *Parliamentary Debates*, Commons, 333 (1938), 1409.

29. Bonnet, *Défense de la paix*, 1:105. See also Nevile Henderson, *The Failure of a Mission* (New York: G. P. Putnam's Sons, 1940), 133.

30. *DBFP*, 3rd series, 1:241–45; also Juliusz Lukasiewicz, "Sprawa Czechoslowacka w 1938 r. na Tle Stosunków Polsko-Francuskich" (Czechoslovak question in 1938 in Polish-French relations), *Sprawy Miedzynarodowe* (London), 1948, nos. 2–3 (6–7), 36.

31. Nuremberg Trials, as quoted by Winston S. Churchill, *The Gathering Storm*, 290.

32. Ministry of Foreign Affairs of the USSR, *Documents and Materials Relating to the Eve of the Second World War*, 2:42–46.

33. *DBFP*, 3rd series, 1:554.

34. For extracts of Litvinov's speech on September 23, 1938, see Degras, *Soviet Documents*, 3:304–5.

35. For the Bonnet-Bullitt conversation on May 16, 1938, and the Lukasiewicz-Bullitt conversation on May 21, 1938, see *FRUS*, 1938, 1:500–4, 507–8, respectively.

36. For the reaction of the British and world public opinion to Chamberlain's role in the Munich agreement, see Ian Macleod, *Neville Chamberlain* (London: Frederick Muller, Ltd., 1961), 256–71.

37. *Parliamentary Debates*, Commons, 340 (1938), 80.

38. Joachim von Rippentrop, *The Ribbentrop Memoirs* (London: Weidenfeld and Nicolson, 1954), 92–93. Two different versions of the Bonnet-Ribbentrop talks appeared eventually in France and in Germany, creating considerable controversy. For an analysis of this subject, see Kazimierz Piwarski, *Polityka Europejska w Okresie po Monachijskim, X, 1938–III, 1939* (*European Politics in the Post-Munich Period, X, 1938–III, 1939*) (Warsaw: Panstwowe Wydawnictwo Naukowe, 1960), 71–87.

39. *DGFP*, series D, 7:258–60.

40. Beck, *Dernier rapport*, 51–52.

41. Szembek, *Journal*, 311; also Beck, *Dernier rapport*, 319.

42. Beck, *Dernier rapport*, 34; 52.

43. Cienciala, "Marxism and History," 60.

44. *AANP-Zespoly MSZ*, 4624, 39.

45. For Lukasiewicz's report dated May 27, 1938, see Lukasiewicz, *Papers and Memoirs*, 90–99.

46. Stefania Stanislawska, *Polska a Monachium* (*Poland and Munich*) (Warszawa: Ksiażka i Wiedza, 1967), 39.

47. Bonnet, *Défense de la paix*, 1:204.

48. Jerzy Kozenski, *Czechoslowacja w Polskiej Polityce Zagranicznej w Latach 1932–1938* (*Czechoslovakia in Polish Foreign Policy During the Years 1932–1938*) (Poznan: Instytut Zachodni, 1964), 268–69; also Józef Chudek, ed., *Wrześniowy Kryzys Czechoslowacki 1938 r. w Raportach Ambasadora Lipskiego* (*Czechoslovak Crisis of September 1938 in Ambassador Lipski's Reports*) (Warsaw: Polski Instytut Spraw Miedzynarodowych, 1958), 40–44, 54.

49. Józef Chudek, "Rozmowy Beck-Göring z 23go lutego 1939r" (Beck-Göring conversations on February 23, 1938), *Sprawy Miedzynarodowe* (Warsaw), no. 5 (1960), 34–35, 48, 53–57; also Lipski, *Diplomat in Berlin*, 345–50, 382–87, 408–12.

50. Kozenski, *Czechoslowacja w Polskiej*, 274–75.

51. *DBFP*, 3rd series, 2:463–73, 499–508. During the second conversation on September 23, Hitler extended the time limit for evacuation until October 1, 1938.

52. Stanislawska, *Polska A Monachium*, 154–55, 196–202, 220, 252.

53. Noël, *L'Aggression allemande contre la Pologne*, 206, 215–16.

54. For the text, Degras, *Soviet Documents*, 3:305.

55. Lipski, *Diplomat in Berlin*, 406–7, 422–24.

56. See Stanislawska, *Polska A Monachium*, 164–66, 201–18; also Bonnet, *Défense de la paix*, 1:364–65.

57. For the full text, see *LJF*, 13.

58. See *DGFP*, series D, 2, map 1.

59. *DBFP*, 3rd series, 3:70–72; also Szembek, *Journal*, 342–43.

60. Lipski, *Diplomat in Berlin*, 435–38; also *DBFP*, 3rd series, 5:80.

61. See Moltke report dated October 1, 1938: *AANA*, 2369/1308/495071-72.

62. See *DBFP*, 3rd series, 3:52–54; Bonnet, *Défense de la paix*, 1:297–98.

63. See Raczyuski, *W Sojuszniczym Londynie*, 21–23; also Bullitt's report on Daladier's comments, *FRUS*, 1938, 1:667–69; also Gamelin, *Servir*, 2:360.

64. Beck, *Dernier rapport*, 162–63.

65. Beck, *Dernier rapport*, 172–75. See also Henryk Batowski, "Rumunska Podroż Becka w pażdzierniku 1939 roku," *Kwartalnik Historyczny* (Warsaw) 65, no. 2 (1958): 423–39.

66. King Carol/Hitler conversation on November 24, 1938: *DGFP*, series D, 5:340; also Beck's memo on his conversation with King Carol sent to Lipski on October 20, 1938: Lipski, *Diplomat in Berlin*, 445–47.

67. For an incisive and positive evaluation of the Polish diplomacy in 1938–1939, see Anna M. Cienciala, *Poland and the Western Powers, 1938–1939* (Toronto: University of Toronto Press, 1968).

Chapter Twelve

France and Poland after the Remilitarization of the Rhineland

FRANCO-POLISH RELATIONS

Soon after the remilitarization of the Rhineland, Hitler embarked upon the construction of the Siegfried Line, a counterpart of the Maginot fortification system. This action was of great significance to France's eastern allies because from then on, in case of a German attack, France would be less capable of coming to their aid. Protected by its own allegedly impregnable fortifications, would it embark upon an all-out offensive against equally protected Germany in the event Hitler turned eastward or southward? This was pondered in Warsaw, Prague, Bucharest, and Belgrade, and, no doubt, in Moscow. It must have been pondered in Paris as well. Flandin, then prime minister of France, confessed to the Polish ambassador Alfred Chlapowski that fortification of the Rhineland would militarily "immobilize" France. If that ever happened, he argued, all of central Europe, Poland included, would have to be left to itself.[1] A prophetic confession! The conversation took place on February 17, 1936, three weeks before Hitler's assault on the Rhineland.

The French domestic political situation did not inspire confidence either. The general elections of April–May 1936 further divided the country. Strikes weakened the national economy and hampered defense preparations. Communism was gaining strength, which, in view of the strength of the rightist parties, dangerously undermined political stability.[2]

Developments in the international arena were no better. On August 29, 1936, King Carol of Romania dismissed his pro-French foreign minister,

Titulescu. On October 14, Belgium abrogated its military convention with France and declared neutrality. On March 27, 1937, Yugoslavia concluded a nonaggression pact with Italy, thus practically abandoning the French camp.

At that time, intimate observers of French affairs opined that France, most likely, would not fight unless directly attacked. The Belgian ambassador to Poland, Count Kerchove, and the American ambassador in Paris, Bullitt, were among them. General Georges, one of the highest-ranking French military leaders, did not conceal his concern while visiting Warsaw in April 1937.[3] To Beck and to his subordinates, France's apparent decline seemed to vindicate their policy. The weaker and more unreliable France was, the greater was the value of Poland's good relations with Germany.

The remilitarization of the Rhineland had a deep effect on the French diplomacy. Now more than ever, France needed friends who would stand by it in order to deter Hitler from further expansion. In the west, this meant primarily Great Britain. Close cooperation with, and eventually dependence on, London ensued. In the east, it meant Little Entente countries and Poland. French political and military leaders believed they should do everything in their power to prevent Poland from falling under Germany's thrall. Poland, after all, was the eastern flank of France's defenses. As long as France nurtured any hopes of making the alliance with Russia effective, Poland's position was crucial.

The latter half of 1936 saw an ostensible improvement in relations between the two countries, at least for a while. From August 12 to 16, General Gamelin, the commander in chief designate, paid a visit to Warsaw, and from August 29 to September 6 Śmigly-Rydz, Gamelin's Polish counterpart, went to Paris.

As a result of the visits the French government agreed to extend Poland financial aid to help in the much-needed military modernization. High-level conversations took place, during which joint measures in the event of German aggression were discussed. Although both visits were highly publicized and the climate of the Franco-Polish relations became warmer, they failed to produce any meaningful improvement.

Poland was promised a loan of two billion French francs ($63,000,000), partly in cash and partly in war matériel. But the loan, inadequate anyway, was never delivered in its entirety.[4] It is likely that France's unstable financial situation, the scarcity of military equipment, and the increasing unpopularity of Beck's policies made French investment in Poland more difficult.

The military conversations accomplished little, only revealing serious differences in the event of German aggression. Śmigly-Rydz wanted the French army to start an immediate offensive, but Gamelin wanted Poland to resist the initial attack, giving France time to gather forces for the second stage of the war. Gamelin insisted on full collaboration with Moscow and Prague, while Śmigly-Rydz opposed any commitments that permitted Soviet military entry into Polish territory under any circumstances, assenting to military cooperation with Czechoslovakia only in the event of French-Czechoslovak war against Germany.[5] He told Yves Delbos, who succeeded Flandin in June 1936, that under no circumstances would Poland attack Czechoslovakia, but he would go no further. In turn, he failed to obtain any precise assurances as to the *automatic* military obligations of France vis-à-vis Poland in case of a *casus foederis*. As a result of these differences, the joint military Franco-Polish cooperation, so badly needed since 1921, again failed to materialize.

In 1937 the situation in France, both internally and internationally, was deteriorating badly. In June, the stock market took a nosedive, and Blum asked for emergency powers. He was defeated in the Senate, and his government resigned on June 21. The rapidly growing rightist groups became so aggressive that the new cabinet, headed by Camille Chautemps, feared an ultranationalist coup d'état.

On the international scene, it was clear that the Versailles system was about to be entirely undermined: Hitler's determination to incorporate Austria into the Reich seemed unshakable, as was his intention to change the status of Czechoslovakia's Sudetenland. Meanwhile, the British government had not comtemplated any effective countermeasures. Undecided as to what should be done, Delbos visited Warsaw, Bucharest, Belgrade, and Prague in December. Rent by civil strife, unable to cope with international problems, and aware of its own crumbling prestige, France looked to its eastern allies for advice and support.

Delbos's visit to Warsaw was a failure. Although Delbos was more acceptable to the Poles than any of the previous French foreign ministers, there was no Polish-French policy on collective security, and no way to establish one. His visits to the other capitals were not much better. In Bucharest, the new foreign minister, Victor Antonescu, publicly hailed Franco-Romanian friendship, then quickly assured the German minister, Wilhelm Fabricius, that his warm speeches about France should not be taken too seriously. In Belgrade, the prime minister, Milan Stoyadinovich, seemed embarrassed and flatly refused any discussions regarding mutual assistance.[6] The Czech foreign minister had nothing to offer.

As soon as Delbos completed his tour, Beck embarked on an official visit to Germany. Again Noël complained, regarding the visit as an even more anti-French gesture than those of the past.[7] His complaints had no effect whatsoever. No wonder! By the end of 1937 Germany's power had grown impressively; France was weak, divided, and ineffective. During his visit to Berlin, Beck seemed more anxious than ever to demonstrate the independence of his policy and to take advantage of the growing confusion and disintegration of the Versailles system.

For the time being, he seemed successful. In March 1936, during the Rhineland crisis, Flandin and Sarraut expressed satisfaction and "gratitude" to the Polish ambassador in Paris. In July of the same year the Quai d'Orsay tried to restrain the French press, which was highly critical of Poland. In November, Daladier spoke favorably about Poland before the Senate Commission on Military Affairs, saying that Poland could be trusted. In the event of war, the Poles would fulfill their obligations according to the Franco-Polish "alliance."[8] In 1938, the year of the Polish ultimatum to Lithuania and Poland's participation in the dismemberment of Czechoslovakia, the Quai d'Orsay refrained from doing anything that might seriously alienate Beck. They did not cease, however, to warn the Poles. In February 1936 Premier Flandin asked Poland for a "clarification" of its foreign policy on the grounds that France and the Soviet Union had the right to know "sur quel pied [la Pologne] saute." In March, the secretary general of the Quai d'Orsay, Alexis Leger, told Ambassador Chlapowski that Poland's policy was "incomprehensible." Soon after, Paul-Boncour warned the Polish chargé in Paris, Mühlstein, that after the remilitarization of the Rhineland, Poland needed France's confidence and respect more than ever, arguing that Hitler made his assault not to threaten France but rather "to fence her in militarily" in order to strike against the east. Polish foreign policy might throw Poland at the mercy of Hitler.[9]

By the end of 1938, the French leaders concluded that Poland of its own volition had thrown its weight on the side of the "New Order." Franco-Polish relations entered a critical stage.

A PROFILE OF POLAND ON THE EVE OF WORLD WAR II

By the end of 1938, on the eve of World War II, Poland had become a pathetic case of paradoxes and contradictions that rendered genuine understanding between Paris and Warsaw impossible. The Polish leaders viewed their country in a way that had little or nothing in common with outside observations. The Polish leadership viewed with pride their domestic and international achievements and were confident of the future. According to governmental data, domestic progress over the past twenty years seemed impressive. The population had increased by almost 27 percent. Forecasts indicated that by 1950 the population might exceed that of France, and it might equal that of Germany by 1975.

Approximately 1,362,000 acres of fallow land were brought under cultivation, and as a result of agrarian reform some 6,650,000 acres of arable land were distributed among 734,100 new farmsteads. No more than 15 percent of the total agricultural area—some 10,000,000 acres—belonged to estates of more than 125 acres, while 81.5 percent belonged to small holdings and 3.5 percent to public bodies and associations.[10] At that time, more than 30 percent of the arable land in Germany and 68 percent in Great Britain belonged to large landowners.

Industrial progress seemed by no means minimal. While in 1921 only 10.3 percent of the gainfully employed were engaged in mining and industry and 72.3 percent tilled the land, by 1931 the corresponding figures were 16.6 percent and 64.9 percent. In 1938 the values of industrial and agricultural output were equal. Poland occupied seventh place in the world in coal production, fifth place in zinc production, ninth in Europe in the production of pig iron, and eighth in the manufacture of steel. In the late 1930s a modern industrial district was established in the central part of the country—as far away from the German and Soviet borders as possible—where heavy industries were being developed.

The value of exports—mostly coal, timber, foodstuffs, iron and steel products, and textiles—reached $231 million in 1938. Some 80 percent of foreign trade eventually became seaborne.

A new harbor, Gdynia, had been built. An unknown fishing village in 1918, twenty years later it became the most modern and largest harbor on the Baltic, with turnover exceeding that of Danzig, Stettin, Copenhagen, or Stockholm. By 1938 shipment of goods through Gdynia amounted to 9,174,000 tons. Gdynia's growth did not take place at the expense of Danzig.

On the contrary, Polish trade made the Free City flourish as never before. It advanced from ninth to second place among the Baltic ports. Its combined incoming and outgoing shipments increased from 2,100,000 tons in 1913 to 7,100,000 in 1938.[11]

Transportation improved. While in 1918 there were no more than 1,750 old locomotives, 3,000 automobiles, and 30,000 freight cars, by 1930, 5,500 locomotives, 11,350 automobiles, and 164,000 freight cars were in use. Some 6,900 miles of standard-gauge and 1,300 miles of narrow-gauge railroad tracks had been laid; highway mileage had been increased by 30 percent.[12]

More than 23,600 new primary schools for children from seven to fourteen years of age were added to the scant 5,000 extant in 1919. By 1938–1939, 91 percent of all children were enrolled. Before 1914, only two universities, both in formerly Austrian Galicia, were allowed to function. By 1938–1939 there were 20 universities and other academic institutions with 50,000 students; 790 secondary schools with 234,000 pupils; and 74 teacher colleges with 6,600 students.[13]

The social security system was one of the most advanced in Europe, and advanced social legislation was adopted long before similar legislation was enacted in France, Italy, or Great Britain. Social insurance covered 2,171,000 persons for illness, 2,523,000 for disability and old age, 1,690,000 for unemployment, and 2,183,000 against accidents. Special legislation protecting industrial workers was passed, regulating overtime pay, paid holidays, working conditions, women's and minors' employment, and protection for pregnant women. Already in 1919 labor unions gained recognition and the right to collective bargaining. By 1938 well over one million members were registered in more than three hundred unions.

Unlike France, Poland appeared politically stable—without parliamentary crises and frequent cabinet changes. The army, maintained and equipped at tremendous sacrifice on the part of the entire nation, commanded popular respect.

On the international scene, the successes of the Pilsudski-Beck diplomacy looked even more impressive. No longer at the mercy of the great powers, Poland had become a significant force in European politics. Its relations with both powerful neighbors appeared stabilized, and it no longer feared the prospect of German-Soviet collaboration. It had freed itself from French tutelage and was able to extricate itself from the minorities' treaties. Poland was strong enough to challenge the authority of the League of Nations whenever its interests or prestige demanded it, and it succeeded in forcing its will on Lithuania and in satisfying its territorial claim against Czechoslovakia.

But whatever progress the Poles had made, detached observers—certainly in the Quai d'Orsay—viewed Poland differently. The country was still underdeveloped, poor, and militarily weak. Its leaders, having forsaken democracy at home, seemed to support destroyers of law, order, and peace abroad.

By 1938 some 18 percent of Poland's population still could not read or write. Urban unemployment was dangerously high and the standard of living appallingly low. More than half of all farmsteads, approximately 2,100,000 so-called dwarf farms, had fewer than twelve acres of land, meaning they were not self-sufficient. Using antiquated farming methods, Poland had an agrarian labor force that was unparalleled in Europe; namely, 154 persons per 1,000 acres of farmland. For Yugoslavia, the corresponding figure was 146; for Germany, 132; for Czechoslovakia, 129; for Hungary, 120; for France, 89; and for Great Britain, 26.

The lack of foreign capital impeded industrial progress, and foreign investors hesitated to invest in a new and unstable economy. Railroad transportation was inadequate; motor roads were proverbially bad. The growth of native capital was slow.

National minorities were becoming more and more alienated from the national mainstream: the Ukrainians, because of their own growing nationalism and because the government failed to grant them autonomy; the Jews, because of growing anti-Semitism; the Germans, because of Nazi influences. To complete the vicious circle, the Nationalists' slogan "Poland for the Poles" was gaining popularity—an irrational slogan for a multinational state.

The army, respected for its gallantry abroad as much as at home, was unprepared for modern warfare. It was not motorized and relied excessively on the traditional cavalry. The national treasury was unable to provide for the much-needed modernization. From 1933 to 1939 almost half of the national budget—some 6,500 billion zlotys—was spent on defense, a terrible expense for an underdeveloped country; it was still inadequate. According to Nazi data, in the same period Germany spent thirty times more on the Wehrmacht![14] Contrary to legend, Pilsudski hampered Polish military strength. He had no understanding of or sympathy for modernization, technology, and motorization of the armed forces. By 1939, Poland had fewer military planes than in 1925.[15]

Poland's political stability was more apparent than real, and the democratic system of government had been long absent. The opposition parties decided to boycott national elections because electoral laws made it impossible for them to obtain fair representation anyway. In the wake of the general elections of 1935 and 1938, the Sejm consisted chiefly of government supporters, and as a result it lost its political significance.

On May 12, 1936, General Śmigly-Rydz was appointed commander in chief by the president of the republic. Two months later, on July 13, he was designated by government decree as the "First Person in Poland after the President of the Republic," and state functionaries were ordered to "honor him and obey." On November 11, 1936, he was made marshal. From then on, he assumed the role of the national leader more and more obviously. His position made the army completely autonomous, free from any public control.

On February 20, 1937, Colonel Adam Koc (Śmigly-Rydz's man) unveiled a new "official" organization, Camp of National Unity (OZON). Moderate as to social and economic programs, the OZON adopted nationalism with anti-Semitic accents. Soon it entered into indirect cooperation with one of the most extremist and most violently anti-Semitic groups, Falanga, led by Boleslaw Piasecki, the man who in 1934—while Pilsudski was still alive—was incarcerated in the "isolation camp" at Bereza Kartuska. The cooperation did not last long, because Piasecki and his men aimed at seizing power rather than cooperating with the Pilsudski-ites. It indicated, however, that those who governed Poland in the name of Pilsudski were ready to embrace nationalistic ideology, which the marshal had opposed all his life.

As to Poland's international successes, the Quai d'Orsay saw in them nothing but the poisoned fruits of Beck's anti-French and pro-German foreign policy.

Beck's denunciation of the minorities treaties in September 1934 was considered a blow to the postwar Versailles system. Poland's refusal to enter the Eastern Pact killed what was considered an extremely important diplomatic offensive. It also made the Franco-Soviet alliance of May 1935 militarily inoperative. Beck's anti–League of Nations policies paralleled those of Hitler and Mussolini. His ostentatious pro-Berlin gestures strengthened Germany's international position and suggested collusion between Berlin and Warsaw. The successes of Poland's ultimata to Lithuania and Czechoslovakia were viewed by the Quai d'Orsay as due not to Poland's strength or right but to international confusion caused by the dictators.

CRISIS IN FRANCO-POLISH RELATIONS

Polish anti-League demonstration of September 1938, as well as Warsaw's ultimatum to Prague, were regarded in Paris as a challenge to its foreign policy. Noël concluded that the time had come to revise French policy toward its erstwhile ally. Besides, as he argued, France was no longer able to defend effectively any eastern European country, and, after the partition of Czechoslovakia, Poland's strategic position became more precarious than ever.

Noël was more critical of Beck than other French diplomats. For some time he tried to use his influence to oust Beck from power but did not succeed. Then he made a more important move. On October 25, 1938, he sent a fourteen-page report to Paris in which he recommended a radical revision of the Franco-Polish alliance.[16]

For all practical purposes, the ambassador reasoned, Poland had ceased to be an ally. The Franco-Polish alliance, far from becoming an asset to France's security, had clearly become a dangerous liability. Polish foreign policy, he wrote, was not only anti-French, it was suicidal; before too long Hitler would certainly confront the Poles with demands concerning the Corridor. Since Poland would undoubtedly reject such demands, war might ensue. If this happened, France, because of its alliance with Poland, would have to declare war on Germany "automatically." It was not in France's interest, Noël reasoned, to honor such an obligation. France's involvement in a war could not depend on people who "almost continuously" supported France's enemies and whose policies contradicted their own long-range interests. In the event Germany attacked Poland, France should have freedom of action. Because the alliance provided for "automatism," the above provision should be formally eliminated and the alliance replaced by a loose "pact of friendship and consultation."

The revision of the alliance, the ambassador continued, would not deprive France of Poland's support in case Germany attacked it. For in the last analysis, Poland's political survival depended on France's strength. The Poles knew it, and on more than one occasion Beck himself admitted it. In case of a Franco-German war, the Poles would have to come to France's support, alliance or no alliance. Furthermore, the ambassador argued, once the "automatism" was explicitly eliminated from the alliance and the Poles were no longer sure of French support in the hour of crisis, Paris might be able to influence Warsaw's foreign policy more effectively.

In May 1938 the Polish ambassador in Paris, Lukasiewicz, notified the Quai d'Orsay that if a Franco-German war broke out as a result of France's military aid to Czechoslovakia, the Franco-Polish alliance would not necessarily come into play, and Poland would have a free hand in pursuing any course it chose. Lukasiewicz also proposed high-level discussions to "clarify" the relations between Warsaw and Paris. Now Noël somewhat sarcastically suggested that his plan be presented to the Poles as the answer to their proposal.

Soon after, Noël went to Paris, where he discovered that opinions were divided on France's policy toward central-eastern Europe. Generals Gamelin and Weygand fully shared his views; so did Bonnet.[17] Daladier, however, apparently considered that whatever happened, France should not abandon its treaty commitments in eastern Europe but, together with the Soviet Union and Great Britain, defend the status quo.[18]

While preparing his unusually elaborate memorandum, Noël had no way of knowing what immediate and deadly significance his recommendations would have for Poland. One day before the dispatch of his report, Ribbentrop secretly confronted the Polish ambassador in Berlin, Lipski, with Germany's demands.

NOTES

1. *AANP-Zespoly MSZ*, 3769, 34–41.

2. For the situation in France, as seen by the Polish ambassador in Paris, see Lukasiewicz, *Papers and Memoirs*, 22–33.

3. Szembek, *Journal*, 226–28.

4. For more details, see Lukasiewicz, *Papers and Memoirs*, 14–21.

5. *PSZ*, 1, part 1, 92; also Gamelin, *Servir*, 2:227–38.

6. *DGFP*, series D, 1:116, 147.

7. Noël, *L'Aggression allemande contre la Pologne*, 180–81.

8. *AANP-Zespoly MSZ*, 3251, 99, 135–44, 205; also 3803, 73–74; 3769, 92–94; 3804, 107–10.

9. Ibid., 3769, 43–44.

10. *Concise Statistical Yearbook of Poland*, 31–32.

11. Ibid., 73, 88.

12. Polish Government Information Center, *Polish Facts and Figures*, no. 9 (1944), 7.

13. *Concise Statistical Yearbook of Poland*, 138.

14. Nicholas Bethell, *The War Hitler Won: The Fall of Poland, September, 1939* (New York: Holt, Rinehart and Winston, 1972), 31.

15. Antony Polonsky, *Politics in Independent Poland, 1921–1939: The Crisis of Constitutional Government* (Oxford: Clarendon Press, 1972), 486. For authoritative data on Polish military preparations, see General Waclaw Stachiewicz, *Pisma. Tom I. Przygotowania Wo-*

jenne w Polsce, 1935–1939 (*Writings*, volume 1, *Military Preparations in Poland, 1935–1939*) (Paris: Instytut Literacki, 1977); *Zeszyty Historyczne*, no. 40 (1977); volume 2, *Zeszyty Historyczne*, no. 1 (1979). General Stachiewicz was chief of staff in the Polish Ministry of War on the eve of World War II.

16. For long extracts, see Noël, *L'Aggression allemande contre la Pologne*, 247–60.

17. Noël, *L'Aggression allemande contre la Pologne*, 257–60; compare with Bonnet, *Défense de la paix*, 2:137–42.

18. Noël, *L'Aggression allemande contre la Pologne*, 247–57; also *DBFP*, 3rd series, 3:365–66.

Chapter Thirteen

Hitler's Demands on Poland, October 1938–March 1939

By October 1938 Poland's standing in London, Paris, and Moscow was lower than ever before. By contrast, Germany, already militarized, fortified by the recent triumphs, seemed at the peak of its power. Hitler decided it was time to clarify Poland's role in his plans and to settle Germany's accounts with the Poles. He wanted to settle peacefully. He still needed Poland and thus offered terms that he considered "extremely modest."

On October 24, less than four weeks after the Munich conference, Ribbentrop invited Lipski to Berchtesgaden for a conversation that was to set the stage for the last act of the Polish-German drama.

The foreign minister reviewed the recent Czechoslovak crisis, which had led to such a "peaceful and happy solution, welcomed by both Germany and Poland." He then spoke about Germany's military power and the decisive importance of German-Italian cooperation. Then he criticized Hungary, which, unlike Poland and "despite the Führer's warning," failed to act resolutely against Prague.

At this juncture, Lipski raised the problem of Czechoslovak Carpatho-Ukraine. He said that it should be given to Hungary because the resulting Polish-Hungarian frontier would be "of great value as a barrier toward the East." It would never be used against Germany, and the "rumors" about an anti-German bloc being formed by Warsaw were just "nonsense," he said—evidently less than frankly. He asked for Germany's support on this matter.

With an equal lack of frankness, Ribbentrop answered that those "ideas" were "new" to him and he "wished to consider them at leisure." Then he came to a much more important point.

It was time, he said, to settle "all possible points of friction" between Germany and Poland. Such a final *Gesamtlösung* would represent a "culmination of the work started by Marshal Pilsudski and the Führer." Danzig, which "had always been German and would always remain German," would return to the Reich. An extraterritorial *Reichsautobahn* and an extraterritorial railroad line would run across the Corridor. In exchange, Poland would receive in the Danzig area an extraterritorial Autobahn, a railroad, a free port, and a guarantee of a market for its goods. Both countries would mutually "guarantee" their boundaries, and the pact concluded in 1934 would be extended to twenty-five years.

Elaborating on these points, Ribbentrop added that eventually Germany might establish with Poland a joint policy on "colonial matters" and cooperate in securing the emigration of Polish Jews. He also indicated that should Warsaw respond positively, the problem of Carpatho-Ukraine might be solved to Poland's satisfaction.

According to Ribbentrop's memorandum, the conversation "took place in a very friendly atmosphere." The foreign minister recommended that the ambassador not make any written report and inform Beck about the "proposals" orally. This would preclude leaks and harmful publicity. Lipski promised to comply, limiting himself to an observation that although "by careful study every point of friction could be eliminated," he "did not consider *Anschluss* [of Danzig] possible." Besides all other considerations, "Beck could never prevail upon the [Polish] people to accept it." Ribbentrop answered that he well understood the difficulties. However "certain reciprocity" should exist. "For the Führer final recognition of the Corridor was also not easy from the standpoint of domestic policy."[1]

Warsaw did not hesitate to reject the demands. In view of the situation in Europe—Germany's extraordinary success and self-assurance, with the vacillation of the Western democracies and Poland's disfavor—the demands had an ominous significance. Poland's acquiescence would mean entering into the Nazi orbit and severing its ties with the West. Beck certainly realized that.

But he did not seem to understand the fateful importance of his refusal. He saw in German demands the beginning of a war of nerves which Berlin had decided to launch against Poland, and which did not necessarily have to lead to a military conflict as long as the Poles stood firm. He also suspected that Ribbentrop's diplomatic maladroitness and intrigues, and not Hitler himself, might have been responsible for what he considered a temporary crisis. For several weeks he seemed confident that the situation would be clarified through direct Warsaw-Berlin negotiations. Therefore he decided to keep the entire matter strictly secret and instructed Lipski to deliver his answer to Ribbentrop in person. To avoid any misunderstanding and to emphasize the importance of the communication, Lipski received a written memorandum from which he would read aloud to Ribbentrop.

In his counterproposals, communicated on November 19, Beck agreed to open negotiations for a bilateral Polish-German agreement on Danzig, which would eliminate the League of Nations from the Free City altogether. Poland was ready, the memorandum stated, to negotiate new and mutually satisfactory solutions. But any attempt to incorporate Danzig into the Reich would "inevitably lead to a conflict." On his own, Lipski "expressed [his] belief" that as far as the demands for transit across the Corridor were concerned, "it might be possible to find a solution." Ribbentrop again was friendly. He assured the ambassador that the chancellor considered "best" German-Polish relations a "necessity," a "fundamental" factor in the Reich's foreign policy. He would communicate the answer to the Führer.[2]

Apparently, Lipski's communication neither made Hitler reconsider nor made him lose hope for a peaceful solution. Because, as Beck saw in Ribbentrop's demands an inauguration of a war of nerves, so apparently Hitler saw in Warsaw's answer an attempt to save face. He was prepared for such a contingency, using methods that never failed him in the past. Only five days after the Lipski-Ribbentrop meeting, the military command was instructed on the Führer's orders to prepare plans for a "surprise" seizure of Danzig, to be submitted no later than January 10, 1939.[3] He pointed out that the contemplated action was *not* to mean all-out war, thinking Warsaw might actually welcome such a move.

A few weeks later, on Ribbentrop's invitation, Beck went to Berlin and saw the chancellor on January 5, 1939. There was no change in Germany's attitude toward Poland, Hitler said. As in the past, he wanted a strong Poland because every Polish division "stationed at the Russian frontier saved Germany just as much additional military expenditure." Germany might help Poland solve the Jewish and colonial problems, but it was a "matter of indifference" to him what would be done with the Carpatho-Ukraine. He appealed to Beck to depart from the "old patterns," to seek "new" solutions along "new" lines, and, above all, not to oppose the incorporation of Danzig into the Reich. He repeated what Ribbentrop had told Lipski before: "Danzig is German, will always be German and will sooner or later become part of Germany." He also confirmed the demand for extraterritorial roads through the Corridor.

Hitler seemed calm but also grave and determined. Although not friendly as in the past, he did not threaten. Rather, he appealed to reason. But he also did not leave any doubts as to his stand. Beck noticed the change in Hitler's behavior and, in communicating his impression to Ribbentrop the next day, said that "for the first time he was in a pessimistic mood." Poland could not compromise, he added, because "in the minds of the whole Polish people Danzig represented a touchstone of German-Polish relations."[4]

The conversations were not stopped, however, although their portentous content was still kept from the public and other governments. Evidently both sides still hoped—though on different assumptions—to end the crisis peacefully and by themselves.

Three weeks later, on the fifth anniversary of the Polish-German pact, Ribbentrop visited Warsaw. On the eve of his visit and in anticipation of the visitor's message, Beck defined the main points of Polish foreign policy in a public interview. He emphasized Poland's determination to maintain "good relations" with both Germany and the Soviet Union, as well as the importance of Poland's alliances with France and Romania. Poland would not take part in any plans of aggression directed against either of its neighbors. Neither would it recognize, however, any unilateral decisions affecting its interests.

As expected, Ribbentrop repeated the demands. Again Beck rejected them. Pilsudski, he pointed out, considered the situation in Danzig a "barometer" of German-Polish relations, and he, Beck, could not do otherwise. Ribbentrop disagreed: Germany's "wishes," he said, were "extremely moderate," and their rejection would not have support in either France or Great Britain. "If 100 Englishmen or Frenchmen were asked, 99 would concede without hesitation that the reincorporation of Danzig and of at least the Corridor as well was a natural German demand," he concluded.[5]

Ribbentrop's visit was inconclusive, and from then on the pace of events quickened. On January 29 a fight between Polish and German students broke out in a Danzig restaurant, Café Langfuhr. Addressing the Reichstag the next day, the chancellor mentioned the importance of German-Polish relations. He said that thanks to his policy, "Germany is happy to possess today friendly frontiers in the west, south, and north." But he did not say anything about the "friendly frontiers" in the east, the omission which Lipski noticed and reported to Warsaw.[6]

In the middle of February, numerous riots between Polish and German students broke out at Danzig Polytechnic University, and classes had to be suspended. Soon after, anti-German demonstrations took place in Warsaw, Poznan, Lvov, Cracow, and other cities. Beck, realizing the danger, apologized to Moltke. On February 25 Ciano arrived in Warsaw for an official visit, offering an opportunity for new anti-German outbursts, mostly led by students. This time—on February 28—Ribbentrop formally complained to Lipski.[7]

On March 1 Lipski was able to exchange views with Hitler and Göring at an official reception for the diplomatic corps. The ambassador explained that the "regrettable" incidents were provoked by anti-Polish elements in Danzig and exploited in Poland by the antigovernment elements. He also pointed out that Germany's "unclear" policy on Danzig contributed to the general excitement of Polish public opinion, "especially touchy" on that matter. Hitler agreed that the "Danzig problems [were] ticklish." That was why, he said, they should be ended "by a solution which would totally remove all complications." As long as he, Hitler, was in power, and as long as Beck, "a very clever and noble man," guided Poland's foreign policy, there would be no conflict. But one day, he observed, both he and the present leaders of Poland might be replaced. Therefore, the agreement should be reached now. Such an agreement "though bilaterally painful, would remove forever all misunderstandings." Germany's final "approval" of the Polish Corridor was "not an easy decision." Still, he, Hitler, was ready to make it. He well realized that the Polish government would be criticized for responding positively to his proposals. But so would he be. There were "many elements [which sought] to spoil Polish-German relations." They should not succeed, he concluded. According to Lipski, the chancellor "closed the conversation in a positive tone."

Göring, who stayed with Lipski a little longer, expressed regret that anti-German demonstrations in Warsaw took place during Ciano's visit. He wanted to have "any information" which could throw light on who provoked anti-Polish outbursts in Danzig, making the ambassador believe that he, Göring, suspected some "provocation" aimed at disturbing good relations between both countries. The field marshal well understood that Poland needed Danzig, and to him Polish interests there were "sufficiently evident."

On the other hand, he added, it could not be denied that Danzig was a German city. He well realized the "great difficulties" the Danzig problem was causing. It was a "misfortune" that Pilsudski was no more, for "only a person like him could make a decision on such a problem." He assured Lipski of Hitler's goodwill, recalling how the Führer, against domestic pressure, agreed that the Czechoslovak Bohumin region should belong to Poland. Like Hitler, Göring expressed his conviction that as long as the Führer and he were in power, no conflict between the two countries over Danzig would break out.[8]

The following few weeks brought German-Polish relations to a climax. On March 14 Slovakia proclaimed its independence. The following day the Nazis seized Prague and proclaimed Bohemia Germany's protectorate. On March 22 Lithuania was forced to cede Memel. One day later a Berlin-Bucharest economic agreement rendered the Romanian economy dependent on the Third Reich. True, simultaneously with the Nazi seizure of Prague, Hungary annexed Carpatho-Ukraine, thus establishing a common Polish-Hungarian boundary, so much desired by Beck. In Poland, the government-controlled press and mass demonstrations hailed the annexation. In the magnitude of the unfolding drama, however, the event was meaningless. With the Nazis controlling Bohemia and Slovakia, the common Hungarian-Polish boundary, although of some sentimental value, had no political or military significance. Germany now surrounded Poland not only to the north and west but also to the south.

By then, Berlin's pressure on Warsaw increased. On March 21, less than a week after Hitler's entry into Prague, Ribbentrop summoned Lipski and told him brusquely that the chancellor was disappointed by the response to his "proposals." He reasserted them and complained of the treatment the German population had been receiving in Poland. He repeated the demands for the incorporation of Danzig into the Reich and for an extraterritorial highway and railroad across the Corridor. Because time was short, he suggested that Beck come to Berlin as soon as possible in order to discuss the matters with the chancellor and himself.[9]

Lipski, realizing that Polish-German relations had entered a critical stage, immediately left for Warsaw to get new instructions, but none were forthcoming. On March 24 Beck summoned the senior officials of his ministry, including Lipski, and formally apprised them of Poland's position. The situation had become "serious," he said, and a "straight and clear line" had been established by the government leaders. Poland would not accept unilateral decisions concerning Danzig, "regardless of what [it] is worth as an object," because "under the present circumstances [Danzig] became a symbol." If Poland, like other countries, accepted Berlin's dictates, no one could be sure "where the matter [would] end." Since Hitler was evidently "losing the measure in thinking and acting," and since, so far, he had never encountered a "determined opposition," it could be that such opposition, if offered by Poland, might actually help him to "recover that measure." If it did not, Poland would fight.[10]

Beck could not know that only one day later Hitler would define his own stand in a secret directive to the commander in chief of the army. The government still hoped, he wrote, for a peaceful solution of differences with the Poles. "The Führer *does not* wish to solve the Danzig question by force," because he "does not wish to drive Poland into the arms of Britain." He amended, however, the November order. A military action limited to Danzig only "could be contemplated" if the Polish ambassador "gave an indication" that such a fait accompli would make a solution "easier" for Warsaw. If such an indication was not given, the military command would have to take under consideration a possibility of an all-out war against Poland. For if Poland did not respond to Germany's demands positively one way or the other, and if "political preconditions" were "favorable," such a war might become necessary. In that event, "Poland would have to be so beaten down that, during the next few decades, she need not be taken into account as a political factor."[11]

When Lipski met Ribbentrop on March 26, he told the foreign minister that Warsaw was ready to conclude a new bilateral agreement on Danzig; Poland would oppose, however, its incorporation into the Reich. Poland would be willing to accord Germany all necessary transit rights in the Corridor, but the Polish government could not agree to the principle of extraterritoriality.[12] The answer, in the main, was the same as that given four months before. And it clearly indicated that the Poles, though they wanted to continue the negotiations, would not surrender to the pressure.

The next day anti-German demonstrations broke out in Bydgoszcz. Ribbentrop availed himself of this opportunity and spoke to Lipski again. He bitterly complained. Obviously well acquainted with Hitler's last directive, he also warned the ambassador that a rejection of the Führer's "generous proposals" might affect the *totality* of German-Polish relations.[13]

This was the last time the German foreign minister spoke to the Polish ambassador with the thought of a peaceful settlement. Their next meeting was to take place five months later, on August 31. By then, the die was already cast. The war started a few hours later.

NOTES

1. *DGFP*, series D, 5:104–7; compare with *PWB*, 47–48. Lipski's report (personal letter) to Beck missing from Lipski, *Diplomat in Berlin.*

2. See *DGFP*, series D, 5:127–29; also Lipski, *Diplomat in Berlin*, 465–69.

3. *TMWC*, 1:198–99; 34:481–83.

4. *PWB*, 53–54; compare with *DGFP*, series D, 5:152–59.

5. For Ribbentrop-Beck conversation, see Szembek, *Journal, 1933–1939*, 411–17; also Beck, *Dernier rapport*, 186–87; compare with Ribbentrop's memo, series D, 5:167–68.

6. For Lipski's report, dated February 22, 1939, see Lipski, *Diplomat in Berlin*, 485–87; also his report of February 7, 1939, ibid., 487–94.

7. *DGFP*, series D, 5:179–81, 172–73, respectively.

8. For Lipski's report, see Lipski, *Diplomat in Berlin*, 496–99.

9. *PWB*, 62; compare with *DGFP*, series D, 6:70–72. Lipski's report missing from Lipski, *Diplomat in Berlin.*

10. Lipski, *Diplomat in Berlin*, 503–4.

11. For the full text of the directive, see *DGFP*, series D, 6:117–19; emphasis in the original.

12. *DGFP*, series D, 6:121–22; Lipski's report missing from Lipski, *Diplomat in Berlin.*

13. *DGFP*, series D, 6:135–36; Lipski's report missing from Lipski, *Diplomat in Berlin.*

Chapter Fourteen

Soviet-Polish Relations, 1934–1938

The German-Polish rapprochement was bound to cause apprehension in the Kremlin because it proved conclusively Hitler's abandonment of the Rapallo course. The Soviet leaders realized this clearly, remembering their own earlier unsuccessful efforts to establish a modus vivendi with the Nazi regime. Now they must have feared that Hitler would try to draw Poland into his schemes for eastern expansion. Thus it became important for the Kremlin to keep Poland from cooperating with Germany and to get it to cooperate with Russia instead, either directly or within a framework of collective security.

Such a cooperation was not in the stars. Pilsudski's policy of maintaining balance between Nazi Germany and Soviet Russia—and, no doubt, his personality as well—would prevent it. His distrust of Russia was matched by his hostility toward Communism and his contempt for Stalin. "I don't congratulate you on your meeting with that bandit," he told Eden, who passed through Warsaw on his way home from Moscow in April 1935. Having failed in his federalist schemes in 1920, Pilsudski had abandoned overt anti-Soviet policies, considering them dangerous for Poland. But he was equally determined not to cooperate with the Soviets politically or militarily. [1]

On the day the Polish-German declaration was signed—January 26, 1934—Stalin publicly praised the new "atmosphere" in Polish-Soviet relations. Although future political "surprises and zigzags" were possible in Poland, "where anti-Soviet sentiments [were] still strong," he said, the improvement could be "noted." He warned, however, against any anti-Soviet plans or coalitions and emphasized his desire to preserve peace. [2]

Good-neighborly relations, based on the principle of nonaggression, with *both* Germany and Russia were the essence of Pilsudski's policy of balance. He was therefore anxious to dispel whatever doubts the Kremlin still had. Only two weeks after the signing of the Polish-German declaration, he sent Beck to Moscow on an official visit, the first such visit of any European foreign minister since Lenin seized power in 1917. He wanted to create a "friendly atmosphere" in Polish-Soviet relations. But he also gave a *mot d'ordre* to Beck not to involve Poland in any "political collaboration" with Russia.[3]

Beck was well received, and as a result of his visit Polish-Soviet relations improved visibly. Soon the diplomatic representations of both countries were raised from legations to embassies. The Polish minister in Moscow, Juliusz Lukasiewicz, was promoted to ambassador, and Iakov Davtian, until then the Soviet minister in Greece, was reassigned to the embassy in Warsaw. On May 5 the nonaggression pact of 1932 was extended to December 31, 1945. In a special protocol the Poles declared that they did not assume any obligations "inconsistent" with the Treaty of Riga, thus alleviating Soviet misgivings about Poland's relations with Germany. In exchange, the Soviet government stated that its formal note to Kaunas of September 28, 1926, should not be "interpreted" as an intention to "interfere" in the Polish-Lithuanian dispute over Vilna.[4] The clouds over Soviet-Polish relations seemed to disappear.

In spite of appearances, the detente was more formal than real, largely because of the Eastern Pact. The Poles, who viewed the pact suspiciously, seemed to have their policy synchronized with Germany's. Pilsudski, it was argued in Moscow, was "still inspired by towering ambitions and the dream of restoring the past grandeur of Poland." He wanted to take advantage of the Russian-Japanese conflict. He probably had some sort of a gentleman's agreement with Hitler. The American ambassador in Moscow, William Bullitt, was assured of it not only by Litvinov, who may have been interested in spreading rumors, but by the French ambassador, Hervé Alphand, as well.[5] An additional factor, which probably contributed to Soviet (as well as Polish) suspicions and fears, was the lack of any direct or meaningful exchanges between Warsaw and Moscow relating to the pact. Throughout all negotiations it was Quai d'Orsay and not Narkomindel with whom the Poles dealt. Eden considered such a procedure faulty and warned Beck against it.[6]

At the end of July 1934 Bullitt reported to Washington on the Soviet press coverage of the Eastern Pact. His press review revealed what great importance Soviet authorities attached to the pact and to the role of Poland. The leading editorial in *Pravda* for July 16 described the pact as "a new and powerful guarantee of peace in Europe." On the same day, *Izvestya* attributed Poland's equivocal attitude "to the influence of Germany" and expressed hope that "the political common sense of Colonel Beck would prevent Poland from procrastination and from imposing impossible conditions which would be equivalent to a negative answer." Germany's unwillingness to enter the pact was due to its "thirst for expansion eastward," wrote Karl Radek. *Izvestya* pointed out that since Poland was the only country "whose frontiers had been seriously questioned," the Eastern Pact represented "the best guarantee" the Poles could have, much better than the temporary and limited guarantees of the Polish-German declaration. According to Bullitt, all Soviet officials considered Poland to be pivotal for the entire scheme, because Germany's refusal to enter the pact would not necessarily kill it, it would only demonstrate Hitler's aggressive intentions. Poland's refusal, however, would inevitably make it "impossible," they all contended.[7]

In February 1935 Litvinov let it be known to both French and British ambassadors in Moscow that Poland's participation in the pact was crucial from a military standpoint. One month later he urged Eden during the latter's visit in Moscow to use his influence on the Poles. Eden did and without delay communicated with the Polish ambassador. He emphasized Germany's accelerated rearmaments and told Lukasiewicz that in the Kremlin fear of German aggression and desire to build an effective collective security system took precedence over any other considerations. His arguments fell on deaf ears. Germany and Russia had no common frontier, argued the ambassador. Poland stood between them. Before attacking Russia, Germany would have to march through Poland, and the German-Polish nonaggression pact precluded this. Poland could not take part in a military aggression against Russia—the Polish-Soviet nonaggression pact precluded that. The Kremlin's fears were "unjustified," concluded Lukasiewicz.[8]

On his way to London, Eden stopped in Warsaw, where he reported on his conversations with Stalin. The Soviet government wanted Poland to enter the pact with or without Germany. If the Poles were "afraid" of its structure providing for mutual assistance, the structure could be changed. In the event of German aggression against any of its neighbors, the Soviet aid, its extent, and its form would be defined by the victim of aggression. The Soviet Union would be allowed to give such "aid"—military, economic, weapons, and so on—as the attacked country asked for. Beck was immovable. Poland would not endanger its good relations with Germany. Unless Germany entered the pact, Poland would not join it.[9]

The admission of Russia into the League of Nations in September 1934 brought Poland to the fore again because its approval, as a nonpermanent member of the council, was required by the League's covenant. Many, particularly the French diplomats, feared that Warsaw would veto the whole matter. Others expected that in exchange for their approving vote, the Poles would demand a permanent seat on the council. There was great excitement in the corridors of the League in the first week of September 1934.

Beck, who headed the Polish delegation to the fall session of the League, did not oppose Russia's entry and had no intention of doing so. Such a show of hostility would not fit into Pilsudski's policy of balance and would hardly be reconcilable with the spirit of the Polish-Soviet agreements. Nor did he ask for a permanent seat on the council—he could not really hope to obtain one. He viewed Russia's entry into the League with apprehension, though, and certainly did not approve of the French-instigated propaganda campaign glamorizing Russia and making its entry a "triumph" for peace and security. He wanted to tone down the atmosphere of jubilation. He also saw an opportunity to enhance Poland's immediate interests and international prestige.

Throughout his tenure as Poland's foreign minister, Beck paid much attention to the problem of prestige and to demonstrations of the "independence" of his policy. This was understandable, considering Poland's unhappy past and its position, until recently, as France's "client," slighted on more than one occasion. Pilsudski and all his men were very sensitive in these matters. Because of Poland's size, its stable government, its allegedly excellent army, and its geopolitical situation, they also tended to exaggerate Poland's importance in European politics. The recently concluded nonaggression agreements with Germany and Russia added to their self-assurance.

Russia's entry into the League of Nations prompted Beck to make two moves. First, he demanded a formal declaration from Moscow that all Polish-Soviet agreements, including the nonaggression pact and the convention for the definition of aggression, would continue to have full validity, regardless of Russia's new obligations as a member of the League. He made such a declaration a *conditio sine qua non* for Poland's affirmative vote on Russia's admission. He held that one day, in some unforeseeable circumstances, using the League's procedures, the Soviet Union might reinterpret its otherwise well-defined commitments vis-à-vis Poland. His move caused a sensation. "All eyes were fixed on us,"[10] he recalled years later. But he was successful.

Moscow agreed, and an exchange of notes promptly took place.[11] Beck's demand, however, was interpreted as lack of confidence in the League and a less than friendly gesture toward Poland's eastern neighbor.

The second move—more important and widely criticized in the international press—concerned national minorities. According to the treaties signed by Poland in 1919, the council of the League had a duty to consider complaints from the ethnically non-Polish populations. No government in Warsaw had ever been satisfied with those procedures, because they suggested certain limitations upon national sovereignty and because none of the great powers had undertaken similar obligations. With Russia's entry into the League's council, Beck argued, the problem assumed new dimensions. From then on, the Soviet government could, via the League, interfere in Poland's domestic affairs. Moscow could also use Poland's minority problems for propaganda purposes, much as Berlin did from 1926 to 1932, which Beck considered "inadmissible." Besides, Russia, itself a multinational state, was not bound by those treaties.

Beck decided to use Russia's entry into the League as an "occasion" for a showdown. First, in need of "justification," he introduced a motion to extend the minorities' obligations to *all* members of the League, knowing that it would be rejected. So it was, with France, Great Britain, and Italy voting against it. Then, on September 13, he addressed the General Assembly and solemnly announced that henceforth the Polish government would cease to be bound by the minorities' treaties and would no longer recognize the League's competence in that matter.[12]

Poland's unilateral abrogation of formally assumed responsibilities represented a direct challenge not only to the League of Nations' authority but to the entire Versailles system. It came less than a year after Germany left the League and coincided with violent anti-League and anti-Versailles Nazi propaganda. One-third of Poland's entire population consisted of national minorities, many of whom considered themselves discriminated against. The Ukrainian "pacification" had just ended, and the Bereza Kartuska "isolation" camp had recently been filled with, among others, Ukrainian extreme nationalistic elements. Poland's rejection of the minorities' treaty also coincided with anti-Jewish excesses at Polish universities, which were widely reported in the international press. The challenge, many reasoned, demonstrated not so much the independence of Polish policy as its internal weakness, fear of international scrutiny, and its solidarity with the Nazi anti-League campaign.

Beck's move was decried even more because the Czechoslovak and Romanian delegates, whose countries were equally bound by the minorities' treaties, sternly criticized his motion. Beneš, Czechoslovakia's popular foreign minister, considered the minorities' treaties and the League's role as "one of the guarantees of his country's security." He always believed that, all things considered, the existence of the new countries in central-eastern Europe depended on the preservation of the Versailles system and on support of the League. [13]

Although Beck scorned his critics, their arguments and reasoning seem to have been correct. Only two days after the Polish declaration, the Auswärtiges Amt sent a secret memorandum to its embassies in London, Paris, Rome, Moscow, and Warsaw. Since Poland's minorities' obligations had been assumed "in return for the acquisition of new territories," by a cancellation of those obligations, "the whole territorial question [would] in fact be re-opened," the memorandum stated. Embassy staffs should proffer this idea in "diplomatic conversations." Caution was recommended because, as the memorandum pointed out, for the time being Germany did not want to raise the argument officially. [14]

In time, Moscow's apprehension concerning Poland's stand grew. As the Polish embassy in Moscow reported, the Soviet press as well as government officials argued that, as a result of Beck's policies, both Germany and Japan might count on Poland's support in their long-range anti-Soviet plans. Were the Poles associated with those plans? [15] On January 28, 1935, Molotov, in a report to the Supreme Soviet, openly criticized Polish foreign policy. [16] The following June, during the government-sponsored mass demonstrations celebrating the fifteenth anniversary of the Red Army victory over the Polish "invaders" of the Ukraine, the Soviet press "warned" Warsaw not to engage in any anti-Soviet activities. At the Seventh Congress of the Comintern (July 25 to August 20, 1935), both Germany and Poland were severely attacked for their "plans" to "invade" and "colonize" the Soviet Ukraine. [17] On August 18, Jan Otmar-Berson, the Moscow correspondent of the semiofficial *Gazeta Polska*, was expelled from Russia amid mutual press recriminations.

Mistrust of Polish foreign policy was not just a matter of propaganda. It apparently reflected the Soviet leaders' actual state of mind. Laval, just back from his trip to Moscow in May 1935, warned Szembek that the Kremlin suspected Poland of aggressive intentions and considered it a German satellite. Stalin, he noticed, became particularly suspicious. The American ambassador in Warsaw, Cudahy, after his own trip to Russia, confirmed Laval's observations.[18]

On May 16, 1936, Neurath told Lipski about "fears" prevailing in the highest quarters of the Soviet leadership. Those in the Kremlin "feared," he said, that Hitler would eventually attack Russia. First, he would destroy Austria. Then, in cooperation with Poland and Hungary, he would partition Czechoslovakia. Then, together with the same partners, he would attack Russia. Neurath, possibly in good faith, called those fears "absurd."[19] The time was May 1936. Most probably until Ribbentrop's appointment, the Führer did not care to inform the Auswärtiges Amt about his far-reaching plans. But those fears, as future events demonstrated, were not entirely groundless.

Nor were suspicions concerning Pilsudski/Beck's policies limited to the Soviet leaders. In his report dated February 4, 1935, Kennard expressed a view that Pilsudski, "gambler" that he was, "probably" gave Hitler some vague assurances of conditional support for the Rosenberg schemes, and Hitler "[had] no doubt taken them at a good deal more than their face value." Such a policy, the ambassador added, was "risky in that it [ignored] the possibility of a German-Russian rapprochement at the expense of Poland." One month later, the British ambassador in Bucharest reported Romanian complaints that the Poles "cherished some fantastic design for a joint German-Polish-Romanian invasion of Russia," out of which Romania was to obtain some Russian territories—"the last thing in the world that she wanted," the ambassador added.[20]

In the spring of 1936 Lukasiewicz was sent as ambassador to Paris; Waclaw Grzybowski took his place in Moscow. When the new ambassador paid an official visit on July 1 to Potemkin, the vice commissar for foreign affairs, he heard comments which left no doubt as to the Kremlin's evaluation of Polish foreign policy:

> The political relations between us could not be worse. We [the USSR] are working to increase the prestige of the League of Nations, and for collective security; we are combating all forms of aggression and all forms of fascism. At the present we are pursuing an anti-German, anti-Italian and anti-Japanese policy. Poland is pursuing a diametrically contrary policy, tending to weaken the League of Nations, combating attempts to realize collective security, supporting Italy and sympathizing with Japan. Poland is within the orbit of German policy.[21]

In April 1937 Grzybowski, evidently alarmed, complained to Szembek about Poland's anti-Soviet course. He expressed disapproval of the frequent and excessive anti-Soviet overtones in the Polish press. All this, he argued, did not fit the official policy of neutrality. Soon after, the Soviet government ostentatiously closed the Polish consulates in Tiflis and Kharkov and recalled its ambassador from Warsaw. Beck became "la bate noire de Moscou."[22]

Moscow's suspicions might also have been aroused by the publicly expounded views of some Polish journalists, writers, and politicians, such as Stanislaw Cat Mackiewicz, Adolf Bochenski, and Wladyslaw Studnicki. Although differing greatly on domestic policies, they usually agreed on Polish-German cooperation, envisaging or advocating a joint Polish-German policy aimed at the dismemberment of Russia. True, they did not represent any specific movements or parties, but they did command a certain influence in right-wing circles.[23]

Furthermore, sympathy and support for various separatist émigré groups that were still seeking independence for their Russian-dominated nations, such as the Ukraine, Byelorussia, Georgia, and Armenia, endured in Poland. A so-called Prometeist movement counted among its members or sympathizers not only prominent intellectuals but highly placed government officials. It published its own periodicals and books, organized seminars, and subsidized émigré leaders. The movement had an extremely loose structure and was not especially widespread, and the government was never officially associated with its program or activities. However, not infrequently, it was used by the Polish foreign ministry and military intelligence. No doubt, Moscow drew its own conclusions.[24]

The Prometeist movement was not representative of Beck's diplomacy. If anything, it was an aggravation, because he wanted to keep Poland away from any international groupings directed against Moscow. When, on November 6, 1937, Italy joined the German-Japanese Anti-Comintern Pact, Beck immediately advised all Polish diplomatic posts that Poland had not been invited to join the pact and, if asked, would decline. Poland's policy of opposing the formation of ideological blocs as well as its proximity to the Soviet Union precluded such participation, he explained, instructing his diplomats to clarify the question wherever necessary.[25]

Beck's instructions no doubt reflected the feeling of the great majority of his countrymen. The Polish nation, regardless of political orientations, wanted peace, not conquests. This was why Beck's pro-German and seemingly anti-Soviet gestures were criticized at home by the main opposition parties. None of those parties, however, favored a *political cooperation* with Russia. Distrust of Soviet-Communist policies and activities were deeply rooted in all political circles. The Comintern's efforts to bring together leftist and liberal forces in a popular front under a Communist aegis found no sympathy or success in Poland. The Polish Communist party—torn by internal rivalries, weak, and soon to be dissolved—was considered Moscow's agent. Fear of traditional Russian expansionism, White or Red, was real. Belief that the Soviets would attack Poland at the first opportunity was widespread.

These fears were not without foundation. On November 14, 1937, William Bullitt, recently reassigned to Paris, told Szembek about his recent conversation with Litvinov. The latter confessed that Moscow "did not attach great importance to the problem of Bessarabia, because anyway Romania would one day be absorbed by Russia." What was worse, as Bullitt reported, Litvinov spoke "in the same terms" about Poland.[26]

That Russia's leaders thought in terms of territorial expansion the Poles eventually learned from Litvinov himself, in circumstances rather characteristic of Moscow's diplomacy. In the spring of 1938, during the Austrian crisis and at the time of Warsaw's ultimatum to Kaunas, the Soviet press was bitingly critical of Poland. Together with the anti-Polish press campaign, Litvinov discreetly approached Ambassador Grzybowski, promoting a division of the Baltic area into Polish and Russian "spheres of interest." The Dvina River was to separate the zones, with Lithuania assigned to Poland. Grzybowski declined on his own initiative, and Beck fully approved his stand.[27]

During the Czechoslovak crisis of September 1938, relations between Poland and Russia had degenerated badly. Polish demands for outright cession of the Teschen area were preceded by troop concentration on the Czechoslovak border, indicating that Warsaw contemplated using force. At the same time, military maneuvers were taking place on the Polish-Soviet frontier, concluded by a spectacular parade. Beck informed Hitler that the maneuvers were designed to let Moscow know that if it chose to intervene on Czechoslovakia's behalf, Poland would oppose that intervention by force. In turn—on September 23—the Narkomindel notified Warsaw that if Poland used force against Czechoslovakia, Russia would abrogate the nonaggression pact of 1932.[28] These posturings did not degenerate into a full-blown crisis because, soon after, Prague bowed to the Polish ultimatum.

Thunderstorms are often preceded by a deceptive calm. Such was the atmosphere surrounding Soviet-Polish relations in the winter of 1938–1939. The Nazi demands, forwarded by Ribbentrop on October 24, certainly alerted Beck to the dangerous course that events had taken. Poland's foreign policy was discredited in Paris and London, and Beck himself was suspected of collusion with Hitler. He was more than unpopular in Moscow. And now, confronted with Nazi demands, Poland was alone. He acted swiftly, approaching the Soviet government for some public reassertion of good-neighborly relations and mutual treaty commitments. Such a reassertion, he apparently hoped, might revitalize his policy of balance, offset Western suspicions, reinstate some normality in Polish-Soviet relations, and, most important, strengthen his hand in dealing with Hitler.

Grzybowski found Litvinov and other Narkomindel officials amenable. Without great delay, on November 26, a joint communiqué was issued, both governments reaffirming the validity of all previously concluded agreements, including the Riga treaty and the nonaggression pact of 1932. In the following weeks, several minor pending problems were settled and, finally, on February 19, 1939, a commercial agreement, based on the most-favored-nation principle, was signed. The annual exchange of goods, until then quite insignificant, was to be increased to some twenty million dollars. Thus, only a few months after the Soviets threatened to repeal the nonaggression pact, relations seemed normal again.

Moscow's responsiveness to Polish initiatives was more than understandable. By the end of 1938, more than communiqués, more than twenty million dollars in trade was at stake. Poland's position vis-à-vis Hitler's anti-Soviet policy became crucial. From Moscow's standpoint, the basic situation had not changed since Hitler's accession to power—the danger had only become more imminent and Poland's role more pivotal. Germany had become strong and more aggressive than ever. Hitler was still intent on pursuing his goal— Lebensraum in Russia—and Nazi policy and propaganda continued to be hostile to Russia. If Germany embarked upon new conquests, Poland's policy of balance, one way or the other, would have to end. Which way would Poland go?

The answer and the assurances had to be conclusive, because in the middle of March 1939 Hitler would strike again. The governments of Great Britain and France would then ask the Soviet government to play a key role in stopping Germany's further expansion, and the course of events would enable Stalin to dictate his own conditions in return for Russia's cooperation.

NOTES

1. Beck, *Dernier rapport*, 91, 95, respectively.
2. For extracts of Stalin's speech to the Seventh Congress of the Communist Party, see Degras, *Soviet Documents*, 3:65–72.
3. Beck, *Dernier rapport*, 54–57, 282–84.
4. For the text, *DPSR, 1939–1945*, 1:21–22.
5. *FRUS*, 1934, 1:504, 498, 497, respectively.
6. See Eden-Beck conversation on April 2, 1935, *AANP-Zespoly MSZ*, 5211, 93–105.
7. *FRUS*, 1934, 1:502–5; also Budurowycz, *Polish-Soviet Relations*, 56.
8. *AANP-Zespoly MSZ*, 3247, 204–7; 5211, 82–83, 87–88, respectively.
9. Ibid., 93–105.
10. Beck, *Dernier rapport*, 68–69.
11. For the texts, see *PWB*, 180–81.
12. Beck, *Dernier rapport*, 67. For Beck's reasoning, see Beck, *Dernier rapport*, 67–72.
13. Beck, *Dernier rapport*, 68n1, 71.
14. *DGFP*, series C, 3:413–15.
15. See reports of the Polish embassy in Moscow for January 1935, *AANP-Zespoly MSZ*, 3245, 4–6.
16. Degras, *Soviet Documents*, 3:111.
17. Budurowycz, *Polish-Soviet Relations*, 74–76.
18. Szembek, *Diariusz*, 1:299, 370, respectively.
19. *AANP-Zespoly MSZ*, 3252, 86.
20. *FO* 371/18896/C1253/465/55, 18897/C1871/1871/55, respectively.
21. *PWB*, 195.
22. See Józef Zaranski, "Diariusz Jana Szembeka za r. 1937" (Jan Szembek's diary for 1937), *Wiadomości* 24, no. 1 (1188) January 1969, 3; Noël, *L'Aggression allemande contre la Pologne*, 169, respectively.
23. For more information on this subject, see Cienciala, *Poland and the Western Powers*, 31–32.
24. For various documentary data, see *AANP-Zespoly MSZ*, 5321, 1–140; for a comprehensive study, see Sergiusz Mikulicz, *Prometeizm w Polityce II Rzeczypospolitej* (*Prometheism in the Politics of the Republic*) (Warsaw: Ksiazka i Wiedza, 1971); also Wlodzimierz Baczkowski, "Prometeizm na Tle Epoki" (Prometheism, Reflection of an Era), *Niepodległość* 17:28–54.
25. For the full text, see *PWB*, 181.
26. Szembek, *Journal*, 251.
27. Beck, *Dernier rapport*, 157.
28. For the text, see Degras, *Soviet Documents*, 3:305.

Chapter Fifteen

The Meaning of the British and French Guarantees, March–April 1939

The Nazi seizure of Prague proved the bankruptcy of the policy of appeasement based on the belief that Hitler wanted only the areas inhabited by Germans. Both the French and the British governments finally concluded that the Nazis could not be stopped but by a display of force. Only one month before, Chamberlain had declared to the American ambassador that he "personally" believed Hitler and that the only way of "doing business" with Hitler was "to take him at his word." Now on March 17, 1939, Chamberlain publicly declared that although his country considered war a cruel absurdity, it was not incapable of taking up a challenge.[1] From then on the British government, previously the leader of appeasement, seized the leadership of the diplomatic offensive.

The decision of the Western democracies to stop Germany brought the complex problem of the Soviet Union and its relations with Poland to the fore. That Soviet participation in any anti-Nazi system of defense had become vital was generally agreed upon in London and Paris after March 15. Hitler had boasted for years that his Reich would never engage in a two-front war. If, therefore, he were faced with such an eventuality, he might abandon the risks of further conquests. On the other hand, if he continued his course of territorial expansion, the effectiveness of the Soviet military contribution hinged largely on the attitude of Poland. Russia had no common frontier with Germany, and any effective anti-German military coalition necessitated cooperation between Moscow and Warsaw.

Just after the seizure of Prague, Berlin presented Bucharest with demands that, though mostly economic, appeared to some Romanians as an attempt to reduce their country, with its rich oil and food resources, to the status of another Nazi protectorate. The Romanian minister in London, Virgil Tilea, hurriedly reported his fears to Halifax. Assuming that the danger was imminent and Great Britain far away, Tilea also suggested that Poland be brought into the system of defending Romania. The suggestion seemed salutary and, without delay, Halifax asked Beck for a public four-power (British-Franco-Polish-Soviet) declaration pledging the signatories to defend the territorial status quo in Europe.[2]

In the meantime, on March 21–22, Chamberlain, Halifax, and Bonnet met in London to discuss means of forging a collective front, with Russia and Poland participating.[3] From the beginning they agreed that in the new situation Poland became extraordinarily important, and that its commitments to assist Romania and cooperate with Russia were indispensable. They knew that Poland was not treaty-bound to come to Romania's aid, because the Polish-Romanian defensive alliance of March 3, 1921, provided for aid only in the event of unprovoked Soviet aggression. Therefore, the three statesmen concurred that their governments would have to undertake new obligations and, if necessary, resort to pressure in order to obtain Poland's cooperation. As Halifax said: "In order to persuade Poland to commit herself to support Rumania, Great Britain and France would have to give Poland a private understanding that, if Poland came in, they would come in also; then it might be suggested to both Poland and Rumania that they should not raise any objection against Soviet participation."[4]

At that time neither London nor Paris knew the extent to which Polish-German relations had deteriorated or where the Poles stood. Some suspected that Poland, under the pressure of events, might be forced into the Nazi camp. In a way Beck contributed to those suspicions. He made Poland the first country to recognize the "independence" of Slovakia and chose not to supply either France or Great Britain with full information concerning German demands. In fact, he downplayed the increasingly evident tension in German-Polish relations.[5] Reporting on his recent conference with Hitler to Noël on January 12, he failed to mention Nazi demands. He used similar tactics on January 30, commenting on Ribbentrop's visit to Warsaw.[6] As late as on March 17, two days after the Nazi seizure of Prague and four days before Ribbentrop's threatening declaration to Lipski, he assured Kennard that rumors of Hitler's plans for Memel and Danzig were due to local excitement, recommending that they should not be considered too seriously. Twelve days later Kennard was rather vaguely informed about German "desiderata." But he was also told that they *did not* represent a direct danger.[7]

The British initiative confronted Beck with an insoluble dilemma. He did not want to shut the door on some understanding with Berlin, hoping that Germany's demands might be part and parcel of a regrettable war of nerves rather than a prelude to a real war. He thus hesitated to make any move that would indicate to Hitler that Poland's foreign policy had been reoriented. The measures proposed by London represented a revival of the collective security system. For more than five years Poland's firm refusal to participate in any such system formed a strong tie between Germany and Poland. Hitler would certainly interpret the four-power declaration as an attempt to encircle Germany. For more than five years Hitler had had assurances from Beck and Lipski that Poland would not take part in such an attempt. The international guarantee for Romania would include Russia. Hitler was given repeated, solemn assurances that Poland would not cooperate with Russia.

Unwilling as he was to make any overt about-face in his policy, Beck viewed the British initiative as a good opportunity to strengthen Poland's security and to engage Britain in his country's defense.

On March 21 Beck explained to Ambassador Kennard that his main policy objective was not to ally Poland with either Russia or Germany but to maintain a balance between them. The proposed declaration, he said, would "definitely place Poland in the Soviet camp," causing a serious reaction in Berlin, and he did not want to provoke Hitler. Besides, he did not trust Moscow, nor did he believe in Russia's military strength. He suggested instead a direct Polish-British understanding.[8]

At this juncture, news of sudden German troop concentrations on the Polish frontier spread all over Europe. Alarmed public opinion in Great Britain demanded immediate clarification of the cabinet's position. In the House of Commons, parliamentary interpellation by the leader of the Opposition was expected on March 31.

Downing Street acted quickly. On March 30, while Kennard was meeting with Beck, a most urgent cable from London was brought to the ambassador, instructing him to ask the Polish authorities if they "had any objection to a British government guarantee to meet any action which clearly threatened Polish independence and which the Polish government accordingly considered it vital to resist with their national forces."[9] The answer had to be given at once, since the prime minister intended to make such a declaration the next day. Beck immediately communicated with the president of the republic and Marshal Śmigly-Rydz and formally accepted the British proposal.

The next day, March 31, Chamberlain made a historic statement in the House of Commons:

> As the House is aware, certain consultations are now proceeding with other governments. In order to make perfectly clear the position of His Majesty's Government in the meantime before those consultations are concluded, I now have to inform the House that during the period in the event of any action which clearly threatens Polish independence, and which the Polish Government accordingly considered it vital to resist with their national forces His Majesty's Government would feel themselves bound at once to lend the Polish Government all support in their power. They have given the Polish government an assurance to this effect.
>
> I may add, that the French Government have authorized me to make plain that they stand in the same position in this matter as do His Majesty's Government. [10]

The declaration, eventually known as a "guarantee," represented an extraordinary step in British foreign policy, which traditionally shunned any fixed commitments to small, central-eastern European nations. Great Britain committed itself to come to Poland's aid not only in case of unprovoked direct aggression but also in case of a "threat" to Poland's independence. Significantly, neither Danzig nor Poland's territorial integrity was mentioned. The emphasis was on "independence," which the *Times* did not fail to note the next day.

The declaration was not the product of a carefully planned policy but of improvisation. In those days, alarm and the general feeling that something had to be done immediately prevailed at Downing Street. [11] Before he created a new fait accompli, Hitler had to be warned that any new aggression would result in a general conflagration. It was believed that such a warning alone might suffice to restrain him. Furthermore, the guarantee was expected to bring Poland into a collective defense of Romania. [12]

When Chamberlain was making his historic statement, Beck had already realized that German-Polish relations had entered a critical stage. He welcomed the guarantee, but he also realized that, being unilateral, it could be revoked at any time. So he aimed at a full-fledged British-Polish alliance. For some time he had planned to visit London in order to tighten up Polish-British relations. Now he offered to go at once. His offer was accepted immediately, and he left Warsaw on April 2.

Beck's visit to London proved to be of fateful importance, not only for Anglo-Polish but also for German-Polish relations. Eventually it became a source of false assumptions and false expectations on the part of the Poles. It also revealed insurmountable difficulties in mounting an effective front against Germany.[13]

Beck thought that a full-fledged alliance with Great Britain was the best guarantee of making the Nazis fight on two fronts from the outset. In this event, he felt, Poland could hold on, and in the end the Anglo-French-Polish coalition would have enough strength to beat Germany. But he still did not want Hitler to know that Poland had in fact decided to take part in Germany's "encirclement." Adamant about not participating in any *public* multilateral agreements, he proposed, instead, a *secret bilateral* Anglo-Polish mutual-assistance pact.

The British disagreed, arguing that if anything could restrain Hitler, it would be his realization that the days of faits accomplis were over, that there existed a united front of powers—France, Great Britain, Poland, and Russia—who were determined and strong enough to defend any prospective victim. For this reason, the British held, any agreement or any declaration should be phrased in unmistakable terms and made public.

Throughout the negotiations in London, Beck kept refusing to join the British guarantees to Romania. Such an act, he said, would alienate Hungary. Hungary was Poland's traditional friend, and the two countries had just established a long-desired common boundary. Antagonizing Budapest made no sense in terms of Polish-Hungarian relations. Furthermore, an open challenge to Germany's expansion that did not *directly* threaten Poland did not fit into the framework of Polish-Nazi relations. There was nothing the British could do, and they finally accepted Beck's position.

Following his traditional course, Beck firmly refused to participate in any political or military bloc of which Russia was a member. As usual citing Pilsudski's opinions, he definitely opposed "any agreement which would have the effect, even if only indirectly, of linking Poland with the Soviet Union." Not only did he not believe that Russia would fight to defend Poland or, for that matter, any country, he was convinced that if efforts were not made to secure Soviet *neutrality* in the event of war, the Soviets might actually invade their western neighbors. He recommended seeking a specific agreement with Moscow to allow Western powers to send war matériel to Poland through Russia and to secure Soviet deliveries to Poland in case of German aggression. Warsaw would not oppose any understanding among

London, Paris, and Moscow as long as it did not impose new obligations upon Poland vis-à-vis Russia. In addition to other risks, he feared that an agreement on Polish-Soviet cooperation might provoke Hitler into an immediate military attack on Poland.[14] The British realized that at least for the time being nothing could be done and dropped the matter. They knew that the Romanians also feared Russia's participation in the declaration—besides, Chamberlain himself had apprehensions about any too-close association with Moscow. He saw in the Soviet Union "a very unreliable friend" and thought that Moscow was "concerned only with getting everyone by the ears."[15]

Eventually the British consented to a mutual-assistance pact with Poland on the condition that it be announced publicly. Their arguments made Beck reflect and led him to a grave decision. He "bypassed" the instructions of his government and, on his own responsibility, agreed. As a result, a public joint communiqué was issued on April 6. It announced an early conclusion of a formal mutual-assistance treaty between Great Britain and Poland and, of utmost importance, specified that should an emergency arise, namely, "any threat, direct or indirect to the independence of either [country]" before the formal treaty was concluded, the communiqué would bind both signatories. For all practical purposes the communiqué itself became a preliminary mutual-assistance pact, a defensive alliance.[16]

The communiqué was regarded in Poland as an extremely important step in strengthening the national security system, because Great Britain had further enlarged the obligations undertaken on March 31. Although the unilateral guarantee covered only "any action which clearly threatened Polish independence," the communiqué referred also to an "indirect threat." From then on, it was up to Poland to decide whether any German move should be interpreted as a "direct or indirect threat." Once Poland decided to counter either "action" or "direct or indirect threat" militarily, Britain's commitment to lend Poland "all the support in [her] power" was to come into play.

By then, the pace of events quickened. On April 7 Italy invaded Albania and the entire structure of Europe seemed to crumble. Many expected that other Balkan countries besides Romania might be directly threatened by the Axis Powers. In a frantic effort to stop further aggression, Great Britain publicly extended the guarantees to Greece and Romania on April 13.

The French, resigned to British leadership, did not remain passive. In order to emphasize solidarity with London, Daladier issued a public declaration the same day assuming identical obligations for France. A special paragraph was dedicated to Poland. It not only confirmed the Franco-Polish alliance but adapted it to new circumstances. "France and Poland," read the declaration, "guarantee each other immediate and direct aid against any threat, direct or indirect, which aims a blow at their vital interest." Thus, France, too, increased its commitments toward Poland, a fact that Daladier emphasized to his cabinet.[17] For while the alliance of 1921 applied to only a *direct* military attack, France was now pledged to assist Poland in the event of any "indirect threat" to Poland's independence or "vital interest."

Interestingly, these commitments did not mean that either France or Great Britain considered Danzig's status as unchangeable. Their declaration aimed at deterring Nazi Germany from further aggression, *not* at guaranteeing the status of Danzig.[18] There was a general feeling at the Quai d'Orsay that Germany's incorporation of the Free City "was a foregone conclusion" and that "there was no reason for France and Great Britain to take action to prevent it." Halifax held a similar view. On May 22, 1939, he told Bonnet that Britain's commitments rested on "general principles" rather than specific obligations. The latter, he thought, could be assumed only after Russia's part in the anti-Nazi collective defense system became clear. He did see the danger in giving Poland the power to involve Great Britain in war, but he also saw a danger in having Hitler believe that Great Britain "should be lacking in resolution" to help Poland "in case of need." Between these two dangers he "had to steer" his foreign policy. As for Danzig, both Paris and London agreed that a specific commitment to defend Danzig should *not* be assumed by either of them.[19] The crux of the matter was *prevention of war*— not a rejection of some possible compromise.[20]

As for the Poles, they saw in the guarantees and preliminary agreement with Great Britain a powerful element of strength. It looked as if Beck again had triumphed as a steward of his country's foreign policy. The French for years had tried to weaken their treaty obligations with Poland and only a few months before had contemplated terminating the alliance altogether. Now they enlarged their commitments. The British traditionally distrusted alliances in central and eastern Europe and were traditionally unwilling to commit themselves a priori in any European conflict. Now they pledged their power to defend a distant nation. And, in an unprecedented turn of events, they left Poland to determine when and under what circumstances they would go to war. Furthermore, Poland had a nonaggression pact with the Soviet Union which, in view of the alleged irreconcilability between Nazism and Communism, was considered an additional factor in the national security system. For reassurances against any surprises from Moscow, there was a defensive alliance with Romania.

All these alliances, treaties, and commitments were enough, the Poles felt, to call Hitler's bluff. If he failed to see the handwriting on the wall and attacked Poland, the British, French, and Polish military riposte, coming simultaneously from east and west, would bring Germany to its knees. Polish leadership felt justified in facing whatever the future might bring with a sense of security.

NOTES

1. *FRUS*, 1939, 1:14; *Times* (London), March 18, 1939, 12–13, respectively.

2. *DBFP*, 3rd series, 4:366–67. Eventually the Romanian foreign minister, Grigore Gafencu, informed the Foreign Office that Tilea "misrepresented the situation," ibid., 369–70, 391, 459–60.

3. For the conference of March 21–22, see ibid., 422–27, 257–63.

4. *DBFP*, 3rd series, 4:459–60.

5. Raczyński, *W Sojuszniczm Londynie*, 26; Noël, *L'Aggression allemande contre la Pologne*, 288, 319.

6. *LJF*, 55–56, 58–59.

7. *DBFP*, 3rd series, 4:362, 543, 548.

8. Ibid., 428, 453–54, 463, 500–503, 5:12.

9. Ibid., 548; also *PWB*, 71–72.

10. *Documents Concerning German-Polish Relations and the Outbreak of Hostilities between Great Britain and Germany on September 3, 1939* (*The British Blue Book*) (London: His Majesty's Stationery Office, 1959), 48. Hereafter cited as *BBB*.

11. Lord Strang, *Home and Abroad* (London: Andre Deutsch, 1956), 161; also Eden, *The Reckoning*, 55–56.

12. The Earl of Halifax, *Fullness of Days* (London: Collins, 1957), 204–5; also Martin Gilbert, op. cit., 236.

13. For the Anglo-Polish negotiations in London on April 4–6, 1939, see *DBFP*, 3rd series, 5:1–19, 30–36, 38–45, 47–49.

14. Beck, *Dernier rapport*, 189–94; also *DBFP*, 3rd series, 5:38.

15. *DBFP*, 3rd series, 5:6–7, 12; also Feiling, *The Life of Neville Chamberlain*, 403–8.

16. For Chamberlain's account on the negotiations and agreement in the House of Commons, see *5 Parliamentary Debates*, Commons, 345, 3002–5; for the text of the communiqué, see *DBFP*, 3rd series, 5:47–48.

17. For the text of the declaration, see *LJF*, 132; also Noël, *L'Aggression allemande contre la Pologne*, 324; Gamelin, *Servir*, 2:424–25.

18. See a contemporary memo by permanent undersecretary of state, Sir Alexander Cadogan: *DBFP*, 3rd series, 5:642; also his reevaluating comments dated January 20, 1964, Sir Alexander Cadogan, *The Diaries of Sir Alexander Cadogan, 1938–1945*, ed. David Dilks (London: Cassell & Co., 1971), 67, 166.

19. See Leger (secretary-general at Quai d'Orsay)/Campbell (British embassy in Paris) conversation on March 18, 1939, *DBFP*, 3rd series, 4:382; also 5:638–39.

20. For a documented study on the British guarantee, see Simon Newman, *March 1939: The British Guarantees to Poland* (Oxford: Clarendon Press, 1976), 253 pages.

Chapter Sixteen

Hitler's Decision to Isolate and Crush Poland, April–August 1939

The British guarantees and, even more so, the Anglo-Polish communiqué failed to produce the results London hoped for. Hitler remained convinced that neither Great Britain nor France would fight Germany in defense of Poland. However, the guarantees did convince him that the Poles would not surrender peacefully, that they would not play the role he had assigned them in his far-reaching plans, but, rather, that they had decided to join the camp of his enemies. Self-centered as he was, Hitler also must have regarded War-saw's move as an unforgivable personal challenge.

He acted with speed indicative of his outrage and frustration. On April 3, the very day Beck arrived in London, Hitler issued secret military directives, Fall Weiss, ordering preparations for war against Poland. Two days later special instructions were sent to Moltke to the effect that German "proposals" to Poland were withdrawn and that he should avoid discussing them with the Polish officials.[1] The German media began an unusually violent campaign. Both London and Warsaw, they said, had decided to encircle Germany, and Poland had undertaken obligations toward Great Britain that were clearly contrary to the spirit and letter of the Polish-German nonaggression pact of 1934.

On April 6, just a few hours before the Anglo-Polish communiqué was published, the state secretary, Baron Ernst von Weizsaecker, summoned Lipski to deliver a stern protest. He charged that the Polish moves could not be reconciled with the declaration of January 1934. Poland, he said, evidently did not understand the magnanimity of the Führer's offer to "guarantee" the

Corridor. Instead of appreciating the Führer's "generosity," the Poles answered with a "strange saber-rattling." Now, the chancellor's proposals, "which could not have been made by any other German statesman," should be considered void.[2]

On April 11 Hitler issued another secret directive and ordered synchronized preparation by the German armed forces for war in 1939–1940. Unimpressed by Great Britain's recently assumed obligations, he pointed out that everything would be done to limit the war to Poland alone. Then on April 28 in his speech to the Reichstag, he denounced the German-British naval treaty of June 19, 1935, and the German-Polish declaration of January 26, 1934. He revealed his "proposals" with regard to Danzig and the Corridor, described them as extremely "modest," "unrenewable," and castigated the Poles for rejecting them. He emphasized that Poland had broken the 1934 declaration by agreeing to a mutual-assistance pact with Great Britain.[3]

Warsaw's answer took the form of a solemn speech, which Beck made in the crowded hall of the Sejm on May 5. Having reviewed the chronological development of Polish-German relations, he expressed his government's determination to preserve the peace Poland needed so badly. He affirmed his readiness for peaceful negotiations in order to find some solutions but left no doubt that Poland would not surrender to Berlin's demands. The conclusion of his speech, received with an ovation, was marked by pathos: "Peace is a valuable and desirable thing. Our generation which has shed its blood in several wars, surely deserves a period of peace. But peace, like almost everything in this world, has its price, high but definable. We in Poland do not recognize the conception of 'peace at any price.' There is only one thing in the life of men and states which is without price, and that is honor."[4]

Because of its patriotism and courage, Beck's speech was enthusiastically received all over Poland. Probably never before had Beck been as popular as in those early days of May 1939. No one knew better than he, however, that the speech reflected the failure of his policy. The stabilization of relations with Germany; peace with security; prestige and independence on the international scene—all these goals, which he had sought so fervently, now seemed to rest on shifting sand. He was still making covert efforts to inform Hitler of his desire to continue good relations with Germany and that he did not intend to enter into any anti-German combination, that the rapprochement with Great Britain was no more than a defensive extension of the Polish-French alliance, and, above all, that Poland would not enter into political collaboration with Russia.[5]

Beck's approaches and efforts were to no avail. Since April Hitler's mind had been set on revenge and war. Once he made a decision, nothing could make him change it. He was spurred on not only by political calculations but by emotions, and among his emotions, hatred was the strongest. Now, as if in self-hypnosis, he focused all his hatred on the Poles. In those last prewar months, Poland replaced Russia in his mind.

On May 23 the Führer summoned his military leaders and unfolded his plans for the immediate future. Germany needed Lebensraum and food, and the Poles had both and were no friends of Germany—they would always take the side of its enemies and try to do it harm. Therefore, Poland had to be destroyed: "There is, therefore, no question of sparing Poland, and we are left with the decision to attack Poland at the first suitable opportunity. We cannot expect a repetition of the Czech affair. There will be war."

Danzig was *not* the real issue in the German-Polish conflict: other greater issues were at stake.

> Danzig is not the subject of the dispute at all. It is a question of expanding our living space in the East, of securing food supplies, and of settling the Baltic problem. Food supplies can be expected only from thinly populated areas. Over and above the natural fertility, thorough-going German exploitation will enormously increase the surplus. There is no other possibility. Colonies are no solution. Germany should beware of gifts of colonial territory. They don't solve the food problem since they can easily be blockaded. The answer, therefore, lies in Poland.

He assured the audience that he would not allow the war against Poland to escalate into international conflagration. "Our task is to isolate Poland. The success of the isolation," he said, "would be decisive" and brought about by "skillful politics." He told them about his conviction that Great Britain would not come to Poland's support. Cautiously, he did not mention that Russia was Germany's ultimate Lebensraum. Instead, he observed enigmatically that "it was not impossible that Russia [would] show herself to be disinterested in the destruction of Poland."[6] By then, secret Soviet-Nazi contacts had already been established.

During June, July, and August 1939 the German media intensified their campaign against Poland—the "skillful politics" of which Hitler spoke. Using false names and fabricating incidents, Nazi propaganda tried to show that the German minority could suffer Polish atrocities no longer and that the status of Danzig was untenable.[7] In Danzig, anti-Polish demonstrations and incidents increased. Local Nazi leaders openly boasted that the unification of the Free City with the Vaterland could wait no longer. On July 23 Alfred Forster, gauleiter in Danzig, was proclaimed by the Free City's senate as "chief of state." In Berlin, all relations with the Polish ambassador, so amiable until recently, were suspended. Worldwide propaganda against Polish "provocations" and "irresponsibility," as opposed to Germany's moderation, blared louder each day.

Realizing that Nazi tactics used previously against Austria and Czechoslovakia were being repeated, many feared that a coup would be administered in Danzig, and Europe would be faced with another fait accompli. The situation became so tense that on July 1 the French government again notified Berlin that if Poland resisted any violent change in the status of the Free City, France would come to its aid. A similar declaration was made by Chamberlain in the House of Commons on July 10. But it was too late. At approximately the same time, Hitler—not without hesitation—finally decided to accept Soviet approaches for cooperation and to conclude the supersecret negotiations (until then ambiguous) concerning the division of spoils in eastern Europe between Germany and Russia.[8]

On August 22, just after the announcement of Ribbentrop's trip to Moscow for the conclusion of the Nazi-Soviet pact, the Führer ordered his generals to prepare an assault against Poland for August 26. War had to be waged at once because, as he said, "now Poland is in the position in which I wanted her." The war was to be merciless and the pretext for invasion conveniently fabricated. Although still doubting that the Western powers would move, Hitler decided to crush Poland even if France and Great Britain declared war on Germany:

> Destruction of Poland is in the foreground. The aim is elimination of living forces, not the arrival at a certain line. Even if war should break out in the West, the destruction of Poland shall be the primary objective. . . . I shall give a propagandist cause for starting the war—never mind whether it be plausible or not. The victor shall not be asked, later on, whether we told the truth or not. In starting and making a war, not the Right is what matters, but Victory.[9]

He was not afraid of the British and French war declarations because he did not believe that they would wage a real all-out offensive against Germany on account of Poland. "I had experience with those poor worms Daladier and Chamberlain in Munich," he said. "They will be too cowardly to attack. They won't go beyond a blockade. Against that we have our autarchy and the

Russian raw materials." Nothing could stop the dictator. He had only one reservation: "I am only afraid that at the last minute some *Schweinehund* will make a proposal for mediation."[10]

The attack against Poland was planned from all directions, including "independent" Slovakia. On August 23 the German envoy in Bratislava received instructions to secure an agreement that would permit the German high command to take over the Slovak army. Poland might "invade" Slovakia, and the chancellor wanted to protect the young country. As a reward for a satisfactory agreement, certain areas seized by the Poles in the fall of 1938 would be given to the Slovaks. On August 29 the Slovak envoy in Berlin, Matus Cernak, expressed his government's approval and appreciation. But he also asked for more real estate—for some areas acquired by Poland as far back as 1920. Two days later he learned that once Germany finished with the Poles, Bratislava's wish would be satisfied.[11] Warsaw's anti-Prague policy had borne poisonous fruit.

On August 22 Chamberlain sent Hitler a letter to reaffirm Great Britain's intention to enter the war if Germany attacked Poland. He appealed to the chancellor not to reject peaceful negotiations. The French ambassador delivered a personal letter from Daladier containing a similar warning. On August 24, 1939, President Franklin D. Roosevelt addressed both the chancellor and the president of Poland, asking them to negotiate their differences. On the same day, and again on August 31, Pope Pius XII appealed for peace.[12] All warnings and appeals were in vain. The dictator had made up his mind, and, in spite of evidence to the contrary, he could not bring himself to believe that either France or Britain would actually fight.

> The men I met in Munich are not the kind that start a new World War. Why should Britain fight? You don't get yourself killed for an ally. France is not directly interested in waging a war.
>
> Russia has no intention of pulling British chestnuts out of the fire, and will keep out of the war. Stalin has to fear a lost war as much as he would a victorious army. Russian aspirations at most extend to the Baltic States.
>
> All these factors argue for the likelihood of Britain and France refraining from entering the war, particularly since they are not under any compulsion.[13]

On August 23 the German-Soviet pact of nonaggression was signed, and everything seemed ready for an attack within three days. That same day Nazi party organizations in Poland were ordered to destroy documents without delay. All German citizens were advised to leave Poland. Demonstrations and provocations in Danzig and anti-Polish riots in Germany and in German-inhabited areas in Poland increased. So did frontier incidents.

Hitler expected that his agreement with Moscow would strengthen the partisans of appeasement and would discourage Great Britain and France from interfering in his war against Poland. Receiving the British ambassador on August 23, Hitler displayed more than his usual self-confidence and castigated London for encouraging the Poles to resist his demands. He kept repeating that Germany did not want to fight Britain, "whose friendship he had sought for twenty years." A few hours later, he handed Henderson his reply to Chamberlain's letter. Again reasserting his determination to use force against Poland, he noted that "all [his] life" he had "fought for Anglo-German friendship," and he certainly did not want a war with Britain now. Two days later, on August 25, he summoned Henderson again and told him that Poland's "irresponsibility," "provocations," and "persecutions" of the German population could be tolerated no longer and that Danzig and the Corridor must be returned to the Reich. Great Britain should withdraw from Polish-German affairs. In exchange, Germany would "accept" the British empire, cooperate with it, and come to an agreement on colonies and disarmament. He was an "artist," and not a "politician," and "once the Polish question was settled, he would end his life as an artist, not a warmonger." Danzig and the Corridor were Germany's last demands. Significantly, he added that "whatever happened, now the fate of Poland would be settled between Germany and Russia."[14] Evidently he had in mind the provisions of the secret protocol of the Nazi-Soviet pact signed just two days before.[15]

A few hours later, Hitler summoned the French ambassador, Robert Coulondre, conveyed his horror at the thought of a war between France and Germany, and asked that Daladier be informed about his feelings. The attack on Poland was scheduled for the next day, August 26.

The same evening, news of the Polish-British pact of mutual assistance and Mussolini's notification that in the event of war Italy would remain neutral reached Berlin. Immediately, Hitler "temporarily" canceled the orders to attack. He wanted to "eliminate" British intervention,[16] still believing that Britain as well as France could be kept from aiding Poland.[17] On August 27 he answered Daladier's letter, saying it was too late for negotiations with Poland, but he did not want to fight France. He indicated that the attack on Poland was imminent and called upon France to stay neutral.

The next day Hitler saw Henderson, who brought him a formal and urgent note, a new attempt on the part of Whitehall to save peace. The note contained an assurance of Britain's desire to reach a general understanding with Germany, providing that Polish-German "differences" could be "peacefully composed." It also contained a solemn declaration that in case of war, Great Britain would come to Poland's aid. His Majesty's government appealed for immediate and direct German-Polish negotiations. Warsaw, the note continued, had already formally notified London of its readiness. The negotiations should not infringe upon Poland's vital interests, and the settlement agreed upon should be internationally guaranteed.

Hitler answered with a harangue against the Poles, bitterly complaining that Britain's and France's support had made the Poles reject his "generous offer" so "contemptuously." These "offers" would not be repeated. Now, not only Danzig but also "the whole of the Corridor" and the Polish Silesia would have to be returned to Germany. He again spoke of his goodwill and friendship toward Great Britain and hinted at his desire to conclude "an alliance" with it. He promised an answer to the note on the following day. [18]

On the evening of August 29, Hitler handed Henderson his official answer. [19] The chancellor "kept saying that he wanted British friendship more than anything in the world." In deference to London's wish, he would agree to direct negotiations with Poland—"skeptical" as he was of their success—provided Danzig and the Corridor were to be united with Germany. Because "no longer days" but "perhaps only hours" remained to settle Germany's claims peacefully, he demanded the presence of a Polish plenipotentiary endowed with "full powers" to sign an agreement in Berlin the next day, August 30. This would be the last chance. Obviously in compliance with the secret protocol of the Nazi-Soviet nonaggression pact signed the week before, the note contained a provision that "in the event of territorial rearrangement in Poland," the Soviet Union could not be ignored.

Henderson had no doubt that if Hitler's demand was not met, Germany would attack Poland any moment and Great Britain would be forced into war. He immediately saw the Polish ambassador and "implored" him to press Warsaw for compliance, fully aware what such compliance would mean to the Poles, but there was no other way to avoid war. He so informed Halifax. [20]

Although Hitler denied that his demand for a special plenipotentiary was an ultimatum, for all practical purposes this was the case. The procedure was reminiscent of the technique used on Chancellor Schuschnigg of Austria in March 1938. Beck refused to go. Kennard agreed with him, and Halifax considered the demand "unreasonable." Subsequently, in the late hours of

August 30, Henderson communicated his government's position to Ribben-trop. In order to start Polish-German negotiations rolling, the German government should first communicate specific demands to the Polish ambas-sador. Only then could Warsaw decide whether to agree to negotiations and propose their procedure. The British government, Henderson stated, could not advise Warsaw otherwise. Ribbentrop answered that it was too late for negotiations, anyway, since the Polish plenipotentiary did not show up.

Then the Reichsminister withdrew a document that he read aloud in Ger-man "at top speed." The document contained a list of sixteen demands, allegedly prepared for the Polish plenipotentiary. When Henderson asked for the document, Ribbentrop refused, repeating that it was too late. When Hen-derson observed that the text should be given to the Polish ambassador, Ribbentrop disagreed, adding that further decisions were in the hands of the Führer.

The main points of the document were annexation of Danzig; a plebiscite in the Corridor to be held within a year, with only those who were born there before January 1, 1918, allowed to vote; participation in the plebiscite of all Germans who emigrated from Pomerania in the last twenty years; Gdynia to remain Polish; both Danzig and Gdynia to be "purely commercial and demil-itarized"; establishment of an international commission to police the Corridor prior to the plebiscite; withdrawal of all Polish civil administration, army, and police from the contested areas; an extraterritorial road through the Cor-ridor for the country that "lost" the plebiscite; and an agreement on national minorities.[21]

The next afternoon Göring saw Henderson and assured him of Germany's friendship, as well as its desire to establish close collaboration with Great Britain. He suggested starting negotiations at once. The British diplomat got the impression that the assurances "constituted an eleventh-hour effort to neutralize Britain in the coming conflict."

The same day Johan Birger E. Dahlerus, a Swedish industrialist and friend of Göring, was suddenly brought to the Polish embassy in Berlin by the counselor of the British embassy and introduced to Lipski as a "neutral intermediary in the confidence of the [British] Cabinet, of the [British] Em-bassy and of the German Government." He read the sixteen points to Lipski and asked him to communicate them to Warsaw and to "press" for Beck or somebody else to come immediately to Berlin for negotiations. Lipski, amazed as he was, told him that the demands, if accepted, would mean a "breach of Polish sovereignty" and their acceptance was "out of the question."[22]

Beck, when informed, agreed with Lipski's reaction. But, still anxious not to miss any opportunity for genuine negotiations, he cabled instructions to seek an interview with Ribbentrop immediately. In a carefully worded message, Lipski was to tell the Reichsminister that the Polish government had just been informed by the British of a "possibility" of starting direct Polish-German negotiations. The Polish government was "favorably considering" the British "suggestions" and would reply within a few hours.[23]

Lipski sought the interview for 1:00 p.m., but he was not received until 6:30 p.m. The meeting was one of the shortest in diplomatic history. Ribbentrop asked whether his visitor had "special plenipotentiary powers to undertake negotiations." On Lipski's negative answer, the conversation ended. Three hours later, Berlin radio broadcast the text of the sixteen "proposals," informing the German people that Poland had rejected them. In fact, the "proposals" were never formally communicated to the Polish government, but Hitler had his "propagandist cause." The first bombs fell on Polish cities seven hours later.

Hitler's diplomatic maneuvers to isolate Poland proved ineffective, because both Great Britain and France declared war on Germany. He succeeded, however, in one respect. Hoping that peace could be preserved and eager to avoid any provocation of the dictator, Paris and London urged the Poles to refrain from ordering full mobilization until the last moment. When a general mobilization was finally ordered on August 29, the British and French ambassadors immediately intervened against it. The orders were revoked for one full day, causing considerable complications in both military and civilian administrations. When, on September 1, the German panzer divisions crossed the Polish frontier, out of forty Polish divisions, ten were not mobilized.[24]

NOTES

1. *TMWC*, 34:380–81; also *DGFP*, series D, 6:195.
2. Lipski, *Diplomat in Berlin*, 528.
3. *DGFP*, series D, 6:223–28; *BBB*, 28–36, respectively.
4. *PWB*, 87–88.
5. See Moltke's report of May 23, 1939, *DGFP*, series D, 6:566–68.
6. Ibid., 549. For the protocol of the conference, see *TMWC*, 37:546–56.
7. See *LJF*, 174–44, 181–84, 213–16, 268–70, 285, 291, 303, 309, 310, 323, 331, 338–39, 344, 357–59, 362. German secret archives (Heinrich Himmler's archives included), seized at

the end of the war by the Allies, revealed the organization of the Nazi provocations, names of the agents used for that purpose, and even the evaluation of the propagandistic effectiveness of particular acts. For documentation, see Edmund Osmanczyk, *Dowody Prowokacji. Nieznane Archiwum Himmlera* (*The Evidence of Provocation: The Unknown Archives of Himmler*) (Warszawa: Czytelnik, 1951), 1–48.

8. "War and Peace in Soviet Diplomacy, 1939," infra, 351–353.

9. *TMWC*, 26:338–44.

10. From the report of one of the participating generals. For the full text of Hitler's speech, see *DBFP*, 3rd series, 7:258–60.

11. *DGFP*, series D, 7:229–30, 458–59, 474.

12. For the texts, see *BBB*, 125–27; *LJF*, 321–22; *PWB*, 98–100; *BBB*, 244–47, respectively.

13. Franz Halder, *The Halder Diaries* (Washington, DC: Infantry Journal Press, 1950), August 14, 1939–September 10, 1939, 1:10–11.

14. For Henderson's reports, see *DBFP*, 3rd series, 7:161–63, 177–79, 227–31, 236, respectively.

15. Infra, 357–58.

16. It was within the framework of this attempt that the services of the Swedish industrialist, Dahlerus, had been used by Göring and Hitler. For Dahlerus's story, see Johan Birger E. Dahlerus, *Der Letzte Versuch, London-Berlin Sommer 1939* (Munich: Nymphenburger Verlagshandlung, 1948).

17. Göring's testimony, *TMWC*, 3:247.

18. Henderson, reports, see *DBFP*, 3rd series, 7:330–32, 351–54.

19. For the full text of the German note, ibid., 388–90; for Henderson's report on the interview, ibid., 376–77.

20. Henderson, *The Failure of a Mission*, 281.

21. For Henderson's reports, see ibid., 432–33, 459–62.

22. Ibid., 445–46. For Dahlerus's account, see Dahlerus, *Der Letzte Versuch*, 109–10.

23. *PWB*, 119.

24. Butler, *Grand Strategy*, 58; also Arnold Toynbee and Veronica Toynbee, eds. *Survey of International Affairs, 1939–1946: The Eve of War* (London: Oxford University Press, 1948), 150ff.

Chapter Seventeen

Nazi-Polish Relations and the Problem of Russia

On December 10, 1938, the Polish ambassador to Moscow, Grzybowski, visited Szembek in Warsaw, and the two reviewed the Polish-Soviet relations.

Grzybowski did not seem perturbed. As he saw it, Russia was essentially weak, and a German-Soviet rapprochement was improbable. Poland should continue its "independent" policy, refrain from showing hostility toward Russia, avoid any association with German and Japanese "pressure" on Moscow, and keep Germany from "penetrating" the Soviet Union. Litvinov, the ambassador thought, *did* want an accommodation with Poland, hoping to find in it a replacement for the weakening France.

Szembek, who had all the information and data, did not share Grzybowski's optimism:

> It is excessively difficult for us [he said] to maintain a balance between Russia and Germany. Our relations with the latter are entirely founded on the theory of the highest personalities in the Third Reich that in the future conflict between Germany and Russia, Poland will become a natural ally of Germany. In these circumstances, the policy of good neighborhood, which originated in the agreement of 1934, could easily prove to be a pure and simple fiction. [1]

What Szembek was saying in December 1938 actually meant that the seemingly solid structure of the policy of balance, erected in January 1934, had no foundation. Hitler's policy toward Poland seems to have been from the outset a function of his plans aimed at the destruction of Russia.

From the early days of his public activities, Hitler had been more than a mere enemy of the Marxist philosophy. He believed that the German master race was entitled to the "soil and territory" inhabited by "inferior" races. He did not see Lebensraum for Germany in the restoration of the prewar frontiers, nor did he look for it in the west or south of Europe. Instead, he wanted to "terminate the endless German drive to the south and west of Europe, and direct [Germany's] gaze toward the lands in the east." The natural Lebensraum for the German master race was in Russia. "If we talk about new soil and territory in Europe today, we can think primarily only of Russia and its vassal border states," he wrote.[2] He did not nurture hostility toward Great Britain or Italy, for he hoped that in cooperating with them, Germany would expand. He considered the destruction of France as a world power a historical necessity, because France was Germany's traditional enemy and also because a powerful France represented a hindrance to Germany's eastward expansion. He wanted to defeat and "isolate" France in order to acquire Lebensraum in Russia.[3]

Once in power, he decided to use Poland in his grandiose scheme, and Pilsudski's approach in 1933 suited him well. The Weimar Republic's Rapallo policy of cooperation with Russia was expected to return to Germany territories lost to Poland after World War I. Hitler rebuked that policy because his territorial ambitions were far greater than the acquisition of relatively small, overpopulated Polish areas. The immensity of Russia was his goal. However, Poland separated Germany from Russia, and according to Hitler's scheme, Poland was a corridor leading to Russia—a corridor that had to be opened one way or another. Until the spring of 1939, he had no plans to do it by force. On the contrary, he expected the Poles to open that corridor willingly by acceding to his anti-Russian plans. In exchange—generously, as he undoubtedly thought—he contemplated recognizing the Soviet Ukraine, one of those Russian "vassal border states," as Poland's sphere of interest.[4]

One day before the declaration of nonaggression was signed—January 25, 1934—Hitler gave Lipski what amounted to his interpretation of the German-Polish rapprochement: The Soviet Union and international Communism represented a growing danger to all of Europe. Germany and Poland were equally threatened, and since the latter was the "last barricade of the [European] civilization in the East," a German-Polish understanding would profit both, strengthening the defenses against the common enemy.[5]

Several months later—on August 27, 1934—Hitler again lectured Lipski, urging that all countries of Europe should unite against Russia, a "colossus of unlimited resources" which was using international Communism as its political weapon. His decision to change Germany's policy toward Poland was a result of the growing "danger coming from the East." Poland, he said, was a "shield against the East," so important to Germany that any "unpleasant divergences" between the two countries should "retreat to the back of the stage." He warned the Poles against the eastern Locarno pacts, launched at that time by Barthou and Litvinov, and asked for German-Polish cooperation in that matter. The proposed pacts, he said, would evidently strengthen Russia—and that was contrary to the interests of both Germany and Poland. Neither of them should provide a "rear cover" or a "shield" for the Soviet Union.[6]

On January 22, 1935, Hitler had a long talk with the Polish ambassador and expressed his belief that the theory of "Polish-German hereditary enmity" had become "unsound." Russia "had made great progress" militarily, and probably one day Germany and Poland would be compelled to fight together "against invasion from the east."[7] He explained how and why he disagreed with the Weimar Republic's politicians, who had wanted to collaborate with Russia against Poland. His words had a particular meaning—Molotov was then publicly calling for improved German-Soviet relations.[8]

Soon after, Hitler entrusted Göring with a special mission—to cultivate German-Polish relations and to help eliminate anything that might endanger them. Göring was to report directly to the Führer. The appointment, made known to Lipski, was unusual. Because Göring was not connected with the Auswärtiges Amt, from then on the Polish ambassador could use two channels in discharging his duties: one strictly diplomatic and the other more intimate, through the intermediary of Göring. The appointment was also significant. Hitler did not always reveal his inner thoughts or his long-range plans to his leading diplomats or to the military leaders. Göring, however, was his closest collaborator and confidant. Göring's views and words had behind them the authority of the Führer himself.

At the end of January 1935 Göring met the highest-ranking political and military leaders on a hunting trip in Poland. As he told Lipski on the eve of his departure from Berlin, the Führer himself briefed him as to his conversations in Warsaw. Following the instructions, Göring told his hosts how General von Schleicher, transferring the office of the chancellor to Hitler in January 1933, advised him to seek an "understanding" with France and Russia and then "with the latter's help to proceed to the elimination of Poland." The Führer's reaction meant a complete reversal of the old policy of Rapallo.

"Und ich werde das Gegenteil machen" (And I will do the opposite), he answered.

Discussing international affairs, Göring became very outspoken, "almost suggesting an anti-Russian alliance and a joint [Polish-German] attack on Russia." He indicated that Poland might establish its "sphere of influence" in the Ukraine, while Germany would do the same in "northwestern Russia." He was so blunt that Lipski recommended through Moltke "some reserve" in Göring's scheduled conversation with Pilsudski. Indeed, when the Nazi leader hinted at a Polish-German attack on Russia and enumerated its advantages to Poland, Pilsudski cut off the conversation, saying: "Nous ne pouvons accepter d'être mis dans une situation qui nous obligerait à coucher avec notre fusil" (We cannot accept a situation that would force us to sleep with our guns).[9]

Three weeks later, on February 14, Neurath, demonstrating his distrust of Russia, assured Lipski that in the event of a Soviet attack on Poland, the Poles could count on Germany.[10] On March 23 he told Lipski that Germany had to rebuild its military forces in view of the growing Russian-Communist danger. Russia "sooner or later" would try to seize first the Baltic states and then, following the old path of tsarist imperialism, the Balkans. Germany and Poland should cooperate because they were directly threatened, he argued. The same ideas, expressed in still stronger terms, had been conveyed to Lipski by Hitler on April 13, and on April 25 Göring returned to the same theme.[11]

In May 1935, just a few weeks after Pilsudski's death, Hitler invited Lipski for a long, important conversation. As the ambassador reported, there were no witnesses; even Neurath was absent. The conversation was informal and the "usual protocol was dispensed with."

The chancellor spoke about his sorrow over Pilsudski's death and his deep concern. Would Poland follow the late marshal's policy toward Germany? Then he gave his ideas about the nature and the future of German-Polish relations.

It was he, Hitler, who had jettisoned the policy of enmity toward Poland. The previous German policy of cooperating with Russia and building its military strength amounted to treason. If not for anything else, General Schleicher and others deserved death just for having done that. Russia was an enemy and a threat not only to Poland but to Germany as well; knowing this, he decided to reverse the Rapallo policy. "The rapprochement with Poland gives much more to the Reich than dangerous relations with Russia," he said emphatically. The Corridor was "of no importance," and one day, perhaps in some fifteen years, some "special railroad and a highway through Pomerania for transport purposes" could be built to solve the problem. *Russia* was important because Germany needed more "room for its population," and it could be found only in Russia.

Pilsudski, he continued, was one of those statesmen who "understood the Russian reality." The chancellor was "obviously pleased" when Lipski pointed out that the Western statesmen were "commonly acquainted with Russia only through literature." He also heard with "visible satisfaction" Lipski's "firm" declaration that "no change [would] occur in . . . [Polish] policy toward Germany."[12]

On December 18, 1935, Hitler told Lipski that National-Socialist Germany was in favor of European solidarity, provided, however, that this solidarity would end on the Polish-Soviet frontier. He condemned France for its recently concluded alliance with Russia. The latter should be kept away from Europe. Great Britain and the Franco-Polish *Rückversicherungsvertrag* represented sufficient guarantees for France's security. By bringing Russia into European politics, France acted against the interests of Europe. The Franco-Soviet alliance endangered Poland, argued Neurath. For in the event of Soviet aggression against Poland, Germany would have to move against Russia. But then, according to the Franco-Soviet alliance, France would have to attack Germany. The French betrayed Polish interests.[13]

On August 14, 1936, Ribbentrop, then the German ambassador in London, spoke to Szembek about the "necessity" for a Polish-German collaboration, because of the "serious danger arising from the fact that the Soviets had not renounced the conception of world revolution." He added that "the only way to counteract this danger and prevent catastrophe was to crush, at its inception, even the smallest sign of communism." He reiterated those views in his conversation with the Polish ambassador in London, Edward Raczyński, on November 5, 1936.[14] The yearly congress of the Nazi party, held on September 9–14, 1936, was marked by extraordinarily violent anti-Communist and anti-Russian outbursts. Goebbels called for an anti-Communist crusade, and Hitler spoke about the Soviet Union in such terms as to provoke rumors that he intended to break diplomatic relations with Moscow.

On November 18, 1936, Moltke, acting under instructions from Berlin, told Beck that the German-Polish agreement "was one of the foundations of German foreign policy," mainly because "of the increasing bolshevisation of Europe and the need for a common defence." A week later, he made a similar statement to Marshal Śmigly-Rydz. The two Polish leaders agreed as to the "Bolshevist danger," although they cautiously pointed out that Poland, because of its geographical position, had to exercise great "restraint." Both assured the ambassador, however, that they would never cooperate politically with Russia. Beck ambiguously added that in the "near future" Poland would take some steps against the "bolshevisation of Europe." [15]

Three months later—on February 16, 1937—Göring, on another hunting visit in Poland, made a new effort to win the sympathy of Śmigly-Rydz for a common policy. He assured the latter that the Rapallo policy of German-Soviet cooperation would not be repeated. Not only Communist Russia, but any Russia, represented a danger to both Germany and Poland. Consequently, they should cooperate not only politically but also militarily. Śmigly-Rydz assured his guest that regardless of circumstances, Poland would never be on Russia's side. Soon after, in August, Ribbentrop tried to use Japanese influence in winning Poland's adherence to the Anti-Comintern Pact. [16]

On November 4 Göring tried to impress upon Szembek that Poland could count on Germany in any "serious difficulties" with Russia, that the two countries should cooperate. Germany needed a strong Poland. A strong Poland could not be satisfied with the Baltic Sea alone. Poland needed a "window" to the Black Sea, he said. Two weeks later, on November 18, he told Lipski that the Nazi leadership would always have a "negative" attitude toward Russia—any Russia, whether Soviet or "nationalist." [17]

In 1938—the year of Germany's international successes—Nazi approaches developed into almost definite proposals. Later, pressure began to be exerted.

On January 14 Hitler spoke to Beck at length about his unchangeable hostility to Communism. He repeated that Russia—any Russia—represented a danger to all of Europe and that the struggle against Communism was the unalterable aim of his policy. Six weeks later, on February 23, Göring, on still another hunting trip to Poland, went one step further and in a conversation with Śmigly-Rydz broached the idea of a war with Russia. He stressed that "while politically the Soviets were a permanent and serious danger," militarily they were still weak, and in the event of war, it would not be difficult to defeat them. Three weeks later, on March 16, just after the Austrian Anschluss, discussing the international situation with Lipski, Göring "came out with an open offer for Polish-German military collaboration against Russia." Two weeks later, Ribbentrop "suggested" to Lipski that Poland accede to the Anti-Comintern Pact. [18]

During the Czechoslovak crisis, the problem of Russia again emerged as a factor in German-Polish relations. On August 10, 1938, Göring informed Lipski that German plans concerning Russia would become "actual" after the "solution" of the Czechoslovak problem. As before, he mentioned approvingly Poland's "direct interests" in the Ukraine. Two weeks later he again mentioned Poland's "legitimate aspirations" in the "fertile Ukraine." On September 20 Hitler told Lipski that "Poland [was] an outstanding factor safeguarding Europe against Russia." One week later, when Germany's attack on Czechoslovakia seemed imminent, Ribbentrop again suggested in a "discreet manner" that Poland join the Anti-Comintern Pact. On October 1, as Warsaw was sending an ultimatum to Prague, he assured Lipski that if the Soviet Union attacked Poland, Germany would take a "more than friendly attitude toward Poland." As Lipski reported, Ribbentrop clearly hinted that the German government would come to Poland's assistance.[19] Moltke extended similar assurances to Beck.[20]

On October 24—the day Ribbentrop raised the demands for Danzig and extraterritorial roads through the Corridor—the proposal for a German-Polish "joint policy toward Russia on the basis of the Anti-Comintern Pact" was added.

In the next few months, the pressure intensified for joint German-Polish policies directed against the Soviet Union. In return for its concessions in the Corridor and Danzig, Poland would gain much more in the east—this was the idea conveyed by the Nazi leaders. On January 5, 1939, Hitler strongly reaffirmed to Beck his hostility toward Russia, "tsarist or Bolshevik," and again pointed to the "community of interest between Germany and Poland."[21]

The next day Ribbentrop elaborated on the subject of Russia. According to his memo, he "condemned" Beck's passivity toward Moscow and "once more appealed" for a Polish-German collaboration against the Soviet Union as well as for a joint policy toward the "Greater Ukraine." Poland might obtain "a special prerogative" there, he said, vowing that Poland could count on Germany's support "in every way." Naturally, he explained, if Poland acceded to the plan, Berlin would expect a "more and more pronounced anti-Russian attitude," and he concluded by asking again if Poland intended to join the Anti-Comintern Pact.

Three weeks later, on the fifth anniversary of the German-Polish nonaggression declaration, Ribbentrop visited Warsaw, where once more he strongly suggested a Polish-German collaboration against the Soviet Union, again drawing his hosts' attention to the possibilities in the Ukraine. He tried hard to convince Beck that Poland should agree to the Anti-Comintern Pact because, as he argued, "if Poland sat in the same boat as we, she could only gain added security." Again he hinted at the possibilities of territorial compensations for Poland in the Soviet Union. "You are very obstinate in maritime questions," he told Beck. "The Black Sea is also a sea."[22] His words carried more weight than Beck probably realized, for Ribbentrop had just suspended German-Soviet negotiations and was even contemplating a rupture of diplomatic relations with Moscow.[23]

On March 21, 1939, Hitler offered the Poles their last opportunity to play a part in his grandiose plan. In a decisive conversation with Lipski,[24] Ribbentrop assured him that the chancellor "still" wanted good relations between Poland and Germany. However, Polish-German relations had to be considered "on a higher plane." Germany and Poland were "dependent on each other." The Poles must realize, he warned, that they could not take a "middle course." They had to cooperate with "Germany and the Führer." Otherwise, "one day there would arise a Marxist Polish government, which would then be absorbed by Bolshevist Russia." From now on, he added, if any Polish-German understanding were to be reached, it would have to have an "explicit" anti-Soviet character. This time, Ribbentrop indicated, the Führer would not tolerate evasiveness or indecision. In order to avoid any "misunderstanding of the Reich's real aims," the chancellor wanted to have "a thorough conversation" with Beck. Evidently, Hitler still hoped that the Poles would cooperate with him against the Soviet Union.

None of the Nazi approaches, suggestions, or offers obtained Warsaw's approval. They could not, because essentially Beck sought peace and not war. Neither he nor any other member of the Polish government entertained aggressive plans against Russia or envisaged territorial aggrandizement at its expense. All realized that adherence to Hitler's plans would put Poland at Germany's mercy for generations to come. Instead, Beck pursued his "policy of equilibrium." He would not enter into any political cooperation with the Soviet Union because he considered it dangerous. But he would not engage Poland in a war against the powerful neighbor, remembering Pilsudski's words to the French ambassador that to do so "serait littéralement travailler pour le roi de Prusse" (would literally work for the King of Prussia).[25]

The conclusion of the preliminary Anglo-Polish alliance in April 1939 finally convinced Hitler that the Poles would not join forces with him. On the contrary, they appeared to be joining the camp of his enemies.

By then his confidence in his own infallibility and providential role had no limits. Whatever action he had undertaken, even against the advice of his generals and diplomats, had brought him victory. By then he considered any questioning of his judgment to be irresponsible. Any opposition to his will meant treason. The Polish attitude must have seemed to him self-contradictory and irresponsible, a betrayal of his goodwill and generosity.

Hitler must have regarded it as self-contradictory because he knew how hostile the Polish leaders were toward Communism, how deeply they distrusted Russia, how much they agreed with him that Russia should be kept away from European politics. He certainly remembered Warsaw's reaction to the Eastern Pact; to the Franco-Soviet and Czechoslovak-Soviet alliances; to Russia's entry into the League of Nations; to Beneš's and Titulescu's pro-Russian policies; and to all initiatives concerning collective security. On numerous occasions, and as late as September and December 1938, Polish leaders were assuring him that they would oppose the spread of Communist Soviet influences in Europe, that they considered Poland a "barricade" against both Communism and Russia, and that they wanted to keep Communist Russia away from European affairs.[26] And yet by deciding to perpetuate their "policy of balance," they actually cast Poland in the role of a barrier *protecting* Russia against his Reich's "historic mission."

Hitler must have regarded the Poles as irresponsible, because every diplomat in the Russian department of the Auswärtiges Amt knew that Moscow had always—before or after Hitler's accession to power—wanted to maintain the Rapallo course. Furthermore, by 1939 Hitler had enough power to break Poland's resistance, anyway, and he was absolutely convinced that neither France nor Great Britain—even if they *did* declare war on Germany—would actually support Poland militarily.

The Führer undoubtedly thought that the Poles had betrayed his goodwill and generosity. After all, his friendly attitude in no small measure had made Poland's successes possible—the normalization of relations with Lithuania, territorial gains in Czechoslovakia, and an international position far beyond Poland's real strength. It was he who offered the history-making Poles opportunities in the Soviet Union. And it was he who reduced Germany's claims on Poland to a degree no German government or German statesman had ever dared to do.

What was more important, however, was that Poland's reticence hampered the strategy he had so carefully planned and so successfully carried out since 1933. Having transformed Germany in accordance with his vision, having secured for Germany a position worthy of its greatness, having united with the Reich the most important German communities in Europe, Hitler was now, at last, ready to enter into the last crucial stages of his policy of conquest: breaking France as a world power and converting Russia into Germany's Lebensraum. To attack France, he needed Poland's neutrality. To attack Russia, he needed Poland's cooperation.

As the Führer explained to his military commanders on August 22, 1939, he had reached the conclusion that "a conflict with Poland" had become unavoidable only in the spring of 1939. Until then he had wanted "to establish an acceptable relationship with Poland in order to fight, first against the West . . . and only afterward against the East." Now he could no longer follow that course, because he had lost confidence in the Poles and had to assume that once Germany became involved in the West, Poland would strike it in the back. He therefore had to eliminate Poland first. This could be done, he concluded, because Poland was weak, the Poles were unreliable, and neither France nor Great Britain really contemplated coming to Poland's rescue. Thus, war against Poland would be short and victory assured.[27]

There is no evidence that Hitler had planned a military attack on Poland before the spring of 1939.[28] His decision seems to have been spontaneous, made in anger and frustration. Once made, it would soon push him to moves equally unplanned and unleash an unforeseen chain reaction: a suicidal cooperation with Russia; a declaration of war by Great Britain and France; an attack on Russia under most unfavorable circumstances; a war on two fronts; expansion far beyond Germany's capacities; and, finally, a confrontation with America's industrial and military might. Eventually, it would lead to the destruction of his Reich and to his own self-inflicted death in its ruins.

Some fifty million people, the dreams and hopes of an entire generation, hundreds of cities, and innumerable monuments to man's genius and travail would perish with him.

NOTES

1. Szembek, *Diariusz*, 4:379–80.

2. Hitler, *Mein Kampf*, 946–51, 182, respectively.

3. Ibid., 183–84, 908, 964–65, 974–79.

4. There is no material on this subject in *The German White Book*. The fact that the book was published in 1940, at the time of the Nazi-Soviet cooperation, would make the inclusion of such material quite undiplomatic. The evidence can be found in Polish sources and *Documents on German Foreign Policy, 1919–1945*, series D.

5. For Lipski's report dated January 25, 1934, see Lipski, *Diplomat in Berlin*, 124–25.

6. *DGFP*, series C, 3:360–61. For Lipski's report, see Lipski, *Diplomat in Berlin*, 153–57.

7. For Lipski's report dated January 24, 1935, see Lipski, *Diplomat in Berlin*, 163–65.

8. David Dallin, *Russia and Post-War Europe* (New Haven, CT: Yale University Press, 1943), 51.

9. Lipski, *Diplomat in Berlin*, 188–92; Szembek, *Journal*, 32–39; Beck, *Dernier rapport*, 34.

10. *AANP-Zespoly MSZ*, 3246, 256–61.

11. For Lipski's reports, see Lipski, *Diplomat in Berlin*, 179–82, 182–92.

12. For Lipski's report, ibid., 202–06.

13. Lipski, *Diplomat in Berlin*, 241–48; also *AANP-Zespoly MSZ*, 3251, 1–4, respectively.

14. *PWB*, 34; *AANP-Zespoly MSZ*, 4622, 81–82, respectively.

15. *AANA*, 1823H/1045/416920-22; 416939-40.

16. Szembek, *Diariusz*, 3:30; *DGFP*, series D, 1:750–52, respectively.

17. Szembek, *Journal*, 246–47; Lipski, *Diplomat in Berlin*, 306–7, respectively.

18. Lipski, *Diplomat in Berlin*, 333–38, 354–60; also Szembek, *Journal*, 276–77.

19. For Lipski's report, Lipski, *Diplomat in Berlin*, 377–78, 382–87, 408–12, 427, 435–38. For Ribbentrop's memo, *DGFP*, series D, 5:79–80.

20. For Moltke's report, *AANA*/2369/495071-72.

21. *DGFP*, series D, 5:153. No report in Lipski, *Diplomat in Berlin*.

22. *DGFP*, series D, 5:153, 160, 167–68, respectively; also Beck, *Dernier rapport*, 186–87.

23. *DGFP*, series D, 4:622–25.

24. *PWB*, 61–64; compare with *GWB*, 210–12 and *DGFP*, series D, 6:70–72.

25. Laroche, *La Pologne de Pilsudski*, 194.

26. See Ambassador Moltke's dispatch concerning his conversation with Beck on September 27, 1938, *AANA*, 1339/747/353357-58; also Lipski-Ribbentrop conversation on December 15, 1938, Lipski, *Diplomat in Berlin*, 477–81.

27. For Hitler's address, see *TMWC*, 26:338–44; for English translation, *DGFP*, series D, 7:200–4.

28. According to Marshal Walter von Brauchitsch's testimony at Nuremberg, no military plans to attack Poland had been prepared before May 23, 1939: *TMWC*, 2:571.

Chapter Eighteen

Hitler-Beck Diplomacy

A Make-Believe World

Because of the undemocratic nature of the German and Polish governments, there was no effective public control and scrutiny, and Nazi-Polish relations were being shaped by a small number of individuals secure in both their "mandate" and their political durability.

On the German side, the decision maker was Hitler and Hitler alone. The party and state officials obeyed him absolutely, even when, as in the case of the military or the Auswärtiges Amt, they might not always be aware of the Führer's stratagems. "When a decision has to be taken, none of us counts more than the stones on which we are standing. It is the Führer alone who decides,"[1] Göring once told the British ambassador.

On the Polish side, the decision maker was primarily Beck. He enjoyed the confidence of the highest government leaders. Even when some of them did nurture apprehensions as to his policies, none stood up against him. This, naturally, strengthened his position and made his chief collaborators in the ministry cater to his views and judgments.

In his encounters with the Poles, Hitler usually spoke in friendly generalities, emphasizing his goodwill, the importance of Poland in his long-range policy, mutual benefits to result from a Polish-German cooperation, and the danger of Russia and Moscow-controlled Communism. Göring, whatever the subject on the agenda, would return as if by habit time and again to the historical imperative of Polish-German cooperation against Russia. The Auswärtiges Amt watched over matters so that the wording of the official and public documents or the daily implementation of the détente would be done in such a way as to make the Polish ambassador and Beck aware that Germany's claims on Poland (and particularly the Danzig problem) were still waiting for some final "solution."

Sometimes in conversations with Lipski, Beck, or Szembek, the chancellor would go too far in assuring the Poles that Germany had no major claims on Poland, or that Danzig's future would not disturb German-Polish relations. This, of course, would produce friction between the Auswärtiges Amt and Lipski. But until the spring of 1939 it never produced a crisis. German diplomats had to become used to the fact that the Führer did not care much for diplomatic precision, nor did he have any great attachment to declarations or commitments. As for Lipski, he always had Göring, who usually was able to smooth out the difficulties. In any event, Hitler, Göring, and the Auswärtiges Amt were always anxious to create the public impression that strong ties of confidence bound Warsaw and Berlin together. This suited the Führer and was apparently—or had to be—good enough for Beck and Lipski as well.

Hitler calculated that his efforts to build up his Thousand-Year Reich eventually would lead Germany into war with both France and Russia. There is no evidence, however, that he considered a war with Poland a necessity, or that he planned for such a war until the spring of 1939. On the contrary, he sought an accommodation with the Poles, expecting that in time it would develop into a firm understanding and cooperation.

The appearance of German-Polish cooperation served Hitler well. It strengthened his position in Europe while he was consolidating Germany's military power. It showed that the Führer, suspected and feared in so many quarters, could be reasonable and generous with those who trusted him and wished him no harm. It strengthened his hand with France. It helped him to shatter the Versailles system of the territorial status quo. It made the collective-security proposals—a potential brake on his expansion—inoperative.

Hitler did not forget Germany's claims on Poland and expected that one day the final *Gesamtlösung* would have to take place. He seemed optimistic, though, for he made plans which apparently made him believe that it would be attained peacefully, if not amicably. First, he decided to postpone the settlement until it came time to implement the final stages of his plans. Second, he decided to reduce Germany's demands to such a minimum that, he believed, the Poles would not dare reject them. He also decided to offer Poland momentous opportunities in Russia.

Postponing the confrontation gave him great advantages. At the end of 1939 Germany was at the peak of its power and successes, while Poland seemed isolated, its foreign policy discredited, and its domestic situation less than stable.

As to Germany's claims on Poland, he reduced them, more than any other German leader ever had. He renounced the Corridor. He forsook Silesia. He left more than eight hundred thousand Germans to what most Germans considered inferior Polish rule. He was ready to declare publicly and unequivocally—something he had never done before—that *all* controversial issues between Poland and Germany had been resolved. He decided to ask only that Danzig be incorporated into Germany and that extraterritorial rail and motor roads be permitted through the Corridor in order to connect Germany proper with East Prussia.

The incorporation of Danzig must have seemed to Hitler more than reasonable and essentially harmless to Polish interests: Danzig did not belong to Poland, and its status as a Free City was only to secure Poland's economic interests. He offered to "guarantee" those interests. True, Danzig was under the League of Nations' protection. But the Poles themselves were critical of this arrangement, and they did not conceal their scorn of the League. Danzig's population was German; the Polish minority was negligible. The Nazi party dominated Danzig's policies—the Polish government never raised any objections on that score. Above all, Danzig's population unmistakably wanted to return to Germany. No German, the Führer must have believed, would ever understand, much less become reconciled to, a permanent renunciation of Danzig.

As for the Corridor, the demands must have seemed to Hitler not only reasonable but generous. The record shows that responsible government leaders in France, Great Britain, and even the United States had long considered the status of the Corridor untenable over the long run. The Auswärtiges Amt knew it, and on at least one occasion the chancellor himself was personally informed of it by Halifax. As late as May 1938, when German-Polish relations still seemed untroubled, Berlin learned that Halifax, in his conversations with Carl Burchkardt, termed the status of the Free City and the Corridor an "absurdity, a most foolish provision of the Treaty of Versailles." Halifax also said that the British government "was quite prepared to play a mediator's role" once Germany formally asked for those areas.[2] These statements had grave significance, because Burchkardt had been the League of Nations' commissioner in Danzig since February 1937, and his solemn duty was to uphold the status of the Free City. Indeed (as Hitler might or might not have known), his "proposal" of extraterritorial roads was not even original. As early as April 1933 President Franklin D. Roosevelt, in a conversation with French premier Édouard Herriot, secretly recommended a similar solution.[3] Moreover, the chancellor on his own initiative offered the Poles compensation by agreeing to Polish extraterritorial roads through East Prussia.

The offer of partnership against Russia, in the Führer's mind, must have represented a unique historic chance for Poland. It would have a free hand in the Ukrainian areas, which the Poles controlled for centuries, and Russia, a traditional enemy in the eyes of every Pilsudski-ite, would disappear as a great power for any foreseeable future.

In offering the Poles what he considered to be tremendous opportunities, Hitler was still playing safe. For once they agreed to go with him to the end, they would throw themselves at the mercy of the Reich for generations to come. He certainly kept that in mind, too.

For more than five years Hitler and his subordinates had been pursuing their goals tenaciously and, as they saw it, successfully. From the very beginning of his mission in Berlin until the end of 1938, Lipski was surrounded by made-to-order sympathy, popularity, and outright friendship. His access to Hitler was unsurpassed among diplomats in Berlin, and his relationship with Göring far exceeded the limits of rigid diplomatic protocol. He was welcomed in the highest government circles—and the Nazi authorities let the entire diplomatic corps know it. The frequent exchange visits between Warsaw and Berlin, the highly publicized hunting parties for Göring—the *Reichsjägermeister*'s passion—and the more than frequent public declarations all indicated that harmony and mutual confidence, if not more, linked Poland and Germany together.

Nazi leaders often emphasized their peaceful, friendly intentions toward Poland; this was especially true during times of either German breaches of international obligations or "peaceful" conquests. A few weeks after the introduction of conscription—on April 25, 1935—Göring, in the friendliest way, suggested more frequent German-Polish contacts and exchange visits. Such contacts and visits, he argued, would bring the two nations closer together and demonstrate that German-Polish rapprochement was not a transitory phenomenon. The Führer's policy toward Poland was not only "tactical" but aimed at long-range goals. And since many people in the

Auswärtiges Amt did not realize or approve it, he, Göring, on the Führer's orders, would take Polish-German relations under his "special protection."[4]

Four weeks later, on May 21, Hitler, faced with hostile world opinion, publicly praised the good relations between Germany and Poland. Those relations, he pointed out, were proof of his peaceful and reasonable policies, of his willingness to cooperate with all those who would show goodwill. The next day, he repeated his assurances to Lipski, emphasizing the importance of Poland for Germany and his determination to establish long-range cooperation with the Poles. Less than two months later, on July 3, he assured Beck that Poland's territorial integrity—particularly its access to the sea—would be respected by Germany. In February 1936 Lipski reported that the political climate in Berlin had become so favorable that General Werner von Blomberg proposed through Admiral Canaris a "very close camaraderie" between the Polish and German armies.[5]

Pilsudski—and, since his death, Beck—considered Danzig a barometer of German-Polish relations. Here, too, Hitler seemed to exercise a salutary influence. The traditionally troublesome attitude of the Free City's authorities toward Poland improved, and the chancellor spared no efforts to show that friendly relations between Warsaw and Berlin were bound to be more effective than the League of Nations' "chattering." On August 12, 1936, he confided to Szembek that the "Danzig question was negligible in comparison with the necessity of Polish-German friendly relations. . . . Polish rights in the Free City, which he [Hitler] knew and understood, could not suffer the least detriment." Three months later—on November 18, 1936—Moltke told Beck about the chancellor's wish to expand the Polish-German agreement and about the chancellor's renewed assurances that Polish rights in Danzig would be respected.[6]

Because the rapid growth of Danzig's bellicose Nazi party was worrying Warsaw, Hitler again went to great lengths to calm the Poles. On January 11, 1937, he assured Lipski that the "growth of national socialism in Danzig would be a guarantee of peace and good relations with Poland," that Poland's rights would not be diminished. In the Reichstag two weeks later, on January 30, he praised the agreement with Poland, "which has worked out to the advantage of both sides." On February 16 Göring assured Śmigly-Rydz that Germany did not want or need the Corridor and would not fight for it; on the contrary, it was in Germany's interest to have Poland strong and with access to the sea.[7]

The incorporation of Austria was also preceded by friendly gestures. On January 14, 1938, Hitler himself assured Beck that "Polish-German rights in Danzig would be in no way violated" and that Polish-German relations were of primary importance. On February 20 he stressed in the Reichstag that German-Polish relations were excellent in spite of "mischiefmakers."[8]

The same pattern was applied during the Czechoslovak crisis. On August 24 Göring suggested to Lipski an extension of the Polish-German declaration for twenty-five years and again assured him warmly of the Führer's goodwill. On September 20 the chancellor assured the ambassador that in the event of a Polish-Czechoslovak "conflict," Poland could count on Germany's full support.[9]

In the seclusion of diplomatic encounters, the Nazi leaders—and particularly the Auswärtiges Amt—repeatedly were telling the Poles that the problem of the Corridor and Danzig should not be considered as settled and that one day it would have to be solved. Until the spring of 1939, however, this was always done discreetly, never threateningly, always accompanied by assurances of peaceful intentions and offers of compensations.

According to the memorandum drawn up by Neurath for the internal record, Hitler, in his first conversation with the Polish envoy, Wysocki, on May 2, 1933, "reserved" Germany's right "at her discretion" to seek a solution of an "untenable situation" resulting from the existence of the Corridor.[10] Two months later on July 13, he again observed that "the authors of the Treaty of Versailles had created the Corridor in order to set an enduring abyss between Germany and Poland." The creation of the Corridor represented an "unreasonable" solution.[11]

Nor did the chancellor fail to explain his stand to the new Polish envoy, Józef Lipski. Receiving him for the first time on November 15, 1933, he spoke about his peaceful intentions. But he also condemned the Versailles decisions and expressed hope that "in the future," in a "friendly atmosphere" with some "compensation," the "difficult problems" between Germany and Poland would be settled. On August 27, 1934, he told Lipski that were it not for the Corridor, Poland and Germany "would long ago have become allies."[12]

On March 16, 1935, the chancellor again indicated to Lipski that Germany's claims on Poland should not be considered settled. German-Polish relations were a model for solving difficult international problems, he said. Since for Germany "it was psychologically impossible to waive so clearly a revindication of [Polish] territories—as could be done regarding Alsace and Lorraine," both countries agreed not to use force in solving this problem, he concluded. As early as May 22, 1935, he told Lipski about building extraterritorial rail and motor roads through the Corridor, probably within some fifteen years. In Warsaw, Moltke, no doubt acting under instructions, raised the same subject with Beck.[13]

Hitler's famous speech—delivered at the time of the remilitarization of the Rhineland, March 7, 1936—contained a reference to Poland, which was received in Warsaw as reassuring. Poland's access to the sea. Passing through once-German territories was "*schmerzlich*" to the German people, he said. Still, "it is impossible and therefore unreasonable to deny a State of such a size as this any outlet to the sea at all." However, at the end of his speech, he inserted a qualifying sentence, the relevance of which Lipski—an experienced diplomat—did notice and so informed Warsaw. The chancellor expressed "hope" that in the future "*schmerzliche*" problems would be "eliminated" peacefully.[14]

At the beginning of November 1936 Göring "most confidentially" told Lipski that the chancellor "would like" to have highway and railway transit across the Corridor.[15] A few days later, on November 12, Lipski himself, in a secret report to Beck, expressed his opinion that one day the "Danzig question would have to be 'solved.'"[16]

On February 16, 1937, Göring, on another hunting visit in Poland, saw Śmigly-Rydz. Expressing satisfaction over the development of German-Polish relations, Göring suggested close camaraderie between the armies of the two countries as well as cultural contacts. Once Polish-German relations were "completely established," he said, one could think about "facilitating" the transit from Germany proper to East Prussia.[17]

Though unannounced, the most positive avowal that Danzig would eventually have to be reunited with Germany came in 1937, during the negotiations for a joint declaration on minorities. The negotiations had been initiated by the Poles, and the resulting declaration was to guarantee proper reciprocal treatment and protection of the Polish population in Germany and the German minority in Poland. Beck wanted the declaration to be accompanied by a *public* and *joint* communiqué affirming that neither government intended to change the statute of the Free City. Not only did he fail, he gave the German officials an opportunity to reemphasize that although Polish economic interests in Danzig were secure, one day the Free City would have to return to Germany.

On September 6 Moltke said flatly that Beck's request "could not be considered." On September 11 Neurath, in answer to Lipski's protestations that it was "imperative to maintain the statute which designates Danzig as the Free City," refused straight out. When, at Lipski's request, Göring tried to intercede on Poland's behalf, Neurath explained that signing the desired declaration would mean that the Third Reich "expressly recognized the settlement of the Danzig question laid down in the peace treaty of Versailles," an act that would be contrary to official policy. This stand, he added, had the full approval of the Führer.[18] Then, on October 7, he told Lipski in unmistakable terms: "We must realize that someday there would have to be a basic settlement of the Danzig question between Poland and us [Germany]. . . . The only possible aim of a discussion on this matter—which to be sure was not at all urgent—would be the restoration of German Danzig to its natural connection with the Reich, in which case extensive consideration could be given to Poland's economic interests."[19]

The joint declaration on minorities was signed on November 5, 1937, and, to emphasize the importance of the event, the chancellor agreed to receive the Polish ambassador on the same day. He was exceedingly friendly, expressed his satisfaction over Polish-German relations, and asked Lipski to assure his government that Poland's rights in Danzig would not be "impaired" and that any surprise step was "out of the question." "Danzig ist mit Polen verbunden" (Gdansk is connected with Poland), he said twice. He also agreed to a joint communiqué about the visit. It contained an apparently assuring paragraph to the effect that "Polish-German relations should not meet with difficulties because of the Danzig question."

Both the declaration and the communiqué were understood by Polish public opinion as evidence of the success of Polish-German rapprochement. But both Beck and Lipski well knew that only the appearance of an understanding had been produced. The original text, as proposed by Lipski, included the statement that "the two governments were in full agreement in their attitude on Danzig affairs."[20] That paragraph was deleted by Neurath, obviously with Hitler's approval. For there was no agreement whatsoever.

On January 13, 1938, Göring met Beck in Berlin. Cordial as usual, the field marshal assured the Polish foreign minister that Nazi leadership did not intend to cut Poland off from the sea and turn a country of "40 million" [*sic*] against Germany. He did point out, however, that eventually Germany "would like . . . to have some convenient communication by railway through Pomerania." He casually added that in such an event, Poland would receive "compensations . . . in the east." He did not elaborate. The next day Hitler assured Beck that "Poland's rights in Danzig will not be infringed upon, and that, moreover, the legal status of the Free City [would] remain unaltered."[21]

During the Czechoslovak crisis, on September 16, Göring again raised the problem of a superhighway connecting Germany with East Prussia through the Corridor. Four days later, Hitler assured Lipski of Germany's support of the Polish claims on Teschen, but he also referred to the *possibility* of recognizing the German-Polish frontier as "definite." He saw the solution in an extraterritorial highway, thirty meters wide, across the Corridor.[22] Then, five weeks later, on October 24, Ribbentrop confronted Lipski with the Führer's "offer" of a general *Gesamtlösung*.

Polish foreign policy must have fortified Hitler in his belief that when the time for the final test came, Poland would comply. Whether or not Beck realized it, his activities in the international arena helped to arouse Hitler's hopes.

Beck successfully opposed the Eastern Pact. His reasons were grave and, as the French ambassador in Warsaw reported, he had the country behind him. Nonetheless he did act in collusion with the Auswärtiges Amt.[23] On May 14, 1935, Göring told Lipski with "great satisfaction" that without Poland as a member of the Eastern Pact, "the Franco-Russian alliance [would] be of little use."[24]

Beck continuously opposed Poland's participation in collective-security measures, and on July 3, 1935, he gave Hitler formal assurances to this effect.[25] This fit into Hitler's own policy. He feared and opposed all initiatives aimed at collective security.

Beck refused to enter into any closer and active bilateral or multilateral political cooperation with Russia. Though, again, his policy commanded popular support at home, isolation of Russia matched well with Hitler's plans.

Beck contributed to the weakening of the already weak League of Nations' authority. Having taken the stability of German-Polish relations for granted, he had no use for the League. With Germany (and Japan) absent and the Soviet Union an important part of it, he saw in the League an instrument of an "ideological bloc." Destruction of the League had been one of Hitler's goals since the beginning of his rule. In time Beck even challenged the prerogatives of the League in Danzig. This again fit into the Nazi plans and created quiet satisfaction in the Auswärtiges Amt.[26]

As Moltke informed Szembek on March 10, 1936, Poland's reaction to the Rhineland crisis pleased Berlin.[27] Polish official attitude toward the Italian conquest of Abyssinia and, later on, toward the Spanish Civil War also generally conformed to that of Berlin.

Beck pursued a policy directed against the Little Entente and Czechoslovakia, and he also supported Hungarian revisionism. The Little Entente and particularly Czechoslovakia were important pillars of the Versailles system of status quo. Hitler's goal was to destroy it. Territorial revisionism was a sine qua non in his strategy.

Taking advantage of the confusion resulting from "peaceful" Nazi conquests in 1938, Beck unwittingly contributed to international decay and thus again strengthened Hitler's hand. True, Beck's policies, acts, and political demonstrations were not of decisive importance in the international arena—Poland was too weak for that. But he created the appearance—eventually taken for reality in Paris, London, and Moscow—that the Poles decided of their own volition to tie their future to that of Nazi Germany. In Berlin, Hitler in all probability took those appearances for reality as well. Having repeatedly told the Poles of his far-reaching goals, of his generosity in respect to Germany's claims on Poland, of the role he assigned Poland in his plans, and then analyzing Beck's policies for over five years, he seemingly took it for granted that the Poles would not fail him. His grand strategy was based on that belief.

What was of greatest importance, however, was that eventually Beck himself took appearances for reality. He believed, until it was too late, that Hitler would not change his policy toward Poland because of Danzig. He failed to realize, until it was too late, that Hitler's accommodation with Poland was no more than a function of his grand strategy of conquest.

With the benefit of hindsight, it seems that Hitler and Beck both lived in a sort of make-believe world. Hitler's expectations that the Poles would eventually accept his demands peacefully and join forces against Russia were without foundation. Some vague and essentially inconsequential statements coming from the Polish side notwithstanding, there is no evidence that Beck ever envisaged such an eventuality. On the other hand, Beck's belief that Hitler considered peaceful relations with Poland as an end in itself, not a means to attain higher ends, was, as Szembek realized so late, a "pure and simple fiction."

Had Beck understood the reasons for Hitler's overtures, their deadly significance, he would have realized that by the nature of things stabilization of

German-Polish relations was bound to be only illusory and transient. He would also have realized that whatever dangers, difficulties, or secondary considerations existed, essentially Poland's security—in fact, its entire future—lay in supporting rather than abandoning the Versailles system of status quo; in strengthening, not weakening, the authority of the League of Nations; in maintaining friendship with and not antagonizing France; in encouraging rather than rejecting collective security; in supporting instead of scorning the Little Entente; in strengthening Czechoslovakia, France's strongest and faithful eastern ally, instead of weakening it.

In September 1934 Beck used the admission of the Soviet Union into the League of Nations as an "occasion" for denouncing the national minorities' treaty binding Poland since 1919. He acted alone, unsupported by any country bound by the same obligations. By that time, the League was hardly able to discharge its responsibilities, but his act could not but further weaken the Versailles system. Destruction of that system was Hitler's goal.

On June 26, 1936, Beck notified the League's council that Poland would not apply economic sanctions against Italy because Abyssinia had ceased de facto to exist as an independent country. He made Poland, which for more than a hundred years had appealed to world conscience not to recognize its de facto nonexistence, the first League member officially to drop sanctions. By then, the anti-Italian sanctions were already dead. They would be lifted formally only a few weeks later.

In 1937 the Polish and Japanese legations were raised to the ranks of embassies and a Polish-Japanese friendship association was inaugurated in Warsaw. The following year Poland recognized the Japanese puppet state, Manchukuo. By then, Japan stood condemned by the League of Nations as an aggressor in China, and Soviet-Japanese relations had deteriorated almost to a breaking point. Pro-Japanese gestures had an exotic flavor but lacked political relevancy.

The ultimatum to Kaunas in March 1938 certainly did not reduce the Lithuanians' resentment or hostility toward Poland. Poland's participation in Czechoslovakia's dismemberment six months later diminished, not strengthened, Poland's security.

In September 1938 Beck notified the League of Nations that Poland refused to be considered for membership in the League's council. Six months later Poland was the first country to recognize the independence of Slovakia. Refusal to be considered for the League's council could not affect that institution one way or the other. By then the League was moribund, with or without Poland in its council. The fate of "independent" Slovakia depended on the strength and support of Germany, not Poland.

All these moves were essentially mere gestures or demonstrations. Intended to generate respect for the "independence" of Polish foreign policy, they instead aroused suspicion about Beck's motives and goals.

Beck considered the Polish German détente a part of Pilsudski's legacy, a legacy he had to preserve. However, Pilsudski probably considered rapprochement with the Nazi regime no more than a short-range expedient, a consequence of his failure to bring the Western democracies into some preventive action *against* Hitler. "Having concluded these two pacts [with Germany and Russia] we are sitting on two stools—this cannot last long. We must find out from which we shall fall down first and when," he cautioned his collaborators on April 12, 1934.[28] Had Pilsudski lived longer, pragmatic as he was, he probably would have tried to adapt, and readapt, and readapt again Polish foreign policy to the changing circumstances.

Beck saw in the Polish-German declaration of 1934 a durable and static factor. Until the end of his life he considered the agreement his master's victory, never grasping that the agreement was no victory at all, since Hitler did not have to be won over. He wanted that agreement as much as Pilsudski did, although for different reasons. Moreover, the agreement as Beck saw it never existed anyway. Hitler never renounced Germany's demands on Poland—he only decided to reduce them to what he considered an absolute minimum and to postpone the settlement. Neither he nor his collaborators made any secret of this in their dealings with Wysocki, Lipski, or Beck himself.

The chancellor was willing, or on occasions even anxious, to reassert publicly again and again that good, peaceful relations between Germany and Poland represented a permanent factor in European politics. He chose that procedure because it strengthened his international position and also because, in his mind, time worked for his Reich. The fact that Polish diplomacy as well as semiofficial Polish press adopted that procedure for both home and foreign consumption only strengthened the Führer's conviction that the Poles would eventually accept his "generous" terms—peacefully.

As for Beck, he not only allowed Hitler to create the *appearance* of a genuine German-Polish understanding, but he himself seems to have taken it for reality. Wishful thinking more than realism guided him in his relations with the Nazis. His subordinates, with a few exceptions, catered to his views.

In his report of May 19, 1933, Wysocki disapprovingly suggested that the Polish public, in its anti-Nazi attitude, was too strongly influenced by the Jews. He himself "understood perfectly well" those Germans who saw danger in Jewish activities and power in Germany. These feelings did not run against Polish interests, because German Jews were generally hostile to Poland. The Nazi movement "undoubtedly" would render a great service to Germany. Furthermore, Hitler was born in Austria and had spent his youth in Vienna and was, therefore, unlike the Prussians, free of "hostility or contempt" toward Poland, the envoy wrote.[29]

In his report of December 18, 1933, Lipski reported that Goebbels had made an "infinitely sympathetic and very good impression" on him as a "great idealist" and a "sentimental man."[30] Two months later he evaluated the chancellor as essentially friendly toward Poland and sincere in his policy of rapprochement. On April 2, 1935, Szembek tried to impress upon Eden that "for the Poles there is no doubt that of all the possible regimes in Germany the present Hitlerian regime is the most satisfactory."[31] Two days later, Szembek and Beck's *chef de cabinet*, Roman Debicki, disapprovingly concluded that rumors about an approaching war resulting from the Nazi expansion were "always" spread by the same kind of people: Jews, Masons, Socialists, and Communists. Hitler made an "excellent impression" on Beck in their conversation on July 3, 1935. The foreign minister considered the chancellor "absolutely sincere." He was convinced that the difficulties in Polish-German relations, particularly in Danzig, were caused by the intrigues of lower echelons of the Auswärtiges Amt, hostile to Hitler's own "Polish policy." The official communiqué mentioned a "far-reaching agreement of views."[32] The strong language could not but arouse suspicions in the Western capitals. Three months later, on October 15, Szembek lectured Noël that of all possible governments in Germany, Hitler's regime was "the most advantageous" to Poland. On August 26, 1937, he said the same to Rickard Sandler, Sweden's foreign minister.[33]

On January 14, 1936, Lipski requested special consideration for Reich's minister, Hans Frank, who was to lecture in Warsaw. Frank, wrote Lipski, "[was] very well disposed towards us and may be useful." Then months later, on October 15, he informed Beck in a "top secret" letter that "clearly" Neurath desired "stabilization" in Danzig and would act accordingly.[34] Lipski considered any weakening of Göring's position in the Reich harmful to Polish interests.[35]

Eventually, the leading Polish diplomats concluded that German expansion, unavoidable as it was, would progress southward, somehow omitting Poland. In the middle of June 1935 Beck told Szembek that sooner or later Austria and Czechoslovakia would "disappear." He thought that Poland should not remain passive, nor should it in any way support either of them. On the contrary, it should take an active part in the reshaping of central-eastern Europe. He looked for "compensations." In December 1936 he thought about seizing Teschen, Danzig, or even Kaunas.[36]

In the midst of the Czechoslovak crisis, on May 26, 1938, Lukasiewicz, warned by Bonnet that destruction of Czechoslovakia would dangerously affect Poland's security, answered that the warning was "pointless" since he had "never heard" of Hitler having such an intention. On September 13 Szembek sharply disagreed with Noël, who warned him that Hitler's assurances "meant nothing." On October 1—that is, three weeks before Ribbentrop presented him with the demands—Lipski reported to Warsaw that the Polish policy during the Czechoslovak crisis was "the surest guarantee of our good relations with the German government."[37]

On November 4, 1938—*after* Ribbentrop's demands—Beck, at a conference with senior officials of his ministry, expressed satisfaction as to Poland's international situation. It was "good," he said. He thought that in the main Ribbentrop's ambition and lack of diplomatic training were responsible for Polish-German difficulties. As late as on February 15, 1939, he told American ambassador Anthony J. Drexel Biddle that "Hitler's eastward-looking ambitions definitely [did] not figure in his immediate program," instead, Hitler would "continue concentrating his attention in the west in his determined colonial campaign." Convinced that the difficulties would be solved peacefully, Beck maintained strict secrecy about the German demands for months. Visiting Warsaw on March 22–23, 1939, and himself in a "highly pessimistic mood," Lipski noticed that his colleagues greatly underestimated the danger of war.[38]

On April 8, Beck—on his way from London to Warsaw via Berlin—met Lipski and the Polish military attaché on the train; the Anglo-Polish communiqué announcing the mutual-assistance pact had just been signed. By then, Lipski, so optimistic only a few months before, was convinced that war had become inevitable. Beck disagreed. He thought that sooner or later Hitler would become reconciled to Warsaw's position on Danzig.[39]

At the end of June 1939 the undersecretary of state, Miroslaw Arciszewski, argued that Germany would not go to war because of Danzig. He was still convinced that Hitler was "bluffing" in his "war of nerves" at the end of August—one week before Germany attacked Poland.[40]

Not only did Beck and his collaborators maintain confidence in the permanence of the German-Polish détente, but they also overestimated Poland's military strength and underestimated Germany's power. On March 24, 1939, Beck solemnly declared at a meeting of the senior officials in his ministry that "the Germans are marching all across Europe with nine divisions; with such strength Poland [in the event of war] would not be overcome." He assured his audience that "Hitler and his associates [knew] this" and concluded that "we . . . [the Poles] have all the trump cards in our hands."[41] The statement was made *before* British guarantees were given to Poland; *before* Britain concluded a preliminary mutual-assistance pact with Poland; *before* Franco-Polish and Anglo-Polish military conversations took place; four months *after* the French ambassador in Warsaw, to the satisfaction of the Quai d'Orsay and France's military leaders, recommended terminating the Franco-Polish alliance.

Commenting ten days later on the imminent Anglo-Polish agreement, Beck told Eden that "Germany would be angry and would bluster, but there was nothing she could do," adding that he thought that "the efficiency of the German army had been greatly exaggerated."[42] In July he considered Poland's military strength as adequate. The army chief of staff, General Waclaw Stachiewicz, believed that Germany "found itself in a very difficult situation." The Nazi regime might collapse. He did not wish that to happen, considering such an eventuality dangerous to Poland.[43]

On August 21, 1939, Beck conferred with Lipski and Stachiewicz. Lipski believed that in the event of war, Poland would be attacked by the Wehrmacht on all fronts, from all sides. Beck was optimistic. According to Lipski, he "praised the anti-aircraft defense of the capital, which allegedly numbered a hundred heavy artillery guns. In general, as usual, he appeared well satisfied with [Polish] military power." Even if Hitler did use force, Beck concluded, he would probably limit himself to the occupation of Danzig.[44]

Throughout most of the period from 1934 to 1939, there was a suspicion, especially among the French, that Beck had some secret understanding with Hitler. There was nothing of the sort. There were no secret agreements between Poland and Nazi Germany, no prearranged cooperation on the international scene, no mutually agreeable solutions of any important problems between the two countries. In the final analysis, Beck's diplomacy toward Germany was mainly one of appearances; of highly publicized, ostentatious visits; of essentially inconsequential—though often provocative—anti-Western and pro-German gestures, all designed to prove the "independence" of his policy, win Hitler's confidence, and force "respect" for Poland among the Western democracies.

Those gestures and those appearances were so much more confusing because, essentially, Beck sought peace and envisioned Poland's role as that of a stabilizer in European affairs. To fulfill that role, he even made some efforts to create his own collective-security system. He encountered, however, insurmountable obstacles.

Some of the obstacles were inherent in the Polish state. Others resulted from Beck's diplomacy. Whether the Poles realized it or not, they were not attractive as partners. Poland was domestically riven, undermined by the insoluble problems of its national minorities, economically underdeveloped, and militarily weak. Internationally, it was threatened by both Germany and Russia; it had to endure the hostility of Lithuania; most of the time Poland itself was less than friendly to Czechoslovakia; its relations with France were stormy; its relations with the Little Entente were nonexistent. Its foreign policy was suspect. Its foreign minister was distrusted.

Beck wanted to revive the old idea of the Baltic bloc. But, as always, Finland gravitated to the Scandinavian countries, Lithuania was adamant, and Latvia and Estonia, with their less than three million inhabitants, could hardly contribute to Europe's stability. He also thought of building up close cooperation with the Scandinavian countries, but they had pursued a policy of neutrality and noninvolvement for generations. They shunned association with a Poland whose own problems, they must have feared, might cause them more trouble than good.

Beck then turned southward, trying to bring together Italy, Hungary, Yugoslavia, Romania, and Poland, all outwardly friendly to Germany, but all certainly apprehensive of the growing German pressure toward the Balkans. Apparently he wanted to foment a sort of third Europe strong enough to bar German expansion and prevent Russia from meddling in the area's affairs. [45]

His efforts intensified in 1938 and resulted in a fiasco. First, Italy never envisaged Poland as an equal partner. Mussolini thought a German-Polish showdown on territorial issues was inevitable and, as the Four-Power Pact showed, he essentially supported Germany's claims on Poland. The Hungarians, anxious to recover what they had lost in World War I, sought to destroy the Versailles system. They hoped to profit from Hitler's revisionist policies, but they also did not want to antagonize the Western powers. On the whole though, they gravitated toward Berlin and believed that some compromise on Danzig and the Corridor had to be made. In August 1938, during the Czechoslovak crisis and at a time when German-Polish relations seemed blooming, Admiral Miklós Horthy, Regent of Hungary, secretly offered Hitler his good services in "[advocating] in Warsaw that Poland return the Corridor to Germany."[46] As for the Romanians, they dismissed Beck's advances less than courteously. Beck made no progress at all in Yugoslavia.

Significantly, not all Polish leaders, even in the government camp, understood or agreed with Beck's policy. Such men as Śmigly-Rydz; General Kazimierz Sosnkowski, inspector of the army; Minister of Finance Adam Koc; and Vice Premier Eugeniusz Kwiatkowski distrusted Hitler and advocated closer ties with France.[47] None of them, however, stood up against the foreign minister. True, he was vehemently and publicly criticized by all democratic political parties in opposition to the government. But, as could be expected, their criticism did not carry weight with Beck.

Eventually, Beck became the most severely criticized of Poland's foreign ministers in the European capitals. Whatever the merits or demerits of his diplomacy, he apparently possessed some genius for making people distrust him. He never commanded respect in any quarter of responsible politicians in Paris. For Moscow, he was *"la bête noire."* He was viewed as an unfriendly intriguer in Prague. In Bucharest they distrusted his initiatives. Even the British, whom he courted, had no confidence in him. In one of his reports, Ambassador Kennard complained that Beck could not be trusted; in another report, he described Beck as "ambitious and unscrupulous"; in still another, as "secretive" and "lacking straightforwardness." According to Kennard, the Polish foreign minister was "full of vanity" and "ambition to pose as a leading statesman."[48]

Beck's personality and methods apart, it is doubtful that another foreign minister could have changed the turn of events, even had he been free of Beck's illusions, seen farther than Beck, and chosen other methods. Situated between Germany and Russia—each stronger than Poland, each dynamic and expansionist—Poland was natural prey. In the event of German-Soviet cooperation, the partition of Poland was bound to become the goal. In the event of German-Soviet hostility, Poland was a corridor to be crossed by either or both of them, with or without the consent of the Poles. Hitler's policy of conquest, aimed at the destruction of Russia, as well as the vacillating policy of the Western powers, made Beck's policy of "equilibrium" essentially inoperative as a long-range solution. The Poles were too weak for that. In the final analysis, they had only two options: either to join the "New Order" led by Hitler or to actively cooperate with the Soviet Union—directly or through the Franco-British-Soviet collective-security system. In either case there was no room for an "independent" Polish policy. Neither option was within Beck's reach. Polish public opinion—progovernment and antigovernment—opposed both.

NOTES

1. Henderson, *The Failure of a Mission*, 297.

2. *DGFP*, series D, 5:48.

3. For Roosevelt-Herriot conversation in the White House on April 26, 1933, see *FRUS*, 1933, 1:111.

4. For Lipski's report, see Lipski, *Diplomat in Berlin*, 188–92.

5. See Lipski, *Diplomat in Berlin*, 202–6; *DGFP*, series C, 4:398–407; Szembek, *Journal*, 159; *PWB*, 32, respectively.

6. *PWB*, 47; also Szembek, *Journal*, 196–98.

7. *PWB*, 35–36; Szembek, *Journal*, 221–23, respectively.

8. *DGFP*, series D, 5:38–39.

9. For Lipski's reports, see Lipski, *Diplomat in Berlin*, 382–87, 408–12.

10. *DGFP*, series C, 1:366–67.

11. *PWB*, 15–16; for parts of Wysocki's report omitted in the *PWB*, see Lipski, *Diplomat in Berlin*, 90.

12. Lipski, *Diplomat in Berlin*, 99, 153–57, respectively; for Neurath's reports, see *DGFP*, series C, 2:128–39 and 3:360–61, respectively.

13. Lipski, *Diplomat in Berlin*, 176–79, 202–6; *DGFP*, series D, 5:20–21, respectively.

14. For Lipski's original reports (not included in Lipski, *Diplomat in Berlin*), see *AANP-Zespoly MSZ*, 3251, 9–15, 92–97.

15. Szembek, *Diariusz*, 2:326; this report is missing in Lipski, *Diplomat in Berlin*.

16. *AANP-Zespoly MSZ*, 4622, 94. This report is missing in Lipski, *Diplomat in Berlin*.

17. Szembek, *Journal*, 221–23.

18. *AANA*, 1723/1007/417009-11; *DGFP*, series D, 5:1–2, 12–13, respectively.

19. *DGFP*, series D, 5:19; compare with Lipski's report, Lipski, *Diplomat in Berlin*, 299.

20. See *AANA*, 147/164/78502-04.

21. For Lipski's reports, see Lipski, *Diplomat in Berlin*, 330–38; compare with Neurath's memo, *DGFP*, series D, 5:38–39.

22. For Lipski's report, see Lipski, *Diplomat in Berlin*, 401–5, 408–12.

23. See Beck-Moltke conversation on June 29, 1934, *DGFP*, series C, 3:102–3; also Hitler-Neurath-Lipski conversation on August 27, 1934, ibid., 360–61; Neurath-Beck conversation on September 2, 1934, ibid., 385–86. For Lipski's report on his conversation with Hitler and Neurath, see Lipski, *Diplomat in Berlin*, 153–57; for Neurath's report, see *DGFP*, series C, 3:360–31. Also Wojciechowski, *Stosunki Polsko Niemieckie*, 132–50.

24. Lipski, *Diplomat in Berlin*, 201.

25. *DGFP*, series C, 4:398–407.

26. See Moltke's evaluation dated October 2, 1936, of Warsaw's role "in getting rid" of the League of Nations' high commissioner in Danzig, Sean Lester: *AANA*, 1724/1016/400599-600.

27. *AANP-Zespoly MSZ*, 3251, 79.

28. Szembek, *Diariusz*, 1:155.

29. Szembek, *Diariusz*, 1:68–70.

30. Ibid., 112–15. This paragraph was deleted from Lipski's report in Lipski, *Diplomat in Berlin*, 112–15.

31. Lipski, *Diplomat in Berlin*, 126–29; also Szembek, *Journal*, 55–56.

32. *PWB*, 30.

33. Szembek, *Diariusz*, 1:262; *Journal*, 106–10; *Diariusz*, 1:122, 372, respectively.

34. *AANP-Zespoly MSZ*, 4623, 49; also 3253, 98–99, respectively. Frank, the wartime governor general in Nazi-occupied Poland, was tried as a major war criminal and hung in Nuremberg in 1946.

35. Szembek, *Diariusz*, 3:161.

36. Szembek, *Journal*, 95, 164, 220.

37. See Lukasiewicz, *Papers and Memoirs*, 91–99; Szembek, *Journal*, 334; Lipski, *Diplomat in Berlin*, 334; Lipski, *Diplomat in Berlin*, 435–38.

38. Szembek, *Journal*, 367–72; *FRUS*, 1939, 1:14; Lipski, *Diplomat in Berlin*, 502.

39. Lipski, *Diplomat in Berlin*, 529–30.

40. *DBFP*, 3rd series, 6:177; and Szembek, *Journal*, 491.

41. For the official memo on the conference, see Lipski, *Diplomat in Berlin*, 503–4.

42. Eden, *Facing the Dictators*, 58.

43. Szembek, *Diariusz*, 4:679, 676, respectively.

44. Lipski, *Diplomat in Berlin*, 566, 587–88.

45. See Ambassador Kennard's report dated October 14, 1938; *DBFP*, 3rd series, 3:178–83. About Beck's plan for a "Third Europe," see Hans Roos, *Polen und Europa, Studien zür polnischen Aussenpolitik, 1931–1939* (Tubingen, Germany: J. C. B. Mohr [Paul Siebeck], 1957), 73ff; also Debicki, *Foreign Policy of Poland*, 104–8.

46. For more information see *DGFP*, series D, 5:74.

47. See Szembek, *Journal*, 34, 152–53, 165, 185, 207, 275, 289–90; see also Laroche, *La Pologne de Pilsudski*, 194–95; Beck, *Dernier rapport*, 150; also German ambassador Moltke's report, dated September 2, 1938; *DGFP*, series D, 5:75–78.

48. *FO* 371/18896/C1253/465/55; *FO* 371/19957/7905/49/55; *FO* 371/19960/9243/317/55.

Chapter Nineteen

Anglo-French-Polish Military and Economic Agreements

Commitments in Bad Faith, 1939

Despite the military convention of 1921, there was no meaningful collaboration between the Polish and French general staffs from 1919 to 1939; of course, there was no basis for such collaboration between the Poles and the British. But by the summer of 1939, the Franco-British guarantees and the danger of war demanded some workable procedures and well-defined mutual military commitments. The Poles were pressing for them, and neither the French nor the British could refuse discussions.

Franco-Polish negotiations concerning the conditions and extent of military cooperation in the event of war took place in Paris in May. Warsaw sent the minister of war, General Tadeusz Kasprzycki; the assistant chief of staff of the armed forces, Colonel Józef Jaklicz; the assistant chief of staff of the air force, Colonel Karpinski; and Polish military, naval, and air attachés to Paris. Speaking for France were the supreme commander designate, General Maurice Gamelin; the commander in chief of the armies, General Alphonse Georges; the chief of staff of the air force, General Joseph Vuillemin; the chief of staff of the navy, Vice Admiral Jean Darlan; and four other high-ranking officers.

The negotiations seemed uneasy from the outset, mainly because the French general staff, particularly Gamelin, tried to avoid specific commitments on an immediate, full-scale offensive once Germany attacked Poland. Later on, in 1946, Gamelin revealed that he was altogether opposed to military negotiations with Poland before a Franco-Soviet military agreement was reached and Poland's cooperation with Russia established. He doubted whether the Poles could resist Germany's attack for long or whether the Western allies could effectively help them unless the Soviet Union cooperated.[1]

On May 19, after four days of discussion, Gamelin was authorized by Daladier to sign a protocol (military convention) in which the French high command assumed the following commitments: (1) In the event of a German attack on Poland, or in the event of a threat to Polish vital interests in Danzig, the French air force would immediately start operations in accordance with a previously established plan; (2) the army would start an offensive with limited objectives on the third day after the mobilization; (3) if the main German forces were directed against Poland, France would start a great offensive with the bulk of its forces ("les gros de ses forces") on the fifteenth day after the mobilization; (4) in the first phase of the war, Poland was to wage only a defensive campaign; (5) if the main German forces were directed against France, the Polish army would attempt to tie up as many German divisions as possible.[2]

The military protocol was followed by an air agreement concluded on May 27. The French air force committed itself to attack Germany at the outbreak of the war. Three bomber squadrons were to be dispatched to the Polish front. A special air mission, led by General Paul Armengaud, was to be sent to Poland in order to command the French air units and to coordinate air activities of the two allies.

The story of the Polish-French military protocol is unclear and controversial. Simultaneous with the military discussions, separate negotiations for a political agreement were conducted, aimed at adapting the alliance of 1921 to the British and French guarantees of March–April 1939. According to those guarantees, France and Great Britain committed themselves to stand by Poland in the event of "indirect" aggression or in the event the Poles decided to use their military forces in defense of their "vital" interests. Negotiations were difficult because the Poles demanded that the incorporation of Danzig by Germany be specifically recognized as a *casus foederis*. But Bonnet refused.[3] He strongly believed that France should not assume any obligations toward Poland that did not bind Great Britain as well. And, as mentioned before, he learned from Halifax himself that the Foreign Office did not consider defense of Danzig obligatory under all circumstances.[4]

As a result, the political agreement was not signed until September 4, one day after France entered the war. The delay eventually caused recriminations among Bonnet, Gamelin, and Lukasiewicz, the Polish ambassador in Paris. Bonnet blamed the British for dilatory tactics and the Polish ambassador for ineptitude, while Gamelin criticized Bonnet severely, calling his attitude "néfaste."[5]

At the time the protocol was signed, both the Polish and the French military representatives assumed that the political agreement would shortly follow. When Gamelin learned that this was not the case, he sent a letter to Kasprzycki, making the validity of the protocol dependent upon the conclusion of the political agreement. Thus, as he stated in his memoirs, France was not bound by the terms of the protocol he signed on May 19.[6]

The Anglo-Polish military discussions took place in Warsaw in May and July, resulting in an understanding which, strangely enough, was never formalized.[7] In the negotiations on May 23–30, the British general staff was represented by Brigadier General Patrick Clayton, navy captain Rawlings, and air force colonel Davidson. Speaking for Poland were the chief of staff of the armed forces, General Waclaw Stachiewicz; Vice Admiral Jerzy Świarski; the chief of staff of the air force, General Stanislaw Ujejski; and Colonel Józef Jaklicz. In the second series, in July, General Sir Edmund Ironside (chief of the imperial general staff after September 1939) arrived in Warsaw and held a long, detailed discussion with the commander-in-chief designate, Marshal Śmigly-Rydz. At the request of the British government, Beck and a representative of the British embassy, Clifford Norton, participated in the discussions.

Ironside considered the war inevitable and assured the Poles that it would be fought to the bitter end by Great Britain.[8] Should Poland be attacked, the British air force would start an offensive against the aggressor immediately, while the navy would confine its task to protecting imperial sea routes. If nonmilitary objectives in Poland were bombed, the British air force would retaliate in the same manner, regardless of the Luftwaffe's moves against Great Britain. British land forces were neither required nor expected to act. To alleviate Poland's need for air force, Ironside promised to send one hundred bombers without delay and to increase the number of Hurricanes previously promised.

Ironside's conversations in Warsaw were carried out in an atmosphere of mutual sympathy and confidence. He made an excellent impression on the Poles, who apprised him of their secret military plans and preparations. Apparently he was awed by the work of the Polish general staff.[9] Reporting on his visit, he described Poland's military effort as "little short of prodigious." He even believed that the Poles were "strong enough to resist" German attack all by themselves![10]

The military commitments undertaken by France and Great Britain during the summer of 1939 were bound to strengthen the self-confidence of the Polish leaders. Immediate bombing of Germany by both the British and the French air forces promised to be commensurate with the German bombing of Poland; an initially limited but then full-scale offensive by the French; French and British air support—these were commitments that would have comforted any nation. Unfortunately for the Poles, these commitments were not to be fulfilled. It is more than doubtful whether they were ever intended to be.

Throughout the negotiations with the Poles, Gamelin apparently realized that he could not start a general offensive in the event of an early German attack on Poland. Only eight months before, during the Czechoslovak crisis (September 13, 1938), General Georges formally informed the cabinet that an attack on the Siegfried Line was impossible. On August 23, 1939, more than three months after the Franco-Polish protocol was signed, Gamelin himself reported at a meeting of the Committee of National Defense that the French army would not be able to mount an effective offensive in less than two years.[11]

Approximately at the same time, in mid-August, Churchill visited the Rhine sector of the French front. Talking to General Georges and other high-ranking French officers, he realized that they neither planned nor intended "to mount a great offensive." They would defend themselves when attacked, but they were not about to take any initiative in the early stages of a war.[12]

When informed about the terms of the Franco-Polish air agreement and his own appointment, General Armengaud protested in Paris, pointing out that neither the plans nor the commitments were realistic. The air chief of staff agreed. But he also argued that some goodwill had to be shown to the Poles. Armengaud was convinced that his superiors well realized that "France's aid to Poland, air as well as land, indirect as well as direct, in practice would be negligible." They wanted the Poles to believe otherwise, however, so Poland would accept Germany's main thrust and France would gain time to mobilize and concentrate its own defenses.[13]

In August, Gamelin dispatched General Louis Faury to Warsaw as head of the military mission. Preparing for his mission, Faury learned that there were no decisions as to any land offensive, anyway. In the event of Germany's attack on Poland, the Poles were to fight alone, he was told. This would give the Western powers precious time to prepare for a long war.[14]

Ironside's evaluation did not differ much from Armengaud's or Faury's. He was well acquainted with French military plans and did not find in them any indication that the French command ever intended an early attack against the Siegfried line. During his stay in Warsaw he learned about French commitments toward Poland. He knew that they would not be fulfilled. "The French have lied to the Poles in saying that they are going to attack. There is no idea of it," he noted in his diary. Unfortunately, he failed to inform the Poles. Moreover, he himself had serious apprehensions about Britain's immediate military capabilities.[15]

There exists further evidence that Franco-Polish and Anglo-Polish military agreements or understandings were meaningless. As early as April 24, 1939, that is, *before* the Franco-Polish and Anglo-Polish military discussions took place, the French and British general staffs jointly "recognized" that "in the first phase of the war the only offensive weapon which the Allies could use effectively was the economic." They also agreed that their "major strategy would be defensive." Soon afterward, in July, they decided that "the fate of Poland [would] depend upon the ultimate outcome of the war . . . and not on our [Franco-British] ability to relieve pressure on Poland at the outset." In the event of war, the Western allies planned to avoid an early, all-out confrontation with Germany to gain time for building up their own national forces. Instead, they intended to apply a naval blockade, which had been so effective in the years 1914–1918.[16] The Poles were unaware of these fateful decisions.

Simultaneous with the military negotiations, the Polish government applied for economic aid in both London and Paris. The growing danger of Nazi aggression and the need to build up its military defense imposed financial burdens on Poland for which it was ill prepared. An internal loan met with success, but it was still insufficient for partial mobilization; purchase of arms, military equipment, and raw materials; and expanded industrial production. Poland's armed forces were obsolete and, according to the British military attaché, needed essential improvement, particularly in artillery and air force.[17] Since efforts to gain financial assistance and military aircraft from the United States had failed, the Poles applied to France and Great Britain for immediate and sizable loans.

Both Paris and London responded, though not to the extent expected in Warsaw. In June the governor of the State Bank, Adam Koc, went to London, but, in spite of strong support from the British embassy in Warsaw, he did not succeed. The British were thinking of their own growing expenses for rearmament, convinced that if a war did break out, it would last for a long time. In such an event, as Halifax told Raczyński, the economic strength of Great Britain would become crucial to all, and Britain's needs had to have priority. Furthermore, Britain's gold reserves were diminishing. Of decisive importance probably was the fact that the Foreign Office still hoped to prevent war by forging an alliance with Russia.

After rather circuitous negotiations, London accorded Poland eight million British pounds—not in cash as requested but in export credits meant chiefly for military purposes. Severe conditions were attached, conditions that even the British ambassador in Warsaw considered "humiliating."[18] The Polish mission placed orders without delay. But time had run out: Before the shipments reached Poland the war was on. It was not until September 7—a week after Germany's attack—that Great Britain accorded Poland 5,500,000 pounds in cash credits. It was too late.

Nor were the Poles successful with the French government, which agreed to an export credit of 430 million pounds but no more. Noël pressed the Quai d'Orsay for more consideration, to no avail.[19]

The economic aid accorded Poland was too little and too late. That, in turn, was understood in Berlin as one more proof that neither France nor Great Britain took their obligations toward Poland seriously, that in fact neither planned to assist the Poles militarily in the event of war. It strengthened Hitler's determination to strike, as he himself told his military commanders on the eve of the war.[20]

Beginning with the spring of 1939 and until the last prewar days, British-French-Polish diplomacy moved in a vicious circle. Commitments or no commitments, neither the British nor the French planned to or considered themselves able to furnish Poland with effective military aid in the event of a German attack. Their guarantees aimed at preventing war, not supporting Poland militarily in the event war did break out. They hoped that their public commitments vis-à-vis Poland would direct Hitler from the path of conquests to the path of rational negotiations. By giving Poland public support and making secret commitments, they also wanted to prevent Poland from total surrender to Hitler's pressure, from becoming Germany's unwilling satellite.

But whether peace could be saved or whether war was inevitable, they considered Russia a decisive factor. To both, an alliance with Russia seemed crucial. Such an alliance would certainly prevent war, they thought; if it failed to prevent war, then such an alliance would certainly win it, they believed. To make such an alliance possible, Poland's cooperation with Russia was necessary, and Poland had to be cajoled, because Poland separated Russia from Germany.

In the event war became unavoidable, neither the British nor the French ever thought in terms of an Anglo-French-Polish alliance. Instead, they sought an Anglo-French-Soviet alliance. Without Russia, they agreed, war would be long and the burden of the war would have to be carried on by Britain and France. As for the Poles, they would have to suffer the first blow, defend themselves for as long as they could, weaken the German machine as much as possible, and give time to the Western allies to prepare themselves. But sooner or later, Poland was bound to succumb. Once victory was achieved by Western democracies, Poland would, of course, be restored.

The Poles had a different view of the situation: Having failed to realize the deadly seriousness and significance of Hitler's demands, they overestimated their own military strength and underestimated Germany's power. But they also missed the strategy and motives of Great Britain and France. They took the British and French commitments at face value. They thought in terms of an Anglo-French-Polish alliance. Such an alliance, they expected, would be enough to call Hitler's bluff and prevent war. Should Hitler embark upon war, a simultaneous riposte by Great Britain, France, and Poland, a riposte on land, sea, and air, would bring Germany to its knees. Their fears and suspicions of Moscow notwithstanding, they did not consider their military and political cooperation with Russia *necessary*. Contrary to the intentions of London and Paris, the Western guarantees and commitments only fortified their assumptions.

In the last prewar months, French-British-Polish diplomacy reached its lowest ebb.

NOTES

1. Gamelin, *Servir*, 2:414–15.

2. For the text, see Waclaw Jedrzejewicz, ed., *Poland in the British Parliament, 1939–1945: Documentary Material Relating to the Cause of Poland during World War 2*, 3 vols. (New York: Joseph Pilsudski Institute of America, 1946–1962), 1:256–57. For negotiations, *PSZ*, 1, pt. 1, 93–101; Gamelin, *Servir*, 2:410–29.

3. For his version, see Lukasiewicz, *Papers and Memoirs*, 210–23; also Bonnet, *Défense de la paix*, 2:224.

4. Supra, 272.

5. Bonnet, *Défense de la paix*, 2:219–21; Gamelin, *Servir*, 2:425–26.

6. Gamelin, *Servir*, 2:422–23; also Noël, *L'Aggression allemande contre la Pologne*, 373–74. For Bonnet's views, see Bonnet, *Défense de la paix*, 2:227–33.

7. Only the Polish *Proces Verbal* seems to be available. See *PSZ*, 1, pt. 1, 101–6. No trace of the understanding in British public documents or postwar memoirs could be found. See Norton's report on Ironside's visit to Warsaw, dated July 20, 1939, *DBFP*, 3rd series, 6:415–19.

8. Beck, *Dernier rapport*, 208–9.

9. See Paul F. Armengaud, *Batailles politiques et militaires sur l'Europe: Témoignages (1932–1940)* (Paris: Éditions du Myrte, 1948), 116.

10. Roderic MacLeod and Denis Kelly, eds., *The Ironside Diaries, 1937–1940* (London: Constable, 1962), 81–82; also Bethell, *The War Hitler Won*, 106–9.

11. See G. Roton, *Années cruciales* (Paris: Charles-Lavauzelle, 1947), 20; Gamelin, *Servir*, 1:33. According to other sources, Gamelin expressed much more optimistic views at the conference. See Bonnet, *Defense de la paix*, 2:313–14.

12. Churchill, *The Gathering Storm*, 384.

13. Armengaud, *Batailles politigues et militaires sur l'Europe*, 91–93.

14. See (Louis-A.) Faury, "La Pologne Terrassée," *Revue Historique de l'Armée* (Paris) 9, no. 1 (1953):132–36.

15. MacLeod and Denis, *Time Unguarded*, 78–85.

16. J. R. M. Butler, *History of the Second World War: United Kingdom Military Series. Grand Strategy. Volume II September 1939–June 1941* (London: Her Majesty's Stationery Office, 1957), 10–12, 55–56, 81. Hereafter cited as Butler, *Grand Strategy*. For the transcripts of the Polish-British General Staffs Conferences in Warsaw, May 1939, see *Protocols of the Polish-British General Staffs Conferences in Warsaw, May 1939* (London: General Sikorski Historical Institute, 1958); also *Protocols of the Polish-French General Staffs Conferences in Paris, May 1939* (London: General Sikorski Historical Institute, 1958).

17. See *DBFP*, 3rd series, 5, enclosure 2, 43.

18. *DBFP*, 3rd series, 6:245–46, 405–9, 557.

19. Noël, *L'Aggression allemande contre la Pologne*, 387–88; for details on negotiations, see Lukasiewicz, *Papers and Memoirs*, 223–33.

20. *TMWC*, 14:64–65.

Chapter Twenty

War and Peace in Soviet Diplomacy, 1939

After the destruction of Czechoslovakia's independence in March 1939, both Great Britain and France—finally recognizing that only force could stop Nazi expansion—approached the Soviet Union in hopes of creating a common front. They encountered a cautious reception and were asked for many clarifications. Because of the complex international situation in the spring and summer of 1939, Moscow had more than one possible course of action. Each possessed advantages and risks.

The Franco-British proposals aimed at both securing Russia's military cooperation in the event Hitler continued his policy of conquest and at preventing Hitler from embarking upon new adventures. Were Hitler confronted with the solidarity of great powers determined to defend any prospective victim, he might well reflect. In either case, the preservation of the status quo in central-eastern Europe, particularly the protection of Poland and Romania, was a basic feature of the early proposals.

The countries lying between Germany and Russia were strongly anti-Communist. In the past, all of them had refused to conclude any mutual-assistance pacts with Moscow; all of them feared and distrusted the Soviet Union. Their protection could hardly have been a goal in itself for the Kremlin, unless it offered some political or territorial gains. If demands for such gains were not approved by Paris and London, Moscow could refuse to join the proposed Franco-British defense system.

Such an act would not necessarily preclude French and British cooperation if Germany attacked the Soviet Union itself. Having no common frontier with Germany, Russia was already protected by the British-French guarantees to Poland and Romania. Before attacking Russia, Germany was likely to attack at least one of these countries first, thus automatically involving Great Britain and France in a war. There was no need, as far as the Soviet government was concerned, to assume new commitments in order to ensure British and French collaboration in case of war. On the contrary, it was the British and the French who, having already committed themselves, now needed Russia's commitments. These commitments Moscow could refuse or assume for a price. Would the Western democracies be willing to pay the price?

The Soviet position vis-à-vis Germany also offered opportunities. Hitler's decision to settle accounts with Poland had been evident since April 1939. Consequently, Russia's neutrality or cooperation was bound to be attractive to him. It would guarantee an easy victory and preclude a two-front war, which he always wanted to avoid. How much was that neutrality worth to him, and what price would he be willing to pay?

The Soviet leaders certainly realized that their refusal to join the Western-initiated defense system could only encourage Hitler to continue his conquests. In view of the Franco-British obligations already assumed, this meant a war in which Germany would have to fight Great Britain and France. Such a war also might offer advantages to Moscow. The enemies of Communism—Nazi Germany and the "bourgeois democracies"—would fight each other, while Russia, if it stayed out of the conflict, would preserve or even increase its strength. Was it not natural for the Soviet Union to stay out of such a war?

The Soviet leaders must have realized as well that if Germany attacked Poland and overran it, Russia's boundaries would become wide open to Nazi aggression. But was it inevitable that Hitler would then give orders to attack the Soviet Union? After all, this would mean opening a second front in his (they hoped) long and exhausting war against Great Britain and France.

All these questions, and probably many others, had to be answered before the Soviet government made decisions. To find the answers, Stalin, the undisputed steward of Soviet policies, began in the early spring of 1939 to engage in a double-decker, history-making diplomatic game.

On the one hand, he entered into discussions, both political and military, with the British and French in order to learn what they had to offer in return for Russia's cooperation. The issue was important and contained an inherent risk. Even if an agreement were reached, and Germany were contained for the time being, Hitler would still remain in power; he would still be able to maneuver; unpredictable fluctuations on the international scene would still be possible. Communist Russia did not have too many friends among the European government leaders, and the men in the Kremlin certainly realized that.

The Soviet government asked for a straight political alliance and for well-defined military commitments on the part of Great Britain and France. Furthermore, since Germany could attack Russia only through its western neighbors—Finland, Estonia, Latvia, Poland, or Romania—Moscow asked for special rights, not necessarily dependent on those neighbors' approval. In the event they were threatened by Germany or their policies reoriented in a way contrary to Russia's interests, Moscow asked for permission to take necessary military measures in order to "protect" them for the sake of Russia's own security. For all practical purposes, Moscow requested recognition of a security zone comprising territory from Finland to Romania.

Simultaneously, and in the greatest secrecy, Stalin initiated negotiations with the Nazis, trying to determine what price Hitler was willing to pay for Russia's neutrality in his intended attack on Poland. It eventually became clear that the Western powers, though ready to conclude an alliance with Russia, were in no position to assume military commitments commensurate with the war effort expected of the Soviet Union if Germany moved eastward.[1] Until very late, they were also more interested in preserving the status quo than in recognizing Russia's "special interests" in central-eastern Europe. Not surprisingly, all countries from Finland to Romania registered their opposition to such recognition.

It was different with the Nazis. Not only did Hitler, after some hesitation, accept Moscow's request for an understanding, but ultimately he agreed to pay for Russia's neutrality, recognizing large areas in eastern Europe as a Soviet sphere of interest. This evidently determined the course of Soviet diplomacy. It also made a Nazi attack on Poland inevitable.

Stalin's first public, though cryptic, initiative for an understanding with Germany took place on March 10, just a few days before the Nazi seizure of Prague. In a speech to the Eighteenth Congress of the All-Union Communist Party held in Moscow, he described the situation in Europe, sharply criticizing the policy of the Western powers, which had substituted for the concept of "collective security" a policy of "nonintervention." The goal of their new policy, he sarcastically observed, was not an attempt to stop Fascist expansion but rather to direct it away from themselves.

The speech was markedly conciliatory toward Germany. Stalin showed readiness to develop economic relations with the Reich and stated that he did not believe Germany planned to seize the Ukraine, in spite of the "hullabaloo raised by the British, French, and American press." He noted that "it looks as if the object of this suspicious hullabaloo was to incense the Soviet Union against Germany, to poison the atmosphere and to provoke a conflict with Germany without any visible grounds." The Communist party, he concluded, "would not allow" Russia "to be drawn into conflicts by warmongers who are accustomed to get others to pull the chestnuts out of the fire for them." He even suggested that the Anti-Comintern Pact was directed against the Western democracies rather than against the Soviet Union.[2] The Congress's deliberations were followed by attacks on France and Great Britain in the Soviet press.

The first Franco-British attempt to establish cooperation with Russia took place three days after the Nazi occupation of Czechoslovakia and amid rumors that Romania was in danger. On March 18 Halifax proposed that France, the Soviet Union, and Poland join Britain in a public declaration of mutual understanding, in case of a "threat to the political independence of any European state." The French government agreed without delay. The Soviets agreed in principle, asking that the Baltic, Balkan, and Scandinavian states participate in the declaration. They also suggested that an Anglo-Franco-Romanian-Soviet conference be summoned first, preferably in Bucharest.[3]

But Poland opposed the plan. So did Romania.[4] And the British initiative came to naught.

Although Bonnet shared apprehensions about Soviet foreign policy, he was determined to bring Russia into the anti-Nazi defense system at any cost. He wanted, first, to conclude a direct Soviet-French military agreement and, second, to secure direct Soviet aid for the eastern European countries in case of German aggression, even against their own wish. Only Moscow's agreement on both points could make the Franco-Soviet pact of mutual assistance (concluded in 1935) operative, he reasoned.[5]

As to the first point, on April 5 the Quai d'Orsay proposed immediate negotiations on the subject of a military convention. Moscow did not refuse but demanded that Great Britain assume the same obligations toward the Soviet Union that France already had or would assume in the future. As to the second point, Bonnet proposed an agreement that would have the USSR assist Poland and Romania in case of war. Since both of them refused to enter into any mutual-assistance pacts with Russia, he suggested that the agreement, as well as the negotiations, be kept secret.[6] The suggestion blatantly disregarded the stipulations of the Franco-Polish alliance prohibiting such dealings. But the stakes were high and the danger imminent. Besides, by that time, Poland's position in Paris was low and Beck's policies were generally held in disrepute. Obviously the Quai d'Orsay did not feel bound by the terms of the alliance.

In London governmental circles, Polish and Romanian opposition to any military collaboration with Russia aroused more understanding than in Paris. But the cabinet felt that the impasse had to be broken. By then a most disquieting message came from the British ambassador in Moscow, Sir William Seeds. He felt that Poland's and Romania's attitude might push Russia into an isolationist, neutral position. The Soviet leaders, he reasoned, were pretty sure that if Germany attacked Poland or Romania, Great Britain and France would go to war regardless of Moscow's attitude. But then, he argued, they might hope that even if Germany overran those countries, Hitler would have no interest in attacking Russia and increasing the number of his enemies. Thus, Moscow had reason to feel relatively safe. Furthermore, once the war broke out, the Soviets could engage in a "profitable business" of selling supplies. The ambassador urged that pressure be brought upon Poland and Romania to enter into a military cooperation with Russia as soon as possible and certainly *before* the war started.[7]

By the time Seeds's message reached London on April 14, the Foreign Office had already dispatched a new proposal to Moscow—a unilateral Soviet guarantee similar to the British and French guarantees. In the event of aggression against any European neighbor of Russia that was militarily resisted by the victim, the assistance of the Soviet Union would be available *if desired*.[8] The proposal recognized Warsaw's and Bucharest's objections and was agreeable to both.

The Soviet counterproposals, put forth on April 18, deepened the impasse. First, Moscow asked that Russia's northwestern neighbors—Finland, Estonia, and Latvia—be covered by the same guarantees as Poland and Romania. Germany might try to expand into that region, it was argued, and thus directly threaten the Soviet Union. The Soviet government had a duty to protect those countries for its own sake. Then Great Britain, France, and Russia would have to conclude a mutual-assistance pact. In the event of a German attack against any of the countries covered by the guarantees, the signatories of the pact would bring all aid, including military, to the victim of the aggression. The form, extent, and circumstances of that aid were not specified, and, more important, it was to be given again regardless of whether the "protected" countries wanted it or not. Ominously, the Soviet government also asked London to inform Warsaw formally that British guarantees were meant to cover *only German* aggression. Moreover, Poland and Romania were either to declare their mutual-assistance pact, covering the eventuality of Soviet aggression, as null and void, or make that pact cover any—not only Soviet—aggression.[9]

Although Moscow's proposals had no chance of being approved voluntarily by any of Russia's neighbors, the French, considering agreement with Moscow absolutely necessary, decided to accept them. But the British dissented, mainly in consideration of the opposition offered by Poland.[10] Some new solutions had to be devised.

Ten days later, on April 28, Halifax presented a new formula that seemed to solve the difficulties. He suggested that Russia, on its own initiative, declare unilaterally that it would render assistance to Great Britain and France if they became involved in a war on account of their previous public guarantees. Neither Poland nor Romania would be mentioned directly, although, in case of war, they would obviously be affected by the content of the declaration. The formula, which left Poland freedom of decision as to cooperation with Russia if war actually broke out, was approved by Warsaw.[11] Moscow, however, rejected it on May 15, arguing that it did not provide for reciprocity and did not cover the Baltic states.[12]

Although the key British government officials did show an understanding of Beck's apprehensions and objections, by then many criticized the Poles. In particular, Lloyd George and Churchill disapproved of Poland's fears and its distrust of Russia and raised their voices in the House of Commons. On May 4 Churchill gave vent to his disappointment over the delay in the British-French-Soviet negotiations by observing that Britain and France had a right "to call upon Poland not to place obstacles in the way of common cause." He urged rapid conclusion of a pact with Moscow. "There is no means of maintaining an Eastern Front against Nazi aggression without the active aid of Russia,"[13] he warned.

Simultaneously with Litvinov's proposal of the triple Anglo-French-Soviet military alliance, on April 17 Weizsaecker was "enigmatically" approached by the Soviet ambassador, Alexei Merekalov. The latter observed that:

Ideological differences of opinion had hardly influenced the Russian-Italian relationship, and they did not have to prove a stumbling block with regard to Germany either. Soviet Russia had not exploited the present friction between Germany and the Western democracies against [Germany], nor did she desire to do so. There exists for Russia no reason why she should not live with [Germany] on a normal footing. And, from normal, the relations might become better and better. [14]

Merekalov's declaration, the significance of which Weizsaecker duly reported, produced immediate and noticeable results. The Nazi press stopped its attacks on the USSR. Even more striking, in a speech on April 28 Hitler failed to denounce Communism, probably for the first time in his public career.

A few days later Moscow took a further step. On May 3 Litvinov—a "champion" of collective security and of British-Franco-Soviet anti-Nazi cooperation, and also a Jew—was dismissed. His successor was Vyacheslav Molotov, a powerful member of the Politburo enjoying a reputation as a Soviet "nationalist." Two days later Georgi Astakhov, counselor at the Soviet embassy, called on Dr. Karl Schnurre of the Auswärtiges Amt to inquire whether the new nomination "would cause a change in Germany's attitude toward the Soviet Union."

On May 17 Astakhov approached Schnurre again and cautiously commented that "there was no reason for enmity" between Germany and Russia. He referred specifically to the Rapallo treaty of 1922 and pointedly expressed skepticism about the Anglo-Franco-Soviet negotiations. Three days later Molotov went further. In his conversation with Schulenburg, he applied some pressure, observing that the "Soviet Government could only agree to resumption of [economic] negotiations if the necessary 'political basis' for them had been found." Molotov was vague and cautious, but Schulenburg easily caught the meaning of the observation and in his report to Berlin commented that "it cannot be understood otherwise than that the resumption of our [German-Soviet] economic negotiations does not satisfy him [Molotov] as a political gesture and that he apparently wants to obtain from us more extensive proposals of a political nature." Molotov's initiative surprised Schulenburg, who recommended that Berlin proceed with "extreme caution." Hitler agreed and instructed his ambassador in Moscow to be careful and to wait for the Soviet side to make more specific proposals. [15]

In the meantime, Anglo-French-Soviet negotiations continued, and it seemed in Paris and London as if some progress was being made. Initially the

British wanted to avoid a direct alliance with Russia, trying instead to commit Moscow to the defense of Germany's neighbors and prospective victims only. Hard-pressed by the French, London eventually gave its basic approval of Moscow's proposals of April 18. The British and the French governments both agreed to come to Russia's assistance in case of either a direct German attack or a war resulting from Russia's aid to a victim of German aggression. Their only condition was that Russia's aid to any country covered by the guarantees would have to be agreed upon by that country or, in the case of a neutral country, would come in response to an appeal for aid.[16] Although the formulation of the draft did not respond entirely to Moscow's demands, both London and Paris were optimistic as to Soviet reaction.

At that time, Hitler was still uncertain whether Germany's policy toward Russia should be reoriented and, if so, to what extent. But he also realized the portentous significance of the Anglo-French-Soviet negotiations. An alliance among those three powers would mean an effective encirclement of Germany and frustration of his decision to break Poland. An alliance among Great Britain, France, and Russia might also preclude any future expansion of Germany. Hitler apparently concluded that only some immediate initiative on his part might prevent Moscow from joining the Western powers. The matter seemed urgent because, on May 24, Chamberlain announced that an agreement between Great Britain and the Soviet Union was imminent.

Three days after the Franco-British draft was forwarded to Moscow—on May 30—Weizsaecker summoned Astakhov and told him that if the Soviet government responded to the British "enticements," any normalization of German-Soviet relations would become impossible. He hinted at such a normalization and assured the Soviet diplomat that Germany had no designs on the Ukraine. The rumors to the contrary were due to Beck's intrigues and his personal "interpretation" of German plans and policies. He pointed out that Germany's agreement to the incorporation of Carpatho-Ukraine by Hungary represented the best "refutation" of suspicions that Berlin wanted to play the Ukrainian card against Russia. He also observed that because of the recent strain on German-Polish relations, Berlin now had more freedom of action against Poland.[17]

The Soviet reaction was instantaneous. The following day, Molotov, in his public report to the Supreme Soviet, sharply criticized negotiations with Great Britain and France and emphasized Moscow's right to conclude an economic agreement with Berlin.[18] Even more important, he also raised new issues in his negotiations with the British and the French.

On June 2 the Soviet government formally proposed its own draft of a treaty with France and Great Britain. It provided for mutual assistance in the event either country was directly attacked or was involved in war resulting from "aggression" against Belgium, Greece, Turkey, Romania, Poland, Latvia, Estonia, and Finland. The "assistance" given to any of these countries would not be conditioned either by their agreement to or request for it. The treaty would not take effect until a special agreement specifying the extent of each signatory's military contribution was also concluded. [19]

The proposals, if accepted, would give Russia a right, in the event of war, to occupy any of its neighboring states under the pretext of protecting them from aggression. That such might be the result all Russia's neighbors were strongly convinced, and when informed about Molotov's proposals, all registered their opposition. Warsaw did it through the Polish ambassador in London, Count Edward Raczyński, on June 10, as did the representatives of Latvia, Estonia, Finland, and Romania. [20] Daladier himself did not hesitate to raise the issue bluntly with the Soviet ambassador in Paris. Both the Quai d'Orsay and the Foreign Office understood the Soviet proposals as a formal demand for a free hand in central-eastern Europe. [21]

At that time, Nazi anti-Polish war propaganda reached its peak. This indicated that Franco-British commitments vis-à-vis Poland did not suffice to make Hitler pause. It was becoming more and more obvious that only Russia's immediate adherence to the Western system of defense might deter Nazi Germany from starting a war. Anxious to secure this adherence, the British government decided to send a special envoy, Sir William Strang, to Moscow.

Strang arrived in Moscow on June 14, and tortuous negotiations resumed. On June 16 Molotov proposed a new alternative, which was mainly a straight defensive alliance between the three powers providing for mutual assistance but only in the event of *direct* aggression against any one of them. [22] This ran against the entire Franco-British policy. The whole idea of the negotiations was to commit Russia to the defense of Germany's neighbors. Hitler had to be convinced that in the event of Germany's aggression against *any* country, Russia, Great Britain, and France would go to war jointly. Informed of the proposal, Halifax declined to consider it "except in the last resort." [23]

By then it became evident to the Western leaders that without serious concessions, the Soviet government would not join an anti-Nazi coalition. As a result, on June 27, new instructions were sent to Ambassador Seeds. Soviet terms for assistance to be accorded to all "guaranteed" countries were accepted. Halifax had only two wishes—namely, that the Netherlands and

Switzerland also be "guaranteed" and that the list of guaranteed countries be kept secret. He feared that some of them might embarrass the signatories by publicly disassociating themselves from the "guarantors." This easily might be the case with any of Russia's neighbors. Molotov was informed about the suggestions from the British and French ambassadors on July 1.[24]

Molotov's reaction surprised the ambassadors because, unexpectedly, he raised a new demand. "Indirect" aggression should also entitle the "guarantors" to give "assistance." Two days later, on July 3, an official Soviet note specified that "an internal coup d'etat or a reversal of policy in the interests of the aggressor" would have to be considered an "indirect aggression." This definition, the note emphasized, should apply to all "guaranteed" countries: Estonia, Latvia, Finland, Poland, Romania, Turkey, Greece, and Belgium. The note rejected the proposal to extend the guarantee to the Netherlands and Switzerland, unless Poland and Turkey agreed to conclude mutual-assistance pacts with the Soviet Union.[25]

The acceptance of the Soviet proposal would give Russia a right to "assist" any of its neighbors under practically any circumstances, even in peacetime, regardless of the wish of the country concerned. Any change of, say, a cabinet minister might be interpreted by Moscow as being "in the interest of the aggressor," and the Red Army might occupy the territory in order to bring "assistance." The British, realizing that the countries concerned would never approve of such an arrangement—and by now more strongly than ever distrusting Moscow's motives—reluctantly declined. The negotiations nevertheless continued, in no small measure due to the insistence of the French. Daladier was firmly convinced that only an alliance among Great Britain, France, and Russia, and the latter's commitment of support in the event of Germany's aggression against Poland or any other country, could deter Hitler from war. So was Bonnet, who sent a personal message to Halifax, dated July 19, urging him to conclude an agreement with Russia on whatever terms.[26]

While forging ever-closer links with the Auswärtiges Amt and simultaneously upping the price for Russia's cooperation with the Western democracies, the Narkomindel did not neglect Poland. On May 7 Molotov congratulated the Polish ambassador, Grzybowski, on Beck's May 5 speech. He "especially emphasized how much he had been impressed by [Beck's] words on national honour."[27] Three days later, Vladimir Potemkin, deputy commissar for foreign affairs, visited Warsaw and—according to a special circular sent by Beck to all Polish diplomatic missions abroad—assured the Poles that the Soviet leaders were ready to support Poland on Warsaw's conditions:

The Soviets realize that the Polish Government is not prepared to enter any agreement with either one of Poland's great neighbors against the other and understand the advantages to them of this attitude. . . .

Mr. Potemkin also stated that in the event of an armed conflict between Poland and Germany, the Soviets will adopt *une attitude bienveillante* toward us [Poland].

As Mr. Potemkin himself later indicated, his statements were made in accordance with special instructions which the Soviet government had sent to Warsaw for him.[28]

Following Potemkin's declaration in Warsaw, the Soviet officials continued to demonstrate their willingness to help Poland in the event of German aggression. There were vague suggestions that Russia might supply Poland with arms. True, a formal agreement on conditions never materialized, but goodwill seemed to be there. On May 31 Molotov included in his report to the Supreme Soviet a paragraph referring to Poland in warm and friendly terms. He referred approvingly to the Polish-Soviet communiqué of November 26, 1938, as "confirming the development of good neighborly relations between the USSR and Poland" and concluded by emphasizing "all-around improvement" in Polish-Soviet relations.[29] Two days later, on June 2, a similar declaration was made by the newly appointed Soviet ambassador in Warsaw. As a result, Beck instructed Grzybowski to seek a special agreement in Moscow for the passage of Western supplies in the event of German attack. Again, although publicly the Soviet government denied committing itself to supply Poland with raw materials in case of war, *secretly* Potemkin assured the Polish ambassador that once Poland *actually* found itself in war, everything would probably change, and Moscow would give permission for the transit.[30]

While the Franco-British-Soviet negotiations were dragging in Moscow, the supersecret Nazi-Soviet contacts in Berlin were taking more and more concrete shape. On June 14, the day Strang arrived in Moscow, Astakhov let the Nazi authorities know through the Bulgarian minister in Berlin that if Germany concluded a nonaggression pact with Russia, the Soviet government "would probably refrain from concluding a treaty with England." Three days later, he told Schulenburg, who was passing through Berlin, that good German-Soviet relations had served both countries well in the past. "The whole course of history had shown that Germany and Russia had always done well when they had been friends, and badly when they had been enemies," he said. Hitler, however, was still hesitant. As late as June 30 instructions were sent to Schulenburg to be noncommittal. But he was also informed that Berlin considered it "important" that Moscow "had taken the initiative for the rapprochement."[31]

Soon after, Hitler did make up his mind. In the second part of July his military command submitted the final plans for an attack against Poland. The attack, if executed in 1939, had to be mounted in a matter of weeks. The usual fall rains might make many Polish areas inaccessible to mechanized divisions. Thus, Russia's neutrality, essential all along, now became urgent. Furthermore, Hitler must have feared that Franco-British-Soviet negotiations might still produce some understanding, impeding all his plans. From mid-July on it was Hitler who would press for a Nazi-Soviet agreement to be concluded as speedily as possible.

On July 22 Schulenburg received instructions "to pick up the threads again," and four days later, in Berlin, Schnurre told Astakhov that the interests of the German and Soviet policies did not conflict and their ideological differences were balanced by their mutual opposition to capitalist democracies. He warned against Russia's understanding with Britain, suggested a full-fledged agreement, and clearly indicated that Berlin was ready to pay a price for it:

> What could England offer Russia? At best, participation in a European war and the hostility of Germany, but not a single desirable end for Russia.
>
> What could we offer on the other hand? Neutrality and staying out of a possible European conflict and, if Moscow wishes, a German-Russian understanding on mutual interest, which, just as in former times, would work out to the advantage of both countries.[32]

This time Astakhov answered without even asking for time to receive instructions. He unhesitatingly indicated Soviet interest in the Baltic countries, in Finland, and in Romania. He inquired cautiously if Germany had any interest in Polish Galicia. Casually, he asked if Germany had any designs on the Ukraine. Schnurre vehemently denied any such interest or designs and, as for the areas enumerated by Astakhov, he assured the Soviet diplomat that Germany would present no obstacles.

Three days later, on July 29, Schulenburg was ordered to inform Molotov officially that Germany recognized Russia's "vital interests" in Poland and the Baltic states, while in Berlin Ribbentrop made a similar declaration to the Soviet chargé d'affaires on August 2. Ribbentrop mentioned that in case of war with Poland, the latter would be crushed in a week. Therefore, he suggested a German-Soviet understanding on the future of Poland. On August 10 Schnurre bluntly asked Astakhov what exactly the Soviet interests in Poland were. This time, Astakhov refused to give the answer without specific instructions. Two days later he informed Schnurre that the Soviet government would like to discuss the Polish as well as other problems and proposed Moscow as the place for negotiations.[33] Informed about the conversation, Schulenburg advised that Ribbentrop go to Moscow immediately.

Molotov received the offer of Ribbentrop's visit with "interest" and a "warm welcome," but he did not seem to be in any hurry. Such a visit, he argued, had to be prepared and, first, preliminary negotiations had to be concluded so that when the German foreign minister came to Moscow, "concrete decisions" could be made.[34] Was Stalin afraid of some trap? Did he still want to continue the negotiations with the French and British missions? Was he still weighing Western and Nazi concessions, biding his time with both?

In the third week of July it seemed to Paris and London that the Franco-British-Soviet negotiations were about to be successfully concluded in Moscow. On July 23 the British and French ambassadors formally informed Molotov that their governments agreed to simultaneous conclusion of political and military pacts. The Soviet demand for the unconditional right to protect "guaranteed" countries in the event of not only "direct" but also "indirect" aggression was accepted. The only demand Paris and London made was a formula of "assistance" that would preclude "interference in internal affairs" of any given country. The countries covered by the guarantees were to be enumerated in a special protocol; all Russia's western neighbors would be included, in addition to Greece, Turkey, and Belgium. The protocol was to be secret, so that the "guaranteed" countries would not be exposed to Hitler's wrath. Thus, after several months of negotiations, Moscow's demands, all of them, were approved.[35]

When the French and British representatives made their declaration, the Soviet leaders were still awaiting Hitler's final answer to their proposals for an agreement. This might have been responsible for Molotov's reaction, because he still demurred. The Soviet government, he said, could not sign the agreement before the military convention was worked out in all details. Paris and London had no choice but to dispatch their military representatives— General Joseph Doumenc and Admiral Sir Reginald Plunkett-Drax, respectively. They arrived in Moscow on August 11—an unfortunate delay under the circumstances.

Three days after their arrival, Marshal Clementi Voroshilov, representing the Red Army, confronted them with demands never before advanced, which created a new situation. In the event of war, the Red Army would have to occupy the main islands and ports of the Baltic states and have free passage through Poland and Romania. In Poland, he specified, the Red Army would have to occupy Lvov and Vilna. It was up to the French and British governments to obtain formal consent from the countries in question. The Red Army could not watch passively while those countries were being destroyed by Germany just because their governments were unwilling to ask for Soviet aid, he explained.[36]

As Voroshilov was making the declaration, the foundation for the Nazi-Soviet agreement had already been laid down and Ribbentrop's visit to Moscow already decided upon. Neither the French nor the British governments had any way of knowing that for Russia's cooperation Stalin was now demanding from them virtually the same price that he already knew Hitler would pay, namely, approval of Soviet expansion into the Baltic states, eastern Poland, and Romania. Did that mean that he still wanted to have alternatives? That if his new demands were approved, there was still a possibility, even at such a late hour, that Russia might accede to the Western system of defense? Without access to the Kremlin's archives, no answer can be offered.

By August, it became evident to the Western leaders that some sort of a dramatic showdown was near unless the new Soviet demands were met. Both the French and the British ambassador in Moscow considered those demands "justified" and strongly advised pressing the Poles and the Romanians for their assent. Without any delay, appropriate instructions were sent to Kennard and Noël, and without any delay they contacted the Polish authorities, arguing that to leave such an important matter as Soviet military aid to the negotiations *after* the German attack would be futile.[37]

The Poles were immovable. Poland's acceptance of Moscow's demands, argued Beck, would probably provoke Germany into a war "immediately." He did not exclude the possibility that even Voroshilov's request might be a provocation. If Poland agreed, the Soviets would probably inform Hitler about it themselves. Besides, he was not convinced at all that once the Red Army occupied the eastern part of Poland, Russia would fight Germany. "This is a new partition which we are asked to sign; if we are to be partitioned, we shall at least defend ourselves," he told Noël. The Poles had no doubt that once the Red Army entered their country, Communism would be imposed. "With the Germans we are risking our freedom. With the Russians we lose our soul,"[38] said Śmigly-Rydz.

Warsaw's stand evoked bitter criticism, particularly in Paris. Daladier considered it folly. As he angrily told Ambassador Bullitt on August 18, the Soviet demands were justified and bona fide. He understood that the Poles were reluctant to have the Red Army in their territories. But he also considered that once Poland had been attacked by Germany, the Poles should be happy to have anyone's assistance. France could guarantee that the Soviet forces would eventually evacuate Poland. Besides, both France and Great Britain could send some of their own land forces to Poland so that there would be an international, not just a Soviet, contingent there. Daladier seemed extremely excited and frustrated. He repeated three times that should the Poles persist in rejecting the Soviet offer, he would not send a "single peasant" to die in defense of Poland.[39]

The next day, August 19, Bonnet instructed Noël to tell Beck that France as an ally had a right to ask just how Poland proposed to resist Germany without Russia's help. Beck's frequently expressed wish for the successful conclusion of the Anglo-Franco-Soviet negotiations was misleading, he argued, since evidently Poland's refusal to cooperate with Russia precluded any possibility of success from the very beginning. He urged Noël to do his best in order to secure some formula for a Polish-Soviet military cooperation. Noël's intervention resulted in a complete fiasco.[40]

The day the Anglo-French-Soviet military discussions started, August 12, the Auswärtiges Amt received information that Molotov was ready to discuss all questions, Poland's future included. Two days later Schulenburg received detailed instructions to solemnly inform the Soviet government that Germany would agree to settle all questions "between the Baltic Sea and the Black Sea" to the "complete satisfaction" of both countries, and that "German-Russian policy . . . has come to an historic turning point." On August 16 Ribbentrop asked for an immediate meeting with Stalin and Molotov. Only three days later, the Soviet draft of the pact was dispatched to Berlin. The next day, the approval, accompanied by Hitler's personal message to Stalin, was sent to Moscow. In answer, Stalin thanked Hitler for the "assent of the German Government to the conclusion of a nonaggression pact."[41] The next day, August 22, Ribbentrop's visit to Moscow was announced publicly. Hitler summoned his commanders the same day to discuss the attack on Poland, which he scheduled for August 26.

The public announcement of Ribbentrop's trip to Moscow fell upon Europe like a bombshell. The same day Bonnet instructed Noël to ask Beck for Poland's "sacrifice." Warsaw, the instruction ran, should immediately give General Doumenc in Moscow carte blanche as to its approval of the passage of Soviet troops through Poland. Otherwise the responsibility for the failure of Franco-British-Soviet negotiations would fall on the Poles. On Paris's request, Kennard received instructions to support Noël in his dramatic representation.[42] Of course, neither the French nor the British knew for certain that the Nazi-Soviet agreement had been decided and the destruction of Poland and the Baltic states as well as the partition of Romania virtually agreed upon.

The joint Noël-Kennard representation made in Warsaw failed. Although this time Beck did not exclude the "possibility" of the German-Soviet agreement "for a partition of Poland," he refused to yield. Realizing the gravity of the situation, he did agree, however, to a carefully phrased formula. General Doumenc was authorized to declare in Moscow that the French government had "learned for certain that in the event of common action against German aggression, collaboration, under technical conditions to be settled subsequently between Poland and the U.S.S.R. [was] not excluded."[43]

The hour was late, and in a frantic attempt to keep Russia away from Germany, Paris went far beyond Beck's authorization. That very evening, General Doumenc, acting under instructions, formally declared to Voroshilov that France was ready to sign an agreement to the Soviet request for military passage through Poland. The declaration was never authorized by Warsaw. Nor was it sponsored by the British government. Nor did it produce any positive results. It was not France's approval but Poland's that was sought, answered Voroshilov, and on this note the discussion ended.[44]

A few hours later the Nazi-Soviet pact was signed. Two days later, on August 25, the Franco-British-Soviet negotiations were officially terminated by Molotov.

The Nazi-Soviet pact, signed in the late hours of August 23 in Moscow by Ribbentrop and Molotov, was a mutual commitment to nonaggression. According to Article 1, in case one party was involved in a military conflict, the other party was to maintain neutrality. The usual formula used in nonaggression pacts—namely, "unprovoked aggression"—was significantly omitted. Regardless of whether one party *was attacked* or *committed an act of aggression*, the other signatory was to remain neutral. Article 3 stipulated that both governments would consult with each other on mutually important problems.

Article 4 stipulated that the signatories would not participate "in any grouping of Powers whatsoever, that is directly or indirectly aimed at the other Party." It was this provision that bound the Soviet Union to break the negotiations with Great Britain and France. They "aimed" at Germany. The pact was concluded for ten years and entered into force at the moment of its signing.

For all practical purposes, the agreement was a pact of aggression. The secret protocol divided eastern Europe into two "spheres of interest," and its provisions directly concerned Finland, Latvia, Lithuania, Estonia, Poland, and Romania. Any political and territorial changes were to be effected by mutual accord. Finland, Latvia, Estonia, the eastern half of Poland, and Bessarabia were recognized as the Soviet sphere. The western half of Poland and all of Lithuania were assigned to Germany. [45]

As soon as the agreement was signed, a champagne party in honor of Ribbentrop took place at the Kremlin. It was marked by a feeling of triumph and mutual satisfaction. "It has been Stalin who through his speech in March of this year, which had been well understood in Germany, has brought about the reversal in [Nazi-Soviet] political relations," Molotov solemnly declared. [46] As for Stalin, he addressed himself directly to his peer in Berlin and proposed a toast to the Führer.

Soviet diplomacy played its role to the end, and its efforts to strengthen Polish opposition to German demands continued even after the conclusion of the Nazi-Soviet pact. On August 24 Sharonov assured Beck that the Nazi-Soviet pact would not change the attitude of the Soviet government toward Poland. On August 27, three days before the German attack and just three weeks before the Red Army invaded Poland, *Izvestya* published an interview with Voroshilov. The highest-ranking Soviet military officer suggested that it was possible for the Soviet Union to deliver raw materials and even military equipment to Poland and that no special agreement of mutual assistance or military convention was necessary for that purpose. On September 2, while German panzer divisions were already rolling into Poland, Sharonov called upon Beck and asked why the Polish government had failed to negotiate with Moscow the matter of Soviet supplies, as the "Voroshilov interview had opened up the possibility of getting them." As late as September 11, just six days before the Red Army marched into Poland, Sharonov still discussed with Szembek the problem of medical supplies from the Soviet Union and discounted the rumors about Soviet mobilization of troops. [47]

Stalin's diplomacy enabled Hitler to start a war in which Nazi Germany on the one side and the "bourgeois democracies" on the other were to fight, while Russia stood to the side, unscathed and well rewarded for its neutrality. "If those gentlemen have such an uncontrollable desire to fight, let them do their fighting without the Soviet Union. We shall see what fighting stuff they are made of," chuckled Molotov to the Supreme Soviet a few hours before the war started. As *Izvestya* reported on September 1, 1939, the audience answered with laughter and applause.

It was a hollow victory. The laughter preceded the agony and death of twenty million Soviet citizens by only twenty-two months. For on that day, Hitler must have felt that, against all odds, the hand of Providence was still guiding his steps toward his final goal—the destruction of Russia. The attainment of that goal had always depended on the Polish corridor to Russia being opened to him. Now he was to open that corridor by war and with Russia's help. In his dreams, Germany's victory would be bought cheaply. Then Russia's turn would come and the indestructible foundations for his Thousand-Year Reich would be finally laid down. "Now I have the whole world in my pocket,"[48] he shouted deliriously upon receiving the news that Stalin had agreed to speed up the conclusion of the pact. The Great Vandal had his great day.

NOTES

1. For the minutes of the Franco-British-Soviet military negotiations in Moscow, see *DBFP*, 3rd series, 7:558–614.

2. Degras, *Soviet Documents*, 3:319–23.

3. *DBFP*, 3rd series, 4:400, 490–91, 467.

4. Ibid., 578–79; also 5:312–13.

5. See the minutes of his conference in London on March 21, 1939, *DBFP*, 3rd series, 4:422–27.

6. Bonnet, *Défense de la paix*, 2:176–80, 190; see also *DBFP*, 3rd series, 5:216.

7. *DBFP*, 3rd series, 5:104.

8. Ibid., 205–6; also Strang, *Home and Abroad*, 162–63.

9. *DBFP*, 3rd series, 5:228–29; also Bonnet, *Défense de la paix*, 2:182. For the text of the proposals, Degras, *Soviet Documents*, 3:329.

10. *DBFP*, 3rd series, 5:268; see also Bonnet, *Défense de la paix*, 2:186–87.

11. *DBFP*, 3rd series, 5:357, 378.

12. For the text of the Soviet note, see Degras, *Soviet Documents*, 3:330–31.

13. Churchill, *The Gathering Storm*, 365.

14. *DGFP*, series D, 6:266–67.

15. Ibid., 429, 536, 547, 558, respectively.

16. Strang, *Home and Abroad*, 167–68.

17. *DGFP*, series D, 6:604–9.

18. Degras, *Soviet Documents*, 3:337.

19. *DBFP*, 3rd series, 5:753–54.

20. Ibid., 6:24–25, 48–49, 95–96, 120–22; 5:746–47, respectively.

21. Strang, *Home and Abroad*, 168–69; for Bullitt's report on Bonnet's and Daladier's opinion, *FRUS*, 1939, 1:266–70.

22. Degras, *Soviet Documents*, 3:349.

23. *DBFP*, 3rd series, 6:103–5.

24. Ibid., 173–74.

25. Ibid., 230–32, 251–52, 313, 450–51.

26. *DBFP*, 3rd series, 6:396–98; also France, *Les événements* 9:2669–74 (Bonnet's testimony).

27. *PWB*, 208.

28. *PWB*, 183; also *DBFP*, 3rd series, 5:657.

29. Supra, 351.

30. Degras, *Soviet Documents*, 3:327, 328; *PWB*, 184, 208, respectively.

31. *DGFP*, series D, 6:729, 741–42, 813, 911, respectively.

32. Ibid., 1008.

33. Ibid., 1016, 1050; 7:17–20, 58–59, respectively.

34. *Nazi-Soviet Relations*, 77.

35. For Seeds's report dated July 24, see *DBFP*, 3rd series, 6:456–60.

36. For the minutes of the fourth meeting of the Franco-British-Soviet military delegates, see *DBFP*, 3rd series, 7:570–75.

37. For the full text of Seeds's memoranda dated August 15, 1939, see *DBFP*, 3rd series, 7:1–5; also 25–26, 39–40.

38. Bonnet, *Défense de las paix*, 2:280–84; Noël, *L'Aggression allemande contre la Pologne*, 423; *DBFP*, 3rd series, 7:53–54.

39. For Bullitt's report, see *FRUS*, 1939, 1:225–26.

40. See France, *Les événements*, 4:861–63 (Noël's testimony).

41. *DGFP*, series D, 7:62–64, 84–85, 150–51, 156–57, 168, respectively.

42. *DBFP*, 3rd series, 7:117, 130.

43. Ibid., 150; also Beck, *Dernier rapport*, 202–4.

44. *DBFP*, 3rd series, 7:609–13.

45. For the photostatic copies of the German and Russian texts of both the pact and the secret protocol, see Szembek, *Diariusz*, 4:752–62.

46. *DGFP*, series D, 7:228. Some seven years later, Göring and Ribbentrop expressed the same views as defendants in the Nuremburg trial, see *TMWC*, 9:345, 10:267–69; see also Ribbentrop, *The Ribbentrop Memoirs*, 111–12.

47. *PWB*, 187–89.

48. Hilger and Meyer, *The Incompatible Allies*, 300.

Chapter Twenty-One

The Anglo-Polish Pact of Mutual Assistance

Poland Misled, August 25, 1939

The announcement of the Nazi-Soviet pact of nonaggression was generally understood as no more than the Kremlin's decision not to join the anti-Nazi coalition but to stay neutral in the event of war. The Western governments did not know that the pact contained a secret protocol on war and Nazi-Soviet war spoils. They did not realize that the protocol made war inevitable. The protocol remained one of the best-guarded war secrets. Neither Stalin nor Hitler dared reveal its contents even after their countries had begun fighting each other. Even as of this writing—some forty-five years after the protocol was signed—the Kremlin has not disclosed its existence in the Soviet Union.

Unaware of the secret Nazi-Soviet understanding, both London and Paris pursued their hopeless efforts to save peace. Even with the Soviet Union's neutrality, they still hoped that Hitler might change his mind once he understood that his new aggression would undoubtedly involve Great Britain and France. Thus, they tried to convince Hitler that they would fight if Poland were militarily attacked. Every hour seemed to count. By then, thirty German divisions had moved toward the Polish borders.

On August 22, the day Ribbentrop's visit to Moscow was announced, Chamberlain solemnly warned Hitler that Britain would stand by Poland. He repeated his warning later in the day in the House of Commons. On August 24, Parliament, in a magnificent display of British efficacy and national solidarity, endowed the government with emergency powers. The measure, introduced by the home secretary, passed through three readings in the House of Commons within a few hours, obtained the consent of the Lords, and was signed by King George VI to become one of the fundamental war laws before the day was over. The next day Henderson warned Hitler again that Great Britain "could not go back on her word to Poland."[1]

On the same day, August 25, the Anglo-Polish alliance was hastily signed in London.[2] The British government leaders considered it the last possible deterrent to war.

The treaty consisted of an open, widely publicized part and a secret protocol.

Article 1 of the open text dealt with a direct aggression:

> Should one of the Contracting Parties become engaged in hostilities with a European Power in consequence of aggression by the latter . . . the other Contracting Party will at once give the Contracting Party engaged in hostilities all the support and assistance in its power.

The secret protocol stipulated that the "European Power" meant Germany.

Article 2 covered indirect aggression:

> The provisions of Article I will also apply in the event of any action by a European Power which clearly threatened, directly or indirectly, the independence of one of the Contracting Parties and was of such a nature that the Party in question considered it vital to resist it with its armed forces.
>
> Should one of the Contracting Parties become engaged in hostilities with a European Power in consequence of action by that Power which threatened the independence or neutrality of another European State in such a way as to constitute a clear menace to the security of that Contracting Party, the provisions of Article I will apply without prejudice, however, to the right of the other European State concerned.

The secret protocol specified that the countries and areas of "vital" importance to the security of both parties were the Free City of Danzig, Belgium, Holland, and Lithuania, as well as (under certain conditions) Latvia and Estonia.

Article 3 provided for mutual assistance in case of economic penetration by the "European Power" (Germany). If a war resulted from such an attempt, the provisions of Article 1 would apply. Article 4 entrusted the application of the methods of mutual assistance to the "competent naval, military and air authorities" of both countries. Article 5 imposed a duty on each party to supply the other with "complete and speedy information concerning any development which might threaten their independence."

Article 6 dealt with the obligations resulting from the pact in the future dealings of either signatory:

> (1) The Contracting Parties will communicate to each other the terms of any undertakings of assistance against aggression which they have already given or may in the future give to other States.
>
> (2) Should either of the Contracting Parties intend to give such an undertaking after the coming into force of the present agreement, the other Contracting Party shall, in order to ensure the proper functioning of the Agreement, be informed thereof.
>
> (3) Any new understanding which the Contracting Parties may enter into in the future shall neither limit their obligations under the present Agreement nor indirectly create new obligations between the Contracting Party not participating in these understandings and the third State concerned.

The secret protocol provided an interpretation of the open text:

> The undertakings mentioned in Article VI of the Agreement, should they be entered into by one of the Contracting Parties with a third State, would of necessity be so framed that their execution should at no time prejudice either the sovereignty or territorial inviolability of the other Contracting Party.

Article 6 of the pact, and particularly its interpretation in the secret protocol, were of great importance in that they imposed serious limitations on the future policies of both countries. From then on, neither country was allowed to undertake any commitments that would affect the other's sovereignty or territorial integrity.

Article 7 contained a clause of no separate peace; Article 8 stipulated that the agreement would be in force for a period of five years. If not renounced six months before the end of the five years, its validity would continue until renounced by either party at any time with six months' notice.

The obligations assumed by Great Britain on August 25 had practically no precedent. The hour, however, was late, and everything had to be done to restrain Hitler from starting a war, it was argued in Whitehall. An attack on Poland meant war with Great Britain—this was the inescapable meaning of the open text.

As in the guarantee of March 31 and the preliminary agreement of April 6, the alliance did not mean that London either opposed or excluded any peaceful compromise between Germany and Poland. On the contrary, until the last prewar days, such a compromise was still sought by the British.

As soon as the alliance was signed, Halifax strongly advised Raczyński that Poland should not oppose a "peaceful modification of the status of Danzig." Two days later Halifax asked Mussolini to inform Hitler that if he had no further demands but Danzig and the Corridor, the British government saw a possibility "within reasonable time to find a solution without war." Mussolini was requested to act as if on his own, without letting Hitler know about London's initiative. Kennard was informed about the matter and instructed to keep the whole affair in strictest secrecy.[3]

As late as August 28, three days before the invasion of Poland, Chamberlain told Dahlerus, Göring's official envoy, that "the maximum the Poles would concede would be Danzig, subject to the retention of the special Polish rights, and extraterritorial roads for Germany across the Corridor, subject to international guarantees."[4] His declaration meant that Great Britain was offering Germany what the Poles had refused to relinquish.

The British initiatives were unauthorized by and unknown to the Poles. But the moves were understandable: Neither London nor Paris considered Danzig and the Corridor crucial. Hitler's faits accomplis, his intractability, his methods, and, above all, his insatiable drive for endless conquests had to be stopped. Both capitals believed if some compromises on local or secondary issues could help, they would have to be made.

None of the British initiatives succeeded, because until the very end Hitler refused to believe that Britain or France would actually fight on account of Poland even if they declared war. Besides, since August 23 he was no longer an entirely free agent on the Polish issue. According to the secret protocol of the Nazi-Soviet pact, Germany could no longer act on its own, independently of Russia. Any territorial changes in Poland on behalf of Germany became inseparable from the Soviet "sphere of interest" in Poland, Finland, Estonia, Latvia, and Bessarabia.

As for the Poles, they did not know—they had no way of knowing—that their pact with Great Britain had no practical meaning. As had been mentioned before, already in April 1939 and then again in July 1939, the French and British general staffs agreed that in the event of war "the fate of Poland [would] depend upon the ultimate outcome of the war . . . and not on [Franco-British] ability to relieve pressure on Poland at the outset."[5]

NOTES

1. *BBB*, 125–27, 140–41, 158, respectively.

2. For the full text of the pact, see Jedrzejewicz, *Poland in the British Parliament*, 1:188–92.

3. *DBFP*, 3rd series, 7:241, 250, 267–68, 329, 336.

4. Ibid., 282.

5. *DBFP*, 3rd series, 7:333–34.

Chapter Twenty-Two

France, Great Britain, and Russia during the German-Polish Campaign

Germany attacked Poland in the early hours of September 1, 1939. Hitler, expecting neither France nor Great Britain to move militarily, sent the whole of his armored and motorized force against the Poles. Some 2,600 first-line aircraft were used. For all practical war purposes, no tanks and only about a thousand first-line aircraft were left on the western front.[1]

Hundreds of aircraft flew over industrial, transportation, and communication centers, troop concentrations, and air bases, destroying them by heavy bombing. Open cities and towns were attacked by the Stuka divebombers, creating panic, which resulted in an aimless, desperate mass movement of the population. This further contributed to general chaos and confusion. The Poles had no more than about 770 aircraft, half of which were used solely for training or were under repair. They had no more than 170 old-type fighters, unsuitable for war operations.[2] It soon became evident that Poland lacked any effective antiaircraft defenses.

Motorized panzer divisions moved in from the north, west, and south, encircling, cutting through, and crushing Polish army units. Polish infantry and artillery were no match for the Germans in modern warfare; the heroic Polish cavalry, so effective in the past, became a pathetic war relic.

Polish strategy was oriented toward defensive operations. It was based on the assumption that Germany's attack would trigger an instantaneous French and British response by land, sea, and air. Already, on September 3, at 9:00 a.m., Poland's highest military leaders informed General Armengaud that without an immediate offensive from the West, Polish resistance would probably collapse.³ No offensive materialized. Declarations of war by France and Great Britain were not even issued until three days after the Nazi invasion.

Some seventeen hours after Germany's attack against Poland—on September 1, at 9:30 p.m.—ambassadors Henderson and Coulondre handed Ribbentrop official notes demanding cessation of military operations and withdrawal of the German armies from the invaded areas. Otherwise, they declared, both France and Great Britain "would fulfill obligations" toward their Polish ally.⁴ It was not an "ultimatum" but a "warning," moderate in tone. The time limit for the withdrawal of the troops was not specified.

The next day, September 2, at 7:30 p.m., Chamberlain repeated the warning in the House of Commons. So did Daladier in the Chambre des Deputés. Chamberlain's speech, in which he expressed hope for the success of negotiations, met with overwhelming disapproval in the House. By then, he feared that his cabinet might be overthrown if he delayed the declaration of war any further.⁵

The delay was caused by expectations that somehow peace could still be restored, and they centered on Mussolini's initiative. Complying with Halifax's request, Il Duce intervened with Hitler on August 28 and then, on his own initiative, on the following day. He pointed out that the Danzig problem might be solved to Germany's satisfaction without a war. Two days later, on the eve of Germany's attack on Poland, he proposed an international conference of great powers with the purpose of revising the clauses of the Treaty of Versailles that had "cause[d] the present grave trouble in the life of Europe." On September 2, with the war already raging, he contacted Berlin, Paris, and London again, proposing the suspension of war activities and an international conference similar in character to the previous year's conference at Munich. Before declaring war on Germany, both Paris and London wanted to explore whether such a conference was still possible and whether it might be successful.⁶

Bonnet fully supported the idea of a conference as the last chance to avoid a general war. The British supported it, too, but on the condition that Poland participate, that Germany suspend war operations, and that German forces be withdrawn from the Polish territories beforehand. These demands, when presented to Hitler, were rejected. In principle, he did not oppose a conference. But he categorically refused to withdraw German forces from areas already occupied.⁷

Bonnet still did not give up. First, he approached the Poles, trying to sound them out. The reaction was not what he hoped for. Beck answered vehemently that it was not a conference that was at issue but the German aggression and Franco-British treaty obligations. Undismayed, Bonnet suggested a "compromise" solution. Let a "symbolic withdrawal" of German troops be made a condition for the conference, he told the Italian ambassador in Paris. Ciano thought, however, that the suggestion had no chance of gaining Hitler's approval. He did not even bother to inform Mussolini about it and refused to approach the chancellor.[8]

On the evening of September 2 Chamberlain and Halifax advised Daladier and Bonnet respectively that London intended to deliver a four-hour ultimatum to Berlin at 8:00 a.m. the next day. The widespread criticism of the government's failure to live up to Britain's commitments vis-à-vis Poland was growing, and Chamberlain deemed it necessary to have the problem of war declaration be resolved the next day. The French answered that they would have to wait: Women and children were not yet transferred to safe areas, mobilization was not complete, the defenses were not yet ready. In addition, Bonnet had promised Ciano to wait until noon on September 3 for the German reply to the British-French note. He would not break his promise. Even if the reply were negative, he argued, a joint forty-eight-hour ultimatum should be presented to Hitler.[9]

Unmoved, the British government decided to act alone. On September 3, at 9:00 a.m., a two-hour ultimatum was presented in Berlin; then, some fifty-five hours after Poland had been invaded, Chamberlain made a radio broadcast to the effect that a state of war existed between Great Britain and Germany. Now the French had to follow the British lead, and at noon Coulondre delivered a five-hour ultimatum to Ribbentrop. The portentous German reply stated that unless French forces actually attacked Germany, the Wehrmacht would not start war operations against France.[10] Hitler, aware of the French war strategy providing for self-defense only, did not intend to open the western front by attacking France. He would do it—successfully—eight months later.

The western front was, consequently, very quiet during the fateful days of September 1939. Neither the French nor the British initiated any meaningful military offensives. Polish appeals, more frantic and more desperate each day, were futile. From the first day of the German attack until the last day of their armed resistance, the Poles fought alone.

The inactivity of the British and French forces was due to the indecisiveness and unpreparedness of the French army command. Later on, the military would be severely criticized by the French civilian authorities, particularly

Bonnet.[11] This "inactivity," however, as was pointed out before, resulted from an inter-Allied war strategy agreed upon at the highest military level even *before* the war started, in the spring and summer of 1939.[12]

On September 4 and 6, inter-Allied military conferences (attended by Gamelin, Ironside, and Marshal of the Royal Air Force Cyril Newall) took place in Paris. All agreed that there should be no general offensive on the eastern front; that Poland would have to bear the main brunt of the German onslaught alone, suffer defeat, and then, after the war, be restored to independence. On September 8 Daladier, Gamelin, and General Vuillemin agreed that French bombers should not bomb Germany except for strictly military objectives. It was feared that bombings might provoke German retaliation against the French civilian population. The next day it was decided that the situation in Poland was desperate and that no practical purpose would be served by bombing the Reich, anyway.[13]

Similar reasoning prevailed in London. According to the British chiefs of staff, one could not establish conclusively "on available evidence" that the Luftwaffe had actually bombed the civilian population in Poland. How could one be sure that bombing Germany would not involve losses in the German civilian population? Hitler should not be provoked. On September 9 the chiefs of staff reported to the war cabinet that "on the available evidence" Germany was "probably not in violation of the generally accepted principles of war, which His Majesty's Government would propose to follow themselves."[14]

As a result, not a single bomb was dropped on Germany by Poland's allies, and not a single German bomb was dropped on France or Great Britain during the entire September campaign. According to Daladier, he did ask the British to bomb German military objectives, especially the Rhine bridges. Chamberlain, however, refused. Such bombing, he argued, could result in Germans bombing British factories. Nothing could save Poland, he concluded. According to Churchill, the French government asked the British *not* to bomb Germany because, if they did, the Luftwaffe might retaliate against French factories. The British air command "deplored" the request but complied with it nonetheless. Instead the Royal Air Force dropped propaganda leaflets over Berlin.[15]

On September 12 the Inter-Allied Supreme War Council, attended by Daladier, Gamelin, Admiral Arthur Chatfield, and General Hastings Ismay (chief of the secretariat of the British national defense), approved Gamelin's decision to end even limited land activities. It was assumed that the outcome of war in Poland could not be changed. Moreover, an argument was advanced that if the French undertook any military land activities of importance, the Germans might transfer their forces from the Polish to the western front. This, the participants agreed, should be avoided. "There is no hurry as time is on our side," Chamberlain summed up the discussions. [16]

The sloth of the Western allies during the September campaign took the Poles by surprise and later on became a matter of controversy and mutual recriminations. Once the war was over it was determined that the initial Franco-British war strategy was badly planned. With the main German forces engaged in Poland, France and Great Britain had impressive superiority over what Hitler had left on the western front. To the 1,000 German first-line aircraft, they possessed almost 3,200 aircraft, including more than 2,200 bombers and fighters. While all German panzer units fought in Poland, the French had not much less than 3,300 tanks, only a few hundred of them obsolete. Against 300 German antiaircraft guns, they had 1,600. With the majority of German divisions in Poland, the French army had tremendous numerical superiority. [17]

At the Nuremberg trials, Field Marshal Wilhelm Keitel and General Alfred Jodl authoritatively stated that the Wehrmacht, so successful in *separate* campaigns against Poland and, later on, against France, might have been unable to withstand a war on two fronts in 1939.

According to Jodl's testimony:

> Up to the year 1939 we were, of course, in a position to destroy Poland alone. But we were never, either in 1938 or 1939, actually in a position to withstand a concentrated attack by these states [Britain, France, Poland] together. And if we did not collapse already in the year 1939 that was due only to the fact that during the Polish campaign the approximately 110 French and British divisions in the west were completely inactive against 23 German divisions.

Keitel testified that British and French military inactivity during the Polish campaign was viewed by the German command as an indication that Britain and France had become reconciled to the Nazi conquest of Poland and had no serious intention of coming to Poland's aid. [18]

The final and unexpected blow to Poland came from the east.

On September 1 Schulenburg asked the Soviet government to include in its broadcasts from Minsk certain codes for German air force use. The request was granted. On September 3 Ribbentrop instructed Schulenburg to ask for the Red Army to move into the areas as defined in the secret protocol of the nonaggression pact. Molotov "agreed," although he considered the moment not yet opportune.[19] On September 8 Molotov informed Ambassador Grzybowski that Voroshilov's declaration of August 27 concerning Soviet supplies for Poland was no longer valid. Nor would the Soviet government allow "transit of a military character." General conditions and the German-Soviet agreement precluded such actions, he said.[20] A few hours later, acting upon false information that the German forces had entered Warsaw, Molotov sent an official note to Berlin conveying "congratulations and greetings to the German Reich Government." On September 14 he informed Ambassador Schulenburg that the Red Army was ready for action and that it would move as soon as Warsaw fell. On September 14 and 15, first *Pravda* and then the entire Soviet press attacked the Polish government for "cruel oppression" of national minorities, particularly the Ukrainians and the Byelorussians. They rose in "rebellion" and demanded "independence." *Tass* reported that Polish military aircraft had violated Soviet territory. Immediately Ambassador Schulenburg rushed a message to Berlin explaining that "the purpose of the article [was] to provide political justification for Soviet intervention."[21]

The Soviet invasion was not expected by the Poles. As in their relations with Hitler's Germany, miscalculations and exaggerated self-confidence prevailed in their appraisal of Russia. The dismissal of Litvinov on May 3, 1939, represented an important decision aimed at forging Nazi-Soviet collaboration. It produced widespread speculation in London and Paris that Stalin and Hitler might eventually agree to partition Poland. Having missed the portentous significance of Litvinov's dismissal, Beck welcomed it as beneficial to Polish-Soviet relations.[22] Having learned about Ribbentrop's arrival in Moscow, Ambassador Grzybowski, guided by his "inner voice," reported that the Nazi-Soviet rapprochement would be "modest" at best. Having learned one day later about the Nazi-Soviet pact, he advised his ministry that German-Soviet cooperation was "improbable." On August 29, two days before Germany's attack, and nineteen days before the Red Army crossed the Polish borders, he sent a secret report directly to Beck. The tone of the report was humorous and cheerful, opining that the pact was without value to Germany. It was signed "for effect" alone and would not stop Hitler in his efforts to negotiate. "In fact," it "considerably" improved Poland's situation.[23] Since the beginning of the German-Polish campaign, news had been coming from Russia about continuing military concentrations in western provinces. But the Poles missed their imminent significance. As late as September 12, a government conference, chaired by the president of the republic, concluded that Soviet military moves were of a preventive nature only, that Russia would not intervene militarily.[24]

Then, five days later, at 2:00 a.m., Stalin personally informed Schulenburg about the imminent Soviet attack on Poland. In a short exchange of views, the two agreed on the content of the Soviet note to be delivered to the Polish ambassador within an hour.[25] Then, at dawn, the Red Army crossed the Polish frontier.

Russia's invasion was accompanied by a joint German-Soviet declaration. Its text had been secretly agreed upon by both parties—although not without difficulties. Molotov proposed a unilateral statement, justifying the Soviet move by the collapse of the Polish government and the "necessity" for Russia to come to the aid of the Ukrainians and the Byelorussians "threatened" by Germany. When informed, Ribbentrop sharply disagreed, since, as he put it, such a declaration "makes the two states [Germany and the USSR] appear as enemies before the whole world." Instead, he proposed a draft for a joint communiqué expressing the decision of both governments "to restore peace and order in . . . their natural spheres of influence and to bring a new order by the creation of natural frontiers and viable economic organizations." At this juncture, Stalin intervened. He approved of a joint communiqué, but he did not like the German draft because "it presented the facts all too frankly." He wanted to eliminate such terms as "spheres of influence" and "natural frontiers." On the evening of September 17 he proposed his own draft, which was accepted by Berlin and immediately released. The Red Army crossed the Polish borders because both Germany and the Soviet Union had decided "to restore peace and order which had been destroyed by the disintegration of the Polish state and to help the Polish population to establish new conditions for its political life."[26]

While the Red Army was crossing the Polish borders, the Soviet press abounded with arguments justifying the invasion. "We are neutral in the Soviet fashion, not in the fashion of neutral bourgeoisie who stuff their pockets with bloodstained money. . . . Our brothers beyond the border, yesterday's slaves, will find that in the future they will live prosperously and happily,"[27] wrote the prominent Soviet writer Alexei Tolstoy.

The Soviet invasion sealed the outcome of the September campaign. A few hours later, the president of the Polish Republic, the government, and the commander in chief left the country for Romania, followed by thousands of Polish troops and civilians. The people of Warsaw still held on for ten more days. Day after day, hour after hour over the radio they implored not only the

Allies but all governments, all nations, for weapons, for food, for medicine. None arrived. Scattered military units fought on in remote areas. All were crushed in the end. After only twenty years of independence, Poland as a state collapsed once again, as it had a century and a half before.

But the Poles cannot be blamed for the fall of their country. They did not hold its destiny in their own hands. Whatever the merits or demerits of their policies, the destiny of Poland depended on the Great Powers. Surrounded by the expansionist Germany and Russia—each stronger than Poland—the policy of *equilibrium*, rational as it seemed, could not suffice. The Poles were too weak to enforce it. Reliance on France and Great Britain—treaties or no treaties—proved to be an illusion. Essentially, Poland was not much more than an object in the policies of the Great Powers—foes and friends alike—and their changeable interrelationships and momentary self-interests, real or imaginary. The Poles had no power to change that.

But the Polish people did not give up. Hardened by painful history, unshaken in their patriotism and love of freedom, they were to carry on the war. The workers and the peasants, the intelligentsia and the businessmen, the enlightened and the simple, political opponents, innocents and those who failed the nation would all join the struggle against tyranny.

Before long the Nazis were to conquer many countries—almost all of Europe. But Poland would be the one nation that would not produce a quisling government.

NOTES

1. Bethell, *The War Hitler Won*, 169–70.

2. Jerzy Kirchmayer, *Kampania Wrześniowa 1939* (*The September Campaign, 1939*) (Lodz, Poland: 1946), 1.

3. Armengaud, *Batailles*, 124–27.

4. *DBFP*, 3rd series, 7:493; also Coulondre, *De Stalin à Hitler*, 307–8.

5. Halifax, *Fullness of Days*, 210.

6. *DGFP*, series D, 7:410; *DBFP*, 3rd series, 7:442.

7. Bonnet, *Défense de la paix*, 2:335; *DBFP*, 3rd series, 7:520–21.

8. See Ciano, *The Ciano Diaries, 1939–43*, 136–37; for a review of events during the three days of war, see also Noël, *L'Aggression allemande contre la Pologne*, 469–97.

9. *DBFP*, 3rd series, 7:524–26.

10. *LJF*, 413.

11. Bonnet, *Défense de la paix*, 2:376–78.

12. Bonnet, *Défense de la paix*, 2:333–34.

13. Gamelin, *Servir*, 3:47–52; also Butler, *Grand Strategy*, 20.

14. Butler, *Grand Strategy*, 567; and Bethell, *The War Hitler Won*, 127, respectively.

15. For Bullitt's report on his conversation with Daladier, dated September 12, 1939, see *FRUS*, 1939, 1:424–25; also Churchill, *The Gathering Storm*, 422–23, 451.

16. Gamelin, *Servir*, 3:65–67; also Bethell, *The War Hitler Won*, 118.

17. For more data, see Bethell, *The War Hitler Won*, 169–70.

18. *TMWC*, 15:350, 10:519, respectively.

19. *DGFP*, series D, 7:480, 540–41, also 8:4.

20. *DPSR, 1939–1945*, 1:86–87.

21. *DGFP*, series D, 8:34, 60–61.

22. Beck, *Dernier rapport*, 175.

23. *AANP-Zespoly MSZ*, 6655, 33, 51; also Szembek, *Diariusz*, 4:770–72, respectively.

24. *PSZ* 1, part 3, 444, 570–71.

25. *DGFP*, series D, 8:60–61, 79–80, 96–97.

26. Ibid., 69, 44, 95, 97, respectively.

27. For this and other comments in the USSR, see *Izvestya* (Moscow), September 18, 1939, 1–3.

Part II

The Great Powers and Poland during the Second World War (1939–1945)

Chapter Twenty-Three

Poland after Defeat

For the Poles, the September campaign of 1939 turned the clock back twenty-five years. Again, Poland ceased to exist as an independent state, partitioned between Germany and Russia. As before, the Poles had to appeal to the conscience of the world for their future.

True, this time their situation seemed better, because the Polish government-in-exile was recognized by all non-Axis powers—except Russia, which cooperated with the Nazis until June 22, 1941. It had formal and still valid alliances with France and Great Britain. It also possessed an army, a navy, and an air force, which, though modest in size, played a significant role, particularly during the critical months of the Battle of Britain. Their government-in-exile commanded the loyalty of most of the population in the homeland and, until the end of the war, its authority was recognized by all underground organizations, with the exception of the Communist groups.

But, because the government had to operate on foreign land, its influence on the policies and strategies of the Western Allies was limited. Throughout the entire war, the Polish government-in-exile, though recognized as sovereign, was unable to carry out or enforce its policies without the full support of the Allied governments—until June 1940, French and British, and after December 1941, British and American. By the nature of things, the Poles depended on the Western Allies, which had to carry the main burden of the war and had real, not just nominal, power.

In other respects, the Polish situation was worse than during World War I. The destruction of life and property carried on by the occupying powers was greater than ever before. Cities, industrial centers, transportation systems, libraries, museums, and monuments of art were destroyed, damaged, or plundered. Almost all Polish Jews were confined to ghettoes, or kept there under inhuman conditions, and then murdered by the Nazis. Millions of people were deported by both the Germans and the Soviets. Underground opposition was made extremely difficult and dangerous: until June 1941 the Nazi and Soviet security forces worked jointly against it.

The collapse of France in June 1940 deprived the Poles of a natural ally and supporter, shifting the decisions to Great Britain and later on, after Pearl Harbor, to the United States as well. For both of these countries, central-eastern Europe was of only marginal interest.

The German attack on Russia on June 22, 1941, transferred the latter overnight into a most valued ally, important in both defeat and victory. In either instance, it was feared that Stalin might seek some new arrangements with Hitler and withdraw from the war, keeping whatever areas Germany had failed to seize or being satisfied with the recovery of prewar territories. Subsequent Soviet military successes increased Russia's importance and prestige, and after the Stalingrad victory in February 1943 the future of Poland in both political and territorial terms was to be decided by the two Anglo-Saxon powers *and* Russia, with France having no voice and the Poles having no strength. This necessarily made Poland's future a function of British-American-Soviet relations.

As a result of the Allied military strategy, all of central-eastern Europe, Poland included, was eventually liberated by the Red Army. That, of course, meant Soviet military and political control, with all its consequences.

When the Red Army entered Poland on September 17, 1939, the highest civilian Polish authorities as well as the commander in chief and his staff resided at Kuty, near the Romanian border. In imminent danger of being captured by the Soviets, they decided to enter Romania to continue the struggle and represent national interests from abroad. According to the treaty of March 3, 1921, Romania had to come to Poland's aid in the event of Soviet invasion. The royal government, however, was in no position to fulfill its obligations and was not even asked by the Poles to do so. Instead, the Poles asked for free passage to France for the president of the republic and the government. Eventually, not only the president and the government but also the commander in chief, with approximately ninety thousand soldiers, crossed the frontier. Free passage had been promised. Then, under strong Nazi-Soviet pressure, Romania interned them all. [1]

In spite of the military debacle, the legal continuity of the Polish state was saved. Unable to exercise his powers, President Mościcki, in accordance with Article 24 of the Constitution, which, in war emergency, gave him a right to appoint his successor, passed the authority on to Wladyslaw Raczkiewicz, chairman of the World Association of Poles Abroad and former speaker of the Senate, who had meanwhile arrived in Paris. On September 30 Raczkiewicz took the oath of office and entrusted General Wladyslaw Sikorski with the post of prime minister and commander in chief.

Without delay, Sikorski formed his cabinet—a coalition of the four most important prewar opposition parties: National, Peasant, Socialist, and Christian Labor. The new president, in accordance with the Constitution, then dissolved the prewar parliament. A National Council consisting of representatives from all political groups was formed under the chairmanship of the venerable Paderewski, then almost eighty. As before, Paderewski gave all his energies and his fortune to the cause of Poland, in a rarely equaled display of selfless patriotism.[2]

Military defeat and sudden collapse plunged the Poles into a state of amazement, shock, and despair. The resulting widespread condemnation of the prewar government and of those who had supported it, as well as constitutional procedures employed to preserve the legality of the government-in-exile, were bound to cause discord. All recognized the government-in-exile as legal. But they differed in their attitude toward its composition and policies.

Though not especially outspoken before the war, Raczkiewicz had occupied high-level government positions and belonged to the Pilsudski-ite camp. No wonder he could hardly win the confidence of the exiled leaders. Hard-pressed, he even had to formally renounce certain constitutional powers on behalf of the prime minister.

Foreign affairs were given over to August Zaleski, Beck's predecessor. Zaleski enjoyed the reputation of an able diplomat and had many friends in the West, particularly in France. In fact, his pro-French orientation contributed to his dismissal in 1932. He was known in international diplomatic circles, had a high standing in Paris and London, and seemed a natural choice. But he was aligned with no party, was also a Pilsudski-ite, and was therefore not too popular with more than a few political leaders.

Command over the secret military organization in the homeland was given to General Kazimierz Sosnkowski. Before the war he was widely respected as an advocate of national unity and opponent of undemocratic forms of government. After Pilsudski's seizure of power, he confined himself strictly to military activities. During the September campaign he fought valiantly, even after the Red Army invaded Poland and the Polish commander in chief withdrew to Romania. But he had been Pilsudski's closest collaborator for many years, and at times was considered by many his most likely successor. He never was able to win the confidence of various exiled political leaders.

The man who enjoyed the greatest prestige was General Sikorski. Pilsudski's antagonist and rival since World War I, and an outstanding military leader, he had a distinguished career behind him. Commander of an army during the Polish-Bolshevik war of 1920, he was soon after appointed chief of staff. In 1922 he became premier at the age of forty-one, and in 1924–1925 he served as minister of war. After Pilsudski's coup he gradually drifted into active political opposition, which by 1928 brought him an unwanted retirement from the army at the age of forty-seven.

Once retired, Sikorski dedicated his time to writing on military matters and keeping in touch with the opposition leaders at home and abroad. An outspoken opponent of Beck's policy, which he considered exceedingly pro-German and harmful, he always advocated cooperation with France, Great Britain, and Czechoslovakia. He acquired many friends in France, where he had lived for extensive periods. As premier and commander in chief he was to steer Polish policies until his tragic death in an airplane crash into the waters of Gibraltar on July 4, 1943. His authority was not challenged by the Poles, whatever their political affiliations, because he represented the continuity of Polish statehood and commanded the genuine respect, if not love, of all.

Probably realizing the essential weakness of Poland's international position—and also, no doubt, because of his personal convictions—Sikorski avoided anything that might endanger Allied unity. Before long, he became highly popular, first in French and later on in British and American official circles, for they felt they had in him a trusted, faithful ally.

By the time the government-in-exile was formed, Germany and Russia had completed the annihilation of Poland. On September 28 Ribbentrop and Molotov signed, in Moscow, the Boundary and Friendship Treaty, which partly amended the territorial clauses of the secret protocol of August 23 and recognized the new partition line in Poland as "definitive."[3] Lithuania, originally to be left to Germany, now was recognized as belonging to the Soviet "sphere of interest." In compensation, the Lublin area and part of the Warsaw Province (the area between the rivers Vistula and Bug) was assigned to

Germany. German nationals were given freedom to leave Soviet-occupied territories, and Ukrainians and Byelorussians could leave areas dominated by the Nazis. In a special secret protocol, both governments agreed to collaborate in suppressing any activities aiming at the restoration of Poland's independence. This was the legal basis for cooperation between the Nazi and the Soviet security forces against the Polish Underground during the period September 1939 to June 1941.[4]

According to the treaty, Germany occupied 72,866 square miles of land inhabited by some 22,140,000 people.[5] Approximately one-half of the area was incorporated into the Reich as the Warthegau. The other half—under the governorship of Hans Frank—formed a *Nebenland*, a sort of subsidiary semi-colonial area. From the very beginning, the population faced the Nazis with implacable enmity.

Interestingly enough, the Nazi-Soviet pact of August 23 did not specify the total extinction of Poland but, instead, provided for the possibility of a rump "independent Polish state." The prewar German ambassador in Warsaw, Moltke, tried to influence Hitler favorably in this respect.[6] Mussolini was also against extreme solutions. As late as January 4, 1940, he advised Hitler that "the creation of a small, disarmed and exclusively Polish Poland . . . could not constitute a threat to the German Reich." On the other hand, he argued, it might end the war and provide an adequate basis for peace.[7] Stalin, however, opposed the idea, and it was under his pressure that the total destruction of Poland was decided upon. On September 20 Molotov pointed out to Schulenburg that Stalin did not wish to have any, even a "residual," Polish state, and five days later, Stalin himself warned the German ambassador that Poland—any Poland, however small—might "create friction" between Germany and Russia.[8]

The Nazi-Soviet collaboration of 1939–1941 had the same result as the collaboration between Prussia and Russia at the end of the eighteenth century. This time, ideologies gave way to power politics. On October 5, 1939, *Izvestya* wrote that "[Hitlerism] is a matter of taste." Four weeks later, on October 31, Molotov boasted to the Supreme Soviet that "one swift blow to Poland, first by the German Army and then by the Red Army, and nothing was left of this ugly offspring of the Versailles Treaty."[9] "It cannot be denied that it was not Germany who attacked France and Britain, but France and Britain who attacked Germany, thus assuming responsibility for the present war," Stalin wrote in *Pravda* on November 30, 1939. By the end of December he cabled Ribbentrop: "The friendship of the peoples of Germany and the Soviet Union cemented by blood, has every reason to be lasting and firm."[10]

In compliance with the treaty of September 28, 1939, Russia occupied an area of approximately 77,620 square miles, 51.6 percent of the entire Polish territory, inhabited by approximately 13,199,000, or 37.3 percent of the entire population of Poland. On October 22, Communist-type elections took place: the voters had only one ballot to cast and voting was obligatory. The "elected" candidates included Molotov, Voroshilov, Kovalev (commander of the Byelorussian front), and other high Soviet officials.[11] The new assemblies, one for the southern part and another for the northern, unanimously "requested" union with the Soviet Ukrainian and Byelorussian republics. To no one's surprise, the Supreme Soviet complied and incorporation was decreed on November 1 and November 2, respectively.[12] Mass deportations soon followed. The new frontier gave the Soviet Union approximately the same territories that Imperial Russia had taken in 1795, in the third partition of Poland. It also corresponded roughly to the so-called Curzon Line, a fact that Halifax brought to the attention of the House of Lords on October 26, 1939[13]—an ominous reminder.

In the meantime, the Polish government-in-exile, with a temporary seat in Angers in France, established its international status. On October 2 it obtained recognition by the United States, and ambassadors Count Jerzy Potocki and Anthony Drexel Biddle were instructed to resume their duties. Two days later the British accorded their recognition. Sir Howard Kennard proceeded to Angers, and Ambassador Raczyński continued his mission in London.

From the very beginning the Poles emphasized that the Soviet occupation was just as forcibly imposed and just as illegal as the German occupation. The first public protest appeared on the very day the Red Army invaded Poland, and soon other similar enunciations followed, most of them pertaining to the "plebiscites" and deportations. The Poles tried hard to obtain official Allied support for their stand, but this proved difficult. At that time, Russia was still formally neutral and neither Britain nor France wished to push Moscow into closer cooperation with Germany. When on September 18 Raczyński formally notified the Foreign Office about the Soviet aggression against Poland and, calling for action, referred to the "treaties now in force," Halifax gently corrected him: the Anglo-Polish alliance concerned only Germany, not Russia, he observed.[14]

The situation changed slightly after the Soviet attack on Finland, which aroused general indignation and finally—on December 4, 1939—resulted in the expulsion of the USSR from the League of Nations. On November 19, 1939, Sikorski stated in a public interview that his government "saw no difference between the seizure of Polish territories by Russia and their seizure by Germany and they had no reason to believe that their Allies took a contrary view." As the British archives reveal, his declaration caused a general dissatisfaction in the Foreign Office and Quai d'Orsay.

At the time, international public opinion overwhelmingly sympathized with Poland—once again beaten, partitioned, subjected to foreign domination. The Soviet invasion carried out in cooperation with the Nazis particularly shocked the world and brought about universal condemnation. A *New York Times* editorial, written one day after the Red Army crossed the Polish border, was representative: "Germany having killed the prey, Soviet Russia will seize that part of the carcass that Germany cannot use. It will play the noble role of hyena to the German lion. . . . Hitlerism is brown Communism; Stalinism is Red Fascism. The world will now understand that the only real ideological issue is one between democracy, liberty, and peace on the one hand and despotism, peril, and war on the other."

The reaction of the American government, though no less sympathetic to the Poles, was conciliatory toward Russia. While the war was still going on in Poland, the president called Congress into special session to repeal the arms embargo stipulations of the Neutrality Law so that Great Britain could buy war matériel in the United States on a "cash and carry" basis. Significantly, the Soviet Union was also excluded from the embargo because, as Hull explained, America did not want to place the Soviets on the same footing as Germany, thus thrusting them further "into Hitler's arms."[15] The American government expected that a Nazi-Soviet clash would come sooner or later and planned its policy accordingly.

From its first days, the government-in-exile acted vigorously, concentrating on rebuilding its armed forces. The navy was nearly intact and in safety. Within a few months an army of one hundred thousand men was formed, consisting of escapees from Poland and internment camps in Romania and Hungary as well as volunteers from among the Poles living in France. By 1940 large Polish forces took part in the Norwegian, and later in the Belgian and French, campaigns.[16]

Poland's military contribution was not limited to its armed forces in exile. At the end of 1939 the Underground began to operate in both the Nazi and the Soviet zones, eventually growing into one of the largest in Europe.[17] The civilian branch, headed by a delegate of the government-in-exile with a rank of vice premier, had the authority of a state administration. The delegate acted under the control of a political council, composed of representatives from the same four major political parties that had formed the government coalition in Paris and, later on, in London.

The military branch, eventually named the Home Army, had an official status and unified command. Throughout the war it carried on sabotage, guerilla warfare, diversion, and intelligence activities with a task to prepare an open uprising at the proper moment.[18] Through the government-in-exile, the Home Army cooperated with the Western allies.

The fourth branch was Justice. Secret tribunals were set up to maintain the morale of the population, to warn potential collaborators, and to punish traitors. In 1942 a special section, Żegota, was created in the office of the delegate with the task of helping the Jews.[19] The tribunals applied a special code, known to the public and generally obeyed. In addition to these government-authorized structures, a great number of loosely organized groups, both civilian and military, tried to combat the enemy. As a whole, the Underground formed a secret *state*, whose government operated abroad.[20]

Financially, the Polish exiles succeeded in preserving a great deal of independence because most of the national gold reserves had been taken out of the country in September 1939. Loans were obtained from France, Great Britain, and the United States. By September 1941 Poland became eligible for American Lend-Lease aid, and in March 1942 the government-in-exile received from the United States 12.5 million dollars in annual credits for government expenses and for subsidizing the Underground in the homeland.[21] British aid for the five and a half years of the war amounted to 120 million pounds.[22]

After France collapsed in June 1940, the Poles continued their struggle on British soil, and the Dunkirk evacuation included a considerable part of their forces as well as their government. Those were desperate days, and men who still wanted to fight were highly valued in London. "We are . . . comrades in life and in death. We shall conquer together, or we shall die together,"[23] Churchill told Sikorski on June 18, 1940, the day after France sued for an armistice. Three days later, King George VI greeted President Raczkiewicz at Paddington Station in London. During the ensuing Battle of Britain, the Polish air force, stronger than the combined air forces of all the other exiled governments, was responsible for 15 percent of all enemy air losses.

With France crushed, Great Britain stood alone against the formidable Nazi war machine, and the following months—July, August, September, and October 1940—were probably the most critical in its history. Everything was at stake, and aid from whatever quarter became invaluable. Particularly the position of Russia—formally neutral but in effect collaborating with Germany—assumed a great importance. To prevent the Soviets from collaborating more closely with the Nazis, or to bring Russia to Britain's side, became a matter of vital importance for London. As a result, the first secret offers to Moscow were made. They concerned central-eastern Europe.

On September 5, Prime Minister Churchill made an important statement in the House of Commons. Referring to recent territorial changes, he declared ambiguously that although Britain could not recognize the implementation of such changes during war, it might recognize them later if "they [took] place with the free consent and good will of the parties concerned."[24] Churchill certainly realized that there was no room for "free consent" or for "good will" in eastern Europe in 1939–1940. His declaration, if it was intended to have any meaning at all, could not be interpreted in Moscow other than as a hint that under certain circumstances, Great Britain might recognize Soviet territorial gains in Europe. Indeed, two weeks earlier, Sir Stafford Cripps, British ambassador in Moscow since June 1940, had secretly offered Stalin Soviet "leadership" in the Balkans in exchange for a "benevolent" attitude toward Great Britain.[25]

Two months later, in the middle of October, Cripps handed a memorandum to Andrei Vishinsky, recently appointed deputy minister of foreign affairs, which contained a proposal for an understanding between the two countries. In exchange for Soviet "benevolent neutrality" toward Great Britain, Turkey, and Persia, the British government was to consult the Soviets as to the postwar settlement; refrain from concluding any agreement "directed against Russia"; and recognize the "de facto sovereignty" of the USSR in Estonia, Latvia, Lithuania, Bessarabia, northern Bukovina, and "those parts of the former Polish State now under Soviet control." In addition, London offered Russia an economic agreement and, if circumstances were favorable, a "nonaggression pact on the lines of the Russo-German pact."[26] At the time, British approaches were shrugged off by Stalin, but he certainly would remember them later on.

When informed of the memorandum, the Polish government registered formal reservations. In his sternly worded letter of December 14, 1940, Zaleski called the attention of Lord Halifax to the stipulations of the Polish-

British alliance and pointed out that Great Britain had no right to make such proposals. It was evident from the terse tone of the letter that the Poles realized the grave implications inherent in the British move. Halifax assured Zaleski that the proposals had been made "on temporary basis, pending a general settlement . . . at the end of the war," and that in no way did they "prejudice" Poland's rights. To smooth the matter, Zaleski was to be sent two official letters, one from Halifax and another from Eden. The handwritten comments and various amendments of the drafts jointly composed by the high officials of the Foreign Office show that Cripps's proposals to Stalin were made in earnest, while the letters to Zaleski were purposefully vague.[27] Soon after, on January 2, 1941, Eden obtained Zaleski's "agreement" that until Russia's position changed, Polish "claims" should be left "dormant."[28] Clearly, long before Russia entered the war, Great Britain's attitude toward Poland had become a function of Anglo-Soviet relations.

NOTES

1. Beck, *Dernier rapport*, 41; for the Romanian attitude, see Alexandre Cretzianu, "Rumania a Wrzesień 1939" (Romania and September, 1939), *Kultura*, no. 3/77 (March 1954): 106–15. M. Cretzianu in September 1939 occupied the post of chief of cabinet in the Romanian ministry of foreign affairs.

2. He died in New York City on June 29, 1941, and by decision of President Franklin D. Roosevelt was buried at Arlington National Cemetery—a temporary haven.

3. For the text of the treaty, see *DGFP*, series D, 8:164–66.

4. For the attitude of the Polish Communists in this respect, see Stefan Korbonski, *W Imieniu Rzeczypospolitej* (*In the Name of the Republic*) (Paris: Instytut Literacki, 1954), 266.

Korbonski was the last civilian head of the Underground in Poland. See also T. Bor-Komorowski, *The Secret Army* (New York: Macmillan, 1951), 46–47. General Komorowski was the commander in chief of the Underground Home Army in the period July 1943–October 1944; also, Kwiatkowski, *Komuniści w Polsce*, 17–18; for the Nazi-Soviet collaboration in military and economic matters, see Bregman, *Hitler's Best Ally*, 94–108.

5. Poland, Ministry of Information, *The Concise Statistical Yearbook of Poland, September 1939–June 1941* (Glasgow: The University Press, 1941), 4.

6. *DGFP*, series D, 7:247, also 8:138–39.

7. *Lettres Secrétes Hitler-Mussolini* (Paris: Editions Pavois, 1945), 52–53; also *DGFP*, series D, 8:105.

8. *DGFP*, series D, 8:105, 130, respectively.

9. Degras, *Soviet Documents*, 3:388.

10. *Pravda* (Moscow), December 25, 1939, 4.

11. For some details, see *Communist Take-Over and Occupation of Poland*, 9–12; also *Pravda* (Moscow), October 15, 1939, 1; 2.

12. For the text of decrees, see *DPSR, 1939–1945*, 1:69–70. For more detailed dates and statistics, ibid., 572–73.

13. *Parliamentary Debates*, Lords, 114 (1939), 1565.

14. *FO* 371/23103/14090/13953/18.

15. Hull, *The Memoirs of Cordell Hull*, 1:685.

16. See Stefan Kleczkowski, *Poland's First Hundred Thousand* (London: Hutchinson Co., 1945), 9–12, 37; see also Arkady Fiedler, *Squadron 303, The Story of the Polish Fighter Squadrons with RAF* (New York: Roy Publishers, 1943), 28.

17. For the structure of the Underground, see Jan Karski, *Story of a Secret State* (Boston: Houghton Mifflin Co., 1944), 124–34, 230–37.

18. Bor-Komorowski, *The Secret Army*, 172–73.

19. See Wladyslaw Bartoszewski, *The Samaritans* (New York: Twayne Publishers, 1966). Bartoszewski was head of Żegota. After the war he was decorated in Jerusalem with a medal of a Righteous Gentile among the Nations.

20. For an exhaustive and authoritative information on the Polish war underground activities, see Stefan Korbonski, *The Polish Underground State: 1939–1945* (New York: Columbia University Press, 1978). After the war, he was decorated with a medal of a Righteous Gentile among the Nations.

21. Hull, *The Memoirs of Cordell Hull*, 2:1270.

22. Winston S. Churchill, *Triumph and Tragedy* (Boston: Houghton Mifflin Co., 1953), 651–52.

23. See *Sunday Express* (London), July 14, 1940, 5.

24. *Parliamentary Debates*, Commons, 365 (1940), 40. The same day Halifax made an analogous declaration in the House of Lords: *Parliamentary Debates*, Lords, 117, 365.

25. *Nazi-Soviet Relations*, 167.

26. Sir Ernest Llewellyn Woodward, *British Foreign Policy in the Second World War* (London: H. M. Stationery Office, 1962), 145–46.

27. *FO* 371/24482/C12458/7177; also *FO* 371/ 24482/C13465/7177/55.

28. *FO* 371/26718/C165/151/55.

Chapter Twenty-Four

The Polish-Soviet Pact of July 30, 1941

June 22, 1941, was probably considered by Hitler the most fateful day in his entire public life. On that day, he threw his might against Russia to gain Lebensraum for Germany and to lay the foundations for his Thousand-Year Reich. Overnight, the USSR found itself on the side of Great Britain. Overnight, the problem of Soviet-Polish relations acquired a new significance.

The Nazi-Soviet collaboration, as well as the Soviet policy of expansion in Poland, Finland, the Baltic states, and Romania in the years 1939–1940 were generally regarded as expressions of either imperialism or unprincipled opportunism. Thus, after June 1941 the Soviet attitude toward Poland became a critical test of the Kremlin's new course. Poland was partitioned in September 1939, and Russia occupied half the country. Would Moscow denounce that partition and recognize the prewar Polish-Soviet frontier? Poland was represented by a government-in-exile in London, recognized by all non-Axis powers. Would Moscow recognize that government? More than one million inhabitants of the Soviet-held Polish territories had been forcibly deported to Russia in the two years preceding. Would the Soviet government restore their freedom? In 1939 large numbers of Polish soldiers had been taken by the Soviets as war prisoners. Would the Kremlin allow them to form their own Polish army in the USSR or let them leave Russia and fight for freedom elsewhere? These were some of the questions asked in Polish quarters.

The problem looked different to the British government, which from the very moment of Germany's attack on Russia did its best to let bygones be bygones and to bind Moscow as strongly as possible to the West. A powerful country had entered the war, and this was considered of paramount importance. Russia's friendship and confidence had to be cultivated. From the outset of the German-Soviet war, Churchill was making supreme efforts to convince Stalin of his sincerity, goodwill, and support. He also had to bring around British public opinion, which until then was critical of or even hostile to Russia. "If Hitler invaded Hell, I would make at least a favourable reference to the Devil in the House of Commons,"[1] he said when asked if he were not going too far in his public support of the Soviets. He considered that the reestablishment of Polish-Soviet relations would be helpful in reorienting British public opinion. It would show that Soviet policies had changed and were trusted even by those who so recently had been wronged by Russia. Eden spoke about this quite frankly to the Polish foreign minister.[2]

The initiative for renewal of Polish-Soviet relations came from Sikorski in his broadcast to Poland the day after Germany attacked Russia. He welcomed the new partner in the common struggle and announced his government's willingness to forget the wrongs perpetrated by the Soviets in Poland. He expressed hope that the Soviet Union would denounce all agreements with Germany partitioning Poland, release Polish war prisoners and deportees, and recognize the prewar Polish-Soviet boundaries. Since there was no reaction from Moscow for several days, he addressed an official letter to Eden on July 4, asking for open support. He wanted the Foreign Office to issue a declaration to the effect that Great Britain had never recognized the Soviet annexation of eastern Poland and that it was "in the interest of war" to reach a Polish-Soviet "settlement."[3]

On the same day, July 4, Eden called Sikorski, informing him of the conversation he had had just a few hours earlier with the Soviet ambassador in London, Ivan M. Maisky. The latter said that his government would be willing to give facilities to the Poles to form a "Polish National Committee" in Russia and organize their own military forces there. All the Polish war prisoners—according to Maisky, no more than twenty thousand—would be freed. As for the territorial questions, although the Soviet government did "favor" the establishment of an independent Polish state, its boundaries would have to follow "ethnographical" lines. The ambassador did not preclude the possibility that certain areas occupied by Russia in 1939 "might return to Poland." He also told Eden that in his country the Polish government was regarded as "reactionary . . . fundamentally hostile to Russia."[4] Eden preferred not to mention that comment to Sikorski.

Sikorski rejected the proposals without hesitation. He saw in them evidence that Moscow had embarked upon the course of "Red" pan-Slavism. He pointed out that the figure of 20,000 Polish war prisoners was shockingly false. According to Soviet statistics, more than 190,000 men, including over 10,000 officers, had been taken prisoner by the Red Army in September 1939. He also drew Eden's attention to the term "Polish National Committee" (instead of "Polish government") and explained its significance. As a condition for any negotiations he demanded unequivocal recognition of the Polish government; annulment of Soviet-Nazi agreements concerning the partition of Poland; establishment of a Polish embassy in Moscow, with authority to care for all Polish citizens in the USSR, including war prisoners and deportees; and, finally, agreement on the formation of a Polish army in Russia under the authority of the government-in-exile. Eden promised to communicate these views to Maisky and agreed that the references to the "National Committee" were "not correct." Otherwise, however, he did not seem to object to Maisky's proposals.[5]

On the same day Eden communicated the Polish proposals to Maisky. He emphasized that "what the Polish government would hope for was a statement by the Soviet government indicating that the treaties of 1939 were nullified."[6]

The next day, Sikorski, accompanied by Zaleski, held the first conversation with Maisky in the presence of Sir Alexander Cadogan, British permanent undersecretary for foreign affairs. According to Cadogan's protocol, the prime minister first stressed that he could not discuss any frontier changes. Probably on Zaleski's advice, he did not repeat the demand advanced in his conversation with Eden, mainly annulment of Soviet-Nazi agreements on the partition of Poland. Instead he asked for explicit recognition of the Treaty of Riga. Maisky disagreed and reasserted that although his government "favored the formation of an independent national Polish State . . . [it] could not explicitly recognize the frontiers of 1939." Then he suggested that "the question might be left open." Sikorski pointed out that Russia had no right to impose ethnographical frontiers on Poland, being a multinational state itself. Eventually, however, after a short exchange of arguments, he approved the formula. The Soviet government would denounce the German-Russian treaties concerning the partition of Poland. No statement would be inserted that the prewar Polish-Soviet frontiers *would not* be restored, but no explicit declaration recognizing the prewar boundary would be made either.[7]

The Sikorski-Maisky conversation was only preliminary—further negoti-ations would follow. From the beginning, British officials assumed the role of intermediary, insisting upon a speedy conclusion of the agreement. Sikor-ski shared this view. But several prominent members of his government strongly objected to the ambiguous formula, which left the question of the Polish-Soviet boundaries open. Sikorski retracted, and three days later, the Polish government handed to the Foreign Office a clarifying note. Having emphasized their determination to fight Germany "as enemy number one," the Poles pointed to the recent Nazi-Soviet collaboration, to the Soviet policy aiming at the destruction of Poland, and to the fact that Russia found itself in the Allied camp "against her will." The note recommended extreme caution in dealing with Moscow. The government-in-exile declared itself ready for reconciliation and collaboration under the condition that all Polish citizens detained by force in the USSR be released and assisted until their evacuation became possible. As for the territorial questions, although the Poles would not demand an explicit revalidation of the Riga treaty, the Soviets would have to denounce agreements with Nazi Germany in such a way that "it will be understood implicitly that all treaties and agreements between Poland and the USSR prior to the Nazi aggression against Poland would be reestab-lished."[8]

On July 11, Eden played host to the second Sikorski-Zaleski-Maisky conference. The Soviet ambassador reiterated the position of his government regarding Poland's independence "within the territorial limits of Polish na-tionality." To Sikorski's protestations he answered that his government did not ask the Poles to agree to the Soviet views, and these views did not have to be either inserted into the pact or formally recognized; he had been in-structed, however, to *register* them. He proposed a joint four-point declara-tion stating that (1) the Soviet-German treaties of 1939 were void, (2) Polish-Soviet diplomatic relations would be restored, (3) a Polish army would be created in Russia, and (4) both governments agreed to fight against Germany. Sikorski, without raising objections, demanded the addition of two more points: release of the Polish war prisoners in Russia and return of the Polish private and public property seized in Poland by the Soviets in 1939–1941. Eden impatiently agreed with Maisky that the last questions should be dis-cussed later, after the general agreement had been concluded. Throughout the conversation the foreign secretary refrained from supporting the Poles and insisted on a *speedy* agreement. He showed an "increased impatience" while discussing the agreement with Zaleski shortly afterward.[9]

The next day Sikorski sent his counterproposals, embodying the views he had expressed during the meeting. The draft specified the manner of the release of the Poles and described the task, status, and structure of the Polish army to be formed in Russia. The Poles should be released and allowed to leave the Soviet Union if they wished, and the Polish diplomatic and consular services should be allowed to help them. With regard to the territorial problems, he proposed the following formula:

> The Government of the USSR considers as null and void the treaties concluded with Germany on August 23, 1939, and September 28, 1939, as well as all other agreements or internal legislation subsequent to these dates and concerning Poland and they renounce all advantages that those agreements had and could have had for the USSR.
>
> Both Governments recognized the reestablishment of mutual relations on the basis of the last bilateral Polish-Soviet declaration in Moscow on November 26, 1938. [10]

On the surface, the formula complied with the Soviet demand not to refer to the Treaty of Riga. Careful reading of the text shows, however, that no more than face-saving was involved. The November 26, 1938, declaration referred to that treaty specifically. [11] In addition, Sikorski asked for a secret protocol in which the independence and territorial integrity of both countries, as of September 1, 1939, would be guaranteed. The draft, differing from Sikorski's stand of July 5, was undoubtedly the result of opposition within the government-in-exile to his concessions. The opposition was led by Foreign Minister Zaleski and included President Raczkiewicz, Defense Minister Sosnkowski, cabinet member Marjan Seyda, and some other prominent leaders.

In the meantime Churchill increased pressure on the Poles to conclude the pact as quickly as possible. On July 15 he informed the House of Commons of the agreement between Great Britain and Russia and emphasized that from then on the Soviet Union was an "ally." He mentioned the Polish-Soviet negotiations, noted that Eden was "instrumental" in bringing them about, and added that, although they had not yet been concluded, he placed great "hope" on the "statesmanship" of General Sikorski. [12] He did not make any appeal to the statesmanship of Stalin, and of course he was well aware of the rift in the Polish government. That same day Eden confronted Sikorski and Zaleski with an ultimatum of sorts, bidding them to agree immediately to the Soviet demands to leave the territorial issue open. "Whether you want to or not an agreement with the Soviet Union has to be signed,"[13] he told them.

Two days later, on July 17, Maisky submitted his own draft that, although conceding to some Polish demands, did not go beyond the annulment of the Nazi-Soviet agreements as far as the territorial issue was concerned. Sikorski still tried to obtain recognition—albeit indirect—of the prewar Polish-Soviet boundary. He failed. As Maisky told Eden, "in no circumstances would the Soviet government recognize Polish-Soviet boundaries as of July 1939." If the Poles persisted in their "obdurance," the Soviet government might organize a Polish National Committee in Russia. "There [are] large numbers of Poles who [have] no love at all for the Polish government," he warned the foreign secretary.[14] By then, it became evident that not only did Moscow consider the annulment of the treaties with Germany as *not* constituting recognition of the Polish prewar boundary, but they attached great importance to the whole problem and had British support. On July 24 the war cabinet instructed Eden to inform Sikorski of its resolution that the Polish-Soviet pact, as proposed by Moscow, "would be in the interest of Poland."[15]

Then the Polish government became irreconcilably divided. Sikorski and the majority of the cabinet members considered signing the pact necessary, even on Soviet conditions. The prospect of saving some one and a half million people imprisoned in Russia; the possibility of organizing a new army; the desire to contribute to Allied unity; reluctance to antagonize the British—these factors seemed paramount. Besides, Sikorski, a soldier, believed that a Polish-Russian comradeship-in-arms would bring the two countries together in time and that the ambiguity of the pact would become harmless. Those who opposed the pact recommended greater efforts to change its ambiguous text, greater resistance to British pressure, or a delay. They hoped that under the impact of military adversities the Soviets would eventually soften.[16] Since Sikorski persisted, Sosnkowski, Zaleski, and Seyda resigned in protest, and in spite of direct British pressure, the president refused to give his constitutional authorization for the agreement.[17]

The pact was signed by Sikorski and Maisky on July 30, 1941, in the presence of Churchill and Eden. As far as the Poles were concerned, it could only be considered a diplomatic defeat. On the subject of the frontiers, the crucial paragraph ran as Maisky proposed: "The Union of Soviet Socialist Republics recognizes that the Soviet-German treaties of 1939 relative to territorial changes in Poland have lost their validity." There was no direct or indirect commitment that the status quo ante would be recreated. The agreement provided for establishment of diplomatic relations between the Polish and the Soviet governments, mutual support in the pursuance of war against Germany, and formation of an autonomous Polish army on Soviet territory. A special protocol stipulated that all Polish citizens imprisoned in Russia, war prisoners as well as deportees, would receive "amnesty."[18] The use of the term "amnesty" was bitterly criticized by the Polish opponents of the pact because it implied indirect recognition of the legality of their deportation and suggested guilt on the part of the deportees, rather than mere justice in releasing them. The term was inserted by the recently appointed British ambassador in Moscow, Sir Stafford Cripps. Charged by Eden to obtain Stalin's approval of the final text, Cripps on his own initiative used the term "amnesty" in exchange for Stalin's firm promise to release "every single Polish citizen who [was] detained anywhere in the USSR." Then, the ambassador appealed to Sikorski through the Foreign Office not to object.[19] Sikorski complied.

Sikorski recognized full well the ambiguity of the wording pertaining to the territorial issue in the pact and, trying to strengthen somehow Poland's position vis-à-vis Russia, asked Eden for a public confirmation that Great Britain recognized no territorial changes effected in Poland since September 1939. He was successful, and on the day of the pact's signing, he received a formal letter from the foreign secretary stating that "in conformity with the provisions of the agreement for mutual assistance between the United Kingdom and Poland of the 25th of August, 1939, His Majesty's Government in the United Kingdom have entered into no undertaking toward the Union of Soviet Socialist Republics which affects the relations between that country and Poland. . . . His Majesty's Government do not recognize any territorial changes which have been effected in Poland since August, 1939."[20]

At the moment it seemed that Eden's formal letter affirmed British recognition of Poland's prewar frontiers with Russia. The illusion lasted only a few hours. Answering a question from the floor in the House of Commons, the foreign secretary observed that the exchange of notes between the Polish and the British governments *did not* involve any guarantee of Poland's frontiers. Moreover, in accordance with Churchill's declaration of September 5, 1940, the future Polish-Soviet frontier would be established by "mutual agreement."[21] The next day, American undersecretary of state Sumner Welles made a similar public statement: although friendly to the Poles in tone, it failed to confirm Poland's right to its prewar boundaries.[22]

Almost immediately after the pact was signed and made public, an open controversy developed between the Poles and the Soviets as to its interpretation. Sikorski, broadcasting to Poland on July 31, said that "[the agreement] . . . does not permit even of the suggestion that the 1939 frontiers of the Polish State could ever be in question."[23] The statement obviously was misleading. And indeed, three days later, on August 3, *Izvestya*, the official government organ in Moscow, sternly took exception, pointing out that the pact *did not* provide for the reestablishment of the Polish-Soviet prewar boundary at all. It was probably no coincidence that simultaneously the same views appeared in the most prominent British and American newspapers.[24]

To the Poles at large, unaware of the background, this divergence was either incomprehensible or seemed an encroachment on the part of Russia. But the situation was more complex. The Soviets made it clear throughout *all* negotiations that they did not intend to recognize the prewar Polish-Soviet frontiers, though they agreed not to say it explicitly and publicly. The Polish government, fully aware of that position, tried to change it, but finally, after a government crisis and under British pressure, agreed to the formula submitted by Moscow.

Churchill's pressure on the Poles not to oppose Soviet terms apparently was more significant than it appeared even to the Polish opponents of the pact. For simultaneous with the Sikorski-Maisky negotiations, difficult and important negotiations between the British and Soviet governments were taking place, with Stalin demonstrating his suspicions and dissatisfaction and Churchill making all-out efforts to win Stalin's confidence and cooperation. On July 9, four days after Maisky had confronted Sikorski with the issue of "ethnographical" frontiers for Poland, the prime minister drafted an important message to Moscow in which he inserted a paragraph that, after the war, the frontiers could be settled "in accordance with the wishes of the people concerned and on general ethnographical lines."[25] Only when confronted with the opposition of his war cabinet did he agree to omit the paragraph. Evidently Churchill had no intention of supporting the Poles in their contention with Moscow. On the contrary, already in July 1941 he essentially approved of the Soviet stand.

NOTES

1. See Winston S. Churchill, *The Grand Alliance* (Boston: Houghton Mifflin Co., 1951), 370.

2. See Rozek, *Allied Wartime Diplomacy*, 59.

3. For the texts, see *DPSR, 1939–1945*, 1:108–12, 114.

4. *FO* 371/26755/C7016/3226/55.

5. For the minutes, *DPSR, 1939–1945*, 1:116.

6. *FO* 371/26755/C7423/3226/SS.

7. For the minutes, see *DPSR, 1939–1945*, 1:117–19.

8. For the text, ibid., 119–22.

9. For the record of the conversation, ibid., 128–32.

10. For the full text, ibid., 132–34.

11. Ibid., 261.

12. *Parliamentary Debates*, Commons, 373 (1941), 464.

13. See Rozek, *Allied Wartime Diplomacy*, 59–60.

14. *FO* 371/26756/C8028/3226/SS.

15. *FO* 371/26756/C8411/3226/55.

16. There were many at that time who expected an early Soviet collapse. The official estimate of the American War Department was that the USSR would hold no more than a "minimum of one month and a possible maximum of three months." Robert E. Sherwood, *Roosevelt and Hopkins: An Intimate History* (New York: Harper and Brothers Publishers, 1948), 304.

17. For valuable details concerning differences of views within the Polish government, see Wladyslaw Pobóg-Malinowski, "O Ukladzie Polsko-Rosyjskim z 30, VII, 1941" (About the Polish-Russian pact of July 30, 1941), *Kultura*, April 1951, no. 4/42, 113–33. Eventually Raczkiewicz withdrew his objections, *DPSR, 1939–1945*, 1:580–81.

18. For the full text, see *DPSR, 1939–1945*, 1:141–42.

19. *FO* 371/26756/C8377/3226/55.

20. *DPSR, 1939–1945*, 1:142–43.

21. *Parliamentary Debates*, Commons, 373 (1941), 1502–4.

22. Jan Ciechanowski, *Defeat in Victory* (Garden City, NY: Doubleday & Co., 1947), 39–40.

23. *DPSR, 1939–1945*, 1:144.

24. See *Times* (London), July 31, 1941, editorial, 5; also *New York Times*, July 31, 1941, 1–4; ibid., August 7, 1941, 7; *New York Herald Tribune*, August 4, 1941, 2.

25. Woodward, *British Foreign Policy in the Second World War*, 152.

Chapter Twenty-Five

The "Four Freedoms" and the Atlantic Charter

The year 1941 was one of trial and anguish. With the defeat of France, Great Britain stood alone against the enemy that controlled most of Europe. In the spring of 1941 Yugoslavia, Greece, and all of the Balkan Peninsula were firmly in Hitler's grip. By the end of the year the whole of the Soviet Union west of the Volga River, with a population of more than seventy million, fell to the Germans, and the Red Army seemed incapable of forestalling the Nazi victory.[1] German U-boats were inflicting heavy damage to Britain's vital supply lines. Egypt and the Suez Canal were in jeopardy. And, in the Far East, Japan was destroying China in an undeclared war.

In enslaved Poland, people lived in abject humiliation, lawlessness, and terror. Concentration camps grew larger and more numerous every month. Nazi atrocities were unspeakable. Forsaken by all and totally helpless, Poland's Jews—three and a half million of them—were about to begin their last exodus, from the ghettoes to gas chambers.[2] Hope seemed futile, the cause of freedom doomed.

In those days of despair, words of hope came from Western leaders and found their way to Polish hearts. The first message came from Franklin D. Roosevelt, the leader of a nation that inspired love and admiration among the poor, the oppressed, and the exploited because it stood for freedom and social justice. The United States was tremendously popular among the Poles because America's stand during World War I was largely responsible for the Great Powers' recognition of Poland's right to freedom and independence. Millions of Poles had migrated to the United States, and their well-being as well as their devotion to the "old country" were proverbial. As for the US president, he called Poland an "inspiration" to the world, and the Poles reciprocated by placing in him a confidence that seemed boundless.

On January 6, 1941, President Roosevelt proclaimed his Four Freedoms upon which the future was to be built. His words passed through all frontiers, prison walls, and barbed-wire barricades because he defined the uncompromising goals of victory in simple and unmistakable terms:

> In the future days which we seek to make secure, we look forward to a world founded upon four essential freedoms.
>
> The first is freedom of speech and expression everywhere in the world.
>
> The second is freedom of every person to worship God in his own way, everywhere in the world.
>
> The third is freedom from want—which, translated into world terms, means economic understanding, which will secure to every nation a healthy peace time life for its inhabitants, everywhere in the world.
>
> The fourth is freedom from fear—which, translated into world terms, means worldwide reduction of armaments to such a point and in such a thorough fashion that no nation will be in a position to commit an act of aggression against any neighbor—anywhere in the world.
>
> This is no vision of a distant millennium. It is a definite basis for a kind of world attainable in our time and generation. [3]

Seven months later, on August 12, 1941, Churchill and Roosevelt signed and announced to the world what later became known as the Atlantic Charter. [4] It was not a treaty and was not submitted to the British Parliament or the American Senate for ratification, but in time both the charter and the Four Freedoms turned out to be among the most widely acclaimed documents of the war.

In Poland, where the feeling of utter helplessness made hope—real or imaginary—the most important driving force in everyday life, the authors of the charter were looked upon as the last defenders and guarantors of everything worth living for. Churchill led an empire that had never been defeated before—a wise, proud, courageous nation—and he was looked upon as the wisest, the proudest, the most courageous of them all. Roosevelt was a great social reformer, an organizer of prosperity and peace, and he led a nation of tremendous power and wealth. Now, in the name of their countries, they agreed on what seemed to be a covenant that all freedom-loving nations were invited to adopt as their own and that would guarantee justice for Poland.

Article 1 of the charter committed the signatories to "seek no aggrandizement, territorial or other." Article 2 stated that the signatories "desire to see no territorial changes that do not accord with the freely expressed wishes of the peoples concerned." Article 3 recognized "the right of all peoples to choose the form of government under which they will live" and called for restoration of "sovereign rights and self-government . . . to those who have been forcibly deprived of them." Article 4 proclaimed freedom of international trade and free access to the world's raw materials. Article 5 imposed a duty on governments to seek "improved labor standards, economic advancement and social security." Article 6 expressed hope "to see established a peace which will accord to all nations the means of dwelling in safety within their own boundaries and which will afford assurance that all the men in all the lands may live out their lives in freedom from fear and want." Article 7 proclaimed freedom of the seas, and Article 8 called for a general disarmament.

On September 24, 1941, in London, the representatives of ten countries—Russia and Poland included—confirmed their adherence to the charter. The Soviet ambassador, Maisky, made a special declaration on that occasion. He did pledge his government's support of the charter's principles. But he also added a rather enigmatic qualification, "considering that the practical application of these principles will necessarily adapt itself to the circumstances, needs, and historic peculiarities of particular countries."[5] World public opinion hailed the Soviet adherence and ignored the qualifications.

On January 1, 1942, twenty-six countries subscribed to the charter, and it eventually became a part of the United Nations Declaration. It was publicized and described as a set of rules binding on the world and a guarantee that the great powers would not abuse the weakness of small countries. Churchill was exuberant in his comments and praise.[6]

The Poles saw in the Atlantic Charter, and particularly in the Soviet adherence to it, a vital achievement. Great Britain and the United States committed themselves to stand guard against the evils that had haunted the small nations for centuries, and the Soviet government finally seemed to renounce its policy of expansion by voluntarily assuming obligations so clearly defined. And, indeed, a few months later, on November 6, Stalin reaffirmed those obligations in a public declaration:

> We have not and cannot have any such war aims as the seizure of foreign territories and the subjugation of foreign peoples whether it be peoples and territories of Europe or the peoples and territories of Asia. . . .

We have not and cannot have such war aims as the imposition of our will
and regime on the Slavs and other enslaved peoples of Europe who are awaiting our aid.

Our aid consists in assisting these peoples in their struggle for liberation
from Hitler's tyranny, and then setting them free to rule on their own lands as
they desire. No intervention whatever in the internal affairs of other nations. [7]

Stalin's words were acclaimed all over the world. They were also taken at
face value.

NOTES

1. Dwight D. Eisenhower, *Crusade in Europe* (Garden City, NY: Doubleday & Co., 1948),
769; also Sherwood, *Roosevelt and Hopkins*, 304.

2. For an eyewitness testimony as to conditions in the Warsaw and Belzec ghettoes, see
Karski, *Story of a Secret State*, 320–54.

3. *Congressional Record*, 1941, 87, pt. 1, 46–47.

4. For the text, see ibid., 1941, 87, pt. 1, 7217.

5. *Documents on American Foreign Relations*, 4:15.

6. Ibid., 4:211. According to Robert Sherwood, the British considered the Atlantic Charter
no more than a "publicity handout." Sherwood, *Roosevelt and Hopkins*, 362.

7. Embassy of the USSR, *Soviet War Documents* (Washington, DC: 1943), 17.

Chapter Twenty-Six

Soviet-Polish Relations, July 30, 1941–April 25, 1943

POLISH DEPORTEES AND THE POLISH ARMY IN THE SOVIET UNION

Following the conclusion of the Polish-Soviet pact, a military agreement was signed on August 14, 1941, which provided for the formation of an autonomous Polish army in Russia.[1] The Poles were to fight in large units under their own command and to receive from Lend-Lease aid, sent specifically for that purpose, the same pay, rations, and maintenance as the Red Army.

Originally, the government-in-exile had planned to organize in Russia an army of three hundred thousand men, an estimate that did not seem exaggerated.[2] On September 17, 1940, the first anniversary of the Soviet invasion of Poland, *Krasnaya Zvezda*, an organ of the Soviet armed forces, reported that by the end of 1939 "ten generals, fifty-two colonels, and seventy-two lt. colonels, five thousand one hundred and thirty-one other senior officers, four thousand and ninety-six junior officers, and 181,223 other ranks" had been captured by the Red Army. Considering an additional number of Polish war prisoners captured under various circumstances and reported in the same issue, it could be concluded that, altogether, some 230,670 Polish soldiers, including twelve generals and more than ten thousand officers, had been taken captive by the Soviets by October 1939. This was not all. From the autumn of 1939 to the spring of 1941, the Soviet government conscripted into the Red Army those inhabitants of the recently occupied areas who had been born in 1917, 1918, and 1919—probably some one hundred thousand men.[3] Apparently nine hundred officers escaped from Poland to the Baltic states. After the Soviet occupation of Latvia, Lithuania, and Estonia in 1940, most of them were captured and deported to Russia. Not a few officers in hiding in the Soviet-dominated part of Poland were eventually arrested and sent to Russia, too. Then, in the years 1939–1941, according to Polish estimates, the Soviets deported more than 1,000,000 men, women, and children, which meant that by the autumn of 1941 approximately 1,500,000 Polish citizens, minus those who had died meanwhile, were somewhere in the USSR.[4] Under the terms of President Kalinin's amnesty decree, all of them were to be released; according to the military agreement, those of proper age were to be incorporated into the army.

By the end of October 1941 about 46,000 men had reported to Polish military headquarters in Buzuluk, and for a short time everything seemed to be going well. However, on November 6 General A. P. Panfilov, deputy chief of staff of the Red Army, informed General Wladyslaw Anders, newly appointed commander in chief of the Polish forces in Russia, that his government could afford food rations for no more than 30,000 men, which meant that further enlistment had to be stopped and 16,000 men discharged.[5] The unexpected decision also meant that every discharged man, deprived of his military ration cards, would be condemned to die of starvation unless he returned to his internment or forced-labor camp, or unless he was somehow fed by his fellow soldiers from their own rations.

There was, however, another and even more serious reason for concern: Only a fraction of the Poles known to be in the Soviet Union had reported to Buzuluk. A great many of the deportees were not permitted to leave their camps, and others could not obtain railroad tickets or establish contact with the Polish embassy, but most of them could not be found at all. Those who had been conscripted into the Red Army were never released, and no communication with them was allowed.[6] Particularly alarming was the absence of more than eight thousand officers. Anxious to find out what had happened to them, the Polish military authorities started an investigation of their own and soon a special office created for that purpose collected voluminous data and evidence of all sorts. As a result, a grave suspicion arose that the missing officers had been killed.

In December 1941 Sikorski went to Moscow to clarify the matter and to obtain Stalin's decision as to the size and future of the Polish forces in Russia. Before he started negotiating with the Soviet officials, Anders informed him that the conditions under which his men had been organized, trained, and equipped were appallingly bad, and the attitude of the Soviet authorities was hostile. In addition, there existed a basic difference between the Soviet and the Polish concepts of the character and the role of the newly organized army. The Poles, in agreement with the pact, wanted to have large units properly equipped and organized, fighting under Polish flags and led by Polish commanders. The Soviets wanted the Poles to go into battle immediately as part of the Red Army's large units. Anders thought that the best solution was to move the troops out of Russia altogether, probably to the Middle East.[7]

In the conversation of December 3 among Stalin, Molotov, Sikorski, Ambassador Stanislaw Kot, and Anders,[8] the Poles complained that the amnesty had not been implemented; that the deportees were not being released; and that those released did not receive adequate food, housing, transportation, soap, tools for construction, lumber, nails, and so on. They also handed Stalin a list of four thousand identified officers who had been captured by the Red Army in 1939 and were still missing. Sikorski proposed at least a partial transfer of troops to the Middle East, where they could be properly organized, trained, and prepared for fighting. The proposal annoyed Stalin, who observed several times that Polish demands were inspired by the British. Finally, however, it was agreed that the army would comprise six divisions of 11,000 men each, with a reserve of 30,000. In addition, 25,000 troops were to be evacuated immediately to the Middle East to join the Polish forces fighting in Libya, and 2,000 airmen and sailors were to be sent to Great Britain. Thus, the total number of Polish soldiers to be recruited in the Soviet Union was 123,000 men.

For the moment, Polish-Soviet relations seemed to be taking a friendly course. Just before Sikorski's departure on December 7, a Polish-Soviet declaration of friendship and mutual aid was signed. On the same day, Sikorski made an optimistic broadcast to Poland from the Moscow radio station. He also wrote Churchill describing his trip to Moscow as a full success. Impressed by Stalin, he described him as "sincere," venturing an opinion that "for the time being Stalin has abandoned the idea of universal communism." He hoped to increase the size of the army to 150,000 men and wanted to have the bulk of it fighting together with the Russians. "I feel my visit to Russia resulted in a solution of nearly all the outstanding Polish-Soviet problems and also resulted in some benefit to the Allied cause" was his overall assessment.[9]

That the agreement was of little consequence soon became evident, because although Stalin displayed his goodwill, the Soviet officials continued to obstruct the release of army men and equipment. Less than four months after Sikorski's visit on March 18, 1942, Anders was notified that the strength of his troops would be limited to 44,000—52,000 men fewer than agreed. There was no recourse for this decision, and the surplus (approximating 30,000 men) was subsequently evacuated to the Middle East. In the spring of 1942 all further release of Poles was halted, causing Ambassador Kot to complain bitterly in his note of May 4. Sikorski, too, had appealed to Stalin on April 9, but received a negative answer.[10]

By July 31, 1942, the Poles were informed that the Soviet government had decided to evacuate the remainder of the Polish forces—approximately 42,000 men—to the Middle East. Simultaneously, the news came that many delegates at the Polish embassy who were supervising the release and distributing assistance to the deportees at various points in Russia had been arrested, in violation of a special agreement of December 23, 1941. Subsequently, all prisoners and deportees (except for those already in the army centers) were cut off from any contact with Polish authorities.[11]

The Soviet decision to evacuate the rest of the Polish forces to the Middle East was accepted and carried out. Altogether, 113,000 men, women, and children had left—a small fraction of the 1,500,000 deportees, war prisoners, forced-labor-camp inmates, so-called free workers, and those forcibly conscripted. Most of them were never to see their motherland again.

THE MISSING OFFICERS AND THE KATYN MASSACRE

According to available sources, the Polish officers were interned in a number of camps, the largest of which were Kozielsk near Smolensk (with some 4,500 officers) and Starobielsk near Kharkov (with 3,920).[12] During the period from October 1939 to the spring of 1940, many of them corresponded with their families in Poland. Then, beginning in May 1940, all communications suddenly ceased.[13]

Of all the officers, no more than 2,300 reported to their army headquarters in 1941–1942, not one among them from either Starobielsk or Kozielsk. Mystified, the Polish military authorities made an extensive investigation among those who did report, and it was established that the internees from those two camps had been evacuated in an unknown direction and to an unknown destiny sometime in the spring of 1940. It was on the basis of that investigation, as well as prewar files, that Sikorski handed Stalin in December 1941 the list of approximately four thousand missing officers.

The Polish government asked the Soviet authorities on numerous occasions to release the pertinent information. In October and November 1941, Kot inquired in conversations with Stalin, Molotov, and Vishinsky about the lists of the internees that he knew had been made by the Soviet authorities. His interventions brought no results. The answers were usually vague or contradictory: the government had set all officers free and did not know where they went, the officers had settled down somewhere, the officers would report any day, and so on. In December 1941 Stalin told Sikorski that perhaps the missing officers had "escaped" to Manchuria.[14]

On January 28, 1942, Raczyński, then acting minister of foreign affairs, delivered a note to Maisky's successor, Ambassador Alexander V. Bogomolov, again requesting some information. Bogomolov reassured him that all Poles had been set free. According to Tadeusz Romer, Polish ambassador to the Soviet Union since 1942, more than fifty formal inquiries had been addressed to Soviet authorities.[15] The Soviet officials never once suggested that the missing officers may have been or had in fact been seized by the Germans in 1941.

Then on April 13, 1943, the German radio and press suddenly announced the discovery of a mass grave of Polish army officers in the forest of Katyn near Smolensk. Several thousand bodies were reported to have been found, all of them shot in the same manner, from the back. The German authorities proposed an on-the-spot inquiry under international auspices and control.[16]

Moscow's reaction was swift. Less than forty-eight hours later, on April 15, the official news agency released a declaration couched in perfervid language:

> The German Fascist reports on this subject leave no doubt as to the tragic fate of the former Polish prisoners of war who in 1941 were engaged in construction work in areas west of Smolensk . . . [and who] fell into the hands of German Fascist hangmen in the summer of 1941 after the withdrawal of Soviet troops from the Smolensk area.
>
> Beyond doubt Goebbels' slanderers are now trying by lies and calumnies to cover up the bloody crimes of the Hitlerite gangsters. In their clumsy concocted publication about the numerous graves which the Germans allegedly discovered near Smolensk, the Hitlerite liars mention the village of Gnezdovaya. But like the swindlers they are, they are silent about the fact that it was near the village Gnezdovaya that the archeological excavations of the historic "Gnezdovaya burial place" were made.[17]

Never before had the Soviet government indicated that the missing officers had been engaged in construction work near Smolensk and subsequently captured by the Germans. On the contrary, Stalin, as well as Molotov and Vishinsky, had maintained consistently that the officers had been released *by the Soviets* or that they had *escaped*. Besides, the Soviet declaration ominously contradicted itself. While one paragraph professed "no doubt as to the tragic fate of the former Polish prisoners," the other referred to the fantastic archeological story, suggesting that the German "discovery" had nothing to do with the missing officers at all. As far as the facts were concerned, the declaration failed to refute German allegations and in fact increased anxiety among the Poles.

Now events moved fast. On April 16 and 17, two official Polish statements were made public. The first, by the minister of national defense, General Marjan Kukiel, contained a factual review of the affair of the missing officers, including data concerning interventions with the Soviet government and the Soviet answers. The second one, by the government, called upon the International Red Cross in neutral Switzerland to investigate the matter.[18] Two days later, *Pravda* announced that the Poles in London had acted in collusion with the Nazis; it branded their appeal to the Red Cross as "direct assistance to the enemy in the fabrication of a foul lie which will fill all people of common sense with repugnance."

The next day, on April 20, the government-in-exile sent a note to Moscow in which it reviewed all of its inquiries from 1941 to 1943, quoted all Soviet answers, and demanded some clarification.[19] None was forthcoming; instead, Stalin sent identical cables to Churchill and Roosevelt, violently condemning the Nazis for their "monstrous crime," denouncing the idea of a "farcical investigation," and accusing the Poles of collaboration with the Nazis:

> The fact that the anti-Soviet campaign has been started simultaneously in the German and Polish press and follows identical lines is indubitable evidence of contact and collusion between Hitler—the Allies' enemy—and the Sikorski government in this hostile campaign.
>
> At a time when the peoples of the Soviet Union are shedding their blood in a grim struggle against Hitler's Germany and bending their energies to defeat the common foe of the freedom-loving democratic countries, the Sikorski government is striking a treacherous blow at the Soviet Union to help Hitler's tyranny.[20]

In conclusion, Stalin warned that the Soviet Union would sever relations with the Polish government-in-exile.

His decision, which took everybody by surprise, anticipated a crisis of incalculable consequences not only for the Poles but for Allied unity as well. Both Churchill and Roosevelt fully realized its potential and its possible impact on world public opinion. On April 23 the Red Cross refused to investigate the matter, because "all parties interested" had not agreed upon the investigation. The next day Eden summoned Sikorski and, emphasizing that he acted under Churchill's instructions, asked for an immediate withdrawal of the Polish request to the Red Cross and for a public declaration that the Katyn massacre was a Nazi "invention." Otherwise, he warned, the Soviet government would break diplomatic relations with Poland. If that happened, Poland and only Poland would be a loser. Great Britain was not going to endanger its good relations with Russia. Sikorski vehemently refused.[21] The next day Moscow did break relations with the government-in-exile. The latter, by then at a complete political impasse and under tremendous pressure of events, *did* withdraw the appeal.[22] To no avail, however. Diplomatic relations between the government-in-exile and Moscow were never to be resumed.[23]

Although the Katyn affair did arouse world public opinion, it was soon forgotten or discounted as just another item of Nazi propaganda. At that time, just two months after the Stalingrad victory, Russia's prestige was higher than ever, and before long Stalin himself made a public gesture that calmed troubled spirits. On May 4, 1943, nine days after the break with the Polish government, he agreed to answer questions submitted to him by the correspondents of the (London) *Times* and the *New York Times*. To the question, "Does the government of the USSR desire to see a strong and independent Poland after the defeat of Hitlerite Germany?" he answered, "Unquestionably it does." Asked "on what fundamentals is it your opinion that relations between Poland and the USSR should be based after the war?" he answered, "Upon the fundamentals of solid good neighborly relations and mutual respect, or should the Polish people so desire, upon the fundamentals of an alliance providing for mutual assistance against the Germans as the chief enemy of the Soviet Union and Poland." The interview received tremendous publicity all over the world, evoked a friendly response in many quarters, and was interpreted as proof of Stalin's statesmanship and goodwill, as opposed to the political irresponsibility of the Poles in London. Less than three weeks later, on May 22, Moscow's announcement about the dissolution of the Comintern appeared and was hailed as conclusive evidence of Russia's loyalty to the Allied cause.[24]

The Katyn affair lowered the standing of the Polish government because it was widely assumed that, unfortunately, the Poles had fallen victim to Nazi propaganda. The fact that the world first learned about the Katyn massacre from Goebbels put the Polish authorities in an extremely difficult position. In order not to weaken Allied unity, hoping for a final settlement with Russia, and well aware that the Soviets were still keeping more than one million Polish deportees, Sikorski's government had not raised the issue of the missing officers publicly, nor did it *officially* notify the Allied governments about it *before* April 1943. Since world public opinion and the Allied governments first learned about the fate of those officers from Nazi sources, subsequent declarations of the government-in-exile lost much weight. Failure on the part of the Poles to inform the public regularly and candidly about the real state of Polish-Soviet relations gave Moscow a great advantage throughout the entire war.

THE PROBLEM OF THE POLISH-SOVIET FRONTIER

In the course of the negotiations of the pact, as well as throughout the entire war, Moscow consistently indicated, directly or indirectly, that Poland's prewar eastern frontiers would not be reconstituted. As the war progressed and Russia's chances of victory grew, those indications became increasingly blunt. On the day of Sikorski's arrival in Russia (December 1, 1941), the Narkomindel informed the Polish embassy that all those former inhabitants of eastern Poland who were of Ukrainian, Byelorussian, and Jewish origin would be considered Soviet citizens and conscripted into the Red Army; only those of Polish ethnic origin would be recognized as Polish citizens. According to the note, the decision was motivated by the fact that "the question of the frontiers between the USSR and Poland had not been settled and is subject to settlement in the future."[25]

Three days later, at a banquet in Sikorski's honor, Stalin vaguely suggested that some settlement of postwar boundaries should be made between Poland and Russia *without* the intervention of the Western powers and *before* the end of the war. "We should settle our common frontier between ourselves and before the Peace Conference, as soon as the Polish Army enters into action. We should stop talking on this subject. Don't worry, we will not harm you," he told Sikorski. The latter refused, arguing that he could not "accept, even in principle, any suggestion that the Polish state frontiers could be considered fluid."[26] Could the Poles have obtained better terms had they accepted Stalin's suggestion and entered into direct negotiations with Moscow during the early stages of the war, instead of waiting and relying on Anglo-American support? There is no way to find out.

Throughout 1942 Moscow indicated on several occasions that they considered the frontiers of June 1941 legally valid—not on the basis of the Ribbentrop-Molotov agreement of September 28, 1939, to be sure, but rather as a result of "plebiscites" conducted under the Red Army's supervision one month later. On January 5 the ministry of the interior stated that the incorporation of Poland's eastern territories was in accordance with the "freely expressed will of the population." The next day, the official communiqué of the German atrocities listed Lvov as a Soviet town. Polish protests brought a reply that in the future any note suggesting that those territories did not belong to either the Ukrainian or the Byelorussian Soviet Republic would be rejected.[27]

On January 16, 1943, the Polish embassy was notified that *all* Polish deportees and former war prisoners remaining in the USSR would be regarded as Soviet citizens, regardless of their ethnic origins. On February 23, the *Radianska Ukraina* published an article in which the Polish refusal to cede the eastern territories was presented as an attempt to "detach" the Ukrainian and Byelorussian territories from the USSR. Since he knew that nothing could be published in Russia without governmental approval, Sikorski sent a stern note to Moscow, and on the night of February 26–27 Romer personally intervened with Stalin. A week later the Narkomindel formally accused the government-in-exile of attempting to "dismember" the Ukraine and Byelorussia, and a public declaration of March 1 accused the Poles of denying the Ukrainian and Byelorussian people the right to be free and "reunited with their brothers" in the USSR.[28] The declaration preceded by only a few weeks the rupture of diplomatic relations with the government-in-exile over the Katyn massacre.

"FRIENDLY" AND "UNFRIENDLY" GOVERNMENTS

Diplomatic relations with the Polish government-in-exile were broken off at the time of great Soviet military successes. The victory at Stalingrad in February 1943 had a tremendous impact within and outside of Russia. Stalin's prestige waxed high all over the world, and he must have felt more independent of British and American policies and aid than at any time before. With the summer offensive in preparation, Russia seemed to be winning the war by itself, without a second front. From 1941 to 1942 Stalin may have feared that the Allies would conclude a separate peace with Germany, but by 1943 he certainly realized that they must nurture a similar fear about him. After all, he might reach a new understanding with Hitler after attaining the frontiers of 1941.[29]

The Red Army's victories opened new diplomatic and political vistas. Throughout 1941 and 1942, Stalin failed in his efforts to obtain formal recognition of Russia's 1941 frontiers from his British and American allies, although he discovered that the British were reconciled to them. The year 1943 made such recognition feasible. It also opened even greater possibilities, namely, extension of Soviet rule over large areas beyond the 1941 boundaries. Beginning in 1943 the Soviets openly pursued two policies on Poland: one, aiming at the British-American recognition of the Ribbentrop-Molotov frontier (to be named the Curzon Line for public consumption), and two, preparing a Moscow-sponsored government for all of postwar Poland.

Most of the Polish Communists who were to become prominent after the war had fled the German-controlled areas to Soviet-occupied Lvov, where they soon formed the Association of Former Political Prisoners. Their situation was difficult and their future uncertain. The Nazi-Soviet secret agreement and war collaboration precluded a Communist anti-Nazi underground in the German-controlled territories. They could not engage in any serious organizational work in the Soviet-controlled areas either, since the Soviet administration concentrated on the support of Ukrainian rather than Polish elements. Thus, in the main, they kept rather quiet until the German attack of June 1941 provided them with opportunities for action.

The handful of Communists remaining in the German-occupied territories had no organization because, ironically, the Communist party of Poland had been dissolved by the Comintern in 1938 as a result of internal rivalries, Stalin's purges, and, probably, ineffectiveness. Even after Germany attacked Russia, the Polish Communists still lacked centralized organization and leadership for several months. Usually they formed loose, small, secret cells that tried to establish some contact with Moscow for help and guidance. Generally concealing their political identity, they also tried to join the non-Communist underground organizations, individually or in groups. Eventually, in the winter of 1941–1942, the first Communist elite units were dispatched from Russia and parachuted to Poland near Warsaw and in Silesia. The first two, dropped in December 1941 and January 1942, were trained in Comintern schools. One of them had been briefed personally by Georgi Dimitrov, secretary-general of the Comintern. Through them, a firm contact with the Soviet authorities was established. [30]

Early in 1942 a unified Communist underground organization emerged under the name of the Polish Workers' Party (PPR). The beginnings were tough. The Moscow-appointed first secretary, Marceli Nowotko, was shot in November 1942. His successor, Pawel Finder, also designated by Moscow, was arrested by the Gestapo one year later. [31] By that time radio communication with Moscow had failed, and the leadership took it upon themselves to elect Wladyslaw Gomulka. He accepted the election results and took over command, thus acting independently from the Kremlin, a fact that would not be forgotten by Stalin.

Gomulka's life was marked by his unswerving devotion to the Communist cause. Born in 1905 to a worker's family, he eventually became a plumber. He joined the Communist party early in his youth and gave all his energies and talents to revolutionary activities. He was arrested in 1926. In 1932 he was wounded by the police in a street demonstration, arrested again, and sentenced to four years' detention. Released in 1934, Gomulka soon left for Russia, where he remained about two years and underwent party training. On his return to Poland in 1936 he was arrested again and given a long sentence. He stayed in jail until the German attack on Poland. Like other political prisoners, he was then released by the Polish authorities, went to the Soviet zone of occupation, and lived in Lvov. A few months after Germany's attack on Russia, he left Lvov and after some delay established himself in Warsaw as a prominent member of the Communist underground.

Although organized, controlled, and partly supplied by the Soviets, the PPR tried to create the appearance of political moderation and organizational independence. Its program for the future Poland seemed moderate, even in comparison with the Socialist and Peasant parties. It emphasized nationalism and sought collaboration with the non-Communist Underground. Its main tasks, according to General Tadeusz Bor-Komorowski (commander of the Home Army since July 1943), were centralization and control of all Communist activities, infiltration of non-Communist underground groups, collaboration with Soviet partisans, and execution of orders from Moscow. Actual fighting against the Germans did not seem to take precedence over these tasks; on the contrary, the PPR apparently avoided the risk of dissipating its meager reserves. [32] Its strength was never impressive compared to non-Communist underground forces: according to their own estimates, by 1944 the combined strength of organized Communists did not exceed twenty thousand.[33]

Those who had sought refuge in the Soviet Union became organizationally active sometime at the end of 1941. Just at the time of Sikorski's official visit in Moscow in December 1941, *Izvestya* reported that a meeting of "representatives of the Polish nation" had taken place two hundred miles away, in Saratov. In March 1943 this group—the nucleus of Poland's postwar government—founded the Union of Polish Patriots.[34]

The more the Polish-Soviet relations deteriorated, the more noticeable became the activities of the Polish Communists in Russia. A few months before Moscow broke off its diplomatic relations with Poland, they began to publish their own organ, *Wolna Polska* (Free Poland), a bimonthly magazine which from the beginning took a stand violently critical of the government-in-exile. The criticism was synchronized with the Soviet diplomatic offensive against the "London Poles."[35] The rupture of diplomatic relations in April 1943 resulted in stepped up activities for the Union of Polish Patriots. Within less than two months, on June 9–10, its first official convention took place in Moscow, with over sixty delegates participating. The convention, supposedly representing all the "democratic" parties from Poland, denounced the government-in-exile as "reactionary," "Fascist," and "pro-Nazi"; called for a Poland with a "parliamentarian-democratic" system of government; emphasized its "friendship" with the Soviet Union; and assumed the representation of all "progressive" Polish elements.[36] Stalin's congratulatory and highly publicized message was a sign of his approval and sponsorship.

Nominal chairmanship of the union was given to Wanda Wasilewska, a colonel in the Red Army at the time, a Soviet citizen, and wife of the assistant commissar for foreign affairs of the USSR, A. Korneytchuk. Most of the elected officers, as postwar official sources have revealed, were those who had directed the Association of Former Political Prisoners in 1939–1941, and who would appear later on as the core of postwar government in Poland. The most prominent among them were Alfred Lampe, Jakub Berman, Hilary Minc, Aleksander Zawadzki, Stanislaw Radkiewicz, Roman Zambrowski, Stanislaw Skrzeszewski, Edward Ochab, Stefan Jedrychowski, and Jerzy Sztachelski.[37]

The convention of the Union of Polish Patriots was preceded by the formation of the Kosciuszko Division, with Colonel Zygmunt Berling, a regular Polish prewar army officer, in nominal command. The ranks of the division were recruited from among those deportees and war prisoners who had not been allowed to leave Russia in 1942–1943, but its actual command as well as its ideological education were entrusted mostly to the Soviet officers, often of Polish descent. Eventually, the Supreme Soviet issued a special decree granting permission to Red Army personnel to accept Polish citizenship—a vehicle for a direct Soviet control.[38]

From the middle of 1943 until the end of the war the Soviet government would use its adherents operating in Poland and Russia effectively against the government-in-exile. The activities of the non-Communist Underground would be minimized or misrepresented and its authority and prestige undermined. Great publicity would be given to those "democratic" and "progressive" forces in Poland and abroad that did not recognize the government in London. The "London Poles" would be discredited as "undemocratic" and "unfriendly" to Russia. Before long, it was Stalin who would actually decide which Poles should or should not be considered "democratic," and why.

NOTES

1. For the text, see *DPSR, 1939–1945*, 1:147–48.

2. R. Umiastowski, *Poland, Russia and Great Britain, 1941–1945* (London: Hollis and Carter, 1946), 27.

3. *Polish-Soviet Relations, 1918–1943, Official Documents*, 26; 38.

4. Dr. Bronislaw Kusnierz, *Stalin and the Poles, an Indictment of the Soviet Leaders* (London: Hollis and Carter, 1949). For conditions of deportations and life in forced labor camps, see Jerzy Gliksman, *Tell the West* (New York: Gresham Press, 1948). Also J. Czapski, *The Inhuman Land* (New York: Sheed and Ward, 1952).

5. *Polish-Soviet Relations, 1918–1943, Official Documents*, 27.

6. See Wladyslaw Anders, *An Army in Exile: The Story of the Second Polish Corps* (London: Macmillan & Co., 1949), 71–79.

7. Ibid., 83.

8. For the minutes, see *DPSR, 1939–1945*, 1:231–43.

9. For the full texts, see *DPSR, 1939–1945*, 1:246–47, 254–57, respectively.

10. Ibid., 320–21, 348–49, 351.

11. Ibid., 257–58, 407–9.

12. *Polish-Soviet Relations, 1918–1943, Official Documents*, 38–39.

13. For a well-documented study of the subject, see J. K. Zawodny, *Death in the Forest: The Story of the Katyn Forest Massacre* (Notre Dame, IN: University of Notre Dame Press, 1962).

14. Anders, *An Army in Exile*, 85; also Stanislaw Mikolajczyk, *The Rape of Poland: Pattern of Soviet Aggression* (New York & Toronto: McGraw-Hill Co., 1948), 22.

15. *DPSR, 1939–1945*, 1:271–72; Zawodny, *Death in the Forest*, 9.

16. For a short but factual review of the matter, see Winston S. Churchill, *The Hinge of Fate* (Boston: Houghton Mifflin Co., 1950), 757–61.

17. For the full text, see *DPSR, 1939–1945*, 1:524–25.

18. For the texts, see *DPSR, 1939–1945*, 1:525–28.

19. *DPSR, 1939–1945*, 1:528–30.

20. *The Correspondence between Stalin-Churchill-Roosevelt*, 1:121; 2:60.

21. *DPSR, 1939–1945*, 2:696–702.

22. *DPSR, 1939–1945*, 1:533–34.

23. After the liberation of the Smolensk area in September 1943, a special Soviet commission blamed the Germans for the crime. For the report and official comments, see *Izvestya* (Moscow), January 26, 1944, 1–4.

At the Nuremberg Trials in 1945–1946, German major war criminals were originally charged with the Katyn murders. After having heard and seen evidence, the court withdrew the charge from the final indictment (Churchill, *The Hinge of Fate*, 761). In September 1951 a special congressional committee was appointed in the United States to investigate the matter. After an extensive investigation, it came to the firm conclusion that the Soviets, not the Germans, murdered the officers. See *Katyn Forest Massacre*. Hearings before the Select Committee to Conduct an Investigation on the Facts, Evidence and Circumstances of the Katyn Forest Massacre, 82nd Congress, 2nd sess., 1952, 7 parts (Washington, DC: US Government Printing Office, 1952).

24. *Times* (London), May 7, 1943, 4; May 24, 1943, 5; *New York Times*, May 30, 1943, 16.

25. For the full text, see *DPSR, 1939–1945*, 1:227–28.

26. For the minutes of the conversation on December 4, 1941, *DPSR, 1939–1945*, 244–26.

27. For the full texts, *DPSR, 1939–1945*, 1:259–63.

28. *DPSR, 1939–1945*, 1:489–502.

29. Isaac Deutscher, *Stalin: A Political Biography* (New York: Oxford University Press, 1949), 480–84, 498–501.

30. Zbigniew K. Brzezinski, *The Soviet Bloc: Unity and Conflict* (Cambridge, MA: Harvard University Press, 1960), 46. For a collection of official Communist documents on the history of the Polish Workers' Party, see H. Kozlowska, ed., *W Dziesiata Rocznice Powstania PPR* (*The Tenth Anniversary of the Polish Workers' Party*) (Warsaw: Ksiazka i Wiedza, 1952).

31. For Nowotko's and Finger's biographies, see *Polska Partja Robotnicza. Kalendarz Robotniczy na 1948 rok* (*Workers' Calendar for 1948*) (Warsaw: Spoldzielnia Wydawnicza "Ksiazka," 1947), 187–88.

32. Bor-Komorowski, *The Secret Army*, 29–30, 70–71, 121–22; also *DPSR, 1939–1945*, 2:91.

33. A. Alster, J. Andrzejewski, "W Sprawie Skladu Socjalnego PZPR" (On the social structure of the Polish United Workers' Party), *Nowe Drogi* 5 (January–February 1951): 235.

34. For Sikorski's reaction, see Stanislaw Kot, *Listy z Rosji do Gen. Sikorskiego* (*Letters from Russia to General Sikorski*) (London: St. Martin's Printers, 1956), 64–65. For details on the origin of the postwar government in Poland, see Select Committee on Communist Aggression, *Communist Take-Over and Occupation of Poland*, Special Report no. 1 (83rd Congress, 2nd sess., 1954, H. Res. 346 and H. Res. 438) (Washington, DC: US Government Printing Office, 1954), 16–20. Hereafter referred to as *Communist Take-Over and Occupation of Poland*.

35. See Hull, *Memoirs*, 2:1268; also *New York Times*, April 29, 1943, 7.

36. *Wolna Polska* (Free Poland) (Moscow), June 16, 1943.

37. Jozwiak, *PPR W walce o wyzwolenie narodowe i spoleczne* (The Polish Workers' Party in the struggle for national and social liberation) (Warsaw: Ksiazka i Wiedza, 1952), 107–8. For short biographical notes on the abovementioned, see *Five Hundred Leading Communists*,

80th Congress, 2nd sess., House Document no. 707 (Washington, DC: US Government Printing Office, 1948), 98–100; also Scottish League for European Freedom, *Who Is Who of the Regime in Poland* (Edinburgh: 130 George Street, 1947), 27–37.

38. On the basis of that decree, a Soviet officer, Marshal Konstantin Rokossovsky, eventually became the commander in chief in postwar Poland.

Chapter Twenty-Seven

The British-Soviet Alliance of May 26, 1942

Churchill's Secret Diplomacy

For Great Britain, the conclusion of an alliance with Russia seemed a matter of vital importance. Russia's loyalty during the war as well as its cooperation at the peace conference had to be secured. The alliance would also become the cornerstone of postwar world order, based on the solidarity of the Great Powers. It was believed that, to achieve these goals, compromises on secondary issues had to be made if necessary.

Informal negotiations started in December 1941 during Eden's visit to Moscow. At that time, Stalin "seemed in a suspicious, even resentful mood," because Churchill had refused his demand to send British troops to Murmansk, Moscow had not been consulted as to the Atlantic Charter, and, finally, because Stalin apparently suspected that Great Britain and the United States planned to exclude Russia from the postwar settlement. Consequently, he insisted that the British-Soviet understanding "should be reached not only on military matters, but also on war aims and on plans for a postwar organization of the peace."[1] Eden was to "smooth out" strained relations and prepare the ground for long-range cooperation.

United States secretary of state Cordell Hull presumed that Stalin would try to exploit British eagerness for an alliance, presenting demands incompatible with the officially proclaimed war aims. Fearing that Eden might yield to those demands, he warned the Foreign Office on December 5 that the principles of the Atlantic Charter would have to be observed, that all territorial questions should be left in abeyance until the peace conference, and that "above all, there must be no secret accords."[2] He pointed out that his government could not be a party to any such agreements. Those were the days when the United States risked a war with Japan because of its refusal to recognize similar Japanese claims in Asia.

Hull's misgivings were fully justified, because in three conversations with Eden on December 16–19, Stalin bluntly asked for an agreement on the postwar reconstruction of Europe. He showed the foreign secretary his own draft of the British-Soviet military alliance and demanded that a secret protocol be made part of it. According to the protocol, Russia would receive slices of Finland; all of Estonia, Latvia, and Lithuania; Bessarabia; and Northern Bukovina. In Poland, the Curzon Line, "with slight variations," would form the Polish-Soviet frontier. East Prussia was to be transferred to Poland and "Tilsit and German territory north of the river Niemen to the Lithuanian Republic of the USSR." The Rhineland was to be detached from Prussia, while Austria and Bavaria were to be made separate states.

In exchange for British approval of Russia's leading position in eastern Europe, Stalin offered to recognize Britain's postwar predominant role in the west. He agreed that Great Britain should establish military bases in Norway and Sweden. Both he and Molotov emphasized that agreement on Russia's western frontiers was of primary importance.[3]

Stalin's demands for an across-the-board recognition of Russia's territorial acquisitions of 1939–1940 contained an apparent exception in the case of Poland. It was not the recognition of the Ribbentrop-Molotov line of September 28, 1939, that he sought but of the Curzon Line "with slight variations." Such a formula allowed him to preserve the appearance that he still adhered to the Polish-Soviet pact of July 1941, making the Nazi-Soviet agreements on the partition of Poland "null and void." It also was bound to make British acceptance easier, because the Curzon Line of 1920 had British approval at the time.[4] For all practical purposes, the formula represented no more than a smoke screen, since there was no significant difference between the two lines. Stalin realized it, and at one of the meetings he asked Eden for an "immediate recognition of Russia's 1941 frontiers as the Soviet frontiers in the peace treaty."[5] He did not even bother to invoke the Curzon Line.

On December 7, 1941, just as Eden was about to leave for Moscow, Japan attacked Pearl Harbor. This was a crucial event for Britain, and Churchill was exuberant in his joy.[6] The US entry into the war affected its course not only with regard to the Axis powers, it also changed the balance between

Great Britain and the Soviet Union. Suddenly Churchill felt stronger in his uneasy relations with Stalin. Territorial concessions in eastern Europe, considered acceptable not long before, now seemed avoidable. American objections to secret treaties assumed special importance.

Eden's cables from Moscow concerning Stalin's demands reached the prime minister at sea en route to Washington, where he and Roosevelt were to lay the foundation for the British-American war strategy. Achieving a community of views and policies between the Anglo-American leaders became a matter of utmost importance, and Churchill wanted to avoid antagonizing the president or Hull at any cost. With a swiftness characteristic of him, he now became a champion of the east European nations. He wired Eden hastily from aboard ship, instructing him to remember that Great Britain was committed because of the United States *not* to enter into any secret pacts with Russia, and that anything done to the contrary would meet Roosevelt's "blank refusal" in addition to other complications of "far-reaching proportions." The same day he cabled the leader of the opposition, Clement Attlee, advising him that Stalin's territorial demands would not be accepted, since they were incompatible with the principles of the Atlantic Charter.

> Stalin's demands about Finland, Baltic States and Rumania are directly contrary to the first, second and third Articles of the Atlantic Charter to which Stalin subscribed. There can be no question whatever of our making such an agreement, secret or public, direct or implied, without prior agreement with the United States. The time has not yet come to settle frontier questions, which can be resolved at the Peace Conference when we have won the war.[7]

Following Churchill's instructions, Eden withheld formal agreement to Stalin's territorial demands. He did not reject those demands per se though but took a formalistic stand, arguing that he had to consult the cabinet, the Dominions, and above all the United States. According to Hull, Eden did indicate that, if Stalin insisted on incorporating the Baltic states, the British government might acquiesce.[8]

Eden had hardly reached London when Molotov inquired about the consultations. Churchill, still in the United States, did not falter. Informed by Eden of Molotov's pressure, he sent another strongly worded message, dated January 8, 1942. "We have never recognized the 1941 frontiers of Russia except *de facto*. They were acquired by acts of aggression in shameful collusion with Hitler. . . . In any case there can be no question of settling frontiers until the Peace Conference. I know President Roosevelt holds this view as strongly as I do, and he has several times expressed his pleasure to me at the firm line we took at Moscow."

He was full of optimism as to the future, confident that the British-American bloc would become a decisive power, and convinced that after the war "the Soviet Union will need our aid for reconstruction far more than we shall need theirs."[9] Suddenly the prospects for Poland seemed bright.

Hull, however, had doubts as to the British stand. When informed by the American ambassador in Britain, John G. Winant, of the negotiations in Moscow and London, he defined American policy in an extensive memorandum prepared for the president's approval on February 4, 1942. He still feared that the British were in sympathy with Russia's demands. This, he reasoned, was bound to result in British efforts to obtain the approval of the United States as well. Consequently, he recommended that the US government should not only refuse to consent to such an agreement, but should restrain the British from making it. Otherwise, "intrigues, mutual suspicions, and the establishment of spheres of influence" would mark the relations among the Great Powers. He believed that firmness had to be used in relations with Russia, arguing that recognition of Soviet demands would undermine the morale of the small nations, strengthen world Communism, "give concern" to the Vatican, and thwart the principles of the Atlantic Charter. It would repeat the unfortunate practices of secret diplomacy of World War I, provide the Nazi propaganda machine with excellent material, and encourage Stalin "to resort to similar tactics later on in order to obtain further and more far-reaching demands."[10]

Hull's apprehensions were well founded, because by then Churchill had begun to change in his attitude toward Russia's territorial demands and the applicability of the Atlantic Charter. He came to the conclusion that what he called a "moral position" could not be maintained any longer. He was a realist, and it seemed to him that the "pressure of events" demanded flexibility.

On March 7, 1942, he cabled the president: "The increasing gravity of the war has led me to feel that the principles of the Atlantic Charter ought not to be constructed so as to deny Russia the frontiers she occupied when Germany attacked her. This was the basis on which Russia acceded to the Charter. . . . I hope, therefore, that you will be able to give us a free hand to sign the treaty which Stalin desires as soon as possible."

In requesting a "free hand," he meaningfully observed that the German spring offensive against Russia was to take place soon and that the Allies could not do much to relieve the Red Army. [11] His appeal did not meet with success. On Hull's insistence, the president refused to give his approval. [12]

Churchill's change of position was remarkable, considering that less than three months before he had branded Soviet acquisitions in eastern Europe as "shameless aggression," irreconcilable with the Atlantic Charter. It was doubtless caused by the military situation. Adversities in Egypt, Japanese victories in the Pacific area, the recent fall of Singapore, disastrous losses inflicted by the German U-boats on the merchant fleet, and the inability to meet Stalin's constant demands for a second front—because of all of these factors, great caution was demanded in dealing with Moscow. Stalin did not hide his disappointment, and Maisky repeatedly inquired about the delay in London's agreement to the Soviet territorial demands. Even more important were the veiled threats coming from the Kremlin. In his order of the day, on February 23, Stalin did not mention the overthrow of the Nazi regime as the war aim but only the liberation of the Soviet territories. This, of course, could be interpreted as meaning that once the Germans were pushed out of Russia's frontiers of 1941, Stalin might lose interest in pursuing the war operations even if he chose not to conclude a separate peace with Hitler. Churchill could not provide the second front Stalin wanted without endangering Great Britain's security. He could, however, try to appease Stalin by granting concessions in eastern Europe, a marginal area as far as Britain's vital interests were concerned.

There were probably other reasons as well for Churchill's change of heart. Stalin's confidence and goodwill might result in bringing Russia into the war against Japan. [13] Furthermore, Eden strongly believed that Russia's "appetites" for aggrandizement were bound to grow once the tide of war changed to its advantage. Consequently, and contrary to Hull's opinion, he considered it prudent to make settlements with Stalin as early as possible, giving him what then seemed reasonable but barring him from asking for more in the future. [14]

The Soviet government was not unaware of the differences between London and Washington, because two days after his telegram to Roosevelt, Churchill sent a message to Stalin informing him about his "urging" the president to approve the Anglo-Soviet secret agreement on Russia's western frontiers. Eleven days later, on March 20, he sent another cable in the same vein. [15] Stalin was displeased with the American intervention. He considered the Anglo-Soviet agreement and its provisions to be the concern of Great

Britain and the Soviet Union alone, and the United States had no right to interfere.[16]

By then the Polish government had learned about the Churchill-Eden stand and also tried to intervene. In the middle of February 1943, acting foreign minister Raczyński went to Washington to sound out the attitude of American authorities. Soon after, on March 9, Sikorski sent a long letter to Eden warning him against making concessions to Russia. Two days later he appealed to Churchill.[17] At the end of March Sikorski himself visited Roosevelt. He informed the president of Eden's assurances that recognition of Soviet territorial demands on Poland would be *excluded* from the British-Soviet agreement and strongly objected to the recognition of Russia's acquisitions in the Baltic area and in Romania. The president seemed to be in sympathy with his views and told him so.[18]

Sikorski returned to London satisfied with his success in Washington and convinced that the British-Soviet plans concerning eastern Europe had been frustrated. Hull was also satisfied, and he left the capital at the end of February for rest and medical treatment. Upon his return some two months later, he found that "events had moved in the wrong direction." During his absence, the president conceived his own plan. On April 1 he forwarded it to London and, of even greater importance, in a special message he let Stalin know about it. The plan contained a recognition of part of Finland and all of Estonia, Latvia, and Lithuania as belonging to the Soviet security zone, under the condition that those inhabitants who did not wish to live under Soviet rule would be allowed to leave their countries and take their property with them. Hull opposed the idea vigorously, told the president about it, and instructed Winant to inform Churchill that the US government continued to oppose recognition of Soviet demands.[19]

On May 20 Molotov arrived in London for final negotiations and the signing of the alliance. Again he put forth territorial demands on eastern Europe, *specifically* including Poland.[20] Informed about this, Hull rushed another memorandum to Roosevelt, even stronger than the one of February 4. This time he went as far as to suggest a public declaration disassociating the United States from the British-Soviet agreement, if it included secret territorial clauses. His views were transmitted to London with a notification that he had the president's support. From then on, in Hull's words, "the British position . . . began to veer."[21] On May 24 Eden rejected Molotov's demands as "incompatible with the Anglo-Polish agreement of August 1939," while Churchill sent a special cable to Stalin pointing out that "we cannot go back on our previous undertakings to Poland, and have to take account of our own and American opinion."[22] This was the last time Churchill and Eden, in their dealings with Stalin, invoked Britain's obligations toward Poland resulting from the Anglo-Polish alliance of August 25, 1939.

Confronted with Anglo-American opposition and solidarity, Stalin gave in, and on May 26 a twenty-year alliance was signed without any reference to Russia's western frontiers. Churchill was jubilant, for he doubtless considered concessions to Moscow a dire necessity and not a matter of choice, and he cherished friendly relations with the United States. The next day he triumphantly cabled Roosevelt that the text of the treaty draft had been "completely transformed, . . . free from the objections we both [*sic*] entertained and [is] entirely compatible with our Atlantic Charter."[23] Hull, too, was more than satisfied: his policy had prevailed over his own president's vacillation. When on June 13 the Polish ambassador in Washington, Jan Ciechanowski, called on him to thank him for American intervention, Hull jokingly told the ambassador that as late as two days before the treaty was signed, Churchill and Eden still did not believe the United States would publicly disassociate itself from the treaty as originally proposed. "We certainly had to give them hell before we could make them realize it," he added.[24]

There cannot be much doubt that in May 1942 both Churchill and Eden intended to recognize—formally, although secretly—Russia's demands in central-eastern Europe, including demands made on Poland. They did not carry out their intentions mainly owing to Hull's opposition. However, Stalin learned again that the British were ready to yield and that Roosevelt was not far away from yielding. Molotov took special care to let London know for the record that the matter was not closed. As soon as he signed the treaty, he told Eden that postwar Poland should receive East Prussia and other German territories, but that its eastern frontier would follow the Curzon Line. Eden did not fail to tell Sikorski about it.[25]

NOTES

1. Hull, *Memoirs*, 2:1165.
2. Ibid., 2:1166.
3. Woodward, *British Foreign Policy in the Second World War*, 191.
4. Woodward, *British Foreign Policy in the Second World War*, 48–51, 58–59.
5. Eden, *The Reckoning*, 342.
6. Churchill, *The Grand Alliance*, 606.
7. Ibid., 630.
8. Hull, *Memoirs*, 2:1168; also *FRUS*, 1942, 3:501.

9. Churchill, *The Grand Alliance*, 659–66.
10. Hull, *Memoirs*, 2:1168–169.
11. Churchill, *The Hinge of Fate*, 327.
12. Hull, *Memoirs*, 2:1171.
13. Woodward, *British Foreign Policy in the Second World War*, 192–93.
14. Eden, *The Reckoning*, 369–72.
15. *The Correspondence between Stalin-Churchill-Roosevelt*, 1:40–41.
16. Hull, *Memoirs*, 2:1171.
17. For the texts, see *DPSR, 1939–1945*, 1:289–94 and 295–99, respectively.
18. Ciechanowski, *Defeat in Victory*, 100.
19. Hull, *Memoirs*, 2:1170–71.
20. Eden, *The Reckoning*, 380–81.
21. Hull, *Memoirs*, 2:1172.
22. *The Correspondence between Stalin-Churchill-Roosevelt*, 1:48.
23. Churchill, *The Hinge of Fate*, 339.
24. Ciechanowski, *Defeat in Victory*, 108.
25. For Eden-Sikorski conversation of June 8, 1942, see *DPSR, 1939–1945*, 1:364–65.

Chapter Twenty-Eight

British and American Attitudes toward Poland, 1941–1943

The attitude of Great Britain and the United States toward Poland stemmed neither from legal or moral principles nor from a priori, determined positions. On the contrary, it was pragmatic and depended on numerous and often changeable factors.

It primarily was a by-product of their relations with the Soviet Union. In London, Russia's entry into the war was seen not only as an immediate salvation but as a condition for a decisive victory over the Axis powers. Many feared that Stalin, like Lenin in 1918, might withdraw from the war and conclude a compromise peace with Hitler. In Washington, military leaders assumed until the end of the war that the Soviets had to be brought into the Pacific war to ensure victory over Japan. Furthermore, in later stages of the war, Roosevelt considered Russia's accession to a postwar international organization vital in securing a durable peace. He therefore deemed concessions on secondary matters necessary. In both capitals, "to keep Russia fighting" took precedence over any single issue—particularly since Stalin eventually made the Western leaders believe that he had abandoned the idea of a Communist world revolution, that he felt nothing but goodwill toward Russia's allies, and that he could be relied upon. Polish interests, whenever in conflict with Russia's demands, rarely seemed important enough to risk antagonizing the Soviet dictator. Stalin realized his worth, and whenever it came to Polish matters, he took full advantage of his position.

Soon after America's entry into the war, another factor of tremendous importance entered the scene—namely, military strategy. One could probably argue that in a way it was the Western military strategy that essentially determined the fate of central-eastern Europe, Poland included.

For a long time there was no agreement between London and Washington as to the most effective way to pursue the war. The American general staff favored an early invasion of France—in 1942. On May 30 of that year President Roosevelt personally authorized Molotov to inform Stalin that such an invasion would take place "this year." Churchill disagreed, and less than two weeks later he told Molotov that it was "impossible to say in advance" whether that would be "feasible." Pressured for a "straight" answer, he refused to make a promise.[1] Instead, he recommended an invasion of North Africa. Had the American plan been put into operation, and assuming it was successful, Germany might have been defeated on the western front *before* the Red Army had time to liberate central-eastern Europe. For at that time the Wehrmacht held large areas east of the Crimean Peninsula.

The British, particularly Churchill, considered the American strategy premature and dangerous. They feared heavy losses and were very skeptical of its potential for success.[2] Their views prevailed, and the invasion of France was postponed, at first until spring of 1943 (Operation Bolero). Eventually it had to be postponed again, because in the meantime, at Churchill's insistence, the invasion of North Africa was ordered for November 1942 (Operation Torch). Then, in the summer of 1943, southern Italy was invaded, with the second front in France still in suspension.

The military operations in North Africa and Italy formed component parts of Churchill's plan to strike at the "soft underbelly of Europe." This plan, pursued since 1942, was never to materialize.[3]

Churchill did not intend to forsake the invasion of France as the principal Allied military action. He wanted, however, to postpone it and then to synchronize it with a diversionary Balkan operation in the direction of Vienna. Less than two weeks after the invasion of North Africa—on November 18, 1942—he recommended his strategy to President Roosevelt. The subject came under discussion again in May 1943.[4] In July of the same year, the British statesman advocated continuing the momentum of the Allied invasion in Italy, as he put it, with "our right to give succour to Balkan patriots." A few weeks later, at the Quebec conference in August, he specifically referred to the Balkans as Europe's "soft underbelly" and, in October of that year, he drew Roosevelt's attention to the possibility of the Balkan countries deserting the Nazi camp.[5]

Roosevelt, trusting that Moscow had no intentions to Sovietize the Balkans, did not appreciate the arguments, considering it "unwise to plan military strategy based on a gamble as to political results." Consequently, the Mediterranean command was prohibited from developing the successful Italian invasion into an all-out offensive toward the Po Valley in conjunction with an amphibious operation aimed at the Istrian Peninsula. On the contrary, seven divisions were ordered to stand in constant readiness after November 1, 1943, to be transported to Great Britain for the future invasion of France.[6]

At the Tehran conference, Churchill again advocated an Allied amphibious landing on the Istrian Peninsula and an attack through the Ljubljana Gap toward Vienna. Faced with Stalin's opposition and American objections, he had to acquiesce.[7] He still argued for his scheme even after the Tehran conference, again without success.

Advocating his "soft underbelly" strategy, Churchill always argued in military terms, most of the time presenting his plan as an effective anti-Nazi diversion in support of the invasion of France. According to Eden, however, whatever the merits of the military arguments, evidently political considerations guided him as well.[8] Roosevelt realized it and disagreed. "Trouble is, the P.M. [Churchill] is thinking too much of the post-war, and where England will be. He is scared of letting the Russians get too strong," commented the president in private at Tehran.[9] Had Churchill's plan been adopted and had it succeeded, at the time of liberation the Western forces would have been present in the Balkan area and thus, no doubt, influenced its political future. That, at least indirectly, would have affected the Soviet position in Poland as well. But the plan was opposed by both Moscow and Washington and had to be abandoned. As a result, the Soviet military presence in all of central-eastern Europe became inevitable—a factor of decisive political importance. At the time of the invasion of France (June 1944), Soviet forces were approaching the Vistula River. A few weeks later they marched into the Balkans.

There is no evidence that either the British or the Americans intervened in Moscow on Poland's behalf in 1941, whether on the question of Poland's postwar eastern boundary or on the subject of supplying the Polish army being formed in Russia.

As for the territorial issue, Churchill had become reconciled to the idea that the Polish-Soviet frontier would be based on "general ethnographical lines," while Roosevelt took the stand that all territorial issues should be decided at the peace conference. Nor did the Poles obtain support on military matters. Arguing that the autonomous Polish army had a right to Lend-Lease aid independent of Russia, they presented the claim in September 1941 when the Anglo-American-Soviet conference was deliberating on the extent, nature, and mode of delivery of Western supplies to Russia. In spite of numerous representations made by Ambassador Kot to the heads of the British and American missions—Lord Beaverbrook and Harriman, respectively—they decided otherwise.[10] All decisions on supplying and equipping the Poles were left to the Soviet government. As Kot pointed out, this could mean only one thing to Stalin: he had been given a free hand in Polish affairs.[11]

From the moment of Germany's attack on Russia, pro-Soviet sympathies grew steadily both in Great Britain and in the United States, increasing after the Pearl Harbor attack and finally attaining their peak after the Stalingrad victory in 1943. After that, the Red Army marched from victory to victory at the cost of tremendous sacrifices. True, the Western Allies in the second part of 1943 had their successes, too: in North Africa, the Mediterranean area, and Italy. But still there was no cross-Channel invasion of western Europe, and only such an invasion was considered by the Soviet government a second front. These realities aroused worldwide sympathy for Russia, mostly for humanitarian reasons. For many it was common sense: Russia was carrying the main burden of war. Certainly in not a few cases the sympathy was ideological. In every case, Polish complaints, criticism, and demands—all directed at the Soviet government—were somehow jarring. They didn't belong in the picture.

In the United States, Ambassador Ciechanowski complained about the radio broadcasts beamed to Poland by the Office of War Information (OWI) because they contained what he considered Communist propaganda. "Notorious pro-Soviet propagandists and obscure foreign Communists and fellow travellers were entrusted with these broadcasts," he noted. In London, the Poles thought American broadcasts "might well have emanated from Moscow itself."[12] The Polish ambassador failed to get any action from the Department of State, since the OWI was apparently under direct control of the White House.[13] The "American Slav Congress" (one of the first organizations to be listed by the Department of Justice as subversive after the war) was officially sponsored by the president and the attorney general. On September 30, 1941, the president pointed out at his press conference that the Soviet constitution provided for freedom of religious worship and freedom of conscience in essentially the same manner as did the US Constitution.[14]

In Great Britain a strict censorship of the press prevented the Poles from appealing to public opinion. The BBC was under far greater governmental control than American broadcasting stations. In addition, British government officials had ample opportunities to exercise effective personal pressure on the Polish cabinet members. Mikolajczyk complained but could not do anything about it, noting: "This was a difficult time for us in London. . . . Prohibited from making even the mildest protests over what was taking place in Russian-Polish relations, we were forced to sit by and watch Russia hailed more and more throughout the world as a democratic liberal government." Sir Owen O'Malley, Kennard's successor as war ambassador to the Polish government-in-exile, realized and deplored the infiltration of what he considered pro-Communist elements into some government agencies and the press. Although sympathetic to the Poles, he could offer no help. [15]

In time, the position of the Poles in London deteriorated still further because the British government showed more and more support for Soviet territorial demands in a manner that, although usually informal enough not to provoke an international incident, clearly indicated the trend in the Foreign Office. In March 1942 Sir Stafford Cripps, by then deputy prime minister and a member of the war cabinet, made a public statement that left little doubt as to his thinking:

> To protect Leningrad it is essential that the Russians should control the Gulf of Finland and the Baltic Coast. It is also necessary that there should not exist small states close to the vital points of Soviet industry which can be made use of by hostile powers as a base for attack. This means that, judging by the strategic necessities of the situation, the Soviet Government must ask for boundaries which it has fought to defend against Germany—the boundaries of June, 1941.

Although he pointed out a possible exception in the case of the Polish-Soviet frontier, he also expressed hope for a "compromise" between Poland and the USSR. He assured the world with "certainty" that the Soviet leaders had no intention of interfering in the internal affairs of any country. [16]

While discussing Russia's postwar frontiers, Sir Stafford emphasized that he was "not speaking from any knowledge of what the Soviet government has actually demanded." He certainly knew that Stalin had made his territorial demands in eastern Europe a condition for concluding an alliance with Great Britain. At that very moment Churchill was asking Roosevelt to approve the secret protocol in the Anglo-Soviet alliance, virtually recognizing

Russia's 1941 boundaries. The deputy prime minister certainly knew that as well. Simultaneously—on March 7—the *Times*, which often reflected government opinion, carried an editorial emphasizing that, after all, the Soviet demands were "in no way incompatible with that security in Europe which the framers of the Atlantic Charter sought to ensure."

In the following months, the military situation of the Western Allies worsened; the increasingly painful reverses continued. In the middle of the year Allied operations in the Mediterranean theater and in Egypt resulted in disaster. Their army in North Africa was decimated, all Egypt was threatened, and the Mediterranean fleet had to evacuate Alexandria. In the Pacific area, the Japanese overran Malaya, Burma, and the Philippines. In May and June, German U-boats sank over a million and a half tons of Allied shipping. The US war production was still lagging. Stalin's demands for a second front in Europe could not be met. His demands for formal recognition of Russia's 1941 frontiers were denied. Fearing the impact of those realities on Soviet-British relations, Churchill decided to see Stalin personally in August. He had to explain the difficulties. He had to tell Stalin not to expect any landing operations in western Europe in the near future. Not having much to offer, he had to win Stalin's confidence and cooperation. On his way to Moscow he felt as though he were "carrying a large lump of ice to the North Pole." He found Stalin extremely disappointed and reproachful, even when the prime minister tried to ease the situation by presenting plans for the North African operation.[17]

These developments could not but adversely affect the position of the Poles in London. More and more often their complaints directed at Russia aroused impatience instead of sympathy. Their demands for support became increasingly embarrassing. In the context of the all-important Anglo-Soviet relations, the Poles and their problems would eventually be considered more of a political nuisance than an asset.

Before long, restrictions—initially informal and discreet—were imposed on the Polish press, which was usually critical of Russia. Later on, restrictions became official and public, applying not only to the Polish but to the British press as well. On March 3, 1943, the censor's office issued a circular requesting all to refrain from discussing, for an unspecified period, Polish-Soviet postwar frontiers. The controls increased—apparently on Churchill's personal order—after the break in Polish-Soviet relations.

In time, the opinion that Russia was destined to play a great role won widespread acceptance. It became fashionable to look for "new" rather than "traditional" solutions in postwar Europe. The most renowned writers, scholars, and commentators in Great Britain and in the United States began to plant the idea that there was no room for genuine sovereignty of small countries and that the Great Powers would have to exercise "leadership."[18] Many exceedingly pro-Soviet books and films appeared, *Mission to Moscow*, by former American ambassador to Russia Joseph E. Davies, surpassing them all. "The bogey that a war would entail communism in defeated Germany and Central Europe is plain bunk," he prophesied.[19] "The word of honor of the Soviet government is as safe as the Bible. . . . The Soviet Union stands staunchly for international morality," he cried at a mass rally in Chicago on February 22, 1942.[20] In an issue dedicated to the Soviet Union, *Life* magazine described Lenin as "perhaps the greatest man of modern times." Referring to the Soviet secret police (NKVD), the magazine explained that it was "a national police similar to the FBI."[21]

The popularity of Russia and praise of Stalin as a leader, an ally, and a man flourished in the United States, especially in political and society circles. "We became victims of our own propaganda; Russian aims were good and noble. Communism had changed its stripes," commented a prominent American politico-military analyst, Hanson Baldwin. Secretary of the Navy James Forrestal bitterly complained about America's irrationally pro-Soviet sentiment:

> If any American suggests that we act in accord with our own interests, he is apt to be called . . . fascist or imperialist, while if Uncle Joe suggests that he needs the Baltic provinces, half of Poland, all of Bessarabia and access to the Mediterranean, all hands in Washington agree that he is a fine, frank, candid and generally delightful fellow who is very easy to deal with because he is so explicit in what he wants.[22]

From December 1942 to January 1943, Sikorski visited Roosevelt to brief him on Polish affairs. The president listened with great interest to Sikorski's arguments in support of the plans to invade Europe from the Balkans. He seemed to like the Polish plans for an east central European federation of small countries and seemed to oppose the Soviet territorial claims, but he would not commit his government in any way. His official letter in answer to Sikorski's memorandum contained no more than amenities.[23]

Soon after, on January 16, Ciechanowski complained to Welles about Soviet policies, asking the United States to intervene in Moscow on Poland's behalf. Although the undersecretary agreed that some action might be useful,

he unexpectedly inquired whether the Polish government "rejected the possibility of making any territorial concessions" on behalf of the Soviet Union.
"Am I to understand," he asked, "that the Polish Government is determined
not to sacrifice even an inch of its eastern territory?" Three weeks later, on
February 5, Welles informed Ciechanowski that the president considered any
immediate intervention impossible because the circumstances were "unfavorable." The only help Roosevelt could give the Poles was the advice that
they "keep their shirts on." Because Ciechanowski persisted, he was finally
informed that the American ambassador in Moscow, William Standley,
would express American "interest" in Polish-Soviet relations but would do
no more. The main intervention would be the president's, during his impending meeting with Stalin.[24]

If Ciechanowski expected any assistance from the imminent Roosevelt-
Stalin meeting, he was certainly mistaken. On March 12–30, soon after Field
Marshal von Paulus's surrender at Stalingrad, Eden visited Washington, and
an informal Anglo-American understanding on eastern Europe was secretly
reached. While discussing eastern Europe and Poland on March 14, Eden
argued strongly for the Soviet Union. He assured Roosevelt that Stalin would
demand "very little of Poland, possibly up to the 'Curzon Line'" and emphasized that this "would not affect Poland unduly from an economic point of
view." He insisted that Stalin wanted "a strong Poland, provided the right
kind of people were running it." He also criticized Sikorski and his government for nurturing "very large ambitions" aiming at the creation of postwar
federations or confederations in eastern Europe. He thought the Soviets had
good and valid reasons for their distrust of Sikorski and his government.[25]

Although Eden expressed the above opinions as his own, in fact they
reflected Soviet views, as communicated to him by Maisky on the eve of
Eden's departure from London. The Soviet ambassador told him about Russia's "determination" to incorporate Latvia, Estonia, and Lithuania, as well
as Russia's demands for military bases in Finland and Romania. As for
Poland, Maisky said that the Soviet Union would incorporate all territories
up to the Curzon Line. That meant, of course, a reconstitution of the Ribbentrop-Molotov line of September 28, 1939. Maisky pointed out that the Soviet
government opposed postwar confederations in eastern Europe. He also mentioned that Moscow's relations with Poland "would depend on the character
of the Polish government."[26]

Eden's argument pleased Roosevelt. He said that he did not like the
attitude of the Poles either. He was of the opinion that the Great Powers—the

United States, Great Britain, and Russia—should decide "at the appropriate time" what boundaries Poland was to have. The Poles would have to accept the decision, since he "did not intend to go to the Peace Conference and bargain with Poland or the other small states." The Great Powers had a duty to "police" small countries.

The discussion resulted in an unofficial, preliminary understanding on the subject of Soviet territorial claims. While both statesmen agreed not to oppose Soviet incorporation of the Baltic countries, Roosevelt favored postwar plebiscites there—not because he thought that the population would vote against Moscow's rule, but because he was convinced that the Baltic peoples would vote *for* Russia and thus satisfy public opinion in the United States. He decided to "appeal" to Stalin "on grounds of high morality," telling him, however, that neither the United States nor Great Britain "would fight Russia over the Baltic States." Both statesmen felt that Russia would retain its acquisitions of 1940 in Finland and Romania. As for Poland, it would have to make concessions in the east, the exact scope of which would be decided later. In compensation, Poland would receive East Prussia, Danzig, and a part of Upper Silesia. The Poles would be allowed to remove the German population from those areas.

While in Washington, Eden got the impression that officials around Roosevelt were skeptical about the prospects of the government-in-exile in postwar Poland. They thought that only Sikorski might be able to play a political role in the homeland, while other members of his government would have to be discarded. Probably to prove his goodwill and confidence, Eden informed Maisky about these impressions upon his return to London. Stalin did not fail to take official note of them and soon afterward wired his satisfaction to Churchill.[27]

Roosevelt's stand on Poland was not known to the Poles, who believed that he intended to defend their cause. In August 1943 a courier from the Polish Underground, Jan Karski, was dispatched to Washington with a mission to report on the situation in Poland and on the Nazi extermination of the Jews. Roosevelt received him with both interest and sympathy. True, he pointed out, Poland would have to concede some territory to Russia, but he was sure that Stalin would demand no more than what was necessary "to save face." Because Poland would have American support, it would not be wronged. East Prussia would be Polish, and there would be no more Corridor. "Tell the Polish Underground authorities," the president concluded, "that their indomitable attitude has been duly appreciated. Tell them that they will never have cause to regret their brave decision to reject any collaboration with the enemy, and that Poland will live to reap the reward of its heroism and sacrifice."[28]

Germany's revelation of the Katyn massacre and the subsequent Polish appeal to the International Red Cross for an investigation disconcerted American officials considerably. Hull feared grave complications and told Ambassador Halifax on April 21 that Churchill and Roosevelt would have to intervene directly with Stalin in order to accomplish anything. Upon receiving information of the imminent Soviet break with Poland, Hull sent a cable to Stalin in the name of Roosevelt, pleading for restraint.[29] Churchill appealed, too, although not without telling Maisky that "the Poles had been unwise" and that they had committed a "blunder." In their personal messages to Stalin, both Churchill and Roosevelt criticized Sikorski's government for the appeal, defended him personally, and blamed some unidentified anti-Soviet Poles for the entire incident. Both appealed to Stalin's magnanimity. None showed any concern over what after all had caused the crisis—mainly the murders of ten thousand Polish officers.

The interventions proved futile, and Stalin broke relations with the Polish government. But having done so, he advanced his own demands. It was the duty of both the British and American governments, he cabled on May 4, to make joint efforts in order to eliminate the "pro-Hitler" elements within the government-in-exile. Churchill responded immediately. He agreed with Stalin and promised to urge changes. But because appearances of "foreign pressure" should be avoided, "discretion" was in order. Anyway, he would "silence" those Polish papers that "attacked the Soviet government." In another cable, he informed Stalin that the "miserable rags" would be suppressed. On May 12 he let Stalin know that "the Polish press [would] be disciplined." Stalin duly thanked the prime minister but expressed doubt about whether the "pro-Hitler" Poles could be disciplined at all.[30] As for Roosevelt, he had decided by then that no immediate attempts to intervene further in the Polish-Soviet dispute should be undertaken, because they might endanger Allied unity.[31] Significantly, after the departure of the Polish embassy staff from the USSR, both London and Washington refused to take care of Polish interests there. Eventually, the Australians undertook the task.

By then, Stalin's attitude had become the source of gravest preoccupation in the White House as well as at Downing Street. He waited for the second front and he waited in vain. He was annoyed and increasingly suspicious. Threats—less and less veiled—appeared in his communications. In a February 16 cable, he expressed disappointment and dissatisfaction over the post-ponement of the cross-Channel invasion until August or September 1943. On March 15 he gave a "most emphatic warning . . . of the grave danger with which further delay in opening a second front in France is fraught."[32] A few days later, as a result of the German concentration of naval forces at Narwik, Allied northern convoys with supplies for Russia had to be suspended, a fact that Moscow could hardly welcome.[33] Then, at the end of May, the British and the Americans decided to postpone the invasion of France again—this time till the spring of 1944. When informed about it, Stalin solemnly pro-tested, refused to approve it, and enigmatically pointed out that the decision "may gravely affect the subsequent course of the war."[34] Sir A. Clark-Kerr, British ambassador in Moscow, considered those vague threats to be taken most seriously. By July the correspondence between the three leaders had almost lapsed, and ambassadors Maisky and Litvinov were recalled.[35] The situation was hardly conducive to any serious intervention on Poland's be-half.

Eventually an Anglo-American intervention of a humanitarian and non-political character was made. The severance of diplomatic relations between the USSR and the Polish government-in-exile deprived the more than one million Polish deportees in the Soviet Union of any protection. The desperate conditions prevailing in forced-labor camps, prisons, and compulsory settle-ments (where most of them lived) were well known in Poland. Poles every-where became agitated, and Sikorski desperately appealed to the conscience of Churchill and Roosevelt. He did succeed, and on August 12, 1943, Lon-don and Washington forwarded a joint plan to Moscow proposing that (1) all "racial Poles" who had Polish citizenship before September 1, 1939, be for-mally recognized as Polish citizens; (2) all other former Polish citizens be allowed to opt for Polish or Soviet citizenship; (3) Polish citizens or those opting for Poland who had relatives abroad, as well as the immediate rela-tives of members of the Polish army, be permitted to leave the USSR; (4) children and women be evacuated; (5) American relief supplies be distrib-uted fairly; (6) all Poles have access to their consular offices, which should be opened. For six weeks Stalin did not even acknowledge the intervention, and then, on September 27, he curtly rejected the proposals in their entirety. That closed the matter.

At that time, Poland suffered a great loss. On July 4, 1943, Sikorski perished in a plane accident. His death dealt a blow to the authority of the government-in-exile. His successor, Stanislaw Mikolajczyk, was relatively unknown at the time and could not aspire to his predecessor's prestige. The prospects for Poland looked gloomy, and Churchill knew it better than others. On July 13 he ordered a transfer of the Polish Second Corps from Persia to the Mediterranean theater of intensive fighting. "Politically, this is highly desirable, as the men wish to fight and, once engaged, will worry less about their own affairs, which are tragic,"[36] he told General Ismay.

Mikolajczyk had been a leader of the Peasant party and, prior to Sikorski's death, was minister of the interior. Unlike many other peasant leaders, he was a genuine farmer. Born in 1901, he lived on a small farm in western Poland until the outbreak of the war and, in spite of his public activities, never abandoned farming. In the early 1930s, he held leading positions in the local agricultural community and gained popular esteem for shunning demagoguery, for his organizational abilities, and for his efforts to speed up agrarian reform. Together with his party, he opposed Pilsudski and his regime, but at times did not hesitate to support government initiatives aimed at strengthening national security. After the departure of Witos into exile in 1933, he assumed one of the leading positions in the party.

Mikolajczyk was a staunch, Western-oriented democrat. Not as colorful, polished, or educated as his predecessor, he eventually won respect in both Allied and Polish quarters because of his dedication, his unassuming personality, and his down-to-earth realism. Like Sikorski, he put all his trust in Poland's British and American allies, and his assumption of the premiership guaranteed a continuity of Sikorski's policies. He saw Poland as a member of the Western community of nations but was firmly convinced—even until his death in the United States in 1966—of the need for Polish-Soviet cooperation.

From October 18 to November 3, 1943, the American-British-Soviet conference of foreign ministers was held in Moscow as a preliminary step to the Big Three Tehran meeting. The Poles nurtured great hopes that Eden and Hull would intervene on their behalf. The Red Army, in its victorious drive, was approaching the prewar Polish-Soviet boundary. What would happen once it entered Poland?

Before Hull left Washington, Ciechanowski pleaded for his support. He asked for an Anglo-American guarantee of Poland's independence and recognition of the Underground's right to establish its own administration in the areas to be liberated. Considering the establishment of Soviet-Polish relations *before* the Red Army entered Poland a necessity, he also suggested that the American-British contingents be placed there to protect the population.

There was a danger, he insisted, that the Soviet forces would try to communize the liberated areas unless controlled on the spot or bound by an agreement. But he also asked Hull not to discuss the Polish-Soviet territorial issues, invoking the Atlantic Charter and the official American stand that those issues would be settled at the peace conference. Hull seemed to agree with Ciechanowski and assured him that he had "decided to defend the cause of Poland as he would defend the cause of his own country."[37]

There were no such amenities in London. On September 9, and again on October 5, Eden told Mikolajczyk that the Poles should immediately agree to territorial changes on behalf of Russia. He thought Lvov might be left in Poland, while the future of Vilna seemed uncertain. In exchange, Poland would receive East Prussia and valuable areas in Silesia. He asked Mikolajczyk for authorization to discuss the Polish-Soviet postwar frontier. Mikolajczyk refused. He expressed fear for the future of the Underground once the Red Army entered Poland and recalled Soviet practices in 1939–1941. He also said that, in the absence of Polish-Soviet diplomatic relations, "the Polish nation would be obliged to adopt measures of self-defense." By the same token, once a genuine understanding had been reached, the Home Army would be ready to stage a military action "carried out on a big scale" and combined with the Allied offensive. Eden "welcomed" Mikolajczyk's declaration concerning the planned military "diversion" by the Home Army but repeatedly raised doubts as to whether Moscow would establish diplomatic relations with the government-in-exile without an agreement on territorial issues.[38]

None among the Polish statesmen realized that, behind the walls of diplomatic secrecy, both the Atlantic Charter and the official policies on territorial questions had been abandoned. Before Hull left for Moscow, Roosevelt told him that at the approaching Big Three meeting he would appeal to Stalin to hold another "plebiscite" in the disputed areas. However, the future Polish-Soviet boundary would follow the Curzon Line.[39] As for Eden, on October 5, the day of his conversation with Mikolajczyk, he himself recommended to the war cabinet that Great Britain should not intervene in favor of the resumption of Soviet-Polish relations unless the Poles agreed beforehand to the Soviet territorial demands and authorized him to inform the Soviet government about their agreement.[40] Churchill heartily concurred and six days later formulated guiding instructions for the conference, leaving no doubt as to British position: "We reaffirm the principles of the Atlantic Charter, noting that Russia's accession thereto is based upon the historic frontiers of Russia before the two wars of aggression waged by Germany in 1914 and 1939."[41]

There are various accounts pertaining to the treatment of the Polish issue at the conference, and they appear contradictory. According to Sumner Welles, eastern Europe was discussed by Stalin and Eden, and the Soviet demand for a "predominant interest" in Poland, Czechoslovakia, Hungary, Romania, Yugoslavia, and Bulgaria in exchange for British "predominant interest" in Greece was "tacitly" recognized by Hull on behalf of the United States. According to Hull, he admonished the Soviets against territorial expansion and spoke against "decisions . . . in favor of areas of responsibility or zones of influence." According to Averell Harriman's report, Hull expressed "hope" that Polish-Soviet relations "could be patched up" but refused to go "into the causes or merits of the dispute." According to Eden, Hull not only failed to bring up the issue of Poland but refused, when pressed by his British colleague, to show his "concern for Poland's future." When Eden himself raised the issue, Molotov observed that "Polish-Soviet relations was the concern almost exclusively of those two countries." He refused to discuss the subject and warned Great Britain against helping the "wrong people" in the Polish Underground.[42]

Indirect evidence supports Welles's account. For as far as central-eastern Europe (Poland included) was concerned, the most important—indeed crucial—result of the conference was the declaration on the liberated areas and the changes Molotov had succeeded in making to the American draft. Hull proposed a formula whereby the Great Powers would "*act together* in all matters relating to the surrender and disarmament . . . [of the enemy] *and to any occupation of enemy territory and territory of other states held by that enemy.*"[43] On Molotov's insistence, the part of the formula had to be dropped. That meant that the Soviets would not have to act "together" with their Western Allies in the areas liberated by the Red Army but would be free to act as they chose unilaterally. Molotov told Harriman that such was his understanding of the formula. That, of course, meant an *implicit* recognition of Russia's dominant position in all countries to be liberated by the Red Army. Soon after, on November 5, Harriman duly briefed the president on the matter.[44]

Whether it was because of the excellent impression Stalin made on Hull,[45] or perhaps because of Stalin's promise to join the war against Japan once Germany was defeated, or—most probably—because he knew what the declaration on liberated areas meant, the fact remains that after October 1943

Hull abandoned his previously unfaltering position that territorial disputes should be settled only at the peace conference. Upon his return to Washington, he told Ciechanowski that without territorial concessions on the part of Poland, the Soviet government probably would not reestablish diplomatic relations and that the United States had become helpless in this matter. He caustically expressed his disappointment over the critical treatment of the Moscow conference by the Polish press. True, neither he nor Eden had pressed the Soviet government hard enough for the reestablishment of Polish-Soviet relations, but that should not be a subject of criticism. "We had gone to Moscow primarily to reach an agreement between Russia and ourselves, not an agreement between Russia and Poland,"[46] he concluded.

Mikolajczyk was no more successful with Eden. When, after the latter's return from Moscow, the Polish prime minister asked him anxiously for news, Eden quoted Molotov: "I want to see a strong, independent Poland, but I cannot collaborate with the Polish government because it has no goodwill." Eden then added pointedly: "and since you had bound my hands by refusing to discuss frontiers, I could do nothing more."[47]

NOTES

1. *FRUS*, 1942, 8:577; Churchill, *The Hinge of Fate*, 342, respectively.

2. Churchill, *The Hinge of Fate*, 313–25.

3. See Sherwood, *Roosevelt and Hopkins*, 617; also Mark Clark, *Calculated Risk* (New York: Harper and Brothers Publishers, 1950), 49; see also Trumbull Higgins, *Soft Underbelly: The Anglo-American Controversy over the Italian Campaign, 1939–1945* (New York: Macmillan Co., 1968).

4. Maurice Matloff and Edwin M. Snell, *Strategic Planning for Coalition Warfare* (Washington, DC: Office of the Chief of Military History, 1953), 363; also Albert C. Wedemeyer, *Wedemeyer Reports* (New York: Henry Holt & Co., 1958), 217, 230.

5. Churchill, *Closing the Ring*, 36, 210.

6. See Wedemeyer, *Wedemeyer Reports*, 241; Churchill, *Triumph and Tragedy*, 63; also Clark, *Calculated Risk*, 368.

7. Churchill, *Closing the Ring*, 345–46, 356. For the minutes of the discussions at the Tehran conference, see Department of State, *Foreign Relations of the United States: Diplomatic Papers. The Conferences at Cairo and Tehran, 1943* (Washington, DC: US Government Printing Office, 1961), 492–97, 535–38, 543–52, 576–78. Hereafter cited as *The Conferences at Cairo and Tehran*.

8. Eden, *The Reckoning*, 533–34, 542.

9. See Elliott Roosevelt, *As He Saw It* (New York: Duell, Sloan and Pearce, 1946), 185.

10. Stanislaw Kot, *Listy z Rosji do Gen. Sikorskiego* (*Letters from Russia to General Sikorski*) (London: St. Martin's Printers, 1956), 110–11.

11. Stanislaw Kot, *Conversations with the Kremlin and Dispatches from Russia* (London: Oxford University Press, 1963), xvi–xvii.

12. Ciechanowski, *Defeat in Victory*, 130; Mikolajczyk, *The Rape of Poland*, 25, respectively.

13. For details, see William Henry Chamberlin, *America's Second Crusade* (Chicago, IL: Henry Regnery Co., 1950), 250–51.

14. See *New York Herald Tribune*, October 1, 1941, 1; *New York Times*, October 1, 1941, 9.

15. Mikolajczyk, *The Rape of Poland*, 19; also Sir Owen O'Malley, *The Phantom Caravan* (London: John Murray, 1954), 231, respectively.

16. Sir Stafford Cripps, "Twenty Russian Questions," *Life*, March 9, 1942, 86–87.

17. Churchill, *The Hinge of Fate*, 475–80.

18. See Edward H. Carr, *Conditions of Peace* (London: Macmillan & Co., 1942), 163–86, 187–209; also Walter Lippmann, *U.S. Foreign Policy: Shield of the Republic* (Boston: Little, Brown & Co., 1943), 137–54.

19. Joseph E. Davies, *Mission to Moscow* (New York: Simon and Schuster, 1941), 434.

20. *Daily Worker* (New York), February 25, 1942, 5.

21. *Life*, March 29, 1943, 29, 40.

22. Baldwin, *Great Mistakes of the War*, 9; Walter Mills and E. S. Duffield, eds., *Forrestal Diaries* (London: Cassell & Co., 1952), 32, respectively.

23. For the minutes of the conversation, see *DPSR, 1939–1945*, 2:688–91.

24. Ciechanowski, *Defeat in Victory*, 139–52.

25. For the entire discussion, see Sherwood, *Roosevelt and Hopkins*, 709–10.

26. Eden, *The Reckoning*, 429–32; also Woodward, *British Foreign Policy in the Second World War*, 203.

27. *The Correspondence between Stalin-Churchill-Roosevelt*, 2:128.

28. Ciechanowski, *Defeat in Victory*, 190.

29. Hull, *Memoirs*, 2:1267–68.

30. For the full texts, see *The Correspondence between Stalin-Churchill-Roosevelt*, 1:123–30.

31. Hull, *Memoirs*, 2:1268–69.

32. *The Correspondence between Stalin-Churchill-Roosevelt*, 1:94–96, 106.

33. Woodward, *British Foreign Policy in the Second World War*, 240.

34. *The Correspondence between Stalin-Churchill-Roosevelt*, 1:132, 2:70–71.

35. Woodward, *British Foreign Policy in the Second World War*, 241; also Herbert Feis, *Churchill-Roosevelt-Stalin: The War They Waged and the Peace They Sought* (Princeton, NJ: Princeton University Press, 1957), 134–35, 143. Hereafter cited as Feis, *Churchill-Roosevelt-Stalin*.

36. Churchill, *Closing the Ring*, 653.

37. Ciechanowski, *Defeat in Victory*, 221.

38. *DPSR, 1939–1945*, 2:49–50, 61–64, respectively. For the full text of the memorandum handed to Eden by Mikolajczyk on the same day, see ibid., 65–68.

39. Hull, *Memoirs*, 2:1266.

40. Woodward, *British Foreign Policy in the Second World War*, 250–51.

41. Churchill, *Closing the Ring*, 283.

42. Welles, *Where Are We Heading?* 151; Hull, *Memoirs*, 2:1297–98; *FRUS*, 1943, 1:667–68; Eden, *The Reckoning*, 482–83, respectively.

43. Feis, *Churchill-Roosevelt-Stalin*, 208 (emphasis added).

44. *FRUS*, 1943, 3:401–2.

45. "I thought to myself that any American having Stalin's personality and approach might well reach high public office in my own country" (Hull, *Memoirs*, 2:1311).

46. Ibid., 1315.

47. Mikolajczyk, *The Rape of Poland*, 45.

Chapter Twenty-Nine

The Tehran Conference

Roosevelt's Secret Diplomacy, November 28–December 1, 1943

The Tehran conference was a turning point in Anglo-American-Soviet policies on Poland because it produced secret understandings among the three heads of government on Poland's eastern boundary and the Soviet position in the areas liberated by the Red Army. Fateful understandings were reached in an unusual way.

Long before the conference took place, Roosevelt had tried to meet with Stalin. He believed such a meeting would bring positive results because of the "terrific power" Stalin represented and because of Roosevelt's own arguments and personality. "I know you will not mind my being brutally frank when I tell you that I think I can personally handle Stalin better than either your Foreign Office or my State Department. . . . He likes me better,"[1] he wrote to Churchill. His hopes were shared and sustained by his closest collaborators.[2]

The Big Three meeting was agreed upon at the time when Soviet military successes made Western strategists advance new ideas about Russia's postwar position in Europe. Just a few months earlier, during the first Quebec conference, Hopkins delivered an important military evaluation of the war situation to Roosevelt and Churchill; it had been prepared by the army "on a very high level." Entitled "Russia's Position," the document forwarded significant conclusions:

Russia's postwar position in Europe will be a dominant one. With Germany crushed, there is no power in Europe to oppose her tremendous military forces. It is true that Great Britain is building up a position in the Mediterranean vis-à-vis Russia that she may find useful in balancing power in Europe. However, even here she may not be able to oppose Russia unless she is otherwise supported.

The conclusions from the foregoing are obvious. Since Russia is the decisive factor in the war, she must be given every assistance, and every effort must be made to obtain her friendship. Likewise, since without question she will dominate Europe on the defeat of the Axis, it is even more essential to develop and maintain the most friendly relations with Russia. [3]

The document's political implications were extraordinary: "Every effort" should be made to obtain the "friendship" of the Soviet government *because* Russia was to "dominate Europe." That "domination" was not to be challenged, although the war was being fought to prevent Germany from accomplishing much the same thing.

By November 1943 the Red Army continued its westward drive and was bound to liberate the Polish areas soon. Liberation meant a military presence, because Poland was once again the corridor between Germany and Russia. Thus, territorial issues were losing their importance altogether, and by then it was not Poland's boundaries that preoccupied Churchill but its independence. There were no relations between the Polish and the Soviet governments; a rival, Stalin-controlled Union of Polish Patriots functioned in Russia; reports concerning the activities of the Polish Communists and the Soviet partisans in Poland were most disquieting. By having his armies in Poland, Stalin would soon control it anyway. Consequently, both Churchill and Eden believed that a formal Polish-Soviet understanding, whatever its terms, should be concluded as soon as possible, *before* the Red Army entered Poland. [4]

Mikolajczyk, too, realized that without Stalin's approval neither his government nor the Underground in the homeland could function in the areas to be liberated. But he was also caught in a terrible dilemma. He knew that the Poles, both abroad and in the homeland, would condemn a partition of Poland resulting in the loss of almost half its territory. Poland was an Ally, and its people were fighting both at home and abroad; the Poles' sacrifices were staggering. Mikolajczyk's formal approval of the eastern boundary resulting from the Nazi-Soviet collusion in September 1939 would certainly render untenable his own and his government's position. He therefore had to find solutions and offer compromises that would restore relations with Russia, win Stalin's genuine cooperation, protect Poland's independence, secure British-American guarantees of that independence, and at the same time have the approval of the Poles at home and abroad. He took it for granted that he would have the support of both the British and American governments in his endeavor.

Raczyński made the first move on November 17. He delivered a memorandum to the Foreign Office urging Churchill (and Roosevelt) to ensure that his government and the Underground authorities would be allowed to assume administration in the areas to be liberated.[5] As long as the Polish government was in exile, it could not enter into discussions concerning "territorial concessions." The memorandum emphasized that as long as Soviet-Polish relations were sundered, the Polish population and the Underground would be in danger once the Red Army entered Poland. According to the British sources, Raczyński not only delivered the memorandum, he said, with some portent, that the memorandum was not Mikolajczyk's "last word." Although his government could not "suggest" territorial concessions on its own, "the position would be different if the friends of Poland were to tell her that she must accept such and such settlement in order to safeguard the future of the country."[6] Apparently Mikolajczyk was trying to place the responsibility for territorial concessions on the shoulders of the British and American governments, an understandable move, inasmuch as he believed both Churchill and Roosevelt would support Poland against Stalin's intractability.

On November 22, a few hours before Eden departed for Tehran, he met Mikolajczyk, Romer, and Raczyński, who complained bitterly about Churchill's refusal to see them. Again they expressed their fears of what would happen in Poland once the Red Army entered. Eden asked for authorization to "explore the ground and to have talks in order to obtain information, without excluding the frontier problems." Mikolajczyk agreed, stressing, however, that no decisions were to be taken without consulting the Polish government. Eden "solemnly" promised to comply with the request.[7]

At Tehran, the first official discussion concerning Poland took place on November 28 when, after a formal dinner, Churchill had a preliminary "heart-to-heart talk" with Stalin. Great Britain, he said, had declared war because of Poland, and Poland was important to Britain. However "nothing was more important than the security of the Russian western frontier." He also said that Britain had never given any pledges in regard to Poland's frontiers and observed that neither he nor Roosevelt had any legislative authority to define frontiers. He nevertheless saw the need for an agreement on "some sort of policy which he could recommend to the Poles and advise them to accept." Poland should "move westward like soldiers, taking two steps 'left close.'" Eden interjected that he was "encouraged" by Stalin's earlier statement that the Poles could go as far as the Oder River. That meant, he said, that what territory Poland lost in the east it would gain in the west.

Stalin cautiously asked if the problem of Polish postwar frontiers would be discussed without the Poles. He received an affirmative answer. Then he assured his visitors that he was not going "to swallow Poland up." He "emphatically" announced that he "favored a Polish western frontier on the Oder." As to Poland's eastern boundary, Stalin said that the Russians did not want anything belonging to others. Both Churchill and Eden considered the exchange of views promising and hoped to "hammer something out" later on, when Poland would be discussed at a formal meeting.[8]

This preliminary exchange of views took place without Roosevelt, who withdrew just after dinner. He probably preferred not to be involved in any specific discussions on the subject of Poland's boundaries—and for a good reason. Eden noticed that the American delegation seemed "terrified" at the prospect. The presidential elections were to take place in less than one year, and Roosevelt's stand, if leaked to the public, could be disastrous. Hopkins, the president's intimate confidant and chief advisor, considered the Polish issue "political dynamite"[9] in the United States. To Americans of Polish descent, Roosevelt was an idol, and they saw in him a willing and sincere supporter of the Polish cause. His record had to be unimpeachable.

The president solved the dilemma in a rather unorthodox way. On December 1—the day scheduled for a full and formal discussion on Poland—he invited Stalin to his quarters; Harriman and Charles Bohlen were at his side, while Stalin was accompanied by Molotov and an interpreter. The conversation that followed was superconfidential, and even Churchill and Eden were not informed of it.[10] The president said he invited Marshal Stalin in order to have a "frank" discussion on a matter concerning American internal politics. There would be presidential elections in 1944, and he might have to run again. There were six to seven million Americans of Polish extraction and, "as a practical man, he did not wish to lose their vote." Although he *did agree* with Stalin's position on Poland's boundaries, he could not participate in any decisions nor "publicly" take any part in any "arrangement" before the end of 1944, that is, until after the elections.

The president also raised the subject of the Baltic states, observing "jokingly" that once the Red Army liberated them, he "did not intend to go to war with the Soviet Union on this point." American public opinion, he thought, would favor a referendum there "someday," once the Red Army liberated the area. He was, however, "personally confident that the people would vote to join the Soviet Union." Stalin curtly replied that he "understood" Roosevelt's situation, adding, in order to avoid any misunderstanding, that should any referendum take place, international control would not be allowed.

The formal discussion on Poland was opened by Roosevelt, who expressed the hope that diplomatic relations between the Polish and the Soviet governments would be resumed.[11] Stalin immediately took exception, observing that Poland's frontiers, not the resumption of diplomatic relations, were scheduled to be discussed. He explained that a distinction between Poland and the Polish government should be made. The latter "joined Hitler" in disseminating slanderous propaganda against the Soviet Union, while its agents in the homeland "were killing the partisans." He would be willing to negotiate with the Poles from London only if they changed their policies. Neither the president nor the prime minister took exception. Instead, they dropped the matter of the government-in-exile and switched the discussion to Poland's postwar boundaries.

Asked by Churchill to state his position, Stalin said that he could not allow the Poles to seize Ukrainian and White Russian (Byelorussian) lands because it would be unfair: those lands had been returned to the Ukraine and to Byelorussia in 1939. Eden inquired if this meant that the Ribbentrop-Molotov line was to be the frontier between Poland and Russia. "Call it whatever you like," Stalin answered.[12] Molotov hastily explained that the line was usually called the Curzon Line. A short argument developed as to where the Curzon Line lay. Eden thought that it was "intended to pass to the east of Lvov," while Stalin maintained that it ran west of Lvov. Churchill interrupted the discussion by saying that the German lands Poland would receive were of much greater value than the Pripet marshes anyway.

Later, there was a prolonged study of the Oder line on a map supplied by the American delegation. Churchill observed that he liked the picture of the new Poland and that he was going to tell the Poles that they would be foolish if they did not agree. He would remind them, too, that were it not for the Red Army, they would have been completely destroyed. He said that if the Polish government did not agree, "then Great Britain would be through with them and certainly would not oppose the Soviet Government under any condition at the peace table." He added that he would not make "a great squawk" about Lvov.[13]

The president carefully abstained from the discussion. He only asked Stalin "whether a voluntary transfer of peoples from the mixed areas would be possible." Stalin answered in the affirmative.[14]

The second part of the discussion is described in Churchill's memoirs in much more detailed and precise terms than in the Department of State publication. The prime minister observed that although he did not ask for a formal agreement on Poland, he nevertheless wanted "something" in writing, and then submitted the following text for acceptance: "It is thought in principle that the home of the Polish State and Nation should be between the so-called Curzon line and the line of the Oder including for Poland East Prussia (as defined) and Oppeln; but the actual tracing of the frontier line requires careful study and possible disentanglement of population at some points."

He explained that he needed such a "formula" because then he could say to the Poles: "I do not know if the Russians would approve, but I think I might get it for you. You see, you are being well looked after." Even with this procedure the Poles might not be satisfied, but "nothing would satisfy the Poles" anyway, he sarcastically observed. Asked whether the "formula" was agreeable to him, Stalin said yes, provided the Soviet Union got Königsberg in East Prussia. When Churchill rather casually inquired about Lvov, Stalin repeated that the Curzon Line would form the postwar Polish-Soviet frontier.[15] The British statesman did not pursue the inquiry.

In considering this informal understanding on Poland's boundaries, one must remember that it was doubtless of secondary importance to both Great Britain and the United States, especially when compared with other vitally important Anglo-American-Soviet agreements concluded at Tehran. In each case, the Western leaders thought Stalin's attitude was reasonable and helpful. The grand strategy of the war was agreed upon: France would be invaded from both the north (Overlord) and the south (Anvil), and a simultaneous, supporting offensive by the Soviets would be effected in the east. Stalin formally committed his government to enter the war against Japan. He gave permission to use Soviet-controlled areas for shuttle-bombing operations. Policies concerning Italy, Japan, China, Iran, Austria, and Finland were established and, what seemed to be of utmost importance, the framework for a future permanent international organization was laid down. True, Stalin was not to abide by many of the commitments he undertook. Some commitments, such as Russia's entry into the Pacific war, proved not to be in the best interests of the Western allies, but at the time, the results were considered more than satisfactory, concessions on secondary matters notwithstanding.

The conference was historically significant for all of central-eastern Europe. The plans Churchill presented for a diversionary Allied operation in the Balkans were rejected by Stalin and Roosevelt. The declaration on the liberated countries, discussed at the Moscow Foreign Ministers' conference in October, was formally agreed upon. Its crucial proviso that the liberating powers would pursue policies in the liberated countries *jointly* was omitted, as Molotov demanded in October.[16] Thus the heads of the British and American governments recognized formally, albeit implicitly, the Soviet Union's right to act *unilaterally* in the areas liberated by the Red Army. Germany had been divided into military operational zones, and the zone assigned to the Soviet Union extended to the Elbe River. The greatest loser was Poland. No pressure was put upon Stalin to reestablish diplomatic relations with the government-in-exile, and an informal, secret British-Soviet understanding was reached, recognizing the Soviet seizure of the eastern half of Poland in 1939. Secretly, the president of the United States became a part to the understanding.

While the agreement on Poland's eastern boundary was specific with the exception of Lvov, the decisions on the western frontier were vague. Churchill apparently was not informed about the geography of eastern Europe and thus did not know the exact locations of the eastern and western Neisse rivers.[17] Maps of the area were not carefully consulted. Poland was to get East Prussia "as defined," but no definition was supplied. Poland was to extend to the Oder River, including "Oppeln," but the city of Oppeln lies on the Oder, while the Oppeln district spreads far to the west of the river.

As soon as the conference ended, rumors spread, particularly in Washington and London, that some secret decisions and understandings concerning Russia's postwar position in eastern Europe had been reached. Roosevelt reassured public opinion to the contrary in his annual message to the Congress on January 11, 1944:

> And right here I want to address a word or two to some suspicious souls who are fearful that Mr. Hull or I have made "commitments" for the future which might pledge this nation to secret treaties, or to enacting the role of Santa Claus. . . .
>
> Of course we made some commitments. We most certainly committed ourselves to very large and very specific military plans which require the use

of all Allied forces to bring about the defeat of our enemies at the earliest possible time.

But there were no secret treaties or political or financial commitments. [18]

Eden was as emphatic in his assurances and, on December 15, 1943, made the following statement in the House of Commons:

> I can also tell the House, lest there is any uneasiness about it, that we have not entered into any kind of secret engagement or treaty or anything which can cause anyone a sleepless night or a sleepless hour. . . . I can give this undertaking, that as long as I have anything to do with the conduct of the Foreign Office, if I made an engagement I shall come and tell the House at once, which is the constitutional practice, and if they do not like it, they can turn me out. [19]

A few weeks later he was asked in the House of Commons whether any decisions had been made on Poland's frontiers that were contrary to the foreign secretary's note of July 30, 1941, and the Atlantic Charter. Again he answered in the negative. [20]

NOTES

1. Churchill, *The Hinge of Fate*, 201; also Eden, *The Reckoning*, 375.

2. Samuel I. Rosenman, *Working with Roosevelt* (New York: Harper & Brothers, 1952), 409.

3. Sherwood, *Roosevelt and Hopkins*, 748.

4. Eden, *The Reckoning*, 495.

5. For the memorandum, see *DPSR, 1939–1945*, 2:83–86.

6. Woodward, *British Foreign Policy in the Second World War*, 252–53; also Eden, *The Reckoning*, 488–89.

7. *DPSR, 1939–1945*, 2:90–93.

8. Churchill's own account, essentially in agreement with the minutes released by the Department of State, is more detailed and more comprehensive. Churchill, *Closing the Ring*, 361; also *The Conferences at Cairo and Tehran*, 512.

9. Eden, *The Reckoning*, 495.

10. For the minutes of the meeting, see *The Conferences at Cairo and Tehran*, 594–96. Churchill was to learn about the meeting only eleven months later. See his telegram of October 18, 1944, to Roosevelt, ibid., 884–85.

11. For the minutes, *The Conferences at Cairo and Tehran*, 596–604.

12. Churchill, *Closing the Ring*, 395.

13. Ibid., 397.

14. *The Conferences at Cairo and Tehran*, 600.

15. Churchill, *Closing the Ring*, 403.

16. Churchill, *Closing the Ring*, 466–67.

17. Churchill, *Closing the Ring*, 406.

18. *Congressional Record*, 78th Cong., 2nd Sess., 1944, 90, pt. 1, 55.
19. *5 Parliamentary Debates*, Commons, 385 (1943), 1651.
20. *5 Parliamentary Debates*, Commons, 386 (1944), 663.

Chapter Thirty

The Entry of the Red Army into Poland, January 1944

On January 4, 1944, the first Soviet detachments crossed the prewar Polish eastern frontier. In anticipation, the government-in-exile sent special instructions to the Underground on October 27, 1943, urging them to avoid any conflicts and to "enter into cooperation with the Soviet commanders in the event of the resumption of Polish-Soviet relations." Simultaneously, the Poles delivered a well-documented memorandum—based on information received from Poland—to the British and American governments.[1]

The memorandum related that the position of the non-Communist Underground had become desperate and seemed hopeless unless diplomatic relations with Russia were established. In numerous instances, local Communists and Soviet partisans provoked bloody Nazi reprisals against the Polish population and then blamed the Home Army for ineptitude and irresponsibility. The Communists constantly attempted to infiltrate, weaken, or destroy the non-Communist resistance forces while preserving their own manpower. In some cases, they even denounced members of non-Communist secret organizations to the Gestapo.[2] The Communist underground press attacked not only the local patriots but also Great Britain and the United States. What official Soviet propaganda did not dare say openly was secretly circulated in Poland by local Communists. The memorandum cited specific cases to this effect. Fear prevailed that once the Red Army liberated the Polish-inhabited areas, the Communists would denounce the non-Communist Underground to the Soviet secret police. The British had little reason to doubt the veracity of the memorandum; independent reports received by the Foreign Office confirmed the charges.[3] To effect some stabilization seemed not only vital but most urgent.

Mikolajczyk's government took the initiative and on January 5, 1944, issued a public declaration that appealed to Moscow to respect the rights and interests of the Polish nation, rejecting "solutions imposed by force." The Poles reaffirmed their determination to continue the fight against Germany, offered full collaboration on the part of the Underground—provided diplomatic relations were resumed—and requested the reestablishment of Polish sovereignty in liberated territories. The original draft referred to "all" Polish territories, but under "strong pressure from the Foreign Office" the word "all" was deleted.[4] Although the declaration was essentially satisfactory to Eden, he was skeptical of its effectiveness. "The truth is that in the present atmosphere of overwhelming Russian victories, there is public impatience with the Poles. This may not be just, but it is the truth," he commented to Churchill.[5] What he had feared and advised the Poles to prevent at all costs was now taking place. The Red Army did enter Poland, but there was no agreement between the government-in-exile and Moscow.

The Soviet answer came one week later, on January 11, and it clearly indicated that nothing short of a surrender would satisfy Moscow. According to a public declaration, the Soviet territorial acquisitions of 1939 were not susceptible to change, since they had been confirmed by the constitution and approved by the local population through a "democratic plebiscite."[6] The government-in-exile was castigated for having failed to organize opposition to the Nazis, and the Union of Polish Patriots received warm praise. Because the declaration contained some vague, general expressions of goodwill, apparently still leaving the door open, it evoked favorable responses, particularly in the British press. The *Times* advised the Poles in several articles to accept the Soviet demands in order to secure "Russia's friendship."[7]

Realizing how fast they were losing ground, the government-in-exile decided to refrain altogether from direct and public discussion and placed the final responsibility on the shoulders of Great Britain and the United States. Still unaware of the Tehran understanding and thus still counting on British and American support, the government-in-exile now proposed that the British and the American governments act as intermediaries in the discussion of "all outstanding questions" between Poland and the Soviet Union. Handing the copy of the statement to the new Soviet ambassador in London, Feodor Gusev, on January 13, the eve of its publication, Eden emphasized that "all outstanding questions" included frontier revision.[8] The statement, formally authorized by Mikolajczyk's cabinet, was the result of tremendous pressure exerted by the Foreign Office. Churchill threatened that "in case the negotiations fail because of the Polish reply to the Soviet note, he [would] consider himself relieved from moral obligations which Great Britain [had] towards Poland."[9]

Three days later Moscow rejected the proposal outright and berated the Poles for not specifically accepting the Curzon Line. Eden considered the Soviet declaration "a blow in the face" and told Gusev so.[10] He also thought, however, that Great Britain was no longer in a position to help the Poles.

The exchange of declarations between the Polish and Soviet governments coincided closely with ominous faits accomplis in Poland. On January 30, 1944, the Kościuszko radio station, broadcasting from Moscow, announced the creation in Poland of the Home National Council—a "parliament" allegedly representing all political groups.[11] Soon after, the station announced that the Peasant, Socialist, and Workers' parties, as well as others, had sent their representatives to the new body. On February 21 *Wolna Polska* (Free Poland), the official organ of the Union of Polish Patriots, declared that "most democratic" elections to the Home National Council had been held in all territories liberated by the Red Army. The manifesto of the new "parliament" proclaimed the full cooperation of all political parties fighting against the Nazis; close cooperation with the Allied troops; cordial relations with the USSR, Great Britain, and the United States; and democracy, freedom, and independence for Poland. The government-in-exile was labeled an "émigré Fascist clique rejected by the Polish people." The chairman of the council, Boleslaw Bierut, was described as having no party affiliations, and the vice chairmanship was given to Edward B. Osubka-Morawski, representing the Socialist party.[12] The whole maneuver was evidently a hoax, because the genuine Socialist and Peasant parties were the main pillars of both the government coalition in London and the Underground in the homeland.

The formation of the Home National Council and the techniques employed could be traced primarily to the organizational talents of Bierut, certainly the most important Polish Communist leader of that period. He was born in 1892 of a lower-middle-class family in Lublin and joined the Communist movement early in his youth. Ever since then, his life had been shrouded in secrecy and evasions.

In the first years of Poland's independence, he operated under the cover of cooperative-movement organizations in various parts of Poland. He made several trips to Russia, though, to participate in party conferences. As a result, a warrant for his arrest was issued in 1923, and from then on he moved under assumed names. In 1924 he went to Russia and underwent advanced party training. On his return to Poland in 1927 he was arrested. Granted bail, he escaped to Russia again. Subsequently, he resided in Berlin, Vienna, and Prague as the Comintern's liaison with the local Communist parties. In 1932 he returned to Poland again—this time under the name of "Biernacki"—sent by Moscow to investigate ideological deviations of the Polish Communists. Arrested in 1933, he received a seven-year sentence. He served only two years; then, in 1935, he was deported to Russia as part of a political prisoner exchange transaction. He remained in the Soviet Union until the summer of 1943 and was then parachuted to German-occupied Poland. Unlike Gomulka, he was one of Stalin's *aparatchiki.*

Bierut had originally intended to bring about a collaboration between the already existing (Communist) Polish Workers' Party (PPR) and other underground organizations. In this he failed, because the most important underground groups considered themselves a part of the secret state structure and recognized the authority of the government-in-exile. Unable to achieve genuine cooperation, he took a one-on-one approach with some leftist members of the Socialist, Peasant, Democratic, and other parties. He encouraged those men—unknown and unimportant for the most part—to abandon their parties. He then put them in touch with his Communist-oriented followers and induced each group to adopt the name of the party from which the dissenters had come. Thus Osubka-Morawski, a minor leftist dissenter from the prewar Socialist party, undertook the task of forming its underground replica.

The conditions of war, of course, required strict secrecy for all underground activities and facilitated Bierut's takeover technique; soon the names of the Socialist, Peasant, and other parties were used by impostors who in fact were controlled by the PPR. The Home National Council itself was a replica of the legitimate Council of National Unity; so was the Communist-controlled military organization, the People's Army, similar in name to the government-controlled Home Army.

From the moment the Red Army reentered Poland, its intention to destroy non-Communist military organizations became evident. According to a plan agreed upon between the Underground and the government-in-exile, the Home Army units, whenever possible, were to stage local uprisings just before the Red Army entered. They were then to reveal themselves to the Red Army commanders and offer to collaborate, declaring, however, their allegiance to the government-in-exile. Whenever they did follow this plan, the Home Army men were either arrested or shot on the spot.[13] These happenings were not sporadic but apparently were part of a policy planned in advance. In his note to Churchill of January 16, Mikolajczyk quoted a relevant confidential circular, which he received from Poland.[14]

After the war it was established that during the first months of 1944, the Soviet military authorities hanged at least twenty Polish Home Army commanders and shot three, solely because they had declared their loyalty to the government in London. In the Lublin area alone, more than fifty thousand Poles were arrested between July 1944 and January 1945.[15] The liquidation of the Underground was followed by mass deportations and enforced conscription into the Communist-controlled army.

World public opinion could not be properly informed about these tragic events because, in the atmosphere of well-earned admiration for Russia's war sacrifices and costly victories, most of the newspapers and magazines either denied publicity to the Poles or refused to believe what was happening. When the information did appear in print, it usually brought severe criticism as "insulting" to Russia or "damaging" to Allied unity. A factual well-documented article, published in London at the end of January 1944 in the *Wiadomosci Polskie* (Polish news), caused public attacks from such respectable magazines as the *Observer*[16] and prompted an official protest from the Soviet ambassador; the entire issue was suppressed by the censor. The minister of information, Brendan Bracken, when asked on February 16 in the House of Commons "how free Polish opinion can be expressed, if one side of the story is suppressed," gave the following answer: "The Poles have a considerable number of papers in this country and I don't believe that British sailors should have to cart paper across the ocean to provide opportunities for foreigners in this country to help German propaganda and sow discord."[17]

The above exchange took place just four days after *Pravda* published in Moscow a vitriolic four-column attack on the Polish government, which was echoed by the *Daily Worker* in London:

> The émigré Polish government and its servants wage no fight against the Germans, do not wish to wage it and cannot wage it. . . . The émigré Polish government, which includes Fascist political cheap-jacks has lost all sense of reality. It lives in a phantom world of Hitler mirage. It has completely severed itself from the real Polish people who are waging a relentless struggle against the German invaders and their Polish assistants. The London Polish political cheap-jacks have nobody to back them in Poland except the pro-Fascist agencies which are helping the Germans, and the simpletons they have misled.

All Poles who value Poland's honor and independence march with the "Union of Polish Patriots" in the USSR.

As a result of the continuous and unrestrained propaganda on behalf of the Soviet policies, and the inability of the Poles in London to present their case, public opinion in the West increasingly considered the "Polish exiles" obstinate, reactionary, or unrealistic. The government-in-exile—unwillingly, to be sure—contributed to the general ignorance and misinformation. Like Sikorski, Mikolajczyk believed strongly that an understanding with Russia was a necessary condition for the success of his efforts to restore and preserve Poland's independence. In order not to antagonize Stalin and desirous to prove his goodwill, he himself on many occasions withheld from the public vital information about Polish-Soviet relations.

NOTES

1. *Polish Documents Report of the Select Committee*, appendix, 67–72.

2. Bor-Komorowski, *The Secret Army*, 71, 118–22, 171–72.

3. Woodward, *British Foreign Policy in the Second World War*, 254.

4. *DPSR, 1939–1945*, 2:12–24; also Woodward, *British Foreign Policy in the Second World War*, 278.

5. Eden, *The Reckoning*, 504.

6. For the full text, see *DPSR, 1939–1945*, 2:132–34.

7. *Times* (London), January 6, 1944, 5; January 8, 1944, 5; January 12, 1944, 5; January 14, 1944, 5.

8. Woodward, *British Foreign Policy in the Second World War*, 279.

9. Rozek, *Allied Wartime Diplomacy*, 190–92.

10. Eden, *The Reckoning*, 506.

11. Deutscher, *Stalin: A Political Biography*, 510. For the Communist Underground, see Korbonski, *The Polish Underground State, 1939–1945*, 110–16.

12. *Daily Worker* (London), February 2, 1944, 1.

13. Bor-Komorowski, *The Secret Army*, 195–98.

14. *Polish Documents, Report of the Select Committee*, appendix, 74.

15. Select Committee on Communist Aggression (House of Representatives), *Communist Take-Over and Occupation of Poland*, Special Report No. 1 (83rd Cong., 2nd Sess., under authority of H. Res. 346 and H. Res. 438) (Washington, DC: US Government Printing Office, 1954), 20–21.

16. *Observer* (London), February 13, 1944, 1. See also *Daily Worker* (London), January 27, 1944, 4.

17. *5 Parliamentary Debates*, Commons, 387 (1944), 171–72.

Chapter Thirty-One

Churchill's Efforts to Implement the Polish "Formula"

British and American attitudes toward Poland after the Tehran conference were directly affected by two factors: (1) the "formula" secretly agreed upon and (2) the Soviet promise to launch an eastern offensive at the time of the scheduled Allied landing in France. It was hoped this would vent the transfer of German forces from the Russian to the western front. Hull later observed that "we could not afford to become partisan in the Polish question to the extent of alienating Russia at the crucial moment [invasion of France]."[1]

Churchill saw the reestablishment of Polish-Soviet relations and Moscow's recognition of the government-in-exile as most important. Once that was done, the government-in-exile and its Underground agencies in the homeland would have a chance, he hoped, to establish their authority in the liberated areas, thus preventing Moscow from setting up its own regime. His plan, however, hinged on Mikolajczyk's approval of Stalin's territorial demands and any further concessions deemed necessary. In its advance into Germany, the Red Army was bound eventually to occupy all of Poland, and the further it went, the more control Stalin would have over Polish matters. Thus, the sooner the government-in-exile became reconciled to Stalin's territorial demands, the more chance it had of returning to Poland and playing an influential role. Any opposition to those demands was doomed anyway, since Churchill himself had already secretly given his approval to them at Tehran. And although at the time he was still unaware of Roosevelt's super-confidential commitment to Stalin, he realized better than anyone else that the president of the United States had no intention of defending Poland's prewar boundaries.

In an effort to fulfill his commitment undertaken at Tehran to make the Poles accept the Curzon Line of "their own free will," Churchill sent Eden a cable from Carthage on December 20, 1943, advising him of the strategy he should use. Churchill had fallen ill and had to take a rest.

Eden was instructed to show the Poles the territorial "formula" without divulging the fact that Churchill and Stalin had already agreed on it. "The Poles should understand, of course, that these are only very broad, tentative suggestions, but that they would be most unwise to let them fall to the ground," he cautioned the foreign secretary. "Even if they do not get Lvov, I should still advise their acceptance," Eden was to say. Remuneration for the eastern territories would consist of "the line of the Oder, including the Oppeln district on the west." If the Poles agreed, they would get "a magnificent piece of country three or four hundred miles across each way and with over a hundred and fifty miles of seaboard even on the basis that they do not begin till west of Königsberg." Acceptance of the "suggestions," Eden was to explain, "would give a chance for the rebirth of the Polish nation brighter than any yet seen." The Poles should "put themselves in the hands of British and American friends to turn this plan into reality," he added.[2]

Confident that the procedure agreed upon at Tehran would work, Churchill cabled Roosevelt:

> This gives the Poles a fine place to live in, more than three hundred square miles with two hundred and fifty miles of seaboard on the Baltic. As soon as I get home I shall go all out with the Polish government to close with this or something like it, and having closed, they must proclaim themselves ready to accept the duty of guarding the bulwark of the Oder against further German aggression upon Russia, and also they must back the settlement to the limit. This will be their duty to the Powers of Europe, who will twice have rescued them. If I can get this tidied up early in February, a visit from them to you would clinch matters.[3]

It seems that Churchill, pressed by his numerous duties, did not have a clear picture of how large the new Poland was to be. While in his message to Eden he contended that the seaboard of the new state would be 150 miles, in his cable to Roosevelt he mentioned approvingly 250 miles.

Following Churchill's instructions, Eden saw Mikolajczyk, Romer, and Raczyński on December 20, 1943, and on January 11, 1944.

In the first conversation[4] he told the Poles that both he and Churchill had the "impression in Tehran that something could be obtained in Polish affairs from the Soviet government." They had the "impression" that the Soviet government would "insist" on the Curzon Line, but, on the other hand, it wanted Poland to extend to the "whole length" of the Oder River and include East Prussia as well as Danzig. "We had to be very cautious in exploring the ground," he said, "as we did not wish to engage ourselves or you."

In the second conversation with the same group,[5] he advised the Poles to take advantage of the Soviet declaration just made public and strongly pressed for the acceptance of Soviet demands as soon as possible. Otherwise, he warned, a rival government might be set up in Poland by Moscow. "What will happen when the Soviet troops advance inside Poland?" he asked. He emphasized that Churchill considered Soviet "proposals" as a "fair basis for negotiations."

Nine days later, on January 20, Mikolajczyk, Romer, and Raczyński were received by Churchill himself.[6] He spoke with greater authority than Eden, and the pressure he applied was more direct. He bluntly asked the Poles to enter into immediate negotiations with Moscow. Before the negotiations started, the government-in-exile would have to agree to the Curzon Line, leaving Lvov on the Soviet side. In exchange, the Poles would receive territories up to the Oder River, if they so "desired"; Danzig; and East Prussia. He made it clear that Great Britain would not oppose the Soviet territorial demands, stating, "It was unthinkable that this country should go to war with the Soviet Union over the Polish eastern frontier, and the United States would certainly never do so." He added that the British government had never guaranteed Polish eastern boundaries. By the same token, he continued, once the Poles accepted the Curzon Line, they could count on the British and American support of Poland's vital interests, such as protection against Germany's revenge, help for population transfers, guarantees for the new Poland, and support of the government-in-exile against Soviet interference.

Churchill asked the Poles for immediate authorization to inform Stalin about their acceptance "in principle" of the Soviet territorial demands. Should they fail to do so, he warned, "we might be overtaken by events which would be difficult to remedy." He himself would prefer to postpone all territorial solutions until the peace conference; however, in the case of the Polish-Soviet dispute, he opined, this had become impossible. "It must be remembered," he reiterated, "that the Russian armies were pressing forward, and if nothing was done it was difficult to know what situation might face us." So far, he warned his guests, he spoke confidentially. However, should the Poles procrastinate, he "would not hesitate" to state his views in public.

From Churchill's arguments it appeared that Poland might receive East Prussia and the Oder frontier in the west, that Poles from the Soviet-incorporated areas would be allowed to settle in the new Poland, and that Germans living in the lands to be given to Poland could be transferred to the new, curtailed Germany. But while the Poles were asked to recognize the Curzon Line immediately and formally, commitments pertaining to Poland's western frontiers were still vague and informal. The Polish government realized the uncertainty of the situation and, three days later, on January 23, forwarded a formal note to the Foreign Office asking for clear-cut answers to several questions, in case a Polish-Soviet agreement were reached.[7]

The note posed the following questions. (1) Would Great Britain guarantee that the Polish government will be permitted to return to Poland and establish its own independent administration? (2) Would Great Britain formally guarantee the territorial integrity of the new frontiers as well as the political independence of Poland and noninterference in Polish internal affairs? (3) Would foreign troops be evacuated from Poland once the military operations were over? (4) Would Great Britain state officially that Poland was to receive the Oder River as its frontier, Oppeln in Silesia, Danzig, and the entire territory of East Prussia? (5) Would Poland's acquisitions in the west and Poland's losses in the east be embodied in the same international document, enacted by the British, American, and Soviet governments? (6) Would the German population be completely evacuated from the newly constituted Poland? (7) Would all the Poles who had been forcibly detained in the USSR be repatriated?

A few days later Churchill submitted the Polish memorandum to the war cabinet, which decided that a special message should be sent to Moscow defining the Polish stand, explaining the position of Great Britain, and asking for a formal Soviet policy statement.[8]

In his telegram to Stalin of January 28, Churchill described his discussions with the Poles.[9] He assured them that the postwar Poland would receive a guarantee from the Allies against any future German attack. He told them that the Curzon Line had to be accepted in exchange for East Prussia and the territories up to the Oder. So far, he had not told the Poles about the Soviet claim on Königsberg. "The Polish Ministers," the telegram continued, "were very far from rejecting [these] proposals but they did submit several questions." He enumerated them and observed that "none of [them] seem to be in conflict" with his own "suggestions." He emphasized that although Great Britain supported Soviet territorial demands on Poland and considered it necessary to depart from the principle of postponing discussions of territorial issues to the end of the war, it opposed "interference in internal sovereignty," that is, the demand for changes in the composition of the Polish government. He warned Stalin that the creation of a Moscow-controlled government in Warsaw would "raise an issue in Great Britain and the United States detrimental to that close accord between the three Great Powers upon which the future of the world depends."

Stalin answered on February 4.[10] He demanded an unequivocal, public, formal declaration by the Polish government accepting the Curzon Line. Confirming his agreement to Poland's territorial gains in the north and east, he reiterated the demand for Königsberg and the adjoining area. As for the composition of the government-in-exile, he refused to compromise. Its "thorough" reorganization would have to take place, and the "pro-Fascist imperialist" elements—not only in London but in the armed forces and within Poland itself—would have to go. He considered the argument concerning "interference in Poland's internal sovereignty" as irrelevant. Only last May, Churchill himself wrote him that the Polish government could be improved and that he, Churchill, "would work towards that end." The message indicated that, regardless of territorial issues, Stalin would not deal with the government-in-exile in its present form.

Churchill immediately (on February 6) informed Mikolajczyk, Romer, and Raczyński about the situation, pressing them again to accept without delay and unconditionally the Curzon Line, as well as the Soviet demand for Lvov and Königsberg.[11] Again Mikolajczyk declined, explaining that his acceptance would be repudiated in Poland anyway. He emphasized that while the Polish Underground leaders had decided to cooperate with the Soviet authorities, thus proving their goodwill and trust, the creation of the Communist-controlled Home National Council brought to light Soviet intentions to set up a Moscow-controlled regime in the liberated areas. Because he recognized the urgency of finding some solution, Mikolajczyk suggested that a demarcation line between Polish and Soviet administration might be agreed upon, leaving the final determination of the Polish-Soviet frontier until after the war.

Although the Polish proposal represented a further concession, it still ran contrary to the Tehran understanding, and Churchill knew that Stalin would never accept it. He did not give up, though, and proposed an approach which, having all the appearances of a compromise, was essentially in agreement with the "formula." The British government would send a note to Moscow informing Stalin that the government-in-exile was ready to negotiate on the basis of the Curzon Line, leaving Lvov to Russia. General Sosnkowski, General Kukiel, and Professor Kot, the three Polish leaders most roundly attacked by Moscow, would be removed. Great Britain and the USSR would both guarantee Poland's independence and its recompensation with the territories of East Prussia, minus Königsberg, and "as much territory up to the Oder as the Polish Government might see fit to accept." For the time being the Curzon Line would serve as a demarcation line between the Soviet and the Polish administrations until Poland "formally" obtained the German areas. Then it would become a boundary. [12]

The procedure as suggested by Churchill was to spare the government-in-exile an immediate, public, and formal cession of half Poland's prewar territory to Russia, thus preserving its standing in Poland. At the same time, the procedure would secure an eventual implementation of the Tehran "formula." He therefore ardently pressed the Poles to authorize the dispatch of the note. Should they refuse or further procrastinate, the British government would have no choice, he threatened, but to make its position public and conclude an agreement with Moscow disregarding the government-in-exile altogether. This, Eden interjected, would preclude the return of this government to Poland.

Soon after, on February 16, another meeting of Churchill, Eden, Mikolajczyk, Romer, and Raczyński took place, at which the Poles made a further concession. [13] By formal authorization of his cabinet, Mikolajczyk proposed an agreement to a demarcation line running between the 1921 frontiers and the Molotov-Ribbentrop line, leaving Lvov and Vilna under the Polish administration. He opposed the Soviet incorporation of Königsberg and also refused to make changes in his cabinet or armed forces "at the demand of a foreign power." Churchill answered that clearly Stalin would reject such a proposal. He insisted that there was no "practical alternative" to accepting the Curzon Line; that no one could stop the Soviet forces from marching through Poland; and that unless a prompt settlement was reached, the Soviets might set up a "puppet government" and "hold a plebiscite in which their opponents would be prevented from voting." He again warned the Poles that the British government considered the Soviet territorial demands justified, even though it was determined to do "whatever it could" to safeguard Poland's independence and to secure territorial remuneration at Germany's expense. Neither Great Britain nor the United States would contemplate using force against Russia for the sake of Poland's eastern frontiers. Once the Red Army liberated the Polish inhabited areas, the Poles would be dependent on Russia's goodwill, as would any Polish government that was operating in Poland—whatever its composition. Acceptance of the Curzon Line was the precondition of Moscow's goodwill.

Concluding the long and tortuous conversation, Churchill gave the Poles forty-eight hours to make up their minds. Should they procrastinate, he would pursue his course without them.

At that time, Mikolajczyk must have concluded that, under the circumstances, further opposition to Churchill's demands or rejection of his advice had become impractical. He seemed to agree with both Churchill and Eden that in view of the Red Army's westward advance, even an unsatisfactory settlement with Moscow was better than no settlement at all. Not only frontiers but Poland's very independence was at stake. Assured of territorial gains, Stalin might leave the Poles to themselves, that is, might recognize the authority of the government-in-exile in the homeland. But Mikolajczyk also knew fully well that, at least for the time being, his stand would not obtain approval by either the majority of his cabinet or the leadership of the Underground in the homeland. Confident of his own Peasant party's support, though, he decided to act on his own.

The next day, Mikolajczyk and Romer informed the Foreign Office that they decided to support the "general line" of Churchill's solution, even though the rest of the cabinet opposed it. They wanted Churchill to know that "although he [Churchill] could not put forward [his] proposals in the name of the Polish Government, he could tell the Soviet Government that he [Mikolajczyk] acquiesced in them and would not later disavow them."[14]

Because of his numerous discussions with the Poles and the above-mentioned notification by Mikolajczyk and Romer, Churchill sent a long and important message to Stalin, dated February 20.[15] The final draft was made in "close consultation" with Mikolajczyk and Romer, and, as Churchill informed Stalin in a separate message, they "agreed" to it. The Polish government, wrote Churchill, was ready to declare that the Polish-Soviet frontier as established at Riga "no longer [corresponded] to realities." The Poles were ready to discuss the new Polish-Soviet boundaries together with the boundaries between Poland and Germany. Because the Polish-German boundaries could not be defined publicly and formally at the present time, he continued, the Polish government "clearly cannot make an immediate public declaration of their willingness to cede territory" to the Soviet Union. Such a declaration "would have an entirely one-sided appearance" and, consequently, would be repudiated by Poles both at home and abroad. The new Polish-Soviet frontier would be "formally agreed and ratified" after the war at the time of armistice or a peace conference. Until then, a "demarcation line" would divide the areas governed by Soviet and Polish administrations. The Poles, Churchill said, were "naturally very anxious" that Vilna and Lvov be placed under their administration. However, they were informed and "clearly understand" that the Soviet government would not allow it. They also learned "for the first time" that Königsberg would belong to Russia.

In order to "facilitate" prosecution of war and establish effective collaboration with the Red Army, the message continued, the Polish government would like to return to the liberated areas "at the earliest possible moment," at which point, in consultation with the British and American authorities, the establishment of the Polish civil administration west of the demarcation line would be carried out.

Churchill assured Stalin that, in the end, the proposed procedure would "inevitably" meet Stalin's objectives. The Polish Underground would collaborate with the Soviet military forces anyway, "even in the absence of a resumption of Polish-Soviet relations," and once diplomatic relations were resumed, only those determined to cooperate with the Soviet Union would be included in the Polish government.

In order to implement and fully guarantee the Polish-Russian settlement, Churchill proposed in the same message that a British-Soviet agreement be concluded, guaranteeing, first, "sovereignty, independence and territorial integrity of reconstituted Poland"; second, incorporation by Poland of the "Free City of Danzig, Oppeln, Silesia, East Prussia west and south of Königsberg and as much territory up to the Oder as the Polish Government sees fit to accept"; third, removal of the German population from the new Poland; and fourth, free exchange of population between Poland and the USSR in the wake of frontier changes. He formally assured Stalin that once this settlement between Poland and the USSR had been achieved, Great Britain would support it at the peace conference and guarantee it in the postwar years. The copy of the message was sent to Roosevelt, who immediately telegraphed his approval to Stalin, expressing hope that all Churchill's proposals would be approved in Moscow as well.

Simultaneous with the message to Stalin, the British ambassador in Moscow, Sir Archibald Clark-Kerr, was instructed to inform Stalin that the message had been sent with the authorization of Mikolajczyk and Romer, and that a rejection of that offer "which had been made with great courage by the Polish Ministers would have a serious effect on British and American opinion."[16] In a separate message, Churchill also "warned" Stalin that the proposals, if implemented, would "very likely split the Polish government."[17]

Churchill was optimistic about Stalin's reaction to his message because, although neither Mikolajczyk nor Romer realized it, their personal initiative offered a possibility to implement the secret Tehran "formula" in *two* stages. The first was to be the immediate, if secret and informal, acceptance of the Soviet demands by Mikolajczyk and his followers, which in turn would be guaranteed by the British and the American governments. The second was the formal and final acceptance of those demands by the Polish government upon its return to Poland, whereupon *all* Polish boundaries would be decided.

Two days later, on February 22, Churchill issued an important statement on Poland in the House of Commons.[18] Using strong language, he informed the House that the "future of Poland" was discussed at the Tehran conference. There, Stalin "resolved upon the creation and maintenance of a strong, integral, independent Poland as one of the leading powers in Europe." He, Churchill, was "convinced" that Stalin's views expressed in Tehran represented the "settled policy" of the Soviet Union. He "reminded" the House that the British government had never guaranteed "any particular frontier line in Poland" and bluntly declared that Soviet demands did not go "beyond the limits of what is reasonable and just." Moreover, Great Britain never approved of the Polish occupation of Vilna in 1920 and did support the Curzon Line in 1919. Although all questions "of territorial settlement and readjustment" should be decided after the war at the peace conference, some "working agreement" would have to be devised as soon as possible in the event of a Polish-Soviet dispute. "The advance of the Russian armies into Polish regions in which the Polish underground army is active" made such an agreement "indispensable." He agreed with Marshal Stalin in Tehran that, for the territories lost in the east, Poland would "obtain compensation at the expense of Germany both in the North and in the West."

Churchill's public and official declaration could not have surprised Mikolajczyk, Romer, or Raczyński. It did shock Polish public opinion, however, both at home and abroad. Like Sikorski before him, so Mikolajczyk, too, either could not or did not consider it wise to inform the Poles at large about the crux of Polish-Soviet relations, the changing attitudes of the British and

American governments, or his own helplessness. Like Sikorski, he adhered to the British and American policy of not voicing public criticisms of Russia. The adverse reaction was particularly strong among the Polish troops fighting alongside the British. Polish armed forces numbered approximately 250,000 men; their losses had passed 60,000. Just eleven days before Churchill's speech, Monte Cassino had fallen to the Polish Second Corps, commanded by General Anders.[19] The Underground leaders cabled that the speech had shocked the entire nation. The tone of the *Wiadomości Polskie* (Polish news) in London was such that the British censorship office suppressed it entirely. The government-in-exile sent a solemn protest.

The surprise of shock was not limited to Polish quarters. Even in the House of Commons, Churchill's speech was severely criticized by several members, including Conservatives. The *Observer*, not unfriendly to Russia in those days, took sharp exception to the speech and Churchill's "cynicism." In New York, the noted writer William H. Chamberlin commented: "One can have the impression that it was Poland who had invaded Russia, occupied the greater part of her territory, established a cruel regime and deported millions of Russians into forced labor. Actually . . . it was the other way around." Referring to the Atlantic Charter's principles, he concluded that "Americans will not underwrite crime."[20]

Whatever the reaction, Churchill must have thought that his speech would advance the successful implementation of the Tehran "formula." He had committed himself at Tehran to make the Poles accept the Soviet demands, hoping to do so without letting them know that he had already agreed to them. For several weeks his efforts failed, but on February 17 he obtained the Mikolajczyk-Romer declaration. Churchill undoubtedly wanted to nail down the understanding (this time, between himself and Mikolajczyk) by registering publicly the extent of the territorial concessions being made to Russia and by publicly committing Britain to secure those concessions at the peace conference. By doing this, he probably also wanted to reassure Stalin *publicly* that the secret proposals sent a few days before would be carried out in full, even though they were not to be executed immediately and formally. He expected to obtain Stalin's approval of the procedure thought out by himself and secretly agreed to by Mikolajczyk and Romer. Most likely, he also expected that his speech would strengthen Mikolajczyk against the intractable majority of the Polish government and the Underground.

The events, however, took a different course. In his conversation with Clark-Kerr, Stalin dismissed "with a snigger" the position taken by Mikolajczyk. "Is that serious?" he sneered, "how handsome of them." He asked for no more than the Curzon Line and a reshuffling of the Polish government. The Poles, however, would not accept the Curzon Line *now* or *formally*, and they were willing to reconstruct their government only upon their return to Warsaw. That meant, Stalin told the ambassador, that they really did not want an agreement with Russia.[21] On March 3 Stalin cabled Churchill that the Poles in London were "incapable of establishing normal relations with the USSR," they were "far from being ready to recognize the Curzon Line," they still "claimed" Lvov and Vilna, and their "desire" to have Polish administration over "Soviet territories" must be considered an "affront to the Soviet Union." He concluded his harsh message by stating that "time is not yet ripe" for his taking up relations with the Polish "émigré" government.[22] The same day he told Harriman scornfully that the problem of the "London Poles" was insignificant altogether, that once the Red Army liberated Poland, the Poles themselves would elect a government anyway, and that he simply had more important things to do than discuss the "London Poles" continuously. He also warned Harriman that the Poles were "fooling" Churchill.[23]

Stalin's unexpected reaction produced most serious apprehensions at Whitehall. Eden had "most disquieting thoughts" about the Soviets' intention to cooperate. The war cabinet considered that having "persuaded" the Poles to make necessary concessions, the British government had also assumed obligations that it could not disregard. As a result on March 7 Churchill sent a new, sternly worded message to Moscow.[24] He bitterly reiterated that his proposals gave Stalin what he wanted. The Soviets would have de facto possession of the area up to the Curzon Line because he, Churchill, "made it clear to the Poles that they would not get either Lvov or Vilna." Soviet occupation would have the "assent of the Poles" and be guaranteed by both Great Britain and "undoubtedly" by the United States. No insult to Russia was intended, either by the Poles or by himself. He hoped that Stalin would agree to a "working arrangement with the Poles which [would] help the common cause during the war and give you [Stalin] all you require at the peace [conference]." He admonished the Soviet leader that "force can achieve much but force supported by the goodwill can achieve more," reiterating Great Britain's resolve to continue recognizing the Polish government-in-exile. In conclusion, he pointed out that all his "hopes for the future of the world [were] based upon the friendship and cooperation of the western democracies and Soviet Russia." The text of Churchill's message was reviewed and approved by Roosevelt.

Following the message, the British ambassador in Moscow was instructed to inform Stalin that the "general sense" of his stand would be communicated to the Poles in London as well as to the House of Commons. If it was negative, there would be great disappointment both in Great Britain and in the United States. Clark-Kerr could not execute his mission because Stalin simply refused to see him. Instead, in a curt telegram of March 16,[25] he pointed out that his messages concerning Polish-Soviet relations had apparently been leaked to the British press "with distortions" and that such violation of secrecy made it difficult for him to continue the correspondence. Because the Foreign Office was convinced that the leakage, which did occur, originated in the Soviet embassy in London,[26] it had become obvious that Stalin had devised a pretext to avoid any negotiated settlement of the Polish-Soviet dispute. He evidently wanted the Polish-Soviet relations to be determined by faits accomplis in Poland.

As far as Churchill was concerned, Stalin's reactions could only be regarded as new evidence that, indeed, Poland's independence, not its borders, was in the balance. The Tehran "formula," his efforts, his public stand on the future of Poland, his successful pressure on the Polish leaders, and the essential though unauthorized concessions made by Mikolajczyk and Romer—everything seemed in vain.

He did not give up, however. On March 21 Churchill sent another message in which he warned Stalin about his coming statement in the House of Commons.[27] He would have to reveal his failure in bringing together the Polish and Soviet governments, and he would have to announce that all territorial changes would have to wait until the armistice or peace conference. Churchill simultaneously instructed Clark-Kerr to call on Molotov and declare that "Soviet rejection of the Churchill proposal might give rise to difficulties in Anglo-Soviet relations, cast a shadow on the carrying out of the military operations agreed at Teheran and complicate the prosecution of the war by the United States as a whole."[28] The ambassador's reference to the "military operations agreed at Teheran" could only mean the commitment to invade France in the summer of 1944. The paragraph in Churchill's cable to the effect that "all questions of territorial changes must await the armistice or peace conference" implied a possible repudiation of the secret Tehran understanding. This time Churchill used the strongest arguments he had.

Stalin understood the implications and retorted with unusual violence. First, he advised Churchill against using threats, since they might lead "to opposite results." He reminded the prime minister that at Tehran the Curzon

Line was agreed upon by all *three* heads of government. He emphasized that he had no quarrel with the Polish people but only with the "Polish émigré government which [did not] represent the interests of the Polish people or express their aspirations." As to the statement in the House of Commons, Churchill was free to make any statement he liked, but if he acted the way he threatened to do, it would be considered by the people of the Soviet Union as a "gratuitous insult," and Stalin would consider it an "unjust and unfriendly act." Although he, Stalin, still favored Allied cooperation, "intimidation and defamation" would not benefit it. [29]

Stalin realized his strength, and he won the round. Churchill never made the statement he threatened to make. Perhaps he never seriously intended to. Preparations for the invasion of France were in their final stages, and the promised Soviet offensive in the east, in support of western operations, was considered vital. The Soviet Union was victorious. Stalin needed the Western Allies as much as they needed him. As long as the USSR stayed in the war—and could still seek a compromise peace with Germany—the occupation of Poland by the Red Army was inevitable. Not an open rift but further concessions might secure Stalin's cooperation, Churchill must have thought.

Eight years later, he chose to ignore the entire incident in his war memoirs.

NOTES

1. Hull, *Memoirs*, 2:1442.
2. For the full text, see Churchill, *Closing the Ring*, 450–51.
3. Ibid., 452.
4. For the minutes, see *DPSR, 1939–1945*, 2:112–16.
5. For the minutes, see ibid., 134–36; see also Eden's account, Eden, *The Reckoning*, 503–4.
6. For the minutes, see *DPSR, 1939–1945*, 2:144–49.
7. For the text, see ibid., 150–51.
8. Woodward, *British Foreign Policy in the Second World War*, 280.
9. *The Correspondence between Stalin-Churchill-Roosevelt*, 1:192–95.
10. For the text, ibid., 195–97.
11. For the minutes of the conversation, see *DPSR, 1939–1945*, 2:165–71; compare with Woodward, *British Foreign Policy in the Second World War*, 282–83.
12. For the text of the proposed note, see *DPSR, 1939–1945*, 2:173–76.
13. For the minutes, see ibid., 180–87; also Woodward, *British Foreign Policy in the Second World War*, 283.
14. Woodward, *British Foreign Policy in the Second World War*, 283–84.
15. For the full text, *The Correspondence between Stalin-Churchill-Roosevelt*, 1:201–4.
16. Woodward, *British Foreign Policy in the Second World War*, 284.

17. *The Correspondence between Stalin-Churchill-Roosevelt*, 1:200.

18. *5 Parliamentary Debates*, Commons, 397 (1944), 697–98. Churchill omitted the above speech in his war memoirs.

19. For the Second Corps's campaign, see Wladyslaw Anders, *An Army in Exile* (London: The Macmillan Co., 1949), 47–130.

20. *5 Parliamentary Debates*, Commons, 397 (1944), 701–804; also *Observer* (London), February 27, 1944; also *New Leader* (New York), March 4, 1944, respectively.

21. Woodward, *British Foreign Policy in the Second World War*, 285.

22. *The Correspondence between Stalin-Churchill-Roosevelt*, 1:207.

23. Feis, *Churchill-Roosevelt-Stalin*, 293–99.

24. For the full text, *The Correspondence between Stalin-Churchill-Roosevelt*, 1:207–8.

25. Ibid., 210.

26. Woodward, *British Foreign Policy in the Second World War*, 286.

27. For the text, *The Correspondence between Stalin-Churchill-Roosevelt*, 1:11–12.

28. Ibid., 391–92n63.

29. Ibid., 212–13.

Chapter Thirty-Two

Roosevelt and the Polish Issue on the Eve of the 1944 Presidential Election Campaign

JANUARY–JUNE

The conversation which the Poles had first with Eden and then with Churchill after the Tehran conference made it clear that the British government had decided to side with Stalin on the issue of the postwar Soviet-Polish boundary. Now, all hopes of the government-in-exile concentrated on the United States and on President Roosevelt.

At the end of January 1944 Ambassador Ciechanowski was instructed to ask officially if the American government thought the final settlement of Europe's territorial problems should take place before the end of the war, and if the United States would guarantee such a settlement. The answer Ciechanowski received was ambivalent on both points. [1]

> The basic position of the United States Government that general discussions of the many European frontier questions during the period of active hostilities against the Axis will run the risk of creating confusion and diverting concentration from the overall objective of defeating Germany is well known. This attitude, however, does not preclude the possibility of any two countries having mutual accord. This Government recognizes that the developments present certain complex and vital considerations which may render it desirable for the Polish Government to endeavor to reach a solution with regard to its territory without delay.

In reply to the second question, "good offices" were offered but without obligating the United States to guarantee any specific settlement. The wording of the offer of "good offices" implied immediate territorial concessions on the part of Poland. Ciechanowski understood the significance of the note and "was taken aback." Although at the time he had no way of knowing about the super-confidential Roosevelt-Stalin conversation, guided by instinct and experience he linked the answer with the Tehran conference. [2]

On January 15, following the exchange of declarations between the Poles and the Soviets, Hull instructed Harriman to intercede with the Kremlin in order to facilitate the resumption of diplomatic relations between Poland and Russia. The intervention proved fruitless. In his answer of January 24 Molotov severely reproved the Poles and contended that the moment was not ripe for American mediation. He implied, though, that if the Poles did reconstruct their government to "include democratic elements" from Poland and abroad, the reestablishment of relations might be possible. [3]

There is no evidence that Hull knew at the time about the Roosevelt-Stalin secret conversation at Tehran, and his intervention in Moscow most probably was made in good faith. But apparently it worried Roosevelt, because he had sent a message to Stalin in early February assuring him that American intervention in Polish matters should not be interpreted as a departure from his "position" at Tehran. Obviously, he was referring to his conversation with Stalin. He noted with approval Churchill's pressure on the Poles and, far from opposing the reorganization of the government-in-exile, he nevertheless recommended caution. There should not be "any evidence of pressure or dictation from a foreign country," he advised. [4] Even more explicit was the telegram he sent to Churchill the next day. Politely but firmly, the president admonished the prime minister for his last message to Moscow on behalf of Poland on the grounds that Stalin might think "that Mr. Churchill was wedded to the present members of the Polish Government in London and was determined to see them become the future government of Poland." [5] Because the president "knew that this was not Mr. Churchill's wish," the prime minister should be more careful.

Roosevelt's attitude toward the government-in-exile was soon demonstrated by a curious incident in April. Early in March Stalin asked that two Americans of Polish descent be allowed to come to Moscow for "discussions" on Polish-Soviet relations. The request was unusual because both of those invited—a prominent university professor, Oscar Lange, and an obscure Catholic priest from a small parish in Springfield, Massachusetts, Reverend Stanislaw Orlemański—were known for their pro-Soviet views.[6] Both Hull and the new undersecretary of state, Edward Stettinius, strongly opposed granting the request. Roosevelt, however, disregarded their objections and ordered that passports be issued.[7]

Reverend Orlemański had two conversations of several hours' duration with the Soviet leader and was greatly impressed. Stalin assured the priest of his religious tolerance and even aroused his hopes for a Soviet-Vatican agreement. Orlemański sincerely concluded that he could contribute not only to a reconciliation of Poland and Russia but of the Vatican and the Kremlin as well. Upon his return to the United States, he extolled Stalin publicly and called for "an understanding" of the Soviet system of government, because Stalin himself had told him that he was ready to collaborate with the Pope against the persecution of religion anywhere in the world!

Orlemański's visit to Moscow and his later activities in the United States created a sort of sensation, for it appeared to many that Stalin was, in fact, seeking a truly independent and democratic Poland, and the American government should help him in his endeavor.[8] The president even weighed the idea of sending Reverend Orlemański to Rome in order to bring the Pope and Stalin together.[9] Above all, it became evident to many that the "London Poles" were now no more than a historical anachronism—sympathetic but irrelevant. Stalin was delighted and, in thanking the president for making Reverend Orlemański's trip possible, addressed him for the first time as "Dear Friend."[10]

In March 1944 Ciechanowski went to London, where he tried to warn his colleagues not to count on Roosevelt.[11] Upon his return to Washington on March 25, he delivered a long, personal letter from Mikolajczyk to the president. The prime minister had tried since January to be invited to Washington, hoping this would demonstrate American support for his policy. In his letter he expressed anew a readiness to come to an understanding with Russia, again emphatically denied Soviet accusations, and voiced fear that the Communist system might be imposed on Poland. He drew Roosevelt's attention to the danger resulting from the widespread belief that the Soviet regime was bringing democracy and political freedom to countries liberated from the Nazi yoke and bitterly complained about the muzzling of the Poles. The letter ended with a dramatic appeal:

> On behalf of the Polish nation and government, I appeal to you, Mr. President, to do all in your power to prevent the creation in Poland of accomplished fact; to safeguard the sovereign rights of the Polish people and its lawful author-

ities; to assure the respect and safety of the lives and property of Polish citizens; to safeguard the Polish Underground Army and administration from the dangers that threaten them from their disclosures to the Soviet forces. [12]

In a short, formal reply on April 3, Roosevelt promised to receive Mikolajczyk, probably in May. He could no longer postpone the visit. Sympathy for the Polish cause was still strong in America. On May 3, Polish Constitution Day, 147 speeches were inserted into the *Congressional Record* on behalf of Poland. That same month the Polish-American Congress was organized and became a powerful center embracing most of the organizations of some six million Americans of Polish descent, dedicating all its activities to the Polish cause. The White House and the Department of State were very conscious of all this, as Hull himself told Ciechanowski. [13] In addition, the presidential elections were approaching, and the electoral campaign was about to start. Roosevelt would soon have to face the problem about which he had expressed such concern in his secret conference with Stalin at Tehran.

MIKOLAJCZYK'S VISIT TO THE UNITED STATES, JUNE 1944

Mikolajczyk arrived in the United States on June 5, 1944, accompanied by the deputy chief of staff of the Home Army, who had been spirited from Poland to London under the pseudonym of General Tabor. The premier stayed at Blair House for nine days and enjoyed an unusually cordial reception. He was attended by the highest government officials, and Roosevelt saw him on four occasions. [14] The attention shown him was exceptional in view of the crucial events stirring official Washington: on June 4, Rome fell; June 6 was D-Day, and the Allied forces were struggling to establish their beachhead on the shores of France; on June 9, the Red Army started its powerful offensive on the Karelian front. Mikolajczyk's visit and the courtesies shown him drew public attention and were extremely well received by Americans of Polish descent.

Each time Roosevelt saw his guest, he assured him of his sympathy for Poland. But he also encouraged his guest to initiate direct conversations with Stalin. Stalin, the president said, was not an imperialist but simply a realist. Mikolajczyk should have "just a human conversation" with him. He dwelt at length and with pleasure on how well he, Roosevelt, got along with the marshal, much better than "his poor friend Churchill." [15]

When Mikolajczyk asked what decisions had been made at Tehran in regard to Poland's frontiers, Roosevelt replied that Stalin was not at all eager to discuss that subject. Unfortunately, however, Churchill suggested to Stalin the Curzon Line.[16] He, Roosevelt, opposed Soviet territorial demands, however he could not at the moment support Poland too overtly. But he hoped eventually to become a "moderator" in the Soviet-Polish territorial dispute. At a state dinner on June 7 he declared that the boundary questions should wait "until a somewhat later time, when this new disease in Europe [Nazism] will be eradicated by the march of time" and "normalcy" would return.[17]

The president pressed Mikolajczyk to reach an understanding with Stalin. "When a thing becomes unavoidable, one should adapt oneself to it,"[18] he said, and asked Mikolajczyk what he thought of this theory. He advised his guest to remember that there were five times as many Russians as Poles and that Russia could swallow up Poland if an agreement on its terms were refused. If, however, the Polish government would make concessions through *direct* negotiations with Stalin, he, Roosevelt, would see to it that the resultant understanding would be advantageous to Poland.

The president went far in his promises. According to Ciechanowski, a participant in the discussions, the city of Lvov and the adjoining oil fields might be left in Poland. The inclusion of Vilna seemed more doubtful, but still the president "did not entirely exclude Stalin's ultimate agreement to leave Vilna to Poland." East Prussia would be given to Poland. When Mikolajczyk interjected that Stalin had claimed Königsberg, the president answered that he might eventually persuade the Soviet leader to relinquish that claim. Mikolajczyk recorded the president's words directly. "Don't worry," Roosevelt told him, "Stalin doesn't intend to take freedom from Poland. He wouldn't dare do that because he knows that the United States government stands solidly behind you. I will see to it that Poland does not come out of this war injured."[19] Both Mikolajczyk and Ciechanowski were most impressed by what they heard at the White House, and both concluded that not only did Roosevelt disagree with Stalin's demands on Poland, but the US government would support Poland at the decisive moment. Roosevelt's gestures of goodwill and sympathy for the Polish prime minister continued until the last minutes of his stay in the United States. At the airport, just before Mikolajczyk boarded his plane, Secretary of State Stettinius delivered a letter from the White House.[20] Although the letter did not refer to any specific issue, its friendly tone was overwhelming. "Our friend Stan [Mikolajczyk] is a regular guy and we shall do all we can to help in his undertaking," the congenial Stettinius told Ciechanowski at the airport, minutes after the prime minister's departure.

When Mikolajczyk informed the British officials about what he considered a highly successful trip, his report caused discontent. The Foreign Office felt that President Roosevelt "not for the first time" was too "vague" and too "optimistic" in his interviews with the Polish prime minister. They considered that such behavior complicated, rather than eased, Polish-Soviet relations. Churchill sternly warned Mikolajczyk not to have illusions as to the inevitability of such concessions as Stalin demanded on the part of Poland. [21] Eden, forwarding minutes of his conversation with the Polish leader to the Foreign Office, commented: "The President will do nothing for the Poles, any more than Mr. Hull did at Moscow or the President himself did at Tehran. The poor Poles are sadly deluding themselves if they place any faith in these vague and generous promises. The President will not be embarrassed by them hereafter, any more than by the specific undertaking he has given to restore the French Empire."

The last reference contained an ironic undertone. Eden knew that Roosevelt was playing with a fantastic idea of dismembering France, detaching Alsace-Lorraine together with northern provinces and incorporating them into a new state, "Wallonia," which he contemplated setting up. [22]

Apparently the British statesmen knew the president's ways and his motives better than the Poles, for the documentary record shows that on the eve of Mikolajczyk's arrival, Roosevelt had instructed Harriman to tell Stalin that the visit had been postponed as long as possible and that the Polish prime minister would be forbidden to make any public declarations while in the United States. He would also be told to jettison those members of his government who would not cooperate with the Soviets. The president thought that Stalin, too, should for the time being refrain from making controversial statements on Polish issues and instead stress "positive" factors like friendship, independence, and religious freedom for Poland so as not to complicate Roosevelt's campaign. He confirmed that the postwar Polish-Soviet boundary should follow the Curzon Line, noting that he was uncertain only about Lvov's situation. Harriman forwarded the message to Molotov on June 3, adding that Roosevelt would not allow any "minor obstacles" to weaken American-Soviet solidarity. A few days later, apparently still during Mikolajczyk's stay in Washington, Roosevelt received a cable to the effect that Stalin was "greatly pleased" with his attitude. [23]

As soon as the Polish prime minister left Washington, Roosevelt rushed a cable to Stalin, again clarifying his stand on Polish-Soviet relations: "You are aware that [Mikolajczyk's] visit was not connected with any attempt on my part to inject myself into the merits of the differences which exist between the Polish Government-in-Exile and the Soviet Government. Although we had a frank and beneficial exchange of views on a wide variety of subjects affecting Poland, I can assure you that no specific plan or proposal in any way affecting Polish-Soviet relations was drawn up." The president added that he encouraged Mikolajczyk to visit Stalin. Even in this matter, however, he made it clear that he was not interceding on Poland's behalf. "I know you will understand," the cable read, "that . . . I am in no way attempting to press upon you my personal views in a matter which is of special concern to you and your country."[24]

NOTES

1. For the full text, see *Polish Documents, Report of the Select Committee*, appendix, 76.

2. Ciechanowski, *Defeat in Victory*, 270–72.

3. Hull, *Memoirs*, 2:1437.

4. For the full text of the telegram, see *The Correspondence between Stalin-Churchill-Roosevelt*, 2:119–20.

5. Hull, *Memoirs*, 2:1440–41.

6. Stalin made his request ten weeks after Reverend Orlemański took part in a New York mass rally, sponsored by the National Council of American-Soviet Friendship. There he sharply criticized American Catholic bishops for their "suspicions" about the USSR and had harsh words for Reverend Fulton J. Sheen: "Whenever the bishops gather and preach morality and dogmas of the Church, then this preaching and teaching should be a law with every one of us, but when they speak of pacts, treaties and policies, then they are nothing else but a clique of politicians, and their pronouncements you and I can accept or reject. . . . [Reverend Fulton Sheen] may possess a doctorship in philosophy but when it comes to politics and diplomacy, he is as ignorant as the oak tree in the woods. I would advise this gentleman to speak more about Ireland and forget Poland." See National Council of American-Soviet Friendship, *We Will Join Hands with Russia* (New York: n.p., 1944), 14.

7. Hull, *Memoirs*, 2:1443.

8. Only for *New York Times*, see March 30, 1944, 3; April 28, 4; April 29, 5; May 1, 5; May 4, 6; May 6, 7; May 7, 1, 12; May 8, 10; May 10, 7; May 11, 7; May 13, 1, 4; May 15, 1, 6; May 16, 10, May 17, 6; see also *Times* (London), May 24, 1944, 3; May 25, 6.

9. Ciechanowski, *Defeat in Victory*, 308–9. Eventually, Reverend Orlemański was silenced by his superiors and sent to a monastery. He obeyed the order. As for Professor Lange, he subsequently renounced his American citizenship, was appointed in 1945 ambassador of the Warsaw government in the United States, approved by the American government, and later recalled to Warsaw to serve as a high dignitary in the Communist hierarchy.

10. *The Correspondence between Stalin-Churchill-Roosevelt*, 2:140.

11. Ciechanowski, *Defeat in Victory*, 276.

12. For the full text, see *DPSR, 1939–1945*, 2:207–11.

13. Ciechanowski, *Defeat in Victory*, 285–86.

14. For Mikolajczyk-Roosevelt conversations, see Mikolajczyk, *The Rape of Poland*, 59–61; Ciechanowski, *Defeat in Victory*, 291–310; Hull, *Memoirs*, 2:1444–445.

15. Ciechanowski, *Defeat in Victory*, 300.

16. Rozek, *Allied Wartime Diplomacy*, 221–22.

17. For the text of the speech, see Samuel I. Rosenman, *The Public Papers and Addresses of Franklin D. Roosevelt*, 13 vols. (New York: Harper and Brothers, 1950), vol. 13, "Victory and the Threshold of Peace," 161. Hereafter cited as *The Public Papers and Addresses of Franklin D. Roosevelt*.

18. Ciechanowski, *Defeat in Victory*, 293.

19. Mikolajczyk, *The Rape of Poland*, 60; Ciechanowski, *Defeat in Victory*, 305.

20. For the text, see *Polish Documents Report of the Select Committee*, appendix, 9; for Mikolajczyk's answer, see *The Rape of Poland*, 79–80; also Ciechanowski, *Defeat in Victory*, 313.

21. Woodward, *British Foreign Policy in the Second World War*, 289.

22. Eden, *The Reckoning*, 539–40, also 432, respectively.

23. See Feis, *Churchill, Roosevelt, Stalin*, 300–1; 374–76.

24. For the full text, see *The Correspondence between Stalin-Churchill-Roosevelt*, 2:146–47.

Chapter Thirty-Three

The Warsaw Uprising, August 1–October 2, 1944

In pursuance of the Tehran conference agreements, the Soviet offensive began in early June 1944, shortly after the Allied invasion of France. The offensive was successful. The central front broke down, and approximately one million German soldiers were killed, wounded, or taken prisoner. On July 12 the Red Army entered Vilna. Grodno was taken four days later. On July 20 the Bug River was crossed, and soon after advance Red Army units penetrated as far as the Vistula River, approaching the suburbs of Warsaw. On July 20 there was an attempt on Hitler's life, and on July 22 the Home Army intercepted a German wireless ordering a general withdrawal to the left bank of Vistula; on July 23–25 the evacuation of German civil offices from Warsaw commenced. Everything indicated an imminent Nazi collapse. During the morning of August 1, the day the uprising started, it was reported on the radio that Kaunas had fallen and, at noon, that Risto Ryti, the war president of Finland, had resigned.[1]

On July 14 the commander in chief of the Home Army, General Tadeusz Bor-Komorowski, reported to London that the Underground could not remain inactive "in the face of German retreat and the Soviet advance, nor in the case of internal collapse of the German troops and the threat of Soviet occupation."[2] On July 25 he informed London that the uprising in Warsaw could break out at any moment. By then, the Polish government had empowered the highest Underground authorities to determine the time and scope of local military actions directed against the withdrawing German armies.[3]

For weeks Soviet radio as well as the Soviet-controlled, Polish-language Kosciuszko radio station had been calling upon the Poles to revolt, and the appeals grew stronger with each broadcast. On July 29 Moscow broadcast a manifesto signed by Molotov and Osubka-Morawski, head of the newly created Committee of National Liberation. The manifesto called for immediate mass action, emphasizing that "there is not a moment to lose." Simultaneous with the radio broadcasts, the Communist-controlled underground groups pressed for an uprising through appeals openly posted on the walls of Warsaw and secretly, by distributing leaflets and newspapers. Similar leaflets were dropped over the capital and its suburbs by the Soviet air force.[4]

The leaders of the Underground in Warsaw had to make grave decisions. They knew that the Nazis were not only building fortifications but were also wiring the city, an important communications center, to blow it up in the event of their withdrawal. An uprising could save the capital. They also realized the seriousness of the Soviet accusation of their inactivity. If the Red Army were to take Warsaw without any help from the Underground, Moscow undoubtedly would declare either that the Home Army was a hoax or that it was hostile to Russia. Subsequently, the Soviet police, usually following close on the heels of the Red Army, would arrest the members of the non-Communist resistance (as they were already doing in other areas), and the Poles would have no defense before world public opinion. There was also another important factor. If Warsaw were liberated by the Poles themselves, the non-Communist administration could be formally established and the Underground authorities brought into the open. Their anonymity would be ended, and the Soviets would not be able to liquidate them as easily as in other areas. The Underground authorities wanted to fill the administrative vacuum created by the withdrawal of the German forces *before* the Red Army entered the capital.

The question of coming out into the open became particularly pressing in the last days of July. On July 22 the Red Army liberated Lublin, the first important city west of the Curzon Line. On the same day the Union of Polish Patriots transformed itself into the Polish Committee of National Liberation, hereafter known as the Lublin Committee. In a highly propagandized manifesto, it assumed a "legal and provisional executive authority" over all liberated territories and denounced the government-in-exile as well as its Underground agencies in the homeland as "illegal." The uprising was to enable the non-Communist Underground to establish in the capital its own authority, in the name of the government-in-exile and without Communist interference.

The Communist groups in Warsaw were rather negligible, and without the Red Army's support they could present no challenge to the government-controlled Underground state.

The leadership of the Underground could not discount the eagerness of its rank and file, either. For years, an uprising had been accepted as inevitable. Large caches of arms were hidden in the capital, and more than forty thousand members of the Home Army in Warsaw alone waited impatiently for action. Together with the rest of the population, they wanted to free their capital themselves, manifesting their determination to be free. Like their leaders, they took for granted that the Red Army would support their action and that air support would come from the West.

But the Red Army's support was not and, considering the circumstances, could not be secured. The government-in-exile had no diplomatic relations with Moscow, and the Home Army's command had no line of communication with the Soviet high command. As to the Western Allies' help, the Polish government *did* formally ask the Foreign Office on July 26 to secure British air support, and two days later they were officially notified that the requested aid could *not* be counted upon for technical reasons.[5] The leadership of the Underground was unaware of this. All hoped that the announced Mikolajczyk visit to Moscow would produce some positive results.

The uprising started on August 1 at 5:00 p.m. The timing was determined by information concerning the Red Army activities in the suburbs of Warsaw.[6] The initial moves of the insurgents seemed more than successful. Within a few hours the center of the city was in their hands. Soon after, the whole city was. The organization of the Home Army looked better and stronger than could have been anticipated.

Then came a shock. As soon as the Poles succeeded in driving the Germans out, the Soviet guns became silent, and a few days later the stunned people of Warsaw saw the Red Army withdraw from the outskirts of the city. Surrounded by eight German divisions, the Poles defied the enemy for sixty-three days. To the end the insurgents did not believe they would be left alone, unaided by either the Allies or the Red Army.

The Soviet action took others by surprise, too. Only a day after the uprising broke out, Churchill, full of hope, announced in the House of Commons that the "Russian armies [which] now stand before the gates of Warsaw, bring the liberation of Poland in their hands . . . offer freedom, sovereignty and independence to the Poles."[7] "Since the beginning of the struggle for Warsaw, the Red Army on its outskirts has discontinued all active operations,"[8] the plenipotentiary of the government in Poland wired to London three days later.

Once the insurgents had seized the city and the Germans had started a powerful counteroffensive, the Communists launched a worldwide propaganda campaign, discrediting the uprising as a conspiracy directed against Russia. The same Moscow station which in the weeks preceding the uprising called upon Warsaw to rise now branded Bor-Komorowski, as well as the Polish government-in-exile, as war criminals responsible for ordering the outbreak without coordinating their plans with the Soviet high command.[9] Mikolajczyk, who implored Stalin for help, received a contemptuous answer on August 16:

> After a closer study of the matter I had become convinced that the Warsaw action, which was undertaken without the knowledge of the Soviet command, is a thoughtless adventure causing unnecessary losses among the inhabitants. In addition, it should be mentioned that the calumnious campaign has been started by the Polish London Government which seeks to present the illusion that the Soviet command deceived the Warsaw population.
>
> In view of this state of affairs, the Soviet Command cuts itself away from the Warsaw adventure and cannot take any responsibility for it.

An almost identical cable was sent to Churchill.[10]

Both the British and the American governments tried to help Warsaw, and in the first part of August several air missions with food and ammunition were sent. Soon, however, it became evident that without landing facilities on the Soviet-held airfields, no effective aid could be given. The British Liberators and Halifaxes had to fly over a strongly defended area totaling some 1,750 miles for each round trip, and the losses were extremely heavy. Since Stalin had agreed at Tehran to the use of Soviet air bases for shuttle-bombing operations from Britain, both Churchill and Roosevelt appealed to him, asking for their Warsaw-bound planes to use the necessary facilities. He steadfastly refused.[11] To a specific request by Harriman, Vishinsky formally replied on August 15 that the Soviet government could not allow the use of these facilities, since the uprising was just the "work of adventurers." The same refusal came on August 17 from Molotov.[12]

Both Roosevelt and Churchill persisted in their efforts to obtain Stalin's cooperation in helping the Poles, and on August 20 they sent another joint appeal. In his answer of August 22 Stalin limited himself to severely castigating the Poles:

Sooner or later the truth about the group of criminals who had embarked on the Warsaw adventure . . . will become known to everybody. These people have exploited the good faith of the inhabitants of Warsaw, throwing many almost unarmed people against the German guns, tanks, and aircrafts. A situation has arisen in which each new day serves, not the Poles for the liberation of Warsaw, but the Hitlerites who are inhumanly putting down the inhabitants of Warsaw.[13]

By August 24 Churchill decided to inform Stalin that Allied planes with supplies would go to Warsaw and land on the Soviet-held airfields unless the Soviet government directly and officially forbade it. The plan fell through, this time because of Roosevelt's opposition. On September 4 Churchill suggested that the American air force carry out the operation, landing on Soviet-held airfields without any permission. The president rejected the suggestion again, on the basis of the information supplied by the Office of Military Intelligence. He was told that the Germans were already "in full control" of the city, that the insurgents had been pushed out of Warsaw.[14] In reality, they fought for thirty more days.

On August 30 the British cabinet formally declared that the Home Army soldiers formed an integral part of the Polish armed forces. The declaration, adhered to by the American government as well, was of value to the insurgents because, by implying possible reprisals against the German war prisoners, it forced the German command to treat them according to international conventions. As far as military operations were concerned, however, it did not help. It was never observed by the Soviet authorities, who continued to arrest the Home Army rank and file, considering them "bandits."

Finally, on September 9 Moscow agreed to the American shuttle operation, and Polish Red Army detachments attacked the suburban Praga, occupying it entirely by September 14. On September 13 and on the following nights, the Soviet air force dropped some supplies on Warsaw. But they were of no use: "The Russian planes, indeed, dropped the ammunition for which Bor-Komorowski's men had cried since the hour of their betrayal. The planes dropped the guns too. But the ammunition did not fit the guns nor did it fit any guns known to be in the hands of the uprising. The planes dropped food in quantity, but dropped it either with defective chutes or with no chutes at all. It smashed against the ruins of Warsaw and was wasted."[15]

A few days later, on September 18, more than one hundred American bombers flew over the fighting capital and dropped supplies. Executed on the forty-ninth day of the uprising, the shuttle operation to Warsaw came too late.

By then, several parts of the city had been recaptured by the Germans, and most of the supplies fell behind enemy lines. The uprising was approaching its agonizing end. Still, the fighting continued for two more weeks while the Germans bombed, dynamited, or shattered house after house with artillery fire. Two hundred fifty thousand defenders were killed, and one of the larger European capital cities lay in ruins. When, on October 2, after sixty-three days of fighting, the insurgents surrendered, the Lublin Committee announced that General Bor-Komorowski had abandoned his men and escaped. Once it became known that he was in Nazi hands, the Communist-controlled press announced that his surrender demonstrated friendship with the Nazis, and he was declared a "traitor."[16]

Long after the war Churchill and Eden criticized Soviet policies and Stalin's attitude toward the Warsaw Uprising. They also revealed their efforts to come to Warsaw's aid.[17] At the time of the uprising, however, their main concern was to not weaken the Anglo-Soviet relations and not antagonize Stalin. With the crucial and coordinated military offensives against Germany progressing successfully on both western and eastern fronts, the Warsaw incident was of no military importance. It had, instead, the potential of arousing British public opinion against Russia, which both statesmen wanted to avoid. In the House of Commons debate on September 24, 1944—just a few days before the fall of Warsaw—the prime minister appealed to the members not to embarrass him by criticizing Russia, and he praised the Soviet government. At the time, Eden even denied that London had ever asked Moscow for airfield facilities.[18]

As for Stalin, one week after the surrender of Warsaw he explained to Churchill that he did not want to cause the destruction of the city and its population—inevitable if he had ordered the Soviet offensive.[19]

The Warsaw Uprising and the motives and calculations of the Polish leadership—civilian and military—subsequently became a matter of international controversy. The controversy will probably continue, for whatever the arguments, the basic truth is undeniable. Without immediate assistance coming from both the Western Allies and the Soviet Union, the uprising never had any chance of success. That assistance had not been secured before orders for the uprising were given.[20]

NOTES

1. For a detailed account of the Warsaw Uprising, see Bor-Komorowski, *Secret Army*, 199–396; also J. K. Zawodny, *Nothing but Honour: The Story of the Uprising of Warsaw* (Stanford, CA: Hoover Institution, 1978).

2. Bor-Komorowski, *Secret Army*, 201.

3. Mikolajczyk, *The Rape of Poland*, 67. There was no uniformity of opinion on the uprising in Warsaw. General Sosnkowski, the then commander in chief, and General Anders, commander of the Polish forces in Italy, were against the uprising and made their views known: Anders, *An Army in Exile*, 208. See also Witold Babiński, "Na Marginesie Polemiki" (On the margin of a polemic), *Kultura*, no. 5/127 (May 1958), 97–106; also Józef Garliński, "Z Perspektywy, Dwudziestu Czterech Lat" (From the perspective of twenty-four years), *Wiadomości* (London), 1147 (March 1968), 4–5.

4. *Communist Take-Over and Occupation of Poland*, 22; also Bor-Komorowski, *Secret Army*, 211–13.

5. For the text of the British note, Edward Raczyński, *W Sojuszniczym Londynie* (*In the Allied London*) (London: Polish Research Center, 1960), 352, 378. Just before the uprising broke out, an emissary of the government-in-exile, Jan Nowak, arrived. On July 29–30 he passed his personal and highly pessimistic opinion as to Anglo-American military aid to the leadership of the Home Army. He, too, however, recognized that the uprising had become unavoidable: Jan Nowak, *Kurier z Warszawy* (*Courier from Warsaw*) (London: Odnowa, 1978), 313–26.

6. For critical evaluation of the Home Army's command—its plans, goals, and lack of political orientation—see Jan M. Ciechanowski, *Powstanie Warszawskie* (*Warsaw Uprising*) (London: Odnowa, 1971), 155, 193, 324–26, and passim.

7. *5 Parliamentary Debates*, Commons, 402 (1944), 1482.

8. As quoted by Umiastowski, *Poland, Russia and Great Britain*, 288.

9. *Daily Worker* (London), August 13, 1944, 3; August 14, 4; August 27, 4; *Izvestya* (Moscow), August 17, 1944, 4.

10. Mikolajczyk, *The Rape of Poland*, 82; also *The Correspondence between Stalin-Churchill-Roosevelt*, 25, respectively.

11. Hull, *Memoirs*, 2:1445–47; also Churchill, *Triumph and Tragedy*, 133–43.

12. Woodward, *British Foreign Policy in the Second World War*, 303.

13. *The Correspondence between Stalin-Churchill-Roosevelt*, 254–55.

14. Woodward, *British Foreign Policy in the Second World War*, 304–5; also Churchill, *Triumph and Tragedy*, 144.

15. Mikolajczyk, *The Rape of Poland*, 85; see also Bor-Komorowski, *Secret Army*, 342; also Churchill, *Triumph and Tragedy*, 144.

16. See Shotwell, *Poland and Russia, 1919–1945*, 71.

17. See Churchill, *Triumph and Tragedy*, 128–45; Eden, *The Reckoning*, 548–49.

18. *5 Parliamentary Debates*, Commons, 403 (1944), 26–27, 489, 556, 1139–1140.

19. Feis, *Churchill, Roosevelt, Stalin*, 389.

20. For a critical analysis of the Warsaw Uprising, see Adam Borkiewicz, *Powstanie Warszawskie, 1944* (*Warsaw Uprising, 1944*) (Warsaw: "Pax," 1964); Jerzy Kirchmayer, *Powstanie Warszawskie* (*Warsaw Uprising*) (Warsaw: Ksiazka i Wiedza, 1973).

Chapter Thirty-Four

The Poles Entrapped in the Homeland and Abroad, August–October 1944

MIKOLAJCZYK'S VISIT TO MOSCOW, JULY 31–AUGUST 9

Mikolajczyk returned to London from Washington reassured that he and his policies had a strong supporter in Roosevelt. Depressed by Churchill's continuous pressure to accept the Soviet demands, he appreciated the president's sympathy, optimism, and advice to seek *direct* contacts with Soviet officials.

Upon his return to London, Mikolajczyk immediately approached the Soviet ambassador to the exiled governments, Victor Lebedev. The two men held their first conversation, exploratory in nature, on June 20. The prime minister assured the ambassador that he and his government sought Polish-Soviet cooperation; he pointed out that the Home Army was supporting the Red Army and would continue to do so "in spite of the deplorable ethics of the latter."[1] Without rejecting Russia's territorial demands, he reiterated that, in agreement with official Allied policy, these matters should be decided after the war, at the peace conference. Lebedev asked for time to receive instructions and then, three days later, delivered the official answer. It was a hard one. The president of the republic, Raczkiewicz, General Sosnkowski, General Kukiel, and Professor Kot would have to be dismissed from the government and replaced by other unspecified "democratic" personalities. The appeal of April 17, 1943, to the International Red Cross (for an investigation of the Katyn massacre) would have to be publicly denounced. The Curzon Line, leaving Lvov to Russia, would have to be accepted formally and without delay. Mikolajczyk thought that the demands, if approved, would mean the end of his government, and he flatly refused.

Meanwhile, the Red Army, pursuing the crumbling German divisions, approached the Curzon Line. It would soon enter the undisputed Polish provinces, which brought up some critical questions—mainly, by whose authority were these provinces to be administered? What was going to happen to the non-Communist Underground? The general suspicion that the Soviets and their Polish collaborators would try to exterminate the Underground and communize the entire country deepened because of stepped-up propaganda from the Communist-controlled Home National Council. Fighting and bloodshed among Poles were generally feared. It became evident that only an immediate understanding between Mikolajczyk and Stalin could bring a solution. Churchill and Eden, who always believed that the government-in-exile should secure an understanding with Moscow, even at the greatest sacrifice, *before* the Red Army entered Poland, urged Mikolajczyk to see Stalin at once. The US Department of State concurred.[2] Realizing that negotiations with Lebedev led nowhere, the Polish prime minister agreed.

The circumstances of Mikolajczyk's trip to Moscow were dramatic. On July 20 Churchill informed Stalin that the Polish prime minister was about to leave for Moscow and expressed hope that "comradeship" would develop between the Soviet forces and the Polish Underground. Two days later the world learned of the establishment of the Committee for National Liberation in newly liberated Lublin and of its formal assumption of "legal and provisional authority" in Poland.[3] Then came Stalin's answer. Referring to the "comradeship," the Soviet leader informed Churchill that the "underground organizations led by the Polish Government in London have turned out to be ephemeral and lacking influence." The only body able to administer the liberated areas was the Committee for National Liberation. He, Stalin, would receive Mikolajczyk if Churchill so desired, but Mikolajczyk should rather contact the committee, which was "favorably disposed towards him."[4]

Mikolajczyk left London on July 26, accompanied by his foreign minister, Tadeusz Romer, and by the speaker of the parliament-in-exile, Professor Stanislaw Grabski. As he reached Cairo en route to Moscow, he learned that the Soviet government had just recognized the Lublin Committee as Poland's official governing body. On first impulse, he wanted to turn back. But, realizing the consequences, he reluctantly decided to continue the ill-starred journey.

And ill-starred it was, for what Churchill and Eden feared most, what they had warned the Poles against, had now happened. There were two rival Polish governments: one acting in the liberated areas in Poland, backed by the Red Army and formally recognized by Russia, the other officially recognized by the Western Allies but separated by hundreds of miles from the homeland.

From the moment of their arrival in Moscow, the Poles were ostentatiously snubbed. No one of importance greeted them at the airport, and while their own visit was not once mentioned in the press, they read in *Pravda* a long article about the official exchange of representatives between the Lublin Committee and the Soviet government. As soon as he arrived, Mikolajczyk, anxious to obtain some briefing, called on the British ambassador, Clark-Kerr. He did not get much information, but he did receive significant advice. The best way to strengthen his position vis-à-vis Stalin was to purge his government of "reactionary" and "anti-Soviet" elements, to accept the Curzon Line as a basis for negotiations, to recognize the Soviet findings on the Katyn massacre as conclusive, and to come to a "working arrangement" with the Lublin Committee.[5] This, of course, meant acceptance of all Stalin's demands.

Molotov received his Polish guest on July 31, asking frigidly: "Why did you come here? What have you got to say?"[6] When Mikolajczyk replied that he had come to see Stalin about Polish-Soviet relations, Molotov told him that Stalin was very busy, and that he should discuss "his problems" with the delegates of the Lublin Committee who, certainly not by accident, were also in Moscow. Mikolajczyk refused and stubbornly waited three days for an audience.

While waiting to be received by Stalin, the hapless prime minister learned about the Warsaw Uprising. The event probably did not take him by surprise, because his office controlled all secret routes of communication with Poland, and before leaving London he was aware that the Underground authorities had been authorized to order an uprising in the capital at any time, depending on the war situation. Suddenly, a new dimension was added to his mission. The future of the uprising evidently was conditioned by outside military aid. If Stalin decided to support it, it might become a historic occasion for Polish-Soviet reconciliation. But, on the other hand, the uprising made Mikolajczyk more than ever dependent on Stalin's goodwill.

Mikolajczyk's audience with Stalin took place on August 3.[7] The Soviet government, Stalin said, had recognized and concluded an agreement with the Committee of National Liberation. He could not deal with two Polish representations. Before negotiating the Polish-Soviet relations, let the Poles first settle differences among themselves. Mikolajczyk should come to some understanding with the Lublin Committee. When asked about Poland's boundaries, the Soviet leader answered that there would be no compromise on the Curzon Line. He was "too old to act against conscience," which dictated that the Curzon Line was right. But Poland would receive boundaries along the rivers Oder and Neisse, plus the bulk of East Prussia. When Mikolajczyk appealed for military assistance in the Warsaw Uprising, Stalin coolly observed that, unfortunately, the Polish Underground had for the most part been inactive during the war, that the Poles were unjustifiably suspicious of the Russians, and that, consequently, he could not trust them. Before any discussion could continue, Mikolajczyk should "get together" with the Lublin Committee. Until then, nothing could be done for Warsaw. He was noncommittal as far as the Soviet military offensive was concerned. True, he had originally expected the Red Army to take Warsaw by August 5 or 6, but now some delay seemed unavoidable. He would not say how long the delay would be.

Mikolajczyk's conversation with Stalin revealed the extent to which all calculations on the uprising had gone wrong. The uprising was expected to strengthen the position of the government-in-exile by proving that it commanded considerable forces in Poland and actually exercised authority in a self-liberated, German-free capital of Poland. Instead, the uprising not only failed to strengthen Mikolajczyk's position in Moscow, it transformed him into a supplicant appealing for indispensable help that might or might not be granted.

On August 6 Mikolajczyk decided on his own authority to see the representatives of the Lublin Committee: Osubka-Morawski, Mrs. Korneytchuk-Wasilewska, Andrzej Witos,[8] General Rola-Żymierski, and, most important, the chairman of the Home National Council, Boleslaw Bierut. He begged all of them to support his plea for Warsaw. They denied that there was any fighting there. Mrs. Wasilewska said that she had just talked with someone who had been in Warsaw as recently as August 4, and that he had not observed any fighting at all. Mikolajczyk told them about Stalin's territorial demands and proposed joint counteraction. They disagreed with him. As far as they were concerned, the Curzon Line was fair and should constitute the Polish-Soviet boundary. The group was merely echoing Stalin.

They met again the next day, and Mikolajczyk implored Bierut to protect Polish interests and sovereignty from Soviet encroachment. Bierut answered that good Polish-Soviet relations were more important than frontiers. He asked Mikolajczyk to resign his position in the London government, return to Poland with his supporters, and recognize the committee as the government of Poland with himself, Bierut, as president of the republic. In exchange, he offered Mikolajczyk the post of prime minister. The new government would consist of eighteen members, and Mikolajczyk would be allowed to give three portfolios in the cabinet to people of his choice. When Mikolajczyk suggested that he might return to Poland on his own, Bierut warned him that he would be arrested if he did so. [9]

On August 9 Mikolajczyk saw Stalin again. This time Stalin told him that there was no uprising in Warsaw. "The Lublin Poles tell me there is no fighting at all," he insisted. He became more congenial when Mikolajczyk hinted at a possibility of some merger with the Lublin Committee after he returned to London and secured the approval of his cabinet. The Soviet leader commended this intention and assured him that he did not want to impose Communism on Poland. On the contrary, he wanted the future Poland to be free, strong, democratic, and friendly with England, France, and the United States. [10]

Mikolajczyk's visit to Moscow showed that he was moving in a vicious circle. Stalin and Molotov told him that he must formally recognize the Nazi-Soviet frontier of 1941, now always referred to as the Curzon Line, before they could discuss any issue with him. As to the formation of a government in Poland, they sent him to the Lublin Committee, which demanded submission to its authority. The people of Warsaw were meanwhile fighting alone, still unaided. On August 9 the Polish delegation left Russia, convinced that only immediate and radical concessions, both territorial and political, could bring some understanding with Moscow, salvage the uprising, and save Poland from total Communist domination.

As soon as they departed, Stalin sent cables to Churchill and Roosevelt, expressing mild satisfaction and optimism. He found Mikolajczyk "inadequately informed" about the situation in Poland but otherwise "not against ways being found to unite the Poles." [11]

THE COMPROMISE PLAN OF AUGUST 30, 1944

After his return from Moscow, Mikolajczyk informed his colleagues and the Underground leadership about the situation, impressing on them all that authorization for workable proposals had become a necessity. But he had to have a consensus. Too much was at stake.

Tortuous debates in London and exchanges of opinion with the Underground took three weeks. A compromise plan was then agreed upon and submitted to the Soviet, British, and American governments on August 30, 1944. The following were its essential points: [12]

1. After the liberation of Warsaw, the Polish government would be reconstructed, and the Polish Workers' (Communist) party would have as many representatives in it as each of the four most prominent prewar democratic parties—Peasant, National, Socialist, and Christian Labor.
2. The new government would establish diplomatic relations with the USSR and conclude an agreement concerning collaboration with the Red Army.
3. All foreign troops would withdraw from Poland as soon as hostilities ended.
4. As soon as possible, the elections to the Constitutional Diet would take place on the basis of a universal, equal, direct, secret, and proportional suffrage; the Constitutional Diet would pass a new constitution; and then the president of the republic would be elected, replacing Raczkiewicz.
5. The new government would institute social, particularly agrarian, reforms.
6. A Polish-Soviet alliance would be concluded "aiming at close political and economic collaboration between Poland and the U.S.S.R. while respecting the principle of sovereignty of both states and the mutual obligation of noninterference in the internal affairs of the other state."
7. As to territorial issues, the plan offered the following formula:

> Poland, which has made so many sacrifices in this war and is the only country under German occupation that produced no Quisling, cannot emerge from this war diminished in territory. In the east the main centers of Polish cultural life and the sources of raw materials indispensable to the economic life of the country shall remain within Polish

boundaries. A final settlement of the Polish-Soviet frontier on the basis
of these principles will be made by the Constitutional Diet in accordance with democratic principles.

Clearly implied was acceptance of territorial changes in favor of the
Soviet Union, but only conditional acceptance was proffered as to the scope
of concessions and the legal procedure. No consensus on further concessions
was possible. The proposals represented a retreat by the government-in-exile,
and Mikolajczyk seemed optimistic. According to his testimony, Eden assured him of support and "endorsed" the plan.

According to British sources, the Foreign Office from the beginning was
skeptical about Soviet acceptance of the proposals.[13] With the Red Army in
Poland and the administration of the Soviet-liberated areas in the hands of
the Lublin Committee, Stalin held the trump card. He no longer needed any
agreement with the government-in-exile. On the contrary, Eden thought it
seemed in his interest "to play for time."[14]

Soon after, another concession followed. It concerned the commander in
chief, General Sosnkowski. Sosnkowski had been given that post by President Raczkiewicz in July 1943, after Sikorski's death, because of his military
rank and the prestige he enjoyed in the armed forces. At the time, Mikolajczyk opposed the nomination, and he had since failed to establish a harmonious relationship with him. Sosnkowski opposed the Polish-Soviet pact of
1941 in its final form, and at the time even resigned in protest from his
cabinet post. He also opposed Mikolajczyk's concessions and did not bother
to conceal his criticism of British pressure on the government-in-exile. This
made him unpopular with the British. Moscow always considered him a
prime enemy.

Then, on September 1, 1944, General Sosnkowski issued a moving order
of the day to the Home Army in Poland. He castigated Allied inactivity,
recalled Polish sacrifices and war contributions, and even implied Great Britain's responsibility for Poland's decision to fight in 1939.[15] His public demonstration served as a pretext, and he was dismissed.

MIKOLAJCZYK IN MOSCOW: CHURCHILL-ROOSEVELT SECRET
DIPLOMACY REVEALED, OCTOBER 10–19

Early in October, five weeks after the Polish August proposals had been
submitted, Churchill, accompanied by Eden, went to Moscow on his third

wartime visit with Stalin. By then, the Red Army had already liberated Finland, Yugoslavia, Bulgaria, most of Estonia, Latvia, Lithuania, central Poland, and part of Hungary. Upon reaching the borders of Greece, it stopped because British forces were already there.

The Soviet authorities acted arbitrarily in the liberated areas, where the Western powers had no access, no voice, and in many cases no direct information. In Poland, the collapse of the Warsaw Uprising caused general frustration, confusion, and despair. The Lublin Committee, backed by the Red Army, was given control of the liberated areas. The government-in-exile and its followers in the homeland were helpless. Churchill thought that some British-Soviet agreement, at least a temporary one, was necessary and urgent. He wanted to establish and somehow define the British and Soviet "spheres of influence" in eastern Europe. He still hoped that some solution for Polish-Soviet relations based on an agreement, not force, was possible, and that once agreement was reached, Stalin would respect it. At that time "agreement" could only mean a merger of two Polish governments: the government-in-exile with the Lublin Committee. This time, Churchill thought, his bargaining position looked better. The Allied offensive on the western front was proceeding well. Anglo-American armies invaded Germany proper on September 11. It was possible that they might reach Berlin before the Russians. Germany was expected to collapse before the end of the year.[16] Thus, he decided to see Stalin immediately.

Despite Churchill's pressure to accompany him to Moscow, Roosevelt, in the midst of an election campaign, refused to go. The exigencies of a political campaign notwithstanding, there was uneasiness in Roosevelt's entourage as to whether the US government should take any part in the proposed conference at all. The Polish issue was extremely delicate. The president's support of Poland and the Polish government-in-exile constituted one of the main themes of his election appeal to Americans of Polish descent.[17] But he knew, of course, that this apparent support contradicted both the secret declaration he made to Stalin at Tehran and his subsequent communications to both Stalin and Churchill. He, himself, still preferred to avoid direct participation in any formal decisions on Polish affairs until *after* the elections.[18] As a result, and on Hopkins's advice, both Churchill and Stalin were notified that the Moscow conference should be considered as a preliminary to the Big Three meeting to take place after the elections and that the American ambassador in the USSR, Harriman, would attend as an "observer" without the authority to commit his government on any issue of importance.[19]

In Moscow, the first session (attended by Stalin, Molotov, Churchill, Eden, Clark-Kerr, and Harriman) took place on October 9, 1944. There, it was decided to summon the representatives of both the government-in-exile and the Lublin group for the purpose of effecting a "merger." Churchill thought the matter should be settled immediately—every day counted. Time worked against the government-in-exile and those Poles whose interests it represented. In his telegram to Mikolajczyk, the prime minister pointed out that no balking would be tolerated. As he put it: "I made it clear that refusal to come to take part in the conversations would amount to a definite rejection of our advice and would relieve us from further responsibility towards the London Polish Government."[20] This was an ultimatum, and Mikolajczyk decided to go without delay, demanding only that the negotiations be conducted on the basis of his compromise plan of August 30. The answer from Eden reassured him—there was a "friendly atmosphere" in the Kremlin, and Churchill "endorsed" his plan.[21]

Mikolajczyk left London on the night of October 9, accompanied by Romer, Grabski, and General Tabor. As in August, the Soviet press ignored their arrival in Moscow, giving front-page coverage instead to the arrival of the Lublin Committee delegation, consisting of Bierut, Osubka-Morawski, and General Żymierski. Throughout Mikolajczyk's stay in Moscow, *Pravda* published daily eulogies of the Lublin Committee and violent attacks on the "London Poles."[22]

Before the official conference with Stalin and Churchill took place, Eden and Clark-Kerr told the Polish delegation of the favorable atmosphere in which a British-Soviet agreement had already been reached, a circumstance allegedly advantageous to Mikolajczyk's mission. They were prudent in not revealing the nature of the agreement, but they were obviously referring to the Churchill-Stalin understanding concerning "temporary" spheres of influence in the Balkans. The Soviets received 90 percent of the "influence" in Romania; Britain received the same proportion in Greece. In Bulgaria, Russia received 75 percent, while in Hungary and Yugoslavia the two powers were to share the influence on a 50-50 basis.[23]

The first official meeting on Poland took place on October 13 and was attended by Stalin; Molotov; the new Soviet ambassador to Great Britain, Feodor Gusev; Churchill; Eden; Clark-Kerr; and Harriman.[24] On the Polish side, there were Mikolajczyk, Romer, and Grabski. Molotov acted as chairman and invited Mikolajczyk, whom he called the "initiator" of the conference, to speak first.

Confident of Churchill's and Eden's support, the Polish prime minister presented his plan of August 30. To his surprise, Churchill opposed the plan. He objected to the Soviet withdrawal of troops after the end of hostilities against Germany and thought that the Communists should get a greater share than any other political party in the new government. He also wanted Mikolajczyk to discuss the problem of the new constitution for Poland with both the Soviet government and the Lublin Committee.

Stalin, who spoke next, told Mikolajczyk to reach an agreement with the Lublin Committee and to recognize the Curzon Line formally. Even before Mikolajczyk had time to answer, Churchill supported the demands. When Mikolajczyk argued that he could not on his own authority renounce half of Poland's territory, Stalin broke in and called him an "imperialist." It was at that moment that the Tehran "formula" was revealed, and Roosevelt's super-secret commitment of December 1, 1943, indirectly mentioned. According to Mikolajczyk:

> However, there was no way of avoiding the matter of the Curzon line and its acceptance, and when I continued to argue against it, Molotov suddenly stopped me roughly.
>
> "But all this was settled at Teheran," he barked. He looked from Churchill to Harriman who were silent. I asked for details of Teheran. And then he added, still with his eyes on Churchill and the American Ambassador:
>
> "If your memory fails you, let me recall the facts to you. We all agreed at Teheran that the Curzon line must divide Poland. You will recall that President Roosevelt agreed to this solution and strongly endorsed the line. And then we agreed that it would be best not to issue any public declaration about our agreement."
>
> Shocked and remembering the earnest assurances I [Mikolajczyk] had personally had from Roosevelt at the White House, I looked at Churchill and Harriman, silently begging them to call this damnable deal a lie. Harriman looked down at the rug. Churchill looked straight at me.
>
> "I confirm this," he said quietly.[25]

Apparently, Molotov's indiscretion was neither scheduled nor expected, because as Mikolajczyk noticed, it made Churchill angry.[26] It also shocked the Polish group, who withdrew, leaving the room to the Lublin delegates.

> According to Churchill, the representatives from Poland merely echoed Stalin:
> It was . . . plain that the Lublin Poles were mere pawns of Russia. They had learned and rehearsed their part so carefully that even their masters evidently felt that they were overdoing it. For instance, Mr. Bierut, the leader, spoke in

these terms: "We are here to demand on behalf of Poland that Lvov shall belong to Russia. This is the will of the Polish people." When this had been translated from Polish into English and Russian, I looked at Stalin and saw an understanding twinkle in his expressive eyes, as much as to say, "What about that for our Soviet teaching!" The lengthy contribution of another Lublin leader, Osubka-Morawski, was equally depressing.[27]

The next day, October 14, Churchill, Eden, and Clark-Kerr saw Mikolajczyk and his companions. The British prime minister was to discuss Poland with Stalin that afternoon, and he wanted to have Polish backing. He scolded Mikolajczyk for not having accepted the Curzon Line earlier and assured him that even if the Poles agreed to that line now, agreement on all other questions—the constitution, the government, the German territories and, above all, the guarantee of postwar independence of Poland—could still be obtained. He warned the Poles that if they did not cooperate, he would have to denounce the government-in-exile publicly. Mikolajczyk in turn reproached Churchill for having sealed the fate of Poland at Tehran. "I am not a person completely washed out of patriotic feeling to give away half of Poland,"[28] he said. Churchill retorted that the Great Powers had fought twice in a quarter of a century to liberate Poland and they were not to be drawn into a conflict again for the sake of quarreling Poles.

Mikolajczyk must now have felt that opposition was hopeless. He also realized, however, that without authorization from his cabinet, he could not take the responsibility for accepting the demands. Apparently in order to salvage the situation, he reverted to Raczynski's suggestion of the previous year.[29] Let the three powers publicly announce that their decision on Poland's eastern frontiers had been reached *without* the participation of the government-in-exile. This suggestion appealed to both Churchill and Eden, and they agreed to propose such a declaration to Stalin. They demanded, however, that if he approved, the Polish government would then accept the Curzon Line as a basis for the Polish-Soviet frontier. Without further delay, they drafted a declaration explicitly leaving Lvov to Russia and showed it to the Poles.[30] Mikolajczyk approved it in essence but still wanted it to be called a demarcation line, not a final state boundary. Churchill raged:

You are no Government if you are incapable of taking any decision. You are callous people who want to wreck Europe. I shall leave you to your own troubles. You have no sense of responsibility when you want to abandon your people at home to whose suffering you are indifferent. You do not care about the future Europe. You have only your own miserable selfish interests in mind.

I will have to call on the other Poles and this Lublin Government may function very well. It will be THE GOVERNMENT. It is a criminal attempt on your part to wreck by your "Liberum Veto" agreement between the Allies. It is cowardice on your part.[31]

The conversation was interrupted by a message that Stalin would receive His Majesty's prime minister in ten minutes. Mikolajczyk just had time to say that the draft *did not* have his approval. Churchill heatedly answered that in that case the Polish delegation had better not return to London, since the British government would probably withdraw their "hospitality."

During a long conference held that same night, Eden and Clark-Kerr brought the news that Stalin refused any compromise. The government-in-exile would have to agree on its own to the Curzon Line, leaving Lvov to Russia without any reservations. Again they pressured the Poles for further concessions and proposed another draft of the British-Soviet declaration for their consideration. Because its essence was still the formal acceptance of the Curzon Line as the basis of the future Polish-Russian frontier, Mikolajczyk again withheld his approval.[32]

The next day, at a conference attended by Churchill, Eden, Clark-Kerr, Mikolajczyk, and Romer, the Poles backed down, agreeing to recognize the Curzon Line as the basis of the Polish-Soviet frontier formally and immediately, under the condition that Lvov and the oil fields remain in Poland, that the Soviets establish diplomatic relations with the government-in-exile, and that the Lublin Committee members receive representation in the new government no greater than that of each of the four other political parties forming the coalition in London and in the Underground. Churchill was calm until Lvov was mentioned; then he repeated his previous reproaches and threats. At the end of a violent discussion, he said that everything was finished between him and the Poles and left without shaking hands.

Three hours later, Eden and Clark-Kerr initiated another conference with Mikolajczyk and Romer and urged them to accept the Curzon Line unconditionally and forget about Lvov. This time Mikolajczyk agreed but reverted to his idea of a demarcation line. If Lvov and the oil fields were left with Poland, he was willing to recognize the Curzon Line as the basis for the Polish-Soviet frontier. Since Stalin refused any compromise on the subject of Lvov, let it be called a demarcation line and leave the question of the frontier to the peace conference. He begged for a new try. Let Grabski, who knew Russian and seemed to be popular with the Russians, speak again to Molotov, and let Churchill do the same with Stalin. Eden was agreeable, but under the condition that if Stalin refused, Churchill would be authorized to present the British formula, which he showed to the Poles. Because the formula meant the acceptance of all of Stalin's demands, Mikolajczyk objected. Eden promised to ask Churchill to intervene once more, anyway.

Neither the Grabski-Molotov conversation of October 15 nor the Eden-Stalin conference (Churchill was "indisposed") of the same day brought any change in the situation. Stalin stood firmly by the Tehran territorial "formula" and, as for the merger of the two Polish camps, he insisted that Mikolajczyk reach an "agreement" with the Lublin Committee. If the terms were acceptable to the committee, they would be acceptable to him, too. He said that he liked Mikolajczyk personally and would support his candidacy for the premiership.

The same evening Churchill and Eden had a friendly conversation with the Polish delegation. It was obvious that Stalin would not yield, and both British statesmen realized how difficult it was for Mikolajczyk to take the sole responsibility for decisions that affected Poland so gravely. They gave him one day to think it over and accept the Soviet demands. If, however, he could not do it on his own responsibility, they agreed that he should proceed to London in order to secure the backing of his colleagues. Once he succeeded, he would then return to Moscow immediately and close the deal. They assured him of their support in his endeavor but insisted on utmost secrecy as to everything that transpired in Moscow. In only three weeks, elections were to take place in the United States and, as Churchill wired the king, until then the Polish matters had to be "hushed."[33]

The next day Mikolajczyk told Eden and Clark-Kerr that he had decided to return to London, consult with his cabinet, and obtain approval of what he now knew was unavoidable. He himself could not make any further concessions. The best proof that he did not avoid decisions and responsibilities, he reminded them, was his consent to the Curzon Line either as a frontier, if Lvov and the oil fields were left in Poland, or as a demarcation line, if Lvov were left to the east of the line. He was afraid that if he granted all that had been asked of him, he would be repudiated by his own people even before he reached London. He stressed that his departure did not mean a "break of negotiations but on the contrary was a continuation of efforts in preparation for an agreement even in the way of the hardest sacrifices on our [Polish] part."[34] He expressed a desire to see Stalin and Bierut again before his departure.

The conversation with Bierut was short and discouraging. The Communist leader said that the boundaries demanded by Moscow were best for Poland. He demanded for his group majority representation in the new government. He would give to the London Poles one-fifth or one-fourth of the seats but no more.[35]

During his last conversation with Stalin on October 18, Mikolajczyk again indicated his agreement to the Curzon Line as a demarcation line and begged the Soviet leader to leave the formal decision on the Polish-Soviet frontier to the peace conference. "I firmly insist on immediate settlement of frontiers which, as I said before, shall follow the Curzon Line," was Stalin's curt answer. "The Polish nation will not object to it. Messrs. Bierut and Osubka . . . declared that this new frontier was just." He added that any opposition was hopeless, since Great Britain and the United States supported the Soviet Union, not Poland.[36]

Before leaving Moscow, the Polish prime minister summarized the situation and his position in a memorandum addressed to Churchill and Harriman.[37] By then it was clear that he considered acceptance of the British-Soviet demands a necessity and that he would say so to his colleagues in London. Upon informing Roosevelt of the conference, Churchill observed in his cable of October 22 that Mikolajczyk was going to "urge upon his London colleagues the Curzon Line, including Lvov, for the Russians."[38] Harriman sent a similar cable to the White House reporting that if Stalin persisted in claiming Vilna and Lvov, Mikolajczyk, together with his foreign minister, Romer, would try to get their cabinet to accept the demands. Harriman had the impression that Romer "much more clearly than Mikolajczyk [saw] the need for an early solution."[39]

Although Churchill expected the Polish delegation to return to Moscow within a few days, he considered even that short delay harmful. He was annoyed by the Poles—their arguments, hesitations, and wavering attitudes. "Our [Polish] lot from London are, as Your Majesty knows, decent but feeble," he concluded his report to the King on Polish negotiations in Moscow.[40]

NOTES

1. Mikolajczyk, *The Rape of Poland*, 65.

2. Woodward, *British Foreign Policy in the Second World War*, 299.

3. For the full membership, see *Polish Documents, Report of the Select Committee*, appendix, 81–82, 85–87.

4. For the full text, see *The Correspondence between Stalin-Churchill-Roosevelt*, 1:242.

5. For the minutes, see Rozek, *Allied Wartime Diplomacy*, 233.

6. Mikolajczyk, *The Rape of Poland*, 71.

7. For the minutes of the conversation, see Rozek, *Allied Wartime Diplomacy*, 237–42.

8. Brother of the former premier and prominent peasant leader Wincenty Witos.

9. Mikolajczyk, *The Rape of Poland*, 76–77.

10. For the minutes, see Rozek, *Allied Wartime Diplomacy*, 245–47.

11. *The Correspondence between Stalin-Churchill-Roosevelt*, 1:250; 2:154.

12. For the text, see Mikolajczyk, *The Rape of Poland*, appendix 24, 287–89.

13. Woodward, *British Foreign Policy in the Second World War*, 309.

14. Eden, *The Reckoning*, 557.

15. For the text, see Kazimierz Sosnkowski, *Materialy Historyczne* (Historical records), (London: Gryf Publications, 1966), 200–203.

16. Sherwood, *Roosevelt and Hopkins*, 832.

17. Woodward, *British Foreign Policy in the Second World War*, 307; also Lane, *I Saw Poland Betrayed*, 60–62.

18. See Feis, *Churchill-Roosevelt-Stalin*, 451.

19. *The Conferences at Malta and Yalta, 1945*, 6.

20. Churchill, *Triumph and Tragedy*, 226–27.

21. Mikolajczyk, *The Rape of Poland*, 93.

22. See *Pravda*, October 12, 13, 14, 15, 16, 18, 19, 21.

23. Churchill, *Triumph and Tragedy*, 227.

24. For the minutes, see *Polish Documents, Report of the Select Committee*, appendix, 115–24.

25. Mikolajczyk, *The Rape of Poland*, 96. See also *Polish Documents, Report of the Select Committee*, appendix, 122.

26. This entire incident was omitted from Churchill's war memoirs.

27. Churchill, *Triumph and Tragedy*, 235.

28. *Polish Documents, Report of the Select Committee*, appendix, 127.

29. Supra, 474–75.

30. For the text, see *Polish Diplomatic Archives*, 2:302–3.

31. *Polish Documents, Report of the Select Committee*, appendix, 130.

32. *Polish Diplomatic Archives*, 2:309–10.

33. Churchill, *Triumph and Tragedy*, 239.

34. For the minutes, see *Polish Documents, Report of the Select Committee*, appendix, 136–37.

35. For the minutes, see ibid., 137–41.

36. Ibid., 143.

37. For the text, see ibid., 142–43.

38. *The Conferences at Malta and Yalta, 1945*, 206.

39. Feis, *Churchill-Roosevelt-Stalin*, 458; also *The Conferences at Malta and Yalta, 1945*, 205.

40. Churchill, *Triumph and Tragedy*, 239.

Chapter Thirty-Five

The Aftermath of the October Conference in Moscow

BRITISH PRESSURE

Mikolajczyk returned to London with the firm intention of convincing his colleagues that concessions of the most serious nature had become both unavoidable and most urgent. The Lublin Committee was expanding its authority daily in the wake of the Red Army's advances, and only an immediate return of the government-in-exile and a formal assumption of power in the liberated areas might protect the Underground and prevent total Communist control. The government-in-exile could not return without the resumption of Polish-Soviet diplomatic relations. That, in turn, presupposed formally accepting the Curzon Line as Poland's eastern boundary, eliminating from the government-in-exile persons unacceptable to Stalin, and, finally, including in that government members of the Lublin Committee.

Mikolajczyk asked for authorization to return to Moscow immediately and negotiate an agreement. He pointed out that although neither Great Britain nor the United States would support Poland on Soviet territorial demands, both would support him getting territorial compensations at the expense of Germany and getting the best deal possible with the Lublin Committee. The discussions were tortuous and bitter. So were the exchanges of radio messages with the leadership of the Underground in the homeland.

While Mikolajczyk was arguing with his colleagues, Churchill pressed for decisions. He knew that bargaining against the Curzon Line had lost all its significance, because not only he but Roosevelt as well had let Stalin know that they supported him. The future of Poland was becoming more and more clouded. He had no illusion about the Lublin Poles and the nature of their activities. But he also knew that neither his own nor the American government could control them. Only Stalin could. He saw the only chance of restraining or controlling the Communists in their merger with the government-in-exile, in obtaining Moscow's recognition of the new government (hopefully headed by Mikolajczyk), and in its functioning in Poland. If this came to pass, Western diplomatic missions could be sent to Warsaw, information might be made public, all democratic elements could come into the open, and then, by their sheer number and strength, they might be able to challenge Communist rule. If Stalin became convinced that the Poles bore Russia no ill will, he might approve of a non-Communist but friendly Poland, Churchill reasoned.

On October 27 Churchill called upon Mikolajczyk in the House of Commons to return to Moscow immediately in order to make a "good arrangement" and form a Polish government on Polish soil. He did not define that "good arrangement" but pointed out that "these are critical days and it would be a great pity if time were wasted in indecision or protracted negotiation." He openly blamed Mikolajczyk's colleagues for the delay, which resulted in the emergence and growing strength of the Lublin Committee. As before, he assured the House that Great Britain as well as Russia and the United States wanted a "strong, free, independent, sovereign Poland." He cautiously qualified that statement, however. Poland was to be "loyal to the allies and friendly to her great neighbor and liberator, Russia."[1] The distinction between "loyalty" to the Allies and "friendship" with Russia was noteworthy.

A few days later, on November 2, Churchill summoned Mikolajczyk, Romer, and Raczyński for what he called a "critical" conference on Polish affairs and impatiently reprimanded them for delaying the formal acceptance of the Curzon Line. Several times he raised his favorite argument of the "Polish Liberum Veto" and threatened "washing [his] hands of Poland." He criticized Mikolajczyk and Romer sharply for still having failed to obtain their colleagues' approval of what had become unavoidable. That meant, he threatened, that in fact "there [was] indeed no Polish government." Finally, he gave the Poles forty-eight hours to accept the Soviet territorial demands in their entirety. After that, Mikolajczyk would have to proceed to Moscow and effect a merger with the Lublin Committee.[2]

Just a few hours before the discussion, Sir Alexander Cadogan, permanent undersecretary of state, handed Romer an official note clarifying Britain's stand as to Poland's postwar eastern boundary and independence.[3] The Poles were formally promised that, in exchange for their territorial losses to Russia, Britain would support them at the peace conference in obtaining German territories up to the Oder River, including Stettin, and would also "guarantee" the independence and integrity of the new Poland "jointly with the Soviet government." The guarantee, as phrased and then orally explained by Cadogan during the discussion, was rather bizarre in view of the conditions prevailing in Poland. When questioned about its meaning, Cadogan answered that "in the event of aggression by Russia on Poland, the British guarantee does not come into play." Thus, the practical value of the note was a formal commitment by the British government to support the Oder River unconditionally as Poland's postwar western boundary. In their future relations with Russia, however, the Poles had to rely on their own and Russia's mutual "friendship."

THE POLISH QUESTION DURING THE 1944 ELECTION CAMPAIGN IN THE UNITED STATES

In the meantime, the American election campaign was reaching its peak, and Roosevelt had to face ticklish complexities on the Polish issue. His super-secret conference with Stalin at Tehran on December 1, 1943, committed him to support Russia's territorial demands on Poland. He had made it clear in his personal cables to Churchill and Stalin that he endorsed Stalin's demand for a "reorganization" of the government-in-exile. He also knew that the Soviet government considered the declaration on the liberated countries as giving Russia a free hand in eastern Europe.[4] Throughout the election campaign, support of the government-in-exile as well as of Poland's independence and territorial integrity represented one of the important elements in Roosevelt's appeal for the votes of Americans of Polish descent.[5] What would happen if the ambiguity of his stand became known?

The difficulties would be somewhat eased if the government-in-exile, under pressure of events but still "of their own will," agreed to the Soviet terms. But they did not and—unaware of his commitment to Stalin—were pressuring him for support. He could not effectively give it but, because of the impact his refusal might have on the elections, he could not reveal where he actually stood, either.

Responding to Mikolajczyk's dramatic appeals for help during the Warsaw Uprising, the president expressed his sympathy but also slipped in some advice:

> In regard to the broader question of the solution of the Polish-Soviet differences, I fully realize the difficulties which confront you, particularly in the light of the heroic and unequal struggle of the Warsaw garrison. I feel, however, that these unfortunate developments should not deter you from presenting reasonable proposals to the Polish Committee of National Liberation, and I am of the firm opinion that if reasonable proposals are not presented to the Committee, and if a crisis should arise in the Polish Government, such developments would only worsen the situation.[6]

The president's message was dated August 24, 1944. By then he was fully informed of Mikolajczyk's negotiations in Moscow of less than three weeks before and knew about the demands of both Stalin and the Lublin Committee. His recommendation of "reasonable proposals" could have only one meaning.

The disparity between Roosevelt's position behind the doors of diplomatic secrecy and in public grew toward the end of the election campaign. On October 11 he granted an interview to the representatives of the Polish-American Congress, who wanted to know before the elections his policy on the Polish-Soviet dispute. When the delegation entered his study, they noticed that behind the president's desk hung a large map of Poland with the prewar eastern boundaries. There was no trace of the Curzon Line. Pictures were taken of the group with Roosevelt seated in front of the map.[7] The symbolic photograph, eventually reprinted and widely distributed, was interpreted as an expression of FDR's support of Poland. After the meeting the president issued a statement stressing his goodwill in general terms, although pointing out enigmatically that "we should all bear in mind that nobody here has accurate information about everything that is going on in Poland."[8]

Several days later, on October 28, during his campaign in Chicago, Roosevelt initiated a conference with Charles Rozmarek, the president of the Polish-American Congress. He assured his guest that the principles of the Atlantic Charter and the Four Freedoms "would under no circumstances be abandoned by him and that the territorial integrity of Poland was his goal."[9] Rozmarek, deeply impressed, immediately announced that in view of the president's stand, he supported his candidacy. His announcement received nationwide publicity.[10]

These incidents occurred simultaneously with the October conference in Moscow, where Harriman, as an "observer," closely followed negotiations on Polish matters. He realized the complexity of Roosevelt's position and was prompt in informing him of everything that transpired. In his cable of October 13, he reported Molotov's indiscretions concerning the president's support of the Curzon Line, adding that he himself did not make any comment. He was, instead, to tell Molotov *privately* not to bring Roosevelt's name into any discussions concerning the Polish-Soviet territorial dispute. Harriman also elaborated on his talk with Churchill with reference to Molotov's statement. That part of the report Harriman must have written tongue in cheek: "he [Churchill] recalls as clearly as I do that although you showed interest in hearing the view of Stalin and Churchill in the [Polish] boundary question, you had expressed no opinion on it one way or the other at Teheran."[11] Thus, Harriman let the president know that the latter's supersecret conference with Stalin on the subject of Poland, a conference in which he, Harriman, participated, was still unknown even to Churchill.

When Harriman dispatched his telegram, he apparently was unaware that Churchill, puzzled by Molotov's statement concerning Roosevelt's commitment on Poland, went straight to Stalin to obtain clarification. Stalin told him all and, after more than eleven months' delay, the British statesman learned about the Roosevelt-Stalin secret understanding on Poland at Tehran. But the prime minister did not want to embarrass the president. On the contrary, he appreciated his difficult situation and wanted to reassure him. In his message, he told the president not to worry. The whole matter would remain secret because there would not be any "indiscretion . . . from the Russian side." Stalin had an "earnest desire" for Roosevelt's reelection, and he would not weaken his chances.[12]

Judging by his reports to the White House, Harriman showed considerable adroitness in Polish matters during the conference. Three days after Molotov's outburst, Mikolajczyk asked the American ambassador officially and in writing for an explanation. He emphasized in his letter that only four months before, the president had assured him that the American government opposed any final settlement of territorial problems before the end of the war and that he, Roosevelt, had argued at Tehran *against* the Curzon Line.[13] In his detailed report to the president, Harriman pointed out that in his conversation with Mikolajczyk, he *denied* Molotov's allegations but succeeded in avoiding written denial. He had also warned the Polish leader that for Poland's as well as his own interests, Mikolajczyk *should not* inform his colleagues in London about the whole incident. [14]

At the time Mikolajczyk was leaving Moscow, he expected (as did Churchill) that the government-in-exile would authorize him to accept the Soviet demands. Both hoped that he would return to Moscow within a few days and sign the agreement. If that happened, however, the Polish issue was certain to explode in the United States just at the end of the election campaign. Once the agreement had been concluded and made public, it was bound to affect the voting, and Churchill realized that full well. He was anxious not to injure his friend's chances in even the smallest way. On his way home from Moscow, he informed Roosevelt that Mikolajczyk had returned to London to "urge" his cabinet to accept the Soviet demands, "including Lvov for the Russians." Although the Polish-Soviet agreement should be concluded "in the next fortnight," it would not be made public until he, Churchill, received word from the White House. Immediately, Roosevelt rushed his answer that, indeed, in the event any "settlement" had been worked out, it might be necessary to keep it secret for about two weeks. "You will understand," he concluded. [15]

ROOSEVELT'S STAND ON POLAND AFTER THE ELECTION

Upon his return from Moscow to London, Mikolajczyk wired Ciechanowski that he was worried by the ambiguous policy of the American government and asked him to deliver his personal message to Roosevelt. "I still cannot believe what Molotov revealed about the secret decisions made by the Big Three at Teheran, in view of the assurances that you gave me at our last [June] meeting," he complained, and entreated Roosevelt to use all his influence with Stalin, so that at least Lvov and the nearby oil fields would be left in Poland. The tone of the letter was desperate. [16]

Simultaneous with Mikolajczyk's personal appeal, the government-in-exile prepared an official memorandum for the Foreign Office and the Department of State: Poland was asked by the Allies to make specific territorial concessions to Russia immediately and formally and was promised German territories and political guarantees in exchange. These promises were, however, both informal and imprecise. Now, in view of the urgency of the situation, the government-in-exile wanted to know exactly what Poland's western frontiers were to be, when they would be decided, whether the three Great Powers would guarantee the independence of the new Poland, and whether the United States would accord economic aid in rehabilitating the country after the war.[17]

President Roosevelt's answer to both the personal message and the formal memorandum did not arrive until almost two weeks after his spectacular election victory.[18] It was, at best, a disappointment. In a formal communication, he passed over most of Mikolajczyk's questions, particularly those concerning Tehran, and withdrew from the Polish-Soviet dispute, leaving the issue to Great Britain, Russia, and Poland. Whatever agreement those three countries would arrive at, the American government "would offer no objection." He declined on behalf of the United States to guarantee any Polish frontiers on a constitutional basis. He approved the transfer of national minorities from and to Poland, and promised US assistance in this respect. Roosevelt's wording implied that Poland would acquire unspecified German lands (transfer of the German minority *from* Poland) as well as the cession of the eastern part of Poland to the Soviet Union (transfer of the Polish population *to* Poland). He also promised assistance in Poland's postwar economic reconstruction. The letter contained the usual clichés about a "strong, free and independent" Poland. Harriman, who delivered it, offered his good services in asking Stalin to leave Lvov and the oil fields with Poland, but since he himself had no hope that the intervention would bring any positive results, Mikolajczyk rejected the offer, on instructions from his cabinet.[19]

Just one day before Harriman delivered Roosevelt's letter, the president summoned Arthur Bliss Lane, his newly appointed ambassador to Poland, to the White House. Lane insisted on the meeting because he wanted political guidance in his mission. He himself was for a strong policy vis-à-vis Russia and an all-out effort on behalf of Poland. "Do you want me to go to war with Russia?" the president asked, adding that he "had entire confidence in Stalin's word, and he felt sure that he [Stalin] would not go back on it." When the ambassador expressed misgivings, Roosevelt, to Lane's dismay, observed that "Stalin's idea of having a cordon sanitaire in the shape of a Poland under Russian influence, as a bulwark to protect the Soviet Union against further aggression, was understandable."[20]

The president's statement, better than any other war document, testified to the changing role of the Polish issue in the policies of the Western powers following World War I. While in 1919 they envisaged the role of a resurrected Poland as a "barbed-wire fence," or a cordon sanitaire *against* Communist Russia, now, in 1944, the leader of the most powerful Western democracy saw Poland's role as that of a "bulwark" for the *protection* of the Soviet Union.

MIKOLAJCZYK'S RESIGNATION

At the end of November 1944 Mikolajczyk found himself in a blind alley. The British government openly supported Soviet territorial demands. Roosevelt's stand after the election showed that, at best, he would leave the Poles to their own fate as far as their eastern boundaries were concerned. Stalin made it clear that formal acceptance of the Ribbentrop-Molotov line was a condition sine qua non for any settlement. The Lublin Committee established its administration in all liberated areas, and there was no doubt that with the Red Army continuously advancing, it would eventually extend its control over all of Poland. The Underground had been terribly weakened by the Warsaw Uprising and was at the mercy of the new masters. The government-in-exile was cut off from the homeland and helpless. No solution was in sight, because it refused to recognize Soviet territorial demands and to surrender voluntarily to the Communist leadership in Poland.

Mikolajczyk was well aware of the enmity of both the Red Army and the Lublin Committee toward the non-Communist Underground. He also realized that no stabilization could be anticipated in the homeland as long as the Underground adhered to the policy of the government-in-exile, which was openly at odds with the Lublin Committee. Time was in favor of the committee, and no one knew this better than Mikolajczyk.

He had personally agreed to all territorial demands in Moscow, trying to save only Lvov and the nearby oil fields for Poland. But at that time he still expected American support. He soon learned, however, that he could not count on Roosevelt, and he perceived that there was no alternative to complete surrender on territorial issues. It became clear that efforts had to be concentrated on saving as much of Poland's political independence as possible and on securing territorial compensation at the expense of Germany. In this, he still felt, both Great Britain and the United States would not fail to help.

His arguments were of no avail. Except for his own Peasant party, which stood firmly behind him, and a few personal followers, the overwhelming majority of the government-in-exile, supported by the leadership of the Underground, refused to sanction the loss of almost half of Polish territory before the war even ended, before the peace conference convened, and before the disposition of German territories had been formally decided. No war government, argued the opponents, had a right to make such a momentous decision, and no government-in-exile could assume such a historic responsibility. If it did, its authority in the homeland would be destroyed, anyway. If a new partition of Poland had become unavoidable, in violation of the Allies' commitments and obligations, the record should show that the Polish nation and its legal representatives did not approve it. Mikolajczyk's opponents also argued that a strong stand by the Polish government might either force Great Britain and the United States to postpone the formal territorial decisions until the peace conference or make them force Stalin to agree to some compromise solutions. [21]

Mikolajczyk had no such illusions. On the contrary, he well understood that such a stand, whatever its merits, was bound to result in political suicide. As long as he had to represent his cabinet's views, he had nothing to take with him to Moscow. But he agreed with Churchill that the Lublin Committee should not be allowed to continue to expand its power unopposed, and that a brake had to be applied by the democratic forces, represented by the government-in-exile and the Underground. At the end of 1944, applying such a brake was possible only through merging the government-in-exile with the Lublin Committee, and through accepting Stalin's territorial demands.

For a few weeks Mikolajczyk hesitated, still hoping that once the American election was over, Roosevelt, whose reelection he expected, might support Poland. But on November 22, after receiving the president's letter, he lost that hope. Mikolajczyk then made up his mind: He would resign as premier and reenter the government only if assured of its support. Otherwise, he would break from that government and act on his own.

Mikolajczyk resigned from the government-in-exile on November 24, 1944, accompanied by the representatives of the Peasant party. He was followed by the foreign minister, Romer, and the speaker of the National Council, Grabski. Because the new cabinet was as uncompromising as the one he had headed, he refused to join it. His party, both abroad and in the homeland, expressed solidarity with him. With his departure, the government-in-exile, already weakened by the turn of events, suffered a mortal blow. Eden announced to the House of Commons only a few days later that the Polish government-in-exile was no longer representative, which, of course, meant that as far as official London was concerned, it had lost its authority in Polish matters.

At the head of the new government, formed on November 29, stood Tomasz Arciszewski. Spirited out of Poland shortly before, he was one of the oldest leaders of the Socialist party and a veteran in the struggle for Poland's independence and democracy. An associate of Pilsudski in antitsarist revolutionary activities before World War I, Arciszewski, together with his party, opposed the marshal's rule after the military coup of 1926, as well as the regime of his successors. A member of the Underground since 1939, he represented his party in the highest councils. A factory worker in his youth, Arciszewski had no formal education. He served socialism and the working class all his life. He opposed Mikolajczyk's policy, still hoping that what he considered a surrender to Russia and the Communist-dominated Lublin Committee was not inevitable. Together with the majority of the political leaders abroad and in the homeland, he thought that, regardless of consequences, no Polish government had the right to absolve Great Britain and the United States of their historic responsibility for agreeing to the partition and abandoning their Polish ally.[22]

Churchill considered Mikolajczyk's decision wise. He did not think Arciszewski's government would last long, nor did he intend to cooperate with it. On the contrary, he expected that the new government would collapse and that Mikolajczyk would return to office soon, with increased authority "as a champion of Poland's good relations with Russia." Then, as Churchill hoped, Mikolajczyk would be able to carry out the policy outlined in the Moscow conferences without any obstruction and in the name of the Polish legal government. He informed Stalin of his views on December 3.

Stalin's reply five days later must have shattered Churchill's hopes. The ministerial changes in the Polish government, Stalin cabled, were of no importance whatsoever. Neither was Mikolajczyk, because he had served "as a cover" for "criminal terror acts against Soviet officers and Soviet people" committed in Poland. The Lublin Committee served well. It carried out reforms and it enjoyed "great prestige" in the liberated areas. That committee and that committee alone should be supported by all Allies in order to "accelerate" the final victory.[23] Evidently, Stalin was preparing the ground for Moscow's recognition of the Lublin Committee as the official government of Poland, a fait accompli Churchill had wanted so much to prevent.

After Mikolajczyk's departure, both the Foreign Office and the US Department of State shunned all contacts with the government-in-exile, turning instead to Mikolajczyk. He was a leader of the influential Peasant party; he was internationally known and enjoyed a reputation as a true democrat as well as a sincere partisan of Polish-Russian reconciliation. Mikolajczyk was also willing to act within the framework of the Tehran decisions and within the limits of the new reality in Poland. They clearly considered Mikolajczyk to be the representative of non-Communist Poland. He accepted that role.

As soon as Mikolajczyk resigned, Osubka-Morawski announced that the Lublin Committee would cooperate with him. The statement evoked favorable comments in both the British and the American press, and Secretary of State Stettinius reported it in a special message to Roosevelt.[24] That the move of the committee was designed to destroy both the government-in-exile and Mikolajczyk himself became evident only later.

NOTES

1. *5 Parliamentary Debates*, Commons, 404 (1944), 494.

2. For the minutes of the discussion, see Rozek, *Allied Wartime Diplomacy*, 305–12.

3. For the full text, see Polish Embassy, *Poland, Germany, and European Peace, Official Documents* (London: 1948), 105; also Rozek, *Allied Wartime Diplomacy*, 303.

4. Rozek, *Allied Wartime Diplomacy*, 466–67, 479–80.

5. Lane, *I Saw Poland Betrayed*, 60–62.

6. Mikolajczyk, *The Rape of Poland*, appendix 23, 207.

7. Lane, *I Saw Poland Betrayed*, 59.

8. *Department of State Bulletin*, October–December 1944, v. 11, 429.

9. Lane, *I Saw Poland Betrayed*, 61.

10. According to Lane, both the Republican and the Democratic parties considered that the votes of Americans of Polish descent might be a deciding factor in such states as New York, Pennsylvania, Illinois, Indiana, Ohio, and Michigan. He also was of the opinion that as a result of Roosevelt's declaration to Rozmarek, most Americans of Polish descent supported the Democratic ticket. See Lane, *I Saw Poland Betrayed*, 58, 61.

11. For a full text of Harriman's report see *The Conferences at Malta and Yalta, 1945*, 202–3.

12. *The Conferences at Cairo and Tehran*, 884–85.

13. For the text of Mikolajczyk's letter, see *The Conferences at Malta and Yalta, 1945*, 205.

14. For the text of Harriman's dispatch, *The Conferences at Malta and Yalta, 1945*, 204–5.

15. *The Conferences at Malta and Yalta, 1945*, 206–7.

16. For the full text, *The Conferences at Malta and Yalta, 1945*, 207–9.

17. Mikolajczyk, *The Rape of Poland*, 103.

18. His answer was dated November 17 but was handed to Mikolajczyk on November 22.

19. For the text, see *The Conferences at Malta and Yalta, 1945*, 209–10; also Hull, *Memoirs*, 2, 1433–39.

20. Lane, *I Saw Poland Betrayed*, 66–67.

21. For the discussions within the Polish government in London, see Rozek, *Allied Wartime Diplomacy*, 294–96.

22. For activities of Arciszewski's government performed in most difficult circumstances, see Jerzy Lerski, *Emisariusz Jur* (*Emissary Jur*) (London: Polish Cultural Foundation, 1984), 179–241. During the war, Lerski acted as the emissary of General Sikorski, Mikolajczyk, and

Arciszewski both in England and, secretly, in Poland. After November 1944 he became Arciszewski's secretary.

23. *The Correspondence between Stalin-Churchill-Roosevelt*, 1:279–80, 282–83, respectively.

24. *The Conferences at Malta and Yalta, 1945*, 213.

Chapter Thirty-Six

Prologue to the Yalta Conference

BRITISH, AMERICAN, AND SOVIET PRELIMINARY STEPS

On December 15, 1944, three weeks after Mikolajczyk's resignation, Churchill spoke again on Poland in the House of Commons. He reminded the House of his previous futile appeals for Polish acceptance of the Soviet demands and deplored the stubbornness of the Poles. He said that if they had followed his advice, Mikolajczyk probably would have been head of the new government in Poland and relations between the Underground and the Red Army would have been straightened out. He praised Mikolajczyk, Romer, and Grabski but censured members of Arciszewski's cabinet. The prime minister reaffirmed his opinion that the "Russians were justly treated and rightly treated" in being granted the Curzon Line as a frontier.

Speaking about the Curzon Line, Churchill specifically referred to its southern prolongation, considered by the Commission on Polish Affairs in 1919, and then called Line A.[1] It left Lvov outside Poland. Those who opposed the loss of a "third of Poland,"[2] he said, were not being reasonable, because Poland would receive East Prussia south and west of Königsberg, Danzig, and two hundred miles of seafront, as well as some territories to the west that he failed to specify. The German population of "several million people" would be expelled from those territories. The Polish-Soviet agreement was necessary, he continued, because of possible clashes between the Red Army and the Polish population. Such an agreement would not contradict the Atlantic Charter principles. "It must not be forgotten that in the Atlantic Charter is, I think, inserted the exception that there should be no changes before the peace table except those mutually agreed."[3] This reference represented such a misstatement that one of the members of the House immediately corrected the speaker.[4]

Eden supplemented Churchill's speech with a short history of the Curzon Line. He pointed out that the Ribbentrop-Molotov boundary of September 1939 corresponded roughly with what Britain had considered a just frontier for Poland in 1919. True, in 1923, the British government recognized the Riga treaty boundary, but that was only "on the Polish responsibility," he explained.[5]

Until then, the American government officially adhered to the Atlantic Charter, leading many to assume that Roosevelt disapproved of Churchill's policy. The prime minister dealt with the matter in cautious language. He explained that there were numerous factors—among others, "the large mass of Poles who have made their homes in the United States"—which "have not enabled" the American government to speak as openly and bluntly as he, Churchill, thought it his duty to do. He wanted the House to know, however, that President Roosevelt was "aware of everything" that had transpired between Great Britain and the Soviet Union. "All I can say is that I have received no formal disagreement in all these long months upon the way in which the future of Poland is shaping itself or being shaped,"[6] he concluded.

The immediate result of Churchill's declaration was a press release issued three days later by the newly appointed US secretary of state, Edward Stettinius. In a remarkable piece of diplomatic ambiguity, he reasserted, on the one hand, the principle that all territorial changes should wait until the end of the war, and, on the other, that a different course might be followed in the case of Poland.[7] The president himself was silent, but the statement reflected his views. For, by then, Roosevelt no longer attached importance to the government-in-exile. Instead, he firmly believed that the forthcoming Big Three meeting should assume formal responsibility for shaping Poland's boundaries and Poland's future. By December 1944 the government-in-exile had lost its authority not only in London but in Washington as well.

At that time the Lublin Committee launched a vigorous campaign for its recognition as the provisional government of Poland. Because such a campaign evidently could not take place without Moscow's authorization, Roosevelt appealed to Stalin to delay any action until the Big Three conference took place. He had to wait a week for the answer. On December 27 Stalin cabled violent accusations against Mikolajczyk and the "émigré" government, confirmed the rumors that he would soon recognize the Lublin

Committee as a provisional government, and advised Roosevelt to do like-wise. On the same day the president sent another message telling Stalin how "disturbed and deeply disappointed" he was. He pleaded with the marshal again not to recognize the committee as a government. Only "a small fraction of Poland proper west of the Curzon line" had been liberated by the Red Army, and the Polish people could not "express themselves in regard to the Lublin Committee." He did not suggest that Stalin "curtail [his] practical relations with the Lublin Committee" nor had "any thought" that Stalin should deal with the "London Government in its present composition." He did request, however, that Stalin refrain from creating faits accomplis before the next Big Three meeting. The president added pointedly that he himself had no "special ties or feeling for the Government in London."[8]

The appeals had no effect. The next day, on December 28,.1944, the Lublin group declared itself the provisional government of Poland, with Bierut as president of the People's Republic and Osubka-Morawski as premier and foreign minister. Then, on January 1, 1945, Stalin curtly informed Roosevelt that the new body would have to be recognized by Moscow. He regretted that he could not comply with the president's wish. The Supreme Soviet, however, had made the decision to recognize the new provisional government of Poland, and he, Stalin, was "powerless."[9] Four days later, on January 5, the Soviet Union announced its official recognition.

THE MEMORANDUM OF THE POLISH GOVERNMENT-IN-EXILE

By January 1945 it became known in diplomatic quarters that the Big Three meeting would take place shortly and that Polish matters would be discussed there. But the government-in-exile was not even consulted on its own position or plans. Still hoping for some solution, but probably also anxious to register its stand for the record, on January 22, 1945, it sent identical memoranda to the Foreign Office in London and the Department of State in Washington.[10]

The Poles argued that, as a matter of principle, all territorial disputes should be settled after the war in agreement with openly enunciated declarations. But they also indicated their willingness to compromise. Should an agreement be reached on the eastern frontier, they wanted a "simultaneous" allocation of the German territories. If the Soviet government refused to negotiate, they demanded that an inter-Allied military commission be established in Poland and that the Underground administration, secretly active during the war, be accorded the right to function openly. Having expressed both their goodwill toward the Soviet Union and readiness to conclude an alliance with it, they emphasized Poland's right to lead an independent life, free from outside dictation. There was no explicit acceptance of the Curzon Line, and the Lublin Committee was not mentioned.

The next day the acting secretary of state, Joseph C. Grew, summarized the memorandum for Roosevelt, commenting that the proposals "do not appear to offer any real basis for an approach to the Soviet government."[11] Cadogan and Eden, having dismissed the document as "unrealistic," again told Mikolajczyk that the Foreign Office would not have any dealings at all with Arciszewski's cabinet and advised him to go to Poland on his own as soon as possible. They assured him that from then on the British government would deal only with him as the representative of the "free Poles."[12]

THE ANGLO-AMERICAN CONFERENCE OF FOREIGN MINISTERS AT MALTA

The long-planned Big Three conference, scheduled for February 1945, was to be held at Yalta, on the Crimean Peninsula. Both Roosevelt and Churchill considered the meeting essential in deciding the final moves against Germany, in bringing the Soviets into the Pacific war, and in settling the problem of the postwar world order. Decisions also had to be made on the future of eastern Europe. The last point did not have a high priority. Roosevelt, in particular, felt that the final victory in Europe and Asia, as well as a stable peace, depended upon maintaining and developing unity among Great Britain, the Soviet Union, and the United States.[13] To achieve that goal, he believed concessions on secondary matters were unavoidable. The Department of State fully shared his views and informed him so.[14]

The moment was favorable to the Soviets. True, Allied forces stood on the Rhine, so Stalin could not complain, as he had at Tehran, that there was no second front. However, by December 1944 the Germans had launched their final counteroffensive in the Ardennes, and for a short time the British-American front was not far from disintegrating. Hard-pressed, the Allied command asked Moscow for a diversionary offensive in the east, and Stalin complied. As a result, both Churchill and Roosevelt went to meet the Soviet leader in a spirit of gratitude.[15] Another factor that enhanced Stalin's bargaining position was the continuous advance of the Red Army. By February 1945 it reached the Oder River. All of Poland was now under Soviet control.

In January 1945 the Soviet-backed provisional government moved into Warsaw, or, rather, its ruins. The Home Army, for its own protection, was officially disbanded by its rump command. The members of the former Underground were disoriented and at the mercy of both the Red Army and the new rulers. The government-in-exile was helpless and isolated, unable to influence the course of events abroad as well as in the homeland.

The Yalta Conference was preceded by the meeting of the US secretary of state and the British foreign secretary at Malta, where they exchanged views on topics to be discussed by the Big Three and agreed on a joint negotiating strategy. Stettinius was accompanied by Charles E. Bohlen, assistant to the secretary of state; H. Freeman Matthews, director of the Office of European Affairs; and Alger Hiss, deputy director of the Office of Special Political Affairs. Eden had at his side Sir Alexander Cadogan and Richard A. Butler, undersecretary of state for foreign affairs. After extensive discussions, on February 1 both sides agreed on a joint policy to be pursued at Yalta in regard to the Polish government and Poland's postwar boundaries.[16]

1. The Polish Government. As Eden reported to Churchill,[17] both secretaries agreed that the Warsaw regime should not be recognized. Instead, *a new government*, consisting of the Lublin group, democratic leaders from Poland, and some Poles from abroad should be formed. The government-in-exile should be discarded altogether. "There are no good candidates from the government in London," Eden thought. The new government should include Mikolajczyk and, if possible, Grabski and Romer. Their participation, Eden held, would facilitate and justify the British-American shift of recognition from the government-in-exile to the new body.

As to the procedure for nominating the new government, Mikolajczyk's suggestion was agreed upon. A special presidential council should be set up, consisting of four personalities, all from Poland: the prominent peasant leader and former prime minister Wincenty Witos; the nationally venerated Archbishop Sapieha; the well-known Socialist leader and advocate of Polish-Soviet cooperation Zygmunt Zulawski; and Bierut, representing the Communists. The main task of the council would be to choose, agree upon, and appoint the members of a new provisional government representing the mainstream of Poland's political life. The main task of the provisional government would be to prepare and organize general elections to be held *under the supervision of a special British-American-Soviet commission.* The result of the elections would decide the political future of Poland. Because it was evident that the Communists represented only a fraction of the Polish people, both secretaries agreed and recommended that *Mikolajczyk and his followers*, and not the Communists, should play the *leading roles* in the new provisional government.

2. Polish Frontiers. The agreement on the Eden-Stettinius recommendation for the Polish-Soviet boundary did not present any difficulty. The Curzon Line, as interpreted by Stalin, should be formally recognized. Lvov would remain with the Soviet Union, although the American delegation "might" attempt to get the city for Poland.

Both secretaries agreed that the problem of Polish-German boundaries was more difficult because of the recent political developments in Poland. According to the understanding reached at Tehran and later confirmed in Moscow in October 1944, Poland was to receive East Prussia without Königsberg in the north and, in principle, the territories east of the Oder River plus Upper Silesia. However, Stalin subsequently advanced a demand that the Oder River and the western Neisse River should form Poland's western boundary, which would include Stettin and Breslau. Both the American and British governments interpreted Stalin's demand as a maneuver to tie Poland to the Soviet Union and decided *not* to approve it.

Both secretaries agreed upon and recommended that Churchill and Roosevelt should demand for Poland East Prussia south and west of Königsberg, the coastal sector of Pomerania, and the whole of Upper Silesia, but no more. On this issue, Eden and Stettinius expected strong Soviet opposition and recommended not giving in. In his report to Churchill, Eden explained that the boundary recommended by him and Stettinius would involve a transfer of approximately 2.5 million Germans. The Oder line, without Breslau and Stettin, would involve a transfer of an additional 2.25 million people, while the western Neisse line would involve the removal of 3.25 million more Germans, making a total of about 8 million people. This should not be permitted to happen.

The Eden-Stettinius recommendation on Poland's western boundary flew in the face of assurances given to Mikolajczyk in Moscow and contradicted those contained in the formal note of November 2, 1944.[18] Eden took it under consideration, but because of the new developments in Poland, he considered a change in Britain's position necessary. As he explained in the memorandum to Churchill:

> We were prepared last October in Moscow to let Mr. Mikolajczyk's government have any territory they chose to claim up to the Oder, but this was conditional upon agreement there being reached between him and the Rus-

sians. . . . We should keep the position fluid as regards the Oder line frontier and take the line that H.M.G. cannot be considered as having accepted any definite line for the western frontier of Poland, since we need not make the same concessions to the Lublin Poles which we were prepared to make to Mr. Mikolajczyk in order to obtain a solution of the Polish problem.[19]

Stettinius fully agreed with his British colleague, and in a special memorandum to Roosevelt recommended:

> If we are unable to obtain Lvov Province for Poland, and if efforts are made to obtain greater compensation for Poland in the west, we should make every effort to keep this compensation to a minimum, particularly because of the large population transfer which would have to be carried out if these purely German areas are included in Poland. We should resist vigorously efforts to extend the Polish frontier to the Oder line or the Oder-Neisse line.[20]

The Anglo-American strategy devised in Malta for use at Yalta did not augur well for Poland. The legal government in London should be dropped altogether; the Molotov-Ribbentrop line of September 1939 should be recognized as Poland's eastern frontier; and Poland's extension to the west should be limited as much as possible. On the other hand, both secretaries agreed on and recommended important safeguards designed to guarantee freedom for the new Poland. The Lublin regime should not be recognized. A special presidential council should be set up to choose and appoint members of a new provisional government. Truly free elections, supervised by a special British-American-Soviet commission, should take place. The Communists should not have the upper hand during the transitory period. On these politically essential issues, Churchill and Roosevelt had been advised *not* to compromise.

NOTES

1. See *5 Parliamentary Debates*, Commons, 406 (1944), 49, 58–59.
2. The Soviet government demanded and obtained almost half of prewar Poland.
3. See *5 Parliamentary Debates*, Commons, 406 (1944), 1481–88.
4. Ibid., cols. 1504–6.
5. For Eden's observations, see ibid., cols. 1563–78.
6. Ibid., col. 1486.
7. For the full text, see *Department of State Bulletin*, December 24, 1944, 11:836.
8. *The Correspondence between Stalin-Churchill-Roosevelt*, 2:175–76, 180–81, 182–83, respectively.
9. Ibid., 184.

10. For the full ext, see *DPSR, 1939–1945*, 2:511–12.

11. *The Conferences at Malta and Yalta, 1945*, 227.

12. For documentation, see Rozek, *Allied Wartime Diplomacy*, 336–37.

13. Stettinius, *Roosevelt and the Russians*, 25. See also Sherwood, *Roosevelt and Hopkins*, 843–44; Churchill, *Triumph and Tragedy*, 331–32.

14. *The Conferences at Malta and Yalta, 1945*, 93–96.

15. See Chester Wilmot, *The Struggle for Europe* (London: Collins, St. James Place, 1952), 580–602. For the exchange of telegrams on the subject between Churchill, Roosevelt, and Stalin, see *The Correspondence between Stalin-Churchill-Roosevelt*, 1:288, 294, 295, 300; 2:184–85.

16. For the minutes of the conference, see *The Conferences at Malta and Yalta, 1945*, 498–507.

17. For the text of Eden's memorandum, see ibid., 508–9; for Stettinius's memorandum, see ibid., 510–11.

18. Ibid., 558–59.

19. *The Conferences at Malta and Yalta, 1945*, 509; also Eden, *The Reckoning*, 597.

20. *The Conferences at Malta and Yalta, 1945*, 510.

Chapter Thirty-Seven

The Yalta Conference, February 4–11, 1945

The official American publication on the conference at Yalta[1] contains three sets of notes covering the discussions on Poland—those of Charles E. Bohlen, then assistant to the US secretary of state; H. Freeman Matthews, then director of the Office of European Affairs; and Alger Hiss, then deputy director of the Office of Special Political Affairs. Hiss's notes are fragmentary and often unintelligible, while Bohlen tended to edit the sometimes too blunt and undiplomatic language used in the deliberations. The most accurate notes seem to be those of Matthews. They include numerous details and, evidently, the original phraseology. As a rule, Matthews's notes are quoted in the following pages.

The records were released by the Department of State at the beginning of 1955 amid international controversy. Soon after, on March 17, both Churchill and Eden criticized the American government for having made the records available to the public.[2]

Poland was discussed at seven of the eight plenary sessions, and the discussions concerned three main subjects: (1) the eastern boundaries, (2) the northern and western boundaries, and (3) the problem of the Polish government.

POLAND'S EASTERN BOUNDARIES

The agreement on Poland's eastern boundary was reached without difficulty or extensive argument. The discussion was opened by Roosevelt on February

6, and judging by Bohlen's and Matthews's notes, he revealed considerable weariness. His comments seemed, at times, almost incoherent.[3] First he stated that he had been supporting the Soviet territorial demands on Poland for a long time, and, evidently referring to his secret conversation with Stalin,[4] observed: "As I said in Teheran, in general I am in favor of the Curzon line." Then he asked Stalin to demonstrate his generosity, adding, however, that the Poles were not so much concerned with saving their eastern provinces as with "saving face." The Soviet government should help them and "give something to Poland," namely Lvov and the nearby oil fields. Such a "gesture," he explained, would help him in his standing with the six or seven million Poles in the United States.[5] He emphasized that he did not insist; he only presented it for the marshal's consideration. According to Churchill's account, he also said that Americans of Polish descent were "generally" in favor of the Curzon Line.[6]

Churchill, who took the floor after Roosevelt, declared himself even more strongly on the side of Russia: "I have made repeated declarations in Parliament in support of the Soviet claim to the Curzon line, that is to say, leaving Lvov with Soviet Russia. I have been much criticized and so has Mr. Eden, especially by the party which I represent. But I have always considered that after all Russia has suffered in fighting Germany and after all her efforts in liberating Poland, her claim is one founded not on force but on right." Having said that, he applauded the president's suggestion for the "Soviet gesture of magnanimity."

Stalin's answer was a lengthy exposé:

> The President has suggested modification, giving Poland Lvov and Lvov Province. The Prime Minister thinks that we could make a gesture of magnanimity. But I must remind you that the Curzon line was made by Curzon, Clemenceau and the Americans in 1918–1919. Russia was not invited and did not participate. This plan was accepted against the will of the Russians on the basis of ethnological data. Lenin opposed it. He did not want to give Bialystok and Bialystok Provinces to Poland but the Curzon line gives them to Poland. We have retreated from Lenin's position. Some want us to be less Russian than Curzon and Clemenceau. What will the Russians say at Moscow and the Ukrainians? They will say that Stalin and Molotov are far less defenders of Russia than Curzon and Clemenceau. I cannot take such a position and return to Moscow.[7]

Though the Soviet leader had evidently done his homework on the history of the Polish-Soviet boundaries, his statement was more dramatic than correct.

At Tehran, Eden himself argued against Molotov's contention that the Curzon Line included Lvov. Clemenceau never favored separating Lvov permanently from the Polish state.[8] In 1919 and 1920 Lenin offered Poland better territorial conditions than the Allies.[9] No one, however, took exception to Stalin's utterances.

The next day, at the fourth plenary session, Roosevelt again opened the discussion on Poland.[10] Having restated that, in the main, he had no intention of opposing Soviet territorial demands, he mildly suggested some compromise. This time Molotov replied and the discussion ended. Subsequently, at the fifth plenary session held on February 8, a formal, unanimous declaration was agreed upon: "The Three Heads of Government consider that the eastern frontier of Poland should follow the Curzon line with digression from it in some regions 5–8 kilometers in favor of Poland."[11]

Thus, finally, the secret Tehran "formula" was sanctioned by a formal agreement of the three Great Powers. The decision deprived Poland of nearly half of its territory and a third of its population.

POLAND'S NORTHERN AND WESTERN BOUNDARIES

There was fundamental disagreement on Poland's western boundary. Both the British and American delegations opposed the Soviet proposal, and, this time, their views prevailed.

The discussion was opened by Stalin during the third plenary session on February 6. He vigorously advocated acceptance of the Oder–Western Neisse line and looked upon Poland's acquisitions in the west as compensation for its losses in the east. He would even be prepared to prolong the war, he said, in order to secure the frontier for the Poles, who, he assured the conferees, all favored his recommendation. Subsequently, Molotov presented a draft declaration for official acceptance: "It was decided that the western frontier of Poland should be traced from the town of Stettin (Polish) and further to the south along the River Oder and still further along the River Neisse (western)."[12]

Churchill spoke forcibly against the proposal.[13] It was true, he said, that he had favored the extension of Polish frontiers in the west. It was also true, however, that he had always qualified his statement by adding that the Poles should take no more than "they wish or can handle." Russia wanted Poland to expand much too far. "I do not wish to stuff the Polish goose until it dies of German indigestion," he chuckled. Many among his compatriots were "shocked at the idea of transferring millions of people [Germans] by force." If Poland received East Prussia and Silesia, six million people would have to be transferred. "That is manageable, but there will be big arguments against it still," he added. "There will be no more Germans for when our troops come in the Germans run away and no Germans are left," Stalin interjected. A short exchange of views on how many Germans were going to be killed before the end of hostilities followed, with Churchill concluding that he was not afraid "of the transfer of population as long as it is in proportion to what the Poles can manage and what can be put in the place of the dead in Germany."

The next day, on February 8, Roosevelt defined the American position in an official memorandum.[14] He agreed to the frontier giving Poland East Prussia south of Königsberg and territories up to the Oder River and Upper Silesia. He decidedly opposed giving Poland territories up to the Western Neisse River, however. Molotov took exception, pointing out that the Soviet proposals had the support of the Polish (Warsaw) government and could not be rejected without consulting the Poles. He suggested that the British and Americans speak to the Poles so that they could see how "categorically" they supported the Soviet demand.

The matter was subsequently sent to the foreign ministers' conference for further deliberation. There, Eden informed his colleagues that he had just received a cable from the war cabinet in London. If the British proposals (which approved the expansion of Poland to the Oder River at the most) were not approved, he did not see any chance for the British government's agreement.[15] The meeting was inconclusive, and the failure to reach an understanding was reported on February 10, at the seventh plenary meeting.[16] Churchill expressed his great disappointment. He strongly believed that all Poland's postwar frontiers should be formally decided by the three Great Powers and publicly announced, thus solving the problem once and for all. He repeated, though, that Great Britain could not and would not agree to Polish expansion up to the Western Neisse River.

President Roosevelt did not like Churchill's insistence on a public announcement of the decision. Although he had no objections to secret decisions on Poland's frontiers, he thought that the public announcement of these decisions should be postponed. The conference should not decide such a fateful issue without knowing what the "new" Polish government thought about it. Since the new government had not yet been formed, it would be better to wait with the public declaration. "It is important to say something,"

Stalin said. Churchill agreed, and Roosevelt became uneasy. He preferred not to have any *public* declaration on Poland's frontiers because, according to the US Constitution, the president could conclude a binding agreement only with the consent of the Senate. Since he did not have it at the moment, he had to insist on postponing the official declaration. In order to break the deadlock, Molotov suggested that since everyone was agreed on the Curzon Line, let this be included in the official public communiqué. Since there was no agreement on the western frontier, let the conference say nothing about it. Churchill again disagreed, offering his own formula. Let the communiqué state that Poland was to get "compensation in the west." Let there also be a clause that the extent of that compensation would be decided later, after the opinion of the future government of Poland became known. Molotov offered no opposition. Roosevelt, however, was still adamant. None of the formulas eased his difficulty.

Eventually the problem of the president's authority to conclude a formal and public agreement was solved with the help of Alger Hiss. During the intermission Roosevelt and Stettinius consulted him and, as a result, a salutary legal formula was agreed upon. In those places of the official declaration on Poland where the expression "Three Powers" had been used, "the Three Heads of Government" should be substituted. Instead of "they [the Three Heads of Government] agree," the expression "they feel" should be inserted. In such a way the agreement, though for all *practical* purposes conclusive, would not contravene American constitutional procedures. Both Churchill and Stalin promptly agreed to accommodate the president, and as a result the following declaration was submitted for acceptance: "It is recognized that Poland must receive substantial accessions of territory in the North and West. They [the Three Heads of Government] feel that the opinion of the new Polish Provisional Government of National Unity should be sought in due course on the extent of these accessions and that the final delimitation of the Western frontier of Poland should thereafter await the Peace Conference."[17]

At the last moment before the declaration was to be accepted, Molotov proposed an amendment. He still wanted to make the extent of Poland's acquisitions more precise by adding "with the return to Poland of her ancient frontiers in East Prussia and the Oder" to the first sentence. The president, apparently having forgotten that only two days before he himself had proposed what Molotov wanted to insert, now asked how long ago these lands had been Polish. Molotov replied that it was very long ago. "This might lead the British to ask for the return of the United States to Great Britain," Roose-

velt laughed, and disapproved. Stalin courteously yielded, the amendment
was dropped, and the declaration was accepted as it stood.[18]

AGREEMENT ON A GOVERNMENT FOR POLAND

The discussions at Yalta on the future Polish government took longer than
any other single subject. All participants realized that the nature of the agreement would profoundly affect Poland's political future.

The most important points of the Anglo-American strategy worked out at
Malta were: (1) a presidential council to be composed of *three* non-Communist leaders and *one* Communist, Beirut; (2) the council to be authorized to
appoint a *new*, representative Polish government; (3) in the new government,
consisting of people from the Warsaw regime as well as Polish democratic
leaders from Poland and abroad, the non-Communist Poles should have a
"leading" position; (4) no one from the Polish government in London would
be included, but Mikolajczyk, Romer, and Grabski proposed instead; (5)
recognition to be withdrawn from the London government and the Warsaw
regime to be dissolved, because the new government was not to be the
continuation of either of them; (6) the new government would hold free
elections as soon as possible; and (7) the elections would be supervised by a
special British-American-Soviet commission. Both Eden and Stettinius
agreed that only these provisions could ensure genuine freedom and independence for postwar Poland and recommended a strong stand.

The discussion on the Polish government was opened by Roosevelt on
February 6.[19] As planned in advance, he advocated the creation of a presidential council with the authority to appoint a government of national unity
consisting of representatives of five political parties—Peasant, Socialist,
Christian Labor, National Democratic, and Communist. The president
praised Mikolajczyk and suggested that he be a member of the new government. As in the case of his "appeal" for the Lvov area, he concluded, however, that the plan he proposed was only a "suggestion." Other "solutions"
might be applied as well. Thus, at the outset, Roosevelt opened the way for
concessions.

Then Churchill spoke.[20] Again he reminded Stalin how consistently he
supported him on the Curzon Line. He did that because he was more interested in Poland's independence and freedom than in its boundaries. He
wanted the Poles "to have a home in Europe and to be free to live their own
life there." It was for this, he said, that the British went to war. Great Britain

had no "material interest" in Poland, its interest was "one of honor." Poland's independence should be limited in one way only. "I do not think that the freedom of Poland could be made to cover hostile designs by any Polish government, perhaps by intrigue with Germany, against the Soviet." If that ever happened, not only Britain but the world organization soon to be created would go to the Soviet Union's aid. He dissociated himself entirely from the government-in-exile. "I have never seen any of the present London government. We recognize them, but we have not sought their company," he said. He had praise for only three Poles—Mikolajczyk, Romer, and Grabski— because these three were men of "good sense." He "cordially" supported Roosevelt's suggestions. The best way to solve the problem was to constitute a new Polish interim government immediately. Then elections should take place.

Stalin answered that for Russia, Poland was "not only a question of honor but also of security."[21] Poland had always been a corridor through which Russia's enemies had attacked it. In the last thirty years, Germany had attacked Russia twice through that corridor. Poland's freedom, independence, and strength was for Russia a question of "life and death." It was because of this that the Soviet Union pursued a policy of friendship toward Poland. The independence and strength of Poland was the "basis" of all Soviet foreign policy.

Then Stalin gave Churchill a lesson in democracy. "The Prime Minister has said that he wants to create a Polish government here. I am afraid that was a slip of the tongue. Without the participation of Poles, we can create no Polish government." To do so, he said, would violate democratic principles which he "respected." "They all say that I am a dictator, but I have enough democratic feeling not to set up a Polish government without Poles."

Then Stalin explained what Poles should be considered, since there were two kinds of Poles: those from London and those from Lublin. The Poles from London were no good. They were "hostile" to the Soviet Union, and they called the Lublin government "bandits" and "traitors." The agents of the London government operating in the Underground in Poland were no good, either. They had killed 212 Soviet soldiers; they were attacking Soviet military bases, they were using the wireless stations, they were breaking "all the laws of war," and then they complained of having been arrested. The Lublin Poles, on the contrary, were fulfilling their tasks "not badly." He had already asked them under what conditions they would come to some agreement with the London Poles. They answered that they would "tolerate" Grabski and

General Żeligowski,[22] "but they won't hear of Mikolajczyk." He, Stalin, wanted Polish unity and was ready to call the Lublin Poles to Yalta or, better, to Moscow to discuss the matter with them.

Apparently Stalin's discourse was too much for Churchill, for, ignoring Roosevelt's adjournment of the meeting, he heatedly observed "for the record" that his government had different information from Poland, that the Lublin government probably did not represent even one-third of the population—though he might be "wrong" on this—and that he feared bloodshed, arrests, and deportations in Poland, and that the Lublin government had no right to represent the Polish nation. In his own report of the incident, Churchill complained that Roosevelt became impatient with his arguments: "The President was now anxious to end the discussion. 'Poland,' he remarked, 'has been a source of trouble for over five hundred years.' 'All the more,' I [Churchill] answered, 'must we do what we can to put an end to these troubles.'"[23]

The same night Roosevelt sent Stalin a letter prepared by the Department of State and Hopkins.[24] The president stated that he was disturbed by the disagreement of the three Great Powers on the "political set-up in Poland," because some solution had to be found. He suggested inviting Bierut and Osubka-Morawski from the Lublin government and "two or three" Poles from the prepared list of five men "at once." The names (atrociously spelled) were those of Archbishop Adam Sapieha; Peasant Party leader Wincenty Witos; Socialist leader Zygmunt Żulawski; and two university professors, Franciszek Bujak and Stanislaw Kutrzeba. All of them were in Poland. This group, the president recommended, would appoint a new provisional government of Poland in collaboration with the representatives of the three Great Powers. The new government should include such Polish leaders from abroad as Mikolajczyk, Grabski, and Romer. Then, Great Britain and the United States would recognize it, and free elections would be held as soon as possible. Of course, the new government would have to be friendly to Russia.

The president's letter marked a serious retreat from the position he had held only one day before. While, according to the Malta strategy, the presidential council was to consist of *three non-Communists* and Bierut, the president now proposed Bierut *and* Osubka-Morawski, plus "two of three" non-Communists. Above all, there was no mention of the essential point that the provisional government would be composed of the leaders of the *five* political parties, only one of them Communist. Roosevelt's only request as to the political makeup of the new government was that it should include Mikolajczyk, Grabski, and Romer. "I am determined that there shall be no breach between ourselves and the Soviet Union" anyway, he concluded the letter, as if indicating that in the event Stalin really made an issue of the Polish government, he, Roosevelt, might compromise further.[25]

The fourth plenary session took place the next day, February 7, and once again the president opened the discussion on Poland.[26] He denounced the government-in-exile and observed that the legal continuity of the Polish constitutional authorities was without importance. "There hasn't really been any Polish government since 1939," he said. Then he called for the establishment of a new government.

In his answer, Stalin informed the participants that he had received Roosevelt's letter only an hour and a half before and had tried immediately to reach Bierut and Osubka-Morawski by telephone. They could not be found. As for Witos and Archbishop Sapieha, he unfortunately could not contact them because he did not know their addresses. Then he called upon Molotov to present the Soviet draft of counterproposals.[27]

Molotov's draft disregarded the British-American plan altogether.[28] It did not provide for the presidential council at all and, instead, proposed an immediate recognition of the Warsaw government by Great Britain and the United States. That government would be "broadened" by some unnamed leaders from "émigré circles." A special commission, composed of American and British ambassadors in Moscow (Harriman and Clark-Kerr) as well as Molotov himself, would take care of the "broadening" of the Warsaw government and agreeing upon the new members to be included. The proposal, if accepted, would mean a total abandonment of the recommendations agreed upon by Stettinius and Eden at Malta, recommendations which they considered vital for Poland's future.

Roosevelt did not object to Molotov's proposals, considered them "definite progress," and asked for time to study them more closely. But he did not like the idea of taking any "émigrés" into the government. There were enough Poles in Poland for that purpose. At that moment Churchill hastily intervened. The president's unexpected objection, if sustained, might block the participation of Mikolajczyk, Grabski, and Romer in the new government, thus undermining the entire British-American strategy on Poland. He politely "agreed" with the president on the use of the word "émigré" and suggested replacing it with the expression "Poles temporarily abroad." Roosevelt resented Churchill's interjection and wanted to adjourn the meeting. "Now we are in for half an hour of it,"[29] he angrily scribbled to Stettinius while Churchill spoke.

The following day, Stettinius presented the American compromise proposals at the fifth plenary session.[30] The idea of a presidential council was still recommended, together with the dissolution of the Warsaw regime and the appointment of a *new* government. Otherwise, the proposals did not differ much from the Soviet draft. When asked to comment, Stalin inquired about the future of the Polish London government once the "government of national unity" was recognized. Churchill answered that recognition would be withdrawn. Then Stalin asked what would happen to the property of the London government. He was told that it would go to the new government. Satisfied with the answers, Stalin called upon Molotov to speak.[31]

Molotov explained that the Soviet proposals originated from "a concrete foundation." One could not ignore the government already operating in Poland. The discussion should center on how and by whom that government should be *extended*, not on how to *replace* it with a new one. The provisional government had great authority among the Polish people and was "enthusiastically" supported by them. The Poles would never allow its extinction, though they would agree to its "broadening." Harriman, Clark-Kerr, and he himself should start conversations with the Polish leaders for that purpose. He proposed discussions with five leaders—*two* from the list proposed by Roosevelt and *three* from the Warsaw government. Mikolajczyk should be excluded, he said, because Poles in Poland would not talk to him. Once the existing government was "enlarged," then "free elections" would take place. The Soviet government wanted these elections to be "absolutely" free because this was "the best way to build stable rule," which "all" considered of "fundamental importance." "I would like to keep the presidential committee," the president interrupted. "It would be better to avoid the presidential committee and to enlarge the national council," Molotov replied.

Then Churchill spoke. In a strong language, he argued for a new government.[32] The question was a crucial one, he said. The present Lublin regime had no support from the majority of Polish people. Great Britain could not switch its recognition from the London to the Lublin government. Poles all over the world would protest unanimously, then there would be a "world outcry," and the Polish army would consider such an action a "betrayal." True, the prime minister continued, he did not agree at all with the London government, which proved to be "foolish," but the public opinion would take such a transition of recognition as an abandonment of Poland. The only solution of the problem was to form a completely *new* government, to make a "new start on both sides more or less on equal terms."

Stalin seemed unimpressed by Churchill's arguments.[33] He did not understand Churchill's fears and assured the prime minister that the Warsaw government was "really very popular." Its members did not leave Poland during the war, and they were from the Underground. People under occupation had a "peculiar mentality"—they preferred those who had remained in Poland. Furthermore, the Poles in Poland had changed. Before, they did not like Russia, but after the Red Army liberated them, they began to like it. Soviet liberation was for them "a great historic holiday." All took part in that holiday, except the Poles from London. The people's will must always be respected. True, the Warsaw government was not elected, and, true, it is always "much better to have a government based on free elections." However, although de Gaulle was not elected in France, the Soviet Union, Britain, and the United States recognized him. The Warsaw government had at least instituted reforms that contributed greatly to its popularity. "Molotov is right," Stalin concluded. It would be better to *reconstruct the present government* than to *create a new one*. The presidential committee, in particular, should not be discussed without consulting the Poles. No one should ever offend Polish "*amour propre* and feelings"; otherwise, "they would accuse us of being occupiers and not liberators," he said.

At that moment, Roosevelt inquired how long it would take to have elections. "About one month," answered Stalin. Then the president adjourned the meeting, suggesting that the problem be referred again to the three foreign ministers. To Eden's annoyance, he also observed that the differences seemed to him unimportant, just "a matter of the use of words."[34]

At the conference of the foreign ministers held the next day, Stettinius pointed out the importance of an *immediate* agreement on Poland, implying that if such an agreement were not reached, US participation in the postwar world organization might become doubtful.[35] With this in mind, the American delegation worked out the new compromise proposals, which he read.[36] The proposals represented further concessions. The idea of a presidential council was dropped altogether. The crucial Soviet formula that "the present Polish provisional government be reorganized" was accepted. Molotov, Harriman, and Clark-Kerr were to consult with members of the Warsaw government and "other democratic leaders from within Poland and from abroad." The government so "reorganized" was to hold "free and unfettered elections as soon as practicable." Once the government of national unity was formed, the three Great Powers would recognize it and send ambassadors who "would be charged with the responsibility of observing and reporting to their respective governments on the carrying out of the pledge in regard to free and unfettered elections." The proposals differed from Molotov's in only one respect: they contained a clause about ambassadors who would "observe and report" on the elections.

Eden, evidently realizing the decisive significance of the American concessions, again defended the idea of a *new government*. He did not think that anybody in his country considered the Lublin government representative of Poland. He thought that the same opinion prevailed in the United States. Because of that, "a new start was necessary." The withdrawal of recognition from the London Polish government would be easier if it were followed by recognition of a completely new government and not a recognition "in favor of the existing Lublin government." He again made forceful appeals for the inclusion of Mikolajczyk in the new government in order to ease British recognition and to convince the British people of its representative character.

Molotov tried to soothe the foreign secretary.[37] The situation in Poland would be stabilized by general elections in no more than one or two months. Why complicate matters by seeking a new government? It was of great importance to the Red Army that Poland remain stable during that short interval, and the Warsaw government had proved capable of maintaining order. As for Mikolajczyk, who knows, perhaps the "question was not as acute as it appeared," after all. Perhaps the matter could be cleared up, and he would become acceptable. The clause concerning the supervision of the elections by foreign ambassadors, however, should be dropped. The Poles would be offended. They would resent the "control of foreign diplomatic representatives." Besides, the ambassadors could observe and report anyway, he explained.

At the sixth plenary session on the same day,[38] Molotov formally recommended three amendments to the American proposals. First, it should be made clear that the presently operating provisional government was to provide the basis for the new government; second, the political parties participating in the elections should be not only "democratic" but also "non-Fascist and anti-Fascist"; third, the reference to the three ambassadors "observing and reporting" on the elections should be dropped. He explained again that "the sensibilities of the Poles" had to be respected.

Roosevelt repeated that he did not see any great difference between Stettinius's and Molotov's proposals but added that he thought "some gesture" should be made to show concern for honest elections. Churchill recommended retaining the paragraph concerning the three ambassadors "in order to see how the Polish quarrels are being settled." He wanted to be able to assure Parliament that elections in Poland would be fair. Parliament, not so much the Poles, was important: "I do not care much about Poles myself," he concluded.[39]

At this point Stalin came to the defense of the Poles. Some of them were "good," and all of them were "good fighters," he said. "In olden times," they had produced many scientists, like Copernicus. He agreed with Churchill, though, that the contemporary Poles were quarrelsome and that there were still Fascists among them. Thus, the stipulation that only anti-Fascist parties would be allowed to take part in the elections seemed to him necessary. The president interjected that the elections should be like Caesar's wife. "I did not know her, but they said she was pure," he chuckled. "They said that about her, but in fact she had her sins," Stalin observed somehow ominously. Then Roosevelt repeated that he did not want the Poles in the United States to question the elections. For him, he pointed out, the whole matter was not only one of principles but also of "practical politics" at home.[40] On that note, the discussion ended.

Poland was subsequently debated at two conferences of foreign ministers, and "after a lengthy but amicable discussion," final agreement emerged.[41] The Lublin government would be "reorganized" and only "democratic" and "anti-Nazi" parties would be allowed to take part in the elections. At the second conference on February 10, Stettinius proposed to drop any reference to the three ambassadors "observing and reporting" on the elections. He said that, personally, he considered the provision necessary. The president, however, anxious to reach an agreement, instructed him to drop it. Eden, now in the minority, bluntly expressed his disagreement. He promised, however, not to raise objections at the plenary meeting.

A few hours later, the seventh plenary session took place,[42] and there final agreement on the Polish government was accepted without discussion. On February 11, at the eighth and last plenary session, the final Declaration on Poland was voted on and confirmed unanimously:

> A new situation has been created in Poland as a result of her complete liberation by the Red Army. This calls for the establishment of a Polish Provisional Government which can be more broadly based than was possible before the recent liberation of Western Poland. The Provisional Government which is now functioning in Poland should therefore be reorganized on a broader demo-

cratic basis with the inclusion of democratic leaders from Poland itself and from Poles abroad. This new Government should then be called the Polish Provisional Government of National Unity.

M. Molotov, Mr. Harriman and Sir A. Clark-Kerr are authorized as a Commission to consult in the first instance in Moscow with members of the present Provisional Government and with other Polish democratic leaders from within Poland and from abroad, with a view to the reorganization of the present Government along the above lines. This Polish Provisional Government of National Unity shall be pledged to the holding of free and unfettered elections as soon as possible on the basis of universal suffrage and secret ballot. In these elections all democratic and anti-Nazi parties shall have the right to take part and to put forward candidates.

When a Polish Provisional Government of National Unity has been properly formed in conformity with the above, the Government of the USSR, which now maintains diplomatic relations with the present Provisional Government of Poland, and the Government of the United Kingdom and the Government of the USA will establish diplomatic relations with the new Polish Provisional Government of National Unity, and will exchange Ambassadors by whose reports the respective Governments will be kept informed about the situation in Poland.

The Three Heads of Government consider that the Eastern frontier of Poland should follow the Curzon line with digression from it in some regions of five to eight kilometers in favor of Poland. They recognize that Poland must receive substantial accessions of territory in the North and West. They feel that the opinion of the New Polish Provisional Government of National Unity should be sought in due course on the extent of these accessions and that the final delimitation of the Western frontier of Poland should thereafter await the Peace Conference. [43]

After the declaration was read and accepted, Churchill gloomily observed that the decisions concerning Poland would be "heavily attacked" in England. "It will be said we have yielded completely on the frontiers and the whole matter to R. [Russia],"[44] he said. Stalin tried to console him.

NOTES

1. *The Conferences at Malta and Yalta, 1945.*
2. *5 Parliamentary Debates*, Commons, 538 (1955), 1456.
3. Leahy called the president's remarks a "splendid presentation of the problem," Leahy, *I Was There*, 304.
4. Supra, 476–77.
5. The president was still preoccupied with the way the Americans of Polish descent voted and brought the matter up on more than one occasion. According to Stettinius, he had observed

two days before at the Big Three dinner that there were "lots of Poles in America . . . vitally interested in the future of Poland." Stalin understood the allusion and consoled him by saying that out of those seven million, only seven thousand voted. He knew because he had "looked it up." Stettinius, *Roosevelt and the Russians*, 113.

6. Churchill, *Triumph and Tragedy*, 367.

7. Matthews's notes on Churchill's and Stalin's comments, in *The Conferences at Malta and Yalta, 1945*, 678–80.

8. Supra, 49–52, 57–59.

9. Supra, 59, 70.

10. For Matthews's notes, see *The Conferences at Malta and Yalta, 1945*, 718–21, 786–93.

11. Ibid., 974.

12. Matthews's notes on the February 7 plenary session, ibid., 718–21.

13. For Churchill's remarks, ibid., 720.

14. For Matthews's notes, see ibid., 786–91.

15. Ibid., 867, also 989. The war cabinet proposed the formula: "and such other lands to the east of the line of the Oder as at the Peace Conference it shall be considered desirable to transfer to Poland." See Woodward, *British Foreign Policy in the Second World War*, 498.

16. For Matthews's notes on the seventh plenary session, see ibid., 906–11.

17. Ibid., 905.

18. For an exhaustive analysis of the Oder-Neisse frontier, see Alfons Klafkowski, *Podstawy Prawne Granicy Odra-Nissa na Tle Umów Jaltanskiej i Poczdamskiej (The Legal Foundations of the Oder-Neisse Frontier on the Basis of the Yalta and Potsdam Agreements)* (Poznań: Instytut Zachodni, 1947); also Friedrich Hoffman, *Die Oder-Neisse Linie; Politische Entwicklung und Volkerrechtliche Lage* (Frankfurt am Main: J. Heinrich, 1949).

19. For Matthews's notes, see *The Conferences at Malta and Yalta, 1945*, 677–82.

20. For Churchill's speech, ibid., 678–79.

21. For Stalin's observations, ibid., 679–81.

22. General Żeligowski—at the time living in London and a member of the National Council—was known for his pan-Slavic orientation.

23. Churchill, *Triumph and Tragedy*, 372.

24. Stettinius, *Roosevelt and the Russians*, 157; for the text of the letter, see *The Conferences at Malta and Yalta, 1945*, 727–28.

25. Chester Wilmot, *The Struggle for Europe* (London: Collins, St. James Place, 1952), 49.

26. For the president's remarks, *The Conferences at Malta and Yalta, 1945*, 718.

27. For Stalin's observations, see ibid., 719–20.

28. For the text, see ibid., 716.

29. Stettinius, *Roosevelt and the Russians*, 184.

30. For the full text, see *The Conferences at Malta and Yalta, 1945*, 792–93.

31. For Molotov's observations, see ibid., 786–87.

32. For Churchill's observations, see ibid., 787–88.

33. For Stalin's arguments, see ibid., 789–90.

34. Eden, *The Reckoning*, 599.

35. For that meeting, Matthews's notes are not available. The Bohlen notes are used instead. *The Conferences at Malta and Yalta, 1945*, 803–7.

36. For the text, see ibid., 803–4.

37. For Molotov's comments, see ibid., 805.

38. For Matthews's notes, see ibid., 850–55.

39. On March 17, 1955, Churchill denied having ever made the above observation. "I think that my record throughout the war and this period will show with what deep sympathy I viewed

the fate of the people of Poland," he declared. *5 Parliamentary Debates*, Commons, 538 (1955), 1456.

40. For the Stalin-Roosevelt exchange of remarks, see *The Conferences at Malta and Yalta*, 853–54.

41. Matthews's notes for these two conferences are only fragmentary. For Bohlen's respective notes, see ibid., 867–68, 872–73.

42. For Matthews's notes, see ibid., 906–11.

43. Ibid., 938.

44. Ibid., 928.

Chapter Thirty-Eight

The Meaning of the Yalta Agreement

Diplomacy and Semantics

Numerous political and military factors affected Churchill's and Roosevelt's attitude at Yalta toward the Polish problem. Politically, Poland was only one and, for that matter, not the most important of the many issues they had to settle with Stalin. Militarily, Russia had the upper hand.

In February 1945 the Red Army had crossed the Oder River and was less than one hundred miles from Berlin; the Allied armies had not yet crossed the Rhine. Finland was already out of the war, and Romania, Poland, and Yugoslavia, as well as the greater parts of Hungary and Czechoslovakia had already been liberated by the Red Army. That, of course, meant Soviet control. In Asia, Japan still dominated Manchuria, Korea, the coast of China, Southeast Asia, and Indonesia. Thus, Russia's support against Japan was highly desired in both Washington and London. The victorious Red Army was vigorous and well equipped.

Going to Yalta, Churchill and Roosevelt were both determined to achieve an agreement with Stalin on all the most important issues. They were also prepared to make concessions on less essential ones. The agreements seemed even more necessary because in the preceding months the Western press had become increasingly critical of the Soviet war aims and Communist practices in eastern Europe. Neither Churchill nor Roosevelt viewed that with indulgence, seeing in it a possible impediment to their policies of continued Western-Soviet cooperation, which they considered vital. Both tried to inculcate the idea that compromise, not rigidity, should guide British-American-Soviet relations. "The nearer we come to vanquishing our enemies, the more we inevitably become conscious of differences among the victors,"[1] the president told Congress on January 6, 1945, just two weeks before he left for Yalta. He pointed out that "nations, like individuals, do not always see alike or think alike, and international cooperation and progress are not helped by any nation assuming that it has a monopoly of wisdom or of virtue." Churchill did not differ in his own attitudes. Although, on January 8, he cabled Roosevelt that "the end of this war may well prove to be more disappointing than was the last,"[2] he, too, considered Western-Soviet cooperation a necessity.

There were two military issues the Western leaders considered vital: coordination of the plans for the final defeat of Germany and Russia's declaration of war on Japan. Roosevelt's military planners impressed upon him the necessity of Soviet war cooperation in both Europe and Asia.[3] The Joint Chiefs of Staff insisted that Soviet help in Asia was imperative. They expected Japan to resist until the beginning of 1947, at which point American fighting forces would have suffered casualties of more than a million, and argued that Soviet war participation would reduce the losses by forcing an early Japanese surrender.[4] The US navy did not agree with this evaluation; however, Chief of Staff General George C. Marshall's arguments prevailed with the president.[5]

The political problems that the Western leaders considered the most important were the future of Germany, establishment of an effective world organization in which the Soviet Union would play a positive role, and coordination of plans for postwar Europe. On the last point, the areas liberated and controlled by the Red Army presented a dilemma. The Soviet authorities acted in central-eastern Europe as if it were their uncontested sphere of influence, not without reason. Both Churchill and Roosevelt certainly remembered that at Tehran they did recognize—secretly and informally—the Soviet Union's right to act unilaterally in the areas liberated by the Red Army.[6] So much depended on Stalin's goodwill. The Dumbarton Oaks Conference, held in Washington, DC, from August to September 1944, had failed to produce an agreement on the charter of the United Nations Organization, and the failure, Roosevelt told Congress, had to be redeemed.[7]

On most of these issues, the agreement reached at Yalta satisfied the Western leaders. On February 8, in a private meeting with Roosevelt, Stalin committed his government to declaring war on Japan approximately three months after the surrender of Germany. In regard to the United Nations

Organization, it was agreed that a constituent assembly would be held in San Francisco in April 1945 and that all nations at war with Germany on March 1, 1945, would be represented. The USSR was to have three votes in the UN Assembly and, together with other permanent members of the Security Council, a veto on all issues under the council's competence.[8] On the subject of Germany, zones of occupation were defined, and German reparations in kind rather than in money were determined. At the time, British and American leaders considered these agreements a great diplomatic victory. Concessions in eastern Europe, including Poland, were undoubtedly viewed as part of the price for that victory. "I've got everything I came for, and not at too high a price," Roosevelt told one of his confidants at the end of his *sejour* at Yalta.

The declaration on Poland, with all its ambiguities and Anglo-American concessions, reveals the complexity of the situation. The opening sentence seemed to justify the Soviet special position in Poland. Since the Red Army had liberated Poland "completely," the Poles owed Russia their national existence. The sentence was proposed by Churchill as "more than ornamental." That it was, since it dismissed the Polish contribution to the war. For the Red Army did not liberate Poland alone. The Polish Underground, its strength best demonstrated during the Warsaw Uprising, collaborated actively and closely throughout the entire war with the Allies. The Polish armed forces fought on both the western and the eastern fronts. The entire nation made sacrifices and distinguished itself by being the only occupied nation that did not produce a quisling. All these, significantly, were disregarded.

While the declaration did not even mention the legal government-in-exile, it clearly stated that the new government would emerge from a "democratic reorganization" of the Warsaw regime. That the Warsaw regime was both Communist and Moscow-dominated Churchill and Roosevelt knew and acknowledged. Still, neither the procedure nor the term "democratic" were defined. According to the Soviet constitution, the government in Moscow was also "democratic." Was the "democratic reorganization" to follow the Soviet pattern?

The term "new government" was used twice in the declaration, the fact of which Eden eventually made a serious issue in the House of Commons,[9] and which eventually became a matter of international controversy. However, the record of discussions shows that this term, as used, was purposefully obscure. For the two Western powers also committed themselves, in the same declaration, to recognizing a "reorganized" Warsaw regime. Both the British and the American leaders opposed the insertion of the term "reorganized" into the agreement but finally became reconciled to it, at Stalin's insistence.

The Communist regime was to be "reorganized" by the inclusion of "democratic leaders from Poland itself and from Poles abroad." The identities, number, and political affiliations of the leaders, and the timing of the "reorganization," were not specified. The "reorganized" Warsaw regime was to hold elections "as soon as possible." How soon, and who was to decide when it would be "possible" to hold them? During the deliberations, Stalin spoke of one month, Molotov of two months, but the elections actually were to take place *two years* later, after the Communists had prepared conditions to hold them in their own way.

According to the declaration, only "democratic and anti-Nazi parties" were to be allowed to participate in the elections. What parties were "democratic" and "anti-Nazi," how many of them were to participate, and who was to pass judgment on their "democratic" and "anti-Nazi" character was not explained.

The elections were to be "free" and "unfettered." What did "free" and "unfettered" mean, and who was to determine the meaning? The difference of view on that subject between the Communist and non-Communist worlds was never a secret. Certainly it was not a secret to the American and British delegations that Stalin considered Soviet elections "free" and "unfettered." Were the elections in Poland to be carried out in the same fashion?

The role of Molotov, Harriman, and Clark-Kerr was to "consult with the members of the present provisional government and with other Polish democratic leaders from within Poland and from abroad." The statement implied that the Warsaw setup was "democratic." Were those "other" democratic leaders to be democratic in the same way? The term "to consult" was in itself vague and ambiguous.

After the reorganization of the Warsaw regime, the three powers were to send to Warsaw their ambassadors, "by whose reports the respective governments [would] be kept informed about the situation in Poland." As Molotov rightly observed, all ambassadors as a matter of routine keep their governments informed about the situation in the countries to which they are accredited; for all practical purposes, the formula had no significance. It was no more than a face-saving substitute for the original British-American demand for international *control* over the elections. That demand, rejected by Stalin, was later dropped by Roosevelt, against the advice of his own secretary of state and over Eden's protest.

The approval of the vagueness and obscurity of the agreement on Poland was not a matter of misjudgment or oversight on the part of the Western leaders. When handed the declaration on Poland to read, Admiral William D. Leahy, one of the key members of the American delegation at Yalta, commented: "I saw the now familiar phrases such as 'strong, free, independent Poland,' Russia 'guaranteeing' the liberated country, 'unfettered elections,' 'universal suffrage,' 'secret ballot,' and so on . . . I handed the paper back to Roosevelt and said, 'Mr. President, this is so elastic that the Russians can stretch it all the way from Yalta to Washington without ever technically breaking it.'"[10] The president did not deny this. "I know Bill—I know it. But it is the best I can do for Poland at this time," he answered.

Originally, neither Churchill nor Roosevelt intended to agree to anything like the wording of the declaration. On the contrary, they deemed strong precautions necessary. They did propose a *presidential council*, with the majority to be held by non-Communists; they did ask for a genuinely *new* government; they did request the inclusion of the representatives of five *specific* political parties, *four* of them non-Communist, in that government; they did demand effective *control* over the elections. Each of their demands was vital to Poland's future, and to each one Stalin said no. Then they ceded, point by point.

Eventually an argument was to be raised by the American and British participants in the Yalta agreement that the agreement itself was good but, unfortunately, was later broken by Moscow. The argument does not seem plausible. The agreement was ambivalent, and its ambivalence was obvious to all parties concerned. So was its failure to provide any effective and clearly defined safeguards for Poland's independence. Its vague and obscure terms allowed Moscow and its Polish supporters to impose their will on the Polish nation. As the record shows, the inclusion of the safeguards was originally intended by the Western leaders, and the significance of the obscure terms was well understood by them. The renunciation of the former and the acceptance of the latter represented a concession to Stalin's demands and a recognition of Russia's role in Poland. As in Tehran, so in Yalta, the agreement confirmed the foreign ministers' understanding of November 3, 1943, which gave each liberating power a free hand in the areas it liberated.

The Western leaders knew both Soviet semantics and Soviet intentions. Less than two months *before* the conference on December 28, 1944, Harriman cabled from Moscow that the Communist use of such terms as "friendly" and "independent" government had a totally different meaning from the

Western interpretation. Anyone who "disagrees with Soviet policies is conveniently branded as a 'fascist,'" he warned, recommending a "firm and
definite stand."[11] On January 10, 1945, four weeks *before* the conference
began, he again informed the White House that the Soviet authorities in
eastern Europe used:

> a wide variety of means at their disposal, occupation troops, secret police,
> local Communist parties, labor unions, sympathetic leftist organizations, spon-
> sored cultural societies and economic pressure—to assure the establishment of
> regimes, which maintaining an outward appearance of independence and of
> broad popular support, actually depend for their existence on groups respon-
> sive to all suggestions emanating from the Kremlin. The tactics are endless in
> their variety and are selected to meet the situation in each particular country,
> dependent largely on the extent and strength of the resistance to Soviet pene-
> tration. It is particularly noteworthy that no practical distinction seems to be
> made in this connection between members of the United Nations and ex-
> enemy countries which have been occupied. [12]

On January 3, 1945, some five weeks before the conference, Roosevelt received General John R. Deane's evaluation of Stalin's policies, his warning
about Soviet methods, and his recommendation for a quid pro quo. Deane
headed the American military mission in Moscow, and he wrote on the basis
of long personal observation and experience.[13] Eden himself had no illusion
about Soviet goals, and said so to Stettinius at Malta on February 1, 1945.

In the final analysis, the Yalta agreement on Poland did not mean an
assumption of responsibilities or commitments by the Western Allies, but a
renunciation of responsibilities and commitments they had previously undertaken. The open and formal decisions made at Yalta scrapped Britain's obligations resulting from Article 6 of the Anglo-Polish pact of mutual assistance, still the legal basis for the war relationship between the Polish and
British governments.[14]

The obligations resulting from the Atlantic Charter seem to have been
discarded by Churchill, Roosevelt, and Stalin at Yalta even more brutally
than at Tehran. While at Tehran a secret, informal understanding had been
reached, at Yalta a *formal decision* was taken. The three leaders formally
agree to partition an ally before the conclusion of the war. According to
Article 1 of the Atlantic Charter, the signatories were not to "seek aggrandizement, territorial or other." At Yalta, the British and American delegations
formally recognized Russia's "right" to incorporate half of Poland. According to Article 2, no territorial changes were to take place without the "freely

expressed wishes of the peoples concerned." No provision for any sort of plebiscite was made, and the Polish government was not even consulted. Article 3, which recognized the "right" of all peoples "to choose the form of government under which they will live," was also violated. Both Churchill and Roosevelt agreed to recognize a government for Poland after Stalin rejected all provisions that could have guaranteed its representative character.

The distinction between Poland's eastern territories to be ceded *at once* and Poland's acquisition of the German territories to be decided *at the peace conference* meant that an ally was put in a worse position than an enemy state. In December 1943 Churchill had instructed Eden to tell the Poles that "by taking over and holding firmly the present German territories up to the Oder, they will be rendering service to Europe." One year later, the government-in-exile obtained an official commitment that Great Britain would support Poland in getting German territories up to the Oder River, including Stettin.[15] At Yalta, the British prime minister said that he did not wish "to stuff the Polish goose until it dies of German indigestion."

The last part of the official communiqué, issued after the conference, referred to the Atlantic Charter.[16] This, understandably, brought protests from numerous quarters. "So far as frontiers are concerned, say what you will, the Atlantic Charter was finally repudiated at Yalta. It started as a principle; afterwards became a guide; tomorrow it will leave off being a guide and will become . . . a 'gesture,'"[17] Churchill was told in the House of Commons on February 28, 1945.

As for President Roosevelt, he apparently was ready to go a long way to get things done. According to Churchill, he stated at Yalta that "most . . . [Americans of Polish descent] were generally in favor of the Curzon line." In view of events during the presidential campaign only a few months before— namely, the interventions of the preeminent organization of Americans of Polish descent, the Polish-American Congress, and the president's assurances to its leaders—such a statement, if not quoted by Churchill, would be hard to believe. On March 9, 1945, that is, nine days after the president reported to Congress on the conference, the Polish-American Congress denounced the decisions concerning Poland in a passionate resolution.[18]

Apparently Roosevelt and his advisors entertained doubts at Yalta about the constitutionality of the president's role concerning Poland's boundaries. The Senate's "advice and consent" was lacking. However, Alger Hiss's suggestion eased this difficulty: Subtle changes were inserted in the final text of the agreement. The term "three powers" was replaced by "three heads of government." The term "they agree" was replaced by "they feel." Thus, as Stettinius put it, the agreement was changed from a "governmental commitment to an expression of views in which Roosevelt concurred."[19] The intricate legalistic formula did indeed protect the president at home, but the full brunt of the agreement fell on Poland.

Reporting to their legislative bodies on the conference, neither Churchill nor Roosevelt was in a position to reveal that he had requested, but had to renounce upon Stalin's insistence, all safeguards as to Poland's future. On the contrary, in order to have the Yalta decisions approved, both had to praise them.

Churchill's report took place on February 27.[20] He emphasized that the "Crimea Conference [found] the Allies more closely united than ever before," repeated that he had always considered the Soviet territorial claims in Poland as "just and right," and extolled the "moderation" of the Soviet government. After all, he said, Russia had had Warsaw in 1914, and Stalin himself told him that Lenin had wanted "considerably" more in 1919 than Stalin had obtained at Yalta. In October 1944 Stalin spoke about the deviation of eight to ten kilometers "in either direction" from the 1941 frontier. At Yalta he agreed that these deviations were to be made only at the expense of the USSR "in order that the Poles might have their minds set at rest once and for all and there would be no further discussion about that part of the business."[21]

He emphasized that the acceptance of the territorial decisions was only one *condition* for a strong, independent, homogeneous Poland. The other condition was Poland's "friendship" toward Russia. Commenting on the government to be formed, he played down some aspects and played up others. He blamed the government-in-exile for the emergence of the Lublin regime. For had the Poles from London "accepted" his "faithful counsel" a year before, or even last October, Mikolajczyk could be prime minister in Warsaw "with every assurance of Marshal Stalin's friendship." He spoke extensively about "consultations" that were to precede the formation of a *new* government in Poland and assured the House that certainly *all* democratic parties would take part in them. Commenting on the elections to be held, he emphasized that the British government would ensure "all democratic safeguards."

Then, the prime minister told the House that Polish-Russian friendship had developed in Poland, that Russian armies had been received by the Poles "with great joy," and that there was "none of that terrible business of underground armies being shot by both sides." Stalin and the Soviet leaders proved to be different from what many thought them to be. "Marshal Stalin and the Soviet leaders wish to live in honourable friendship and equality with the Western democracies," he said. He cautiously admitted, though, that the provisions of the Yalta agreement on Poland were vague and could be interpreted in different ways, but he also assured the House that the Soviet government could be trusted. "I know of no government which stands to its obligations, even in its own despite, more solidly than the Russian Soviet government," he stated, and "absolutely" declined to discuss Russia's good faith.

Eden echoed the prime minister's arguments and added his own. He recalled that Great Britain as early as 1919 had favored a Polish frontier roughly similar to that agreed upon at Yalta. He also had unusually harsh words for those who thought that Yalta decisions on Poland violated the Atlantic Charter: "As I listen to some of the speeches, I could not help feeling that some of my Honourable friends, in talking about Poland, had not only Poland in mind, but the fear that Russia, flushed with the magnificent triumphs of its armies, was also dreaming dreams of European domination. This, of course, is the constant theme of German propaganda."[22]

In his address to Congress on March 1, 1945, President Roosevelt expressed satisfaction with the agreement on Poland, adding "we know everybody does not agree with it—obviously."[23] He was careful about the constitutional aspect of his own part in the agreement and observed that the decisions on Poland had been agreed to "by Russia, by Britain and by me." Praising the compromise on Poland's new frontiers, he failed to point out that while the eastern frontier had finally been fixed, western boundaries were to be decided later. He was ambiguous on the subject of the Polish government. Once he stated that "steps were taken at Yalta to recognize the existing provisional government in Poland on a broader democratic basis." Then he spoke about a "new" government to be recognized in the future by the United States.

He was expansive in his optimistic comments on the overall results of the conference:

> I think the Crimean conference was a successful effort by the three leading nations to find a common ground for peace. . . . It spells and it ought to spell, the end of the new system of unilateral action, exclusive alliance, and sphere of influence, and balances of power, and all the other expedients which have

been tried for centuries and have always failed. . . . Never before have the major allies been more closely united, not only in their war aims but also in their peace aims. And they are determined to continue to be united, to be united with each other, and with all peace-loving nations, so that the ideal of lasting peace will become a reality.

He concluded by saying that he had achieved with the Soviet leaders a "unity of thought" more important than the "agreement of words."

The president's aides and assistants who participated in the Yalta conferences echoed his enthusiasm. Upon his return to Washington, Stettinius passed the word that the conference provided "every evidence of the Russian desire to cooperate along all lines with the United States."[24] He advanced a theory that the "Soviet Union made greater concessions at Yalta to the United States and Great Britain than were made to the Soviets." He considered the agreement on Poland "a concession by Marshal Stalin to the Prime Minister and the President." As a matter of fact, he revealed, some members of the president's staff believed Stalin had "difficulties" with the Politburo. "Certain members of the Politburo may well have taken the line that the Soviet Union had been virtually sold out at Yalta."[25] He described the conference as a "diplomatic triumph" for the Western democracies.

Even more outspoken in his praise was Hopkins:

We really believed in our hearts that this was the dawn of the new day we had all been praying for and talking about so many years. We were absolutely certain that we had won the first great victory of the peace, and by "we" I mean all of us, the whole civilized human race. The Russians had proved that they could be reasonable and foreseeing and there wasn't any doubt in the minds of the President or any of us that we could live with them and get along with them peacefully, for as far into the future as any of us could imagine.[26]

He saw in Stalin a powerful pillar of peace and feared what might happen to the Soviet-American friendship should Stalin disappear.

It has often been argued that at Yalta the Western leaders were helpless as far as eastern Europe was concerned because the Red Army was there, and Stalin could have had his way, agreement, or no agreement. Stettinius, for one, put forth such a proposition.[27] However, at Yalta, the Western leaders not only failed to secure Poland's rights, rightly or wrongly feeling unable to do so, but they also indirectly, though not less effectively, *sanctioned* the Soviet position in Poland. Upon Stalin's insistence, they agreed to replace firm and precise safeguards for Poland's independence with purposefully obscure or meaningless formulas. In doing that, they contributed to general confusion concerning the nature of the Communist activities in Poland—a fact of great importance, as the future would show.

The concessions were apparently made in the hope that Stalin, impressed by their extent, might somehow feel obligated not to disappoint the Western leaders. This was particularly true in the case of Roosevelt. When William Bullitt warned him about Stalin's goals, the president answered:

> Bill, I don't dispute your facts, they are accurate. I don't dispute the logic in your reasoning. I just have a hunch that Stalin is not that kind of man. Harry [Hopkins] says he's not and that he doesn't want anything but security for his country, and I think that if I give him everything I possibly can and ask nothing from him in return, noblesse oblige, he won't try to annex anything and will work with me for a world of democracy and peace.[28]

While these opinions and evaluations were being expressed, a grim reality was setting in in the Soviet-controlled areas.

When Churchill was reporting on the Yalta conference to the House of Commons, the Foreign Office already possessed authoritative information that the "Lublin Poles were carrying out measures of liquidation on a large scale in order to terrorize and destroy their opponents. These measures were taken with the connivance, and indeed the active help, of the Russians."[29] Already, by March 5, the Harriman–Clark-Kerr–Molotov commission found itself in a "complete deadlock" due to the Soviet "interpretation" of the Yalta agreement. As early as the beginning of April, Eden came to the conclusion that the commission had become a "farce" and considered a withdrawal of the British member.[30] Then, on April 6, Harriman sent the following message from Moscow to the president:

> It may be difficult for us to believe, but it still may be true that Stalin and Molotov considered at Yalta that by our willingness to accept a general wording of the declaration on Poland and liberated Europe, by our recognition of the need of the Red Army for security behind its lines, and of the predominant interest of Russia in Poland as a friendly neighbor and as a corridor to Germany, we understood and were ready to accept Soviet policies already known to us.[31]

When the message reached the White House, Roosevelt had less than one week to live. He died of cerebral hemorrhage on April 12, 1945, two months after the Yalta conference.

NOTES

1. "Victory and the Threshold of Peace," in *The Public Papers and Addresses of Franklin D. Roosevelt*, 13:498.

2. *The Conferences at Malta and Yalta, 1945*, 1.

3. Stettinius, *Roosevelt and the Russians*, 90–91, 304–5.

4. See the memorandum of the Joint Chiefs of Staff to the President dated January 23, 1945. *The Conferences at Malta and Yalta, 1945*, 396–400; also US Congress, Senate, *Military Situation in the Far East: Hearings before the Committee on Armed Services and the Committee on Foreign Relations*, 82nd Cong., 1st. Sess., 5 parts (Washington, DC: US Government Printing Office, 1951), pt. 1, 562.

5. Leahy, *I Was There*, 317; see also Pulestone, *The Influence of Force in Foreign Relations*, 166–68.

6. Supra, 466–67, 479–80.

7. *Congressional Record*, vol. 91, pt. 2, 1945, 1621.

8. *The Conferences at Malta and Yalta, 1945*, 766–71, 660–67, respectively.

9. See *5 Parliamentary Debates*, Commons, 408 (1945), 1503.

10. Leahy, *I Was There*, 315–16.

11. The *Conferences at Malta and Yalta, 1945*, 65.

12. Ibid., 450–51.

13. For the text of Deane's report, see ibid., 447–49.

14. For the provisions of the pact, see supra, 359–70. For the incompatibility of the Yalta decisions and the Polish-British pact, see also Petherick's statement in the House of Commons on February 28, 1945, *5 Parliamentary Debates*, Commons, 408 (1945), 1421–28.

15. Supra, 558–59.

16. *The Conferences at Malta and Yalta, 1945*, 975.

17. *5 Parliamentary Debates*, Commons, 408 (1945), 1492.

18. For the text of the resolution, see *Congressional Record*, vol. 91, pt. 2, 1945, A1702–03.

19. Stettinius, *Roosevelt and the Russians*, 270–71.

20. For the three-day House of Commons debate on the Yalta agreement, see *5 Parliamentary Debates*, Commons, 408 (1945), cols. 1267–1345, 1416–1516, 1579–1672.

21. The "deviations" represented less than 2 percent of the area acquired by the Soviet Union.

22. Ibid., col. 1427.

23. For the full text of Roosevelt's report on the Yalta conference, see *Congressional Record*, vol. 91, pt. 2, 1945, 1618–22.

24. Millis, *Forrestal Diaries*, 44.

25. Stettinius, *Roosevelt and the Russians*, 295, 303, 309–310, respectively.

26. Sherwood, *Roosevelt and Hopkins*, 870.

27. Stettinius, *Roosevelt and the Russians*, 301.

28. William C. Bullitt, "How We Won the War and Lost the Peace," *Life*, August 30, 1948, 94.

29. Woodward, *British Foreign Policy in the Second World War*, 501.

30. Eden, *The Reckoning*, 606; 608.

31. Millis, *Forrestal Diaries*, 40.

Epilogue

Following the Yalta decisions, the fate of the Polish nation was left at the mercy of the Soviet government, which, at that time, meant Stalin. He was fully aware of the background of the decisions reached at Yalta—still unknown to the general public—and he certainly realized the extent of his political power. And he was deadly determined to use that power not only in Poland but in all areas liberated by the Red Army. It is hard to imagine that Roosevelt and Churchill did not expect the Soviet Union to pursue its policies unilaterally in the liberated countries.

Both the Polish government-in-exile and the Underground were ignored at Yalta. Thereafter, the Polish government in London, headed by Tomasz Arciszewski, became not much more than a political shadow insofar as the policies of the three Great Powers were concerned. As for the Underground in the homeland, the Yalta agreement signaled its physical extinction. There Stalin had his Red Army, Soviet secret police, and Polish sycophants renamed as the provisional government of Poland.

The collapse of the Warsaw Uprising constituted a terrible blow to the Poles, resulting in a national sense of despair and helplessness. The resignation of Mikolajczyk was another political setback for Poland, because it weakened still further the country's constitutional government. The resignation also served to weaken the Underground, which had depended on and was loyal to the government-in-exile. Thereafter Polish public opinion and leadership at home and abroad became divided, causing two politically contradictory orientations to emerge. One supported the government-in-exile and its intransigence, the other viewed Mikolajczyk as the only Pole capable of influencing the future of the country.

Having learned of the Yalta declaration, the leaders of the Underground decided to preserve its structure and continue their activities. Unaware of the real meaning of the American-British-Soviet decisions on Poland, they believed their activities would work to strengthen the government-in-exile, provide leadership for a disoriented nation, enable the Underground to participate in forming a new, democratic government, and lead them out of a deadly impasse.

As for the Home Army soldiers, they found themselves trapped. In the areas still controlled by Germany, they faced an enemy they had been fighting since 1939. But once the Red Army advanced and the Home Army soldiers either revealed themselves or were discovered, they were arrested, deported, or shot by either the Soviet secret police or the Polish Communist-controlled regime. There was no way out. Subsequently, on January 19, 1945, on the eve of the Yalta conference, General Bor-Komorowski's successor, General Leopold Okulicki, dissolved the Home Army and released its soldiers from their oaths. Some fifty thousand of them laid down their arms; all were arrested.

Two months later, on February 21, the Underground political council, headed by a Socialist leader, Kazimierz Puzak, passed a resolution to be communicated to the participants at the Yalta conference. The opening paragraph read:

> The Council of National Unity declares that the decisions of the Crimean Conference, made without the participation and agreement of the Republic of Poland, impose on Poland the burden of new, extreme and inequitable sacrifices. The Council of National Unity protests in strongest terms the one-sided decisions of the Conference, although it finds itself compelled to submit to these decisions prompted by its desire to see in them the only avenue—under the present circumstances—of salvaging Poland's independence, of preventing further destruction of the nation, and of building the foundations permitting the mobilization of national strengths and the conduct of future, independent Polish policies.

In the final paragraph of the resolution, the council announced its readiness to take part in negotiations designed to lead to the creation of the Provisional Government of National Unity—as prescribed by the Yalta decisions.

Approximately two weeks later, Government Delegate Jankowski and General Okulicki received through secret channels some messages from Soviet colonel Pimenov proposing an exploratory meeting. Pimenov alleged to be acting on behalf of Colonel General Ivanov, who represented the Soviet high command. Although suspecting a trap, both Poles also realized that their rejection of the proposal would lay them open to accusations of hostility toward the Soviet Union. They therefore responded cautiously, sending an intermediary. He returned safely and rather impressed. The colonel had sounded genuine, and the proposed conversations with General Ivanov seemed promising. The intermediary also transmitted Colonel Pimenov's request that the entire council, together with General Okulicki, attend the negotiations; this would make the discussions "formal." The Poles complied, only to be kidnapped, trundled onto an airplane, and flown to Moscow, where they were incarcerated in the notorious Lublyanka prison.

That the Underground's political and administrative structure did not disintegrate after the imprisonment of its leaders was due in no small measure to Stefan Korbonski, a man of indomitable courage and unusual organizational abilities. One of the Peasant party's leaders, Korbonski had been active in the Underground since 1939. In 1941 he became head of the Directorate of Civil Resistance, and in this capacity issued a code of patriotic behavior and organized secret courts that warned, punished, or executed collaborators, traitors, and criminals—especially those who blackmailed or denounced Jews in hiding to the German police. Throughout the war, Korbonski maintained constant covert radio contact with the government-in-exile—by far one of his most dangerous tasks. Following the arrests of the council leaders, he quickly reorganized the council and replenished it with new representatives designated by their respective political parties.

Meanwhile, in London, Churchill and Eden were pressuring Mikolajczyk to take part in the formation of a "new" government, while in Moscow, Harriman and Clark-Kerr urged Molotov to recognize Mikolajczyk and some of his followers as "democratic" and "friendly to the Soviet Union." Subsequently, on April 16, 1945, Mikolajczyk publicly declared his unequivocal acceptance of the Yalta decisions on Poland.

Six days later, the Soviet government signed a formal treaty of friendship, mutual assistance, and postwar cooperation with Poland's existing, Communist-controlled government—clearly as a signal that, with or without "reorganization," he considered his men in Poland *the* government. By then Eden had come to realize that the ambassadorial commission had become a "farce."

The official negotiations on the creation of the Provisional Government of National Unity had been scheduled for June 17, 1945. They were to take place in Moscow and be formally sponsored by the tripartite ambassadorial commission. Mikolajczyk decided to go.

Then, on June 14—the eve of Mikolajczyk's departure from London—the Soviet press announced the upcoming trial of sixteen Polish leaders imprisoned in Moscow. Mikolajczyk began to vacillate. In a dramatic conversation with Churchill on June 16, the British leader urged Mikolajczyk to go, assuring the Pole of his personal safety, of the support by Harriman and Clark-Kerr, and of the full backing of the British and the American governments. He appealed to Mikolajczyk's courage and patriotism, saying that only he, Mikolajczyk, could provide effective leadership for patriotic Poles. Churchill argued that once Mikolajczyk joined the "new" government, other genuinely democratic parties and individuals would have a chance, and the "Lublin Poles" might lose their monopoly of power. Free elections would then demonstrate the strength of the democratic elements in Poland. Mikolajczyk decided to go.

The Moscow negotiations lasted four days. Neither the American nor the British ambassador played a significant role, and on June 21, 1945, the "new" government was formally created. The Communist-controlled bloc received seventeen portfolios—state security included—while Mikolajczyk and his associates received five portfolios and the title of vice premier for Mikolajczyk. That was the way the Yalta decisions had been implemented.

Simultaneously, only a few blocks away, the highly publicized trial of the leaders of the Polish Underground proceeded. Charged with illegal activities, hostility toward the Soviet Union, collaboration with the Germans, and sabotage and diversion carried out against the Red Army, they were all found guilty on June 21. General Okulicki was sentenced to ten years in prison; Jankowski, eight. The others were given sentences ranging from four months to five years.

The Polish Underground had become by then a tragic anachronism and was dissolved in a pathetic declaration by its political council on July 1, 1945. Four days later the American and British governments withdrew their recognition of the government-in-exile and declared formal recognition of the new government.

An intense campaign ensued, encouraging expatriate Poles—especially Polish soldiers who had fought in the western campaigns—to return to Poland. The campaign failed. Some 150,000 Poles refused to return to a captive country. Likewise, the government-in-exile refused to disband.

The Potsdam Conference followed. As at Yalta, the American and British delegations insisted on reducing Poland's territorial acquisitions at Germany's expense. Stalin and the Polish delegation that was invited to present its own demands supported them. As at Yalta, Stalin's will prevailed.

In the new government of Poland, neither Mikolajczyk nor any of his associates had any power. Arrests, trials, and executions were rampant. Desperate underground groups emerged, only to be pitilessly crushed. Finally, two years after the conclusion of the Yalta agreement, the Communist leadership declared the country ready for general elections, scheduling them for January 19, 1947. The Peasant party and associated groups—all led by Mikolajczyk—challenged the Communist-led bloc of various political organizations and presented their own candidates.

The elections, more than any other single event, showed the futility and tragedy caused by the Yalta decisions. Believing the American and British commitments to "free and unfettered elections" would somehow be enforced, the surviving democratic leaders, as well as the general population, openly campaigned against the Communist slate. Opponents of Communist rule, who otherwise would probably have been silent, not only declared their political sympathies but became outspoken. This only served to help the Communist security organs. Arrests, kidnappings, assaults, murder, and terror followed. Mikolajczyk appealed to the British, American, and Soviet ambassadors, providing them with proof of the abuses and the names of those arrested or murdered. The British and American ambassadors filed protests in Moscow, but these were rejected. They were told that the Soviet government had no jurisdiction in Poland, a sovereign state. The ambassadors then protested to the Polish Communist leaders, only to hear that their inquiries constituted interference in Poland's domestic affairs. Because of his maintenance of contacts with and complaints to foreigners, Mikolajczyk was labeled a traitor and a foreign agent.

On the day of elections, the democratic groups succeeded in gathering information on how the votes were being cast. They had no doubt that more than 60 percent of the vote was being cast for the democratic candidates. The official returns told another story: out of 444 seats, the democratic bloc was entitled to 28. The returns had been falsified.

Once the elections were over, a ruthless, nationwide campaign was perpetrated against Mikolajczyk and his associates. They were branded as Fascists, agents of imperialist capitalism, enemies of democracy and progress. It soon became evident that, as in other Soviet-dominated countries, show trials were in the making. Mikolajczyk learned of his imminent arrest in October 1947, and he hastily fled in secret, soon to be followed by the former head of the Underground, Korbonski, and a few others. Those who stayed behind or were foiled in their attempts to flee were either arrested or had to reconcile themselves with the Communist monopoly of power.

One year after his escape from Poland, Mikolajczyk published a book about his experiences and ultimate defeat. It was entitled *The Rape of Poland*. Shortly thereafter, the first US ambassador to Poland, Arthur Bliss Lane, chronicled his own experiences and firsthand accounts. He entitled his work *I Saw Poland Betrayed*.

Bibliography

I. DOCUMENTS

1. American

Auswärtiges Amt Archives. Microfilm. National Archives, Washington, DC.

Congressional Record, The Proceedings and Debates of the Congress of the United States. Senate; House of Representatives. Washington, DC: US Government Printing Office, 1917–1945.

Department of State Archives. National Archives. Washington, DC.

Department of State. *Foreign Relations of the United States: Diplomatic Papers, 1931–1939*. Washington, DC: US Government Printing Office, 1931–1939.

———. *Foreign Relations of the United States: Diplomatic Papers, 1941*. 7 vols. Washington, DC: US Government Printing Office, 1941.

———. *Foreign Relations of the United States: Diplomatic Papers. The Conferences of Berlin (The Potsdam Conference), 1945*. Washington, DC: US Government Printing Office, 1960.

———. *Foreign Relations of the United States: Diplomatic Papers. The Conferences at Cairo and Tehran, 1943*. Washington, DC: US Government Printing Office, 1961.

———. *Foreign Relations of the United States: Diplomatic Papers. The Conferences at Malta and Yalta, 1945*. Washington, DC: US Government Printing Office, 1955.

———. *Nazi-Soviet Relations 1939–1941*. Edited by James Sontag and James Stuart Beddie. Documents from the archives of the German Foreign Office. Washington, DC: US Government Printing Office, 1948.

———. *Papers Relating to the Foreign Relations of the United States, The Lansing Papers, 1914–1920*. 2 vols. Washington, DC: US Government Printing Office, 1939.

———. *Papers Relating to the Foreign Relations of the United States: The Paris Peace Conference, 1919*. 13 vols. Washington, DC: US Government Printing Office, 1943.

Goodrich, Leland M., and Marie J. Carrol, eds. *Documents on American Foreign Relations*. Norwood, MA: Princeton University Press, published annually.

Rosenman, Samuel I., compiler. *The Public Papers and Addresses of Franklin D. Roosevelt*. 13 vols. New York: Harper & Brothers Publishers, 1950.

Select Committee on Communist Aggression (House of Representatives). *Communist Take-Over and Occupation of Poland.* Special Report no. 1. 83rd Congress, 2nd Session, H. Res. 346 and H. Res. 438. Washington, DC: US Government Printing Office, 1954.

———. *Five Hundred Leading Communists.* 80th Congress, 2nd Session. Washington, DC: US Government Printing Office, 1948.

———. *Katyn Forest Massacre.* Hearings before the Select Committee to Conduct an Investigation on the Facts, Evidence and Circumstances of the Katyn Forest Massacre. 82nd Congress, 2nd Session. 7 parts. Washington, DC: US Government Printing Office, 1952.

———. *Polish Documents, Report of the Select Committee on Communist Aggression, Appendix to Committee Report on Communist Take-Over and Occupation of Poland.* 83rd Congress, 2nd Session. Under Authority of H. Res. 346 and H. Res. 438. Washington, DC: US Government Printing Office, 1954.

Nuremberg Trials

Office of the United States Chief of Counsel for Prosecution of Axis Criminality. *Nazi Conspiracy and Aggression.* 10 vols. Washington, DC: US Government Printing Office, 1947.

The Trial of the Major War Criminals before the International Military Tribunal. 42 vols. Nuremberg: 1947–1949.

Trials of War Criminals before the Nuremberg Military Tribunals under Control Council Law No. 10. 15 vols. Washington, DC: US Government Printing Office, 1950.

2. British

Foreign Office Records. London: Public Records Office.

Great Britain, Foreign Office. *British and Foreign State Papers, 1919.* Vol. 112. London: H. M. Stationery Office, 1923.

———. *Documents Concerning German-Polish Relations and the Outbreak of Hostilities between Great Britain and Germany on September 3, 1939.* New York: Farrar & Rinehart, 1939. (*The British Blue Book.*)

Parliamentary Debates. House of Lords; House of Commons. London: H. M. Stationery Office, 1917–1945.

Wheeler-Bennett, J. *Documents on International Affairs.* London: Institute of International Affairs, 1930–1939.

Woodward, Sir Ernest Llewellyn. *British Foreign Policy in the Second World War.* London: H. M. Stationery Office, 1962.

Woodward, Sir Ernest Llewellyn, and Rohan Butler, eds. *Documents on British Foreign Policy, 1919–1939.* London: H. M. Stationery Office, 1946–1955. 1st series, 5 vols. for the year 1919; 2nd series, 7 vols. for the years 1930–1939; 3rd series, 9 vols. for the years 1938–1939.

3. French

Assemblée Nationale. *Les événements survenus en France de 1933 à 1945.* 9 vols. Paris: Imprimerie Nationale, 1974–1951.

Documents Diplomatiques Français, 1932–1939. Paris: Imprimerie Nationale, 1963–1966. I-ère Série (1932–1935). Tome I; 2-ème Série (1936–1939). Tomes 1–3.

Journal Officiel de la République Française. Débats Parlementaires. Chambre des Deputés. Paris: Imprimerie Nationale, 194?.

Ministère des affaires ètrangères. *Le Livre jaune francais, Documents Diplomatiques, 1938–1939.* Paris: Imprimerie Nationale, 1939.

4. German

Department of State. *Documents on German Foreign Policy, 1918–1945.* Series D, vols. 2–7. Washington, DC: US Government Printing Office, 1957.

———. *Documents on German Foreign Policy, 1919–1945.* Series C, vols. 1–5. Washington, DC: US Government Printing Office, 1958.

German Foreign Office. *Documents on the Events Preceding the Outbreak of the War.* New York: German Library of Information, 1940. (*The German White Book.*)

German Foreign Ministry. Microfilmed documents. Deposited in the National Archives, Washington, DC.

Titles of Serials:
1723 Politische Abteilung V: Danzig, Politische Beziehungen zu Polen.
1823H Politische Abteilung V: Polen, Politische Beziehungen zu Deutschland.
2860 Büro des Reichsministers: Russland.
2945 Büro des Reichsministers: Polen.
4556 Büro des Staatssekretärs: Russland-Randstaaten.
4562H Büro des Staatssekretärs: Russland.
4569 Büro des Staatssekretärs: Polnische Angelegenheiten.
6609H Geheimakten 1920–36: Russland, Politische Beziehungen Russland-Deutschland.
9183 Geheimakten 1920–36: Polen, Politische Beziehungen Polen-Deutschland.
K179 Geheimakten 1920–36: Polen, Politische Beziehungen Polen-Russland.
K290 Geheimakten 1920–36: Russland, Sicherheitspakt: Nichtangriffspaktverhandlungen mit Frankreich, Polen and anderen Staaten (Handakten des Direktors).
1339 Politische Beziehungen zwischen Polen and der Tschechoslowakei, von 15 Marz 1936, bis 5 Okt., 1938.
147 Polen, von 1 Jan., 1936, bis 31 Dec., 1938.

5. Polish

Archiwum Akt Nowych, Zespoly Ministerstwa Spraw Zagranicznych (New Records' Archives, Folders of the Ministry of Foreign Affairs). Warsaw: National Archives.

Zespoly Ministerstwa Spraw Zagranicznych (MSZ)
Zespoly Placówek
Zespoly Prezydium Rady Ministrów

General Sikorski Historical Institute. *Documents on Polish-Soviet Relations, 1939–1945.* 2 vols. London: Heinemann, 1961–1967.

Horak, Stephen, ed. *Poland's International Affairs, 1919–1960; A Calendar of Treaties, Agreements Conventions, and International Acts with Annotations, References, and Selections from Documents Texts of Treaties.* Bloomington, IN: Indiana University Press, 1964.

Jedrzejewicz, Waclaw, ed. *Poland in the British Parliament, 1939–1945. Documentary Material Relating to the Cause of Poland During War II.* 3 vols. New York: Joseph Pilsudski Institute of America, 1946–1962.

Komisia Historyczna Polskiego Sztabu Głównego w Londynie. *Polskie Sily Zbrojne w Drugiej Wojnie Swiatowej* (The Polish Armed Forces in the Second World War). 3 vols. London: General Sjkorski Historical Institute, 1950–1951.

Kumaniecki, Kazimierz W. *Odbudowa Państwości Polskiej, Najwazniejsze Dokumenty, 1912–Styczeń, 1924* (*The Reconstruction of Polish Statehood, Basic Documents, 1912–January 1924*). Kraków: Ksiegarnia Powszechna, 1924.

Memorandum on the North and South-Eastern Frontiers of Restored Poland. Paris: Polish Office of Political Publications, 1919.

Polish-Soviet Relations, 1918–1943, Official Documents. Washington, DC: Polish Embassy, 1944.

Polska Akademia Nauk. *Materialy Archiwalne do Stosunków Polsko-Radzieckic* (Archive Materials on Polish-Soviet Relations). Warsaw: Ksiazka i Wiedza, 1957.

———. *Dokumenty i Materialy do Historii Stosunków Polsko-Radzieckich* (Documents and Materials on Polish-Soviet Relations). Warsaw: Ksiazka i Wiedza, 1961.

Polish Diplomatic Archives. *Stosunki Polsko-Sowieckie* (Polish-Soviet Relations). 2 vols. London: Ministry of Foreign Affairs, 1946.

Polish Embassy (London). *Poland, Germany and European Peace: Official Documents, 1944–1948.* London, 1948.

Polish Ministry of Foreign Affairs. *Documents on the Hostile Policy of the United States Government towards People's Poland.* Warsaw, 1953.

Polish Ministry of Information. *Concise Statistical Year-Book of Poland, September 1939–June 1941.* Glasgow: The University Press, 1941.

———. *The Black Book of Poland.* New York: G. P. Putnam's Sons, 1942.

Protocols of the Polish-British General Staffs Conferences in Warsaw, May 1939. London: General Sikorski Historical Institute, 1958.

Protocols of the Polish-French General Staffs Conferences in Paris, May 1939. London: General Sikorski Historical Institute, 1958.

Republic of Poland. *Official Documents Concerning Polish-German and Polish-Soviet Relations, 1933–1939. The Polish White Book.* London: Hutchinson & Co., 1940.

6. Russian/Soviet

Browder, Robert P., and Alexander F. Kerensky. *The Russian Provisional Government, 1917. Documents.* 3 vols. Stanford, CA: Stanford University Press, 1961.

Degras, Jane, ed. *Soviet Documents on Foreign Policy, 1917–1941.* 3 vols. London: Oxford University Press, 1951–1953.

———. *The Communist International 1919–1943: Documents.* 2 vols. London: Oxford University Press, 1956, 1960.

Embassy of the Union of Soviet Socialist Republics. *Soviet War Documents: Addresses, Notes, Orders of the Day, Statements.* Washington, DC: Soviet Embassy, 1943.

Golder, Frank A., ed. *Documents of Russian History, 1914–1917.* Gloucester, MA: Peter Smith, 1964.

Ministry of Foreign Affairs of the USSR. *Correspondence between the Chairman of the Council of Ministers of the USSR and the Presidents of the USA and the Prime Ministers of Great Britain during the Great Patriotic War of 1941–1945.* 2 vols. Moscow: Foreign Languages Publishing House, 1957.

———. *Documents and Materials Relating to the Eve of the Second World War, Dirksen Papers.* 2 vols. Moscow: Foreign Languages Publishing House, 1948.

Schapiro, Leonard, ed. *Soviet Treaty Series.* 2 vols. Washington, DC: Georgetown University Press, 1950.

II. SEMIPUBLIC DOCUMENTARY PUBLICATIONS, MEMOIRS, BOOKS

Alexander, Frederick. *From Paris to Locarno and After*. London: J. M. Dent and Sons, Ltd., 1928.

Anders, Wladyslaw. *An Army in Exile: The Story of the Second Polish Corps*. London: The Macmillan Co., 1949.

Armengaud, Paul F. *Batailles politigues et militaires sur l'Europe: Témoignages (1932–1940)*. Paris: Éditions du Myrte, 1948.

Avon, Earl of. *The Eden Memoirs: Facing the Dictators*. London: Cassell & Co., 1962.

Baczkowski, Wlodzimierz. *Towards an Understanding of Russia: A Study in Policy and Strategy*. Jerusalem: Hamadpis Liphshitz Press, 1947.

Bailey, Thomas A. *Woodrow Wilson and the Lost Peace*. New York: The Macmillan Co., 1944.

Baker, Ray S. *Woodrow Wilson and World Settlement*. 3 vols. Garden City, NY: Doubleday, Page and Co., 1922.

Balcerak, Wieslaw. *Polityka Zagraniczna Polski w Dobie Locarna* (Polish foreign policy during the era of Locarno). Warsaw: Wydawnictwo Polskiej Akademii Nauk, 1967.

Baldwin, Hanson W. *Great Mistakes of the War*. New York: Harper & Brothers, 1949.

Ball, Adrian. *The Last Day of the Old World: 3rd September 1939*. London: Frederick Muller, 1963.

Bartoszewski, Wladyslaw. *The Samaritans*. New York: Twayne Publishers, 1966.

Basiński, Euzebiusz. *Stosunki Polsko-Radziecki w Latach 1917–1945. Dokumenty i Materialy* (Polish-Soviet relations, 1917–1945). Warsaw: Ksiazka i Wiedza, 1967.

Basler, Werner. *Deutschland Annexions Politik in Polen und in Baltikum, 1914–1918*. Berlin: Ruetter & Loening, 1962.

Batowski, Henryk. *Agonia Pokoju i Poczatek Wojny* (*The Agony of Peace and the Beginning of War*). Poznan: Wydawnictwo Poznanskie, 1969.

Baumont, Maurice. *La faillite de la paix (1918–1939)*. 2 vols. Paris: Presses Universitaires de France, 1951.

Beaufre, André. *Le drame de 1940*. Paris: Librairie Plon, 1955.

Beck, Joseph. *Dernier rapport. Politique polonaise, 1926–1939*. Neuchatel: Éditions de la Baconnière, 1951.

Beitzell, Robert. *The Uneasy Alliance: America Britain, and Russia*. New York: Knopf, 1973.

Beneš, Edward. *Memoirs*. London: Allen & Unwin, 1954.

Beneš, Vojta. *The Mission of a Small Nation*. Chicago: Czechoslovak National Council of America, 1941.

Benoist-Mechin, Jacques. *Histoire de l'armée allemande depuis l'armistice*. Paris: Michel, 1936.

Berber, Friedrich, ed. *Europaeische Politik, 1933–1938: Im Spiegel der Prager Akten*. Band VIII. Essen: Essener Verlagsanstalt, 1942.

Bethell, Nicholas. *The War Hitler Won: The Fall of Poland, September 1939*. New York: Holt, Rinehart and Winston, 1973.

Bielecki, Tadeusz. *W Szkole Dmowskiego. Szkice i Wspomnienia* (*In Dmowski's School: Essays and Souvenirs*). London: Polska Fundacja Kulturalna, 1968.

Bierut, B., and J. Cyrankiewicz. *Podstawy Ideologiczne PZPR* (*The Ideological Foundations of the Polish United Workers' Party*). Warsaw: Ksiaka i Wiedza, 1952.

Bilmanis, Alfred. *Baltic Essays*. Washington, DC: Latvian Legation, 1945.

Bluhm, Georg. *Die Oder-Neisse Linie in der deutschen Aussenpolitik.* Freiburg im Breisgau, 1963.

Bolshaya Sovietskaya Enceeklopedya 1940. Vol. 46. Moscow: Gosudarstviennyi Institut, 1940.

Bonnet, Georges. *Défense de la paix.* 2 vols. Geneva: Les Éditions du Cheval aile, 1946–1948.

———. *Le Quai d'Orsay sous trois républiques, 1870–1961.* Paris: Librairie Arthème Fayard, 1961.

Bor-Komorowski, T. *The Secret Army.* New York: The Macmillan Co., 1951.

Borkiewicz, Adam. *Powstanie Warszawskie, 1944 (Warsaw Uprising, 1944).* Warsaw: "Pax," 1964.

Bregman, Alexander. *Najlepszy Sojusznik Hitlera (Hitler's Best Ally).* London: Orbis, 1958.

———. *La Politique de la Pologne dans la Societé des Nations.* Paris: Librairie Felix Alcan, 1952.

Bretton, Henry L. *Stresemann and the Revision of Versailles.* Stanford, CA: Stanford University Press, 1953.

Breyer, Richard. *Das Deutsche Reich und Polen 1932–1937: Aussenpolitik und Volksgruppenfragen.* Würzburg: Holzner Verlag, 1955.

Briault, Édouard. *La Paix de la France, Les Traités de 1918–1921.* Paris: Librairie du Revueil Sirey, 1937.

Broszat, Martin. *200 Jahre deutsche Polenpolitik.* Munich: Ehrenwirth Verlag, 1965.

Browder, Robert P., and Alexander Kerensky. *The Russian Provisional Government 1917.* Documents. Stanford, CA: Stanford University Press, 1961.

Brzezinski, Zbigniew K. *The Soviet Bloc: Unity and Conflict.* Cambridge, MA: Harvard University Press, 1960.

Buchanan, Sir George. *My Mission to Russia.* 2 vols. London: Cassell & Co., 1923.

Budurowycz, Bohdan B. *Polish-Soviet Relations, 1932–1939.* New York: Columbia University Press, 1963.

Buell, Raymond L. *Poland, Key to Europe.* New York: Knopf, 1939.

Bullitt, William G. *The Great Globe Itself.* New York: C. Scribner's Sons, 1946.

Bülow, Prince Bernhard von. *Memoirs of Prince Bülow.* 3 vols. Boston: Little, Brown & Co., 1932–1936.

Burian von Rajecz, Graf Stephan. *Austria in Dissolution.* London: E. Benn, 1925.

Butler, J. R. M. *September 1939–June 1941.* Vol. 2 of *History of the Second World War. United Kingdom Military Series. Grand Strategy.* London: H. M. Stationery Office, 1957.

Byrnes, James F. *Speaking Frankly.* New York: Harper & Brothers, Publishers, 1947.

Cadogan, Sir Alexander. *The Diaries of Sir Alexander Cadogan, 1938–1945.* Edited by David Dilks. London: Cassell & Co., 1971.

Callwell, Major General Sir C. E. *Field-Marshal Sir Wilson, His Life and Diaries.* 2 vols. New York: C. Scribner's Sons, 1927.

Cameron, Elizabeth Ripley. *Prologue to Appeasement. A Study in French Foreign Policy.* Washington, DC: American Council of Public Affairs, 1942.

Cannistraro, Philip F., Edward D. Wynot, and Theodor P. Kovaleff, eds. *Poland and the Coming of the Second World War: The Diplomatic Papers of A. J. Drexel Biddle, Jr., US Ambassador to Poland, 1937–1939.* Columbus, OH: Ohio State University Press, 1975.

Carr, Edward H. *The Bolshevik Revolution, 1917–1923.* 3 vols. New York: The Macmillan Co., 1953.

———. *Conditions of Peace.* London: The Macmillan Co., 1942.

———. *German-Soviet Relations between the Two World Wars, 1919–1939.* Baltimore, MD: Johns Hopkins University Press, 1951.

Castellan, George. *Le Réarmament clandestin du Reich, 1930–1935*. Paris: Librairie Plon, 1954.

Chamberlain, Neville. *In Search of Peace*. New York: G. P. Putnam's Sons, 1939.

Chamberlin, William Henry. *America's Second Crusade*. Chicago: Henry Regnery Co., 1950.

Chudek, Józef, ed. *Wrześniowy Kryzys Czechoslowacki 1938r. w Raportach Ambasadora Lipskiego* (*Czechoslovak Crisis of September 1938 in Ambassador Lipski's Reports*). Warsaw: Polski Instytut Spraw Miedzynarodowych, 1958.

Churchill, Winston S. *The Aftermath*. New York: Charles Scribner's Sons, 1929.

———. *Closing the Ring*. Boston: Houghton Mifflin Co., 1951.

———. *The Gathering Storm*. Boston: Houghton Mifflin Co., 1948.

———. *The Grand Alliance*. Boston: Houghton Mifflin Co., 1951.

———. *The Great War*. 3 vols. London: G. Newness, Ltd., 1933–1934.

———. *The Hinge of Fate*. Boston: Houghton Mifflin Co., 1950.

———. *Their Finest Hour*. Boston: Houghton Mifflin Co., 1949.

———. *Triumph and Tragedy*. Boston: Houghton Mifflin Co., 1953.

Cialowicz, Jan. *Polsko-Francuski Sojusz Wojskowy 1921–1939* (*Franco-Polish Military Alliance, 1921–1939*). Warsaw: Państowe Wydawnictwo Naukowe,1970.

Ciano, Conte Galeazzo. *The Ciano Diaries 1939–1943*. Garden City, NY: Doubleday & Co., 1946.

———. *Ciano's Hidden Diary, 1937–1938*. New York: E. P. Dutton & Co., 1953.

Ciechanowski, Jan. *Defeat in Victory*. Garden City, NY: Doubleday & Co., 1947.

Ciechanowski, Jan M. *Powstanie Warszawskie* (*Warsaw Uprising*). London: Odnowa, 1971.

Cienciala, Anna M. *Poland and the Western Powers, 1938–1939: A Study in the Interdependence of Eastern and Western Europe*. Toronto: University of Toronto Press, 1968.

Cieslak, Tadeusz. *Historia Polskiej Dyplomacji w latach 1926–1939* (*History of the Polish Diplomacy in the Years 1926–1939*). Vol. 2. Warsaw: n.p., 1960.

Clark, Mark. *Calculated Risk*. New York: Harper & Brothers Publishers, 1950.

Clemenceau, Georges E. *Grandeur et misères d'une victoire*. Paris: Plon, 1930.

Coates, William P., and Zelda K. Coates. *Armed Intervention in Russia 1918–1922*. London: Victor Gollancz, 1935.

Cocks, Seymour F. *The Secret Treaties and Understandings*. London: Union of Democratic Control, 1918.

Coulondre, Robert. *De Stalin à Hitler: souvenir de deux ambassades, 1936–1939*. Paris: Hachette, 1950.

Craig, Gordon A. *The Politics of the Prussian Army, 1640–1945*. New York & Oxford: Oxford University Press, 1956.

Craig, Gordon, and Felix Gilbert, eds. *The Diplomats, 1919–1939*. Princeton, NJ: Princeton University Press, 1953.

Czapski, J. *The Inhuman Land*. New York: Sheed & Ward, 1952.

D'Abernon, Edgar V. *An Ambassador of Peace: Pages from the Diary of Viscount D'Abernon*. 3 vols. London: Hodder & Stoughton, 1929–1930.

———. *The Eighteenth Decisive Battle of the World: Warsaw, 1920*. London: Hodder & Stoughton, 1931.

Dahlerus, Johan Birger Essen. *Der Letzte Versuch, London-Berlin Sommer 1939*. Munich: Nymphenburger Verlagshandlung, 1948.

Daladier, Édouard. *In Defense of France*. New York: Doubleday and Co., 1939.

Dallin, David J. *The Real Soviet Russia*. New Haven, CT: Yale University Press, 1947.

———. *Soviet Russia's Foreign Policy, 1939–1942*. New Haven, CT: Yale University Press, 1942.

Dalton, Hugh. *The Fateful Years 1931–1945*. London: Frederick Muller Ltd., 1957.

Davids, Jules. *America and the World of Our Time*. New York: Random House, 1960.

Davies, Joseph E. *Mission to Moscow*. New York: Simon & Schuster, 1941.

Davies, Norman. *White Eagle, Red Star: The Polish-Soviet War, 1919–1920*. New York: St. Martin's Press, 1972.

Debicki, Roman. *Foreign Policy of Poland, 1919–1939*. New York: Frederick A. Praeger, 1962.

Deutscher, Isaac. *Stalin: A Political Biography*. New York: Oxford University Press, 1949.

Dirksen, Herbert von. *Moscow, Tokyo, London: Twenty Years of German Foreign Policy*. Norman: University of Oklahoma Press, 1952.

Dmowski, Roman. *Polityka Polska i Odbudowanie Państwa* (*Polish Policy and the Rebuilding of the State*). Warsaw: Perzyński, Niklewicz, 1925.

Dodd, W. E., Jr., and Martha Dodd, eds. *Ambassador Dodd's Diary*. Introduction by Charles Bear. New York: Victor Gollancz, Ltd., 1941.

Driault, Édouard. *La paix de la France les traités de 1918–1921*. Paris: Librairie du Recueil Sirey, 1937.

Dugdale, Blanche E. C. *Arthur James Balfour*. New York: G. P. Putnam's Sons, 1937.

Dyck, Harvey Leonard. *Weimar Germany and Soviet Russia, 1926–1933: A Study in Diplomatic Instability*. New York: Columbia University Press, 1966.

Dziewanowski, M. K. *The Communist Party of Poland: An Outline of History*. Cambridge, MA: Harvard University Press, 1959.

———. *Joseph Pilsudski: A European Federalist, 1918–1922*. Stanford, CA: Hoover Institution, 1969.

Eden, Sir Anthony. *Facing the Dictators: The Memoirs of Anthony Eden*. Boston: Houghton Mifflin Co., 1962.

Eden, Anthony, Earl of Avon. *The Reckoning*. Boston: Houghton Mifflin Co., 1965.

Erickson, John. *The Soviet High Command: A Military-Political History, 1918–1940*. London: St. Martin's Press, 1962.

Eisenhower, Dwight D. *Crusade in Europe*. Garden City, NY: Doubleday & Co., 1948.

Epstein, M., ed. *Statesman's Yearbook 1922*. London: Macmillan Co., 1922.

Fabry, Phillip W. von. *Der Hitler-Stalin Pact 1939–1941. Ein Beitrag Zür Methode Sovjetischer Aussenpolitik*. Darmstadt: Fundus Verlag, 1962.

Farley, James A. *Jim Farley's Story: The Roosevelt Years*. New York: Wittlesey House, 1948.

Feiling, Keith G. *The Life of Neville Chamberlain*. London: The Macmillan Co., 1946.

Feis, Herbert. *Between War and Peace: The Potsdam Conference*. Princeton, NJ: Princeton University Press, 1960.

———. *Churchill-Roosevelt-Stalin: The War They Waged and the Peace They Sought*. Princeton, NJ: Princeton University Press, 1957.

Filasiewicz, Stanislas, ed. *La Question polonaise pendant la Guerre Mondiale*. Paris: Section d'Études et de Publications Politiques du Comité National Polonais, 1920.

Fisher, Louis. *Men and Politics*. New York: Harper & Row, 1941.

———. *The Road to Yalta: Soviet Foreign Relations, 1941–1945*. New York: Harper & Row, 1972.

———. *The Soviets in World Affairs*. 2 vols. Princeton, NJ: Princeton University Press, 1951.

Fisher, Ruth. *Stalin and German Communism*. Cambridge, MA: Harvard University Press, 1948.

Flandin, Pierre Étienne. *Politique francaise, 1919–1940*. Paris: Les Editions Nouvelles, 1947.

Francois-Poncet, André. *Souvenirs d'une ambassade à Berlin*. Paris: Flammarion, 1946.

Freund, Gerald. *Unholy Alliance: Russian-German Relations from the Treaty of Brest Litovsk to the Treaty of Berlin*. London: Chatto and Windus, 1957.

Freytagh-Loringhoven, Axel von. *Duetschlands Aussenpolitik, 1933–1940*. Berlin: O. Stollberg, 1940.

Gafencu, Grigore. *The Last Days of Europe*. New Haven, CT: Yale University Press, 1948.

Gamelin, Maurice Gustave. *Servir*. 3 vols. Paris: Plon, 1946–1947.

Garlinski, Józef. *Politycy i Żolnierze (Politicians and Soldiers)*. London: Odnowa, 1971.

Garthoff, Raymond L. *How Russia Makes War (Soviet Military Doctrine)*. London: George Allen & Unwin Ltd., 1954.

Gathorne-Hardy, G. M. *A Short Study of International Affairs 1920–1939*. Issued under the auspices of the Royal Institute of International Affairs. London: Oxford University Press, 1950.

Gatzke, Hans W. *Stresemann and the Rearmament of Germany*. Baltimore, MD: The Johns Hopkins University Press, 1954.

Gaulle, Charles de. *Mémoires de guerre. L'Appel, 1940–1942*. Paris: Plon, 1954.

———. *Mémoires de guerre. L'Unite, 1942–1944*. Paris: Plon, 1956.

Gibson, Hugh, ed. *The Ciano Diaries, 1939–1943*. Garden City, NY: Doubleday & Co., 1946.

Gilbert, Martin, and Richard Gott. *The Appeasers*. London: Weinfeld & Nicolson, 1963.

Gliksman, Jerzy. *Tell the West*. New York: Gresham Press, 1948.

Goerlitz, Walter. *Der Deutsche Generalstab, 1657–1945*. Frankfurt: Verlag der Frankfurter Hefte, 1950.

Grabski, Stanislaw. *The Polish-Soviet Frontier*. New York: Polish Information Center, 1943.

Gromada, Thaddeus V. *Essays on Poland's Foreign Policy, 1918–1939*. New York: Joseph Pilsudski Institute of America, 1970.

Grosfeld, Leon. *Polityka Państw Centralnych Wobec Sprawy Polskiej w Latach 1914–1918 (The Policy of the Central Powers toward the Polish Question in 1914–1918)*. Warsaw: Państwowe Wydawnictwo Naukowe, 1962.

Haines, C. G., and R. J. S. Hoffmann. *The Origin and Background of the Second World War*. London: Oxford University Press, 1943.

Halder, Franz. *The Halder Diaries*. Washington, DC: Infantry Journal Press, 1950.

Halifax, Viscount. *Fullness of Days*. London: Collins, 1957.

———. *Speeches on Foreign Policy, 1934–1939*. London: Oxford University Press, 1940.

Heike, Otto. *Das Deutschtum in Polen 1918–1919*. Bonn: Selsverlag des Verfassers, 1955.

Helbig, Herbert. *Die Träger der Rapallo-Politik*. Göttingen: Vandenhoek und Ruprecht, 1958.

Henderson, Nevile. *The Failure of a Mission*. New York: G. P. Putnam's Sons, 1940.

Hesse, Fritz. *Das Spiel um Deutschland*. Munich: P. List, 1953.

Higgins, Trumbull. *Soft Underbelly: The Anglo-American Controversy over the Italian Campaign, 1939–1945*. New York: The Macmillan Co., 1968.

Hilger, Gustav, and Alfred G. Meyer. *The Incompatible Allies, a Memoir-History of German-Soviet Relations, 1918–1941*. New York: The Macmillan Co., 1953.

Hitler, Adolf. *Mein Kampf*. New York: Reynal & Hitchcock, 1940.

Hoffman, Fredrich. *Die Oder-Neisse Linie: Politische Entwicklung and volkerrechtliche Lage*. Frankfurt am Main: J. Heinrich, 1949.

Höltje, Christian. *Die Weimarer Republik und das Ostlocarno-Problem 1919–1934*. Würzburg: Holzner Verlag, 1958.

House, Edward M. *The Intimate Papers of Colonel House*. Arranged as a narrative by Charles Seymour. 4 vols. Boston: Houghton Mifflin Co., 1926–1928.

House, Edward M., and Charles Seymour. *What Really Happened in Paris*. New York: C. Scribner's Sons, 1921.

Hudson, G. F. *The Hard and Bitter Peace: World Politics since 1945*. London: Pall Mall Press, 1966.

Hull, Cordell. *The Memoirs of Cordell Hull*. 2 vols. New York: The Macmillan Co., 1948.

Jedruszczak, Hanna i Tadeusz. *Ostatnie Lata II Rzeczypospolitej (1935–1939) (The Last Years of the Second Republic, 1935–1939)*. Warsaw: Polski Instytut Spraw Miedzynarodowych, 1970.

Jedrzejewicz, Waclaw, ed. *Diplomat in Berlin, 1933–1939: Papers and Memoirs* (of Józef Lipski). New York: Columbia University Press, 1968.

———. *Papers and Memoirs: Diplomat in Paris, 1936–1939* (Juliusz Lukasiewicz). New York: Columbia University Press, 1970.

———. *Poland in the British Parliament, 1939–1945*. New York: Columbia University Press, 1946–1962.

Józwiak, F. *PPR w Walce o Wyzwolenie Narodowe i Spoleczne (The Polish Workers' Party in the Struggle for National and Social Liberation)*. Warsaw: Ksiazka i Wiedza, 1952.

Jurkiewicz, Jaroslaw. *Pakt Wschodni (Eastern Pact)*. Warsaw: Ministerstwo Obrony Narodowej, 1963.

Karski, Jan. *Story of a Secret State*. Boston: Houghton Mifflin Co., 1944.

Kennan, George F. *Russia and the West under Lenin and Stalin*. Boston, Toronto: Little, Brown & Co., 1960.

———. *Soviet Foreign Policy 1917–1941*. Princeton, NJ : Van Rostrand, 1960.

Kerensky, Alexander. *The Crucifixion of Liberty*. New York: John Day Co., 1934.

Kirchmayer, Jerzy. *Kampania Wrześniowa 1939 (The September Campaign, 1939)*. Lódź, 1946.

———. *Powstanie Warszawskie (The Warsaw Uprising)*. Warsaw: Ksiazka i Wiedza, 1973.

Kirkien, Leszek. *Russia, Poland and the Curzon Line*. London: Caldra House, Ltd., 1945.

Kimche, Jon. *The Unfought Battle*. London: Weidenfeld & Nicolson, 1968.

Klafkowski, Alfons. *Podstawy Prawne Granicy Odra-Nysa na Tle Umów Jaltańskiej i Poczdamskiej. (The Legal Foundations of the Oder-Neisse Frontier on the Basis of the Yalta and Potsdam Agreements)*. Poznań: Instytut Zachodni, 1947.

———. *Umowa Poczdamska z Dnia 2 Sierpnia 1945r. (The Potsdam Agreement of August 2, 1945)*. Warsaw: Pax, 1960.

Klein, Fritz. *Die Diplomatischen Beziehungen Deutschlands zür Sovjetunion, 1917–1932*. Berlin: Rutten and Loening, 1952.

Kleist, Peter. *The European Tragedy*. Isle of Man: Times Press and Anthony Gibbon Phillips, 1965.

Klochowicz, Kazimierz. *Cztery Niedotrzymane Pakty (Four Un-Honoured Pacts)*. London: Gryf, 1966.

Kochan, Lionel. *Russia and the Weimar Republic*. Cambridge: Bowes and Bowes, 1954.

Koch-Weser, Erich. *Germany in the Postwar World*. Philadelphia: Dorrance & Co., 1930.

Komarnicki, Tytus, ed. *Diariusz: Teki Jana Szembeka* (Diaries and Papers of Jan Szembek). 3 vols. London: Polish Research Center, 1964–1969.

———. *Rebirth of the Polish Republic: A Study in the Diplomatic History of Europe, 1914–1920*. London: William Heinemann, Ltd., 1957.

Konovalov, S., ed. *Russo-Polish Relations: An Historical Survey*. Princeton, NJ: Princeton University, 1945.

Korbel, Josef. *Poland between East and West: Soviet and German Diplomacy toward Poland 1919–1933*. Princeton, NJ: Princeton University Press, 1963.

Korboński, Stefan. *The Polish Underground State: 1939–1945*. New York: Columbia University Press, 1978.

————. *W Imieniu Kremla (In the Name of the Kremlin)*. Paris: Instytut Literacki, 1956.

————. *W Imieniu Rzeczypospolitej (In the Name of the Republic)*. Paris: Instytut Literacki, 1954.

Kordt, Erich. *Wahn and Wirklichkeit*. Stuttgart: Union Deutsche Verlagsgesselschaft, 1948.

Kot, Stanislaw. *Conversations with the Kremlin and Dispatches from Russia*. London: Oxford University Press, 1963.

————. *Listy z Rosji do Gen. Sikorskiego (Letters from Russia to General Sikorski)*. London: St. Martin's, 1956.

Kowalczyk, Józef. *Za Kulisami Wydarzeń Politycznych z Lat 1936–1938 (Behind the Political Events in the Years 1936–1938)*. Warsaw: Ksiazka i Wiedza, 1976.

Kowalski, Wlodzimierz T. *Polityka Zagraniczna RP, 1944–1947 (Foreign Policy of the P[olish] R[epublic], 1944–1947)*. Warsaw: Ksiazka i Wiedza, 1971.

————. *Walka Dyplomatyczna o Miejsce Polski w Europie, 1939–1945 (Diplomatic Struggle for Poland's Place in Europe, 1939–1945)*. Warsaw: Polski Instytut Spraw Miedzynarodowych, 1967.

————. *Wielka Koalicja 1941–1943 (The Great Alliance, 1941–1943)*. Warsaw: Ministerstwo Obrony Narodowej, 1973.

Kozeński, Jerzy. *Czechoslowacia w Polskiej Polityce Zagranicznej w Latach 1932–1938 (Czechoslovakia in the Polish Foreign Policy During the Years 1932–1938)*. Poznań: Instytut Zachodni, 1964.

Kozlowska, H., ed. *W Dziesiata Rocznice Powstania PPR (On the Tenth Anniversary of the Polish Workers' Party)*. Warsaw: Ksiazka i Wiedza, 1952.

Krasuski, Jerzy. *Stosunki Polsko-Niemieckie 1926–1932 (Polish-German Relations 1926–1932)*. Poznań Instytut Zachodni, 1964.

Kukiel, Marian. *Dzieje Polski Porozbiorowe, 1795–1921 (The Post-Partitions History of Poland, 1795–1921)*. London: B. Swiderski, 1961.

Kukulka, Józef. *Francja a Polska po Traktacie Wersalskim, 1919–1922 (France and Poland after the Versailles Treaty, 1919–1922)*. Warsaw: Ksiazka i Wiedza, 1970.

Kutrzeba, Tadeusz. *Wyprawa Kijowska, 1920 (Kiev Expedition, 1920)*. Warsaw: Gebethner i Wolff, 1937.

Kwiatkowski, J. *Komuniści w Polsce (The Communists in Poland)*. Brussels: Polski Instytut Wydawniczy, 1946.

Lane, Arthur Bliss. *I Saw Poland Betrayed*. New York: The Bobbs-Merrill Co., 1948.

Langer, William L., and Everett S. Gleason. *The Challenge to Isolation, 1937–1940*. Vol. 1, *The World Crisis and American Foreign Policy*. New York: Harper & Brothers Publishers, 1952.

————. *The Undeclared War: 1940–1941*. New York: Harper & Brothers Publishers, 1953.

Lansing, Robert. *The Big Four at the Peace Conference*. London: Hutchinson & Co., 1922.

————. *The Peace Negotiations: A Personal Narrative*. Boston: Houghton Mifflin Co., 1921.

Lapter, Karol. *Pakt Pilsudski-Hitler (Pilsudski-Hitler Pact)*. Warsaw: Ksiazka i Wiedza, 1962.

Laroche, Jules Alfred. *La Pologne de Pilsudski: Souvenirs d'une ambassade, 1926–1935*. Paris: Flammarion, 1953.

Leahy, William D. *I Was There*. New York & Toronto: McGraw Hill, 1950.

Leczyk, M. *Komitet Narodowy Polski a Ententa i Stany Ziednoczone 1917–1919 (Polish National Committee, the Entente and the United States)*. Warsaw: Państwowe Wydawnictwo Naukowe, 1966.

————. *Polityka II Rzeczypospolitej wobec ZSSR w Latach 1925–1934 (Policy of the Second Polish Republic toward the USSR, 1925–1934)*. Warsaw: Państwowe Wydawnictwo Naukowe, 1976.

Lenin, Vladimir Illich. *Sotchinenya* (*Works*). 3rd ed. Vol. 25. Moscow: Gosudarstvennoe Izdatelstvo, 1935.

Lerski, Jerzy. *Emisariusz Jur* (Emissary Jur). London: Polish Cultural Foundation, 1984.

Librach, Jan. *The Rise of the Soviet Empire: A Study of Soviet Foreign Policy*. New York: Frederick A. Praeger, 1964.

Lippmann, Walter. *US Foreign Policy: Shield of the Republic*. Boston: Little, Brown & Co., 1943.

Lipski, Józef. *Diplomat in Berlin, 1933–1939: Papers and Memoirs*. Edited by Waclaw Jedrzejewicz. New York & London: Columbia University Press, 1968.

Litvinov, Maxim. *Against Aggression*. New York: International Publishers, 1939.

Lloyd George, David. *The Truth About Peace Treaties*. 2 vols. London: Victor Gollancz Ltd., 1938.

———. *War Memoirs*. 6 vols. London: Ivor Nicholson & Watson, 1933–1936.

Lukacs, John. *The Last European War, September 1939–December 1941*. Garden City, NY: Anchor Press, 1976.

Lukasiewicz, Juliusz. *Papers and Memoirs: Diplomat in Paris, 1936–1939*. Edited by Waclaw Jedrzejewicz. New York: Columbia University Press, 1970.

Lutz, Ralph Haswell. *The Causes of the German Collapse in 1918*. Stanford, CA: Stanford University Press, 1934.

———. *The Fall of the German Empire*. 2 vols. Stanford, CA: Stanford University Press, 1932.

Mackiewicz, Józef. *The Katyn Wood Murders*. London: Hollis & Carter, 1951.

Mackiewicz, Stanislaw. *Colonel Beck and His Policy*. London: Eyre and Spottiswoode, 1944.

Macleod, Iain. *Neville Chamberlain*. London: Frederick Muller Ltd., 1961.

Macleod, Roderic, and Denis Kelly, eds. *Time Unguarded: The Ironside Diaries, 1937–1940*. London: Constable, 1962.

Manteyer, G. de. *Austria's Peace Offer, 1916–1917*. London: Constable & Co., 1921.

Markert, Werner, ed. *Osteuropa-Handbuch, Polen*. Koln/Graz: Boehlau Verlag, 1959.

McIntire, Ross T. *White House Physician*. New York: G. P. Putnam's Sons, 1946.

McSherry, James E. *Stalin, Hitler and Europe 1933–1939: The Origins of World War II*. Cleveland & New York: The World Publishing Co., 1968.

Meissner, Otto. *Staatssekretär unter Ebert-Hindenburg-Hitler: der Schicksalsweg des deutschen Volkes von 1918–1945, wie ich ihn erlebte*. Hamburg: Hoffman und Campe Verlag, 1950.

Michowicz, Waldemar. *Walka Dyplomacji Polskiej Przeciwko Traktatowi Mniejszościowemu w Lidze Narodów w 1934* (*Struggle of the Polish Diplomacy against the Minorities Protection Treaty in the League of Nations in 1934*). Wroclaw: Instytut Ossolińskiego, 1953.

Mikolajczyk, Stanislaw. *The Rape of Poland: Pattern of Soviet Aggression*. New York & Toronto: McGraw-Hill, 1948.

Mikulicz, Sergiusz. *Prometeizm w Polityce II Rzeczypospolitej* (*Prometheism in the Politics of the Second Republic*). Warsaw: Ksiazka i Wiedza, 1971.

Miller, David Hunter. *My Diary at the Conference of Paris, with Documents*. 21 vols. New York: Printed for the author by the Appeal Printing Co., 1924.

Millis, Walter, and B. S. Duffield, eds. *Forrestal Diaries*. London: Cassel & Co., 1952.

Montamus, D. *Polish-Soviet Relations in the Light of International Law*. New York: University Publications, 1944.

Norris, Robert B., ed. *Encyclopedia of American History*. New York: Harper & Brothers Publishers, 1953.

Namier, Sir Lewis Bernstein. *Diplomatic Prelude 1938–1939*. London: The Macmillan Co., 1948.

————. *Europe in Decay: A Study in Disintegration 1936–1940*. London: The Macmillan Co., 1950.

National Council of American Soviet Friendship. *We Will Join Hands with Russia*. New York: n.p., 1944.

Newman, Simon. *March 1939: The British Guarantees to Poland*. Oxford: Clarendon Press, 1976.

Nicolson, Harold. *Curzon: The Last Phase, 1919–1925*. Boston: Houghton Mifflin Co., 1954.

Noël, Leon. *L'Aggression allemande contre la Pologne. Une ambassade à Varsovie, 1935–1939*. Paris: Flammarion, 1946.

Nowak, Jan. (Zdzislaw Jezioradski). *Kurier z Warszawy* (*Courier from Warsaw*). London: Odnowa, 1978.

O'Malley, Sir Owen. *The Phantom Caravan*. London: John Murray, 1954.

Osmańczyk, Edmund. *Dowody Prowokacji. Nieznane Archiwum Himmlera* (*The Evidence of Provocation: The Unknown Archives of Himmler*). Warsaw: Czytelnik, 1951.

Pajewski, J., ed. *Problem Polsko-Niemiecki w Traktacie Wersalskim* (*The Polish-German Problem in the Treaty of Versailles*). Poznań: Instytut Zachodni, 1963.

Paleologue, Maurice. *An Ambassador's Memoirs*. 3 vols. London: Hutchinson & Co., 1923–1925.

Papen, Franz von. *Memoirs*. New York: E. P. Dutton & Co., 1953.

Paul-Boncour, Joseph. *Entre deux guerres. Souvenirs sur la III-e Republic*. 3 vols. New York: Brentano's, 1946.

Pietrzak, Michal. *Rzady Parlamentarne w Polsce, 1919–1926* (*Parliamentarian Governments in Poland, 1919–1926*). Warsaw: Polski Instytut Spraw Miedzynarodowych, 1969.

Pilsudska, A. *Pilsudski: A Biography by His Wife, Alexandra*. New York: Dodd, Mead & Co., 1941.

Piszczkowski, Tadeusz. *Anglia a Polska 1914–1939 w świetle Dokumentów Brytyjskich* (*England and Poland in the Light of British Documents*). London: Oficyna Poetów i Malarzy, 1975.

Piwarski, Kazimierz. *Polityka Europejska w Okresie Po Monachijskim. X.1938–III.1939* (*European Politics in the Post-Munich Period, X.1938–III.1939*). Warsaw: Państwowe Wydawnictwo Naukowe, 1960.

Pobóg-Malinowski, Wladyslaw. *Najnowsza Historja Polityczna Polski, 1864–1945* (*Modern Political History of Poland, 1864–1945*). 2 vols. London: B. Swiderski, 1967.

Polonsky, Antony, ed. *The Great Powers and the Polish Question 1941–1945: A Documentary Study in Cold War Origins*. London: School of Economics and Political Science, 1976.

————. *Politics in Independent Poland, 1921–1939: The Crisis of Constitutional Government*. Oxford: Clarendon Press, 1972.

Polska Partja Robotnicza. *Kalendarz Robotniczy na 1948* (*Worker's Calendar for 1948*). Warsaw: Spóldzielnia Wydawnicza "Ksiazka," 1947.

Potemkin, Vladimir Petrovich, ed. *Istoriia Diplomatii* (*History of Diplomacy*). 3 vols. Moscow: Gosudarstvennoe Izdatelstvo Politicheskoy Literatury, 1941–1945.

Przybylski, Adam. *La Pologne en lutte pour ses frontières*. Paris: Gebethner & Wolff, 1929.

Pulestone, W. D. *The Influence of Force in Foreign Relations*. New York: D. Van Nostrand, Inc., 1955.

Rabenau, Friedrich von. *Seeckt, Aus seinem Leben, 1918–1936*. Leipzig: Verlag Hase und Koehler, 1941.

Raczyński, Edward. *The British-Polish Alliance, Its Origin and Meaning*. London: Melville Press, 1947.

———. *W Sojuszniczm Londynie (In Allied London)*. London: Polish Research Center, 1960.

Reddaway, W. F., J. H. Penson, O. Halecki, and R. Dyboski, eds. *The Cambridge History of Poland: From Augustus II to Pilsudski (1967–1935)*. Cambridge: Cambridge University Press, 1941.

Reed, Douglas. *Disgrace Abounding*. London: Jonathan Cape, 1939.

Reshetar, John S., Jr. *The Ukrainian Revolution, 1917–1920: A Study in Nationalism*. Princeton, NJ: Princeton University Press, 1952.

Reynaud, Paul. *Au coeur de la melée, 1939–1945*. Paris: Flammarion, 1951.

Rhode, Gotthold. *Kleine Geschichte Polens*. Darmstadt: Wissenschaftliche Buchgesellschaft, 1965.

Rhode, Gotthold, and Wolfgang Wagner, eds. *The Genesis of the Oder-Neisse Line: Sources and Documents*. Stuttgart: Brentano Verlag, 1959.

Ribbentrop, Joachim von. *The Ribbentrop Memoirs*. London: Weidenfeld and Nicolson, 1954.

Riekhoff, Harald von. *German-Polish Relations, 1918–1933*. Baltimore, MD: Johns Hopkins University Press, 1971.

Ripka, Hubert. *Munich: Before and After*. London: Victor Gollancz Ltd., 1939.

Roos, Hans. *A History of Modern Poland: From the Foundation of the State in the First War to the Present Day*. London: Eyre and Spottiswoode, 1966.

———. *Polen und Europa, Studien zür polnischen Aussenpolitik 1931–1939*. Tübingen: J. C. B. Mohr (Paul Siebeck), 1957.

Roosevelt, Elliott. *As He Saw It*. New York: Duell-Sloan & Pierce,194.

Rosenbaum, Kurt. *Community of Fate: German Soviet Diplomatic Relations, 1922–1928*. Syracuse, NY: Syracuse University Press, 1965.

Rosenfeld, Günther. *Sovjetrussland und Deutschland, 1917–1922*. Berlin: Akademie Verlag, 1960.

Rosenman, Samuel I. *Working with Roosevelt*. New York: Harper & Brothers Publishers, 1952.

Rossi, A. *The Russo-German Alliance, August 1939–June 1941*. Princeton, NJ: Princeton University Press, 1945.

Roth, Paul. *Die Enstehung des Polnischen Staates*. Berlin: O. Liebmann, 1926.

———. *Deutschland und Polen*. Munich: Isar Verlag, 1958.

Rothschild, Joseph. *East Central Europe between the Two World Wars*. Seattle: University of Washington Press, 1974.

———. *Pilsudski's Coup d'Etat*. New York: Columbia University Press, 1966.

Roton, Général G. *Années cruciales*. Paris: Charles-Lavauzelle, 1947.

Roucek, Joseph S. *Contemporary Europe*. New York: D. Van Nostrand Co., 1947.

Rowse, A. L. *Appeasement: A Study in Political Decline, 1933–1939*. New York: W. W. Norton & Co., 1961.

Rozek, Edward J. *Allied Wartime Diplomacy: A Pattern in Poland*. New York: John Wiley Sons, 1958.

Rubin, Harry H. *Armistice, 1918*. New Haven, CT: Yale University Press, 1944.

Sazonov, Sergei D. *Vspominanya (Memoirs)*. Paris: E. Cyaliskoy, 1927.

Schacht, Hjalmar. *Account Settled*. London: G. Weidenfeld and Nicolson, 1949.

Scott, William Evans. *Alliance against Hitler*. Durham, NC: Duke University Press, 1962.

Seekt, Hans von. *Aus Seinem Leben, 1918–1936*. Leipzig: Verlag Hase & Koehler, 1941.

Senn, Alfred Erich. *The Great Powers, Lithuania, and the Vilna Question*. Leiden, Netherlands: E. J. Brill, 1966.

Seton-Watson, H. *Eastern Europe between the Wars, 1918–1941.* Revised ed. Cambridge: Cambridge University Press, 1946.

Sforza, Carlo. *Diplomatic Europe since the Treaty of Versailles.* New Haven, CT: Institute of Political Publications, 1928.

Sherwood, Robert E. *Roosevelt and Hopkins: An Intimate History.* New York: Harper & Brothers Publishers, 1948.

Shotwell, James T. *Poland and Russia, 1919–1945.* New York: King's Crown Press, 1945.

Shtein, B. E. *Burzhuaznye Falsifikatory Istorii (1919–1939).* Moscow: Izdatelstvo Akademii Nauk, 1951.

Sikorski, Wladyslaw. *General Sikorski's Speeches during His Visit to the United States in December, 1942.* New York: Polish Information Center, 1942.

Simone, André (pseudonym of Otto Katz). *J'Accuse: The Men Who Betrayed France.* New York: The Dial Press, 1940.

Skaryński, Aleksander. *Polityczne Przyczyny Powstania Warszawskiego (Political Causes of the Warsaw Uprising).* Warsaw: Państwowe Wydawnictwo Naukowe, 1969.

Skrzypek, Stanislaw. *The Problem of Eastern Galicia.* London: Polish Association for the South-Eastern Provinces, 1948.

Smogorzewski, Casimir. *About the Curzon Line and Other Lines.* London: Free Europe Pamphlet, 1945.

Sobczak, Janusz. *Propaganda Zagraniczna Niemiec Weimarskich Wobec Polski (International Propaganda of the Weimar Republic against Poland).* Poznan: Instytut Zachodni, 1973.

Sosnkowski, Kazimierz. *Materialy Historyczne (Historical Records).* London: Gryf Publications, 1966.

Stachiewicz, Waclaw. *Pisma. Tom I. Przygotowania Wojenne w Polsce 1935–1939 (Writings: Volume 1, Military Preparations in Poland, 1935–1939).* Paris: Instytut Literacki, 1977. *Zeszyty Historyczne* no. 40 (1977); volume 2, *Zeszyty Historyczne*, no. 50 (1979).

Stahl, Zdzislaw. *Najazd od Wschodu (Invasion from the East).* London: Polska Fundacja Kulturalna, 1971.

Stanislawska, Stefania. *Polska A Monachium (Poland and Munich).* Warsaw: Ksiazka i Wiedza, 1967.

Stalin, J. V. *On the Great Patriotic War of the Soviet Union.* Moscow: Foreign Languages Publishing House, 1944.

———. *Report on the Work of the Central Committee to the XVIII Congress of the Soviet Union.* London: Modern Books, 1939.

Starzewski, Jan. *Polska Polityka Zagraniczna w Latach 1914–1939 (Polish Foreign Policy in 1914–1939).* London: Szkola Nauk Politycznych i Spolecznych, 1950.

Stettinius, Edward R. *Roosevelt and the Russians: The Yalta Conference.* Garden City, NY: Doubleday & Co., 1949.

Stimson, Henry L., and McGeorge Bundy. *On Active Service in Peace and War.* 2 vols. New York: Harper & Brothers Publishers, 1948.

Strang, Lord. *Home and Abroad.* London: Andre Deutsch, 1956.

Stresemann, Gustav. *Vermächtnis.* 3 vols. Berlin: Ullstein Verlag, 1932–1933.

Stroński, Stanislaw. *Pierwsze Lat Dziesiec 1918–1928 (The First Ten Years, 1918–1928).* Warsaw: Gubrynowicz i Syn, 1929.

Stypulkowski, Zbigniew. *Invitation to Moscow.* London: Thomas and Hudson, 1951.

Sutton, Eric, ed. *Gustav Stresemann, His Diaries, Letters and Papers.* 3 vols. London: The Macmillan Co., 1935–1937.

Światlo, Józef. *Za Kulisami Bezpieki i Partji (Behind the Coulisses of the Security Police and Party).* New York: Free Europe Press, 1955.

Szembek, Jean Comte. *Diariusz i Teki Jana Szembeka* (*Diary and Archives of Jan Szembek*). 4 vols. First three volumes edited by Tytus Komarnicki. Fourth volume edited by Jan Zaranski. London: Polish Research Center, 1964–1972.

———. *Journal, 1933–1939*. Trans. by J. Rzewuska and T. Zaleski. Preface by Leon Noël. Paris: Plon, 1952.

Tabouis, Geneviève. *They Called Me Cassandra*. New York: C. Scribner's Sons, 1942.

Tansill, Charles C. *Back Door to War: The Roosevelt Foreign Policy, 1933–1941*. Chicago: Henry Regnery Co., 1952.

Tarulis, Albert N. *Soviet Policy towards the Baltic States*. Notre Dame, IN: University of Notre Dame Press, 1959.

Taylor, A. J. P. *The Origins of the Second World War*. New York: Atheneum, 1961.

Temperley, Harold W. V., ed. *A History of the Peace Conference of Paris*. 6 vols. London: Frowde, Hodder and Stoughton, 1920–1924.

Templewood, Viscount (Sir Samuel Hoare). *Nine Troubled Years*. London: Collins, 1954.

Thompson, John M. *Russia, Bolshevism and the Versailles Peace*. Princeton, NJ: Princeton University Press, 1967.

Thorne, Christopher. *The Approach of War: 1938–1939*. London-New York: Macmillan and St. Martin Press, 1968.

Tissier, Pierre. *The Riom Trial*. London: George G. Harrap & Co., 1942.

Tolishus, Otto D. *They Wanted War*. New York: Reynal and Hitchcock, 1940.

Tommasini, Francesco. *Odrodzenie Polski* (*The Resurrection of Poland*). Warsaw: F. Hoesick, 1928.

Toynbee, Arnold J., ed. *Survey of International Affairs, 1920–1923*. London: Oxford University Press, 1925.

———. *Survey of International Affairs, 1936*. London: Oxford University Press, 1937.

———. *Survey of International Affairs, 1939–1946: The Eve of War*. London: Oxford University Press, 1948.

Truman, Harry S. *Memoirs*. 2 vols. Garden City, NY: Doubleday & Co., 1955.

Turlejska, Maria. *Prawdy i Fikcje. Wrzesień 1939–Grudzień 1941* (*Truths and Fictions: September 1939–December 1941*). Warsaw: Ksiazka i Wiedza, 1966.

———. *Rok Przed Kleska I Września 1938–I Września 1939* (*The Year before the Defeat, 1 September 1938–1 September 1939*). Warsaw: Wiedza Powszechna, 1962.

———. *Spór o Polske* (*Quarrel about Poland*). Warsaw: Czytelnik, 1972.

Turner, Henry Ashby, Jr. *Stresemann and the Politics of the Weimar Republic*. Princeton, NJ: Princeton University Press, 1963.

Umiastowski, R. *Poland, Russia and Great Britain, 1941–1945*. London: Hollis & Carter, 1946.

Vandenberg, Arthur H., Jr., ed. *The Private Papers of Senator Vandenberg*. Boston: Houghton Mifflin Co., 1952.

Vansittart, Lord. *The Mist Procession*. London: Hutchinson & Co., 1958.

Villard, Oswald G. *The German Phoenix*. New York: Harrison Smith and Robert Haas, 1933.

Wagner, Wolfgang. *Die Enstehung der Oder-Niesse Linie*. Stuttgart, 1953.

Waite. Robert G. L. *Vanguard of Nazism: The Free Corps Movement in Postwar Germany, 1918–1923*. Cambridge, MA: Harvard University Press, 1952.

Walters, F. P. *A History of the League of Nations*. London: Oxford University Press, 1952.

Wambaugh, Sarah. *Plebiscites since the World War, with a Collection of Official Documents*. Washington, DC: Carnegie Endowment for International Peace, 1933.

Wandycz, D. S., ed. *Polish Americans and the Curzon Line: President Roosevelt's Statement at Yalta*. New York: Joseph Pilsudski Institute of America, 1954.

Wandycz, Piotr S. *France and Her Eastern Allies, 1919–1925: French-Czechoslovak-Polish Relations from the Paris Peace Conference to Locarno*. Minneapolis: The University of Minnesota Press, 1962.

———. *Polish-Soviet Relations 1917–1921*. Cambridge, MA: Harvard University Press, 1969.

———. *The United States and Poland*. Cambridge, MA: Harvard University Press, 1979.

Watt, Richard M. *Bitter Glory: Poland and Its Fate, 1918–1939*. New York: Simon and Schuster, 1979.

Wedemeyer, Albert C. *Wedemeyer Reports*. New York: Holt, 1958.

Weinberg, Gerhard L. *The Foreign Policy of Hitler's Germany: Diplomatic Revolution in Europe, 1933–1936*. Chicago: University of Chicago Press, 1970.

Weizsäcker, Ernst von. *Memoirs of Ernst von Weizsäcker*. London: Victor Gollancz, 1951.

Welles, Sumner. *Seven Decisions That Shaped History*. New York: Harper and Brothers Publishers, 1951.

———. *The Time for Decision*. New York: Harper & Brothers Publishers, 1944.

———. *Where Are We Heading?* New York: Harper & Brothers Publishers, 1946.

Werth, Alexander. *The Last Days of Paris*. London: Hamish Hamilton, 1940.

Weyers, I. *Poland and Russia*. London: Bernard & Westwood, Ltd., 1943.

Wheeler-Bennett, J. *Munich, Prologue to Tragedy*. New York: Duell, Sloan and Pearce, 1948.

———. *The Nemesis of Power: The German Army in Politics 1918–1945*. London: The Macmillan Co., 1953.

———. *The Treaty of Brest Litovsk and Germany's Eastern Policy*. Oxford: Clarendon Press, 1940.

Wiewióra, B. *Granica Polsko-Niemiecka w Świetle Prawa Miedzynarodowego* (*The Polish-German Frontier in the Light of International Law*). Poznan: Instytut Zachodni, 1957.

Wilmot, Chester. *The Struggle for Europe*. London: Collins St. James Place, 1952.

Wiskemann, Elizabeth. *Germany's Eastern Neighbours*. London: Royal Institute of International Affairs, 1956.

Wojciechowski, Marian. *Stosunki Polsko Niemieckie, 1933–1938* (*Polish-German Relations, 1933–1938*). Poznan: Instytut Zachodni, 1965.

Wolfers, Arnold. *Britain and France between Two Wars*. New York: Harcourt, Brace & Co., 1940.

Wynot, Edward D. *Polish Politics in Transition: The Camp of National Unity and Struggle for Power 1935–1939*. Athens, GA: University of Georgia Press, 1974.

Zabiello, Stanislaw. *O Rzad i Granice* (*For a Government and Frontiers*). Warsaw: Instytut Wydawniczy, 1964.

Zauski, Zbigniew. *Czterdziesty Czwarty* (*Forty Fourth*). Warsaw: Czytelnik, 1968.

Zawodny, J. K. *Death in the Forest: The Story of the Katyn Forest Massacre*. Notre Dame, IN: University of Notre Dame Press, 1962.

———. *Nothing but Honour: Story of the Uprising of Warsaw*. Stanford, CA: Hoover Institute, 1978.

Zevin, B. D., ed. *Nothing to Fear: The Selected Addresses of Franklin Delano Roosevelt, 1938–1945*. Boston: Houghton Mifflin Co., 1946.

Zimmerman, Ludwig. *Deutsche Aussenpolitik in der Ära der Weimarer Republik*. Göttingen: Musterschmidt Verlag, 1958.

Zoltowski, Adam. *Border of Europe: A Study of the Polish Eastern Provinces*. London: Hollis & Carter, 1950.

III. CHAPTERS IN A FULL-LENGTH WORK, PAMPHLETS, AND JOURNAL ARTICLES

Alster, A. i Andrzejewski, "W sprawie skladu socjalnego PZPR" (On the social structure of the Polish United Workers' Party). *Nowe Drogi*, January–February 1951, vol. 5.

Anonymous. "Silva Rerum: Eppur si volle movere." *Wiadomości* 8, no. 43 (395). October 25, 1953.

Babinski, Witold. "Jeszcze o Powstaniu" (More about the Uprising). *Wiadomosci*, 1942–1943 (January 1970).

———. "Na marginesie polemiki" (On the margin of a polemic). *Kultura* 5, no. 27 (May 1958).

Baczkowski, Wlodzimierz. "Prometeizm na Tle Epoki" (Prometheism Reflection of an Era). *Niepodleglość* 17 (1984).

Batowski, Henryk. "Rumuńska Podróż Becka w październiku 1938 roku." *Kwartalnik Historyczny* 65, no. 2 (1958).

Beneš, Edouard. "Memoirs." *Nation*, July 17, 1948.

Bocheński, Feliks. *The Economic Structure of Poland*. Birkenhead, UK: Polish Publications Committee, 1943.

Bregman, Aleksander. "Legenda czy Fakt Historyczny?" (A Legend or a Historical Fact?). *Dziennik Polski*, January 4, 1954.

Bromke, Adam. "Poland and Czechoslovakia: The Hesitant Alliance." *Central European Federalist* 15, no. 1 (June 1967).

Bruening, Heinrich. "Ein Brief an R. Pechel." *Deutsche Rundschau* 70 (July 1947).

Bullitt, William C. "How We Won the War and Lost the Peace." *Life*, August 30, 1948.

Burmeister, A. "Tragedia Polskich Komunistów" (Tragedy of the Polish Communists). *Kultura*, no. 51 (January 1952).

Buzinkai, Donild I. "Poland and The League of Nations, 1934–1939: A Political Analysis." *Polish Review* 10, no. 4 (Autumn 1965).

Carman, Harry J. "Russia and the Reversal of Allied Policy." *Journal of International Relations* 10 (April 1920).

Challener, Richard D. "The French Foreign Office: The Era of Phillipe Berthelot." Chapter 2 in *The Diplomats, 1919–1939*, ed. Gordon A. Craig and Felix Gilbert, 49–85. Princeton, NJ: Princeton University Press, 1953.

Chocianowicz, Waclaw. "Sejm Wileński w 1922 Roku" (Vilna *Sejm* in 1922). *Zeszyty Historyczne*, no. 4, August 1963.

Chudek, Józef. "Rozmowy Beck-Göring z 23go Lutego 1938r." (Beck-Göring Conversations on February 23, 1938). *Sprawy Miedzynarodowe*, no. 5 (1960).

Cienciala, Anna M. "Marxism and History: Recent Polish and Soviet Interpretations of Polish Foreign Policy in the Era of Appeasement. An Evaluation." *East European Quarterly* 6, no. 1 (March 1972).

Cretzianu, Alexandre. "Rumunia a Wrzesień 1939" (Rumania and September 1939). *Kultura* 3, no. 77 (March 1954).

Cripps, Sir Stafford. "Twenty Russian Questions." *Life*, March 9, 1942.

Dallin, A. "The Month of Decision: German Soviet Diplomacy, July 22–August 22, 1939." *Journal of Central European Affairs* 9 (April 1949).

Deshanel, Paul. "La Politique éxterieure de la France." *Revue des Deux Mondes*, June 18, 1922.

Dumont-Wildon, L. "L'Évolution de la Pologne." *Revue Politique et Litteraire*, no. 23 (November 17, 1923).

Dyck, Harvey L. "German-Soviet Relations and the Anglo-Soviet Break, 1927." *Slavic Review* 25, no. 1 (March 1966).

Dziewanowski, Marian K. "Joseph Pilsudski, the Bolshevik Revolution and Eastern Europe." Chapter 2 in *Essays on Poland's Foreign Policy, 1918–1939*, ed. Thaddeus V. Gromada, 13–29. New York: Joseph Pilsudski Institute of America, 1970.

———. "Pilsudski's Federal Policy, 1919–1921." *Journal of Central European Affairs* 10, no. 3 (1950).

Faury, Louis A. "La Pologne Terrassée." *Revue Historique de l'Armée* 9, no. 1 (1953).

Garliński, Józef. "Z Perspektywy Dwudziestu Czterech Lat" (From the Perspective of Twenty-Four Years). *Wiadomości* 1147 (March 1968).

Gasiorowski, Zygmunt J. "Did Pilsudski Attempt to Initiate a Preventive War in 1933?" *Journal of Modern History* 27, no. 2 (June 1955).

———. "J. Pilsudski in the Light of American Reports, 1919–1922." *Slavonic and East European Review*, no. 116 (July 1971).

———. "J. Pilsudski in the Light of British Reports." *Slavonic and East European Review*, no. 121 (October 1972).

———. "The Russian Overture to Germany of December 1924." *Journal of Modern History* 30, no. 2 (June 1958).

———. "Stresemann and Poland before Locarno." *Journal of Central European Affairs* 18, no. 1 (April 1958).

———. "Stresemann and Poland after Locarno." *Journal of Central European Affairs* 18, no. 3 (October 1958).

Gatzke, Hans W. "Gustav Stresemann: A Bibliographical Article." *Journal of Modern History* 36 (March 1964).

———. "Russo-German Military Collaboration During the Weimar Republic." *American Historical Review* 63, no. 3 (April 1958).

———. "Von Rapallo nach Berlin: Stresemann und die deutsche Russlandpolitik." *Vierteljahrshefte für Zeitgeschichte*, no. 1 (January 1956).

Jedrzejewicz, Waclaw. "The Polish Plan for a 'Preventive War' against Germany in 1933." *Polish Review* 11, no. 1 (Winter 1966).

———. "Rokowania Borysowskie w 1920 Roku" (Borisov Negotiations in 1920). *Niepodleglość* 3 (1951).

Jeleński, Konstanty A. "Wywiad z generalem Weygand" (An Interview with General Weygand). *Kultura* 6, no. 68 (June 1953).

Johnson, B. E. W. "Poland Plays a Dangerous Game." *North American Review* 238, no. 3 (September 1934).

———. "Something New in Peace Machinery." *North American Review* 238, no. 4 (October 1934).

Komarnicki, Tytus. "Pilsudski a polityka wielkich mocarstw zachodnich" (Pilsudski and Great Western Powers' Politics). *Niepodleglosc* 4 (1952).

Kruszewski, Charles. "The German-Polish Tariff War (1925–1934) and Its Aftermath." *Journal of Central European Affairs* 3 (October 1943).

Kukiel, Marian. "Letter to the Editor." *Kultura*, no. 4/174 (April 1962).

———. "Rzad generala Sikorskiego a Soviety" (General Sikorski's Government and the Soviets). *Wiadomosci* 10, no. 471/472 (April 1955).

Kulski, Wladyslaw W. "The Anglo-Polish Agreement of August 25, 1939: Highlight of My Diplomatic Career." *Polish Review* 21, no. 102 (1976).

Kunicki, Tadeusz. "Problemy Polsko-Niemieckie" (Polish-German Problems). *Niepodleglość* 4 (1952).

Lerski, Jerzy J. "A Polish Chapter in the Russo-Japanese War." *Transactions of the Asiatic Society of Japan*, 3rd series, vol. 7 (1959).

Lipski, Józef. "Przyczynki do Historji polskoniemieckiej deklaracji o nieagresji" (Addenda to the History of the Polish-German Declaration of Non-Aggression). *Bellona*, in two installments: first, in 1/2 (January–June 1951); second, in 3 (July–September 1951).

―――. "Stosunki Polsko-Niemieckie w Świetle Aktów Norymberskich" (Polish-German Relations in the Light of the Nuremberg Documents). *Spprawy Miedzynarodowe*, nos. 2–3 (1947).

―――. "Trzecia Podroz" (The Third Journey). *Wiadomości* 4, no. 39 (September 1949).

Lukas, Richard C. "Russia, the Warsaw Uprising and the Cold War." *Polish Review* 20, no. 4 (1975).

Lukasiewicz, Juliusz. "Sprawa Czechoslowacka w 1938 r. na Tle Stosunków Polsko-Francuskich" (Czechoslovak Question in 1938 in the Polish-French Relations). *Sprawy Miedzynarodowe*, nos. 2–3 (6–7).

Matthews, H. P. S. "Poland's Foreign Relations." *Fortnightly*, no. 860 (August 1938).

Miedziński B. "Pakty Wilanowskie" (Milanow Pacts). *Kultura* 3, no. 190 (July–August 1963).

―――. "Polityka Wschodnia Pilsudskiego" (Pilsudski's Eastern Policy). *Zeszyty Historyczne* 31 (1975).

Millerand, Alexandre. "Au secours de la Pologne." *Revue de France* 12-e année, 4 (1932).

Mühlstein, Anatol. "Świadectwo Ambasadora Larocha" (Ambassador Laroche's Testimony). *Kultura* 6, no. 68 (June 1953).

Nowakowski, Zygmunt. "Wspomnienia Przedjaltańskie" (Pre-Yalta Souvenirs). *Dziennik Polski i Dziennik Żolnierza* 16, 41 (February 17, 1955).

Okulicz, Kazimierz. "Umowa Sikorski-Majskij z 30 VII 1941" (Sikorski-Maisky Agreement of July 30, 1941). *Niepodleglośc* 2 (1950).

Pankratowa, Anna Mihailovna. "Zakhvat Fashistami vlasti v Germanii i padryvaia Rabota Nemetsko-Fashistskoy Diplomatii v Europe (1932–1933)" (The Fascist Seizure of Power in Germany and Disruptive Activities of the German-Fascist Diplomacy in Europe [1932–1933]). Chapter 19 in *Istoriia Dyplomatii*, ed. Vladimir Petrovich Potemkin, vol 3. 3 vols. Moscow: Gosudarstvennoe Izdatelstvo Politicheskoy Literatury, 1941–1945.

Pinon, R. "La Visite de M. Barthou à Varsovie et à Prague." *Revue des Deux Mondes*, May 15, 1935.

Pobóg-Malinowski, Wladyslaw. "O Ukladzie Polsko-Rosyjskim 30 VII 1941" (About the Polish-Russian Agreement of July 30, 1941). *Kultura* 4, no. 42 (April 1951).

Pomian, Andrzej. "Plany Stalina a Zryw Stolicy" (Stalin's Plan and the Outbreak in the Capital). *Wiadomości* 962 (September 1964).

Pragier, Adam. "Droga do Klęski" (The Road to Defeat). *Wiadomości* 1242–1243 (January 1970).

―――. "Katyn w Radzie Narodowej" (Katyn in the National Council). *Wiadomości* 950 (June 1964).

―――. "W Dziesieciolecie" (Tenth Anniversary). *Wiadomości* 465 (February 1955).

Rhode, Gotthold. "Die Entstehung der Curzon-Linie." *Osteuropa* 5, no. 2 (1955).

Roberts, Henry L. "The Diplomacy of Colonel Beck." Chapter 19 in *The Diplomats, 1919–1939*, ed. Gordon A. Craig and Felix Gilbert, 579–614. Princeton, NJ: Princeton University Press, 1953.

Roos, Hans. "Die Präventive Kriegspläne Pilsudskis von 1933." *Vierteljarshefte für Zeitgeschichte* 3 (October 1955).

Rousselet, S. "Ou sont les Relations Franco-Polonaise?" *L'Europe Nouvelle*, December 11, 1934.

Scottish League for European Freedom. *Who's Who of the Regime in Poland.* Edinburgh, 1947.

Seeckt, Hans von. "Deutschlands Stellung zum Russischen Problem; Antwort auf ein Promemoris des Grafen Br[ockdorff]-R[antzau] an den Reichkanzler, II, 9, 1922." *Der Monat* 1, no. 2 (November 1948).

Siemaszko, Z. S. "Powstanie Warszawskie" (Warsaw Uprising). *Wiadomości* 1242–1243 (January 1970).

Silva Rerum. "Eppur si voile movere." *Wiadomości* 395 (October 1953).

Skrzypek, J. "Ukraińcy w Austrii i Geneza Zamachu na Lwów" (Ukrainians in Austria and the Origins of Their Coup in Lwow). *Niepodległośc* 19.

Sontag, Raymond J. "The Last Months of Peace, 1939." *Foreign Affairs* 35 (April 1957).

Sopicki, S. "Przyczynek do polskiej akcji prewencyjnej" (An Addendum to the Polish Preventive Action). *Niepodległośc* 4 (1952).

Staar, R. F. "The Military Potential of Communist Poland." *Military Review* 36 (July 1955).

———. "The Polish Communist Party, 1918–1948." *Polish Review* 1, nos. 2–3 (Spring–Summer 1956).

Sworakowski, W. "An Error Regarding Eastern Galicia in Curzon's Note to the Soviet Government." *Journal of Central European Affairs* 4, no. 1 (April 1944).

Wandycz, Piotr S. "August Zaleski, Minister Spraw Zagranicznych RP 1926–32 w świetle wspomnień i dokumentów" (August Zaleski Foreign Minister of Poland 1926–1932 in the Light of Memoirs and Documents). *Zeszyty Historyczne* 52 (1980).

———. "Beneš and Beck." *Central European Federalist* 9, no. 1 (June 1961).

———. "Secret Soviet-Polish Peace Talks in 1939." *Slavic Review* 24, no. 3 (September 1965).

———. "Stany Zjednoczone a Europa Środkowo-Wschodnia w okresie miedzywojennym 1921–1939" (The United States and Central-Eastern Europe between the two World Wars, 1921–1939). *Zeszyty Historyczne* 37 (1976).

———. "Trzy Dokumenty: Przyczynek do Zagadnienia Wojny Prewencyjnej" (Three Documents: A Contribution to the Problem of the Preventive War). *Zeszyty Historyczne*, vols. 3–4.

Wheeler-Bennett, John. "Twenty Years of Russo-German Relations, 1918–1939." *Foreign Affairs* 25 (October 1946).

Wiskemann, Elizabeth. "Germany's Eastern Neighbors." *Survey*, October 1962.

Wojciechowski, Marian. "How It Really Was with the Polish Corridor." *Poland* 10 (October 1972).

Woytak, Richard A. "Polish Military Intervention into Czechoslovakian Teschen and Western Slovakia in September–November 1938." *East European Quarterly* 6, no. 3 (September 1972).

Index

About the Author

Jan Karski (1914–2000) received a degree in law and diplomatic science in 1935. He was a young diplomat when war broke out in 1939 with Hitler's invasion of Poland. Taken prisoner by the Soviet Red Army, which had simultaneously invaded from the east, Karski escaped and joined the Polish Underground, acting as a liaison and courier between the Underground and the Polish government-in-exile. He infiltrated both the Warsaw ghetto and a German concentration camp and then carried the first eyewitness accounts of the Holocaust to a mostly disbelieving West, meeting with President Roosevelt in 1943 to plead for Allied intervention. After World War II, Karski earned a PhD from Georgetown University, where he served as a distinguished professor in the School of Foreign Service for forty years. Karski has been recognized as Righteous Among the Nations by Yad Vashem. In 2012, he was posthumously awarded the Presidential Medal of Freedom by President Barack Obama. His books include the bestseller *Story of a Secret State: My Report to the World*, first published in 1944 and reissued in 2013.